9- Portland OR

to Earl
the best
boss
ever
— Tim

"But you are a chosen generation,
    a royal priesthood,
        a holy nation,
            a peculiar* people;
                that you should show forth the praises of God
                    who has called you out of darkness
                        into God's marvelous light"
                                  ... I Peter 2:9

*something separated to one's own use; unlike anything else or anything of the same class or kind; singular; select; special; distinguished

Copyrighted 2006 by David Grant Kohl
Printed in the USA
by Witham and Dickey

ISBN 1-893075-54-0

Cover Art and Design by WhipLash Design
Christian Messer and Ethan Firpo

Book Design by Spirit Press
Front Cover Photo by David Kohl
Back Cover Photo by Bill Barry

This book may not be reproduced by electronic or any other means which exist now or may yet be developed, without permission of Spirit Press, except in the case of brief quotations embodied in critical articles and reviews.

Depiction or mention of any person in this work should not be construed as an implication of said persons sexual orientation.

Metropolitan Community Church of Portland
2400 NE Broadway
Portland, Oregon 97232
www.mccportland.com

Spirit Press
PO Box 12346
Portland, Oregon 97212
www.spiritpress.org

A Curious and Peculiar People

A History of the Metropolitan Community Church
of Portland, Oregon and the Sexual Minority
Communities of the Pacific Northwest

by

David Grant Kohl, M.A.

Spirit Press
Portland, Oregon

Dedication

Dedicated to all people who take a stand
for what they believe,
and act on it.

The Road Not Taken

Two roads diverged in a yellow wood,
And sorry I could not travel both
And be one traveler, long I stood
And looked down one as far as I could
To where it bent in the undergrowth;

Then took the other, as just as fair,
And having perhaps the better claim,
Because it was grassy and wanted wear;
Though as for that the passing there
Had worn them really about the same,

And both that morning equally lay
In leaves no step had trodden black.
Oh, I kept the first for another day!
Yet knowing how way leads on to way,
I doubted if I should ever come back.

I shall be telling this with a sigh
Somewhere ages and ages hence:
Two roads diverged in a wood, and I –
I took the one less traveled by,
And that has made all the difference.

-Robert Frost

Table of Contents

Foreword - Rev. Troy Perry....**ix**

Introduction and Acknowledgments....**xi**

Chapter 1. Prelude 1853–1971....**1**
    I. The Homophile community in Portland
    II. Civil Rights
    III. Spirituality

Chapter 2. Early MCC Groups 1971–1973....**59**
    Rev. Ken Jones
    Rev. Ken Adams

Chapter 3. Portland Community Church 1974–1975....**79**
    Rev. Frank Fortenberry
        Denis Moore - Nita Gates - David Rushong
        Becoming an MCC - 1975

Chapter 4. Rev. A. Austin Amerine January 1976–June 1979....**89**
    Establishing Traditions
    Buying the Building
    Rev. Arlene Ackerman - June 1978; Interim pastor June '79 - October '79

Chapter 5. Interlude: The Church of Good Tidings **121**
    I. Ownership History
        1909 - First Universalist Church of Good Tidings
        1919 - Grace English Lutheran Church
        1963 - Church of Divine Science
        1977 - Metropolitan Community Church
    II. Architecture (descriptive and analytic)
    Style(s) & Architect(s)
    Components and Furnishings

Chapter 6. Rev. Don Borbe September 1979–January 1981....**165**
    Inclusion and Language
    Rev. Claudia Vierra - Interim Pastor January 1981-September 1981

Chapter 7. Rev. Jim Glyer October 1981–September 1983....**189**
    Exhorters and Student Clergy

Chapter 8. Rev. Delores Berry September 1983–November 1984....**223**
    Music at MCC

Table of Contents

Chapter 9. Laity Leadership December 1984–March 1986....**247**
Dave Dishman & Marguerite Scroggie

Chapter 10. Rev. Gary Wilson March 1986–February 1993....**265**
Politics and Ballot Measures
AIDS - Discovering Community Resources
Rev. Kate Zon

Chapter 11. Rev. Dennis Chappell September 1993–March 1994....**303**
Rev. Mary Frantz (March 1993-August 1993)
Changing Directions
Rev. A. Austin Amerine (April 1994-September 1994)

Chapter 12. Rev. Roy Cole October 1994–October 2001....**317**
Community Outreach - Esther's Pantry - Rainbow Youth
Ecumenical Ministries of Oregon
Rev. Marsha Dempsey

Chapter 13. Rev. Glenna Shepherd February 2003–Present...**353**
Rev. Michael Nikolaus and Laity (November 2001-January 2003)
Community of Welcoming Congregations
Issues around same-sex marriage
Rebuilding Our Home and Our Mission

Chapter 14. Postlude....**385**

Appendix....**392**
History Project Patrons
Historic Gay Venues in Portland
Historic GLBT Organizations in Portland
What Is Metropolitan Community Church
What does Jesus say about Homosexuality?
Familiar Christian Literature
Gay Christian Manifesto
In Memoriam

Bibliography....**423**

Abridged Index....**430**

Forward

MCC
METROPOLITAN
COMMUNITY CHURCHES

8704 Santa Monica Boulevard, Second Floor
West Hollywood, California 90069   www.MCCchurch.org
Phone 310.360.8640   Fax 310.360.8680

Mementos of 37 years of ministry and memories—photographs, plaques, awards, and correspondence—have all been packed and moved into my home office. What I am feeling on this day as I close one chapter of my life, is a deep sense of gratitude. I am so thankful for the calling God placed upon my heart so long ago…thankful for God's guidance, grace, and strength that have sustained me along every step of the way.

As a child growing up in Georgia, Florida, and Alabama, I sensed God's presence and guidance on my life. But I scarcely dreamed of the journey my own life would take, of the doors God would open.

On October 6, 1968, the first service of a Metropolitan Community Church was held in Huntington Park, California. From that small beginning, with a group of twelve, meeting in my home for the first time, the UFMCC has grown to almost 300 congregations world-wide with a membership of over 42,000 people.

On October 24, 1971, the first official meeting of a Portland MCC was held, making MCC-Portland a part of one of the first groups of MCCs that were started outside of the state of California.

There is no greater joy in my life than knowing that on this journey of nearly four decades, we've — together—touched lives, inspired hope, and helped people discover their value and meaning through the life and teaching of Jesus Christ. This founding and leading of the Metropolitan Community Churches would not have been possible without the love and prayers and faithfulness of friends in the family of God.

I'm not only reflecting on God's blessings of the past, I'm doing what we've always done in the UFMCC: I'm looking with faith and anticipation to the future. I believe the words of the Hebrew prophet that God is blessing us with "a future and a hope."

Forward

In your hand, you are now holding a wonderful history book, written by David Kohl. In this book, David has done an incredible job of telling the history, not only of this congregation, but some of the history of the GLBT movement in Portland. This is an exceptional book on the genesis of a modern denomination that was born out of a political protest movement that had started in the gay community. Drawing on interviews and archival research, David reveals the political tensions and the growth of MCC-Portland, which was one of the organizations that helped lead this fight. Included in his work are the stories of wonderful clergy, laity, and friends of MCC-Portland who made this such an incredible read.

I leave you with two thoughts. First, the words from my original MCC sermon: "Be true to you. Be true to yourself, just as God created you. And be true to God, who loves you just as you are." And the text from my final sermon as UFMCC moderator: "You are a chosen people. A royal priesthood, A holy nation, A peculiar people."

Rev. Troy D. Perry
Founder / Moderator
UFMCC
September 15, 2005
Los Angeles

Introduction

*" Let my words and my thought be pleasing to you, Lord,
because you are my mighty rock and my protector.*

Psalm 19:14 (Contemporary English Version)

This book has come about as the evolution of a simple idea I had in the fall of 2004. Realizing many founders of Metropolitan Community Church of Portland were advancing in years, and having lost several significant figures in the congregation like José Montoya, Bob Jackson, and Don Strausbaugh, it seemed the time had come to at least record some oral histories. Then I realized that our 30th anniversary was less than two years away, and that our building is approaching its centenary...thus the excuse to delve into our congregational history.

It wasn't long before I realized that I could not get too far into the congregation's activities without relating their history to the greater gay-lesbian-bisexual-transgendered and straight communities of the Rose City. That opened a delightful can of worms, which has taken my research into the roots of gay culture in Portland, the religious discussion over the morality of sexual orientation, and the changing attitudes of folks inside and outside the sexual orientation issue. Thus a longer chapter on the prelude than I had anticipated. Please bear with it, I think you'll find the roots of the homosexual subculture in this city to be an amazing blend of diverse influences, activities, characters, and locations. Portland is often referred to as Rose Town, the Rose City, Bridgetown, Portlandia or Stumptown, an endearing term leftover from the timber-clearing days of the 1850s.

Throughout this book, I use "gay" generically to include all forms and genders of alternative sexual orientation–male, female, or otherwise. Politically correct terminology has changed in 30 years. "Gay" originally included everyone, then distinctions were made between gay men and lesbians. Soon bisexuals were identified separately, as were transgendered. In 2006, "queer" is often used to include all of the above, plus intersexual and questioning people. For variety and simplicity, I often use GLBT to indicate inclusion.

A disclaimer: Mention of individual names anywhere in this book in no way implies or infers reference to their sexual orientation or practices. MCC-Portland has attracted friends and members of all sexual persuasions since day one. Similarly, supporters of the gay community or of MCC-Portland come from all orientations. MCC of Portland is not a gay church...it is a ministry to all believers, but especially to those of the gay, lesbian, bisexual, and transgendered lifestyles.

MCC is also a user-friendly congregation. Throughout this book, pastors and leaders are commonly referred to using first names, as has been the practice in the daily workings of the congregation. It is a sign of both respect and positive association, and dates from the earliest pastors.

Metropolitan Community Church is certainly the most physically visible piece of Portlandia's gay culture, although there are groups that can claim more longevity as far back as 1958. The many organizations that have in the past, and do now, compose, the gay community in Portland number well over one hundred. The most significant have been the Gay Liberation Front, The Second Foundation, the Portland Town Council, Equity Foundation, the many AIDS organizations most notably Cascade Aids Project, The Imperial Sovereign Rose Court, and the Portland Gay Men's Chorus. Ecumenical Ministries of Oregon and the Community of Welcoming Congregations have played monumental roles in bringing about healing and acceptance between straight and gay peoples, and establishing dialogue between mainline congregations and other communities of faith.

Introduction

Hand-in-glove has been the involvement of gay-owned and gay-friendly businesses. Early tavern owners allowed, supported, or encouraged an atmosphere not only of fun and escape, but provided venues where small groups planned and large groups celebrated and mourned. Names like The Harbor, Dahl and Penne's, The Other Inn, The Half Moon, Embers, Riptide, JR's, Flossie's, CC Slaughter's, Scandals', Starkey's, JOQ's, The Cadillac, Old Wives' Tales, Wilde Oscars', Jonah's, Roxy Harts, the Fox and Hounds, and so many more remind Portland's gay community members of their pivotal role as meeting places.

Within the gay community, Portland has had a disproportionate number of active, energetic, talented, and persistent individuals who have emerged in good times and bad to provide inspirational leadership. A short list of these would have to include John Baker, Terry Bean, Gary Coleman, Darcelle, Glen Dugger, Sandy Director, Steven Fulmer, Holly Hart, Donna Redwing, Neil Hutchins, George Nicola, George Oberg, Susie Shephard, Steve Suss, and Jerry Weller.

Portland's religious community has played a major role in advancement of human rights, diversity, and support for gay individuals, organizations, and churches. That list has to include Art Buck, Joe Dubay, Kiernan Healey, Charles Hinkle, Robert McNeil, Rodney Page, Harper Richardson, Pat and Gene Ross, Pat and John Schwiebert, Rita and Charles Knapp, and Ann and Bill Shepherd.

The progress of the gay community could not have happened without the support and active leadership of elected politicians at many levels. The community has been blessed with the friendship and services of Connie McCreedy, Bud Clark, Neil Goldschmidt, Vera Katz, Gretchen Kafourey, Gladys McCoy, Mike Lindberg, Sam Adams, Tom Potter, and Barbara Roberts, Gordon Smith, and Ted Kulongoski to mention just the higher office holders.

Assembling a comprehensive picture of this congregation and the sexual minority community from which it emerged is the goal of this book. The church will never be known for its ability to keep and preserve archives. Even after days of digging into dust-covered storage boxes in the church tower, the archaeology of MCC-Portland is incomplete. There is no complete set of service bulletins or church newsletters. Many objects of interest and history have deteriorated, grown legs, or have been discarded by well-meaning (?) committees making space for something else.

Personal interviews, phone and e-mail conversations, skimming 35 years of mainstream and community newspapers, combing the existing old service bulletins and monthly newsletters have all helped this history come into focus. Archives at the Oregon Historical Society, the Multnomah County Library, and several private libraries have provided a wealth of background material. And there's been a significant amount of prayer.

My research has led to the Multnomah County Library, the City of Portland Archives, and some jumbled storerooms. The Oregon Historical Society, its research staff, and Susan Seyl in particular, have been of enormous help. Fortunately, many savers and hoarders of historic papers and tidbits have become friends and advisors –Gregg Pitts and his wonderful photo and newspaper collection, Neil Hutchin's photos and complete run of the *Cascade Voice*, Dick Burdon's files of MCC and Methodist memorabilia; Steven Stone's research on Portland Theaters; Tom Cook's boxes of research and writing; photos from Marty Davis and the *Just Out* archive, Ann Mussey at Portland State University, Rob Douglass and Pat Young of the Gay and Lesbian Archives of the Pacific Northwest collection, stored at the OHS.

Without exception, individuals previously unknown to me have agreed to interviews and provided the corrections, details, and tidbits that have made this process so fascinating to me. Nearly everyone I interviewed recommended at least one other person to contact, resulting in the discovery of unassuming individuals tucked away in Portland with marvelous stories to tell. I regret that I ran out of time and space for more.

Introduction

Thankfully, I've been able to benefit from several individuals who have been with MCC since its inception–Bill Barry, Dan Brown, Eric Cordingly, Neil Curry, Dave Dishman, Chuck Harvey, Denis Moore, Betty Nelson, Larry Foltz and Troy Perry. Four former senior pastors have been very helpful–Don Borbe, Jim Glyer, Delores Berry, and Roy Cole. I have been unable to contact Gary Wilson, so his chapter had to be written without the benefit of his input. Current senior pastor Glenna Shepherd has been so supportive of this project. For their reading of parts of the manuscript, I owe a debt of thanks to many people. Verna Dice, Dave Dishman, Rich Kibbons, Betty Nelson, and Frank Myers generously gave of their time to proofread. My patient editor and *ho pang yau*, Bruce Richards has endured my foibles of poor grammar, spelling, and innuendo. Maggie Rogers offered invaluable insight into the indexing process. Pamela Martin's services as proofreader have eased my mind. Bill Dickey's generosity and advice have been instrumental, and I appreciate the publishing experience of Suzanne Deakins and marketing counsel from Elizabeth Doggett.

It has been a marvelous adventure. I hope you enjoy the tale. I've tried my best to put this together factually. For all errors in date, detail, or substance, I accept full responsibility. I welcome comments and corrections through the church's website: www.mccportland.com or by phone at 503-281-8868. Correspondence and inquiries about copies of the book can be addressed to MCC History Project, 2400 NE Broadway, Portland, Oregon 97232.

Dave Kohl
Portland, Oregon
January, 2006

Charles M. Schulz...as found in a 1977 MCC *Chalice* newsletter.

The Portland Metropolitan area, spreading into parts of three counties, straddles the Willamette River from Oregon City and West Linn until it joins into the Columbia River north of St. Johns. This 2005 real estate map identifies the major areas by their common designations. Some are separate municipalities like Beaverton and Lake Oswego. Others are neighborhoods, like Irvington, Concordia, and Ladd's Addition.

While the GLBT community is spread throughout the Metro area, there are concentrations of gay men in the Northwest, Beaverton and Irvington, and lesbians in Sullivan's Gulch, Ladd's Addition, and Buckman. The Pearl District is a recent development, a conversion of inner industrial and rail yards into new high rise condominiums and converted warehouses into loft and live-work spaces. Burnside Street divides the area into north and south, and the Willamette divides east from west. The wedge between Williams and the Willamette is designated North Portland, but there is no South Portland since the urban renewal of the 1960s and 1970s.

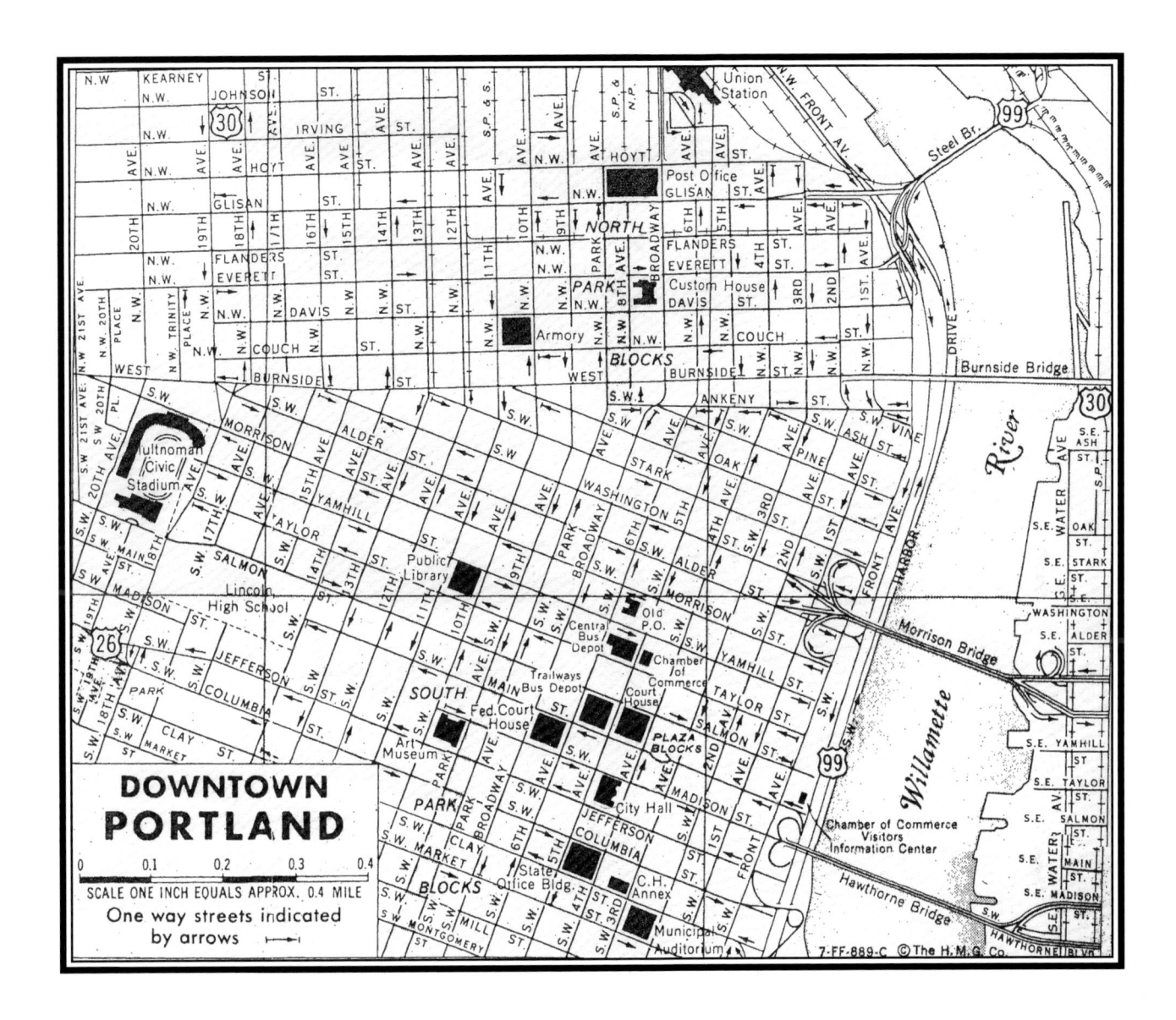

Downtown Portland Street map of 1958, prior to the development of any freeways. Four draw-bridges feed traffic into the city from the east side, where light industrial manufacturing and storage businesses take advantage of riverside docks and rail spurs. Most commercial activity, entertainment facilities, and finer night spots are located south of Burnside and east from SW 18th to the Willamette. Portland State College (later University) is south of Market, straddling the Park Blocks.

Significant gay gathering spots were concentrated around the bus depots. The YMCA was two blocks west from the stations on Taylor, and an area commonly known as "The Camp," was 2 blocks east at Taylor and SW 3rd. North of Burnside was Old Town, then called the North End, the vice district, or Skid Row. Chinatown occupied the zone between 3rd and 4th, from Burnside toward Union Station. Many gambling establishments, flop houses, and itinerant boarding houses were located in the area, as were several transient hotels. The then-new post office marked the eastern edge of rail yards and industrial activity as far as 18th, sometimes called Slabtown. That area would be dissected along 14th by the I-405 and approaches to the Fremont Bridge in 1973. The area began a slow transition in the 1980s, reaching a fervent transformation into the trendy residential and shopping zone, The Pearl District, by 2000.

Photo by Irv Ewen

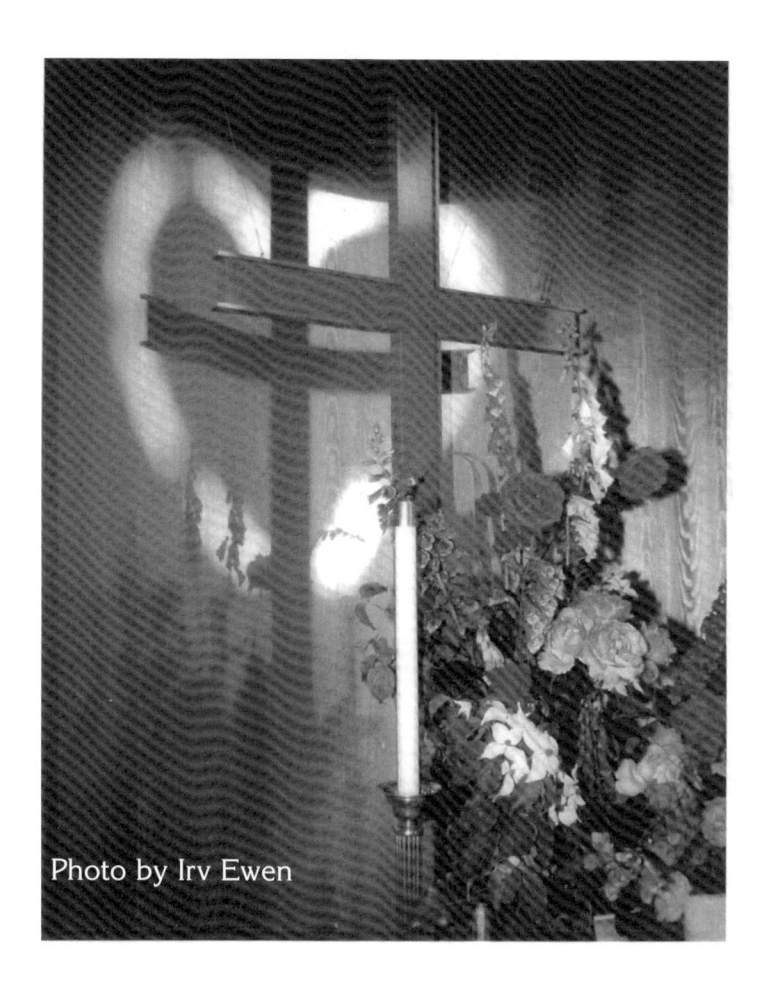

- Lyndon Baines Johnson was the U.S. President;

- Charles DeGaulle ruled France;

- Americans watched the Tet Offensive nightly from Viet Nam on the three networks;

- Martin Luther King Jr. and Bobby Kennedy were assassinated;

- Three days of riots accompanied the Democratic National Convention in Chicago;

- Stanley Kubrick changed filmmaking with *2001-A Space Odyssey*;

- *Hair* opened in New York, celebrating hippies, nudity, drugs, and rebellion;

- *Laugh-In, Mayberry RFD,* and *Family Affair* were the top television programs;

- National Public Radio was going on air with *All Things Considered* and *Sesame Street*;

- The "Cultural Revolution" had just begun in "Red" China;

- A gay minister held a worship service with homosexual Christians in Los Angeles;

- Homosexuality was branded as deviant behavior by the American Psychiatric Association...

It was 1968.

Chapter One
Prelude ~ 1853~1971

"To everything there is a season, and a time for every purpose under heaven"
Ecclesiastes 3:1 (King James Version)

In Portland, Oregon, a small cluster of gay and lesbian Christians started meeting at the YMCA in 1968. In San Diego, a group of frustrated homosexual Roman Catholics were preparing to form an association of worshiping gay Catholics. In Los Angeles, a Pentecostal preacher gathered a dozen gay Christians together for an October worship service in his living room. Troy Perry had resigned from his congregation when his homosexuality was discovered. His new group continued to meet and grow, organizing as the Universal Fellowship of Metropolitan Community Churches. It would expand into a worldwide denomination, the fastest growing American church in the late 20th century.

Nine months later, on June 28, 1969, riots in New York City at the Stonewall Inn would ignite a national liberation movement of gays and lesbians, with far-reaching effects on sexual minority populations in the U.S. and around the world. Their fight for rights and recognition would impact mainstream culture in the last quarter of the 20th century.

Civil rights campaigns and the anti-war movement aligned to challenge the status quo of domestic American life. College students across the Nation questioned traditions on and off campus, demanding new solutions, new definitions, and new understandings from their families, schools, and government.

The interplay of these factors and the energies of determined individuals in the Pacific Northwest would lead to the emergence of a unique Christian congregation on Portland's east side. After two attempts, it would materialize as Metropolitan Community Church of Portland - a community of faith welcoming all people, with special outreach to the gay, lesbian, bisexual and transgender communities.

How that assembly grew through the efforts of individuals, committees, pastors, laity, deacons, student clergy and business people in two run-down relics is a fascinating case study. Involvement of cross-dressers, leather-people, drag shows, bar nights, picnics, renovations, bazaars, potlucks, pinochle sessions, spiritual renewals, congregational meetings, conferences, AIDS, political battles within and without, PRIDE celebrations, music groups, soloists and a 100-man chorus makes a most unusual tale.

It's a story of faith, of course. But this story also includes boldness, courage, naiveté, failure, intrigue, altruism, drama and theater, lots of mistakes, mostly wise planning, determined financing, some predictable quibbling, hurt feelings, emotions, compromise, forgiveness, reconciliation, and healing...and lots of prayer.

And now, for the rest of the story...

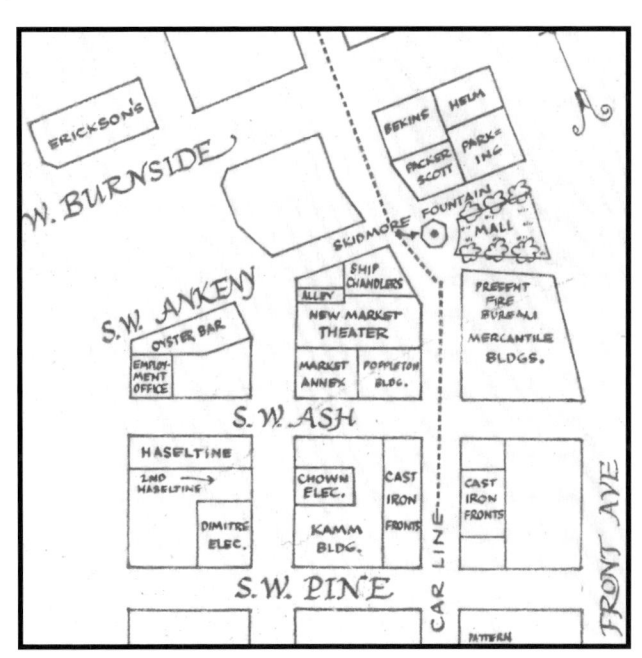

Courtesy of Multnomah County Library

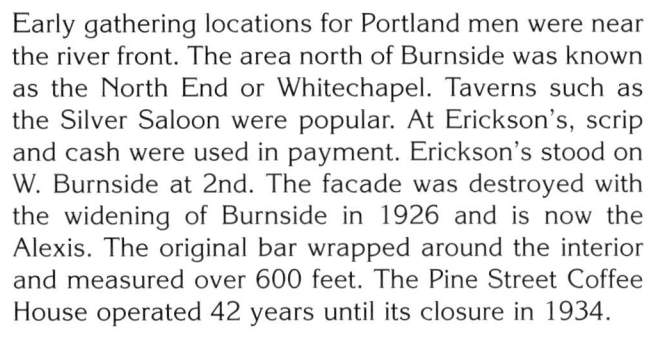

Early gathering locations for Portland men were near the river front. The area north of Burnside was known as the North End or Whitechapel. Taverns such as the Silver Saloon were popular. At Erickson's, scrip and cash were used in payment. Erickson's stood on W. Burnside at 2nd. The facade was destroyed with the widening of Burnside in 1926 and is now the Alexis. The original bar wrapped around the interior and measured over 600 feet. The Pine Street Coffee House operated 42 years until its closure in 1934.

OrHi neg 50614

OrHi neg 21750

OrHi file 1737

OrHi neg 38157

Prelude 1853 - 1971

Records of the early days of MCC-Portland are sketchy. However, it is possible to reconstruct the milieu in which these determined Christians came together to organize, worship, evangelize, party, falter, and eventually thrive as a congregation. In order to focus a full picture of the times, three elements will be considered:

I) Portland Homophile History - 1853 - 1971
II) Civil Rights - Gay Rights
III) The quest by individual gay Christians to find spiritual meaning in their lives, despite being shunned or rejected by their mainline denominations

I. Portland Homophile History

Gay individuals living in Portland in the mid 1960s were a scattered lot. Almost all intimate activity was clandestine, whether meeting at bars, frequenting several bath houses, finding "tricks" on the streets or in the recesses of movie houses; enjoying certain beaches on the Columbia and Willamette Rivers, or gathering to watch semi-annual drag-shows. At some levels, gay activity in Northwest cities – Seattle, Boise, Tacoma, Vancouver BC, and Portland – had been noted since the early 1900s. Two distinct historic *cultures* of homosexuals have been identified:

A. Working class ethnic minority populations of itinerant mostly seasonal laborers ("outsiders"), and;

B. Predominantly white middle class educated men among Portland's more elite society ("insiders").

When Oregon's first Criminal Code was formulated in 1850, no mention of sodomy appeared in the statutes, hence meaning that it was legal. But new criminal codes in 1853 specifically contained an anti-sodomy provision. Beyond this, no notation of same-sex concerns appears in print for the next forty years of Oregon history.

The first mention of same-sex activity in *The Oregonian, The Oregon Journal,* or *The Evening Times* appeared in 1895 with international coverage of the Oscar Wilde trial in London. The well-known author of *The Importance of Being Earnest* was tried and convicted of committing "the love that has no name" with his younger companion, Lord Alfred "Bosie" Douglas.

Careful to avoid specifics but anxious to portray the evil aspect of such activity, a variety of terms were used in Portland's newspapers to refer to such men and their activities, including "degenerate, sot, queer, dandified men, street scourings, inverts, deviates, fairies, and fruiters." Officials often used the term "sodomite." Court language preferred the Latin phrase *pecatum illud inter christianos non nonimandum* (the sin that must not be named among Christians). Although the term "homosexual" had been used clinically since 1869, it was not a word in common use at the turn of the 20th century, and certainly not in the press. The term "gay" would not emerge until the 1930s; nor would "lesbian" become common until the 1950s.

Rose City police had been dealing with same sex activity since the arrival of migratory men in the mining, logging, and fishing populations. Lone men spent "off-season" time living in Portland's North End, off Burnside Street near the rail yards and west of the Willamette River –the area equivalent with today's "Old Town." Portland attracted a concentration of individuals who over the years migrated to the city where the overall atmosphere was relatively more permissive than surrounding rural areas. Because of the high amount of unsavory behavior and subsequent police concern, the area was called "Whitechapel," referring to the infamous area of Victorian London known for similar activity and the legend of Jack the Ripper (1888). Prostitution in all forms was well known there. In Vancouver, BC, the equivalent area was Hastings Street, and in Seattle, it was Skid Road or First Avenue, with its South End Baths.

Many social reformers saw alcohol and its misuse as the root of all evil, including immorality and the decline of the family. Men who sought the bottle were thought to sabotage the family unit in two ways – by being less productive when drunken or recovering, and by frittering away much-needed family money.

Many Portland restaurants were known to have small hidden back rooms where men could "have their way" with available young women.

OrHi neg 53799

OrHi file 1662

Gambling was common in Chinatown, originally on SW 2nd, but moved to NW 4th after the 1894 floods. Chinese clan associations, gambling halls, and opium dens were located in both buildings, the Bow Yuen is now a parking lot at Everett, and the Fong Chong burned(except for the corner) in 1979.

OrHi neg CN 015406

Portland City Archives

Chinese men left families behind to build railroads, then work in Portland. Italian steelworkers built the Hawthorne Bridge in 1910. Italian farmers and vegetable sellers set up shop on Yamhill Street at the produce market. Japanese shopkeepers headquartered where today's Chinatown is located.

OrHi neg 28945

OrHi neg 28933

4

Prelude 1853 - 1971

Taverns, or beer halls, were equated with crime – especially gambling and prostitution. The prohibition movement was headed nationally by the Anti-Saloon league. An Oregon Temperance Society had existed since 1836, founded by Methodist missionary Jason Lee. The State Temperance union formed in 1873, and praying women marched in front of saloons in 1874. Despite these efforts, there were 430 taverns and saloons in Portland by 1910. In that year, Dr. Clarence Wilson of Centenary Methodist Church railed against alcohol and its connection with gambling dens run by Asians. "If we don't Christianize them, they will Paganize us," said the young minister who soon quit Oregon for Chicago, where he became field secretary of the national Temperance Society. Oregon voted to become a dry state in 1916.

Male-male sexuality was a part of the migrant road life, and some men preferred the "road culture" and the variety of men and settings possible with seasonal labor. Newspaper and police reports of the early 20th century mention same-sex activity in Portland and surrounding areas. Men frequented the bars, taverns, card rooms, and poolrooms of the North End, living in cheap housing there as well. Most of these men were from minority ethnic groups –especially Greeks, other European "foreigners," as well as Asian Indians and Chinese from Canton and Hong Kong. They were employed as railroad workers, miners, woodsmen, agricultural workers, or were fortune hunters. (Boag, Peter, *SameSex Relationships*, 2003)

The Vice Clique Scandal of 1912

A more hidden secluded group of homosexuals were white, and part of the mainstream culture of upstanding citizens – primarily clerks, salesmen, office staff, and a few professional men. Portland high society played down the scandal in 1912 involving men of higher rank connected in a ring of sexual "improprieties" with younger men. Despite evidence to the contrary, newspapers of the time consistently chose to name the "victims" as "boys," rather than as "young men," who were over the age of consent. That November, the YMCA building on SW 6th was named as a site of questionable same-sex liaisons, and as the residence of four of the 68 suspects.

The YMCA movement began in London in 1844 and was first established in America in Boston in 1851. Aiming to improve the moral choices available to young men in urban settings, they were non-denominational efforts of Christian volunteers from many local Protestant churches within a community. The city was branded as a moral cesspool, especially because of the temptations of the saloon, brothel, and worst of all, the theater. YMCAs were established in many east coast cities by the time of the Civil War. After the War Between the States, many more "Y's" were established throughout the country. Student YMCAs were opened near many colleges, and "Railroad Y's" were established near urban rail stations. The Portland YMCA dates from 1868, originally in the Gilman Building near the river front.

Portland's YMCA, beginning in an upstairs room near the river front on 1st Street, eventually occupied an entire building. By 1909, a new facility was opened on SW 6th and Taylor, boasting meeting rooms, gymnastic facilities, the Parker Chapel, and hotel-like rooms which young men could rent for $1 per night, or by the month. The new building was evidence of a strong local Association.

A YMCA in a city often drew the local denominations together in the collective effort. Not content with only introspective pietistic prayer meetings, or with revivals for their own sake, energy was directed toward the reformation of male character, the improvement of human relationships, and the inculcation of simple virtues of behavior and morality. YMCAs often became involved in issues around observing the Sabbath; the obliteration of obscene literature and vice activity; and temperance, often combining efforts with the WCTU (Women's Christian Temperance Union).

Solutions to alcoholism included rescuing drunkards, providing public drinking fountains, closing saloons on Sundays, redeeming men's paychecks so they would not have to cash them in a saloon, helping men find employment, and providing temperance tracts and books. Boys who had taken pledges of temperance formed "Cold Water Brigades" to encourage their peers into activities other than

OrHi neg 99069

OrHi neg 12997

The Nob Hill baseball team in 1891 predated the construction of the YMCA on S Broadway in 1909. The YWCA is the smaller half, built a few years later and facing Broadway across from the Fox theater. The YMCA Glee Club of 1915 was composed of both men and boys who sang primarily Christian and patriotic tunes and ballads.

Bicycling became a craze at the turn of the century, providing an outlet for adventurous women and teams of men who pedaled throughout Oregon. One team visited Salem en route to New York. The capitol building was destroyed by fire years later.

OrHi file 1874

OrHi neg 17929

OrHi neg 44011

6

Prelude 1853 - 1971

drinking. Gymnasiums and bowling alleys were added to many "Ys", but recreational activities were discouraged. Courses were offered to educate young men in language, geography, history, religion, and various fine arts.

When the scandal broke, involving some men living at the "Y" as well as young men from the streets and from Whitechapel, the unwelcome news initiated controversy. This was the first revelation that the Portland "Y," founded and publicized "to prevent moral, social and physical deterioration" of young men moving into Portland was, in fact, a venue which enabled the antithesis of its stated values...and even on the premises!

The episode became known as the *Vice Clique Scandal*, "vice" being the popular term encompassing prostitution, gambling, and drug dens.

Newspapers identified the thirteen men arrested as part of a "clique," or "brotherhood" of perverts in an underground "association." Much of the hype was, in reality, a battle between newspapers seeking increased circulation, and several key details were later found to be fabrications of *The Portland News*. *The Oregon Journal* of Nov. 21, 1912 reported an investigation of wholesale acts of "degeneracy and depravity" involving about 50 men and boys. One case reached a sensational trial, defaming an until-then noted local attorney, E.S.J. McAllister. From these events emerged a local popular belief that homosexual men were somehow organized to convert or victimize underage boys. The "Y" experienced a major slump in both membership and financial support for many years thereafter. Yet, in the swimming pool, boys were required to swim in the nude well into the 1940s, for "sanitation" purposes.

Another "affair" was reported in the newspapers in 1913, the same year Portland changed its charter to the Galveston Plan of city management. Five commissioners would be elected citywide, one of whom would be the mayor. This piece of Progressive Era legislation set the format for Portland city government to the present day.

Unsavory Behavior

Author Laurence Pratt relates that in 1915, the Plaza blocks at SW Third and Main were known as places where homosexual pick-ups were possible – which he claimed to discover quite inadvertently. In 1924, to protect innocent women and children from being exposed to any unsavory activity in the two adjacent parks, Chapman Park to the south of Main was designated for women and children only. This left Lownsdale Park north of Main as a defacto men-only area. The brick restroom facilities in each park were boldly identified with bronze letters set into the cement sidewalks – Men in Lownsdale and Ladies in Chapman Park. Ironically, in the attempt to protect society, authorities had created an area perfect for cruising, complete with bricked-in privacy.

Several bars opened within a short distance of the park, the first being the Manhattan Club in 1911 (later to be Dahl and Penne's). The Lotus Cardroom opened on SW 3rd in 1928, followed by Dinty Moore's Tavern next door, and the Little Brown Jug. It was not until the 1970s that the gender restrictions on the parks were lifted.

Women's Issues

Harry Allen was arrested in 1912 on a vagrancy charge. It was found that "he" was a "she" named Nell Pickerall. The sentence was for 60 days in jail. For about twelve years, her dress and exclusive behavior had been that of a man, and she had "fooled many a saloonkeeper." She was typical of several thousand "passing women" that appear in old police records nationwide. Police noted that she walked, talked, swore, drank, and smoked like a man. She also had worn her cowboy garb when she was previously jailed in Spokane on a bootlegging charge. There were unsubstantiated rumors that two girls had fallen in love with Harry, and both committed suicide upon learning his true identity.

In 1912, Oregon also adopted women's suffrage, eight years before the 19th amendment to the U.S. Constitution. The cause of Women's Liberation had received a major boost

OrHi file 1786

Some Portland women set high social standards, like the Women's Convalescent Assn.

OrHi neg 5740

The Floradora girls danced at the 1905 Fair. They were touring performers, like the Beef Trust girls.

Dr Alan Lucill(e) Hart   Harriet Speckhart (OrHi neg 60817) and Dr. Marie Equi (OrHi neg 23494)

OrHi file 1798a

The Nortonia Hotel and lobby (now the Mark Spencer) where Marie and Harriet lived.. Female impersonator Julienne Eltinge came to Portland often in the 1920s and also stayed at that hotel.

OrHi neg 97147

8

Prelude 1853 - 1971

in Oregon when Susan B. Anthony spoke at the unveiling of the Sacagawea sculpture by Alice Cooper during the Lewis and Clark Exposition on July 6, 1905. Noted women's rights activist Inez Milholland Boisevain spoke in Portland and stayed in the Multnomah Hotel on October 10, 1916.

By 1916, the anti-saloon league was also very successful, culminating in the adoption and implementation of statewide prohibition. The Portland Directory listed 406 taverns and beer halls in the Rose City that year. Progressives also pushed for the initiative and referendum system which, when adopted, became known nationwide as the Oregon System. Oregon also began the direct election of Senators. It was an era of great change in the state.

Just south of Burnside at SW 2nd and Ankeny was Dan and Louis' Oyster Bar, a popular eatery under the temporary Portland City Court offices. The area was filled with men on official business as well as out for a good meal. Sporting a red handkerchief in the lapel pocket meant the wearer was open to meeting men for "other purposes," and if a red tie was also worn, this indicated the owner was quite serious about finding a liaison.

Quietly living in Portland at this time were several women living out various sexual identities. Dr. Marie Equi practiced medicine in her offices in the Lafayette Building. She was a lesbian and lived with her longtime partner Harriet Speckhart at five different locations over time, including the Nortonia Hotel on SW 11th, now called the Mark Spencer. She also raised an adopted daughter, Mary. Dr. Equi provided abortions and early medical care for women in "desperate" situations. These patients were often indigent or immigrants, commonly without the means to pay. Dr. Equi was popularly known as a "Good Samaritan" but she also held radical political beliefs, which brought her eventually into court on charges of sedition, for which she was temporarily imprisoned.

Another well-known medical doctor was Alan Lucill(e) Hart. As a medical student at Albany College (later Lewis and Clark) about 1917, she had sought psychological analysis with Dr. Allen Gilbert in the Selling Building. Dr. Gilbert had suggested that Lucill(e) deal with her "sexual inversion" by living as a man, rather than to try to convert or cure herself. She underwent a hysterectomy and as Dr. Alan Hart, dressed and lived the role of a male, first marrying Inez Stark. They were divorced in 1925 and he married Edna Ruddick a schoolteacher. Dr. Hart specialized in the study of X-rays (discovered by another woman in France, Marie Curie) and their application in the diagnosis of tuberculosis. Hart was also a novelist, penning *Dr. Mallory, The Undaunted, In the Lives of Men,* and *Dr. Finley Sees It Through,* published by Harper and Brothers. Dr. Hart lived to age 74, dying in Connecticut in 1962. Inez outlived Lucill(e), dying at age 92 in 1986.

Some well-known visitors to Portland also raised same-sex issues. On August 7 and 8, 1915, noted lecturer Emma Goldman spoke at the Turn Verein Hall, located on the NE corner of SW 4th and Yamhill. She regularly toured and spoke on controversial topics of the day–birth control, socialism, Russian drama, and Frederick Nietzsche – and was often categorized as an anarchist. Her topic that August, however, was on *The Intermediate Sex,* being a reference to a term then made popular by her friend Edward Carpenter, who had published a book by the same name a few years earlier. *The Oregonian* advertisement for her talk aroused major objections, but she did present two lectures. In her autobiography *Living My Life,* she regarded her lecture as an extraordinary defense of the homosexual to live his/her life without society's stigmatization. Many "inverts" thanked her for the presentation. But her critics also had their way. The Rose City police later arrested her on charges of distributing "obscene" birth control literature.

Another regular visitor to Portland was the famous vaudevillian Julian Eltinge, bringing his musical extravaganzas to the Heilig Theater (later renamed the Fox) on Broadway. Eltinge is considered the most famous female impersonator of the live stage show era, and always included Portland on his West Coast tours in the 1920's, where he was received by sold-out enthusiastic audiences.

The bell staff at the Imperial Hotel in 1912.

Imperial Hotel on S Broadway after the 1922 addition, including a popular men's restroom.

Portland police on their new motorcycles in front of the new 1928 headquarters building on SW 2nd, at the edge of old Chinatown.

Some women became machinists, others joined the Women's Ambulance Corps or gave up their latex swimsuits for the war effort.

Prelude 1853 - 1971

Same-Sex Activity Between World Wars

Another series of Rose City police investigations occurred during the "Roaring 20's." In 1928, it became well known among white middle class men interested in same-sex liaisons that the first floor men's room of the Imperial Hotel on SW Broadway was a reliable cruising spot. The wearing of a green suit was an indicator of availability for a same-sex "adventure." In an effort to curtail this activity, the Imperial imposed a dime charge to use the facility, a fee that continued well into the 1980s. Apparently the 10-cent fee was a major deterrent! The most popular residential area for single men at the time was conveniently near that hotel in rooming houses and apartments off Broadway. City records indicate an abnormally high percentage of single men residing in the area, where there were many boarding houses and restaurants.

Portland experienced the rush of energy known as the Roaring 20s, with several "speakeasys" and lots of vaudeville acts passing through town. Several local theaters were constructed expressly for vaudeville shows. High society had its men-only clubs, and well-to-do women were sure to be found at the Japanese Tea Room in the Multnomah Hotel mezzanine viewing the afternoon fashion shows put on by Lipman's Department Store. It was also the only venue in town where women could smoke cigarettes in public.

Any issues around homosexuality and individual homosexuals were caught up in a greater matrix of conflict between the economic classes of Portland society during the first third of the 20th century. Prohibition and the Great Depression brought on changing times. Immigration patterns and racism, especially towards European and Chinese reinforced a socioeconomic hierarchy. Portland's African-American population was basically confined to the Albina neighborhood near the Union Pacific railyards, one primary source of employment. Urbanization and industrialization changed the face of local neighborhoods. Many Portland neighborhoods experienced decline to near - ghetto status, and many homeless lived under the bridges over Sullivan's Gulch during the Depression.

The turmoil of World War I and the devastation of the 1918 influenza epidemic decimated the population significantly. Geographic mobility was made possible by the mass production of the automobile. The women's suffrage movement, and the growth of unionized labor in the build-up to another World War affected societal roles for both men and women.

When America mobilized after the unprovoked Japanese attack on Pearl Harbor on December 7, 1941, many social changes took place within weeks. The U.S. was in sore need of the machines of war– tanks, airplanes, and ships of all sizes. Domestic production of cars and appliances was placed on hold during the war years.

During World War II, millions of service men passed through Portland. Over 72,000 workers came to work in the Portland and Vancouver shipyards from across the country– from city, town, and farm. The Hoyt Hotel was the first lodging place many men found after getting off the train at Union Station. In the tight housing market, a man could get a space at the Hoyt only if he agreed to work for the Hoyt's favored shipyard.

Included in the migrant groups were a large number of women, working at many jobs in the Oregon Steel shipyards and Kaiser plants, previously held by men. *Rosie the Riveter* flourished, and many women established homes and often raised children as single parents, especially in the Vanport area near the docks of North Portland.

One opportunity for women to help with national defense in 1939 was joining the new Oregon Women's Ambulance Corps, in anticipation of a Japanese attack on the west coast and a need for emergency services. The women practiced driving the Packard ambulances, marched in formation at parades, and became accustomed to military drills by marching on Duniway Field. This appealed to many gay women, who accounted for at least half of the sign-ups in 1942. In 1943, many of these women soon enrolled in the Women's Army Auxiliary Corps, an Army regiment proposed by Missouri Senator Oneta Culp Hobby. Recruits

OrHi neg 75228

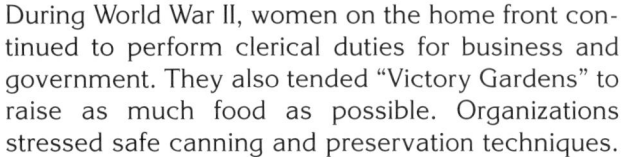

OrHi neg 66729

OrHi file 1786

During World War II, women on the home front continued to perform clerical duties for business and government. They also tended "Victory Gardens" to raise as much food as possible. Organizations stressed safe canning and preservation techniques.

The old Linnton bus parked on NW 11th, near present-day Powell's Books. Many people took shelter in the Foster Hotel on NW 3rd after the 1948 Vanport Flood. The awning marked "Suits" became Demas' Tavern, later bought by Darcelle XV. After WW II, women became more independent, even doing delivery jobs on motorcycles.

OrHi neg 78285

Portland City Archives

Portland City Archives

12

Prelude 1853 - 1971

from colleges and groups like the OWAC entered with instant rank. The women performed primarily office jobs, and assisted with medical work when injured men returned after the June 6, 1944 D-Day invasion.

WACs and WAVs supplemented many previously male-only postings during and after WW II, some serving in the Korean Conflict as well. Several of the women veterans formed the Dana King American Legion *Post* in Portland, one of only two female American Legion posts in the entire country. The bonds these women formed became one backbone of the viable lesbian community in Portland. A few of them would later attend MCC in the late 1970s.

The U.S. Army also brought together legions of gay men, who had to lie when asked if they were homosexual during intake. Documentation and oral histories from these soldiers did not surface until many years after the men returned to civilian life. Military men and women served with honor, but in fear of being found out and receiving a "blue discharge," usually eliminating any GI benefits. It also made it difficult for such a discharged man to get a civilian job.

Portland's population grew by 160,000 over the war years. This situation brought together a huge, largely single, new population, and if Alfred Kinsey's later 1948 study is correct, statistically 5% to 10% of them were same-sex oriented. Being away from their traditional home roots, they were more likely to explore their inclinations in the anonymous new world of urban venues along the banks of the Willamette, especially in the setting of personal and societal upheaval during wartime.

Portland's entertainment industry supported theaters, dance halls, restaurants, illicit gambling joints, and other legal and non-legal entertainment establishments. City officials were concerned in 1942 about "taverns which have been getting out of hand," referring to bootlegging and other alcohol-related problems. Prostitution was giving Portland the reputation as a "wide open town," a situation that was only finally controlled in the 1980s. Many lower class movie houses became known as hangouts for individuals seeking anonymous sexual encounters in the climatically controlled dark recesses of the upper balconies. Downtown, the Circle, Capitol, Blue Mouse and Round-Up theaters were notorious for their balcony smoking sections where clandestine sexual encounters in-volving both sexes were common. Most balconies had a defacto men-only area. Farther to the east, the Walnut Park and Bob White theaters were especially popular (notorious?).

After World War II

Mainstream Americans were shaken in their images and definitions of male sexuality with the 1948 publication of Dr. Alfred Kinsey's *Sexual Behavior in the Human Male*, a study based on over 12,000 interviews with men from all walks of life and from all parts of the country. For closeted and isolated men with homosexual leanings, it was an academic avalanche of validation. Over 50 pages were dedicated to men's homosexual outlets.

It was estimated that over 37% of American men had experienced a same-sex encounter to orgasm, and that 5-10% of men were exclusively gay in their sexual practices. Kinsey noted the difficulty in securing factual data on the nature and extent of male-male activity, due to the Jewish and Christian branding of abnormality and immorality. Anglo-American legal practices and penalties made men reluctant to share their innermost sexual secrets until the anonymity of Kinsey's study, supported in part by the Rockefeller Foundation, made it safe to tell all.

Kinsey's book, and his later study, *Sexual Behavior in the Human Female* (1950), did liberate men and women to start cracking open their personal closet doors.

Stumptown's older bars, which had been quiet "gay" gathering places, received increased business, and new bars opened to serve the wartime and post-war crowds. With a setting of relaxed morality, several gathering places were popular–the Cupboard and the 19th Hole in the Broadway Theater building the Rathskeller near the Greyhound terminal and the YMCA; the Buick Cafe; the Music Hall Club; the Harbor Club; and Dinty Moore's Tavern, next to the Lotus on SW 3rd.

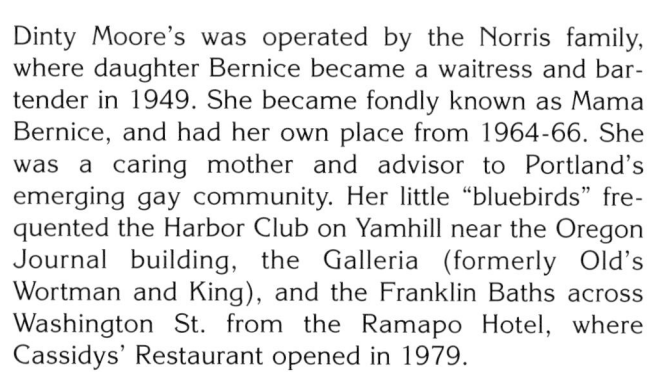

Portland City Archive

Greg Pitts Archive

Dinty Moore's was operated by the Norris family, where daughter Bernice became a waitress and bartender in 1949. She became fondly known as Mama Bernice, and had her own place from 1964-66. She was a caring mother and advisor to Portland's emerging gay community. Her little "bluebirds" frequented the Harbor Club on Yamhill near the Oregon Journal building, the Galleria (formerly Old's Wortman and King), and the Franklin Baths across Washington St. from the Ramapo Hotel, where Cassidys' Restaurant opened in 1979.

OrHi neg 50421

Portland City Archive

Portland City Archive

Prelude 1853 - 1971

Swollen rivers overflowed their banks on Memorial Day, 1948, inundating and destroying the North Portland community of Vanport within hours. Fifteen people died and the Vanport Flood left 18,500 homeless. Refugees from the raging Columbia found shelter with friends and family throughout Portland, or took up residence in low cost hotels. The Foster Hotel on NW Davis housed many of these victims. It would later be the home of Demas' Tavern (Darcelle's), Odyssey (CC Slaughters), and Dobie's (Fox and Hounds).

Portland's Own Mama Bernice

In 1949, working mother Bernice Norris began tending bar at Dinty Moore's. Although straight, she soon endeared herself as "Mama Bernice" to her patrons, especially gay men. When in 1964 Arthur Brannen opened a bar in the Old Phoenix, he hired Mama to tend his bar, naming the new business Mama B's Inn. From this perch, Mama kept an eye on young men (she called them her bluebirds) frequenting the Aero Vapors Bath House directly across 3rd.

Near the bus depot, other taverns were the Reed, Brown Jug, Rose City, and Buddy's Post. Nearer to the Willamette were the Transfusion Inn, the sleazy Old Glory (Glory Hole) and a mysterious eatery known fondly as "Mother Featherstone's Finishing School for Frustrated Faggots." Two of the Transfusion Inn lady barkeeps had done time for theft. It and the downstairs of the Harbor Club became popular with independently minded women. The story is told of one day when a group of lesbians became upset with harassment from gay men at the Harbor. They exited the Club, found a Volkswagen belonging to one of the men, picked it up, and set it up against the doorway, trapping the men inside. Portland police were called to remove the vehicle.

Also popular were several bathhouses. Public baths were once essential, many lower income homes lacking indoor plumbing and the luxury of a bathtub until after World War I. Baths were built as part of the Civic Auditorium in 1918 and in the basement of many hotels constructed before the War, such as the Franklin, Cornelius, and the Royal Palm. The oldest baths date from 1903–the McMahon Mineral Baths at SW 4th and Washington, which later became the downtown Olympic Baths. There were Turkish baths in the basement of the Multnomah Hotel, operating as a separate business from the hotel. Several spas were located in the Portland Hotel and the Dekum Building. Many of these had disappeared or were in decline by the 1960s.

The Aero Vapors at 1237 SW 3rd was the best known, with twenty-two canvas bunks and a maximum capacity for sixty-seven "guests." Until Mama Bernice's closed in 1966, the observant and quick-tongued Bernice kept an eye on her patrons heading in and out of the Vapors. The Aero was demolished as part of the South Auditorium Urban Renewal Project and is now the site of Terry Schrunk Plaza–named for Portland's anti-gay mayor. Competing for bathhouse patrons was the Olympic Baths on Morrison. When urban renewal took down the Olympic, it relocated downtown in the old McMahon Baths on SW 4th and Washington, and uptown on SW 12th across Alder from First Presbyterian Church, later to be called The Workout. The Majestic Hotel Baths at SW 12th and Stark also drew men interested in afternoon delights. Other baths were under the Franklin Hotel, under the Cornelius Hotel, later converted into the Continental baths with an outside entrance on Park Ave., and at the Aero Club, an exclusive members-only "old boy's" club on Taylor near Hamburger Mary's.

North of Burnside were Japanese baths in Chinatown, and the Finnish Baths under the Royal Palm Hotel and Seamen's Center, both on NW 3rd.

The YMCA reentered public awareness as a sexual depot in 1951 where nearly one hundred of the city's supposedly best residents were "indulging in a modern Sodom and Gomorrah play." A system for connecting men with boys of their favorite type was expedited using a card index system. The "male prostitutes on call" were cataloged by age, price, and physical qualities. The index keeper supposedly lived in the adjoining YWCA. Many indictments led to time in the hoosegow. Some of the accused committed suicide rather than being "found out." Scores of boys were sent to "reform school."

OrHi neg 52847

OrHi neg 60095

The Harbor Club opened in 1946, earning a reputation so bad as to be off-limits to sailors. It became very popular with lesbians and gay men. Many women of the time worked in large numbers for Pacific Telephone, and single women could reside at the Martha Washington Hotel, on SW 11th, later known as the Rajneesh Hotel. Cross dressing men at the Music Hall in 1950 earned the ire of Mayor Dorothy McCullough Lee, who learned about the atom bomb from a friendly boy scout.

Portland City Archive

OrHi file 643a

GLAPN Archive

Prelude 1853 - 1971

Women's Neighborhoods

An area that attracted many women was around Hawthorne Boulevard from Ladd's Addition eastward. A large number of women-owned businesses opened and flourished along the Boulevard, making the area attractive to female households on into the 1960s. The displacement caused by the South Portland urban renewal and the construction of Portland State University destroyed much of the Lair Hill neighborhood, transferring many "hippie-types" to the low cost Hawthorne area. "Head shops," cafes, coffeehouses, and shops catering to female tastes and interests continue to set the tone for this now-trendy zone of southeast Portland. Farther south, closer to Milwaukie, Bertie Lou's Cafe opened in 1943, a small hole-in-the-wall eatery owned and run by women. In the 1970s, Bertie Lou advertised monthly in gay community newspapers. It still exists with the motto "good food and bad service since '43."

In the late 1950s, women's baseball in Portland was dominated by a team supported by florist Irv Lind. The women achieved championship status. Proudly named The Florists, they drove to Chicago in a three-car caravan in 1962 to compete in national playoffs. One of the drivers was Pat Cach, later to join MCC and serve as church secretary.

The women had a marvelous time on the team, and while all the lesbians knew who each other were, they selectively shared that information with the other players. A number of the gay women happened to work in the shipping room at Monkey (oops) Montgomery Wards catalog store on NW Vaughn. The bonding there was more-or-less equivalent to the scores of men who staffed Meier & Frank.

Most women tended to socialize via potluck meals, coffee klatches, and backyard gatherings, although women did begin to gather across the Willamette in downtown Portland at the Transfusion Inn, the Model Inn, the Milwaukie Tavern on Burnside, and at the Harbor Club, which was also a gay men's watering hole upstairs. In Old Town on NW 4th there was the Magic Gardens, known affectionately as the "Plastic Fern."

Under the east side Hawthorne Bridge approach was The Other Side of Midnight, a women-only bar, originally called The Ramp. It was well known that men were only welcome (tolerated?) if they were escorted by a woman. Another popular establishment was the 927, also a lesbian mecca for many years at, where else...927 SE Morrison. In spite of these many choices, women often spent weekends in Seattle, where bars could stay open two hours later than Portland watering holes.

Sometime in the early 1970s, a group started making sounds on washboards, comb-and-tissue paper, and various ad hoc instruments, including an old stoneware jug. Soon the group evolved into a decent-sounding ensemble, performing as Pearl Stewart and the Rock Mountain Mamas. You guessed it - they became the Portland Women's Jug Band, which continued for many years, and performed at MCC women's events in the early 1980s.

Official Harassment – The Axe Lady

From 1949 to 1952, Mayor Dorothy McCullough Lee relentlessly tried to expose illegitimate activity, but was only able to convince the OLCC (Oregon Liquor Control Commission) to close down impersonation acts. As Portland's first female mayor, she claimed that she had eliminated "lewd customers to protect Portland society."

The Music Hall club was located on SW 10th at Washington, near the Bohemian Restaurant. There, live "impersonator" shows were staged as early as 1938, which often included local and traveling burlesque performers. The upstairs stage also featured drag shows to a loyal audience "in the know." The Backstage Bar and Zebra Supper Club were also connected under the same liquor license. However, when the Music Hall double-booked the Mills Brothers with an opener drag performance in 1949, several unenlightened patrons there to see the well-known black singing group were outraged. They made a fuss to City Hall, bringing the negative investigations of Mayor Lee, and the eventual closure of the Hall in 1950. Oregon Liquor Control Commission records noted "lewd and indecent entertainment on premise and failed to serve bona fide meals to public as

Rathskeller

DINE & DANCE Every Night

Featuring the BEST STEAKS in Town!

Mike Kokich & Joe Kralovich, Prop.

★ ★ ★

722 S.W. Taylor   BEacon 1737

The Rathskeller was located on Broadway and Taylor in a former horse stable, near the Fox Theater and the YMCA. This photo was taken in 1948, the year before it became the Rhumba Room, which did not remain in business very many years.

Portland's most elegant hotel in the 1950s was the Multnomah on SE 4th and Pine St. Fashion conscious women socialized and smoked there in the 1930s, but it became popular with single men seeking an afternoon "pick-me-up" after the opening of the Jester Bar in 1954. In that year, Oregonians were granted OLCC permission to buy liquor by the glass for the first time. A full contingent of service staff proudly served presidents and other visiting dignitaries in starched uniforms.

MULTNOMAH HOTEL

This 1952 staff photo was provided by Joe Gimarelli (second from the right in the upper row). Now retired, he still offers professional advice to bellmen of the Embassy Suites, which re-opened the hotel in 1995, after 30 years as a government office building.

Joe Gimarelli archive

Prelude 1853-1971

required by law." Mayor Lee was not reelected in 1952, but in 1953 the National Hurricane Center began using women's names for tropical cyclones. Surely this was coincidence?

The Rathskeller, over an old horse stable at 722 SW Taylor, was closed in 1949 for lewd behavior by patrons and for serving minors. It evolved into the Rhumba Room, but it, too, was another targeted closure, reputedly because of the play in the restroom rather than the action onstage. Mayor Lee was also well-known for taking an axe to pinball machines in taverns, intent on driving out gambling and corruption. She had several unsavory nicknames.

Anti-homosexual campaigns were launched in many American cities, including nearby Seattle during and after the anti-communist hearings led by Wisconsin Senator Joseph McCarthy in Washington, DC. Portland authorities, however, decided to be less threatening, reasoning that it was better to leave the gays alone than to bust up their gathering places and then not know where they could be found.

Portland Police worked to entrap gay men in parks and public restrooms with some success. Joe McCarthy's witch hunts for communists expanded to include perverts, the two groups being nearly synonymous in the minds of the authorities. It was assumed/implied that gays could not hold government jobs, since they would be subject to blackmail, lest they be "exposed." Actor Jack Webb, playing Herbert J. Philbrick in the popular 1950's TV series *I Led Three Lives*, could have led four–Communist spy, U.S. double agent, mild-mannered citizen ...and a closeted homosexual. But America wasn't ready to even think about it.

The Multnomah Hotel Sets A Standard

The Multnomah Hotel at SW 4th and Pine became the first Oregon hotel to serve liquor by the glass in 1954 after State liquor laws were changed. The Multnomah had eclipsed the Portland Hotel as the fashionable site for local events and visiting dignitaries (Charles Lindberg stayed there in October, 1927; President Eisenhower in 1952, etc.). Luncheon meetings usually filled the Multnomah each working day, and grand events were held in the downstairs Arcadian Garden.

With the change in Oregon Liquor Control Commission rules, a bar was carved out of the lobby-level Stirrup Room known as the Jester. The name was in keeping with the medieval theme of the hotel's Golden Knight room and Cafe Baron (where the "Baron of Beef" originated). Immediately popular in those days of near-paranoia about public drinking, the Jester soon had a piano bar, and music by Bart Woodrow or Jack Baine. The Jester was described as a pleasant drinking room, with an unobstructed view into the lobby, which featured "pick-me-ups" for the downtown business crowd. The concept that would become the "happy hour" had been born.

Soon discovered by discrete gays, the Jester served as an ideal venue to see and be seen, and to meet "friends of Dorothy." Dorothy refers to Dorothy Parker of the New York City Algonquin round-table, not Dorothy Gail, and her little dog Toto, of Kansas. To aid in communication, interested men usually wore a green coat, often sporting a pinkie ring on the small finger, and smoking Pall Mall cigarettes. Pall Malls became the fag of choice since their motto was *for men of distinction*.

Several other hotel bars emerged as popular rendezvous venues, including the London Bar at the Benson, the Lanai Room at the Paramount-Heathman, and the Driftwood Bar at the Mallory.

Meier & Frank's 10th floor Georgian Room and the adjacent coffee shop served no alcohol, but became known in the gay underground as a spot to find men interested in casual anonymous encounters. The hairpin-shaped counters in the department store's coffee shop made eye contact easy, if not inevitable. When two men established a mutual unspoken interest, one would leave to use the convenient nearby men's room, where he would most likely be joined by his person of interest.

OrHi neg 76689

OrHi neg 95295

Many gay men held jobs at Meier & Frank's flagship department store downtown and frequented the Georgian Room or the adjacent cafe for lunch. Lippman's was also a popular employer (later sold to Frederick & Nelson). Portland retailer Fred Meyer opened his downtown store on Alder at SW 6th in 1928.

The Star Theater just north of Burnside on NW 6th was one popular venue where live performers augmented scenes on film. Run by the Portland "mafia," it closed shortly after the debacle and scandal of 1957.

Portland City Archive

OrHi neg 103391

20

Prelude 1853 - 1971

Fred G. Meyer

Unique to Portland, Fred Meyer department stores sold groceries, hardware, and more variety of goods and clothing than Meier and Frank or Sears to the middle class. The flagship store was built downtown in 1928. In most Fred Meyer stores, men often waited in the men's room stalls for someone to use the adjacent cubicle, and if contact and interest evolved, they would meet in one closed stall. To eliminate suspicion, one of the two could stand in an empty shopping bag or brief case; hence only one pair of legs would be visible to the curious on the other side of the stall door. Years later with greater bathroom surveillance but larger parking lots, men would catch each other's eye in the parking lot, adjourning to a handy RV or camper for intimacies.

Busted!

In the mid-fifties, newspapers launched campaigns against "sex-deviates," creating an anxiety about perceived child molesters, stating that suspicious characters should be reported around playgrounds and parks. *The Oregonian* ran many anti-homosexual stories, spotlighting men of questionable character, insinuating danger to children and other victims. Men interested in other men used secretive codes to find similar men. Clothing, smokes, jewelry, and "the look" were a few tricks used when venturing into the world beyond wearing *"the mask"*.

The Portland Police Juvenile Division claimed to have broken up four homosexual "rings" by 1956. As fashions changed, girls who wore ducktails and leather jackets were whispered to be lesbians, and were often severely ostracized by teachers and peers. Newspaper articles created an atmosphere of near paranoia over association with anyone who fell into questionable categories because of their dress, appearance, or speech.

Until 1956, Portland's darkest and best kept secret was that there were at least two layers of corruption involving a mafia-like underground that ran much of the city, with the benevolent acquiescence of City Hall and the Police Bureau. Investigations by a U.S. Senate Rackets Committee lawyer named Bobby Kennedy investigated about two dozen Portlanders and subpoenaed them to Washington, DC. Committee hearings were televised locally on Channel 8, featuring Bobby and John Kennedy, and local Portland crime luminaries Jim Elkins, Terry Schrunk, and Nate Zusman. Zusman's club was the Desert Room on Stark Street, which after several changes of ownership later became the Silverado. Multnomah County's District Attorney William Langley pled the Fifth Amendment. New mayor Terry Schrunk, formerly the sheriff under mayor Fred Peterson, failed a polygraph (lie detector test). Other testimonies were questionable or inconclusive.

About 115 indictments were issued by three grand juries to the Portland men. Most of the trials did not lead to convictions. Several of the accused were determined to be criminal psychopaths. Elkins got off because he blackmailed a closeted homosexual judge known to take young men out of the county jail. (Read Phil Stanford's *Portland Confidential*, Westwinds Press, Portland, 2005, for the complete stories.)

Bobby Kennedy went on to pursue Jimmy Hoffa and the Teamsters Union. Most local "businessmen" soon moved their gambling, prostitution, and alcohol-related operations to Las Vegas or Reno. There was a breath of fresh air in the Rose City in the late '50s.

National Homophile and Civil Rights Movements & Literature

A small number of "inverts" in California in the 1950s chose not to go further underground, but rather to form nascent organizations that became known as the homophile movement. In 1948, a "bachelors" support organization formed to promote far left Presidential candidate Henry Wallace. His campaign was unsuccessful. In 1950, some of the Bachelors-for-Wallace men met and formed The Mattachine Society on in Los Angeles under the leadership of Harry Hay. The founders chose to use the term "homophile," believing this new term with its incorporation of the Greek word for love, could help counter the stereotype of homosexuals as purely sexually motivated. Headquarters moved to San Francisco in 1953. The Society

MEN

Men had their own park and toilet ("T" room) in Lownsdale Park near the Camp. Favorite stores included Rich's Cigar Store, originally on Morrison, then on Alder. Besides smokes, they could ask for copies of both One Magazine and the Mattachine Review, publications from California which provided early information about homophile organizations and topics.

Dave Kohl photos

OrHi neg 26917

Tom Cook Collection

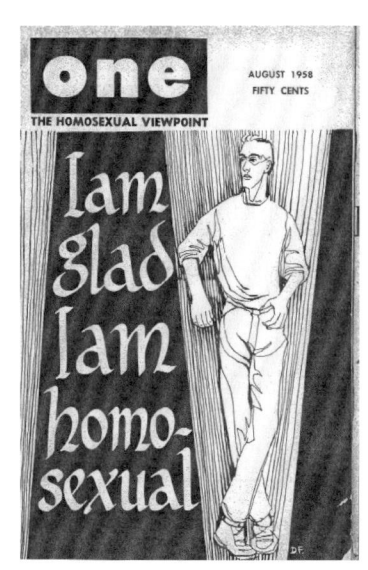

Portland City Archive

22

Prelude 1853 - 1971

began publishing its monthly *Review*. Mattachine was the name of medieval Italian societies wherein clowns, mimes, and jesters would entertain crowds, while hiding true feelings from those in power. (Carter, David, *Stonewall*, St. Martin's Press, NY, 2004)

Dorr Legg started the organization ONE in 1952, growing out of the Mattachine Society. Using Carlyle's quote "...a mystic bond of brotherhood makes all men one," their purpose was education, enlightenment, and encouragement for homosexuals living throughout the country. Their stated purpose was "to aid in the social integration and rehabilitation of the sexual variant...and to aid in the development of social and moral responsibility in all such persons." (*ONE Magazine*, Vol. IV No. 1, Jan. 1956, p4)

By 1959, *ONE Magazine* editor Don Slater clarified his position:

1. Homosexual acts between consenting adults are neither anti-social nor sinful;
2. Legal attempts to regulate such behavior violate American principles of personal freedom, (and) are therefore immoral;
3. Those practicing homosexuality are not doing so because they are either mal adjusted or sick;
4. No scientific verification for such folklore has ever been presented;
5. Homosexuality is a desirable "Way of Life" for many, despite social disapproval and pressure;
6. It is the right of anyone, in a free society, to live according to his (her) convictions, so long as they do not demonstrably harm others;
7. Those who, by reason of judicial, political, scientific, journalistic, or administrative position, use their positions to impose ignorant views to the detriment of homosexual men and women merit only pity and contempt;
8. Time, scientific, and social advances will support each of these points, one by one.

In San Francisco, two Seattle lesbians (Phyllis Lyons and Del Martin) founded the *Daughters of Bilitis (DOB)* in 1955, publishing a journal known as *The Ladder*. That newsletter, *ONE Magazine*, and the *Mattachine Review* could be purchased in Portland only at Rich's Cigar Store, located at 539 SW Washington, before 1961, then at 734 SW Alder. A copy was obtained by asking for one of the hidden copies stored under the counter. An average of 15 copies were sold per month. No one would risk having an issue coming through the mail. Plain mailing wrappers were still in the future. Rich's was one of the few places where condoms were discreetly available in the Rose City.

In 1964, the Society for Individual Rights *(S.I.R.)* formed in San Francisco to promote homosexual awareness, and began publishing the magazine *Vector*, which included articles on gay issues, interviews, creative sexual fiction, and provocative photos. It was a popular publication, with bold photography of full frontal naked men (with only one to a picture). Articles were intellectual, and focused on presenting answers about coming out, pride, and the success of many gay individuals. Also interested in spirituality, the *Vector* carried a large article and review on Troy Perry's *The Lord is My Shepherd and He knows I'm Gay* in September, 1972.

Students at Columbia University in New York formed the first student homophile league in 1967, which then became *NACHO* (North American Conference of Homophile Organ-izations*)*. In February 1967 a Los Angeles homophile group organized *PRIDE (*Personal Rights in Defense and Education). Its newsletter was renamed *The Advocate* in September of that year. By December of 1968, its circulation was 7,000 copies. Changing ownership in 1969, it became the major voice of the homosexual community nationwide.

In England, the Earl of Arran became a hero to British gays by successfully sponsoring the 1966 Sexual Offenses Act in Parliament, which legalized homosexual acts between consenting adults in England. The milestone went pretty much unnoticed in America.

In the 1970s, free thinkers opened food co-coops, like this one in SE Portland. At Vortex, they monitored quality control over local drug supplies. Women found outlets for their own interests, including the 927 bar on SE Morrison and and the Club Northwest (aka the Magic Fern), later called the Magic Gardens in Chinatown, and opened a shelter for homeless and abused women in nearby Old Town.

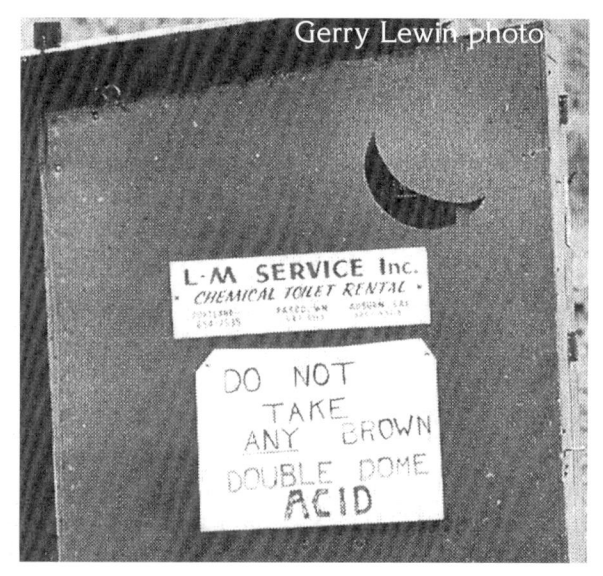

Portland City Archives

Gerry Lewin photo

Dave Kohl photos

Prelude 1853-1971

On newsstands, copies also appeared of the first issue of the *National Lampoon Magazine* in April of 1970. Inspired by *MAD Magazine*, but with more directed purpose, the monthly took an irreverent look at society, using satire and other intellectual humor to rail against the institutions and individuals held responsible for the perceived failures and frustrations of American life. No aspect of American life was immune from satiric ridicule, and these publications would influence the offbeat thinking of a generation. *The Lampoon* soon produced the film *Animal House*, the top-grossing comedy of its time, which satirized American idioms and institutions. It would usher in later gross-out film comedies such as *American Pie*. Wits the likes of Bill Murray, John Belushi, and Christopher Guest were propelled into the national spotlight. But we digress...

Music, Poetry, and Altered Minds

Nationwide, changes were also happening in the popular music culture that would affect social attitudes. The quiet comfort of the post-War "Pax Americana" was about to be altered. In 1954, Elvis Presley made his first soon-to-be epic recording *That's Alright, Mama*. In his first live concert, his legs shook nervously in rhythm with the music, setting his audience a twitter. The rest is history. He also appeared live in Portland in September 1957, in the company of Mayor Schrunk.

Capitalizing on the popularity of folk music and the good feelings generated by group singing, Mitch Miller launched his weekly *Sing-Along* on national TV. Families sat and sang in their living rooms. There were just three TV networks. Radio star and bandleader Ozzie Nelson and wife Harriet starred in their own TV show, which soon began to feature their guitar strumming younger son Ricky. He gave popular music a real garden party, and an alternative to crooner Pat Boone's ballad of *April Love*.

In the late '50s, an American "beat" poet said, "I sleep with men and with women. I am neither queer, or not queer, nor am I bisexual. My name is Allen Ginsberg and I sleep with whoever I want." Ginsberg's adherents became known as "beatniks" (a term perhaps inspired by the launch of the Soviet Union's "Sputnik" satellite in 1957). Known as "drop-outs," or non-conformists, most lived primarily in "pads" (rooms) in New York City's Greenwich Village and the Montgomery Block in San Francisco. Many were "laid-back," non-confrontive, and accepting of just about any philosophy or practice, including homosexuality. Social conformity was seen as an evil. Opposite in philosophy were the "squares," those who stayed within societal boundaries, dressed traditionally, and participated in the concentrated scientific education triggered by the USSR's lead in the "Space Race." In other words, they were "nerds," "pencil-heads," or later, "geeks."

At the same time, experimentation with a mind-altering chemical began to surface. Even Henry Luce, editor of *TIME Magazine*, took several "hits" of Lysergic Acid Diethylamide (LSD), claiming he once "talked to God on the golf course and found that the Old Boy was pretty much on top of things." Other intelligentsia to try this hallucinatory drug, which the government had discovered in 1938 as part of its search for a non-invasive "Truth Serum," were Ginsberg, Christopher Isherwood, Aldous Huxley, and Mrs. (Clare Booth) Luce, the Grande Dame of postwar American politics.

What began as a civilized afternoon soiree soon came to the attention of psychology doctor Timothy Leary, who did not want to interpret ecstasy as mania, or serene calm as a catatonic state. Psilocybin (mushrooms) was administered to prisoners to see if it would alter their criminal thinking. Mushroom pills were given to theology students to focus on the relationship between drug-induced and naturally occurring religious experiences. Some post-trippers felt a rush of messianic philosophy, wanting to teach the world to stop hating and to start a movement of love and peace.

Near San Francisco, volunteer graduate students were paid $75 a day to be part of a study group using psychotomimetic drugs. One was a graduate writing student named Ken Kesey. After the study was completed, Kesey became an attendant in the psychiatric ward at Veterans Hospital in Menlo Park. Psychedelic

Portland City Archive

Portland City Archive

OrHi file 608

The Lovejoy Viaduct over the NW rail yards were little-known locations popular with migrant artists who also found shelter there until their destruction in the 1990s, with the development of the Pearl District. While the Kennedys set social standards in Washington, counterculture hero Ken Kesey wrote of drug trips, traveling U.S. highways in a converted pre-war bus like this one outside Portland's Central Bus Depot on SW 6th, which later became the Trailways depot.

OrHi neg 24223

Just Out Archive

Prelude 1853 - 1971

drugs like LSD, Mescaline, Ditran, and IT-290 were soon circulating among his friends, and Kesey's first novel *One Flew Over the Cuckoo's Nest* came into being. With earnings from the highly successful book, he purchased a country home fifty miles south of the Bay, which became a mecca for dopers ("acid heads"), beatniks, and intellectuals. He toured the country in a refurbished 1939 International Harvester bus named "Further," complete with bunks, shelving, a sink, and a fridge. Nineteen "Pranksters" dressed in tattered clothing patched with parts of American Flags tripped their way to Phoenix and New York City in 1964.

"Dope" became widely available. Its use was made political by the very fact that it was illegal. That it was fun and illegal made it even more tantalizing. Consumption, possession, selling, and ownership of the full range of mind bending substances were thus destined to dominate legislative and judicial agendas for decades. Auxiliary materials like black lights, Peter Max posters, pipes, papers, jewelry, crystals, beads and bubble lamps were commonly found in "head" shops. Like alcohol at the beginning of the century, drug use was blamed on the deterioration of society in general and the American nuclear family in particular. When an experience was good, it was a "high" and when it was bad, it was a "bummer."

College students, dropouts, hippies, and advocates of free love traveled a circuit on the West Coast along the Interstate-5 corridor. Besides hitchhiking and driving older used cars and hand-painted vans with peace signs and psychedelic patterns, travelers could also ride the *Gray Rabbit*. This single bus drove the circuit from Portland to San Francisco, with numerous planned and unplanned stops in most college towns along the way–Eugene, Corvallis, Ashland, Chico, and Sacramento. The schedule was erratic. Backpacks and guitars were stashed in the modified bus which had several rows of seats removed. But the fare of $25 was unbeatable. In the later 1970s, the *Green Tortoise* ran a similar operation–a happening on wheels, which inspired by Ken Kesey's Merry Pranksters.

The Free Speech Movement appeared on the UC Berkeley campus in the fall of 1964. Students launched a two-pronged mission, challenging the establishment to change institutions and policy-making systems. But they also wanted to lead lives that would embody the kind of society they espoused. There was no meaningful strategy. Hence communes, concerts, coffee houses, and radical music inspired by Bob Dylan came to identify the movement.

Folk singers, inspired by Woody Guthrie and Pete Seger, performed songs pointing out the sins of the establishment and what was seen as a repressive, bigoted, and insensitive government. Bob Dylan holed up at an artist's colony in upstate New York. From Woodstock, his 1965 album *Bringing It All Back Home* put out the message that drugs were "where it was at." *Mr. Tambourine Man* had as many levels of interpretation as there were interpreters.

Disaffected youth quickly adopted his music, along with that of Peter, Paul, and Mary, Simon and Garfunkel, The Byrds, Buffalo Springfield, the Lovin' Spoonful, and the Grateful Dead. The idealism of folk was melded with the emotion and energy of rock music. The times... they were a-changin'!

Leave it to Beaver gave way to The Beatles following their appearance on the *Ed Sullivan Variety* TV program in 1964. American popular music became fascinated with the boys from Liverpool and with anything from England. It was sometimes called the British Invasion.

Portland Gay life in the mid-1960s

Oregon was thought to have a statewide homosexual ring when many "homosexual-type sex-magazines" were seized in gay and lesbian bars in 1963. Portland Mayor Terry Schrunk launched a morality campaign the following year against perverts, deviates, and "congenital inverts" to prevent Portland from becoming a "small San Francisco." His Committee for Decent Literature and Films wanted to deny Oregon Liquor Control Commission alcohol licenses for eight establishments – which included the Old Glory Tavern, the Model Inn, the Tel and Tel, the Half Moon, and the Harbor. These

Dave Kohl photo

OrHi neg 59950

OrHi file 1731

Favorite Portland "hang-outs" in the 1960s: the Ming Lounge in Chinatown, Jolly Joan on Broadway, the Tik Tok on E. Burnside, Henry Thiele's and Bonnie's Burgers in NW, and Barts Drive-In on SW Morrison in Uptown.

OrHi neg R-57

Portland City Archives

Neil Hutchins photo

28

Prelude 1853 - 1971

were generally regarded as a "disorderly premise." Since at least the years of the Great Depression, alcohol had been associated in the public mind with criminality and/or the Mafia. At a public hearing, commissioners voted in agreement with the Mayor, and the demise of the eight taverns appeared inevitable.

Many bar owners were known to have paid bribes to police to be left alone in the past, but now they united and hired a lawyer to present their case. The bars in question appealed the decision to the Oregon Liquor Control Commission, which determined that the city wanted bars closed because of the nature of their patrons, not because they had violated any laws. The Oregon Liquor Control Commission determined to grant the licenses. Mayor Schrunk urged Governor Mark Hatfield to review the liquor license situation.

The Governor took no action. The only bar to close was the Harbor, when it lost its license to serve food in 1965. John Honegger soon reopened it at the Riptide many blocks north at 933 SW Stark, the earliest of several bars to "colonize" the so-called "gay-triangle" that would develop between W. Burnside and SW Stark Street. The Riptide sought to be respectable venue, and they developed a reputation of alleged persecution of homosexuals. Women were denied entry if they were wearing long pants. The Riptide became far more successful when purchased a few years later by Roman Wydra and advertised in the emerging gay press.

On SW Oak Street, the Tel and Tel Tavern (so-named because the Pacific Telephone and Telegraph building was across the street) operated at the corner of SW 8th since the late 1950s, where G.I.s were dropped off on leave, or upon mustering out of the service. The watering hole became a natural venue for lonely and curious men to gather at the spot that had once been a station for the Linnton Trolley. Although not a gay-owned establishment, the nearby Ming Lounge on NW 4th in Chinatown stayed open after hours when bars closed at 2:30 am. The Ming did, however, advertise in gay publications. Located mere blocks away from several North End bars, patrons could have a few more drinks until the Ming's 4 am closing.

Jolly Joan's was a 24-hour eatery on Broadway, just south of the Benson, across from the Imperial. It was popular day and night, and while large, was still often overcrowded with theater and late night customers in its art deco split level atmosphere.

Gay men could also choose to frequent popular gathering places in the straight and alternative communities like Quality Pie, Yaws, Waddell's, The Tik Tok, Henry Thiele's, Huber's, Bonnie's Burgers, or Bart's Drive-in.

The Hill Group

In the hills above southwest Portland, a group of semi-closeted men living in Portland Heights between SW Vista and SW Skyline Drive began meeting. In San Francisco, they would have been dubbed "the cufflink crowd" – men of means with an education and social prominence. Gatherings were held in the privacy of their large homes and apartments, usually around drinks and a meal. Events were always for the entire group, not to slight anyone by holding a more intimate gathering. They called themselves the Hill Group. While staying mostly to themselves, an occasional new man would enter the club, usually having been initially picked up down on SW 3rd, among the young hustlers of *The Camp*.

One unique Portlander at the time was Gloria Lavon, a "fashion consultant" who operated a local beauty salon and school. In the early 60s she organized a week long summer *Dream*, a "T-V" Charm school at Lincoln City for cross-dressing men from all over the U.S. Maximum attendance allowed was 100 participants. There she taught individuals how to maximize their features. This led to the establishment of the *IFGE* (International Foundation for Gender Education) this later inspired the Northwest Gender Alliance. Some Portlanders also attended Charles Pierce's 1962 *Fantasia Fair*.

As was the case in New York and several other American cities, no specific statute outlawed being homosexual in Oregon, but real or perceived "deviant" acts were illegal. Men could be picked up on a variety of charges– vagrancy, loitering, disturbing the peace, even J-walking. "While the law classified homosexuals as crimi-

Greg Pitts Archive

Tricycle races were held during campaigns for Empress. Teams pedaled from The Embers on SW Park to Dahl & Penne's on SW 2nd., downing a drink and doing a trick before moving on. The Side Door, seen behind the bikers, was the entrance to the original gay area of the bar.

Neil Hutchins photo

Neil Hutchins photo

The Riptide became the first bar of the gay triangle in 1969, when Roman Wydra bought it from John Honnegger. A popular role for female impersonators was Lily Tomlin and her persona as Ernestine from "Laugh-In." Drag shows raised funds for charity, with costumes from Helen's Costumers or Goodwill. Revelers often adjourned to after hours at Hubers', the Rose City's oldest eatery.

Portland Archives

Greg Pitts Archive

30

Prelude 1853 - 1971

nals and the scientific establishment used psychology to 'medicalize' homosexuality into an illness, gay men and lesbians found almost universal moral condemnation from religions, whether mainstream or obscure. Thrice condemned–as criminals, as mentally ill, and as sinners–homosexuals faced a social reality in post-World War II America that was bleak, if not grim." (Carter, *Stonewall*, p 16).

Oregon in the '60s and '70s became a more socially progressive state, making issues from land-use planning to no-fault divorce part of the national conversation. The bottle bill was passed, inspiring early ecologists and giving kids a motive for cleaning up their back porches and neighborhoods. Rebel Governor Tom McCall invited tourists to savor Oregon's culture, but also encouraged them to return home .

Portland gays were basically a bar culture, not organizing to resist police harassment as had happened in Seattle. Some knew about gay organizations such as the Mattachine Society in other West Coast cities. They had not responded to outside attempts to organize. Primary gathering places were the Harbor Club (later, the Riptide), Milwaukie Tavern, Dahl and Penne Tavern, Derek's Tel and Tel Tavern, the Half Moon Tavern (later, The Tavern), and the Other Inn. None of these bars advertised themselves as "gay." The clientele just happened to be of that bent.

In 1968, two partners from Seattle purchased a downtown tavern known as the Focal Point. Steve Suss and Roman Wydra were destined to have a major influence on the bar scene when they dissolved their partnership in 1971. Steve held a third interest in the Atlas Baths in Seattle, but acquired a restaurant behind the Focal Point at SW 9th and Yamhill called The Embers. He attempted to balance his gay and straight customers by designating his exit door on Yamhill as the "Side Door" for homosexuals, and his main door on SW 9th for "normal" customers. It didn't work. The two crowds did not mix well, and Steve made the decision to turn his place into an "out" gay establishment, the first in Portland.

Roman acquired the Riptide on SW Stark, which had been bought by John Honnecker when his Harbor Club was shut down by the City in 1965. Honnecker had attempted to keep the Riptide high class straight, but when it became Roman's Riptide, it grew into the first "out" gay bar on Stark Street–the area that by the 1980s became the mecca for gay bar culture with at least eleven establishments and a bathhouse within the "gay triangle."

Early Portland Gay Organizations

About 1958, some frequent patrons of the Half Moon Tavern came up with an idea for a social phenomenon to be eventually known as The Rose Court. Partially as a spoof on the golden anniversary of the city-wide Rose Festival and its princess court, a fantasy imperial kingdom called Transylvania was devised with a Rex Regina (Queen). Some called her Salmon-Ella. Queen Samuel was the first Mother Superior, taking an oath as Empress Eugenie I. Playing with words and titles, there were eventually designations for a Lord High Sheriff, Prosecutor Archbishop, Grand Dukes and Duchesses, and a Mother Superior known as The Immaculate Assumption, Sister Mary Wanna of the Order of the Holy Smoke. Note: The stereotypical American male in 1958 was contentedly entertained by such popular TV fare as Wanted: Dead or Alive; Gunsmoke; Wagon Train; The Rifleman; and Have Gun, Will Travel.

The Portland Imperial Court became the first court system on the West Coast. Annual charity blowouts began in 1961.

A theatrically-oriented group emerged in 1966 as semi-comic relief against City Hall attempts to close eight bars in 1965. Organizational gatherings happened in homes on upper College Drive, in the hills south of downtown known as the "swish alps." Calling themselves The Pruitts of Portland, after a popular television program called The Pruitts of South Hampton, they produced several semi-annual stage (drag) shows:

"Road to Ruin"– Halloween 1966
 at Beaver Hall
"April in Portland"–Spring 1967 -
 at Neighbors of Woodcraft
"Pot Pourri" Fall 1967 -

OrHi neg 53054

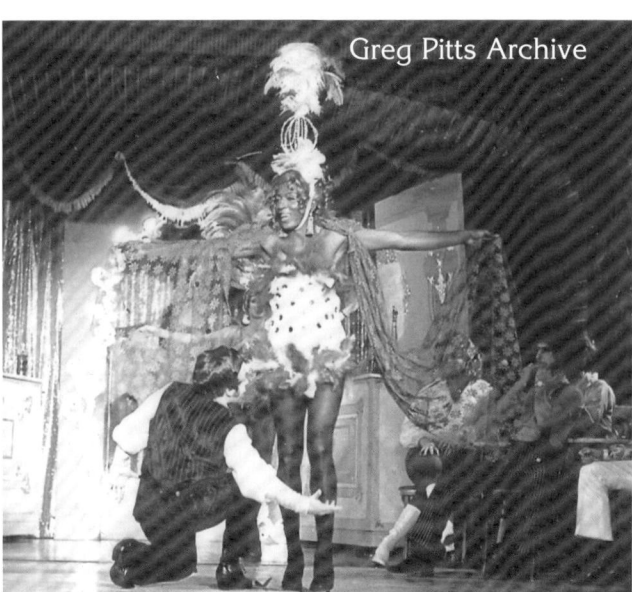

Neil Hutchins photo

OrHi neg 003200

The Hoyt Hotel was built near Union Station about 1910. In 1948, it was nearly flooded, as was the neighboring Boyd Hotel. Harvey Dick had it restored and furnished with his art collection in the mid-1960s. Seattle singer Gracie Hanson and her show made the Hoyt a popular night spot with Portlanders, featuring shows in the Roaring '20s Room. The early shows of the Pruitts and several early drag shows were presented on the stage, which pneumatically rose in Buzby Berkeley fashion to the gasps of audiences.

Greg Pitts Archive

OrHi neg53055

32

Prelude 1853 - 1971

in Hoyt's Roaring '20s Room
"Mama B(Bernice)'s Sweetheart Ball"
　　Winter 1968 in the Pythian Ballroom
"Wine and Roses"–Spring 1968 -
　　in the Masonic Temple Ballroom
"Anything Goes"– Halloween 1968–
　　in the Hoyt's Roaring '20s Room

The Portland Forum developed in 1969, filling the dramatic needs for another segment of the gay population. Three survivors of The Pruitts, which had disbanded in late 1968, were determined to continue the follies of earlier events. Their creation, The Forum, was registered with the State of Oregon as the first gay organization in Portland. The title of Queen was changed to Empresses of the Inland Empire.

Their social events, primarily drag functions, and the annual picnics were most sucessful and came to be anticipated as an important part of gay life in Portland. Volunteers donated hours of time in set design and construction, costuming, hair and make-up, lighting, interior design, and floral work. New Queens were crowned at the fall events, but were called *Empress*, and a princess royale was elected each spring.

Each year's event has to be entitled "something" of the Rose, honoring Portland's Rose-oriented culture. Hence:

　　Celebration of the Rose
　　Ecstasy of the Rose
　　Faith of the Rose
　　Harmony of the Rose
　　Legend of the Rose
　　Pride of the Rose
　　Unity of the Rose　etc.

Some monarchs became institutions of service to the community, serving the court far beyond the years of their actual reigns. The best known include Vanessa XIII, Darcelle XV, Candi Wrapper XX, Esther Howard XXIV, Champagne XXV, Rosey Waters XXVI, and Lady Elaine Peacock XXIX, and emperors Kim I, Harold II, Blaine IV, and Gary X. The Roman numeral behind their name indicates their chronological rank.

The expectation of each monarch was performing community service, fundraising, representing Portland in other cities' gay functions, and establishing long range beneficial programs for the gay and lesbian community.

The Rose Court became a separate entity around 1970, and changed the voting for nobility to a popular vote. Proudly, the Imperial Sovereign Rose Court of Oregon has been the parent to many smaller regional Courts, which now co-exist within the Pacific Northwest, like Salem and Eugene.

The Hoyt

Entertainer Gracie Hanson sang and danced in the opulent "Roaring '20s" room of the Hoyt Hotel on NW 6th. The Hoyt had become a seedy residential hotel near Union Station before Harvey Dick began an extensive restoration program on the interior in 1963. The gaslight era of San Francisco was emulated in the Barbary Coast Room with magnificent antique wooden mirrored bars brought in from the old Idaho mining town of Wallace. Elegant wood paneling, Dick's collection of original artwork, and a plastic replica of an old steam locomotive all added to the atmosphere. The plastic locomotive later became famous in the opening scenes of TV's *Petticoat Junction*. There was an old-fashioned men's bar, with a running water trough at the base of the bar (for the convenience of overzealous male drinkers).

Most well known, however, was the full - size replica of Cuban dictator Fidel Castro, set in a cavernous urinal in the men's room. When enough liquid filled his open mouth, alarms sounded and flashing lights were activated, to the amusement of the donor and his friends. In the women's lavatory, a live harpist performed while patrons did their business seated on wicker seats positioned over the commodes. Gracie used to love to give tours of both "facilities."

Gracie drew in sell-out crowds and kept the Hoyt supplied with customers. Competition included other well-known Portland nightclubs like the Clover Club on SW 10th, Amato's on Broadway at SW Main, and the Embassy Club on SW 3 rd which became Fathers, then Ruth's Chris Steak House).

Portland City Archives

Darcelle is the creation of Walter Cole and partner Roxy Neuhardt. They first met at the Hoyt Hotel across from Union Station in 1969. Darcelle became *Empress XV*, reigning in 1973, and re-naming her club at the former Demas' Tavern where she welcomed Christine Jorgensen in 1975. Long time supporters of the GLBT community, they participated annually in *Peacock in the Park* shown here in 2003.

Neil Hutchins Archive

Greg Pitts Archive

Marty Davis/Just Out photo

Neil Hutchins Archive

34

Prelude 1853 - 1971

The Hoyt became the venue of several drag shows of the Imperial Rose Court before it suddenly closed 1972, over a tiff with Dick's former business partner. Bought by the city for offices, which never materialized, it was sold to Greyhound and Pacific Trailways bus lines in 1976 and fell to the wrecking ball. It has been a vacant lot across from the new bus terminal for 30 years. And the only remaining men's bar with a trough in Portland is at Jake's on SW 12th and Stark.

Darcelle XV

Businessman Walter Cole operated Portland's first gourmet coffee house at the Cafe Espresso at SW 12th and Montgomery in the mid-1960s. He also owned the Cafe Trieste on SW 5th and Harrison near PSU. He became interested in female impersonation in 1968 when he met Roxy Neuhardt, who had come from Las Vegas to dance with Gracie Hanson at the Hoyt.

Walter and Roxy soon became partners. With David Hamilton (*Mame*), they invented "Darcelle" in 1971 as an act to attract customers at Demas' Tavern on NW Third. The tavern, purchased by Walter in 1967, had been only moderately successful, with a long bar and six booths, catering to the pensioners living above the bar in the Foster Hotel during the day, and a more sophisticated crowd in the evenings.

With stage experience in Las Vegas, "Rock" danced in Walter's troupe and advised "Madame D", Darcelle's first incarnation. She became the hit of the show. Attracting a mixed audience, early favorable reviews brought success and an expansion of the club. He first became popular with a crowd of leather-clad lesbians, who enjoyed Darcelle's give-and-take stage banter. Word quickly spread about the entertaining shows, and the place became popular with gays and straight audiences alike, with the resulting interaction of the two.

Drag—men dressing as women—had been a part of the entertainment scene in Portland since the 1930s. Mickey Rooney, William Powell, and other mainstream actors had played female roles in such films as *Babes on* Broadway and in *Love Crazy* and were commonly seen in many of Portland's forty movie houses. For viewers, these were a comedic escape from the more grim realities of post-depression America during the era of rising tensions in Europe as Hitler's threat became increasingly manifest.

Seattle also had supported a cabaret bar with shows by female impersonators. This was the Garden of Allah, open from 1946 to 1956 at the North end of First Avenue in the basement of the Victorian-era Arlington Hotel. Jackie Starr, Skippy La Rue, Paris Delair and several other regular impersonators wowed audiences with their feminine charms, often emceed by a woman in male drag, Nick Arthur. The Garden is generally regarded as Seattle's first gay-owned gay bar, eventually closed down by the city over both liquor rules and morality issues stemming from the McCarthy hearings.

From the 1950s to the 1970s, the accomplished cross dresser and female impersonator Charles Pierce brought his traveling show to Portland. He did an impeccable Bette Davis. *But you are in drag, Blanche, you are!* Working out of the Club La Vie in Los Angeles, the Echo Club in Miami Beach, and then the Gilded Cage Theater in San Francisco, Pierce made a career recreating Mae West, Kathryn Hepburn, Tallulah Bankhead, Joan Crawford, and Marlene Dietrich. Later he mastered Barbara Stanwyck, Carol Channing, Joan Collins, and Lucille Ball.

Darcelle and Roxy agree that Pierce's *Evita* was his all-time best. He even came out of retirement in 1993 to make a special appearance with the Los Angeles Gay Men's Chorus.

Darcelle competed unsuccessfully for the role of Empress in 1971, but was voted Empress XV in 1972. After her reign during 1973 ended, she renamed her club Darcelle XV. The place has been a Portland legend for over thirty years.

Darcelle and Roxy became especially vocal and active supporters of gay rights and the Portland gay community in the decades to follow. St. Mary's Boys Home became the focus of the Court's charitable efforts with Darcelle's leadership. Several Metropolitan Community Church events and fundraisers have been staged at Darcelle's Old Town club.

Portland City Archives

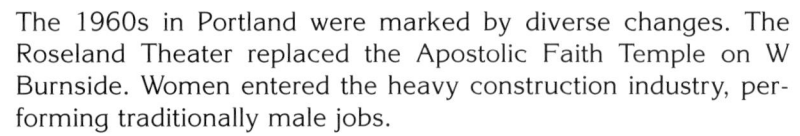

The 1960s in Portland were marked by diverse changes. The Roseland Theater replaced the Apostolic Faith Temple on W Burnside. Women entered the heavy construction industry, performing traditionally male jobs.

In 1963, 300 members of the National Association for Colored People (NAACP) marched 1.5 miles on North Williams Ave. in memory of Medgar Evers, NAACP field secretary slain by snipers in Mississippi on June 12. President Kennedy would be assassinated November 22.

OrHi neg 38665

Prelude 1853 - 1971

Attempts to Organize

In Seattle, a few men who had been receiving the *Mattachine Review*, contacted the San Francisco based Society about becoming an official Chapter. It took from 1960 until 1967 for this to happen. The Seattle group named itself the Dorian Society in 1967, published a newsletter, opened a counseling center for sexual minorities, speakers were provided to the community.

A representative from San Francisco's Tavern Guild and several Seattle Dorians proposed organizing Portland gays with a conference in February 1968 at the Park Haviland Hotel. A month before the scheduled conference, hotel reservations were canceled, and the so-called Northwest Homophile Conference failed to materialize. Perhaps they were distracted, watching the remarkable just-released Stanley Kubrick film *2001 - A Space Odyssey*, or even Mel Brooks' classic that year, *The Producers*.

Many men, in recalling their personal history, speak of "wearing the mask" and living a double life. Fear of discovery and the resulting loss of job, family, and church, was a powerful deterrent to honesty. With little support beyond companions in the Hill Club, at the bars or drag shows, and even less in bathhouses, individuals felt isolated and without support. Popular literature had nothing positive to say about homosexuals, or their perceived activities. When the Oregon legislature passed Senate Bill 40 legalizing all private sexual activities between consenting adults in 1971, it joined only four other states with such laws that de facto allowed homosexual activity. Its implication for gays created no groundswell. Closet doors remained essentially closed.

II. Civil Rights–Gay Rights

The spirit of civil rights had long been brewing throughout the country, precipitated by the Brown v. Board of Education case in 1954; Rosa Parks and the ensuing Montgomery Bus boycott of 1955; and the 1963 March on Washington with Martin Luther King's *I have a Dream* speech. When Medgar Evers, the National Association for the Advancement of Colored People field secretary in Mississippi was slain by snipers on June 12, 1963, over 300 Portlanders held a march of mourning. The peaceful parade was routed over North Vancouver and North Williams Avenues, and ended at the Church of the Living God on North Stanton without any violence. Civil rights issues caused much dissension nationwide, culminating in the Civil Rights act of 1964, prohibiting discrimination in public places for reason of color, race, religion, or national origin.

1965 was a significant year in the civil rights and gay rights struggle nationwide. In March, Rev.. Martin Luther King, Jr., led the march from Selma to Montgomery, Alabama that would open ballot boxes to African Americans across the South. Singer Harry Belafonte also joined in that march. President Lyndon Johnson signed the Voting Rights Act into law later that year. A peaceful march took place in Portland in support of these national issues.

That July 40 gay people staged the first gay and lesbian demonstration against repression in front of Independence Hall and the Liberty Bell in Philadelphia, starting a movement that would erupt four years later in a Greenwich Village bar in New York City.

Several anti-Viet Nam war protests and the riots at the Democratic National Convention in August 1968 in Chicago's Grant Park demonstrated the frustration that divided the country when President Lyndon Johnson escalated theAsian war. In civil rights, the emergence of such groups as the Students for a Democratic Society (SIDS) and the *Black Panther Party* galvanized political thought. The Panthers, with their Ten Point Program for economic and social equality for the African American community, were alternately seen as criminal thugs or high-minded social reformers.

1968 was the year that "negroes" became "blacks," "hippies" became "yippies," and Arab guerrillas became "Palestinians." In Cuba, Che Guevara was canonized for his martyrdom in Bolivia. Dr. King was assassinated in Memphis by escaped convict James Earl Ray.

Locations familiar to Portland gays in 1968 were the Masonic Temple on the South Park Blocks, site of several presentations by the Pruitts, and the Other Inn Tavern on SW Alder. For six months in 1972, the space above the Inn was the Gay Community Center, operated by the Second Foundation especially for the use of young people seeking alternatives to the Camp.

Robert Kennedy was assassinated by a Jordanian Arab named Sirhan Sirhan. A bitter election campaign brought Richard Milhouse Nixon to the Presidency.

It was the United Nations' *International Year for Human Rights*. The "war baby" generation was being drafted to fight in a distant Asian war that was hated so universally that it provided a focus for just about all rebels seeking any cause. The civil rights movement was maturing after years of incidents and confrontations. And the technology of same-day broadcasting of news made events around the country and world immediately available on the 5 and 10 o'clock news. Television's first war was nobly covered by newly trained journalists scrambling to make sense of skirmishes and drawn-out sieges, mixed with scenes of devastated civilians and napalmed geography.

Seeing parallels with the civil rights issues for racial minorities, gay individuals and leaders began to take heart in the late 1960s that their cause was just and their time of liberation was eminent. America was in domestic turmoil and social definitions were being rewritten. Gay activists found particular encouragement by participating in the anti-war protests and marches as individuals and groups, upset with the political and social status-quo, found voice in song, literature, and activism.

The Summer of 1969

America and the world were mesmerized, with ears and eyes focused on screens, to exprience Apollo 11 landing on the moon July 20, 1969. Neil Armstrong was the first human to take a lunar walk. And in Europe, the Anglo-French supersonic Concorde made its first real test flight.

That summer, two seemingly unrelated events occurred in New York State that would influence American culture for the remainder of the century — Woodstock and Stonewall. They would both have distinct direct and indirect results in Oregon.

The now-famous 3-day Woodstock musical gathering took place near Bethel, New Yorkexposing 400,000 Americans on site to free

Prelude 1853 - 1971

love, "hippies," the drug culture, and innovative music. At the time, the general population viewed "hippies" with cynicism, regarding them as unwashed hirsutes flaunting their freedoms without taking responsibility for duty, tradition, civility, religion, and "doing things the way we did." *Woodstock* was glorified in the release of audio tapes (yes, even 8-tracks), vinyl albums, and a full-length semi-documentary movie, which came out the following spring. The musical *Hair* did much to modify and extrapolate understandings of the "hippie" culture, as did Arlo Guthrie's song and movie about *Alice's Restaurant*.

Stonewall

Secondly, in New York City, a group of homosexuals resisted police harassment on a summer evening at an unlicensed Greenwich Village bar called the Stonewall Inn.

The Stonewall Inn was a popular bar on Christopher Street in the Village. Despite the large size of the New York City gay community, individuals and their meeting places had long been subject to extreme harassment by police. Many, if not most, establishments catering to the gay crowd were owned by the Mafia, including the one-time Bonnie's Stonewall Restaurant. The place had been popular with lesbians before it was gutted by fire and closed in the mid-'60s. Mafia owner "Fat Tony" Lauria reopened the Christopher Street business as a dance bar in 1967, also serving illicit mafia-provided watered-down expensive alcohol.

It had been assumed that newly elected mayor John Lindsey would ease up on police harassment of gays, but this did not happen. In the early morning hours of June 28, 1969, six days after the untimely death of gay icon Judy Garland, a large group of police entered the Inn as part of their ongoing harassment program to eliminate public assemblies of homosexuals and to close down businesses catering to gay clientele. They escorted patrons outside, and then began to lead the owner, employees, some drag queens, and a lesbian into squad cars and paddy wagons. The crowd of exiled patrons became restless and began tossing coins at the remaining cops after those arrested were hauled to the police station. Gays pushed against the Inn's door until one of them was dragged inside by the police and severely beaten. By most accounts, it was the drag queens and lesbians who were the most outrageous in their defiance of the police. Police reinforcements arrived as trash barrels were being ignited and several Molotov cocktails were being hurled at the building.

A second night of rioting ensued Saturday evening. Since homosexuals had rarely dared to resist, much less fight back against police, the event came as a shock to the establishment. A new sense of militancy soon arose. Dissatisfied younger members of the Mattachine Society of New York broke away to form the first Gay Liberation Front (GLF), which spawned chapters throughout the country, bringing homosexuality into the open all over the U.S. Others formed the Gay Activist Alliance (GAA), which often used militant tactics of disruption and civil disobedience to confront politicians. Within a year, several lesbian feminist groups had formed, often aligning themselves with the growing Women's Liberation Movement.

The Portland Gay Liberation Front

The first direct result in Portland from the summer of 1969 occurred at Centenary-Wilbur Methodist Church, where nine months after Stonewall, on March 10, 1970, the first organizational meeting of the Gay Liberation Front was held. At the time, Portland was a hotbed of political dissent centered on civil rights, opposition to the war in Viet Nam, and a general questioning of the status quo in the relatively Puritanical city.

One Portland voice of dissent was a weekly newspaper called *The Willamette Bridge*. It was, literally, an underground publication, being produced in a basement space in Old Town on West Burnside. On the staff was John Wilkinson, who editorialized that gays needed to get beyond the bars, baths, and streets.

The Bridge had turned down a personal ad because the editor thought it was sexual in nature. It read: "Gay longhair, young, lonely, seeks meaningful relationship with same. Answer with ad in the *Bridge*."

OrHi neg 36980

OrHi neg 01708

OrHi file 1737

Dave Kohl photos

In the tradition of open-minded independent booksellers, Walter Powell opened his shop in 1971, inspired by his son Michael's Chicago bookstore. When Michael moved to Portland in 1979, they combined operations and moved into the old American Motors dealership building on W Burnside. The City of Books is the largest independent bookstore in the nation with seven stores and on-line service.

OrHi file 1737

Prelude 1853 - 1971

Wilkinson wrote a response to "Young, Gay, and Lonely" in the next edition, and lesbian feminist Holly Hart wrote the first lesbian article soon after. She padded the paper with other articles about lesbianism, using a nom de plume. John and Dave Davenport joined with Hart in the March 6 *Bridge* to call the first meeting of the Gay Liberation Front of Oregon, part of the national activist movement then picking up momentum.

Hart was a 1970 Reed College graduate who volunteered to help start the group. Gay-informative articles were written for *The Bridge*, suggesting places for gays to meet, such as the Ninth Street Exit coffee house at Centenary-Wilbur. The result was a consciousness-raising support group.

Four days later, the meeting at Centenary-Wilbur drew about 35 attendees, and a movement was born. Decisions were made to become an active group for gay rights in Oregon. The *GLF* eventually helped operate the coffee house certain evenings.

The Power of the Press!

The Bridge ran a center pullout section on Gay Liberation in its July 17, 1971 issue. The GLF began a hotline and sent speakers to address church and community groups about gays and gay liberation. Activists were heard on *KBOO* radio programs.

KBOO had become Portland's listener-supported non-profit radio voice in 1968, a 10 watt mini-station run by volunteers. The community radio movement dated back to 1949 with *KPFA*, begun by WW II draft resistors in Berkeley who had learned about broadcasting bandwidth reserved by the FCC for non-profit educational stations.

Portlanders modeled *KBOO* radio after Seattle's *KRAB*, on the air since 1965. Portland classical music buffs had recruited David Calhoun, an ex-monk from the Washington city, to help start the station. *KBOO*'s first transmitter was in a member's garage, gaining subscribers and loyalty enough to grow into a storefront studio in 1971. Definitely grassroots, it was the 1970s!

KBOO's support and involvement with the *GLBT* community began with its earliest broadcasts. Gay-friendly talk shows, interviews and features, and eventually nationally syndicated National Public Radio and GLBT programming became part of the KBOO mix. Live interviews with visitors such as the Berrigan brothers and Joan Baez, augmented readings by local poets, and performances of local musicians. Howie Baggadonutz, Barbara Bernstein, Dave Laurence, and several other hosts are still familiar names to *GLBT* listeners.

The Gay Liberation Front organized and grew locally, and within a year sent a delegation to San Francisco for the Christopher Street West Parade on June 27, 1971. This was the first Gay Pride weekend, with simultaneous gatherings in New York, Los Angeles, Chicago, and Boston. Eventually, dissension within the Portland group weakened the GLF and meetings ceased, but the awareness had begun and *The Bridge* articles had spread the word that there were gays in Portland and they were normal citizens. Gay groups started at Reed College and at Portland State University. Hart went on to law school at UC Berkeley and returned in 1975 to a solo law practice in Portland, handling mostly gay-related domestic cases.

Centenary-Wilbur

Centenary-Wilbur United Methodist Church, where the *Gay Liberation Front* first met, was unlike any other institution in Portland. It was on the original site of the first Methodist church built on Portland's east side at SE 9th and Pine. Methodism in Oregon was very strong in the 19th century since it was not a church based on ethnicity or theological dogma, but social involvement as preached by John Wesley. The damaged and dry-rotten 1890 sanctuary was torn down in 1963, following the destructive the previous fall, but the 1929 educational wing and gymnasium continued to serve multiple purposes. The gym be-came the Sanctuary for worship—a decision that in 1963 saved the small congregation the expense of rebuilding a church.

Newly arrived Pastor Harper Richardson had visited a very unusual San Francisco church

Portland General Electric's Trojan nuclear power plant at St. Helens was 45 miles north of Portland, and the object of much protest

Dave Kohl photo

Centenary Wilbur Methodist Church, once a congregation of 1500, was an inner city congregation by 1965, popular with alternative culture people and, at times, under police surveillance.

Portland City Archives

Prelude 1853 - 1971

in the Tenderloin district in 1965. Glide Memorial Methodist welcomed hippies in the church, sponsored jazz worship, and served its local community with food and shelter, ministering to "street people." Beginning about 1966, Centenary-Wilbur began similar programs of neighborhood outreach and advocacy.

The church, just off Sandy Blvd. at Pine and SE 9th, existed on the momentum of its once glorious days when in the 1890s it built its magnificent graystone Sanctuary and served 1500 neighborhood Christians. But by the 1960s, the area had become industrial, the Sandy Blvd. extension had cut the neighborhood in two, families with enough funds moved to the suburbs, and the remnant congregation numbered about 200, some of whom lived in the suburbs. And it didn't look like a church because of the Sanctuary demolition.

While the San Francisco congregation was basically funded by an endowment from the Glide family, C-W had only the meager donations of its members for income. Richardson and the congregation decided to get involved in the "real work" of the church, foregoing their "silk-stocking" heritage for a less glamorous destiny of service and involvement, at the risk of financial distress. Philosophically, this was a combination of the parables of the widow's mite and the mustard seed and Christ's exhortation that "as you have done it to the least of one of these, you have done it unto me."

When approached about the possibility of opening a coffee house at the church, the congregation designated an unused old choir room on the ground floor, spent $600 to cut a doorway onto the street, and called it the Ninth Street Exit. A coffee house in the 1960s implied lots of music and rap talk, smoky atmosphere, and loud counterculture discussions on topics from war to taxes and sexuality, and drug usage.

No alcohol was served at the Exit, just coffee, juice, and pastries. Donuts from a local shop supplemented baked goods donated weekly by a lady from the C-W congregation. Pastor Richardson told Paul Libby, the manager, that everything at the coffee house had to be legal, above reproach and accusation by critics. It was the young people's chance to prove they could manage such an atmosphere. They were successful, but this was not a Sunday School!

Monday evenings evolved into men's night, and Tuesdays became reserved for women only. Soon, the men's groups attracted a large number of gays. The women's evenings became a caucus for women's liberation *movements,* with both lesbians and the National Organization of Women (NOW) eventually holding sessions at the same time, but in different rooms. C-W became popularly known as the alternative culture building.

Harper Richardson continued to welcome community action groups, neighborhood improvement groups, and organizations that helped the poor and elderly. Other groups that challenged the Establishment and the current Viet Nam war soon came to rely on C-W as a meeting place, as well. One colorful group that were known to frequent C-W was the Gypsy Jokers, a motorcycle group that on occasion actually drove their machines into the sanctuary. This behavior also was noted at the J and J Tavern on West Burnside.

Koinonia House

On the west side of the Willamette, Ecumenical Ministries of Oregon (EMO) established and built Koinonia House on the campus of Portland State University in 1965. The Centenary-Wilbur congregation took out a $50,000 loan on their property to pay 5/6 of the Methodist contribution to the Campus ministries building. Five other church bodies participated in the joint effort–the Baptist Church, the ALC Lutherans, the Disciples of Christ, Presbyterians, and a union of the Roman Catholics and Episcopalians.

Originally conceived to serve traditional college students and their faith life, by 1969 Koinonia house had changed the direction of its ministry. The nearby First Unitarian Church had transferred its Cherix Coffee House from Outside In to the basement of K-house to mollify police pressures on its street clients. Agora was the resulting meeting spot. As the Viet Nam war intensified, draft counseling at K-house emerged. Together with Centenary-Wilbur, a joint draft card burning "party" was held. A crisis intervention

OrHi neg 17568

Centenary Wilbur, circled was just west of the Sandy Blvd. extension. The large tapered building in the foreground was the Oriental Theater on SE Grand Ave.. By 1962, most of the once-fine homes in the area had been replaced by light industrial buildings and warehouses. Three blocks east on Pine is St. Francis Catholic Parish, a church where Dignity met in the 1980s.

The corner choir room became the 9th St Exit coffeehouse, with a separate entrance from Ash Street through a new doorway and staircase. C-W became a popular live theater and music venue known for years as the Pine Street Theater and La Luna. In 2005, the building became the Pine Street Studios.

The 9th Street exit was actually on SE Ash Street.

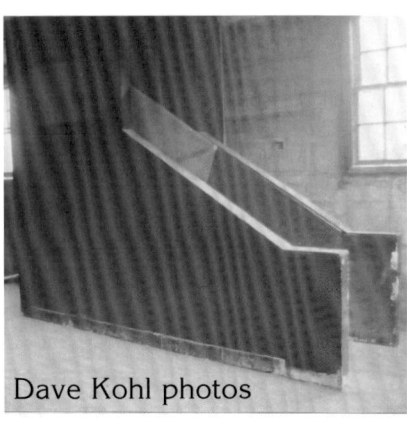

Centenary Methodist Church, built in 1883, later became Centenary-Wilbur United Methodist Church. The house on the right was replaced with the 1928 Education Building. The 1962 Columbus Day storm blew down the steeple.

Dave Kohl photos

Prelude 1853 - 1971

and run-away center evolved, called the Contact Center. During the summers of 1969 and 1970, about 15 street workers were funded to help and counsel young people in financial, housing, or drug crisis. K-house and its staff, managed by Will Newman II, became neutral middlemen between hippies and street youth and the police concerned with tension and behavior during protests and strikes.

In May, anti-war riots at Kent State University in Ohio resulted in U.S. National Guardsmen killing four students there. In sympathy, PSU students put up a hospital tent on the Park Blocks and launched a strike to take over the University President's office. An atmosphere of tolerance and defense of student rights had been fostered by Dean of Students Channing Briggs, but Portland police, under orders from Mayor Terry Schrunk, intervened, injuring 32 people while dismantling the tent. K-house held its place as a center of peaceful resistance just two blocks from the confrontation.

The Portland State Gay Men's Union chose to meet at Centenary-Wilbur in the early 1970s. This group worked to elevate the visibility of gay students on campus; to promote self-respect; and to foster social respect of the individual. The desire was to see the day when the label "homosexual" would no longer be an anti-social label, nor would there be fear of job security. They also protested negative and stereotypical images of gays, as portrayed when the PSU drama department staged *The Boys in the Band* in May, 1971.

Throughout the 1970s, Centenary-Wilbur would continue to provide venues for radical political and social groups to meet, including anti-war groups, the National Organization of Women, the Trojan Decommissioning Alliance, Portland Tenants Union, Oregon Solar Institute, and the Portland Nicaragua Support Committee. Rose Town police are now known to have staked out Centenary-Wilbur, at the behest of the HUAC (House Un-American Activities Committee) and to have taken surveillance photos of individuals entering or leaving the building. An alternative school called the Willamette Learning Center opened and functioned there for several years, with a student group of about 40 youngsters annually under arrangements with Portland Public Schools.

Years later, in 1974 and 1975, Centenary was the meeting place of the Portland Community Church, the group that predated Metropolitan Community Church. Centenary was also the first home of MCC, which met there from January 1976 through August 1977 under its first pastor, Rev. A. Austin Amerine.

Throughout the Portland gay sub-culture in the late '60s, concerns were also evident over job security. Myths equating homosexuality with child recruitment and molestation caused the public to become suspicious if educators were found to be gay. Homosexual teachers were particularly careful that they were not discovered. Rumors that gay government employees could be held up for blackmail created another negative myth in the civil service community. And dating back to the "Red scare" of the 1950s and McCarthy's witch-hunts, there was certain paranoia over national security that led to other murmurings about homosexuals. Widespread discrimination led many younger gays to lower their horizons on job choices, often despairing of any high profile or high paying careers. Even though the ACLU helped get the Oregon legislature to pass Senate Bill 40 in 1971 abolishing sodomy laws, this had no impact on the gay movement. *Oregon Journal* columnist Doug Baker played on and perpetuated fears and misconceptions about gays through his own brand of shaded journalism.

Vortex

The second major result in Oregon from the New York happenings of the summer of 1969 was a "far out" rock festival held on the banks of the Clackamas River at Milo McIver State Park. *Vortex* I has gone down almost unacknowledged in U.S. history as the only state-sponsored rock festival in the nation. While never gaining the national fame of Woodstock, nearly 100,000 concert goers passed through the gates near Estacada over five days from August 28 to September 3. Its story is fascinating, and its indirect influence on the gay community is rarely noted, and undocumented.

Dave Kohl photo

Dave Kohl photo

Gerry Lewin photo

Holly Hart helped organize the Gay Liberation Front at Centenary Wilbur in March 1970. Four months later, Governor Tom McCall gave his blessing to the Vortex I Festival at McIver Park, 25 miles south of Portland. During that week in August, American Legionnaires met few protests as they supported the military and the Viet Nam War. Others spent the summer cooling off at the Jantzen Beach pool.

Lee Meier photo

Portland Archives

46

Prelude 1853 - 1971

Vortex came about as a compromise. Government officials were concerned that a large counter-culture group called the People's Army Jamboree was planning to disrupt the American Legion Convention in Portland, meeting the week prior to Labor Day, 1970. President Richard Nixon was slated as the keynote speaker. Protesters threatened to create havoc and to damage property in Portland.

A group of "peaceniks" including individuals from Outside In, Reed College, and PSU came together with a different idea. First meeting at Koinonia House and then at C-W, they called themselves The Family, and proposed staging a rock festival for the same dates, to siphon off the energy of violent protest, since groups including the Black Panthers, several student groups, and some self-identified Marxists had affiliated with the People's Army.

Outside In played a role in *Vortex*. One of the first young men helped by Outside In was 20-year old Sam McCall, whose dad happened to be the Governor. His friends Lee Meier and Mike Carr, of The Family, proposed having a rock festival to the Governor. The *Woodstock* movie had been showing in local theaters, and most states had banned rock festivals on private land to thwart such large unmanageable gatherings. Tom McCall, 57, a former journalist, correspondent, and Navy veteran, was in his first term as governor. He listened to his son's advice and took the risk of backing the idea on August 6, and provided McIver Park, 25 miles south in Clackamas County.

The park's camping restrictions were lifted. Anxiety over a Woodstock-type event with nudity, drugs, free-love, and police interference was balanced by assurances of the peace-pushing hippies and the Governor's right hand man, Ed Westerdahl. It became known as *Vortex I: A Biodegradable Festival of Life*. (Love, Matt, *Vortex I*, 2004)

Word of the planned event spread rapidly via the underground press throughout America. Oregon business people rallied to donate staging, portable toilets, food, water, and medical supplies. The state park near Estacada was transformed by August 28 into camping areas, with an institutional-style cooking zone, an elevated stage and loudspeakers, and additional parking areas rented from neighboring farmers. Additional food was stored at K-House and prepared in the Centenary-Wilbur kitchen, then trucked out to the festival. The National Guard and Clackamas County law enforcement agreed to stay out of McIver as long as participants caused no trouble, but several tanks were quietly parked in southwest Portland near Wilson High School as back-up. The largest material expense was $15,000 for chemical toilets.

Close cooperation with Dr. Charlie Spray and Willamette Falls Hospital in Oregon City proved essential. Dr. Cameron Bangs of Oregon City set up a volunteer medical unit at *Vortex I*, with donated medical supplies that treated at least 2000 people during the event, mostly for drug-related problems. Dr. Bangs became quickly experienced in the treatment of drug overdoses, techniques that he passed on to others. Later in his career, he became expert in treatment of hypothermia and cold-related injuries. News articles at the time of his retirement in 2005 made no mention of his work at *Vortex*, but he was honored in a video documentary about *Vortex I* made in 2005. (Clackamas County Government Cable, *Vortex I*, 2005)

Several live local bands performed, including a Portland group known as *Jacob's Ladder*. Two commercial rock festivals the same weekend in Washington State drew off most name bands in the area. *The Sky River Festival* was staged in Washougal, and another festival happened in Seattle. That didn't matter.

For participants, *Vortex I* wrapped up the hopes and goals of a generation of Northwest youth. *Vortex I* has come to symbolize the activism and innovative nature of Oregonians, who could combine responsible ecology and open-minded discussion of social change. It probably marks the peak of the counterculture movement, certainly in Oregon, if not in the whole country.

That season, Jim Morrison, Jimi Hendrix, and Janis Joplin all passed from the world scene. For those who knew its origins, *Vortex* represented the possibility of collaborating for

7 days of peace action!
PEOPLES PORTLAND ARMY JAMBOREE
aug. 28 - sept. 3

Vortex countered the negativism of the Peoples Army, who planned to disrupt the convention.

Lee Meier photos

Vortex was the last major rock festival staged anywhere without promoters or commercialism, and brought together volunteers, businesses, churches, medical personnel, and about 100,000 attendees. Some Portlanders visited out of curiosity for a few hours, most were there four days, and many stayed up to two weeks. The spirit of cooperation and mutual support between participants, organizers, and community groups was an alternative to anti-social protest. It influenced the lives of many of those present for years to come. Several future MCC members were part of the crowd.

Lee Meier photo

Clackamas County photo

48

Prelude 1853 - 1971

peace with the governor's office and other authorities. It was peace, love, and anti-war sentiment safely wrapped up and packaged, liberally sprinkled with LSD and a lot of grass.

Participants returned to Eugene, Salem, and Portland with memories of a good time and hope for the future of their various causes, be they anti-war, Jesus People, ecology, or gay freedom. It added significant momentum to the women's movement. While there is no documented presence of gay political groups at *Vortex*, numerous gays were there, and many spontaneous gay gatherings took place. Members of the emerging *GLF* were not prepared to stake out an identity there. Several gay men report their presence at *Vortex*, noting that no one really seemed to care who was with whom in the sea of sleeping bags. At least three of these men, Dwayne Downing, Ron Powell, and Russ Howerton became founding members of MCC. An atmosphere of acceptance and freedom, unlike any previous West coast experience, set another example for the emerging gay movement in Oregon.

No efforts were made to present itself at *Vortex* by the Gay Liberation Front. The organization was too new and focused on gaining members and other issues to see the potential audience they would have had at the Festival.

But just one month after *Vortex*, David Larsen, Randy Shilts, Terry Bean, and Larry Monocle held the first meeting of the Eugene Gay People's Alliance in the basement of the Wesley Center at the University of Oregon in September of 1970. Taking an activist's stance, the 87 members at the initial meeting expressed frustration at the political winds ablowing across the land. Trials were in process in Chicago and New Haven, as well as for the Catonsville Nine, the Manson Trial, and the Calley Trial. Frustration with second-class status, public derision, and discrimination was obvious.

Robert Peters was the Director of the Wesley Center, a Methodist minister, and Chairman of the Lane County American Civil Liberties Union. He admitted that much soul-searching went into the decision to allow the *GPA* to use their campus facilities. He freely admitted that he did not understand homosexuality. U of O Student Personnel Services Dean Robert Bowlin expressed the hope that public education through the *GPA* would ease the animosity between the community and homosexuals. Homosexuals were seen, like many others in American society, as someone who by quirk of nature or milieu, found himself or herself tagged with a label, which was also a dirty word, simply because of some quality, which was neither shared nor understood by the majority of the population. Each homosexual, however, like all persons, had to come to an understanding and acceptance of themselves in the individual dark night of their own heart, or forever live a life hacked down the middle by confusion and self-deception.

The GPA hoped to be an undertaking of welcome with a difficult assignment, the results of which would be to give the homosexual self-respect, and their valid place in society. The group published a newspaper. *The Women's Press* began publication in December 1970 and put out monthly publications until 1981. The GPA launched many affirming programs, influencing attitudes and politics in the Willamette Valley and in Portland, 100 miles down river, where it eventually became more influential than the *GLF*.

III. Spirituality and Religion

Several homosexual Christians first gathered in the downtown YMCA's Parker chapel at 831 SW 6th in 1968 to exchange ideas, share experiences, to discuss, and worship. It is not known who organized the group, or how long they met, but it is significant that they organized themselves before Stonewall and the resulting Gay Liberation movement, and before Rev. Troy Perry formed the Metropolitan Community Church. It is possible that they were an off-shoot from K-House, but this is not documented. The personal renaissance which motivated people to recognize themselves as worthwhile individuals began with new understanding that 1960s concepts such as "born free," "equal opportunity," and "justice for all" applied to gays and lesbians.

The historic irony of meeting at the "Y" was probably not apparent to either the man-

Lee Meier photo

Clackamas County photo

The *Vortex* stage was built from donated Weyerhaeuser lumber, 20 feet above the ground to discourage people climbing onto the stage. This had been a problem at *Woodstock* one year earlier. Many small groups quietly enjoyed the festival including several spiritual groups.

YMCA archive

Portland's downtown YMCA, built in 1909, was located between Broadway and SW 6th Street (on the right) and Taylor St. Despite its mission to keep boys out of the theater, the Fox cinema, earlier known as the Heillig, and then the Mayfair, it was just across SW Broadway. Inside the "Y" was The Parker Chapel, used by several groups, including the 1968 gathering of gay Christians.

Next to the "Y" was the YWCA, a smaller brick building on the Broadway side. Both buildings were razed in the 1970s.

Prelude 1853 - 1971

agement of neither the YMCA nor the individuals who rented the chapel. YMCAs across America in the '60s were much different than the religion-dominant associations described previously of the early 1900s. Witness their immortalization by *The Village People* song of the same name in 1977.

No individuals who were in the 1968 group are known by name, but their action to meet and worship was referred to in accounts written eight years later when the Metropolitan Community Church in Portland recounted its early history. More research needs to be done on this group and its pioneering actions. The YMCA building was razed in 1973. The Metro Y, its reincarnation on SW Barbur Blvd., has scant records from the earlier building, and no extensive written history of the Portland YMCA seems to exist in published form.

Origins of the Second Foundation

For perspective, 1970 was the year that *Sesame Street* reached national acclaim as effective children's educational television. It was the year of the first Earth Day involving 2000 events and 20 million Americans on April 22. Wisconsin senator Gaylord Nelson had taken the idea of anti-war teach-ins and applied the concept to the environmental issue. The Environmental Protection Act, the Clean Air Act, the Clean Water Act, and the Safe Drinking Water Act were some of the results.

In Portland, during October 1970, less than two months after *Vortex* I, an informal group met at PSU's Koinonia House to discuss the need for a homosexual counseling service. At this time, students seeking counseling about gay issues on campus were encouraged to "go straight." One PSU student reported in *The Vanguard* that he was offered a middle-aged woman to go to bed with, which would teach him how to have good relationships with women.

Chaired by Father Kiernan Healy, Julia Saslow of the PSU counseling department met with Neil Hutchins and Dennis Kennedy. Neil had been involved with SIR. when he lived in San Francisco and was familiar with gay activism. Much discussion produced a consensus that a counseling program was needed, but even more importantly, a positive organization for homophiles would be advantageous. Father Healy appointed a committee, which met several times to produce a constitution by February 9, 1971. Terry Tunnell suggested that the organization be called The Second Foundation, and papers were filed with the State of Oregon to register as a non-profit corporation, which became official on August 5, 1971. Meetings were most often held at Zorba the Greek's, a popular gay night spot just off the South Park Blocks.

The name, Second Foundation, originated with Isaac Asimov's classic trilogy known as the Foundation Series: *Foundation*, *Foundation and Empire*, and *Second Foundation*. In this series about a future universal human society, the First Foundation is composed of technicians, economists, and other business-minded people (responsible for material prosperity, physical safety, and the everyday function of organized society). The Second Foundation is composed of psychologically-minded people who understand human emotions, drives, needs, and potentials. These are factors responsible for the intangibles of life–personal freedoms, morale, goals, and confidence of the people. This Second Foundation developed a feeling of unity and community, a trust in each other, and anticipation for a better future.

Among the goals of Portland's Second Foundation was the counseling program, a free service offered to any who needed help understanding their sexual identity. The second major goal was to establish a Gay Community Center where groups could gather for meetings, plays, social events, dances, and games. Employment counseling, lawyer referral, legal aid, and housing help were also proposed. The first newsletter, typed on a manual typewriter with several strike overs, was mimeographed on standard 8-1/2 by 11 paper and dated March 1971. It was called *The Fountain*, and carried a logo of the Skidmore Fountain in the masthead.

Officers were George Oberg, Larry Beck, Dave Fredrickson, and Neil Hutchins, who also edited *The Fountain*. George brought the structure of his military reserve experience. Dave was a landscape architect with the Port of Portland,

Gay students and supporters of gay causes were active and ready to take some type of action in 1970. Neil Hutchins, recently returned from San Francisco, the *SIR* Foundation, and work with *Vector Magazine*, participated in initial organizational sessions at Koinonia House.that led to establishing The Second Foundation in February, 1971.

Dave Kohl photos

Just across SW Broadway from K-house is the Smith Center, hub of student social activity on the urban campus just south of downtown. *The Fountain* ran cartoons by Snickers LaBarr and advertising for gay-friendly KBOO radio.

52

Prelude 1853 - 1971

and had connections with the City. Neil brought energy, enthusiasm, and his experience in publishing. Jim Schnelling, Ken Strebling, LeRoy Kinler and Dwayne Downing brought other strengths in organizational experience to the group. Critics believed The Foundation couldn't accomplish much, since it was composed almost entirely of ex-drag queens, straight-uptight vocal conservatives, liberal closet cases, and scattered remnants of the defunct Portland Gay Liberation Front. They were wrong.

The prominent opinion piece in that first issue of *The Fountain* addressed the issue of Homosexuality and the Church. In his article, Downing, a former missionary in Corbett with the Full Gospel Sunday School Union, wrote:

"For too long, homosexuals have alienated themselves from the presence of God because they have felt rejected. Recently, I have come to believe that this rejection is not from God, but rather from the church... The homosexual usually feels ostracized from the traditional Christian society because we withdraw ourselves from the church rather than to develop a personal relationship with God within an ununderstanding church... In Portland, there are hundreds of gays who would have a church home if they could attend and not feel like hypocrites or different... We can only hope someday there will be a church in Portland with a good fundamental doctrine that will accept a relationship based on love and fidelity as a gift of God regardless of the sexuality of the relationship."

The Fountain continued to publish dialogue and articles about religion, civil rights, sexuality, and emerging gay culture. Membership swelled quickly in the Second Foundation to 150 in the first six months, drawn by the moderate nature of the group and its goals of working within the mainstream establishment to better the lives of gays and all minorities. Psychologist Dr. Tom Cherry gave training sessions in ways to generate positive attitudes. George Orber and Dave Frederickson were featured guests on the *KGW Dick Klinger* radio show representing The Foundation and its efforts to organize a positive gay community.

The Foundation rented the Pythian Ballroom as part of the first National Gay Prid*e week* in June of 1971, holding a dance for 200 with a live rock band, the Sound Syndrome. Dancing lasted all night. It was the beginning of Portland's annual Gay Pride celebration*s*.

In June of 1971, Neil Hutchins and George Nicola borrowed recording equipment from the Riptide Bar and put together an hour-long program on gay history and culture that aired on *KBOO* radio during Pride Week. The station offered a regularly scheduled weekly gay program as a result. Dave Laurence became the new *Fountain* editor in October, and began the weekly radio program *on* KBOO called the *Homophile Half-Hour,* airing every Thursday evening at 8 pm. It turned into the longest running weekly gay radio program in the nation and became an important outreach to gays, closeted gays, and mainstream communities.

Annual Second Foundation dues were suggested at $10. Attendance grew so that by 1972, it had become one of the largest and most active homophile organizations on the Pacific Coast, working with other Portland and Seattle gay organizations, and supporting what would become Metropolitan Community Church. Most members were law-abiding non-confrontive people who wanted to work within the system to elevate the status and role of gays.

Among the committees formed early on were a membership committee, a health committee dealing with issues around venereal diseases (VD), and a religion committee. This committee regularly searched news services, national press, and professional journals for articles relating to gays and their churches. These were often reprinted in *The Fountain* along with original articles and opinion pieces around religion. Many letters-to-the-editor continued the dialogue over spirituality, historic episodes with various churches, and the need for a spiritual base for Christian homosexuals.

Homosexuality in 1970s Churches

Spirituality was a topic that had been receiving increased attention in the gay press

Second Foundation leader George Oberg says he just happened to be at the right meeting to be elected first president. Working with Dave Fredrickson and Neil Hutchins, they led the Foundation towards its goal of establishing services and counseling for underage gay youth. The Foundation sponsored several social gatherings, some at the Imperial Roller Rink at the east end of the Hawthorne Bridge (now an indoor soccer facility).

Foundation leaders attempted to set standards for the gay community, providing alternatives for youth, who often looked old enough to patronize gay and straight bars. Kelly's dates to 1902, and was for many years known as a place to hook up with longshoremen when there were still active docks a few blocks east on the Willamette River. It was called the "Olympian" because it sold Olympian (WA) beer.

PREAMBLE

THE SECOND FOUNDATION OF OREGON is a charitable organization established in the State of Oregon — dedicated to the aid and growth of the person through counseling services, social encounters, religious experiences and the building of community support and spirit.

What does it mean "To be a person"? Could you say it means "To be that self which one truly is." That self with all its marvelous parts and attitudes and talents brought together in the human being we call a "person". What if someone answers that statement with — "I am a homosexual person" — Can that statement really include all that society, psychology, and church mean when speaking of *personhood*?

We of THE SECOND FOUNDATION OF OREGON believe it can mean just that. We believe in the beauty and goodness of the person, without any qualification. We are a homophile organization, called into existence by the needs of real persons, some very confused, some very much in need of others and community and some ready to help their brothers and sisters with the same needs.

But above all, we are striving for community — for it is only in the atmosphere of a loving community that one can grow as a person, and experience his unique worth. It is only through real human love that the person can grow, blossom and achieve that state of personhood he has within him.

We of THE SECOND FOUNDATION OF OREGON believe that we can strive to achieve that community. We believe that we can help men and women grow. We believe we can say something important not only to the homophile community, but to our own society in general and to the community of Oregon in particular.

Dave Kohl photos

Portland Archives

Prelude 1853 - 1971

and main-line Christian denominations had begun addressing issues around gay Christianity in the early 1970s.

Roman Catholics since the mid-'60s were in turmoil over the changes made at the Vatican II Council called by Pope John XXIII. Over a 3-year period, their familiar, ritual-oriented Latin-speaking church altered the practices of 2000 years. Services were conducted in the vernacular (in America, that meant English or Spanish). Habits were changed, as were robes. Laymen took over roles from Brothers, Friars, and Priests in schooling and worship. Financing of local parishes now became a local responsibility. Church policies on homosexuality and birth control became debatable topics.

The Roman Catholic Church hoped to open windows of understanding to enlighten and encourage the membership; but many people left through those open windows, relieved of strict structure and dogmatic limitations. The opportunity to question and explore articles of faith and practice led to individual journeys of faith, the study of alternative meditation practices, and a spirit of ecumenism. Hence, the cooperation in Portland of the Catholics in the founding of Koinonia House at PSU was possible.

Dignity became the Roman Catholic grass-roots gay organization in 1969. Never sanctioned by the Church, this national group provided support, education, worship, and socialization for thousands of Catholic gays and lesbians who did not want to leave the church, but who could not openly worship within it. Chapters opened in all major cities where a sympathetic priest or parish would make its facilities available. Such places in Portland were St. Philip Neri on SE Division and St. Francis on SE 12th at Oak, four blocks east from Centenary-Wilbur, across Sandy Blvd.

St. Herman's Liberal Catholic Church met at various churches, including Centenary-Wilbur, St. David's Episcopal at SE 28th and Harrison, and in the large home of Nestor Perala at 2229 SE Market. Gay attendees were invited in 1971 to their 9 am Sunday masses, which also proclaimed an open communion. Their theology came out of the *Theosophical Society* in Ojai, California, keeping the rituals and customs of the pre-Vatican II Catholic Church, but changing the accompanying theology.

The Church of St. Joan of Arc at 43rd and NE Broadway offered a ministry to non-sexist Christians at St. Michael and All Angels Episcopal parish. Sunday meetings involved Holy Eucharist, coffee hour, and rap groups. Father David Rich-Miller led that group.

Boxed advertisements for all the above were placed in the monthly *Fountain*.

The Second Foundation established a Religious Committee by February of 1972, and Father David led that committee on a *Day of Recollection* event March 12. He later became active with another gay support group called the Portland Town Council, which formed in late 1975, and participated in later MCC services. (See chapter 3)

Elsewhere, religion and homosexuality had been involved in a courtship dance for several years. In San Francisco, a coalition of homophile leaders and clergy formed the Council on Religion and the Homosexual (CRH) in 1964. The hope was that by involving men of the cloth, an aura of credibility could be added to the activities of the Society for Individual Rights (SIR) and the League for Civil Education (LCE), two early San Francisco gay activist groups that had been growing since 1961. SF bar owners and employees had formed the Tavern Guild in 1962, and together with the SF chapter of the Mattachine Society formed the largest homophile organization in the country.

The San Francisco Council on Religion and the Homosexual organized a New Year's Eve ball in 1964 to raise money for the gay community. Despite their promise to the clergy to not interfere with the event, police showed up in force to film individuals as they entered California Hall, and then found a pretext to enter the ball and arrest several of the organizers. The result was that clergy now further understood that tales of police harassment and oppression were not exaggerated.

The first fully gay publication in Portland was *The Fountain*, the publication of the Second Foundation.

Troy Perry's early autobiography gave him instant fame, He was recognized in the LIFE magazine article in 1973, and appeared on several TV talk shows. He would also participate in several demonstrations, fasts, and protest events.

THE FOUNTAIN

VOLUME 1 NUMBER 1   MARCH 1971

THE FOUNTAIN
The Official Publication
of THE SECOND FOUNDATION
of OREGON

Published monthly in the intrest of the Homosexual community.

EDITOR
Neil Hutchins

CONTRIBUTORS
Duayne Downing
Paul Bearden
Jennie Crawford
Terry Tunnell

OFFICERS OF THE SECOND FOUNDATION OF OREGON

PRESIDENT
GEORGE OBERG

SECRETARY
LARRY BECK

TREASURER
DAVE FREDRICKSON

BOARD OF DIRECTORS
NEIL HUTCHINS

Articles represent the viewpoint of the writers and are not necessarily the opinion of the Second Foundation of Oregon.

THE SECOND FOUNDATION OF OREGON

IN THE BEGINNING..

In October 1970 a group of interested individuals headed by Neil Hutchins and Dennis Kennedy met for the first time to discuss the needs for a homosexual counseling service. The first meeting was held at The Koinonia House and was haired by Father Healy, and attended by Julia Saslow of the PSU Counseling Service. Much was discussed at this meeting and the consesus came that the need did exist for this service. The group decided the best way to become involved was to organize. Many saw the need for more than a counseling center and so the idea of a homophile organization grew. A committee was appointed by Father Healy and the wheels were set b motion. At the fllowing meetings things were voted on and discussed and on Feb. 9th a costitution was adopted and proceedings started to file The Second Foundation of Oregon with the State as a non-profit corporation. The name of the Organization was suggested by Terry Tunnell along with other names, but this name was selected by a vote of the members. Many people have come to me and asked what The Second Foundation is and where it is going. I can only answer, "attend some of our meetings and find out."
I can state some of the long range ideas for The Second Foundation. The first and most important being a counseling service. This service would be free of charge to anyone that would like to understand better his sexual identity. The second Foundation also islooking to the future in the terms of a gay community center. A center that would be large enough to hold meetings, plays, social events, dances along with offices and meeting rooms. We are hoping to b able to provide many community services like employmen counseling. lawyer referral services legal aid, housing help and many other areas of need by the gay community. As you can see our hopes are high and that's where they will stay. Because we are sure we can accomplish many of these projects, but not without your help. Please Help Us and yourself to a more rewarding and meaningful life...Join The Second Foundation.

The Lord Is My Shepherd and He Knows I'm Gay

By Reverend Troy Perry
Founder, Metropolitan Community Church
With Charles L. Lucas

Opinions shared in *The Fountain* often revealed deep thought, anger, hurt, and patience:

• "The movement should emphasize the right to love, rather than the right to have sexual encounters..."

• "The gay community runs around screaming for recognition by the straight community, but they will not give their own people the recognition they deserve..."

• "We cannot expect active support from our black gay brothers until we integrate our own heads... there is a clear lack of understanding for the position of blacks and women in the Gay Liberation movement..."

• "The basis of gay oppression is the homosexual's refusal to cooperate in the sexual-political class stratification of our society..."

• "It seems that psychologists are more concerned with adjusting people to fit into an immoral society rather than changing that society...Now that homosexuality is not so much regarded as a crime or a sin, many gays see our real enemy as being the sickness theory..."

• "We need cooperation between the men and women very much. There is more that can be done by cooperation than segregation..."

• "Whenever I have seen gay women and men trying to work together, the women almost always end up getting screwed over. It is a shame, because gay men can profit a lot from the new lesbian awareness..."

• "Gay people are the tragic victims of this caste system - where all men are to rule women, and some men are to rule other men, be it monarchy, democracy, or socialism...

Prelude 1853 - 1971

Glide Memorial Methodist, the church in the Tenderloin area, became increasingly active in trying to meet the social needs of street people, gay youth, runaways, and itinerants. Three ministers and yearly interns in 1965 and 1966 worked to establish credibility with their clients and to use the Gospel as a basis for social action. The group named itself as Vanguard. Individual self-criticism and self-help was as important as group action. The church provided spiritual and philosophical help to support SF gays and transvestites in a confrontation at Compton's Cafeteria on July 18, 1966.

Methodist churches in several other communities also supported individual rights. Capitol Hill Methodist in Seattle provided worship facilities for MCC Seattle from 1972 until the mid-1980s. Portland's Centenary-Wilbur provided meeting space for several religious and activist groups in the politically turbulent 70's, especially groups protesting the unpopular war and the government seen as responsible for so many of the social evils of the day.

Ads also appeared in the *NW Gay Review* for several other religious groups, one being Evangelicals Concerned. Not a church, this was a National Task Force and Fellowship for gay Christians and concerned Evangelicals. Their Northwest chapter headquarters were in Seattle.

Good News

On a national level, the topic of homosexuality was presented in an eleven-page spread in *LIFE magazine's* end-of-the-year issue in December 1971. *LIFE* surveyed the phenomenon of gay revolts stemming from *Stonewall* and other protest activities, especially in New York City. Various aspects of the gay movement were explained in a neutral non-judgmental photo essay. Profiles of individual gays and lesbians included propagandists, communalists, activists, writers, politicians, and ministers.

Two pages of the *LIFE* spread were dedicated to Rev. Troy Perry, the MCC denomination of 20 churches, and Troy's involvement in protests against California's archaic sex laws with a fast during a six-day march of 109 miles.

Addressing the "normalcy" of homosexuality, *LIFE* presented a balanced and reasoned discussion at a time when 45 states had sodomy laws and the American Psychiatric Association still regarded homosexuality as a disease.

Metropolitan Community Church was about to make its first appearance in Portland.

Metal pendant worn by many early MCC church members from various cities.throughout the country.

1971 Thanksgiving Eve–NW Airlines Flight 105 from Portland skyjacked by D. B. Cooper, bailed out with $200,000. None of the money was ever found.
- Church of England and Vatican agree on the meaning of the Eucharist.
- Daniel Ellsberg releases his Pentagon Papers about U.S. involvement in Viet Nam.
- *Godspell* and *Jesus Christ* Superstar both are hits on Broadway.
- 26th Amendment to the Constitution lowers voting age to 18.
- *All in the Family* makes Archie Bunker and "meat-head" household names.
- Communist "Red" China admitted to United Nations.

1972 Military draft ends; armed forces become volunteer.
- Mark Spitz swims to seven gold medals in the Sapporo Summer Olympics.
- Richard Nixon visits China; reelected president; break-in discovered at the Watergate office complex.

1973 Juan Peron reelected Argentine President.
- *The Exorcist* horrifies viewers with visions of demons and the occult.
- Roe v. Wade Supreme Court decision legalizes abortion.

Chapter Two

Early MCC Groups

October 1971-December 1973

"If you had faith the size of a mustard seed, you could say to this mulberry tree, 'Be uprooted and planted in the sea,' and it would obey you."
Luke 17:6 (An Inclusive Version)

Metropolitan Community Church Effort #1

On October 24, 1971, the first official meeting of Portland Metropolitan Community Church was held at Centenary-Wilbur Methodist Church at 215 SE 9th Ave. The meeting was conducted by Rev. Ken Jones, a former minister of the Assembly of God, who was a missionary for the MCC. He lived in San Francisco, and commuted to Portland.

Origins of the UFMCC

Metropolitan Community Church was a fellowship of churches rather than a denomination at this time. Begun in 1968 by Rev. Troy Perry in Los Angeles, the church had grown into a fellowship of about 35 congregations spread across America. Perry's story is best told in his 1990 autobiography *Don't Be Afraid Anymore*. In summary, Troy's tale began when his secret same-sex orientation and activities were revealed by his then-bishop in the Church of God of Prophecy. He had resigned his pastorate in 1963, accepted his then-wife's request for divorce, spent a hitch in the U.S. Army, and after a time of soul-searching determined that God wanted him to study scripture for answers to the supposed Christian v. homosexual dilemma, and start a church for homosexuals.

Placing an announcement in a local Los Angeles gay newspaper called *The Advocate*, he held a living room gathering for interested gay Christians in his pink house in Huntington Park, on Sunday, October 6, 1968. Among other concerns, he feared the arrival of protesters and the loss of his job at Sears, where he had a job in the yardage department. With the support of his mothe,r and roommate Willie Smith, the afternoon service attracted 12 attendees. The Spirit was infectious. The group multiplied rapidly, moved to a Los Angeles Women's Club, then the Echo Theater, before purchasing an old church building on Union Avenue at 22nd in Los Angeles by March 1971. It had held services in a gay bar near Disneyland and been the subject of news articles in *The Advocate* and *The Washington Post.* Troy had held an impromptu prayer service in the National Cathedral. The evolving Metropolitan Community Church proclaimed:

"Liberation for all, a church which extends its ministry to all nationalities, a church in which women and men are one in Christ, a church in which there is a mingling of rich and poor, old and young, handsome and homely, butch and fem, transvestites and transsexuals, a church which welcomes gay people and straight people to worship together, to witness together, and to work and serve together." (*NW Fountain*, September 1978, p.7)

Rev Troy Perry first invited gay Christians into his house in Huntington Park in October 1968. The group quickly numbered in the hundreds and soon purchased an old church on Union Ave. in Los Angeles. They restored the old building and worshiped there until destroyed by an arsonist in 1973.

✝ Metropolitan Community Church

Portland

The first meeting of the Metropolitan Community Church was held Sunday, October 24, at the Centenary Wilbur Methodist Church, 215 S.E. 9th Ave., to form the foundation of a homophile Christian community in Portland. The meeting was conducted by Rev. Ken Jones, a former minister of the Assembly of God and now a missionary for the MCC which is an interdenominational congregational Christian church.

Rev. Jones refers to the MCC as "a fellowship of churches rather than a denomination. A church which upholds the basic Christian tenets of faith. The goals of the MCC are to unite the homophile community in Christian fellowship."

MCC's purpose is basically to minister to the homosexual community in both a religious and social basis. The MCC views homosexuality not as a sin but as a variation in the many ways that human beings used to express affection, if that affection is in terms of an act of love and not mere lust.

The MCC was founded in 1968 by Rev. Troy Perry in Los Angeles and now has 21 active churches in almost every major city in the U.S. It is a Christian church, however, those who do not believe in the divinity of Christ may become "friends of MCC", and can participate in regular activities but will be ineligible to vote at congregational meetings or to serve on the board of the church. Straight members are welcome and many members of MCC, acording to Rev. Jones, are heterosexual. The pastor of Portland's MCC has yet to be selected but he will be empowered to perform homosexual marriages which Jones refers to as "committments of a Holy Union."

The MCC's goal is to integrate the homosexual back into every area of society especially the church.

Services will be held every Sunday at the Centenary Wilbur Church at 2 P.M. Inquiries about MCC, for the time being, should be sent to Rev. Ken Jones, 317 Northhaven Drive, Daly City, California, or The Second Foundation, 227-5651.

Early MCC Groups 1971 - 1973

Troy published the results of his Biblical search in 1971, as *The Lord is My Shepherd and He Knows I'm Gay*. It became a best seller, and eventually Troy was featured on several TV talk shows and in publiations such as *Time, Life, Newsweek, Playboy, Esquire,* and *Cosmopolitan* magazines. His Gospel program involved three aspects:

Salvation–God so loved the world that God sent Jesus to tell us that whoever believes shall not perish but have everlasting life; and that "whoever" included me as a gay male, unconditionally, because salvation is free–no church can take it away;

Community–for those who have no families who care about them, or who find themselves alone or friendless, the church will be a family;

Christian Social Action–We would stand up for our rights, secular and religious, and we would start fighting the many forms of tyranny that oppressed us. (Perry, Troy, *Don't Be Afraid Anymore,* p. 38)

Portland's first involvement with the Metropolitan Community Church came about through the efforts of Neil Hutchins, who had also been instrumental in the formation of *The Second Foundation*. Neil had lived in San Francisco, been a part of *SIR* (Society for Individual Rights) and had been on the staff of *Vector, SIR's* monthly magazine. Having attended MCC-San Francisco, Neil contacted that church about sending someone to help start an MCC in Portland.

Most MCC congregations began as study groups or missions of other MCC churches. Many first met in bars, and critics often noted the transient nature of several "iffy" congregations. The Portland group assembled in the liberal east side building also housing the Ninth Street Exit. Centenary-Wilbur Methodist in inner southeast Portland was the common meeting ground for activists and open-thinkers. The Portland State Gay Men's Union met there on Monday evenings. The Gay Liberation Front had organized there in 1970, as did the *Vortex* group. The site was well known in the underground community.

Rev. Jones promoted MCC as a church that upholds the basic Christian tenets of faith. Although a Christian church, those who did not believe in the divinity of Christ were also welcome to become friends of MCC. MCC's goal was to integrate the homosexual back into every area of society, especially the church. Straight members were also welcomed.

On the controversial issue of the morality of homosexuality, Rev. Jones represented the MCC viewpoint that homosexuality is not a sin, but is a variation on the many ways that human beings use to express affection, if that affection is in terms of an act of love and not mere lust.

Although a regular pastor had not been selected, the group met each Sunday at 2 pm. Contacts for Rev. Jones were listed in Daly City, California. The Second Foundation also served as a contact point from its offices at 1017 SW Morrison, and carried an article and ads about worship services in *The Fountain*. Dwayne Downing headed The Foundation's Religion Committee and coordinated their Sunday morning meetings with MCC services.

Radio programs featured interviews with several religious personages of Portland and on April 13, *KBOO* aired an interview with MCC's Pastor Jones discussing the role of the church. *The Oregon Journal* ran a story on the gay community and its connection with churches on August 30.

Services were moved to the Parker Chapel in the YMCA building on SW 6th. In the March 1972 Fountain, an article stated that Pastor Fred Seferrazzo had recently taken over the MCC services. He had moved from Los Angeles recently, and was adding his organizational talents to the group. Times and dates of weekly Sunday afternoon services were listed on the calendar of events for the gay community in *The Fountain*, with a special large ad for the Easter celebration.

Sometime during this interval, MCC was visited by a minister from San Francisco familiar with the MCC there. He was passing through Portland on a business trip. As he drove east

Portland's first Gay Community Center was upstairs in this building at 258 SE Alder, where an Italian Restaurant had been located. Above the Other Inn near Dahl & Penne's, it was easy to find. Second Foundation leaders hoped to provide a better place for young gay men to socialize, rather than looking for pick-ups a few blocks south in the "camp" or at the Greyhound depot, where the restrooms were very popular.

Portland City Archive

OrHi neg 020615

Portland City Archive

OrHi neg 66372

OrHi neh 88697

62

leaving Portland, he had a strange feeling that someday he would be back in Portland, doing some type of ministry. His name was Austin Amerine.

A few months later, Pastor Seferrazzo returned to the MCC mother church in Los Angeles. Rev. Jones had found the commuting arrangement from San Francisco too difficult, and Fred Seferrazzo was also unable to continue. By July, there was no mention of, or worship schedule posted for, MCC in *The Fountain*, but there was a listing in the community services section for the Portland Community Church. Services were conducted at Parker Chapel at the old YMCA, ironically the focus of the 1912 sex scandal, and the same venue where the first gay Christians in Portland had met in 1968.

Opinions On Christianity and Homosexuals

• The Church and the Homosexual continued to be a frequent topic in dialogues and articles in *The Fountain*. The full range of viewpoints were expressed. What follows are a few of the various comments on the issue:

• "We should point out that the short-tempered St. Paul never knew Jesus in the flesh, while the gentle John did."

• "The Bible-thumping church for centuries has cried that natural homo-love was not normal and was condemned by Paul."

• "The Bible is undeniably anti-woman... St. Paul even blamed Eve for the fall of the human race."

• "Paul did discuss the problem of synchronistic churches who were incorporating forms of pagan sex worship into their churches... Paul condemns only promiscuous sex."

• "Paul wrote not only from a Jewish point of view, but also against a background of debauchery, especially in Corinth that would make book store regulars on SW 3rd blush."

• "The term Christian means a follower of Christ, not a person indoctrinated with 'churchianity'...the *Christian gay* who seeks God and finds Him knows that there is so much more to knowing Him than a Sunday ritual."

• "Women's Liberation has not made religion a part of their movement like gays have, since Christianity throughout history has reinforced the inferior position of women."

• "For too long gays have listened to ministers telling them they are sinners, police telling them they are criminals, and psychiatrists telling them they are sick."

• "The Bible is full of sexual curses aimed at women, homosexuals, and those who dare to spill their seed on the ground... If religion is a crutch...Troy Perry is a brand new wheelchair."

• "There is no question that most of homosexual oppression stems directly from the Judeo-Christian heritage... Among the peoples of the ancient Mediterranean, only the Jews forbade homosexual activity."

• "We have no actual words attributable to Jesus on the subject of homosexuality...It does not seem that the church is treating the homosexual as Jesus would want it to...The Christian religion has been a leaven of compassion throughout its history."

• "If the church would adopt the attitude that perhaps the homosexual is the man sinned against rather than the sinner, there might not be the so-called "homosexual problem." Many Gay people have a deep sense of religious responsibility and sincerely wish to belong to a religious organization. Is it possible that just because of their sexual orientation, these people will not be allowed to follow what they feel is right and thus be denied serving Jesus Christ as they feel called to do?"

Portland's Gay Community Center

A two-page interview with Allen Ginsberg ran in the April 2, 1971 *Fountain*, wherein the beat poet linked protest and liberation movements with rock musicians such as The Doors, and Jefferson Airplane. He also expounded on the path each person takes to discover their soul, either "naturally by God's finger's touch or (through) psychedelic drugs." He set both American and Asian Indians as a model of sitting and waiting in tranquility long hours for gods to come into one's consciousness. He said, "Sit down an hour every morning from now on. Otherwise, there will be a growing credibility gap between inflated revolutionary violent rhetoric and the so-called spiritual revolution which is also part of the inflated violent revolutionary

Portland City Archive

Neil Hutchins Archive

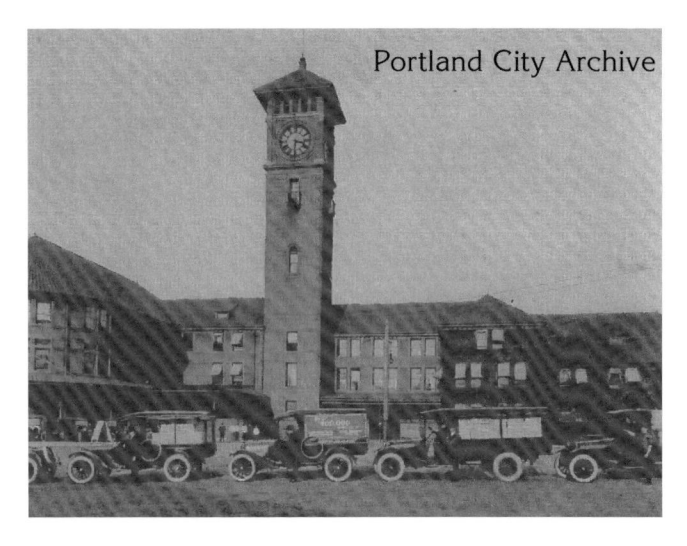

George Oberg photos

Single men arrived by bus and train at Union Station. The Second Foundation hoped to help young men coming out to avoid unsavory experiences. Neil Hutchins edited *The Fountain*, which carried advertising for MCC monthly.

Skits and plays were part of the entertainment at the Second Foundation, introducing a different level of drag to the community, which often adjourned to the nearby Lotus for refreshments.

Portland City Archives

64

Early MCC Groups 1971 - 1973

rhetoric." More good stuff to talk about at the Ninth Street Exit!

Since the inception of the Second Foundation, one major goal had been to establish a Gay Community Center. In November of 1971, actions were undertaken to search out a location. One major goal was to establish a place where under-21 gays could meet others like themselves, feel safe, and engage in counseling and other positive activities. Many younger gay men had been involved in several programs of the Foundation, but they had no legal social outlets in a culture that revolved primarily around alcohol.

For many years, an area commonly referred to as Camp or The Camp had been the domain of underage boys looking to meet men for various intimacies, often involving money. New York City had the Port Authority. In Boston it was called the Combat Zone. Hollywood's area was the Golden Cup. Portland's corner was at SW 3rd and Taylor.

The Oregonian reported that boy prostitutes–known as hustlers or chickens–would provide a variety of sexual acts when paid between $10 and $50 by customers–known as "tricks." Initially a hangout for local young men, soon there was a group of out-of-state fellows who came to cash in on the "skin" trade. The area included SW Yamhill and SW Taylor between 2nd and 3rd Avenues. The sleazy character of the zone attracted the attention of the police, and an Officer Murphy often patrolled the area, making arrests on occasion for vagrancy, loitering, J-walking, or disturbing the peace. (*The Oregonian*, September 11, 1977, p G7)

Boys between the ages of 14 and 21 were known to line up along walls of vacant parking lots, watching the passing parade of potential customers–single men driving, repeatedly through the "camp." Some boys were "trade," supposedly straight, but willing to be passive in an oral encounter. *The Oregonian* story noted that customers were often clergymen, stockbrokers, truck drivers and schoolteachers, ranging from white to blue collar. Some were regular clients who took their hustler to motels, apartments, the clients' homes, or to downtown parking structures, where the sex acts were performed. The adult gay community abhorred such activity, both because of the fact that older men were taking advantage of youngsters, and because it perpetuated the common myth that all gay men were predatory pedophiles. There were many incidents involving confrontations with straight boys taunting the younger gays. Trouble often involved fast cars, knives, tire irons, and lots of verbal abuse.

Gay bars were the subject of a large *Oregon Journal* article. The Riptide was listed as a popular gay hangout. Observing that there had been a recent proliferation of gay bars in Portland, twelve bars were referenced including The Embers, Dahl and Penne's, the Other Inn, Half Moon Tavern, Pink Cat (actually a bookstore), Club Northwest, and Zorba the Greek's. The other five bars were not named.

Individuals seeking sexual gratification in an anonymous setting often visited several movie houses, some being lower class theaters showing standard and B-grade films, and others specifically catering to men seeking pornography. Some of the older theaters in downtown Portland had lost their glitter and offered cheap showings of 2nd run films. The Circle and Blue Mouse on SW 4th, the Capitol on Broadway, and the Round Up on Morrison were popular. The Capitol and Circle Theaters both had balconies well known as venues for anonymous encounters. On the Eastside, the Oriental, Egyptian, Irvington and Walnut Park Theaters had well-deserved sleazy reputations.

"Peepshow" movie houses also existed. In the days before videos, 8 mm and 16 mm films and film loops were viewed in booths in "select" theaters. Live dancers performed erotic numbers at several spots, the most popular with gay men being the Tom Kat at 425 NW Glisan. Popular porno theaters included the Adult Flick at 24 NW Broadway, the adult-only Oregon Theater on SE Division, and several "sin city" type shows on SW 3rd near the "camp." Much of this area was disappearing by 1972 with urban renewal. Destruction of a large area south of Jefferson and near the Civic Auditorium pro-

Common places to "hang out" in Portland included the Round-Up Theater, located on Morrison, between SW 3rd and SW 4th. In the adjacent building was the Blue Mouse Theater, once the Capitol. Also in that building was the Olympic Baths. The block was torn down in 1977 to make way for a parking structure. The Mayfair Theater on SW Broadway became the Fox, until it was torn down to become the new Fox Tower in 2003. In south east Portland, the Oregon Theater on SE Division had declined greatly since the silent film era. The Bob White was a neighborhood cinema on SE Foster, near 64th. Both were known by the 1970s as places for boys to play while seeing cheap films.

Early MCC Groups 1971 - 1973

duced new steel and glass architectural landmarks such as the 40-story First National Bank Tower, completed in 1972.

So it was in May 1972, that the Second Foundation of Oregon opened its first Gay Community Center, and moved their offices from SW Morrison. The Center was located in the Chambers Building, and occupied the entire second floor, with a private entrance at 258 SW Alder Street. With about 4500 square feet, there was room to divide what had been an elegant Italian restaurant with vaulted embossed ceilings into three spaces. There would be offices for the Foundation, for counseling, and for *The Fountain*; a drop-in center and reception area; and meeting rooms. There was enough space for large socials and dances. Volunteers came forth to repair, clean, paint, and donate furnishings. Finally the gay community had a visible and identifiable space, and one they were proud of.

The Fountain continued to be the voice of the gay and lesbian community, expanding to include Seattle, Spokane, and Vancouver, BC in its coverage. A *Fountain* representative reported from each of those cities monthly, and the pastor of MCC Seattle, Rev. Robert Sirico, wrote a regular column. Sirico had served a stint in the U.S. Military, and his messages were plain and common sense. His columns provided sound advice on topics such as coming out, revealing one's orientation to family and friends, and acceptance of Christ as the *Great Liberator*. For about a year, through July of 1973, his monthly columns encouraged readers to seek alternative avenues by which gays could achieve liberation; to realize that unity and education were crucial; to know that until all are free, none will be free. He reminded readers that, "God is no respecter of persons–Christ died for all...by placing one's faith in Him, you will become a new creature–a new homosexual, a new heterosexual!" There is a promise in the Bible for those who will dare to trust in God. It says, "Casting all your care upon Him, for He careth for you." God is interested in our well being, and He stands ready to help in time of need.

The Lord is My Shepherd and He Knows I'm Gay

The October *Fountain* carried Sirico's review of Rev. Troy Perry's newly-released book, *The Lord is My Shepherd and He Knows I'm Gay*. The review recommended the book as one that "you cannot put down" as it traced Perry's journey through childhood, the fiery accidental death of his father, early ministry, marriage and two children, the armed forces, a shattered gay relationship, to the founding of the Los Angeles Metropolitan Community Church in 1968. Another reviewer in January 1973, R.L. Sanderstrom, observed the fact that Perry being homosexual didn't bother Jesus. "Christ did not say even once, 'Come to me all you heterosexuals, who, if you have sex or intercourse, (must) have it in the missionary position with a hetero'." Placement of the book in public libraries caused controversy, and even legal battles in Niles, Michigan.

The book came out at a fortuitous time for Portland gays, as a team of "Jesus People" had been distributing anti-gay literature at the Lloyd Center, and the current issue of the Jehovah's Witness *Awake Magazine* had published an article condemning homosexuality as an "abomination," calling for gays to be "put to death."

On a brighter note in September of 1972, Rev. Rodney Page, Associate Director of the Greater Portland Council of Churches, proposed that his organization should host a conference on religion and the homosexual. Page had been the campus minister at the PSU campus ministry as a Disciples of Christ pastor. He was also Director of the Center for Urban Encounters. The conference was scheduled to be held at Augusta Lutheran Church on NE Knott, but was postponed, and ultimately canceled.

Medical professors and marriage counselors were beginning to see homosexuality as just a biological variation. Dr. Joseph B. Trainer noted, "It is no more possible for them to change, by persuasion or harassment, than it is for a straight person to become homosexual." (*Journal*, Aug. 31, 1972 p8). He also made it

Neil Hutchins Archive photos

Greg Pitts Archive

Neil Hutchins Archive

Dahl & Penne's became the "home bar" for most young emerging gay men in Portland during the 1970s. Purchased by Gene and Sam (on the left and right of the top photo) in 1972, its back room soon became the venue for drag shows. The Vanessa, Empress X of the Imperial Sovereign Rose Court, held sway there for over ten years. The back room was the "Royal Flush Corral" and site of many drag shows. These fundraising events were often held to benefit the Portland Town Council or other causes advancing gay rights. Drag queens donated their time and efforts many times. One popular bartender was Lida, pictured here in 1973. Sunday mornings at D&P's was called "Sunday Mass," featuring waiters on roller skates serving up breakfast as early as 7am.

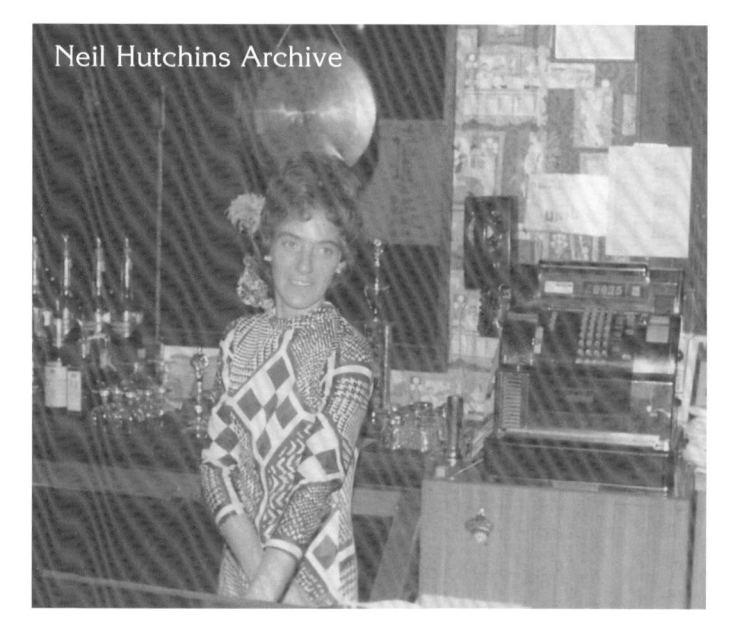

Dahl & Penne's popularity dates back to the 1960s, prior to its acquisition by the Landauers. It was built as the Montana Assay Company. in 1884. Originally Dahl and Penne was a soft drink company. This view is looking north, with 2nd Ave. on the right. The cross street is Alder. The Other Inn and Grand Oasis were a block west, forming the "dirty triangle."

OrHi neg 51949

Early MCC Groups 1971 - 1973

clear that it usually took a man about two years to go through all the steps of "coming out," and that many homosexuals are not sexually active at all, merely preferring the company of persons of the same-sex. "The public somehow has the idea that the homosexual is a sex fiend of some kind, but this is not often the case. Some get married because society is pretty ferocious to people like them."

In July, the Portland Forum and the Second Foundation hosted a joint picnic at McIver Park, site of *Vortex I*. The all-day event featured lots of food, an auction, and a carnival –all designed to build a greater sense of gay community among members of the two groups.

Portland Gay Bar Culture in the 1970s

Portland was an appealing mecca for Northwest men hoping to explore their sexuality and orientation in the mid-1970s. The attractions of the City included basically clean bars that one could enter through a front door without having to use a password. Bars were located throughout the city, not just in a sleazy part of town. There was no mafia activity and the bars were not beholden to payoffs or police harassment. One could dance with a same-sex partner in bars without having to worry about watching for a signal should police arrive. In other towns, such a warning system alerted dance partners to switch to an opposite sex friend when officers would show up.

A straight California couple decided to purchase a dilapidated tavern at SW 2nd and Alder. It had been called Dahl and Penne's since 1914 and was tacky at best. But they wanted a change from their California careers and a challenge. Mama Bernice Norris met them, was charmed, and sent The Vanessa, her dancer and decorator, over to help them redecorate and start up a few shows. The rest is Portland gay legend... D&P's soared in popularity, becoming the venue of countless drag shows, Mr. Leather contests, the meeting spot for out-of-town men-seeking-men, a few MCC events, "Sunday Mass," and nearly 11 years of traditions.

"If this is Sunday, this must be Portland," was a common expression among Portland gays. Many even stayed home Saturday nights to rest up for a full day of socializing on Sunday, starting at 7 am at D&P's. Waiters dressed as nuns on roller skates began serving cocktails before dawn. The place was packed with eaters and drinkers. Many tipsters would relocate to Wilde Oscar's for brunch. By 3 pm, the crowd had reassembled at the Family Zoo for drinks and dancing to music reminiscent of Woodstock.

Problems facing gays in 1972 involved civil rights – housing and job discrimination – noted the Second Foundation's lobbyist, George Nicola. Gays felt the stigma of society, creating an identity crisis for homosexuals and fears of persecution. The internal battle to resolve one's gay tendencies was compounded by society's judgment that gays were degenerate. The Second Foundation wanted to be more than social, continuing the battle for laws more indulgent to homosexual behavior...where the "unstructured" Gay Liberation movement had left off.

Then in September, five representatives from the Second Foundation had a short meeting in Salem with Governor Tom McCall, who had been reelected either because of, or in spite of, his support of *Vortex I*. The men requested that a gay representative be placed on the Governor's Committee on Human Rights, and also requested an executive order that could ban discrimination in state employment. Two of those speakers were Neil Hutchins, editor of *The Fountain*, and George Nicola.

On the national scene, 1972 was the year Shirley Chisholm became the first black woman to seek the Democratic Party nomination for President.

1973

1973 was a tumultuous year for America in general and for the gay community in Oregon and nationwide. It would include the Watergate revelations over President Nixon's misuse of power, as well as much anti -Viet Nam War protesting.

Well known movie houses of the 1970s included the old Blue Mouse, which relocated into the former Capitol Theater with its infamous balcony, The Egyptian and Walnut Park Theaters on NE Union, and the Roxy. The Circle, on SW 4th, also had a balcony, divided into sections for couples and singles.

OrHi neg 4711

Portland City Archive

Portland City Archives   OrHi neg 91253

70

Early MCC Groups 1971 - 1973

It was a year of anti-gay activity that would come to include the June 20 arsonist attack on the Upstairs Lounge in New Orleans, killing 30 and critically wounding eight members of the gay community. MCC New Orleans had offices in the same building. Among the dead were several members of MCC-New Orleans and its pastor Rev. Dave Larson. The 16-minute gasoline-fueled holocaust was one of the worst in that city's history. Troy Perry was in the city within a day. He organized local support, relief for survivors, and advised on legal issues. MCC churches around the country rallied to send financial and emotional support.

On July 27, arsonists successfully set fire to the MCC-San Francisco building for the second time. The congregation had been using Steward Memorial Presbyterian Church at 23rd and Guerrero. It was the sixth burning in that city of a gay-oriented institution in seven months, including the headquarters of the Society for Individual Rights (SIR). In a display of community support, Sheriff Richard Hongisto and City Supervisor John Molinari launched a campaign to raise $100,000 needed to rebuild the church.

On October 2, the MCC-Indianapolis became the first congregation anywhere in the gay denomination's history to be raided. Police entered the home where worship was held after the completion of a communion service, expecting to find a "happening." Pastor Bo Daniels eventually convinced the interlopers as to the nature of the infant church, and the intruders backed off. Several press conferences, the involvement of the *ACLU*, and work with the MCC District coordinator in Atlanta, turned the event into a catalyst to solidify the gay community there and throughout the MCC Fellowship.

In Seattle, the Episcopal Church denied the priesthood to John Rowe when he was about to take Holy Orders. He became a minister with Seattle MCC instead. Several alternative national religious movements originated in the early 70s, including the Metropolitan Community Temple, organized in Los Angeles by Jerry Small and Jerry Gordon in 1972. The summer of 1973 saw several national conventions of national church groups addressing the topic of homosexuality and Christianity.

There were several high points for the Oregon gay community that year. Peggy Burton, a high school teacher from Turner, who had been fired for perceived "immorality," won her lawsuit against her school district with a judgment from Senior Portland Federal District Court Judge Gus Solomo. Charles Hinkle was her attorney. TV station KGW carried a five-part feature series on Portland's Gay community from Monday to Friday January 8-12 on both the noon and 5:30 evening news. Each "spot" was about five minutes long. The series included:

Monday–*Coming Out*, with Andrew Henry, John Wilkinson, and Dawn Anderson
Tuesday–*Legal Problems* - George Nicola and attorney Jere Webb
Wednesday–*Lesbian Issues* - Elise Rosenbaum; Mary Furnari, Barb Aehle, and Robin Wright
Thursday–*Ego-Destruction*–Steve Fulmer, Nicola, and Charles Hinkle
Friday–*The Second Foundation* and its work–Neil Hutchins, Roy Bouse, Doris Stubblefield, Nicola and Ray Thompson

Politics

In Eugene, an activist student and avowed homosexual gained the leadership of the University of Oregon's million-dollar Incidental Fees Committee. He reassigned funds so that women's sports received 50% of the athletic fund; the campus bowling alley had to give same-sex couples the same couples discounts as straight couples; and he worked towards acceptance of gay liberation. His name was Randy Shilts...later to become known as the powerful and outspoken author of such gay issue works as *And the Band Played On*.

In Salem, newly elected representative Vera Katz proposed a Gay Rights Bill. She allowed lobbyist George Nicola to use her office as he sought support for the Bill. He had become involved through his work with County Commissioner Gladys McCoy, the first African American to be elected to any office in Oregon. In Portland, he rallied supporters to a meeting at the Family Zoo, where letters were penned and sent to representatives. Working with Steve and

The Lord Is My Shepherd and He Knows I'm Gay

The Autobiography of the Rev. Troy D. Perry

As told to Charles L. Lucas

With a Foreword by Mrs. Edith Perry

Nash Publishing, Los Angeles

Rev. Troy Perry wrote about his understanding of a loving Christ in his 1973 autobiography. It was widely reviewed, and gained recognition on a national level. He appeared on several TV shows. It went through several printings.

When the Second Foundation was unable to pay rent for their Community Center on SE Alder, Metropolitan Community Church needed to find a new space in which to worship. For a few weeks, worship was held at Holy Rosary Catholic Church on NE Union (MLK Jr Blvd). First Methodist Church was the next location. Adams insisted on using the larger sanctuary rather than the smaller intimate chapel that was also available. When Six Under rented the Pythian Building, services were moved to the fifth floor ballroom there.

Dave Kohl photos

Early MCC Groups 1971 - 1973

Gretchen Kafoury, he also found support from Norma Paulus, Barbara Roberts, Lloyd Kinsey, and Nancy Fadely. When presented to the Hearings Committee, the strongest speaker in favor of the bill was Rita Knapp, a Portland mother of a lesbian and one of the founders of *Parents and Friends of Lesbians and Gays (P-FLAG)*. On the floor of the House, the final count defeated the Bill by one vote, 28-29. It was to be the closest that any Oregon gay rights bill has come to passage as of 2005.

And in Portland, there was a second beginning for Metropolitan Community Church.

Metropolitan Community Church Effort #2

Rev. Ken Adams was a former Lutheran national youth director living in Seattle. Adams had begun attending the newly formed Seattle-MCC there in 1972. He participated in services and became good friends with founding head pastor Rev. Bob Sirico. Although not an MCC clergy, in those "collar happy" days of the early UFMCC, it was decided that Adams would come to Portland and investigate the possibility of starting an MCC.

His plans were to attract over 200 members in the downtown area "where the homophile community is located." His plans included going to bars and "the street" to meet and counsel people. In planning, Rev. Adams summarized Portland as a venue where there was cooperation between the homophile and majority communities, different than most cities at the time. (*Oregon Journal*, April 16, 1973)

Several women from the Seattle church planned to come to Portland to help establish the church. Women at MCC-Seattle were particularly active, led by Ann Montague. They had attended the Northwest District Conference, and were planning their own Women's Conference for May of 1974, to be held in Sacramento.

The first worship service occurred on May 13 in the "ballroom" of the Gay Community Center on Alder Street. Both *KOIN-TV* and *the Oregon Journal* had covered an earlier press conference with Rev. Adams. The Second Foundation had been barraged with phone calls requesting information, and about 50 persons attended the initial service. Present were many people who had become alienated from their own churches because of being told that homosexuality was immoral. Some Christians still sought peace with their home churches, while others were ready for a new beginning.

Pastor Adams spent much of his time in counseling in his office at the Second Foundation Community Center. He also performed at least one wedding, which took place on Sunday, August 26, in the ballroom of the Second Foundation Center. Donna Kepler and Pat Kelly exchanged vows and spent their honeymoon at the Second Foundation's Labor Day Campout at Silver Creek Falls, (*Fountain*, Vol. 3 No. 9, September, 1973)

Involvement at the District level began almost immediately, as Portland representatives attended the May 27-29 Northwest District Conference in Seattle, where Rev. Sirico was officiate. And on June 23, women members of Seattle and Portland MCCs held a joint meeting in Portland. At the time, about half of the deacons and half of the board of directors of the Portland MCC were women. Seattle women held another conference in July, featuring acting Assistant Pastor of MCC-Seattle Val Valrejean speaking on *Jesus Christ Super-feminist*.

Worship services were moved in early June to Holy Rosary Roman Catholic Church on the east side at 375 NE Clackamas when attendance outgrew the space at the Gay Community Center. Pentecost Sunday was the first worship in the beautiful church on NE Union near Lloyd Center. The worship folder from that service listed a mixture of traditional and contemporary hymns:

> What a Friend We Have in Jesus
> Holy, Holy, Holy
> Reach Out to Jesus
> In the Garden
> He Touched Me

After a few weeks, services were moved again. The reasons for moving from Holy Rosary included tension between the Dominican Order

73

The Knights of Pythian building on Yamhill and SW Park contains three large ballrooms. Rev. Ken Adams secured the fifth floor space for the use of the Metropolitan Community Church. The climb up five flights of stairs was no deterrent to about twenty-five worshippers. But when rent money disappeared from the gay consortium that had rented the entire building in December of 1973, Rev. Adams discontinued the church. Other groups that shared in the rent included Mildred's Palace, the youth club and disco named for them City Councilwoman Mildred Schwab. It later relocated to the corner of SW 3rd and Burnside.

Dave Kohl photos

that was supportive of MCC and the Roman Catholic Archdiocese, which was not. To avoid internal strife for the Catholics, Rev. Adams moved the services out of their space. A smaller issue had been the discomfort with some gay Catholics over the holding of Protestant worship in a Catholic church.

In the process of seeking a new worship space, Rev. Adams contacted First Unitarian Church, but their leadership at the time felt that supporting a group associated with gay liberationists would injure their good reputation.

By June 24, services had been moved to First United Methodist Church at SW 18th and Jefferson. Numbering less than fifty worshippers, the MCC group felt overwhelmed in the massive sanctuary, but Rev. Adams preferred the large space rather than a smaller chapel. This building was also the site of many community ministries, as well as the headquarters for the Bishop of Oregon's United Methodist Diocese.

Reaching the Community

Rev. Adams spoke a number of times on the *Homophile Half Hour* program on *KBOO* radio, on July 19, 23, and 26. Rev. Sirico, who had once run a radio ministry out of Bremerton, substituted for Adams in May as the featured guest on a 10 pm *KOIN-AM radio* session of *Dialogue*. This regularly scheduled program was a telephone talk show on Sunday evenings. The radio host, Gene Still, fielded many calls, as all lines were busy with interested callers during most of the show. The program was dedicated to topics about gay people as well as the role of MCC in the gay community. Later that summer, Rev. Sirico left Seattle to start an MCC church in Cincinnati, Ohio. He eventually joined the Catholic Church.

Rev. Adams wrote a monthly column in *The Fountain*, replacing the regular MCC pieces that had been provided by Seattle's Bob Sirico. Adams often focused his gospel-based messages on understanding how the heart of mankind is often antagonistic to peacemaking. He pointed out passive behavior in getting along as opposed to making peace actively...one who goes out of his way to make peace. He quoted St. Paul in Colossians pointing out that Christ "made peace through the blood of His cross." The connection to gay and lesbian issues in a somewhat negative culture was implicit.

In another column (Dec. '73), Rev. Adams retold Christ's parable of the Wedding feast. In this story, none the invited guests to a great feast attended, so the King sent messengers to invite others from the highways and byways. The wedding hall then became filled with these new guests, who had been provided with the proper festive garments by the host. One guest tried to attend without donning the appropriate attire, as provided. The King found him and threw him out! The point is that even though God opens the gates of heaven to all, accepting sinners and Pharisees, he would not save a soul by the scruff of its neck. There is no room for carelessness or evil in heaven. Without being cleaned up, there is no staying at the Feast. If one made no effort to be worthy of the great honor of being called, they would be denied. A man would be a fool to be called into the Kingdom and come without the garment of holiness and grace that Christ freely offered him. There are some who think that the invitation is a guarantee, but it is not a "carte blanche." Many are called, but few are chosen, and God is grieved when the invitation is ignored.

On June 20, Ken Adams participated in a meeting at Concordia College with the Missouri Synod's Northwest Conference of Lutheran Pastors, where the discussion centered on new types of family units. Adams had been invited to speak on the gay lifestyle. Mixed with some mild hostility, the majority of participants expressed the desire to know more about the topic, realizing that they were bound to meet homosexuals in public and in the workplace.

MCC-Portland sent representatives to the General Conference of MCCs in Atlanta. The September meeting was concerned with revision of the bylaws of the nascent church. With 52 congregations, many of the early bylaws drawn up by the original four churches in 1968 needed revision. Upon his return, Adams noted that sev-

Rev. Ken Jones held MCC worship services in the fifth floor ballroom of the Pythian Building in the fall of 1973. Several gay groups were attempting to purchase and use the entire building, which would have housed the Second Foundation, offices for *The Fountain*, and several gay businesses. Financing, however, fell through at the end of 1973 and the vision vanished, as did MCC and Rev. Adams. The space is one of three ballrooms in the Pythian. One of them was the site of Portland's first Gay Pride celebration.

The advertisement and photo are from *The Fountain*.

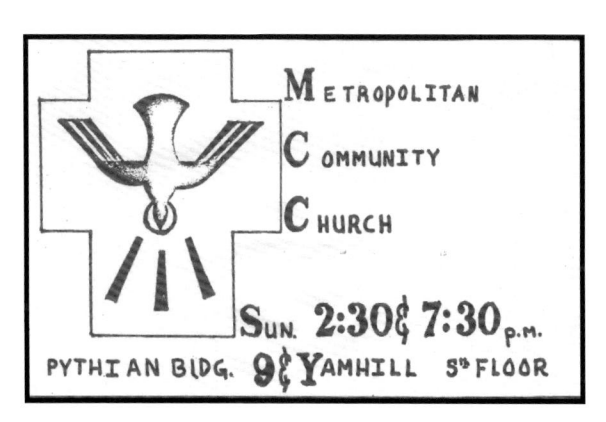

Dave Kohl photo

NW Fountain reprint

METROPOLITAN
COMMUNITY
CHURCH

Sun. 2:30 & 7:30 p.m.
PYTHIAN BLDG. 9 & YAMHILL 5th FLOOR

Portland's newest bridge, the Fremont Bridge, was completed in 1973 with the raising of the pre-fabricated central arched section to bridge the Willamette River. It carries I-405 northbound traffic towards Mt. St. Helens (pre-eruption) on its lower level, and southbound on the upper deck. It is one of ten bridges that cross the Willamette within the city of Portland.

OrHi neg 38937

OrHi neg 97023-0a

76

Early MCC Groups 1971 - 1973

eral Portland personalities were well known within the MCC circuit - Mama Bernice, and Empresses Darcelle, Blaine, and Mame.

Endings

Turmoil in late 1973 at the Second Foundation was precipitated by the disturbing disappearance of $3000 and the threat by the Portland Fire Department to close down the Gay Community Center due to violations of code. By October, financial issues were under control and a new home was found for the Community Center and several gay organizations. This was the Pythian Building at 918 SW Yamhill. MCC worship was moved to the fifth floor there from the First Methodist Church, services being held at 2:30 pm each Sunday. Evening services at 7:30 pm were added in November.

The Pythian was rented due to work by Jim Bee and Mrs. T. Dobson. Offices of The Second Foundation and *The Fountain* were on the second floor. The Portland Forum, the Second Foundation Youth Organization, *and* MCC were part of a corporation entitled "Six Under Incorporated." Spaces were available for dances, parties, banquets, receptions, proms, lectures, and meetings. Four halls were available with adjacent kitchen and dining facilities. One of the two ballrooms also had an elaborate balcony. Again, the gay community had a visible and identifiable space, a community center prominently located downtown. It was also very close to the Rafters, Embers, and several other bars. But the finances did not work out, and the gay community center and all other related groups had to move out in December.

Although the church met successfully for many months, when Rev Adams returned from a Los Angeles trip in December, a sign was placed on the meeting room door stating that "MCC No Longer Meets". The only reason given was that the group was unable to maintain itself, although this may have coincided with the loss of the lease on the entire Pythian building.

In Portland, while MCC and the Second Foundation struggled to survive, construction crews completed the Fremont Bridge over the Willamette. The 6000-ton center arch assembly was lifted 170 feet from river level and placed into position within a few hours. Engineers from around the world came to witness the event.

Dave Kohl photo

First meeting place of the Portland Community Church.

1974 - Watergate investigation and hearings lead to President Nixon's resignation; Gerald Ford is President;
- Gene Wilder stars in Mel Brook's *Blazing Saddles*;
- Freon discovered to damage ozone layer;
- First synchronous orbiting satellite launched;
- Streaking becomes a popular craze;

1975 - Union boss Jimmy Hoffa disappears, never found;
- Shana Alexander becomes first woman anchor on *Point/Counterpoint of CBS 60 Minutes*;
- *Jaws* and *One Flew Over the Cuckoo's Nest* (filmed at the Oregon State Hospital) dominate theaters;
- *A Chorus Line* opens on *Broadway*;
- Viet Nam war ends; Americans learn about the *Cambodian Killing Fields*;

Chapter Three
Portland Community Church
January 1974 - December 1975

"And they, continuing daily with one accord in the temple, and breaking bread from house to house, did eat their meat with gladness and singleness of heart."
Acts 2:46 (Authorized King James Version)

Remnant members from the Rev. Ken Adams group decided to continue meeting without any affiliation to MCC in Los Angeles or Seattle. On January 13, 1974, they voted to remain outside the MCC fellowship, feeling that the denomination had not shown the personal concern that Portland needed, most likely due to lack of communication and the distance from Seattle or other MCC congregations. The feeling was that a local church was needed to meet local needs.

Portland Community Church (PCC) was actually a continuation of a search by several members who had formed a living room fellowship at the home of Nita Gates and Fran Hamilton in Dundee, a very small Oregon hamlet about 45 minutes' drive west of Portland. In the late 60s, these women began fellowshipping with a few women in Seattle. There were also about six children in the group. Nita had rediscovered God when she experienced a total healing from multiple sclerosis in 1967. She held strong fundamental beliefs and had many charismatic experiences. After raising her children, she met and fell in love with Fran. With the blessing of her former husband, she and Fran became partners. Her strong faith and will are still her trademarks.

The Portland group saw itself as more conservative than MCC. They described themselves as "charismatic, very fundamental, full gospel, and evangelical." Feeling that MCC was too ecumenical, their focus was on a more narrow range of Christian backgrounds and practices. Pastoring the group was Rev. Frank Fortenberry, of the Pentecostal tradition, who observed that at least one MCC congregation, was breaking away from the Fellowship over doctrinal issues. Although primarily a church of homosexuals, straights were welcomed as well. Advertisements about services were placed in the *NW Gay Review*. (*NW Gay Review* Vol. 1, No. 1, Feb. 1974)

Officers of the church were identified as Pastor Fortenberry, Assistant Pastor Walters, Secretary Fran Hamilton, and Treasurer Jeri White. Eleven deacons were elected at the January meeting, Pastor Fortenberry's southern preacher style and music were greatly appreciated, and the group regularly gained new members.

The group of about 15 members met in a rented space at 615 SE Alder, called the East Side Commercial Building in the second floor auditorium. The gay youth center called "Stairs Down" was meeting in the same building, and the church subsidized the rent. At Easter, the church hosted an Easter Pageant, which was a musical and dramatic presentation enlisting several groups in Portland for the orchestral, organ, piano, and choral performance. Someone had forgotten to build the cross, so it was being hammered together backstage during the production. The sound of the pounding added an unplanned haunting tone to the passion play.

The East Side Commercial Building on SE Alder (p. 80) was used by the gay youth club known as "Stairs Down" for several years. Second Foundation connections made the building a logical choice for a meeting place for the Portland Community Church. Today the building is known as the Melody Ballroom.

Portland City Archive

Dave Kohl photo

Portland Community Church Pastor Frank Fortenberry arranged with Centenary-Wilbur United Methodist Church to use an upper room in their education building on SE 9th. Pastor Harper Richardson's library office was in the oriel window over the arched doorway on the right. The square door was the entrance to a coffeehouse which operated there since the mid-1960s, called "9th Street Exit." The building was a popular musical venue known as *La Luna* and was also known as the Pine Street Theater. The church sold the building about 1980, and merged with Sunnyside United Methodist . That congregation made a reputation for feeding homeless people despite complaints from neighbors over bringing such people into the area. In 2005, the Centenary-Wilbur building was refurbished into the Pine Street Studios.

Epicenter was a youth club operated in connection with the *Portland Town Council* for several months in 1975.

Portland City Archive

Roger Troen photo

Three gay bars in the same ancient building–The Foster Hotel building became the site of Darcelle's when Walter Cole purchased Demas' Tavern on NW 3rd (left). The Daisy Kingdom became the Odessey, which became the new CC Slaughters. Fox & Hounds is around the corner.

80

Portland Community Church 1974-1975

Later in 1974, the group moved to an upstairs room a few blocks west at Centenary–Wilbur Methodist Church in their Tudor-style education building. After the demise of their sanctuary in 1963, the Methodist congregation used this building as worship and meeting center. David Rushong, a Methodist, knew of the supportiveness of C-W to alternative communities. Pastor Harper Richardson, their open-minded and community oriented minister, found an upper room to rent to the Portland Community Church. A circle of chairs were arranged so that everyone could see, hear, and be heard. Over the next months, the circle continued to expand in the upper meeting room, with attendance reaching about 25.

Frank Fortenberry also serviced the Eastwood Community Church at 3950 SE Lincoln. Billed as inter-racial and non-denominational, the motto was *The end of your search for a friendly church*. The group also operated a non-drug disco for gay youth (14-140) called "Epicenter" in a rented shop front at 4620 SE 67th, off Foster Road. A lot of volunteer effort went into cleaning and remodeling the space, carpeting it with colorful patches and samples, and creating a positive atmosphere. They had previously met in 1975 at the Contact Center at 1532 SE Morrison, a venue connected with Koinonia House and Outside In.

Epicenter aimed to serve vulnerable, questioning, and wayward underage gay youth seeking a safe place to "hang out." Plans for the non-profit club included an art gallery; a TV and lounge room; space for dances, office quarters, and library; and vending machines for pop, candy, and snacks. Rent and other costs were to come from bake sales, a crafts fair, auctions, and sales of buttons and tank tops. The center eventually succumbed to financial problems and the inability to find gay-friendly landlords in 1976.

Publicity and Politics in Portland

Local issues over representation of gays in the media were uniting several gay organizations. Ron Powell representing the Second Foundation, Roger Troen with Gay Liberation Front, Lanny Swerdlow with the Portland Association for Gay Equality, and Jerry Gayken of Gay Males Together met with KATU station manager Tom Dargan and Program Director Charles Gingold to protest the airing of an episode of the *ABC Marcus Welby program*. The show in question, entitled *The Outrage* centered on a fourteen-year-old male student who is raped by an older male teacher. The portrayal of male homosexuals as child molesters advanced the negative stereotype of gay men. Protests of the episode had caused TV stations in Philadelphia and Boston to cancel that segment and advertisers Colgate-Palmolive, Shell Oil, Lipton, and Gillette to withdraw sponsorship. *KATU* did not cancel, nor did *KOMO* in Seattle.

Young gays in Portland were dealt a sad blow when the Portland Youth Alliance Community Center and Youth Night Club had to close down. An independent outgrowth of the Second Foundation, "The Stairs Down," was open about six months in the basement of the Eastside Commercial Center, where the Portland Community Church also had met. Rents had been raised from $400 to $950 per month. Weekly dances raised enough money to barely pay the bills. One summer evening, after a dance, the building was broken into, the safe pried open, and all dance receipts taken. It was the final blow.

Combined with problems of volunteer staffing, the Board of Directors decided to close the Center at the end of August. It had been the venue for dances, meetings, social events, and a coffee house. This left the "Ninth Street Exit" at nearby Centenary-Wilbur as the only gay-supportive gathering spot on the east side for underage persons. On the west side, Outside In was the gathering spot, although focused on homeless youth.

To help with counseling, the Portland Town Council had established the *Counseling Center* for Sexual Minorities as part of its office space at 320 SW Stark. Mayor Neil Goldschmidt had encouraged funding through the government's Comprehensive Employment and Training Act (CETA). politicians like Commissioners Mildred Schwab and Francis J. Ivancie (aka Frank "I can't see") would have withheld CETA funding, rather than support a service for gays. Staffed primarily by volunteers, the center operated a "hot line"

OrHi neg 89972   Portland City Archive

Mayor Neil Goldschmidt became convinced of gay rights issues through contacts with the Portland Town Council. The Town Council met regularly at the old Congress Hotel at SW 5th and Main, before its destruction. Many gay men also met regularly in the dark balcony of the Blue Mouse, which was closed and taken down in 1975. The Oriental, on SE Grand Ave., also became a parking lot. Few of those pioneer men recognize the place with the lights on.

Goldschmidt was the first mayor to march in a Gay Rights Parade. He appointed Sandy Director as Portland's honorary "gay mayor," seen below left of Gov. Vic Atiyeh.

Neil Hutchins photo

Steven Stone Archive

Gregg Pitts Archive

Neil Hutchins photo

82

Portland Community Church 1974-1975

and referral service. Many individuals were alone, feeling the incredible stigma attached to being a sexual minority because of fears and stereotyping in the general population.

Incidentally, Mayor Goldschmidt, before he left for Washington, DC to be U.S. Transportation Director, appointed an honorary "gay mayor" for Portland–Sandy Director, scion of the local furniture dynasty. He was the very active Sandra Dee of several fundraising drag shows. Sandy became the public figurehead of the gay community for nearly 10 years before his untimely death from heart disease.

Other youth centers and clubs would appear in the later '70s, but for the moment, underage gays were adrift, and the "Camp" became more appealing. When boys made themselves available for sexual encounters in such a public arena, there was a much higher risk of running afoul of the law on various charges. And meeting anonymous partners included the possibility of engaging with unsavory characters, which could mean mental and/or physical injury.

The Blue Mouse, a popular theater where men could "mess around" in the balcony was closed after many years of offering a seedy alternative to the Camp for public sexual activity. Another similar cinema, the Round-Up was in the same block. The closure of the entire block was hotly debated in the press, as it was the sight of several small businesses, which were popular. It was replaced by a multi-story car park, needed by the downtown Meier and Frank department store.

Changing Leadership of Portland Community Church (PCC)

Two of the regular worshippers at PCC were partners David and John Rushong, who had relocated to Portland from Indianapolis in 1974, where they had attended the MCC church in that city, and had heard Rev. Troy Perry preach there. On one occasion, the local police had raided that church. David, a retired College professor of education, had officially adopted his much younger partner in Indiana as a legal alternative to marriage. They had expected to find an MCC in Oregon, but the Ken Adams church had closed.

There was a study group meeting in Eugene as the MCC of the Willamette Valley under the leadership of Rev. Ann Montague from Seattle's MCC. The Rushongs joined the Portland Community Church, finding the group very social, with a lot of potluck suppers, Thursday prayer meetings, and often gatherings after functions at the Sambo's restaurant at 8th and E. Burnside. David became an elder, along with Nita Gates and Denis Moore.

1974 was the year that the Portland City Council passed a resolution protecting homosexual city employees from discrimination due to sexual orientation. Controversial as this move was, the edict was challenged, reversed, but eventually reinstated. This was also the year of the Watergate hearings, leading to the resignation of President Richard Nixon because of apparent abuse of Presidential powers, and the elevation of Gerald Ford to the Presidency.

In early 1975, Rev. Fortenberry found the obligations of leading the Portland Community Church overly stressful and he asked Denis Moore to pilot the group. Denis was a former Baptist who had studied for two years at Bob Jones University in Greenville, SC. Denis had visited MCC-Seattle and knew Rev. Robert Sciricco. He had done some college level teaching at Portland State, was married with a young daughter, and he was coming out. With the support of his soon ex-wife and daughter, he became part of the leadership team with David Rushong and Nita Gates. The congregation voted their approval of this new arrangement. On several occasions played on the piano and later on the organ accompanying the congretional hyms.

The format of services led by Denis, Nita, and Rushong consisted of gathering the group in a circle of chairs. There was no advance order of service, and anyone could request a hymn. Concerns and sharing often led to spontaneous prayer. Denis usually brought a short message of hope and encouragement. They called themselves "a little band of fugitive believers." At this time, there was no communion served, apparently for lack of an ordained clergy.

Roger Troen Archives

Rev. Frank Fortenberry at the pulpit.

Frank Fortenberry and two members at C-W.

Meeting in the "upper room" at C-W. Upper photo shows Fran Hamilton, John Laidlaw, and John Rushong. In the lower photo is Denis Moore, who with Fran and John piloted the group towards membership in the Universal Fellowship of MCCs.

Early MCC members wore a distinctive metal cross on a chain around their neck. These were often given by pastors as a sign of membership. MCC tee shirts of the 1970s were worn with pride in bars and at parades.

Dave Kohl photos

Nita Gates photos

84

Portland Community Church 1974-1975

One individual who found the ad in the *Review* showed up one Sunday to find the doors locked. Another man was also there waiting. But no pastor or congregation was evident until about 10 minutes after the time posted for worship, then they saw a group walking towards them from the Sambo's Restaurant two blocks away on E Burnside. That morning, everyone had gathered for breakfast before worship and had paid little attention to the time. But the new men were warmly welcomed, worship was spontaneous, and afterwards, Nita and Fran invited the whole group out to their place for an impromptu potluck. The party didn't break up until after 9 pm. Quite an experience for two shy men just coming out. It had been a powerful and positive day. Don Howse returned the next week and eventually became a Board member and leader. Bob Fulton also became a regular attendee.

The Southeast Asian war ended with the fall of Saigon (now Ho Chi Minh City) in April 1975. The Viet Nam experience would continue to have ripple effects in personal and community lives for years to come. In Portland, a return to simpler ways and an emphasis on holistic living and crafts led that same spring to the opening of Saturday Market–a food and crafts fair now running every Saturday and Sunday from Easter until Christmas.

During this period, the PCC remained a small, uncomplicated fellowship. Focus was on interspiritual development. With no concerns about worship folders, liturgy, hierarchy, or budget, it was an era of simplicity. Distractions of a mainline church did not exist. There were few day-to-day problems, few expenses, no concerns about building maintenance, and no obligations to a larger church body. Denis Moore met Dan Brown at a meeting of "Gay Males Together" at Portland State University and invited Dan to come to services. There were about 20 attendees at the time. Dan helped establish a checking account and became treasurer of the group.

Courting the UFMCC

John Rushong in particular missed the formality and structure of a mainstream Christian worship experience. And having experienced the Indianapolis MCC, proposed that the Portland group should consider joining the Universal Fellowship of Metropolitan Community Churches. David and John had heard Troy Perry preach and felt that the energy and message of MCC would move the PCC to greater goals. The group also realized that they had a choice to either become a religious clique, or they could reach out into the greater community.

Steve Jordan, a member of MCC-LA visited Portland to see a Rose Court-sponsored drag show at Dahl and Penne's. In the audience he spotted a man on whose shirt was embroidered with an MCC *Chi-Rho* symbol. This started a conversation with Dan Brown, since Steve was also wearing a similar MCC logo. Dan invited Steve to worship at Centenary-Wilbur the next day, where John and David Rushong and Denis Moore were leading the service.

Noting their interest in becoming affiliated with MCC again, Steve returned to Los Angeles and shared what he had learned in Portland with Troy Perry and Jim Sandmeier, pastor of MCC-LA.

Several discussions took place at the Half Moon Tavern between the Rushongs, Glen Scott, and Jim Chambers. A full-time pastor with the ability to fashion unity out of diversity was in order. After much deliberation and discussion, a delegation of Dan Brown, David Rushong, and Denis Moore went to Seattle to meet with Wally Lanchester of MCC Seattle. Lanchester had only recently been installed as MCC Seattle's pastor in a service on October 20, 1974. Troy Perry, founder of the UFMCC had officiated at the Service of Ordination. At that time, Perry had been reported in the *NW Gay Review* as saying "I think we have given gay people something. There has to be something in the gay community more than the four B's - bars, baths, bushes, and beaches. This church has given you something that you've never had before, and that is a feeling of community."

Coincidentally on the national scene, October 10-14 was the Bicentennial Gay Conference in Washington, D.C., organized by the *Gay Activists Alliance*. Representatives heard many messages with several themes:

MCC Archive photos

Centenary-Wilbur's basement kitchen was used by both the Portland Community Church and later by Metropolitan Community Church. Most events around food were potlucks or spaghetti suppers.

Early leaders in the Portland Community Church at a later MCC conference–(l to r) Denis Moore, Glen Scott, and Nita Gates.

Nita Gates photo

Vector Magazine was published in San Francisco and available by mail or in certain bookstores in Portland. Published by the Society for Individual Rights (SIR), it gave encouragement to individual gay men through stories, letters to the editor, articles about gay life in various U.S. cities, and with photographs of happy wholesome gay young men in various natural settings.

Cover of the first issue of the *NW Gay Review* from February, 1974, published by Lanny Swerdlow and Neil Hutchins. Several of the staff were members of the Metropolitan Community Church, and wrote articles about spirituality as well as news and events of the congregation.

Portland Community Church 1974-1975

- Gay Americans needed to rededicate themselves to a new revolution for liberty, as our patriot forefathers did;
- Gays could celebrate diversity while working in a unified manner to achieve liberation for all;
- Separatist women needed to rejoin the larger gay liberation movement and unite for an end of oppression and discrimination on all levels
- The MOVEMENT had come of age with the formation of the National Gay Task Force;
- West Coast delegates realized they were happily ignorant of the internal politics and turf battles of East Coast organizations.

The UFMCC had established an office in Washington by this time, obtaining space in the Methodist Building directly across from the Capitol. Small world–the Methodist building was the direct result of leadership by Clarence True Wilson, the Portland temperance enthusiast of 1910.

Back in Portland, Rev. Lanchester began visiting regularly, taking the train with his partner once a month, to hold services, preach, and administer Holy Communion. He worked closely with the three deacons, and called the church "the group of twelve."

Some women in the group had become concerned that one of the men had behaved inappropriately towards one of their sons, and an undercurrent of distrust eroded unity. The rumors got out of proportion to the event, and it was never resolved A small number of women left the group to form another church.

Discussion about forming an MCC study group was passionate and the vote was not unanimous. The division fell mostly along gender lines. The final vote determined that the Portland Community Church would request affiliation with UFMCC.

Rev. Lanchester was approached about becoming Portland's first pastor, but he felt that he had not fulfilled his commitment to Seattle. Because of earlier unsuccessful MCC experiences, members were bold in their request for a dynamic minister and church-builder. Wally Lanchester knew of the availability of a minister in San Francisco who might be well suited to Portland. His name was Aaron Austin Amerine.

Rev. A. Austin Amerine had joined the MCC fellowship and was minister of music at the San Francisco MCC congregation while working for Colonial Penn Insurance in the Bay area. He was a gifted musician and had penned several hymns. He was open to changes in his life. David Rushong went to the District Conference in Sacramento in the summer of 1975 to meet with Austin. After visiting Portland, leading worship and communion, and several meetings with the Portland Community group, it was decided that Austin would accept the position as minister of Portland's third attempt to form an MCC. He began his work in Portland on January 6, 1976, the date MCC Portland now uses as its founding date.

The membership at this time included:

Mary Klepser	David Rushing
John Rushong	Don Howse
Glen Scott	Bob Fulton
Gary Coleman	John Laidlaw
Mel Hamilton	Bob Jackson
Dan Brown	Joe Maher
Oren Hornbeck	Denis Moore

Wendell Gleason photo

1976 U.S. celebrates the Bicentennial (of the *Declaration of Independence*)
- Mao Tse-tung and Chou En-lai die ending China's Cultural Revolution; *Gang-of-Four* purged
- Cease-fire halts fighting between Christians and Muslims in Lebanon
- Erma Bombeck writes *The Grass is Always Greener Over the Septic Tank*
- MCC-Portland begins as a Study Group becomes a Mission

1977 Portland Trailblazers (starring Bill Walton) win NBA Championship
- President Jimmy Carter makes "human rights" part of U.S. foreign policy
- *Star Wars* introduces C-3PO and R2D2, it spawns an entire genre of film
- John Travolta disco-dances *Saturday Night Fever*
- California debates the Briggs Initiative; Anita Bryant campaigns in Florida
- Portland Mayor Neil Goldschmidt proclaims Gay Pride Day for 3rd annual event
- MCC-Portland Chartered January, Church building purchased September
- Parents of Gays begun by Charles and Rita Knapp and Ann and Bill Shepherd
- Sweet Spirit MCC-Salem chartered in October
- Eugene passes gay rights ordinance, referendum filed to overturn
- Tri-Cities defense fund formed with Minneapolis and Wichita

1978 Congress extends ratification of 1972 *Equal Rights Amendment*
- Mass murder-suicides kill 911 at People's Temple, Jonestown, Guyana
- Mary Simpson is first woman to preach at London's Westminster Abbey
- San Francisco Mayor George Moscone and Supervisor Harvey Milk murdered
- Cardinal Karol Wojtyla of Krakow, Poland elected as Pope John Paul II

1979 Mother Teresa awarded *Nobel Peace Prize* for work with poor of India
- Jane M. Byrne elected first woman Chicago Mayor
- 50 Americans taken hostage at U.S. Embassy in Teheran, held 444 days
- *Kramer vs. Kramer* wins Oscars for Meryl Streep and Dustin Hoffman

Chapter Four
Rev. A. Austin Amerine
January 1976 - June 1979

"Then they that gladly received his word were baptized: and the same day there were added unto them about three thousand souls. And they continued steadfastly in the apostles' doctrine and fellowship, and in breaking of bread."
Acts 2:41-2 (The Dartmouth Bible)

Reverend Austin Amerine was a consummate and successful organizer. His bubbly and charismatic character won many new attendees to the MCC study group's evening meetings in the parlor at Centenary-Wilbur. All new MCC churches at the time began as "study groups" then grew into "missions" before qualifying as full-fledged churches with a charter from MCC headquarters in Los Angeles. In joining the UFMCC fellowship, Portland became one of 18 study groups around the country in January 1976. There were 15 "missions" in the Fellowship and 48-chartered churches, including three in Australia and one in England. Membership in the greater UFMCC at this time numbered about 18,000, and was growing rapidly.

Austin was born in 1921 and raised in Tulsa, Oklahoma. After college, he became an Assemblies of God minister and pastored several churches in the Pentecostal tradition. A marriage and two children, Dorothy and Robert, were part of his life until he divorced in the late 1950s. Being divorced, he could no longer be clergy in his denomination and became a businessman.

In 1969, he discovered MCC in Los Angeles as part of his quest to reconcile his sexual orientation with his faith. He had brief stints in churches located in Long Beach and San Francisco, where he used his musical gifts to lead the choir and play piano for services. He wrote several hymns that are in print. In 1975, he indicated to Troy Perry that he might be open to a full-time ministry position, and the connection with Portland Community Church was made through Rev. Wally Lanchester of MCC-Seattle.

Bill Barry and Don Howse drove to San Francisco to help Austin pack and move his household to Portland in the early winter. As usual, moving was an unorganized ordeal, carrying household goods and furniture down two flights of circular stairs and finding places in the truck for a huge hide-a-bed and piano. At a pause in the packing of the piano, Austin sat down and played a rousing version of *Onward Christian Soldiers,* with the sound echoing down Guerrero Street.

Austin lived in the home of John and David Rushong before permanently locating himself, and the church telephone number was actually the home phone. The Rushongs reported that they always thought there were more people in the house, because Austin was always talking to God and himself–they called it the "Austin - Aaron Syndrome." He frequently answered himself as well. They were also suspicious that Austin had imported some of California's earthquakes, until they realized it was just their rotund houseguest creating a 6.9 on the Richter Scale as he moved through the house.

The Lord's Prayer

And when thou hast shut thy door, pray to the Father... — Matthew 6:6

MALOTTE
Albert Hay Malotte
Arranged by Fred Bock

Matthew 6:9-13

Our Father, which art in heaven, hallowed be Thy name. Thy kingdom come, Thy will be done on earth as it is in heaven. Give us this day our daily bread, and forgive us our debts as we forgive our debtors. And lead us not into temptation, but deliver us from evil, for Thine is the Kingdom and the Power and the Glory, forever. A - men.

Alfred Hay Malotte's "Lord's Prayer," reprinted with permission. CCLI #1021630

Rev. A. Austin Amerine   1976 - 1979

Since the previous two MCC attempts in Portland had failed, Austin kept many of his church building secrets to himself, lest he should fail. Once he was sure his "method" would work in Portland, the early church group began to relax and accept his foibles.

The Study Group

The enthusiasm of members spilled into the gay community, and soon flyers advertising MCC and its worship times were posted in several bars along Stark Street and at Dahl and Penne's at SW 2nd and Alder, near the *Camp*. The worship space at Centenary-Wilber was limited by its multiple functions. To create a more sacred atmosphere, David and John Rushing crafted a large simple wooden cross to hang in the space. This same heavy unadorned cross still hangs above the altar at the current MCC church on NE Broadway.

An early member noted the wide diversity of backgrounds represented in the growing congregation. New members were challenged to lay aside their denominational backgrounds and heritage of ritual long enough to learn about and accept the practices and beliefs of others. Toleration would lead to acceptance, finding a common ground in the knowledge that all were worshiping the same God. Salvation is lived out each day in how people treat each other.

Austin's background in music began to influence worship. He played piano, sang heartily and with repetition. Gary Coleman volunteered (actually, Austin recruited him) as choir director. Soloists alternated with hearty congregational singing. Every service included the congregational singing of the Alfred Hay Malotte version of *The Lord's Prayer*, with members holding hands. Austin warned members not to miss Sunday worship, as that might be the Sunday that the message was meant just for them.

With newfound excitement and pride, members distributed more information cards in the bars, baths, and beaches. Articles and ads appeared in the *NW Gay Review*. A notice was posted on the bulletin board at the Embers, using the Rushong home phone number, where Austin lived for several months. It was agreed that Austin's salary would be based on a percentage of the offerings until better financing would materialize. Eventually he was offered a salary of $800 a month.

Austin had the appearance of a jolly Friar Tuck, wearing a white Roman clerical collar on his blue shirt. It wasn't long before he adopted a simple humorous drawing of an overweight friar as his logo, using it on stationery, notes, and twenty-seven years later, it was lovingly placed on the cover of his memorial service program in 1998. He became known fondly to several as *The Reverend Mother*. Perhaps it was Austin's approachability that set a pattern at MCC, where pastors have usually been addressed by their first name as often as by the more traditional "Rev........" title.

Membership continued to grow, mostly among men. Austin was a vivacious and well-liked person, and he attracted many people to the congregation by merits of his personality. He specifically tried to recruit professionals, business people, and generous givers. Shortly after Austin's arrival in town, Rev. Arthur Buck took him to lunch at the Koinonia House at PSU. They discussed the role of the church in the homosexual community and possibilities for involvement with the Ecumenical Ministries of Oregon. MCC was a controversial entity to the EMO, and the idea of membership was not seen as a possibility at the time. However, Art Buck did become a regular attendee at MCC.

Steve Jordan, an MCC-LA member, met with Austin Amerine at the General Conference in Washington DC. He then returned to live in Portland and was soon interviewed by the *NW Fountain* because of his connections with Troy Perry. Steve made it perfectly clear that this time MCC-Portland was here to stay.

At this time of the Women's Liberation movements, tension existed between the sexes for several historic reasons, not the least of which was each gender's focus on independence from gender roles and social expectations. Individuals recently released from unhappy relationships with an opposite sex partner were

Neil Hutchins Archive

Terry Bean Archive

Founders of the Portland Town Council included Jerry Weller and Terry Bean (pictured on the far right with Oregon State Representative George Eighmey. The Town Council led the campaign for establishing protection for Oregon gays and lesbians through legislation on the state level.)

OrHi neg 21696

An outline of the South Portland Urban Renewal area, just south of Civic Auditorium. Italian and Jewish neighborhoods would be wiped out, as would many gay bars and baths along SW 3rd. The upper white line follows SW 4th. Hawthorne Bridge is in the foreground with offramps to Harbor Drive. The Transfusion Inn was located at the foot of *The Bridge* on SW 1st. What would become Tom McCall waterfront park is warehouses, boatyards and industrial land in 1976. Note *the Oregonian* building, lower right, which was the Portland Central Market at the foot of SE Yamhill.

Rev. A. Austin Amerine 1976 - 1979

often suspicious and downright hostile to socializing in mixed company. Austin often held coaching sessions, particularly with the men, to help them get along with females as friends and fellow worshippers.

Betty Nelson learned about the church from a notice posted at Dahl and Penne's. She and a friend ventured into the room at Centenary-Wilber their first Sunday, perceived that it was all men, and turned around to leave. Mary Klepser stood and emerged from the group to welcome the women. Women did begin to join the church, including Kathy Walden, Vi Leagjeld, and the Jeans (Dant and Conner). A new female member in 1977 noted that there was about one woman for every 20 men at services.

Austin began involving himself in the lives of his parishioners immediately. There were times when he would be awakened at 3 or 4 o'clock in the morning to go help somebody in distress. He spent inestimable hours in hospital calls. If an emergency or crisis arose, he was immediately accessible. To his detriment, he often subjugated his own personal needs as secondary to the needs of those to whom he was shepherd.

Early on, it was felt that the congregation needed to remain above politics, fearing that any sort of political involvement might offend potential members. More significantly, definitions of the church's non-profit status might be in jeopardy. Those concerns would eventually dissipate.

Portland Town Council

Around the time Portland Community Church was transitioning into Metropolitan Community Church, another significant organization formed in the gay community. The Portland Town Council was put together by Larry Copeland and Jerry Weller in 1975. More politically oriented than the Second Foundation had been, the PTC took a keen interest in the promotion of a statewide *Gay Rights Bill*. The Oregon Legislature had defeated the first such bill, proposed by Rep. Vera Katz, by one vote in 1973. They hoped to add the phrase, "No one shall be discriminated against on the basis of sexual orientation," into Oregon law.

To raise the issue in the eyes of the general population, lesbians in particular began leaving business cards on buses, in restaurants and anywhere else they could. These stated in large type *I am a Lesbian*. The concept was that after they had been served or been in a discussion, that they would leave to card to let people know that they were just average people. The campaign was the subject of a positive story in *The Oregon Journal* of June 23, 1976, in advance of Gay Pride Fair on the waterfront that Saturday.

Monthly PTC meetings were held at the Mallory Hotel, and several after-meeting groups met in the hotel's Driftwood Bar. Mainstream political and cultural leaders spoke regularly to the assemblies, which often numbered over one hundred. George Nicola worked as a lobbyist in Salem to advance anti-discrimination legislation.

Several men from PTC became involved in State and national groups and committees. Terry Bean worked in Washington, D.C. with the *National Gay Rights Lobby* as did Jerry Weller, who also founded the Human Rights Campaign. Jerry Weller first met Troy Perry at a conference in Denver. They became good friends and worked together for gay rights. Both had an interest in leather and in the Court system, and helped MCC members better understand the elements of the gay community known as "leather and lace." In later years, Jerry would name and help form the *Right to Privacy PAC (Political Action Committee)*, which became *Right to Pride* and changed into *Basic Rights Oregon*. (See Chapter 12)

Hopes were high for success in another legislative season. Donations were raised with weekly drag shows at Dahl and Penne's, and from the 680 members on the *PTC* mailing list. G*ay Pride* was organized by *PTC*. Their *Oregon Gay Rights Report* newsletter printed opinion pieces, news articles, and schedules of local gay activities, including upcoming MCC worship and activities.

Co-founders of *P-FLAG*, Ann and Bill Shepherd at an early rally. Sambo's Coffee Shop was a favorite eatery for early MCC people. This one was on W Burnside at NW 23rd.

Centenary-Wilbur's worship space was a converted gymnasium with an industrial skylight. Pews were from the destroyed 1883 original gray stone church. On the exterior wall still stands this stone statement of philosophy, which perfectly fit the mission of the re-vitalized neighborhood church.

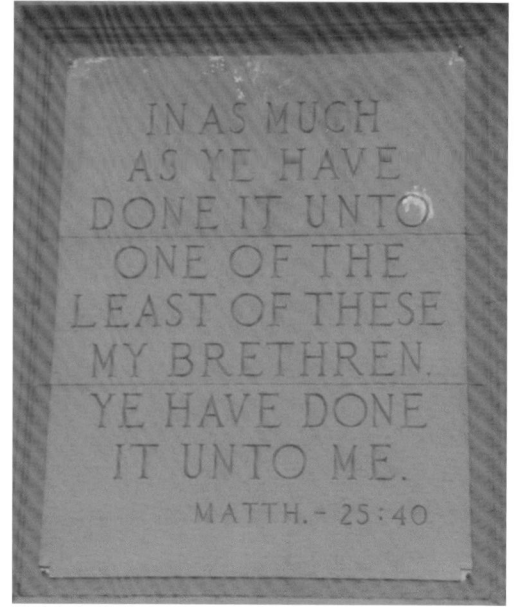

Susie Shepherd photo

OrHi neg 83684

Oregon Journal reprint

Dave Kohl photos

IN AS MUCH AS YE HAVE DONE IT UNTO ONE OF THE LEAST OF THESE MY BRETHREN, YE HAVE DONE IT UNTO ME.
MATTH. - 25:40

Rev. A. Austin Amerine   1976 - 1979

Parents of Gays and P-FLAG

Two mothers from First Presbyterian Church supporting their lesbian daughters came forward to testify in Salem. Rita Knapp testified for the ill-fated House Bill in 1973. Her well-reasoned testimony drew spontaneous applause in the Chamber, which had been forbidden in the session ground rules. When the issue was again raised in 1975, Ann Shepherd, once a reporter for *The Oregon Journal,* boldly spoke in Salem. Her daughter Susie was an MCC founding member, and active in the emerging Portland leather community.

In 1976, Governor Bob Straub organized a statewide task force to determine levels of discrimination in the state. Austin Amerine was invited to join, as was Ann Shepherd, whose visability had been raised in the gay community by her 1975 testimony in Salem. Portland lawyer Holly Hart, Libby Anderson, and Portland City Commissioner Gladys McCoy were also members of the Gay Task Force. Holly Hart eventually left the legal profession, opening the Old Wives Tales Restaurant on East Burnside, which is still a gay mecca, especially with women–a site for meals and meetings, with childcare.

One of the task force recommendations when it was finished in 1978 was that a parental support group was needed for gays. Ann Shepherd volunteered to get it going. She and her husband Bill formed the *Parents of Gays* organization, with Charles and Rita Knapp, announcing their organizational meeting for July 11, 1978 in the MCC Sunday bulletin. *POG* merged in 1980 with *P-FLAG,* the national friends and family support group (*Parents and Friends of Lesbians and Gays*). In 1985, the Portland chapter of *P-FLAG* hosted the *national P-FLAG convention.*

The Mission

In mid-1976, regular attendance rose to over 50, which qualified a change in status for MCC, from a study group to a mission. A letter was sent to District Coordinator Rev. Gary Wilson requesting the elevation in status to a MCC Mission. Attendees who signed this letter of request were:

A. Austin Amerine	Cindy Dahlgren
Denine Moore	Jean Ringena
William Barry	Robert Fulton
Denis Moore	Craig Root
Greg Basford	Gerald Grosenheider
Donald Morrison	H. David Rushong
Deborah Betron	Mel Hamilton
C. Nugent	John Rushong
Hazel Blanton	James Hibbs
Betty Nelson	Bud Schneider
Roberta Blanton	Michael Hoffman
Mark Parkisen	Jonathan Schneider
Jacquie Bogle	Oren C. Hornbeck
Linn Payne	Mary Klepser Schneider
Daniel Brown	Donald Howse
Nestor Perala	Jerry Sowards
Keren Byrdon	James Johnson
Karen Plamondon	Susan Starkey
Marge Clark	Mary Jane Kamm
Susan Plamondon	Roger Stigen
Gary Coleman	John Laidlaw
Michael Quimby	Darl Synoground
Barry C	Virgil Miller
Ron Raz	Gary Wilcox
Neal Curry	Mark Moody
Daniel Reed	Raymond Worthy
Cathy Dahlgren	

Services continued to be held on Sunday evenings in the upper room in the Centenary-Wilbur Methodist education wing. Denis Moore often played the piano while Austin conducted service and preached. Occasionally another soloist would show up and play the violin, sometimes spontaneously. The room had no decor and it was difficult to create a worshipful atmosphere. Even so, attendance rose and it soon became overcrowded.

Centenary-Wilbur's minister, Harper Richardson, agreed to make the large downstairs auditorium / gymnasium available around Easter 1977. But it was already doubling as a stage for community plays (it later became the Pine Street Theater and La Luna). So worshippers were sometimes distracted by sets and backdrops that had no religious connections. Sometimes "church" happened on the sets. One set that many members remember was an old-

The Universal Fellowship of
Metropolitan Community Churches

The Northwest District

by the authority of the Annual Conference and on
action of the District Committee confers on the

Metropolitan Community Church of Portland
Portland, Oregon

the status of

Chartered Church

with all attendant rights, honors and privileges
IN THE NAME OF THE CREATOR
AND OF THE CHRIST
AND OF THE HOLY SPIRIT

The Rev. David M. Pelletier
coordinator

Rev. A. Austin Amerine   1976 - 1979

time diner with a soda fountain counter. Austin usually incorporated references to the sets into his messages.

The services were healing, obviously full of love and concern for fellow worshippers. These folks were politically and religiously motivated. Most were involved in either the Second Foundation, The Portland Town Council, or knew someone who was. The relative smallness of this worshiping community meant there was much crossover and involvement. There were few strangers. Everything was brought in for service, and removed at the end of the evening. The circle of chairs gave way to rows of chairs and pews. The wooden cross continued to serve as the focal point. It was Austin's desire to create as much of a church-like atmosphere in the auditorium as possible.

Austin was quite aware of the vast range of denominational backgrounds of the membership. For a number of Sundays, he took on a different format each week in the service wherein he presented the service in the style of a particular tradition such as Lutheran, Methodist, Charismatic, Roman Catholic, etc. As part of that practice, he would then explain the historical reasons for those particular rubrics, hence increasing everyone's appreciation of the various historical traditions, and bridging potential areas of doctrinal misunderstanding.

In a similar spirit, Austin tried to accommodate the interests of various individuals. If someone came up with an idea for a new group or way of doing things, he would find a way for that to happen. This proved to be a blessing and a curse. Austin's accommodation and enthusiasm drew members of a wide spectrum and kept them enthralled with good sermons and high spirit. The need for individual counseling and healing, for resolution of differences with other members, and for unity of direction as a church could have been a higher priority. Unresolved differences would lead to challenges for his successors.

On July 4th, Austin encouraged all military veterans to wear their uniforms, even though the recently concluded Viet Nam conflict was still a bitter and divisive memory to many. Returning veterans and films about the war reminded Americans of the unpopular debacle. Former conscientious objectors and soldiers were forced to co-exist, and in most cases resolved their differences.

One particularly successful program was a women's group, proposed by Jacquie Bogle. The women used an upstairs "parlor" following service for social sessions, where they could freely discuss issues and concerns that didn't seem of interest or appropriate to the men.

Austin could also be innovative. In setting up for a Eucharist service one Sunday it became apparent that the elder in charge had forgotten to check the supply of communion wafers on hand. When Austin learned of the short supply, he substituted Oreo cookies, which he broke into small pieces for distribution. No situation was too challenging!

On another Sunday, a long-lasting thunderstorm rained outside. As Denis Moore was playing a hymn, he noticed moisture on the inside of an exterior wall. Austin soon became aware of the trickle of water down the surface and shortened his message considerably as the flow increased. By the time of benediction, the wall was solid water and puddles several inches deep were rising on the floor as worshippers made a hasty exit, with cross and communion ware in hand.

The Charter

When regular attendance reached about 60 in the Sunday evening services, the Mission qualified for its MCC Charter as a congregation. Mike Hoffmann headed a by-laws committee to prepare this required document for chartering.

The founder of the MCC Fellowship, Rev. Troy Perry, was the guest speaker at the 2 pm service held January 9, 1977 at the recently restored historic Old Church (formerly Calvary Presbyterian) at SW 11th and Clay. The mixed-voice choir performed, Oren Charles Hornbeck played the organ, and "Papa" John Hose of MCC-Los Angeles was an honored guest. Several deacons, including Steve Jordan, were appointed at this service. At the reception was a

The Old Church originally Calvary Presbyterian, in 1977, before the carriage porch was restored.

Lloyd Porter and Don Howse met at the Chartering service, and are still together in 2005.

David Kopay's coming out was newsworthy, controversial, and broke a stereotype of gays.

Rev. A. Austin Amerine   1976 - 1979

4-tiered cake crafted by member Mel Hart. Because of protests and unrest in other cities over gay activities at this time, a self-appointed "security team" of members kept Troy Perry as protected as they could without looking obvious or drawing undue attention to their efforts. Portlanders were gracious, and there was no negative episode.

Many in the gay community had been anticipating that the third MCC incarnation would also be unsuccessful. So when the chartering was announced in the gay and straight press, the critics were proven wrong, and a massive outpouring of support resulted in a large crowd. Many came to see Troy Perry. Troy's book *The Lord is My Shepherd...and He Knows I'm Gay*, and his social activism throughout the country on behalf of the gay community made him a celebrity to be seen and heard. Darcelle and Roxy made the event complete with their support. At least one couple met at the service who later became life-long partners, Don Howse and Lloyd Porter. They never have trouble remembering their anniversary date.

The congregation grew rapidly in numbers. By June the possibility of registering with the State of Oregon as a corporation emerged, and on July 12, 1977 the Articles of Incorporation were signed by the Board of Directors. It was Austin's goal to include successful business people on the church's Board of Directors. The seven board members whose names appear under Article V of that document are:

   Daniel Brown
   Don Howse
   Michael Hoffman
   Mary Klepser
   Mary Jane Kamm
   Denis Moore
   David Rushong
   A. Austin Amerine, Moderator

A most prominent transsexual at this time was Paula Nielsen, living as a woman since 1963. She found MCC in early 1977. Sister Paula eventually would become church secretary, submitting monthly articles for the *NW Fountain* newspaper, and studying for the ministry in the Exhorter program. In addition to her day job as a legal secretary for Kathryn English, she wrote monthly news items for the Fountain about doings at MCC. Austin's living room was the church office, and there Paula typed out early bulletins and correspondence. When the church moved into its own building later, she would insist that her office be equipped with an IBM Selectric II self-correcting typewriter, then the top of the line. When Board members balked at the expense, she quipped, "The best that there is, is none too good for God!" She got her typewriter!

As she became more and more theological and thought provoking in her writing, she began a regular column in *The Fountain,* then *The Oregon Gay News, Cascade Voice* and the *Eagle Newsmagazine* over the years. She launched a cable access television ministry on *Rogers Cable Access* Channel 21 in 1984. *Just Out* ran a feature article on her TV evangelism. Paula helped others, like Snickers LaBarr, start their own programs. Sister Paula also became good friends with Darcelle when she first went to the tavern to meet visiting transvestite Christine Jorgenson. For much of the '80s and '90s, Paula performed at Darcelle XV's NW 3rd Ave. dinner club with her well-received emulation of Sophie Tucker. She also became Darcelle's secretary and publicist.

Anita Bryant and Anti-Gay Ordinances

Anita Bryant was a popular singer in the mid-1970s who was hired by the Florida Citrus Commission to become their National advertising figurehead. On screen she touted the merits of orange juice in nationwide ads. She was also a mother and resident of Dade County Florida, where a gay rights ordinance had been passed for the Miami urban area. Miss Bryant began a vociferous campaign to repeal the measure, based on her fundamental interpretations of Biblical texts and the backing of conservative Christians and politicians.

During the same period, NFL player and hero David Kopay had come out positively. Kopay had been a guest on talk shows like *Today* and the *Phil Donahue Show,* talking about his recently released autobiography *The*

Rev. Austin Amerine was larger than life, in many ways. He could easily spoof himself with the jolly friar logo, become earnestly serious in his Assemblies of God preaching style. His love of food was well known and obvious, requiring the services of MCC tailor George DeLand. Most people fondly remember his habit of raising his glasses on his forehead.

His underpowered Mercedes diesel was "snowflake," whose engine he blew up several times. The rear end raised up in reverse gear and back seat passengers often felt they were riding a cat in heat. He fell asleep at the wheel once in California and took out several fence posts in a median. Not trusting himself to stay awake, he usually had his roommate Andrew Dixon do the driving for short or long distances.

MCC Archive photos

Rev. A. Austin Amerine   1976 - 1979

David Kopay Story. Florida, and eventually most of the country, became embroiled in verbal and media battles over homosexuality issues. Three other municipalities in the country also had gay-rights issues on upcoming ballots, one being Eugene, Oregon. Editorial pages reflected the wide range of positions on the issue.

In the course of the election season, many closeted or quiet homosexuals spoke up for their rights, coming out to family and friends. A *Gaycott* was organized nationwide against Florida orange juice. *Ban Anita Bryant* buttons and tee-shirts appeared. This became a major watershed in the lives of many gays.

Ultimately, on June 7, 1977, the ordinance to provide equal rights to gays in Florida was repealed, as eventually were the ordinances in other states. The campaign had exposed the undercurrent of homophobia in many parts of the nation. The Bryant crusade exposed a witch hunt designed to push gays back into the closet; to finance John Birch Society chapters, Fundamentalists, and Ku Klux Klan attacks on American Democracy; and to persecute or "cure" gays, pot smokers, ERA supporters, abortionists, and birth control advocates. More than ever, gay rights groups mobilized to encourage coming out and other individual acts; to work for the election of pro-gay candidates; to initiate referendums and initiatives on future ballots; and to use the court system to expose and fight "official discrimination."

Acquiring the Building

During the summer of 1977, Mel Hamilton, a member with connections in real estate, became aware that an old church building was for sale at the corner of NE 24th and Broadway. Bob Fulton, a member of the search committee for a building, had spotted the "For Sale" sign on the brown shingled old church at NE 24th and Broadway, near Lloyd Center.

The 1909 wooden structure originally constructed by the First Universalist Church of Good Tidings was being used by the Church of Divine Science, a group espousing the teachings of a 19th century American healer named Malinda Elliott Cramer. The Scientists had purchased the building in 1963 from Grace Lutheran Church. Numbering about 300 members in the '60s, they had dwindled to fewer than twenty regular attendees by 1977. To keep the church from defaulting on payments, Mr. Art Lind and his partner Mr. Abbott (of Abbott and Lind Printing) purchased the building, but when his partner died suddenly, Mr. Lind became interested in liquidating the property.

When Austin first saw the church building, he felt instantly that it was to be the future home of the congregation. Negotiations were begun with Dan Brown and Mel Hamilton representing MCC. As the final purchase price of $87,000 was agreed upon, MCC members felt it was important to tell Mr. Lind that MCC served a homosexual population. It was with relief that the team heard Mr. Lind voice, "No problem, I know all about you." The purchase was one of the wisest decisions in MCC history. It not only gave MCC a stable home, but it represented permanence and *pride for the gay* community.

Hamilton also advocated for the purchase, at $5000, of the parking lot on the northwest corner of 24th and Broadway. An elegant home from 1910 on the site had been torn down about 1930, replaced with a Savemore Gas Station, which had also been recently bulldozed. The Second Foundation had used the station's lot as a locale for fundraising car washes in the early 1970s. Robertson's Pharmacy and a barbershop sat directly across Broadway in a 1928 streetcar-era commercial block. The barbershop is still owned by the same family in 2005.

The suggestion to purchase the vacant lot was rejected, and even the vote to purchase the church was not unanimous. Sitting in a meeting at Centenary-Wilbur, leaders debated the merits and negatives of taking on responsibilities of indebtedness and having a facility, run-down as it was, to call home. Bob Jackson recounted the dilemma of donating $1000 to the down payment on his $800 monthly salary. He looked around the room to see newfound friends, companions in the faith, and the energy of a new venture and signed the pledge slip. $18,000 was pledged that night and the future of MCC-Portland decided. For a new congregation with 160 members, taking on such debt was for-

When Metropolitan Community Church of Portland became the owner of the former Church of Good Tidings, the building immediately became a symbol for the congregation. Member artist Patti Magee drew several versions for use on letterheads, bulletin covers, and for the monthly newsletter, *the Chalice*. The building's once-bright colors had been painted a dour chocolate brown by previous owners, the Church of Divine Science, and remained another 18 years, until re-painting was inspired by Rev. Roy Cole in 1995 got it the current three-color motif.

Reprint of committee tasks and responsibilities from a 1977 Chalice (continues next 2 pages).

About the Finance Committee

By Dan Brown

The Finance Committee consists of members of the congregation with knowledge and experience in the world of finance. It is chaired by a committee member elected by the committee itself.

The Church Treasurer serves as liaison between the committee and the board of directors — without vote.

The responsibilities of the Finance Committee are:

1. Preparation of an annual budget;
2. Recommendations on all matters of finance to the board of directors;
3. To serve as a clearinghouse for planning and proper timing of all fundraisers;
4. To serve as a guide for all purchases related to the church which may require future funding; and
5. To recommend special areas for consideration as "Designated Funds."

All Finance Committee decisions require approval by the Board of Directors before their enactment.

The recommendations of this committee serve as a great aid and give professional guidance to the members of the board of directors and church treasurer in all finance decisions.

Portland City Archive

September-October, 1977

the Chalice

Rev. A. Austin Amerine   1976 - 1979

midable, but faith prevailed over reason, and the contract was signed. The contract was for $77,000. It would be 1993 before the final payment was made. For many years, MCC rented the parking lot for $5 a month.

During one of the last worship services at Centenary-Wilbur, a fire broke out in another part of the building, and congregants hastily exited the smoky structure. The fire was contained, and the worship space untouched, but nonetheless the congregation was glad to move into the Broadway location a few weeks later.

MCC-Portland thus became the fifth MCC congregation to purchase its own property. In 2005, it is one of only four MCC congregations in Region I to own their own building. About 70 congregations in the UFMCC fellowship out of 300 own their buildings. The arrangement was made that the Divine Science congregation would continue to use the sanctuary for Sunday morning services, while MCC's services would continue on Sunday evenings and Thursdays.

The first MCC service was held in the building on September 4, 1977. There was literally nothing to move over to the new sanctuary except for communion ware and the Cross built by the Rushongs.

Little thought was given to making major changes to the new old church. MCC used the existing hymnals and altar furniture. The building was not in the best repair. Oiling the dried pews to restore a luster took four applications and far more elbow grease than volunteers Vi Leagjeld and Harry Sherburne had anticipated. The carpeting was old and worn. The shingled exterior was a dull brown, with no accent color.

Real estate people in Portland commented that it was a shabby church in a rundown neighborhood–good enough for the gays, since few other churches would want it. Irvington in the 1970s was dotted with decaying former mansions converted into rooming houses and hostels, with tie-dyed sheets often hung in the windows for curtains.

The church has rarely been marked with anti-gay or gang graffiti. One time in particular during a political campaign, a black *God Hates Your Sin* was spray painted on the retaining wall. "Sin" was painted in red. There have been a few incidents of tagging as rival factions tried to mark territory. The era of gay gentrification of the 'hood was about to begin.

The dedication service was held in January 1978, as part of the Western Ministers Conference, hosted by the congregation. The conclave was a major assembly of UFMCC clergy and it gave the energetic congregation an opportunity to share their spirit and blessings of acquiring their own building in record time. For the next few years, MCC-Portland was known within the denomination as the "Cathedral" church, a reference to the building's size and architecture. The founder and moderator of UFMCC, Rev Troy Perry, returned to Portland for the conference and ceremony.

Development of Programs

MCC now had a physical visible identity, and word spread quickly through the community of its location. After the demise of the two Second Foundation community centers in 1972-1973, the gay people once again had a physical identity in Portland. Political, social, religious, and 12-step groups began using the facility on a regular basis. It was an historical building to be proud of, with a cornerstone laid by U.S. President William Howard Taft. See Chapter 5 for details of the building's colorful history and architectural significance.

Within the larger Portland community, it became popularly known as the "queer church."

Members proudly spread flyers and put up signs and church business cards at several local bars and other gay gathering places, even the baths. Several members who joined at this time report that when they were first considering coming to a gay church (hence partially "coming out") they often took several Sundays of driving to the church, cruising around the block, maybe even parking, before deciding not to go in, and returned home to try again the following week. Stepping over the threshold for the first time was a transforming experience in the lives of several members–finding a legitimate sanctu-

Our Social Committee
Actually four-in-one

**By Jacquie Bogle
& Kathy Byrdon-Eyer**

This is one of the largest and most varied committees within the church.

The Social Committee is actually four committees under one Social Director, Larry Wormington.

If you're interested in becoming involved in any of these, we have listed below the committees and their respective chairpersons:

1. Coffee Hour — Jack Hobson, chairperson.(See article, *Your Coffee Hour.*)

2. Large Social Functions — Jacquie Bogle, Kathy Byrdon-Eyer, co-chairpersons. Plans church-wide functions for special holidays — Halloween, Thanksgiving, Christmas and New Year's Eve. This committee is responsible for such events as the Fourth of July and Labor Day picnics, the monthly Bingo game, and film night, which last month included a bake sale presented by the Choir.

If you're interested in participating in this type of activity, we welcome any suggestions or help. Please talk to Jacquie, Kathy, or Larry. Jac and Kath's phone number is 643-7194, "if you can't reach us at church."

3. Socials for Fund-raising — Frank Meyers and Neil Neilsen, co-chairpersons. Works in conjunction with Large Social Function Committee planning fund-raising events. If you have ideas for fund raising, or wish to be involved in the planning and presentation of these events, talk to Frank, Neil, Kath, Jac or Larry.

4. Subcommittee for Theater Parties, Camping and numerous other outings — Steve Wombig, chairperson. If this is your thing, talk to Steve.

The Social Committee wants to meet your needs and this is only possible if we have your input. See any of us with your ideas. . . or to help.

Thanks in advance!

Board of Directors

By Pastor Amerine

The Board of Directors, consisting of eight members, is elected by the Congregation. Except for the first elected class, the term of office is three years. Since this is the case with the Board which will be installed January 1, 1978, three will serve three years, three will serve two years, and two will serve one year.

This group serves with the Pastor in determining the goals and direction of the Church. They conduct the business affairs for the church body between congregational meetings. They also implement the decisions of the congregation as determined at such meetings.

The members of the Board also act as enablers for the various committees of the church, primarily for the time, space, counsel and resources necessary to their function.

Your Coffee Hour

By Jack Hobson

The success of our coffee hour so far is directly related to the wonderful response from you, the congregation, for sponsors.

Many thanks to all of you!

The committee is always open to suggestions for any new direction that individuals, couples, or groups of friends would enjoy sponsoring.

I can't think of a more Christian way to say "Hello," or "Have a nice week," than to sponsor the coffee hour in our House of God.

The responsibilities of the sponsors are to bring, prepare and serve the refreshments, and assist in the cleanup.

The committee's responsibility is to set up the coffee hour, assist in preparation and do backup work in the kitchen while you're serving, furnish coffee cups, plates, napkins, etc., tear down and clean up.

We can always use more volunteer workers on our coffee hour committee.

And. . . if you're interested in sponsoring a coffee hour, please feel free to contact me during coffee hour.

About the Altar Committee

By Dan Brown

The Altar Committee consists of members of the Diaconate.

The primary functions of this committee are the preparation of the Altar for the celebration of the Eucharist — washing (by hand), ironing and proper keeping of all Sacristy linens, and the orderly supply of all Sacristy supplies.

Great care is given to the service of the Altar with the utmost of reverence and respect . . . for it's The Lord's Table.

Rev. A. Austin Amerine   1976 - 1979

ary where they were accepted as both gay and Christian. One early attendee, a policeman, felt he had to disguise himself when attending, to protect his identity and job. So he did.

NE 24th and Broadway became the choice place to hold meetings for several gay organizations, most notably the Portland Town Council, which held monthly meetings the first Tuesday of each month. They held their first major fundraiser shortly after adopting MCC as their regular meeting place. Gay Pride planning meetings, Parents of Gays (P-FLAG), the Portland Gay Men's Chorus, and numerous other groups found MCC the logical if not ideal place to gather. The building also provided privacy for the meetings of an early transgender group, who felt the need for complete secrecy. Those attendees changed clothes after coming into the building, and again before leaving.

Moving headquarters from his home to the church office enabled Austin to more fully fulfill the role of pastor in counseling, program direction, and service planning. The church finally got its' own telephone number–ATwater 1-8868. Sunday service bulletins were typed by church secretary Paula Nielsen, on her new Selectric II, printed on blank Lutheran covers bought just down NE Broadway at the Augsburg Bookstore (now Kinko's).

Austin's girth was such that finding clothes presented a real problem. Early member George DeLand, a tailor by trade, became Amerine's one-man clothing store. George, who lived a block from MCC, took on other sewing functions for the early congregation, but not vestments or liturgical garb. His goal for the congregation was that it would offer a positive alternative to gays and lesbians, whose primary social outlet was the alcohol-oriented culture of the bars and taverns. Pinochle and Bridge were two card games popular at the time, and George started groups around each activity, with several tables of players at each event.

Austin's penchant for music influenced many members to volunteer their talents in singing. The choir was directed by Gary Coleman, son of an Iowa preacher. The first Sunday Gary came to MCC in 1976; Austin picked out his voice in the congregation, and proposed to Gary that he direct the church choir. As a "PK" (preacher's kid), Gary could hardly refuse. While he claimed a modest musical background, Gary held the choir together through several major festivals and services until the arrival of Jack St. John in 1978, when Gary became the Music coordinator. Together, they went shopping for a baby grand piano, purchased in 1980, to be played in concert, and with the organ for congregational singing.

Jack St. John brought keyboard energy into the congregation to match that of Austin and Denis Moore. Coincidentally, Jack had grown up in the same Olympia Baptist church as Denis Moore and B J Wilkinson. In September, Jack gave a concert that was publicized in the *NW Fountain*, inviting the gay community to the MCC auditorium. He performed his own compositions as well as other favorites. Jack also composed liturgical music that became part of MCC services. Jack composed original cantatas for several years at Christmas. He wrote music for *Simon of Cyrene* in 1979, a script that Paula Nielsen rewrote from a Kathryn Kuhlman radio program. Jack's most successful work was Esther the Queen in 1980, again with a script by Paula. David Pelletier designed the program cover. Esther was so professional that the choir performed it later in Eugene and Vancouver, BC.

St. John worked with Rev. David Pelletier to compose *The Church Alive*, for MCC of the Willamette Valley in Eugene. The spirited tune and specific words have made it a favorite choice for celebrations and anniversaries. The hymn has since become the thematic hymn for the UFMCC fellowship.

Since the Lutherans had taken their pipe organ with them in 1963, a donated used Rogers electric organ was initially used to accompany hymns. An Allen Organ, belonging to the First Church of the Nazarene, was acquired but its system of tubes and amplifiers required most of the space in the adjoining storage room near the console. It was rebuilt and maintained by Paul Wirth, but performers reported that it was a cantankerous instrument, at best. A rotation of organists took turns "on the bench" - Denis

Deacons and Exhorters

By Pastor Amerine

The function of the Diaconate in a church varies according to the theological traditions and Church government of the group with which it is affiliated.

M.C.C. has opted to use the office of Deacon as a vehicle of service and assistance in certain aspects of Pastoral care, concern and responsibility.

The Diaconate is responsible for a Deacon's Closet, out of which material needs of people are provided, such as food, clothing and lodging referrals. Deacons are also active in visitation, both hospital and home, as well as attempts to do follow-up contact of visitors to our services and absentees from Church services. They are frequently called into counseling situations so it is important that they have a positive attitude about their Christian testimony, the Church and their lifestyle. Finally, the Deacons serve as enablers to the various parishes and parish officers representing the Pastor and acting as resource people.

The Exhorter is at a level of the ministry recognized by the Universal Fellowship of Metropolitan Community Churches. An exhorter is a person who is either a student minister or a lay minister recognized by the local congregation. Most exhorters have either been Deacons or have been through the Diaconate training program where they have learned the fundamentals of Christian service and are responding to the leading toward a broader, or professional, ministry.

Anyone may become a candidate for these programs after counseling with the Pastor and who is willing to expend the effort and energy in time and study.

Christian Social Action Committee

By Pastor Amerine

The Christian Social Action Committee, although not provided as a standing committee in our local Bylaws, is being formed as a result of recommendations from both the 7th and 8th sessions of the General Conference of U.F.M.C.C.

Its purpose is to serve as a consciousness - raising tool within the church in matters of Human Rights — providing us with relevant information and encouraging us to explore our questions about women's liberation, men's liberation, racism and other related areas.

This committee also would be a source of reports back to the congregation about the developments in the field of legislative and political effort and participating on a volunteer basis in these endeavors.

Special Ministries

"And the King will answer them, 'Truly, I say to you, as you did it to one of the least of these my brethren, you did it to me'."

By Donald Howse

Now that we have our own home, and have time to reflect on our mission and outreach, we need to remember that our service is to Jesus Christ.

We have no better method to demonstrate that service, than through service to fellow Christians, who are in need of our love and concern.

I feel there are three areas which need are attention:

Aged, Infirm, Handicapped

Bob Jackson and a few other people, both members of Portland MCC and not, have met to discuss this ministry and lay groundwork for its development. These Christians can use your love and concern, your input of ideas, your helping hand.

If you have an interest in this area, contact Bob Jackson. To participate in this ministry, one does not have to be old, infirm or handicapped, but have love to share with those who are.

Alcoholics

In our community are many individuals who freely admit to their alcoholism, but must fight their battle alone because of their lifestyle.

I propose we organize a group called 'Gay Alcoholics Together.' This group has been formed in other MCC congregations with good (attested) results.

Gay Alcoholics Together operates progarms similar to those of Alcoholics Anonymous.

Anyone interested in helping to form such a group at MCC Portland, contact either Rev. Austin Amerine or Don Howse.

Several people have casually expressed an interest, now we need to find, together, our resources and activate our ideas.

Prison Ministry

People in correctional and penal institutions need to be made aware of our love and concern for them. One way to achieve this is by initiating a correspondence ministry.

Many of these people are very lonely, and have no friends or relatives outside the prison walls. A simple letter can be a useful tool in expressing God's love for them.

If you feel you could serve God through a ministry of correspondence, give me your names and I will proceed to establish contacts inside the prison.

With each of these ministries, may we always keep Jesus in mind, and know assuredly that we, too, will be ministered to in our time of need.

Rev. A. Austin Amerine   1976 - 1979

Moore, Mark Parkinson, Oren Charles Hornbeck, and Jack St. John. John Phillippi also joined the ranks, playing in concert style until he lost one leg as a result of bone cancer. In those pre-transistor days, the old Allen had a peculiar habit of blurting out unexplained booms, occasionally during the sermon when there wasn't even an organist in place!

Gary Coleman was given the opportunity to select new hymnals for congregational use, and suggested *Hymns for the Family of God,* copyrighted the previous year by *Paragon Associates* in Nashville, Tennessee. The hymnal represented a balance of hymns from many Christian traditions plus many contemporary songs and spirituals, printed in full score. Another bonus for experienced singers was that music often included optional descants for the last verse. Congregational singing occasionally bordered on symphonic. The book was commonly referred to as the "*Gaither Hymnal.*" MCC continued using these hymnals for about 20 years.

Small groups formed to contribute to the music program. In addition to the choir, a women's trio performed on occasion, as did a "Quartet," a chamber ensemble, and an MCC orchestra assembled for special occasions.

Many members provided special music during services–instrumental or vocal–as soloists or small groups. A partial list, gleaned from Sunday bulletins, includes the following performers: Rob Birchard, Jacquie Bogle, Kathy Brydon, Gary Coleman, Casey Elliott, Howard Hannon, Mel Hart, Ron Ivans, Richard Loganbill, Denis Moore, Frodo Okulam, John Rushong, Jack St. John, Bill Samuels, Bob Sherwood, Richard Strange, and BJ Wilkinson.

The Chalice

Austin originated a bimonthly newsletter in 1976, christened as *the Chalice,* which was distributed to all members and mailed to individuals and churches in the Northwest. A volunteer staff began helping with publication. Bill Barry, Glen Scott, and Paula Nielsen were early editors. In addition to the Pastor's column and articles of local interest, contributing writers often dealt with the larger issues of homosexuality and Christianity, understanding different denominational backgrounds, explaining doctrines of the church, and, naturally, providing recipes.

Calendars of up-coming events included announcements for concerts, bingo nights, potluck suppers and MCC District One events. Educating old and new members on church procedures, traditions, and conduct at congregational meetings was another function of *the Chalice.* One particularly influential article was "*The Gay Manifesto,*" penned by Denis Moore in 1977.

Within months of acquiring the building, Patti McGee, another *Chalice* staffer, drew up a view and design of the building which came to represent the church on bulletins, stationery, note cards, and in the *NW Fountain*, the newspaper that succeeded the original Fountain of the Second Foundation.

Committees

What is a church without committees? They enable the mission of the congregation to reach full development, spread out the effort and time commitment, and involve members in the work of the organization. Many hands make light work. Just two months after moving into their permanent home, members had organized at least ten committees to better carry out both the daily workings of the congregation and the larger outreach and ministry of MCC Portland. These committees were:

Social Committee (notice which one they listed first)
- Coffee hour
- Large social functions
- Fundraisers
- Subcommittee for "off-campus" events

Records and Membership Committee
Publications Committee–the *Chalice*
Finance Committee
Altar Committee
Christian Social Action Committee

Special Ministries Committee:
- Aging

Portland began a conscious program of historical preservation in the 1970s. Old Town buildings like the Merchant Hotel were restored. Hobo's occupies the space with the awning on the far right.

Portland City Archive photos

Railroad turntable north of Union Station was destroyed, but the Naito family purchased and restored several historic properties in Old Town.

OrHi file 1903

Innovative ideas in urban planning typified the progressive nature of Portland under Mayor Neil Goldschmidt. The nation's first transit mall was created when SW 5th and SW 6th were converted into one way streets, with restricted bus-only lanes and widened sidewalks encouraging a greater pedestrian presence in the downtown commercial core.

Rev. A. Austin Amerine   1976 - 1979

Addictions
Prison
The Diaconate
Deacons
Exhorters
Board of Directors

Traditions

Many of the programs and traditions so familiar to MCC members began during this period. While some no longer exist and some have changed form or title, several key aspects of MCC congregational life were taking form, now that the congregation had space to hold meetings, game nights, film nights, bingo nights, fundraisers, concerts, special events, and potlucks, of course.

Annual Bazaars began in 1977. Various combinations of events and sales became the trademark. Robin Hixon, a professional chef, catered remarkable meals while raffles were drawn for crazy quilts, door prizes, and much more. Craft tables abounded. Often the bazaar became equated with rummage sales and other fundraisers. This is a firmly entrenched MCC tradition, requiring hours of volunteer work and organizing, and an extraordinary amount of both humor and patience. Attendance by members and neighborhood friends has always been rewarding and countless dollars have been raised for general fund and specific campaigns.

BJ Wilkinson developed unique presentations known as *Chalk-Talks* which involved much more than colored chalk. Often done in connection with Christmas dinners, programs were sponsored by MCC's Women's Group and the dinners were cooked by the Deacons. Benefits from ticket sales went to the Deacons' Closet –a collection of food to be given to those in the church family with special needs. Carol singing, narrations, and other holiday presentations went into these evenings.

The first congregational picnic was held at Larry Wormington's Vancouver home. It was called Larry's Big Bang, and it was. Congregational picnics soon became a tradition on Memorial Day, 4th of July, Labor Day, and just some regular weekends. While never reaching the magnitude of *Vortex I,* they were nonetheless events to remember. Picnics and camp outs were held at Lewisville Park and Beacon Rock State Park in Washington, and several city parks in Portland. Members Don Howse and Lloyd Porter hosted one early picnic. Their eight-acre private nursery near Sandy provided a rural setting, an open expanse, plenty of room for potluck fare and a keg. Later that evening, a neighboring farmer spotted an errant VW bug stranded in his ditch, complete with at least one MCC member therein, who needed the cow manure hosed from his body and car before others would help him return to town. He earned quite a reputation for a board member. Although he's a great photographer, only mental images of this adventure remain.

Special evenings were targeted as social high points. Halloween nights became a tradition. And then there were the Valentines Disco Dance Evenings!!

While Austin had a penchant for organizing, he was also known to have the endearing quality of forgetfulness. Significant in some early parishioners' memories is the Sunday that Daylight Savings time went into effect, with Austin showing up a full hour late for worship. Equally charming was the Reverend's Mercedes, affectionately dubbed "Snowflake." Member Andrew Dixon soon became Austin's chauffeur. Adding further to Austin's charm was his ability to control his temper, but when it was safe, to let go and use any or all of the seven invectives then banned on broadcast television. At least once during Holy Communion Austin's enthusiasm for the sacrament sometimes meant flinging his arms while wearing his robe. One Sunday, the resultant distribution of wine went on the floor. He was mortified!

In those early days, when some "emergency" situation requiring major amounts of money would arise, Austin's solution was to simply tell the congregation they needed "X" amount of money for the leaky roof, haywire electrical, or whatever...and it would get donated! In order to use the electric typewriter in the office, for instance, all the lights had to be switched on in the Sanctuary, since both rooms were one circuit.

Liturgical artist Bryan Paatz, a friend of Dan Brown, designed and embroidered a com-

Portland City Archives

Dave Kohl photo

Favored rendezvous spots for closeted gay men included the old McMahon baths (now closed) under today's Greek Cusina. Restrooms in the Galleria and Lippman's were well used. In 1977, Dick Lawson opened the Continental Baths under the Cornelius Hotel, the classiest bathhouse in the city. Art films and second run favorites could, and still can, be viewed at the art deco Roseway.

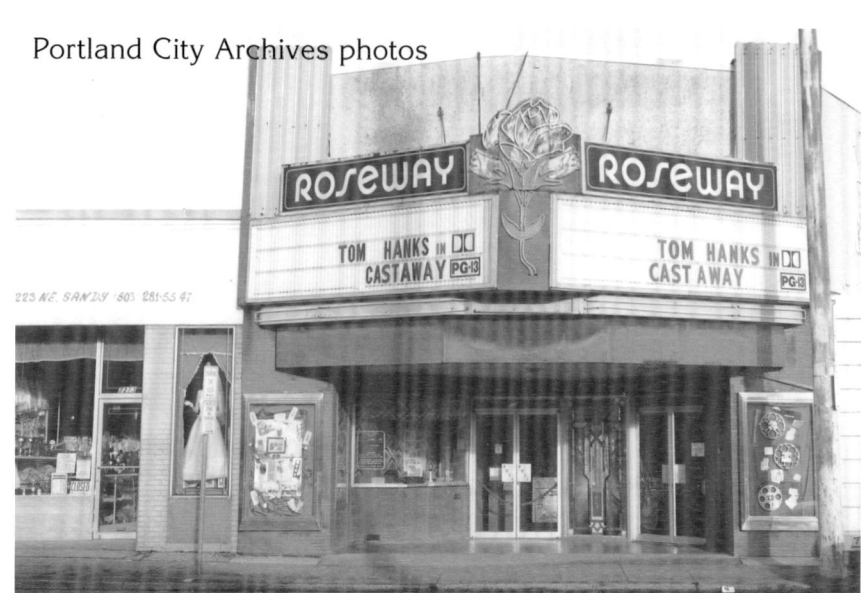

Portland City Archives photos

110

Rev. A. Austin Amerine   1976 - 1979

plete set of very elaborate seasonal stoles to be worn as part of the pastor's liturgical appointments. Brian, a Lake Oswego fabric artist of national renown, outdid himself, adding more pomp to Austin's already pompous frame. Termed "ecclesiastical drag" by Brian, Austin considered it his "holy armor" although at other times, it seems to have been more like "holy hardware" or "divine drag." Twenty years later, Rev. Roy Cole self-admittedly carried this concept to extremes during his pastorate in the 1990s. He acknowledged good-naturedly that his stoles and capes competed with Darcelle's outfits, and made Austin's look like drab drag. Roy just loved those robes! What is it about gay clergy and ecclesiastical garb? (See chapter 12)

Portland Environmental Progress

Portlanders took time from the rigors of political warfare to celebrate the victories of the *Trail Blazers* marching toward the National Basketball Association championship in 1977. It was a time of reflection on the progress of the *City of Roses*. The Willamette was clean enough again to support a fish population. Occasionally, a salmon would be caught in front of Waterfront Park, now named for sainted Governor Tom McCall. New tall buildings of glass and steel filled the urban renewal blocks. New commercial areas had arisen in salvaged old buildings like the Galleria (once the Olds, Wortman and King Department Store) and John's Landing (former warehouses). McCormick Pier had developed as a posh river front residential complex where industrial buildings had once stood.

Old neighborhoods were revitalized with active neighborhood associations in areas like Lair Hill, Sellwood, Buckman, and Irvington, just north of MCC. Chinatown and Old Town became respectable once again. Though a small town in population, Portland could boast of big-time entertainment, including the *Oregon Symphony, Chamber Music Northwest, Double Tee Promotions, Celebrity Attractions,* the *Trail Blazers* Basketball and *Timbers Soccer.* (Stein, Harry, *Portland*, 1980)

Portlanders were proud of their city, its architectural beauty and its natural setting. They axed the idea of a grid of freeways chopping up the town in favor of a below surface by-pass on the west (the I-405 Stadium Freeway) and replaced Harbor Drive with a full-length city park. The city was ringed with an Interstate, not bisected by one. The nation's first transit mall restricted one-way traffic on SW 5th and SW 6th to busses, with widened tree-lined sidewalks to make downtown an attractive and functional commercial and entertainment center.

Appreciation of historical and heritage buildings increased with restoration of century-old cast iron fronted commercial blocks in Old Town and alternative uses for other buildings. Several underappreciated buildings, like the Swedish Evangelical Mission Covenant Church at 1624 NW Glisan were nominated and entered into the *National Register of Historic Places*. It became the Mission Theater, and with over 20 other historic structures salvaged by two brothers from the upholstery industry, turned into successful movie houses and brew-pubs throughout the city. The McMenamins actions have saved buildings and rejuvenated entire neighborhoods for 25 years. (*The Oregonian*, October 29, 1982, p.C3)

Gay Rights in 1978

Portlanders were sympathetic to land use planning, school desegregation and to the gay rights cause. The January 17, 1978, *Oregonian* ran a half-page feature story on a gay couple celebrating their 25-year 'marriage.' Eric Marcoux and Gene Woodworth went public with their quiet but proud lifestyle in their Northwest Portland neighborhood. In telling their story, they gave a face to the possibility that same-sex couples could form long-lasting committed relationships. At ages 47 and 49, it had taken years for them to reveal to neighbors and friends that they were lovers, not brothers. Beginning in 1974, they had become active leaders in the Portland chapter of *Dignity* and had become involved with Lifespring Inc.'s self-awareness seminars. One hope they shared was that they could be a positive role model to young gays, and show that the stereotype of gays being exclusively promiscuous was not valid.

Chuck Short, an early board member. After service, a group of early members surveys Broadway and the possibilities of brunch. Included are Bill Barry, Austin Amerine, and Andrew Dixon.

Austin Amerine performed several Holy Unions during his three and a half years. This couple owned Jonah's, a popular restaurant with gays. It was a popular venue for after church brunch many Sundays.

MCC Archives photos

Rev. David Pelletier pastored the MCC in Eugene. Austin left MCC-Portland to become the first NW District co-coordinator, a position eventually held by David Pellatier. Jane Sandmeier served in many roles at MCC.

Connie McCready completed Neil Goldschmidt's term as Portland mayor. Lunch with her was a prize in the building fund campaign.

MCC Archive photos

Rev. A. Austin Amerine   1976 - 1979

The Oregonian featured Austin in a January 1978 article, as part of a week-long series on various aspects of the local gay community. Photographed in front of the west window, the portly minister appears even larger than life. Austin hastened to clarify that MCC was not a gay church, but was a Christian church that ministers to the gay community. The church provided a comfortable setting for gay people to worship and at the same time, be themselves. He did relate that the majority of members were homosexual. The balance of social activity was also pointed out, recognizing needs of people newly out of the "closet," to meet others in settings beyond bars and baths. "The church is the first step out of the closet for a lot of these people," he noted.

There was some concern expressed by MCC members that raising the profile of the church might bring on some anti gay persecution or picketing. None happened.

Austin classified MCC worship experiences as ecumenical. "Since our members are from a number of different religious backgrounds, we try to have something for everybody." Austin explained that he had combined parts of a number of religious services and beliefs to create the worship template. To overcome basic differences in dogma, he encouraged individual church members to interpret the service themselves and to experience God in their own way. Austin also explained to *The Oregonian* that MCC did not depend on literal interpretations of Bible passages that condemn homosexuality. Rather, the church viewed those passages in their context. He pointed out that many "proof" texts against homosexuality were written by Paul, who also condoned slavery, abhorred inclusion of women in religious services, and condemned believers who wore gold jewelry.

Even in this congregation of mostly 20-somethings, there were a few funerals, including that of Bill Knapp. Killed in an auto accident near his Vancouver home, he was 31 when he died. He was a generous member in his financial, emotional, and spiritual support of the MCC family and had made many friends after moving to Oregon from New York City. His family donated funds, which were eventually used for a Lexan covering over the large stained glass window as a practical gift in his memory.

Rev. Arlene Ackerman

Reverend Arlene Ackerman came to Portland on March 15, 1978 to be the Assistant pastor. MCC had five pastor "A" names - Aaron Austin Amerine and Arlene Ackerman! Austin had advocated for a woman minister almost since his arrival, recognizing that he was unable to meet all the needs of the congregation. Regular attendance was nearing 200. Arlene was hired part time to specifically work with the women of the church and to create some staff balance.

With a background as minister-in-residence for MCC-Stockton, Arlene worked in crisis-intervention and short-term counseling. Austin's reputation of strong leadership in the building of new congregations particularly attracted Arlene. By her account, they worked very well together and complimented each other's skills. This was her first pastoral role after credentialing with the UFMCC.

Along with her partner, Jane Sandmeier, Arlene established a women's study group, and continued the tradition of yearly women's retreats at Camp Adams near Molalla in rural Clackamas County. An annual women's service became tradition, held in August at the church. Women also set up their own after-services coffee hour, which continued for several years. From their point of view, women were not so much trying to separate from the men, as they were interested in addressing what they saw as their own unique issues.

Arlene was also Director of the *Exhorter Training Program,* designed for individuals who felt called to develop pulpit skills, administrative and leadership skills, and learn about other areas pertinent to the professional ministry. The program served as a screening experience whereby people could find out whether they had a calling in professional or lay ministry. Classes were held on evenings and weekends, covering topics from Holy Communion to Church

Austin Amerine's story of frogs was told many times, and inspired this cover for *the Chalice*, the last issued during his tenure as pastor at MCC. The drawing was done by church members and artist Patti Magee, pictured in the center of the photo below. Her husband Randy is to the left.

Early social adventures set the tone for MCC social life for three decades. Picnics and outdoor weekend renewals meant lots of opportunity to bond with members of the church, and members of other churches like MCC in Boise.

the Chalice

The business of the church is kissing frogs

March-April, 1979
Metropolitan Community Church of Portland

Dave Dishman photos

114

Rev. A. Austin Amerine   1976 - 1979

Financing. Several Exhorters went on to become student clergy and pastors in the UFMCC including Jack St. John, Denis Moore, Ron Bergeron, Phil Crum, Betty Pederson, Paula Nielsen, Frodo Okulam, Teresa Nunn, Joyce Baxter, Marguerite Scroogie, Jodi Mekkers, Mary Frantz, and LaPaula Turner.

Outreach ministries of MCC grew to include groups not directly sponsored by the church, but related to it. These included the *Live and Let Live Group*, for men with an alcohol or drug history; *Up and Over* for women with similar situations; the *Continuity Guild*, an organization serving senior citizens; and a *Gay Emergency Services Shelter*, located at 5026 NE 17th, which provided temporary food and lodging in a Christian family atmosphere. A large number of new church members came to MCC by first attending the alcohol and drug groups.

Several social and educational groups also formed. Deacon Bob Jackson, an experienced broadcast journalist who also used American Sign Language on TV, volunteered to teach a sign language class at MCC. Robin Hixson cooked fantastic meals for church suppers and special events, he also taught cooking classes. Several social groups met regularly for pinochle, bridge, banner making, and pasting-up the monthly *Chalice*. Prayer breakfasts were held on Tuesdays at 7 am, downtown at either the International House of Pancakes cater corner from the Embers on SW Park Ave., or at the Riverside West Motel on SW Front, where the original Half Moon tavern had stood. In addition to the Continuity group for seniors, there was a youth group that regularly met with Arlene Ackerman. Special occasions were always an excuse for Larry Wormington's social committee to plan a wing-ding, such as the MCC Halloween party at the Heathman Hotel Georgian Room in 1978.

Austin and his Frogs

Kissing Frogs was Austin's favorite message. He'd say "you gotta kiss a lot of frogs in life before you find your prince!" He summarized this message in 1979 for one of his last columns for *the Chalice*:

"In his book *Ask Me to Dance*," Bruce Larson introduces an adaptation of the old story about the ugly frog who was put under the spell of a wicked witch, but later turned into a handsome prince when kissed. (This was shared with him by an Episcopal priest [Wes Seelig] who had used it in a pastoral letter to his congregation.)

"Do you ever feel like a frog? Frogs feel slow, low, ugly, pudgy, drooped — you want to be bright but you feel dumb; you want to share but feel selfish; you want to feel thankful but instead feel resentful; you want to feel great but feel small; you want to care but are indifferent. You want to be challenged by life but you are too froggish to budge. It's like you, too, have been put under the spell of the wicked witch. What is the business of the church? Kissing frogs.

"Many of us were once frogs; under the spell of a 'wicked witch' — turned out of our churches, our families, our society — rejected as Christians.

"If the job of the church is indeed to kiss frogs, then we have to look around us and see the frogs. There are old ones, ugly ones, poor ones, dull ones; there are dependent ones; there are unhappy ones. There are frogs that are rejects — there are frogs that are prisoners — there are frogs that are rich. Why do we withhold the testimony and witness of the Lord to people around us? If we believe that the task of any church ministering in the name of Christ is to change the lives of people, then we must look at the unlovely, the unloved, and the unlovable, and offer them that 'magic kiss' — the power which will change their lives. Stop and think — the power that will change their lives. Stop and think — where would you and I be if someone had not kissed us?

"It is not always easy to meet the challenge, or to fulfill this obligation. Those who are most effective in kissing frogs are usually those who have been kissed themselves, and in this kiss received a transforming communicable experience of the living Christ — in its wake we felt a tremendous passion to pass it on to someone else. In Christ we recognize this as 'compassion' and, really, we are simply following in the steps of Christ when we demonstrate this compassion to those around us. Another demonstra-

MCC Archive photos

Lewisville, Laurelhurst, and several other parks were popular early MCC picnic sites. Inevitably, food was involved. Austin enjoyed celebrating his birthday with cake, while secretary Paula Nielsen and Steve Jordan look on. Paula came to MCC after working and studying at the Angelus Temple in Los Angeles, home of radio evangelist Aimee Semple McPherson. While working as a legal secretary, she also began her cable TV ministry.

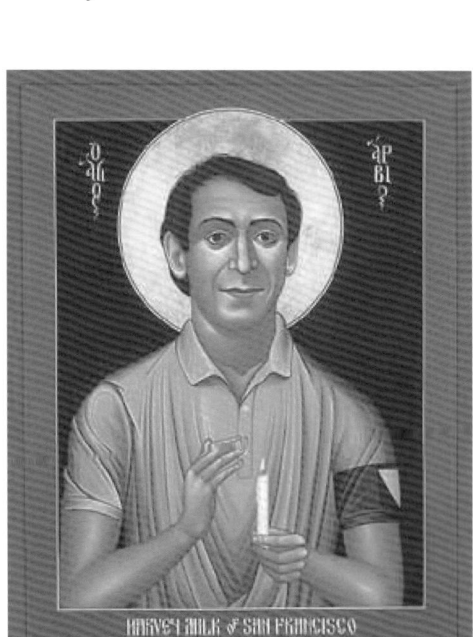

Harvey Milk's death galvanized the gay population of San Francisco, and of the nation. It was a turning point. He is seen by many as a martyr to the cause of gay liberation.

Paula Nielsen Archive

116

Rev. A. Austin Amerine 1976 - 1979

tion of this urgency is to share with others that transforming kiss in that we find within us a love for others that is not dependent on being loved, liked, or flattered, in return. This concern for others is the basis for an unbreakable fellowship we feel with others who are also busy kissing frogs.

"While it is true that it may not be easy to kiss a frog, still it is made easier when we possess a serenity and a peace not dependent on things we are doing or feeling a need to do. This, in turn, gives one a deep sense of joy.

"We are part of the MCC family because somebody took the time to kiss us when we didn't even like ourselves. Therefore, may we never withhold this kiss to others who have suffered, who are estranged or feel they are unlovely.

"Yes, the Episcopal priest was right — THE BUSINESS OF THE CHURCH IS KISSING FROGS."

Harvey Milk & George Moscone

San Francisco policeman Dan White stormed into City Hall and fatally shot Mayor George Moscone and openly gay County Supervisor Harvey Milk in November 1978. Milk was a financial analyst who became a leader in the protest against intervention by the United States in Cambodia. He embraced broad support of human rights, and had been recently elected to the Board of Supervisors as the highest ranking elected gay official at the time. George Moscone had been a lawyer, spent 3 years on the San Francisco Board of Supervisors, became a California State Senator for 9 years, and was elected San Francisco Mayor in 1976.

San Francisco Was in Shock

A spontaneous memorial gathering on the City Hall steps formed within hours of the shootings. News spread throughout gay and straight communities. Nationwide this produced a mixture of anger and sadness at the loss of good men and frustration at latent bigotry, and a resolve to address the mistreatment of homosexuals. Many new movements and groups grew from this misfortune, after *Stonewall* probably the most significant event in modern gay liberation history. A group of gays assembled to sing for his memorial, and soon decided to form the *San Francisco Gay Men's Chorus*. This began the nationwide gay and lesbian choral movement. Within a year, Portland become the fifth city in the nation to have a gay-identified men's chorus (See Chapter 6)

Austin Amerine was approached by Jerry Weller of the *Portland Town Council* about holding a memorial gathering at MCC. About 200 Portlanders filled the MCC sanctuary on Sunday, December 3rd for memorial services honoring the slain leaders. It was a somber gathering, with an organ meditation by Denis Moore, an original song written and sung by Jack St. John, an invocation from Arlene Ackerman, and personal reflections from Austin, who had lived and worked in San Francisco. The church was overflowing with gay and straight people.

Three local political leaders gave messages. Barbara Roberts, then a Multnomah County Commissioner, spoke on the challenge to public life. She would go on to become Oregon's first female governor. Holly Hart, who had helped found the Gay Liberation Front, spoke on the call to come forward in such times. She would continue to influence Portland alternative culture by opening her Old Wives Tales Restaurant in 1980. Jerry Weller, founder of the Portland Town Council, spoke eloquently of Harvey Milk's dream of a society where all gay people could be out and accepted. Jerry went on to serve the *National Gay Task Force* in Washington, D.C. and worked closely on this committee with Troy Perry. Those who attended the memorial report a feeling of solidarity, and left with the resolve to honor the slain leaders by making a difference for gay rights.

MCC-Portland took an active role in the Northwest District of the denomination, sending representatives to all conferences in the district and to General Conference in Denver ('77) Membership at that time was 110. In January of 1978, Portland hosted the Western Ministers Conference, which coincided with the dedication of the church building. At the 1978 District Conference, one of the decisions made was to elect a full-time coordinator for the District. Portland delegates were both proud and sad to vote for the first person to fill that position, because it was their own Austin Amerine who had been nominated.

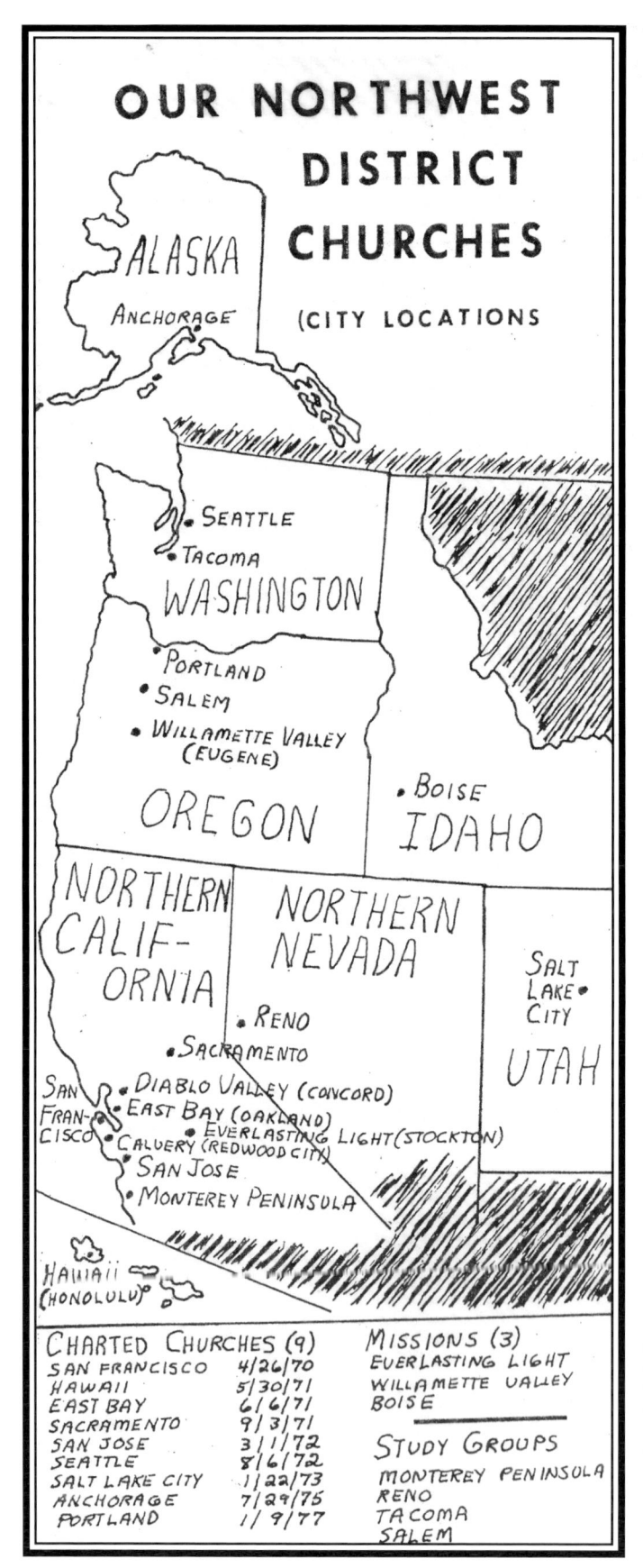

OUR NORTHWEST DISTRICT CHURCHES
(CITY LOCATIONS)

- ALASKA — Anchorage
- WASHINGTON — Seattle, Tacoma
- OREGON — Portland, Salem, Willamette Valley (Eugene)
- IDAHO — Boise
- NORTHERN CALIFORNIA — Sacramento, San Francisco, Diablo Valley (Concord), East Bay (Oakland), Everlasting Light (Stockton), Calvary (Redwood City), San Jose, Monterey Peninsula
- NORTHERN NEVADA — Reno
- UTAH — Salt Lake City
- HAWAII (Honolulu)

CHARTED CHURCHES (9)
SAN FRANCISCO	4/26/70
HAWAII	5/30/71
EAST BAY	6/6/71
SACRAMENTO	9/3/71
SAN JOSE	3/1/72
SEATTLE	8/6/72
SALT LAKE CITY	1/22/73
ANCHORAGE	7/29/75
PORTLAND	1/9/77

MISSIONS (3)
- EVERLASTING LIGHT
- WILLAMETTE VALLEY
- BOISE

STUDY GROUPS
- MONTEREY PENINSULA
- RENO
- TACOMA
- SALEM

Dave Dishman photos

Two district co-coordinators, David Pelletier and Austin Amerine. Austin enjoyed his work with the District, but after three years, determined to re-enter parish ministry and start a new congregation in Spokane, Washington.

The Northwest District of the Universal Fellowship of Metropolitan Community Churches when Austin became co-coordinator.

Rev. A. Austin Amerine   1976 - 1979

Austin remained in his pastoral role in Portland through June 10, 1979, continuing to nourish the congregation as membership continued to climb. There were many farewell events sponsored by various groups and committees. The men hosted a major steak BBQ as a farewell from the males in the congregation. Reverend Ackerman became the interim minister upon Austin's departure. Her internship lasted almost four months.

Austin had helped found three other MCC congregations while he served the Portland church. These were in Salem; Roseburg, in southern Oregon; and in the Tri-Cities of Pasco-Richland-Kennewick, Washington. He served as District Coordinator for three years, but could not resist the opportunity to help found another congregation, which he did in Spokane, Washington in 1983. When that group was well established, he moved to Bellevue, Washington, and founded MCC-Overlake. Several years later, he moved again to Sacramento to help with the music program at MCC-River City, working with Rev. Elder Freda Smith. He retired there at age 72, but within two months, Portland called him back to be the interim pastor when Rev. Dennis Chapell resigned in 1994. When Rev. Roy Cole arrived four months later, Austin retired again and moved back to Bellevue. He passed away in November 1998 at the age of 76.

MCC-Portland celebrated Austin's life with a memorial service on Saturday, December 5, 1998, with Rev. Elder Troy Perry as the speaker. True to Austin's character, the ceremony was followed with an ice cream social, augmented with many tales of Austin's life, gifts, foibles, and adventures.

At his request, memorial funds donated in his name became the seed money for one of Austin's dreams–a retreat center in Northern California. The concept had originated in 1985 at District Conference. Rev. Ed Sheriff and Keith Philpott donated 20 acres of land in Washington that year. That plot was eventually determined to be unsuitable and sold for seed money. Combined with many generous gifts, the Retreat Center fund eventually purchased a property in Northern California. The Austin Amerine Center opened in 1997 and dedicated in 2003.

OrHi neg CN 018599

Water is a key element in Portland geography. In 1894 floods submerged Washington at 4th. The Dekum building is on the right. The mouth of Sullivan's Gulch was also flooded. The old Steel Bridge is to the north. The Gulch runs diagonally across the view of the eastside, with the new 1895 Union Station to the lower right. Drainage pipes kept the gulch dry for rails.

OrHi neg CN 018595

OrHs file 1680

OrHi neg 25587

120

Chapter Five
Interlude: The Church of Good Tidings
1909 - Present

"I was glad when they said unto me, Let us go into the house of the Lord"
Psalm 122:1 (Revised Standard Version)

I. Ownership and Legal History

The Neighborhood

On April 8, 1909, ground was broken for a new picturesque English design church at the corner of Broadway and East 24th Avenue in Northeast Portland. The edifice was to be built as the First Universalist Church of Good Tidings. Metropolitan Community Church became its fourth owner when it was acquired in 1977. To appreciate the rich religious and aesthetic heritage of the building, it is helpful to look back into Portland's early east side history.

East Portland was one of several communities developing on the right bank of the Willamette River in competition with the deeper-harbored City of Portland across the river. Originally a small clearing in the dense forests of old-growth fir trees in the 1850s, small developments there and in Albina, Sellwood, and Milwaukie had languished until Portland's commercial and residential growth had filled up the alluvial plain at the base of the West Hills.

The shallow riverbank of the east side did not make an appealing town-site, as compared with the west bank. Sullivan's Gulch effectively separated north and south portions of the Willamette's right bank as far east as East 33rd Street. The 60-foot deep gulch was named for Timothy Sullivan's donation land claim there of 1851. That claim gave him 320 acres; 640 since he was married. The Gulch was subject to occasional flooding during the years of 1853-54 and 1861-62 when the Willamette rose over 55 feet from its summertime low level. Sullivan built his house on the claim in 1863. When he died, much of his claim passed to his daughter, a Roman Catholic nun, and upon her death, that land became the property of the Sisters of Charity for many years.

In 1869, the end of the Oregon and California railroad line was established on the east bank at East 3rd and Morrison. By 1883, a rail line also ran east from Portland, utilizing the watercourse of Sullivan's Gulch for its easy east-west grade. The creek was channeled into cement pipes, keeping the track bed dry. Originally laid by Henry Villard's Oregon Railroad and Navigation Company, the tracks became part of the Union Pacific mainline east in 1884. The Northern Pacific line into Portland was completed from the north in 1883. In 1887, rail connections with San Francisco were finished, eliminating the need for a stagecoach over the Siskiyou Mountains. By 1904, there were five transcontinental connections into Portland. Steamboats hauled passengers and cargo up rivers as far as Eugene or Boise, and to coastal and transpacific ports through Astoria.

The 1905 Lewis and Clark Exposition celebrated the 100th anniversary of American ownership of the Louisiana Purchase. Oregon Territory was not part of that acquisition, but the journeys of Lewis and Clark formed a major claim on the territory in later years. Portland was only 50 years old when it mounted the World Fair. The Forestry Building was constructed of solid logs, set into rows reminiscent of the Greek Parthenon. Most other buildings were constructed of wood framing and stucco to resemble Mediterranean architecture. Both structures influenced the Church of Good Tidings.

The Lewis and Clark monument, dedicated in 1908 by President Teddy Roosevelt, overlooks the entrance to Washington Park above the city.

These two men first met at the unveiling of the Sacajawea sculpture at the 1905 fair. They set a date to meet again 50 years later under the statue. The story in *the Oregon Journal* gave no more details. By that time, the sculpture was permanently installed in Washington Park. The park is the second largest urban park in the U.S. and the only urban park containing an old-growth forest, miles of hiking trails, and a well-known cruising area known as "the fruit loop."

Interlude: The Church of Good Tidings

The Stark Street ferry was used to cross the river until completion of the first Morrison Street Bridge in 1887. Real estate development followed, tracts or additions were laid out, and Albina and East Portland were joined with the City of Portland in 1891. In 1892, the First Universalist Church of Good Tidings started meeting in Albina under the leadership of Rev. Q. H. Shinn. Prosperity was set back for several years following the national silver crisis and recession of 1893.

The Lewis and Clark Fair

The city on both sides of the Willamette witnessed a burst of new building activity and growth following the successful Lewis and Clark Exposition of 1905. The Lewis and Clark Centennial and American Pacific Exposition and Oriental Fair marked the 100th anniversary celebration of the Louisiana Purchase and resultant exploration by the Corps of Discovery. It brought 1.5 million visitors in 1905 and revitalized Portland business with local visitors as well as guests from throughout the nation. Featured in various exhibit halls were new electrical inventions and appliances, displays from several foreign countries, especially Japan, and immense examples of Oregon native products. One purpose of the fair was to establish Portland's preeminence in the region as a shipping hub and commercial center.

The fair site was Guild's Lake in Northwest Portland, between Upshur and St. Helen's Road at the head of 28th Street. The noted American landscape architect John Olmstead, son of Frederick Law Olmstead who designed New York City's Central Park, was brought to Portland by the Parks Bureau and the Exposition planners to make suggestions on landscaping Guild's Lake. He didn't much care for the site, but made proposals that were carried out. More significant to Portland, John Olmstead recommended many changes in the City Parks and the development of Forest (Washington) Park.

Most of the buildings were designed in a colonial Spanish Renaissance style, influenced by James Knox Taylor, best known for his U.S. Treasury Building. He designed the U.S. Government Building at the Fair. Exposition structures were built quickly and cheaply from wood framing covered with lath, plaster, and ornamentally decorated stucco. The only permanent building was the massive 100 x 200 foot Forestry Building, constructed of newly cut logs 6 feet in diameter and 60 feet long. The exterior had the appearance of a log cabin with shingled upper walls and jettied, or overhanging gables, but the interior emulated the Parthenon of Classical Athens with colonnades of 32 ton logs. After the fair closed in October of 1905, all other buildings were demolished and the lake was drained to become the NW industrial district, a very controversial decision at the time. Sitting near the Montgomery Ward Retail store, the wood *Parthenon* was neglected, refurbished in 1952, and used irregularly for exhibits until fire destroyed it in 1964.

Planners of the Exposition wanted a large Amusement Park-Midway, based on the success of Coney Island in New York. Designers were brought from New York who engineered and built the successful attractions, including a scenic railway (roller coaster), "carry-us-all" (carousel), and the Ferris Wheel first popularized at the Chicago Columbian Exposition of 1892. Ironically, too many designers were present, and another competing amusement park was constructed farther south along the Willamette, and opened as the Oaks Park on May 31, 1905, two days before the Lewis and Clark Site opened.

After the Fair Was Over

Portlanders collected and sent a large financial contribution to the survivors of the San Francisco earthquake in 1906. Stumptown swelled with civic pride, and began the annual Rose Festival in 1907. President Theodore Roosevelt visited in 1908 to dedicate the Lewis and Clark Monument. Buffalo Bill Cody brought his Wild West Show the same year. In 1909, Seattle organized the Alaska-Yukon-Pacific Exposition, which brought even more notoriety and prosperity to the Northwest.

The population of Portland doubled in the period from 1905 to 1912. It was a period of

Portland City Archives photos

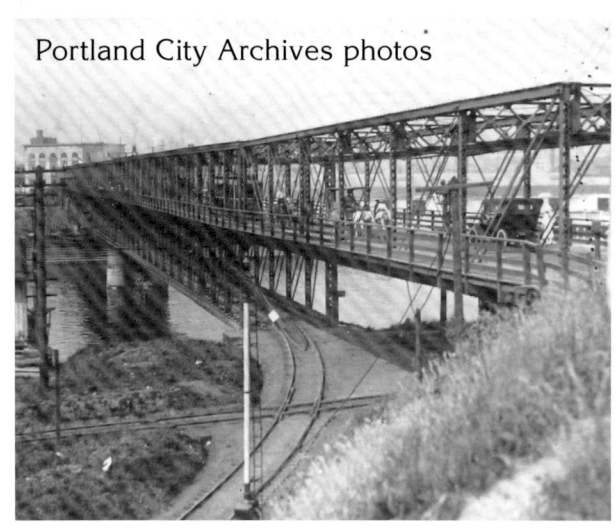

The Steel Bridge was the first permanent crossing of the Willamette, used for railroads from the south and east since 1883. It was replaced by the current lift span Steel Bridge in 1912

Mt. Olivet Baptist (1901) and Westminster Presbyterian (1912) Churches, and the Doernbecker Plant (1900) with Mt. St Helens.

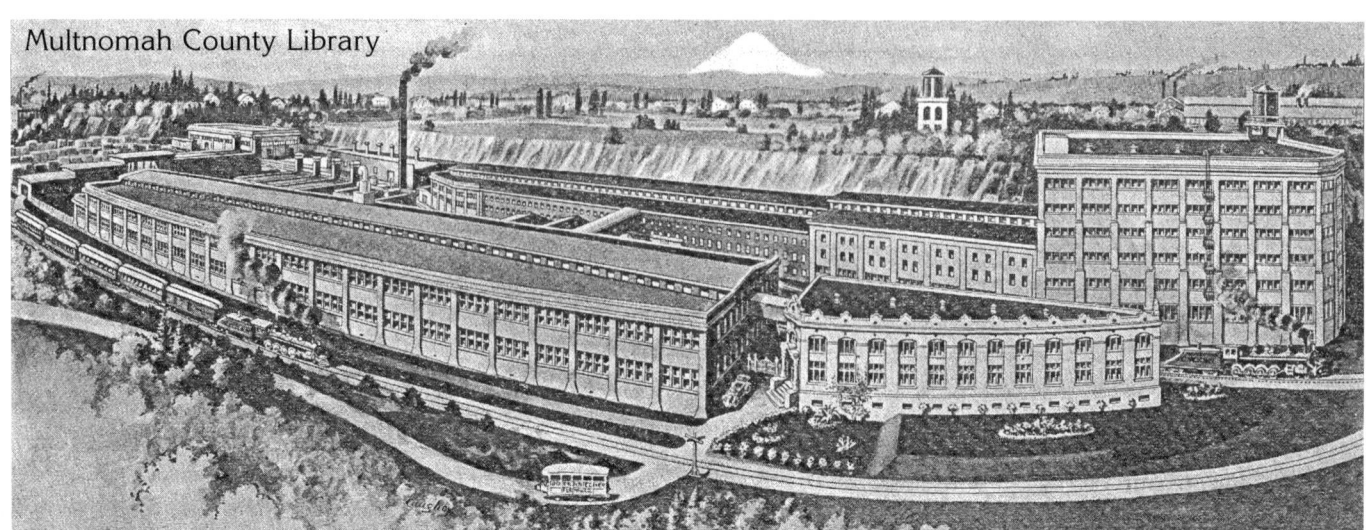

Multnomah County Library

Interlude: The Church of Good Tidings

unprecedented prosperity for the City of Roses. Real estate values rose well over 25 percent; street car usage quadrupled; many new 12-story hotel and office block "skyscrapers" were built; and 2500 new dwellings were added to the city. The Madison Street Bridge was rebuilt using steel and was renamed in honor of Dr. J. Hawthorne who had operated a large asylum on the east side. He had also been an energetic advocate for bridges.

In 1912 the new Steel Bridge was completed, replacing the first 1888 metal bridge. Its lower deck, for trains, was raised over 50 times each day. Its upper deck, allowing autos and electric trolleys to access the east side, could be raised up to ninety feet. The new connection facilitated the development and expansion of residential neighborhoods on the east side.

Irvington, Piedmont, Eastmoreland, and Ladd's Addition had been laid out on the east side and streetcar service reached its greatest extent about 1910. Citywide, there were about 100 miles of streetcar and trolley tracks. From Grand Avenue, the Broadway/Halsey line extended as far as East 22nd. Another line on East 28th extended north from Morrison as far as the Ankeny line and the Doernbacker plant across the 28th Street Bridge at Sullivan's Gulch. The city limits had expanded eastward all the way to East 24th Street on the north side of the Gulch in 1889, to 42nd Street in 1893.

Among cultural buildings built downtown around this time were Trinity Episcopal Church (1905), the YMCA on W 6th in 1909, the First Church of Christian Science (now the Northwest Neighborhood Cultural Center) in 1911, and the Central Library (1912). Meier and Frank opened their grand store annex on Morrison in 1909 and three blocks east, Olds, Wortman, and King opened in 1910, the first department store to occupy a full city block–oday it is known as *The Galleria*. Several new hotels were built downtown, such as the Seward (Governor) and Benson. Commercial blocks like the Wells Fargo Building and the Pacific Telephone and Telegraph building were built of steel girder framing, clad with brick, stone, or terra cotta in styles emulating Italian and Spanish Renaissance styles.

On the east side, churches like Mt. Olivet Baptist at East 1st and Schuyler (1901), Piedmont Presbyterian (1906) at N Cleveland and Jarrett, Grace Memorial Episcopal (1908) on Weidler, East Side Baptist, now Hinson Memorial (1910) at E 20th and Salmon, Westminster Presbyterian (1912) on E Hancock, and St. Philip Neri Catholic (1913) at Hickory and E 16th, were all built within a short streetcar ride of residential areas.

Ground Breaking

The building site for the new sanctuary of the Universalist congregation was the vacant lot # 3 and 4 of Tract 25.02 Block 2, owned by Mrs. Mary Ross, who purchased lots 3-7 in that block from Elisa B. Brimson in 1907. Like nearly all churches of the era, it was to occupy one-quarter of a city block.

Located in Carter's Addition, at the time considered a suburb, this was a nine-block development, platted separately from Holladay's Addition and Irvington. It does not line up with the surrounding street pattern, with its east-west streets about 15 feet north of the grid. Broadway westbound was originally called "Clay," and the portion passing through Carter's Addition was originally designated as "Third." The church building site hence effectively is at the head of Broadway, making the church visible from the length of lower Broadway. In later years, the city would align Broadway across this offset, with the church losing a triangular wedge of its northern easement, paving over its oil tank, and sacrificing the original grand staircase.

In nearby Sullivan's Gulch, Frank Doernbecker had built a revolutionary mass-production furniture factory of poured reinforced concrete by 1905 off E 28th Street. Bedroom furniture was the sole product of the plant, using wood from its own nearby forests. (That plant eventually became the Hyster plant, partially torn down when the Hollywood Fred Meyer Store was built in the 1990s).

City of Portland building permit #16,722 was registered in the *Portland Daily Abstract* on August 5, 1909 to the Universalist Church for a one-story frame church at East 24th between Broadway and Weidler.

President William Howard Taft, standing on a temporary platform in front of the building, spoke after he laid the cornerstone on October 3, 1909. Note Portland City Police uniforms, similar to English uniforms of the same era. Background shows balloon frame construction with ship lap boards set in at a 45 degree angle. Photo of the building in that day's *Oregon Journal* presented a silhouette of simple truss and beam roof. Hammerbeams would be added after the roofing was in place.

The McGivern house stood at 769 Broadway, catercorner from the new church. It was taken down in 1930, a victim of widening Broadway.

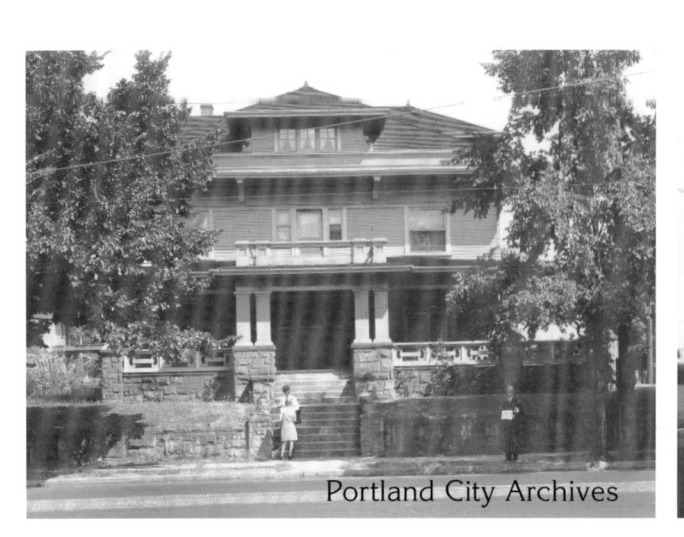

Interlude: The Church of Good Tidings

The church address would be 348 East 24th Street, but the corner lot was also numbered 790 East Broadway. Each block east of the Willamette contained 20 numbers, but with no more than 5 addresses. So it took five blocks to reach each 100 of numbering. Hence the building's location was 33 blocks east of the Willamette. Current numbers, some street names, and the changing of numbered streets to avenues, were part of a very controversial transition on the east side between 1929 and 1931. Following the changeover, the church was addressed 1644 NE 24th Avenue. There were large fir trees on adjacent lots of the 8374 square foot property until 1930, when the El Capitan apartment block was constructed to the south.

The new church was to be open for prayer and service every day of the week. Connected to the church would be a parish house for the use of the Sunday School and other branches of congregational work. Other spaces within the church building included a reading room and library, a choir room, and several classrooms, in addition to a kitchen and dining room facility on the lower level. As a modern building, it would be electrified, but also have pipes for less expensive gas lighting (these are still in place).

At the groundbreaking, Reverend James Dimond Corby welcomed "citizens who wish to meet to consider bettering their section of the city." Dr. Corby had been a businessman in the East, moving to Portland to pastor the church two years earlier. It was perhaps his arrival and business acumen that stimulated the congregation to act on its long-held plans to build a sanctuary. Dr. Corby envisioned a church "responding to all human needs- educational, physique building, and adding a vision and inspiration that will kindle a light to shine upon and make the world brighter." He felt a church needed to serve every man with everyday necessities, and to provide equipment for the modern work that a liberal church is called to do.

Unitarian officials present at groundbreaking included the Rev. T. Elliot, DD, and pastor emeritus of the Church of Our Father, the Unitarian congregation in Portland. The Rev W. H. McGlauflin, general superintendent of the Universalist Church from Chicago, gave a message of congratulation from the Universalist General Convention, whose aid made possible the new building.

President Taft Lays the Cornerstone

Sunday October 3, 1909, was a monumental day in Portland history, as the President of the United States William Howard Taft conducted the cornerstone laying for the church. Taft, of the Progressive movement, visited Portland for the weekend, staying in the opulent Portland Hotel (now the site of Pioneer Courthouse Square). This was exactly half way through his two-month rail tour of the nation.

He spoke at Multnomah Field near the Athletic Club on Saturday, October 2, after his morning arrival from Tacoma, to a gathering of 20,000 school children. Almost 5000 students formed a "living flag" wearing red, white, and blue clothing and hats. The President spoke to the youngsters, calling them the "human roses" of the Rose City. Later that day, he played a round of golf at Waverley. His caddy, a 15-year old Washington High School boy, reported that Mr. Taft was "one of the jolliest men I ever saw He just beamed at all of us out on the links."

Accounts in *The Oregon Journal* and *Oregonian newspapers* of the weekend supply numerous articles and photographs to paint a detailed image of the visit of the President, the advance planning, and the efforts of local citizens and politicians to ensure a nearly flawless and noteworthy visit. The invitation from the Universalist Church was among over 15,000 invitations received in the 8 months preceding the visit. When the President included Portland on his 13,000-mile excursion, it was one of only 25 cities so honored. He traveled in a special unmarked six-car train of New York Central Railroad cars. In the baggage car was his favorite automobile, a White Steamer, which could run on gas, kerosene, alcohol, wood, charcoal, or coal.

Sunday, after attending church at the downtown Unitarian Church of Our Father on Morrison and 7th Street (now the site of Fox

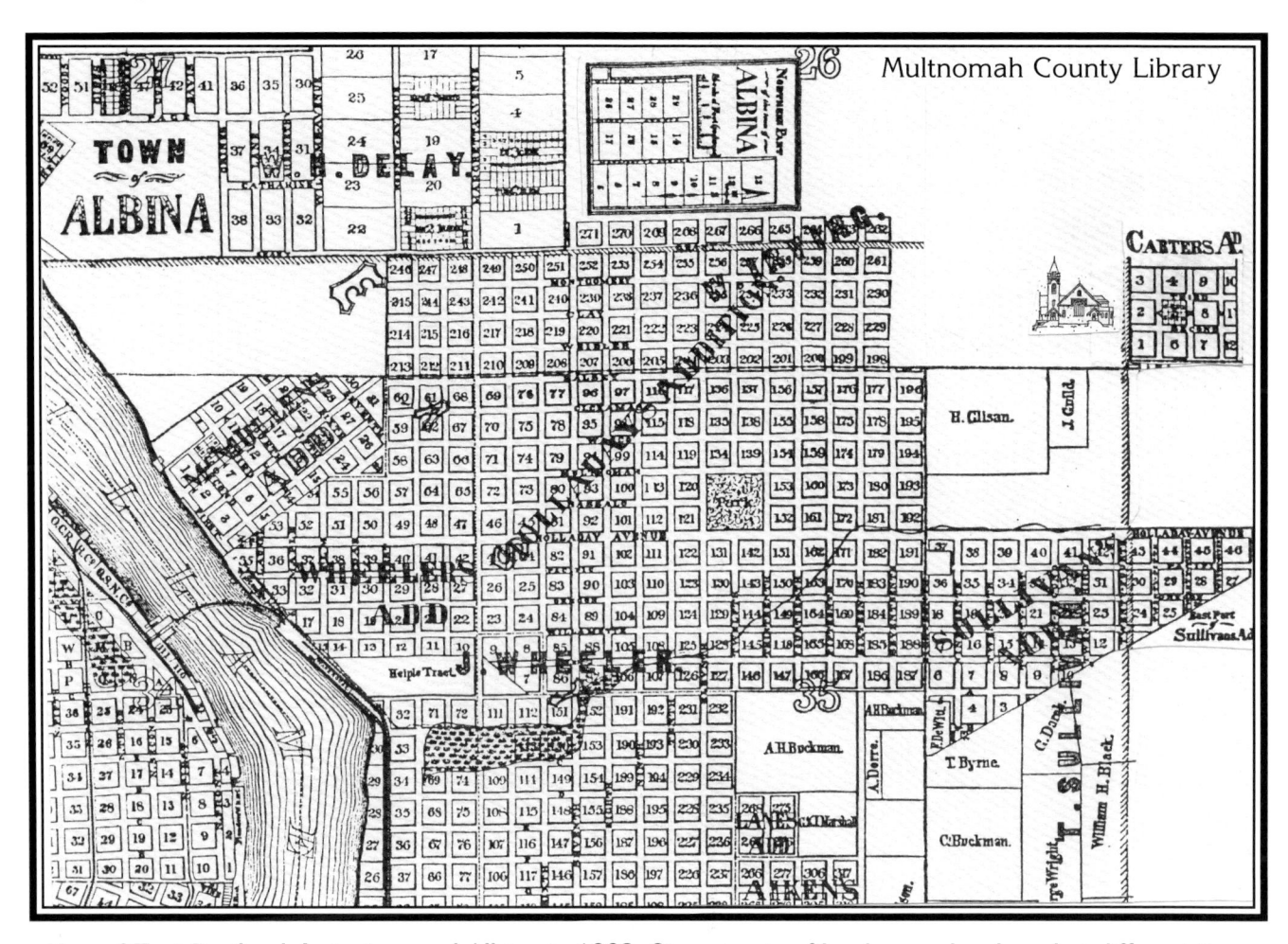

Map of East Portland, Irvington, and Albina in 1882. Since tracts of land were developed at different times, not all "additions" line up with a uniform grid. The Church of Good Tidings would be built on lot 2 on the western edge of Carter's Addition, the most northeasterly development. Open, undeveloped land lay between Carter's and Holladay's Addition to the west. The street which would become Broadway is identified as "Clay" in Holladay's section, and as "Third" in Carter's. Schuyler is labeled "Montgomery." The Stark street ferry is the only crossing of the Willamette River.

President Taft rode in his own White Steamer, pictured here outside the Portland Hotel with Pioneer Courthouse in the background. It was Portland's first grand "railroad" hotel. Torn down in the 1950s, the site was a parking lot before it became Pioneer Courthouse Square in 1985.

128

Interlude: The Church of Good Tidings

Tower on Broadway), the President, in his White Steamer, and an 11-car motorcade, crossed the river on the Morrison Bridge. (It would be another year before the new Hawthorne Bridge would be completed, and the new Steel Bridge would follow in 1912.) The automobiles most likely included high class cars of the day–Essex, Maxwell, Packard, La Fayette, Buick, Stevens-Duryea, Studebaker, and Franklin–and were proudly supplied by the Portland Automobile Club to enable the crowds to see the President clearly. Three Secret Service men were in attendance as well.

Riding in the open phaeton, the President's handlebar mustache was neatly curved and waxed and he wore a smart straw hat. He rode past elegant homes on Wasco Street, which had been built since about 1903 in the then-popular neoclassic box or Colonial style. Some homes were built by local carpenters from kits supplied by Sears and Aladdin. Several mansions were false-fronted to resemble various English medieval traditions. There were several representing the late Victorian "Stick" style. Some houses reflected newly fashionable Bungalow, Craftsman, and Prairie styles.

An estimated crowd of about 15,000 people was waiting at the intersection of East 24th and Broadway. Onlookers choked the street in four directions and overflowed onto lawns and vacant lots. Gathered under clear skies, men sat on rooftops and porch roofs, while women and children were seated in the upper windows of the houses, some watching through opera and field glasses. Church members sat in a temporary tier of seats on the west side of the church.

At intervals, flags were suspended from wires strung across the street, and at several points white-clad young girls showered the President with roses and other flowers. It was a dry and sunny afternoon, rare perfect fall weather in Portland. It was described in *The Oregonian* as a "bully day."

Upon arrival, the President stood on the elevated entrance platform of the church, well above the crowd, with the unfinished structure of the main round arch in the background. Flags, bunting, and mottoes decorated the open framework of the building, as they did from several nearby residences. Recently elected Portland Mayor Joe Simon shared the dais. The ceremony began about 3 pm with several speeches of welcome given by city and church dignitaries.

The cavity for the cornerstone was soon filled with a small metal box containing several artifacts commemorating the day–a history of the Albina congregation; lists of members and Sunday school classes; letters of greeting from church officials; photographs of the old church building; a list of major contributors; several old coins and a spoon once belonging to Ethan Allen (no one seems to understand the connection with the Universalists and the Colonial hero).

Observers were impressed that the President himself handled the silver trowel "with a practiced hand," expertly setting two flat slabs of stone into the mortar, one facing north, and one facing west. One of these stones is still in the original position at the northwest entrance to the church, proclaiming "Placed by William H. Taft, President of the United States." The north stone, lettered "First Universalist Church 1909," was covered up in 1993 with a new stone reading "Metropolitan Community Church 1977."

Upon completion of the masonry work, the President addressed the crowd in his unamplified strong bass voice:

"I do not know that anybody questions the propriety of my attendance on this occasion, or that it is necessary for me to enter into an explanation. I conceive it to be the duty of the President of the United States to welcome and encourage and support every instrument by which the standard of morals and religion in the community shall be elevated and maintained." (Applause)

"It was my pleasure and my opportunity to take part in the dedication of an orthodox Congregational Church in Washington in the Spring; my pleasure to take part in the ceremony of a Jewish tabernacle in Pittsburgh (applause); to officiate as the layer of the cornerstone of a Roman

OrHi neg 68646

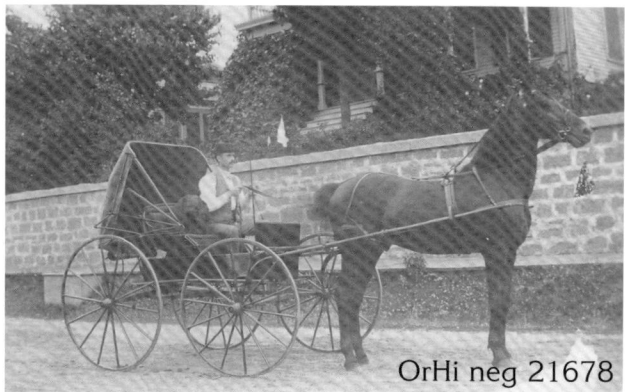

OrHi neg 21678

In 1890, street car rails were set in dirt or cobblestone roads. Electrification came later. Horsepower provided transportation for higher class Portland and Irvington residents in 1905, Horse rings are still set in curbs around MCC.

The Church of Good Tidings as built differed somewhat from the original plans. The tower received the final touches of a wooden crenelation pattern above the cornice. The walls were covered with a rough textured stucco which set off the wooden beams and archwork. Those exposed wood elements were purely decorative. Wide bargeboards and eaves gave the building its distinctive markings as an Arts and Crafts structure. Shingles in the triangular gable above the beams added the rustic appearance of the shingle style. The pattern in the Povey Brothers stained glass windows added a Prairie element, influenced by Frank Lloyd Wright's early work in the mid-West.

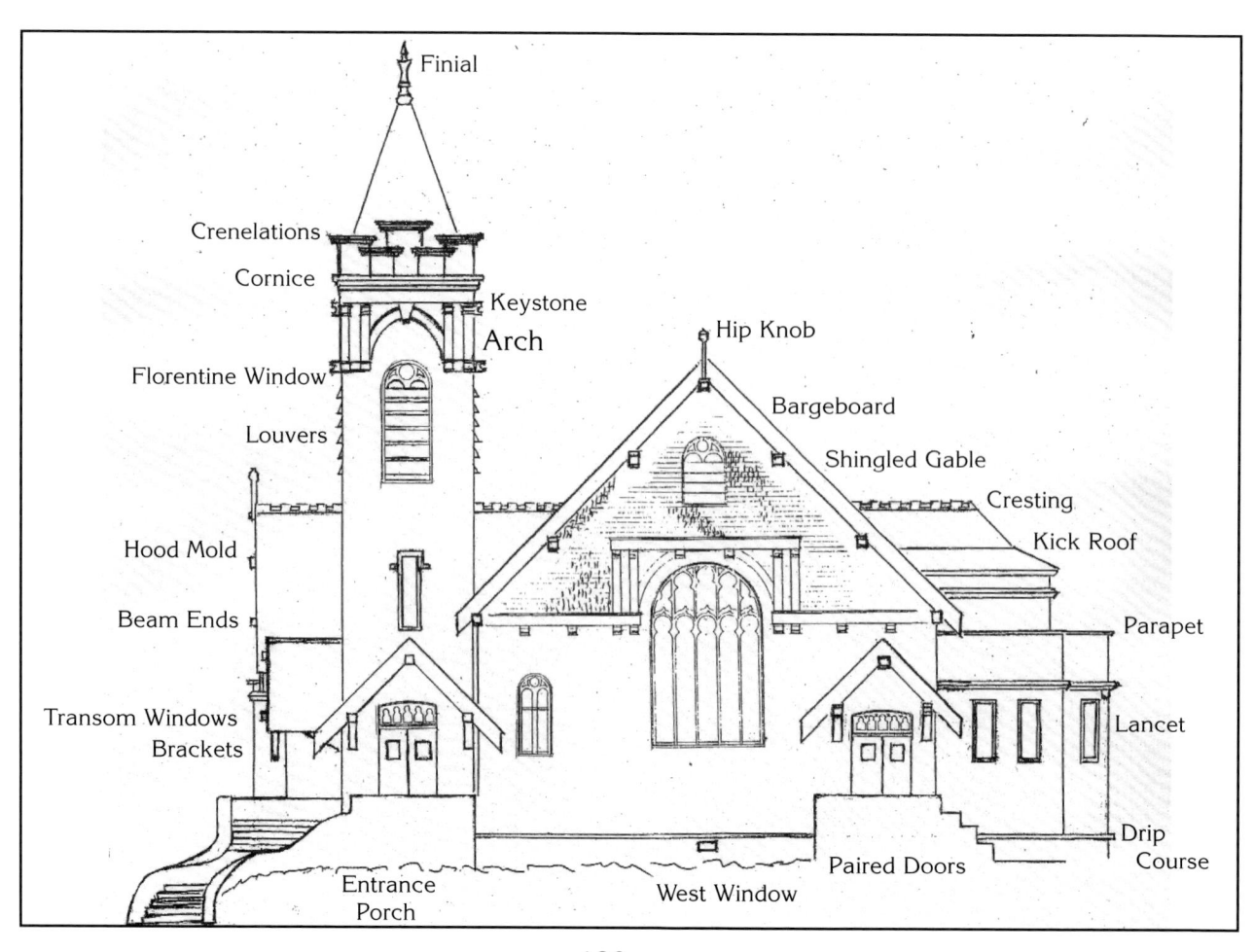

Interlude: The Church of Good Tidings

Catholic University at Helena; and now to take what part I may in the ceremonies of laying the cornerstone of the Universalist Church in this beautiful suburb of Portland (applause). And I do it because I believe that the cornerstone of modern civilization must continue to be religion and morality." (Applause)

"We have in our Constitution separated the civil from the religious. It was at one time my good fortune to visit Rome in order by negotiations to effect a settlement of a number of questions, which had arisen between the Roman Catholic Church and the civil government in the Philippines. The government of the Philippines under Spain had illustrated that system known in the Spanish government as the union of church and state. Their interests were so inextricably mixed that it seemed almost impossible to separate them; but, with the consent and acquiescence of all denominations in the country, I was authorized to go to Rome to meet the head of the great Roman Catholic Church in order to see if those matters might not be amicably settled. I am glad to say that the result of the visit was a satisfactory settlement, equitable and just to both sides."

"But I started to mention it for the purpose of saying that at that time, to the Pope, His Holiness, I ventured to say that the division between church and state in this country and their separation was not in the slightest degree to be taken as an indication that there was anything in our government, or in our people, that was opposed to the church and its highest development; and I ventured to point out that in the United States the Roman Catholic Church had flourished and grown as it had not grown in many European countries; that it had received at the hands of the government as liberal and as just and as equal treatment as every other church–no better, no worse; but that that was not to be taken as an indication that every officer of the government, properly charged with his responsibility, would not use all the official influence he had to encourage the establishment of churches, their maintenance, and the broadening of their influence in order that morality and religion might prevail throughout the country. (Applause)

"This is a Universalist Church, known as a liberal church. My own church is the Unitarian Church, also known as a liberal church. I think it must have been a Universalist who said that the Universalists believed they would be saved because God was good. (Laughter) But whatever the creed, we have reached a time in this country when the churches are growing together; when they are losing the bitterness of sectarian disputes; when they appreciate it is necessary, in order that their influence be felt, that they stand shoulder to shoulder in the contest for righteousness." (Applause)

"They believe in the fatherhood of God and the brotherhood of man, and the really broad Christian statesman is glad to accept from every quarter the assistance, which will elevate people and lead them on in that progress we all believe the American people are making. If they are not, if they are not going to a higher moral standard, then all this material progress, this entire advance in luxury and comfort, is worth nothing."

"I am an optimist. I believe we are better today than we were 50 years ago, man-by-man. (Applause) I believe we are more altruistic. I believe that each man is more interested in his fellows than he was 50 or 100 years ago. I know you can point to instances of self-depravity and selfishness and greed; but I believe those instances are made more prominent because we condemn them more, and because by being made prominent, the happening of them again is made less likely.

"I am glad to be here. I hope this church will thrive. I hope it will maintain its high principles of being a good man and good citizen and mixing them together. I welcome the opportunity to be able, as President of the United States, to say that there is no church in this country, however humble, which, preaching true religion, which, preaching true morality, will not have my support and my earnest effort to make it more successful whenever opportunity offers. (Prolonged Applause)   (*Oregonian,* October 4, 1909, pp. 1 and 9)

With less than two hours remaining before his train was to leave for Salem, a quartet led the audience in the singing with vim of

The Church of Good Tidings nears completion in May 1910. The frame structure was covered with a rough-cast stucco/cement coating, with exposed or "expressed" beam ends protruding from the walls and under the roof to give the impression of a craftsman open construction system. Italianate arch motifs were used in the fenestration pattern of the window heads. Gothic cresting edged the roof ridge and tall hip knobs marked the tips of the gables. Simple massive bargeboards gave a clean line to the roof overhangs. The grand staircase of concrete was different from the original plans, using many more stairs to reach the worship level. That stairway was lost in the 1930 widening of the corner. Retaining walls replaced the gentle slope between building and sidewalk. The street was not paved until 1921. Reverend Corby's house is in the left background behind the Sunday School rooms. This photo was discovered in 2005 in a folder of miscellaneous Portland churches at the Oregon Historical Society and has become a favorite view.

Interlude: The Church of Good Tidings

"America," and the events were over. The President's motorcade headed west on Thompson, then south on Grand. While the chief of police's car sped on ahead, the steamer chugged at the then-breakneck speed of 25 mph. A major disaster was narrowly avoided when a Southern Pacific freight train, heading out from the station at 3rd and Morrison, cut across the Presidential path. Taft's alert driver "threw on the emergency brakes, and brought his car to a stop within a short distance from the train." The President and his aide had seen the danger and were standing, ready to jump from the car if need be. An investigation a few days later found that the gates were not closed, the bell was not ringing, and in fact, the gates were out of order and could not be operated.

Two days after President Taft left town, an equally large event captured the attention of huge crowds downtown by the old post office — it was the new greater Meier and Frank department store at 5th and Morrison, holding its grand opening amidst a frenzy nearly matching that of the Presidential visit! Celebrants and shoppers were invited to see "every convenience and invention that human thought could devise to make shopping something more than shopping has ever been before in this Far West."

William Howard Taft was not reelected in 1912, losing to Woodrow Wilson. Taft did, however, complete a life of public service by serving as Chief Justice of the Supreme Court from 1921 to 1930.

First Universalist Church of Good Tidings

E M Rasmussen, the building contractor, had the balloon framing complete by October 29. The Universalist congregation left its former home at East 8th and Couch and moved in even before the scaffolding was taken down in June 1910. It was to be a show piece in a new part of the city, and many pricey details were included, most notably stained glass windows on the north and west walls, designed and built in Portland by the renowned Povey Art Glass Company at the cost of about $1000. Building cost was estimated at $20,000. At the time, average carpenters were paid $3.50 per 8-hour day; the plumbers earned $5 a day; rough lumber cost about $14 per 1000 board feet; and nails ran 4 cents per pound.

A former minister of the congregation, Rev. Asa M. Bradley, sent a most timely message of congratulations in time for the dedication, which ironically portends the eventual multiple uses and owners that the building has seen over the years. He wrote in 1909:

"Perhaps at no distant day, this house may be outgrown. This is our Father's house it is for the conduct of His business; we should plan for enduring work; but be willing to tear down what we have builded whenever it is good for the cause we would serve. We must always be ready to move forward and to put aside whatever retards growth."

The Universalist doctrine of universal salvation–the belief in the final salvation of all souls–continued to attract a large congregation under Rev. Corby's leadership. Universalist teachings originated in England about 1750 with the teachings of Rev. James Relly. Universalists became well established in Colonial America, but their growth was hindered by internal doctrinal divisions in the late 19th century. They taught that there is one God, whose nature is Love, revealed in one Lord Jesus Christ by one Holy Spirit of grace. They believed that holiness and true happiness are inseparably connected, and that believers ought to be careful to maintain order and practice good works. Among other institutions, their best known school is Tufts College, founded in 1852 at Medford, Mass.

Access to the new church building was by foot, on paved concrete sidewalks, which connected with the closest streetcar line at E 16th and Broadway. That line was extended to run past the church, turning the corner at E 24th to head north as far as Fremont. Broadway (originally Clay) was no wider than Wasco, Weidler, or any other nearby street until 1930. Horsedrawn carriages or riding horseback on the unpaved streets was also common into the 1930s, eventually phased out by automobiles, which required paved streets.

Worship services were at 10:45 am and at 7:45 pm. On Sundays, the Sunshine House of Bible Study met at noon, and the Young People's Christian Union gathered at 6:30 pm.

Dr James Corby finished his house next to the church in 1910 at 802 Broadway, when it was pictured in the Sunday *Oregon Journal*. In 1928, a Mediterranean-style shop front was built at the corner of 25th in the popular "streetcar commercial" style with large clerestory panes placed above plate glass shop windows. The corner store was Halls Grocery. The pastor's house still occupied the adjacent lot. Widening of Broadway in 1930 took away much of the easement. In 1935, the shop front was continued westward, incorporating the house into the new part of the building. The Honey Dew Ice Cream Shoppe occupied the space nearest the church, which must have made Ice Cream Socials an easy affair for the Walther League Young Lutherans.

Multnomah County Library

Halls Grocery occupied the new shop front in 1928. In 1935 an addition was built to the west, incorporating Dr. Corby's house into the Honey Dew Ice Cream Shoppe (now Healing Waters).

Looking east from 24th and Broadway during widening in 1930. Note church is on the right.

Interlude: The Church of Good Tidings

Dr. Corby was a kindly and benevolent minister, greatly appreciated by the congregation and by the surrounding neighborhood residents and businesses. His house was constructed in 1910 next to the church, at 802 E Broadway (in the numbering system used before 1929), where he lived with his wife, the former Lena A. Salls of St. Lawrence County, New York, whom he married in 1887. They left the congregation sometime later to take charge of the Boys Farm in Gresham, a project that failed for lack of financial backing. In 1916, Dr. Corby moved to Spokane, and passed away on May 14, 1917. His one-time highly regarded house was later incorporated into shop fronts on Broadway east of his church in 1935. The business in front of his fine house became the Honey Dew Ice Cream Shoppe.

Rev. Frank Scott succeeded Dr. Corby and later conducted his funeral service. Six months into this ministry, on October 21, 1917, Rev. Scott closed the church doors, having decided to go into another field of business. It may be that the financial burden incurred in constructing the church was eventually unmanageable. Apparently, most remaining members became affiliated with the Unitarian church. The elegant church building remained shut during the hard times of World War I and the influenza epidemic of 1918.

Grace English Lutheran Church

Following World War I, an east side English-speaking Lutheran congregation sought to purchase the shuttered Universalist church. They had been worshiping on Mason, between Albina and Borthwick, under Rev. Ernest Probst. Most Lutheran churches at the time had been German speaking, but due to wartime hostility and anti-German sentiment in the United States, the majority switched to English during and after the Great War. Many Germans lived between Sullivan's Gulch and Albina, since Frank Doernbecker had recruited them as workers in his factory, even supplying them with homes. To make this easier, he simply deducted the house payments from their paychecks.

Lutherans, following the 16th century Reformation teachings of Martin Luther, held scripture as the sole source of doctrine (Sola Scriptural); believed that man is saved only by faith (Sola Fede); and only by the forgiving grace of God through Jesus Christ (Sola Gratia). Evangelism and education of all believers are strong tenants of the denomination. A German Lutheran academy had been founded in 1905 north of Killingsworth Street in the Kennedy addition, which became today's Concordia University.

Grace English Lutheran occupied the building in 1919 and used it more than 40 years. The streetcar line on Broadway had been extended to 24th, where it turned north until it terminated at Mason. Until 1920, the streets on both sides of the church, and in much of the neighborhood were still unpaved, although permanent concrete sidewalks were put in between 1903 and 1912. Many streets in Irvington and Sullivan's Gulch were paved during 1921. Bridges crossing the nearby gulch were completed by 1921 on E 21st and E 28th, greatly improving north-south transportation in the neighborhood.

Carl H. Bernhard was the new pastor, having previously served Lutheran churches in New York, New Jersey, Texas, and California. He had been a chaplain during the World War, and while in school in Chicago, had met and married Helen, a graduate of the Chicago Art Institute, who designed in the current Art Deco style.

The Lutherans thrived at their new location, filling the sanctuary for its 10:30 morning services. Sunday School took place before service, and there were often potluck suppers following. The Sunday School met in several keystone-shaped rooms on the eastern end of the main level, separated by a wooden partition from the worship space. Several circles of small chairs accommodated more Sunday School groups in the basement.

In December 1923, a small fire in the wall behind the fireplace in the pastor's study caused minor damage. $1500 was spent in non-structural repairs, mostly new lath and plasterwork, and $167 paid for an all-new brick flue from the ground up.

The fire apparently did not damage the large pipe organ whose pipes were on the backside of the fireplace. Organ pipe work and wind

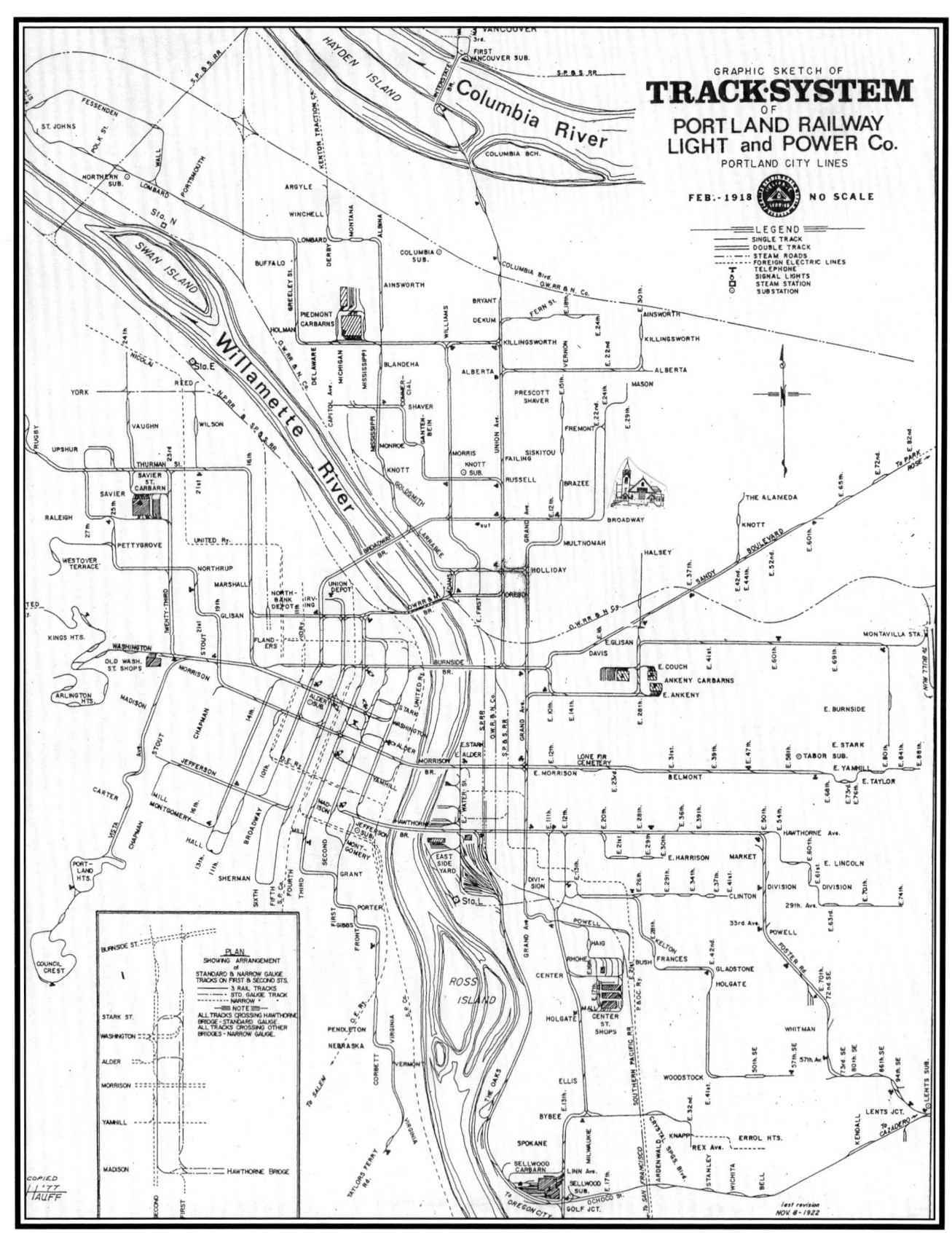

Portland City Archives

Street car lines came as far east on Broadway as 15th when the church was built in 1909, and extended to 24th in 1918, two years before Grace English Lutheran bought the building.

Interlude: The Church of Good Tidings

chests occupied almost half of the choir "loft." Enclosed boxes in the area above the arches housed additional pipes. Louver doors controlled their volume. The console extended several feet into the sanctuary, with the organist's back to the congregation so that he could direct the choir from the bench.

Helen Bernhard began supplementing the pastor's salary to help with household expenses of their three children. In 1924 she converted the front room of the parsonage at 1725 E Broadway into a bakery sales room for her decorated cakes. While in Chicago, she had worked with a new product called oleo-margarine in making tasty and beautifully decorated cakes. She applied the same techniques using local butter, and found an enthusiastic following in Portland. The bakery thrived so that she expanded, moving the sales room behind the house, but never regained their living room until she and her son Benjamin designed and built the current bakery and sales room west of the old house at 1717 Broadway in 1940.

A major remodel of the church exterior became necessary in September 1930, when NE Broadway was widened. The "Cities Beautiful" movement had begun across America with the writings of John Nolen, a city planner in the first decade of the 20th century. The corner at NE 24th and Broadway was clipped to enable a more gradual right turn onto Broadway eastbound and Broadway was brought into alignment by angling that street north of the church. This meant the elimination of the original grand concrete staircase leading from the corner to the twin entrance porches, and a reduction of the easement to allow for the sidewalk. The oil tank for the furnace was covered with the new pavement and sidewalk, leaving the filler sleeve cover flush with the concrete. A poured concrete retaining wall was necessary at the edge of the sidewalk. The new landing and staircase was centered beneath the large Povey Stained Glass window on the NE 24th Avenue facade.

Apparently the north entrance was closed off at the same time, as it was too close to the new sidewalk on Broadway. The entire roof and wooden supports of that entrance portico were moved to a new double doorway on the west side, thus turning the original choir room into the southern vestibule. A smaller doorway, which had opened into the Sanctuary, was eliminated, and much of that single door opening made into another stained glass window to match the opposite smaller window on the facade. This gives the facade its current symmetry, with the large central stained glass window and two smaller windows balanced on either side. All but the largest stained glass windows are paired within a round headed arch and a tondo or circle resting on the shoulders of the paired arches, giving a Roman, Florentine, or Mediterranean design element–one of the motifs leading to the designation of 20th century Italianate style.

It was probably at this time also that the lower half of the coarse stucco exterior walls of most of the building was covered with grooved wooden shingles, known as "rake shake". Areas in the gables and above the exposed massive false beams are covered with traditional sawn shingles, perhaps the originals. The 50-foot-tall tower was also clad with rake shake shingles, and all of its ornamental wooden crenellations at the top removed, leaving a simple and classic cornice. The tower roof and finial were left intact. This finial remains as evidence of the Universalist origin of the building, for it is in the form of a flame, which represents wisdom and truth. Some architectural features of the tower and church facade were covered by the shake siding, while other bold wood elements were allowed to show through the new exterior.

In 1946, the wooden porch landing and steps on the north side entrance were removed and replaced with poured concrete. A 1963 photo in the *Oregon Journal* shows the exterior to be painted in several contrasting tones, emphasizing the bold wooden beam work and architectural details.

Pastor Bernhard became the part-time emeritus pastor shortly after World War II, preaching on occasion and making sick calls while the new pastor, Rev. Luckel, assumed full-time responsibilities. Carl Bernhard was very content to become the "fix-it" guy for Helen's Bakery, and was often seen in his shop and around the

Looking east on Broadway in 1924 (above) and after the 1930 widening and re-numbering (below)

The church is visible 9 blocks east from the corner of 15th. Hamburger Mary's and Dugan's once occcpied the soda fountain and ice cream shop on the far left. In 2005, it was Peet's Coffee.

Interlude: The Church of Good Tidings

store in his dungarees or overalls. Helen thrived on the business, becoming a leader in the 50/50 Club, a women's business organization. She was well known in Portland's high society, and took delight in her role as one of the rare female business owners in the city. Not one to relinquish control, she avoided involvement with union activity by hiring only women staff.

Helen's sister Ann Schiele came to Oregon and operated a well-known bakery on NE 42nd. Her specialty was pastries and cookies, so there was never competition between the sisters. Of Helen's three children, Benjamin took over the business, and his son David assumed leadership in 1969. Grandpa Carl had died in 1965, but Helen baked another 9 years before her passing in 1974. Although David sold the bakery to Dick Laufer in 1988, he continued baking until his retirement in 2004.

During their tenure, the Lutherans also changed affiliation from the Missouri Synod to the more conservative Wisconsin Synod. In 1963, they further expanded their congregation with a new church at NE 76th and Fremont, selling the 53-year-old building on Broadway for $35,000 to the Church of Divine Science.

Among the items they took with them was the pipe organ, which had occupied the back half of the choir space. Exposed pipes had provided a backdrop for choirs, and the console actually extended a few feet in front of the raised platform. Some damage may have been done at this time to the varnished wooden columns of the choir area, as they were painted over with a thick coating of black and swirling white "veins" to simulate marble. The same faux covering was painted on the square pilasters and beam surrounding the altar.

The neighborhood also changed dramatically during those 40 years. Nearby at 41st and NE Sandy, entrepreneur grocer Fred Meyer opened his first east side location, the Hollywood Public Market in 1931. It remained a Fred Meyer store through several remodels for over 70 years.

In 1926, Ralph Lloyd had begun purchasing land in Holladay's original plat between NE 12th and NE 21st, eventually creating the commercial complex regarded as America's first Shopping Mall by 1960. In the construction of Lloyd Center, most of the magnificent homes and the Holladay school were razed. Sullivan's Gulch was excavated and what had been a golf course was paved by 1958 to become the Sullivan's Gulch freeway, later named the Banfield after the Oregon State Transportation director. This became the main route into Portland from the east, designated as Interstate 84 under the Eisenhower Highway System Act. It was connected to the I-5 in the mid-1960s. The MAX light rail line was built along the same route in 1986. The golf course clubhouse became a popular restaurant for many years, Ireland's, then Sweet Tibbie Dunbar's, and finally, Polo's. It is now the Point West Credit Union on NE 12th.

First Church of Divine Science

Dr. Irwin Gregg, president of Divine Science International, was the featured speaker at the dedication of the congregation's new home on Sunday, October 13, 1963. Rev. William J. Atzbaugh was the minister of the Portland church, which numbered about 350 members, when the building was sold to them on July 2 of the same year. The Divine Science group had been meeting in the Pythian building on SW Morrison St.

Three paintings by Elmer House, a member of the congregation had been donated by the artist. Two of the paintings were replicas of well-known Christian paintings, a Last Supper and an Annunciation. The third was an original work. At least two of these large panels were left behind when the Divine Scientists disbanded, one of them in the arched choir/organ loft. Early MCC members remember looking at a slightly cross-eyed Jesus staring at them across the Last Supper's table during worship.

The church was completely renovated after purchase from Grace Lutheran. About $7500 was spent redecorating the interior and refurbishing the exterior. The entire exterior was coated with a dark brown paint, which minimized the exposed wooden beams and architectural trim.

Divine Scientists followed teachings of Malinda Elliott Cramer. Healed from an incur-

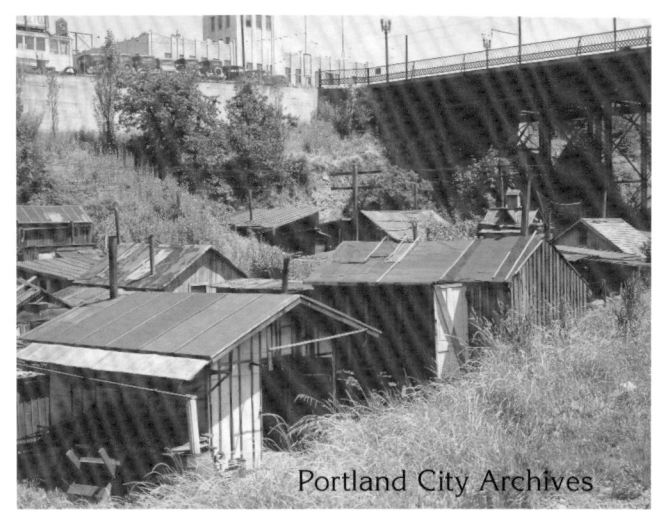

"Hooverville" shanty town under the Grand Ave. Bridge and at the Sandy and 39th overpasses were transformed into the Banfield Freeway. This meant the disappearance of the Lloyd Golf Course. Its clubhouse became Sweet Tibbie Dunbar's Restaurant near the 12th Ave. overpass.

Two large paintings, painted by a member of the Church of Divine Science were left behind. These seem to be the only two photos existing of them.

140

Interlude: The Church of Good Tidings

able invalid condition in 1885, she formalized her teachings into "Divine Science," and founded a school in 1888. Believing in universal spiritual laws, emphasis was placed on God's omnipresence – a universal energy that is perfect Wisdom, Love, Understanding, Peace, and Goodness. Rooted in Genesis 1:26, humanity is seen as endowed with a full complement of divine qualities and powers. Man's true identity is God's image. A person's self-image determines their self-fulfilling prophecy, and the possibilities are unlimited. There is no belief in hell or eternal damnation, reasoning that if God the Good is everywhere, where could a "Hades" exist? Miss Cramer died in 1906, as a result of injuries she sustained in the San Francisco earthquake.

The Portland congregation later fell upon hard times as their aging membership declined. Arthur Lind and his partner Mr. Abbot, of Abbot and Lind Printing, purchased the church in order that the congregation could continue worshiping there without fear of foreclosure. By 1977, there were less than 20 active members, most of them elderly.

Metropolitan Community Church

Sometime after his partner's death, Arthur Lind placed the building on the real estate market in 1977. Mel Hamilton and Darl Synoground of MCC became aware of this property and notified Austin Amerine, who almost immediately felt this building was destined to be the new home of MCC Portland.

The agreed-upon selling price was $ 87,000. An agreement was made so that the Divine Scientists could continue to hold Sunday morning worship at the church, while the MCC congregation would continue to hold Sunday evening services, as had been their tradition since their founding. This arrangement continued until 1981.

The church was in a prominent location on the edge of the Lloyd District. When the Lloyd Center and Memorial Coliseum were built in the 1960s, Broadway had been made into a one-way street heading west, and Weidler, a block south, had been configured into the parallel one-way street headed east. Weidler's one-way segment ended at NE 24th and all eastward traffic had to turn left onto 24th for one block, then a right turn at the corner where the church stands to continue eastward. On the NW corner of the intersection stood a Savemore gas station, and Robertson's Pharmacy occupied the corner on the Northeast.

Prior to the balloon payment deadline in 1987, several fundraising efforts aimed at $50,000 for debt retirement. $30,000 of this was to pay off the mortgage and $20,000 was designated for repairs and renovations. A major campaign was launched in November of 1986. Besides individual donations and pledges, garage sales, home dinners, bake sales, movie nights, and several other activities were used to raise funds. Advertisements were placed in the local gay and community newspapers, encouraging tax-deductible 1986 contributions. This campaign was not a total success.

On September 30, 1987, a land contract was negotiated at 11% to be paid to Arthur Lind and the Estate of Gordon Guild, his sons Terry and Frederick Guild through Columbia Pacific Bank. Monthly payments of $439.79 were due against a principle of $23,105.40 with a balloon payment to be made on September 10, 1993.

A Christmas Eve fire destroyed the large west window and some of the wood wall facing NE 24th Street in 1988. An alert neighbor, (or taxi driver–the story varies) saw flames about 3 am Christmas Day and called in the fire alarm, almost certainly saving the entire church from destruction. Insurance paid most of the costs of a new window created by local stained glass artist David Schlicker. Repainting and carpeting also utilized the settlement funds.

The congregation paid off the final mortgage payment in 1993. Soon thereafter, a spontaneous group of volunteers took it upon themselves to renovate and redecorate the southeast corner room, known as the Family Room. Its dedication was occasion for a musical presentation based on the film *Sister Act*.

It has been said that a church without a debt is a church that is not vital. In spite of paying off the mortgage, by 1995 it became appar-

Just one light fixture remains from the original 1910 church. It was re-wired and restored by Rick Nye, and hangs in the Friendship Room, which is also called the Al Williams Chapel-pel.

The new paint scheme accentuates the architectural features of the exposed beams, beam endings and corbelled brackets supporting the bargeboards. The rake shake shingles were not part of the original lower facade. The 1910 furnace was dismantled in 2005. It burned wood and charcoal before its conversion to oil about 1930. Five gas units replaced the behemoth, each ducted to a different zone of the building. MCC's sexton Matt Matuskey kept busy cleaning.

Dave Kohl photos

Interlude: The Church of Good Tidings

ent that major maintenance and some remodeling work was essential. Rev. Roy Cole consulted with Portland architect and historian William Hawkins III, and plans were made to redesign the Broadway entrance, make repairs and paint the exterior, reroof the structure, and meet the requirements of the Americans with Disabilities Act with a new elevator and restrooms. The church address changed from 1644 NE 24th Avenue to 2400 NE Broadway when the office entrance was expanded.

In order to finance these improvements, the church was reappraised at a market value of $575,000, and a mortgage was taken out. Robertson Hay and Wallace were engaged as the contractor, and scaffolding was in place around the entire structure by November 1995. New roofing and a 3-tone paint scheme greatly enhanced the exterior. Not all of the proposals suggested by Mr. Hawkins were implemented, in order to stay within budget.

As the congregation grew under Rev. Roy Cole's leadership, the seating in the sanctuary became inadequate. Gordon Branstator, a member since YMCA days, having retired in 1997, volunteered to head up a construction squad to redesign the interior space. The massive wooden wall with panels, which raised and that divided the sanctuary from the rehearsal area and stage to the east, was disassembled. The aged wooden panels were reused as backdrop in the arched choir area. The stage was dismantled and the entire altar platform and colonnaded surround were flattened against the wall backing the old pastor's office. A ramp was added to provide wheel chair access to the altar, and a wall was built to mask the entrance to the founder's room and stairway.

Carpeted platform risers were built at the east end of the enlarged worship space for choir use, and the Allen organ console moved nearby. At the same time, the reception, office and secretarial rooms were modified, creating more privacy for counselling, offices for church musicians, clerical work, committees, church nurse, and a more secure machine room. All this work was done with the services of many volunteers and only one paid carpenter, Chuck Carlisle, and was completed by Christmas of 1998, at a cost of under $22,000.

The nemesis of the basement and several persistent sewer problems came to a head in the winter of 1998 when the old clay pipes fully collapsed, necessitating the digging of an all new 8-foot-deep sewer line. Porta-potties were set up outside the southwest entrance for a few weeks. There has never been any plumbing on the upstairs level, although a capped pipe is located in a storage area. In the kitchen sat a commercial stove without a hood or venting system. A commercial dishwasher was purchased, sat in its crate several years, and was later sold without ever being hooked up.

Three large new halogen lighting fixtures replaced ancient chandeliers in the main sanctuary in 2002, eliminating inadequate antique fixtures. Rick Nye painstakingly rewired one of the ancient candelabras and it is now installed in the hospitality area with its original hand-blown tulip globes. The small morning-glory lights that hang from the hammer beam brackets in the main sanctuary are the original 1910 fixtures, still on 1910 knob-and-tube lines.

Steady payments had been reducing the 1995 mortgage, but the interest drain on the annual budget limited the congregation's ability to fully fund the community and out-reach programs that are part of its mission. At the end of a Sunday service in Spring 2004, Rev. Glenna Shepherd proposed that with one major commitment from members, the church could eliminate the remaining $30,000 debt. Following two worship services on that Sunday in April, members raised their hands and filled out pledges to fulfill those commitments within a month. The final check was written on May 27, 2004, and the church is now debt-free.

The oil furnace, water heater, inadequate bathrooms, and sub-code kitchen situation was finally addressed during the "Rebuilding Our Home and Our Mission," campaign in 2005. With the congregation's 30th anniversary less than a year away, motivation existed to complete upgrades in time for the January 2006 celebration.

William Hawkins III was reengaged to draw up modified plans. He also reconfigured the back staircase, and expanded and brought the bathrooms up to ADA code. The 95-year old furnace was cut up and removed, volunteers

OrHi drawing by Gracie Campbell

Original architects drawing, MCC Archive

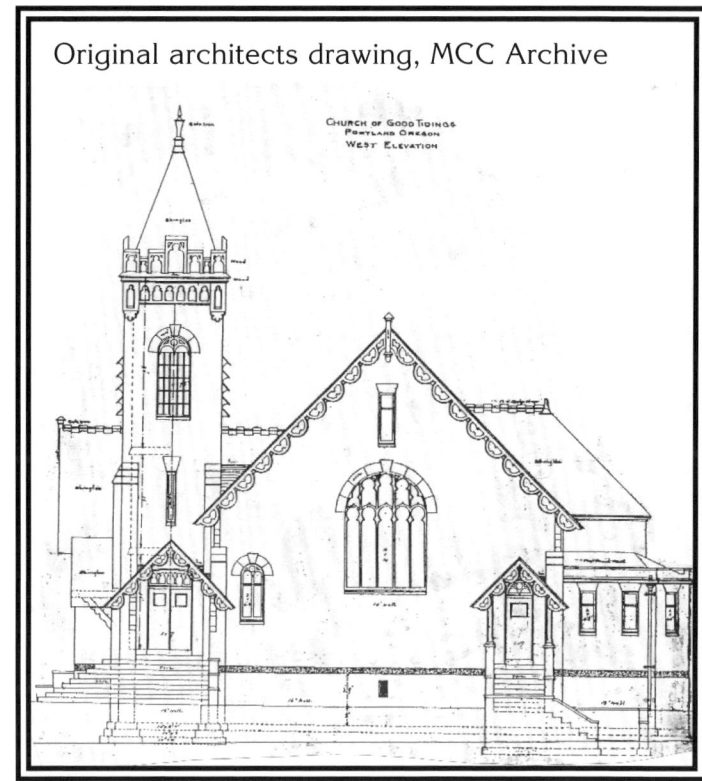

Multnomah County Library

Calvary Presbyterian Church, on SW 11th, was the classic exemplar of Carpenters Gothic or English Picturesque architecture in Portland. It still stands, restored as "The Old Church," for community performances. The original plans for the Church of Good Tidings incorporated many Picturesque motifs, including scroll-cut bargeboards on the eaves, cresting on the roof ridge with a hip knob on top, and an arched opening with louvers in the bell tower.

The photo from a June 1910 *Oregonian* shows the church near completion, modified by architect or builder in several ways. The bargeboards reflect the newer bungalow style, the gabled walls exhibit beamwork and structural elements similar to the Stick Style and Arts and Crafts architecture. The arch and keystone motif from the original plans is eliminated, and shingles cover the upper gabled walls. The staircase was redesigned to take advantage of the slope, presenting a grand entrance. The Universalist flame tops the tower in both plan and finished building.

Interlude: The Church of Good Tidings

dug out 3 truckloads of dirt to make way for a new furnace pad, and four units were installed, each ducted to a separate zone within the building for efficiency. Centralized cooling is also part of the plan. See Chapter 13.

II. Architecture and Furnishings

"Architects of all times and places give the interpreter a seemingly infallible insight into the lives of their creators" (Jamieson Parker, OHQ, March 1934 Vol. 35 #1, p. 38)

While the original blueprints have gone missing, copies of them were made in 1995 by William Hawkins so that much is known about the original design of the building. The style of the exterior was noted as "English Picturesque" at the time of groundbreaking, and there are many elements in the original plans that reflect late Victorian motifs. These would include the battlemented tower with trefoil arches in the crenellations, a corbelled entablature below the cornice, a keystone over the narrow lancet window, and buttresses supporting the lower portion. On the sanctuary eave, there is a hip knob at the apex, an incised and scalloped bargeboard, similar bargeboards over the three entrance porches, and trefoil arches in the transoms over the two main entrances. Window and vent openings in the facade and tower are Romanesque round-headed openings. There are false or engaged buttresses at the corners of the sanctuary.

The "Picturesque" style was first made popular in Oregon about 1855, appearing in several houses at Fort Dalles. The design of several buildings there reflect the style made popular at the time through the design books of Andrew Jackson Downing. His "Victorian Cottage Residences" of 1842 and "The Architecture of Country Houses" of 1850 feature wooden buildings of a romantic and medieval style with ornamental bargeboards; steeply gabled roofs; and quaint and picturesque porches, brackets, chimneys, and window styles. Downing also promoted the structural technique known as "balloon-framing," the now-common method of building a wood structure from 2 x 4 studs covered with shiplap or tongue-and-groove sheathing for strength.

Influences from these books are directly visible in many buildings of the late 19th century in Portland. Calvary Presbyterian Church (now called the Old Church) of 1882, a tall steepled wooden masterpiece of high Victorian Gothic, is a notable and local example of this style. The pitch of the roof exceeds 45 degrees, and it is ornamented with pinnacles, pointed arches, incised gableboards, a roofed porte cochere with exposed truss work, vertical wooden siding, locally-made stained glass windows by the Povey Brothers, and many other elegant touches typical of the "carpenter's gothic" style.

Examination of the original exterior plans for the Church of Good Tidings reveals several decorative elements of this Victorian Queen Anne Style, including bargeboards at the end of eaves with incised designs, cresting along the roof ridge, and finials at the top of gables and the tower. The pitch of the roof, however, is not nearly as steep as the typical Victorian building, creating more of a cozy, less vertical design, perhaps indicating the influence of concepts from the Bungalow Movement in western America, starting about 1905. The pitch of the church's roof is nearly identical to the Forestry Building from the Lewis and Clark Exposition.

However, the Church of Good Tidings, as constructed in 1910, does not stay true to the original exterior plans. *The Oregonian* of 1909 described the design as generically "English Picturesque." Architecture historians would more likely classify the initial design as "Gothic Revival, Romantic or Medieval," but that is not the style of the finished edifice. Many significant changes were made to the style and appearance between the initial design and the actual construction:

1. Bargeboards (also called vergeboards) are plain and massive, with extended raftertails, not scalloped and incised or pierced Victorian "gingerbread."
2. Archivolts of stone-like voissoirs and keystones were eliminated over arched doors and windows in the facades and tower.

OrHi neg 57274

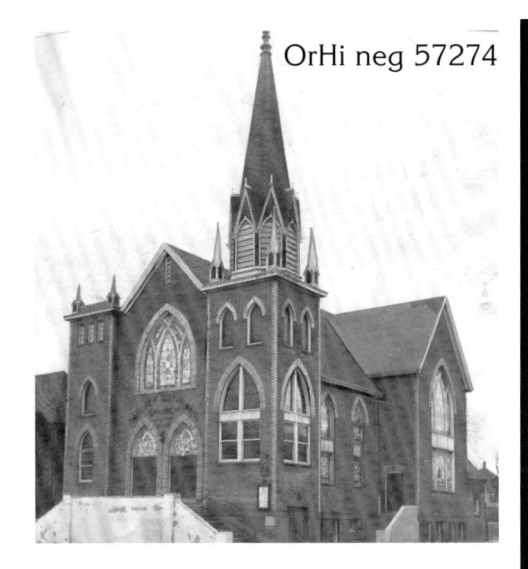

Drawing by Dave Kohl

Trinity Lutheran Church on N Ivy was built in 1920 by a member of that congregation from plans sent from church headquarters.

The Church of Good Tidings was not built as drawn in the original architect's drawings. It was modified from a Picturesque English Gothic design into a "modern" eclectic combination of new styles, especially Arts and Crafts, Bungalow Craftsman, Prairie, and Italianate. This seems to have suited the church's philosophy.

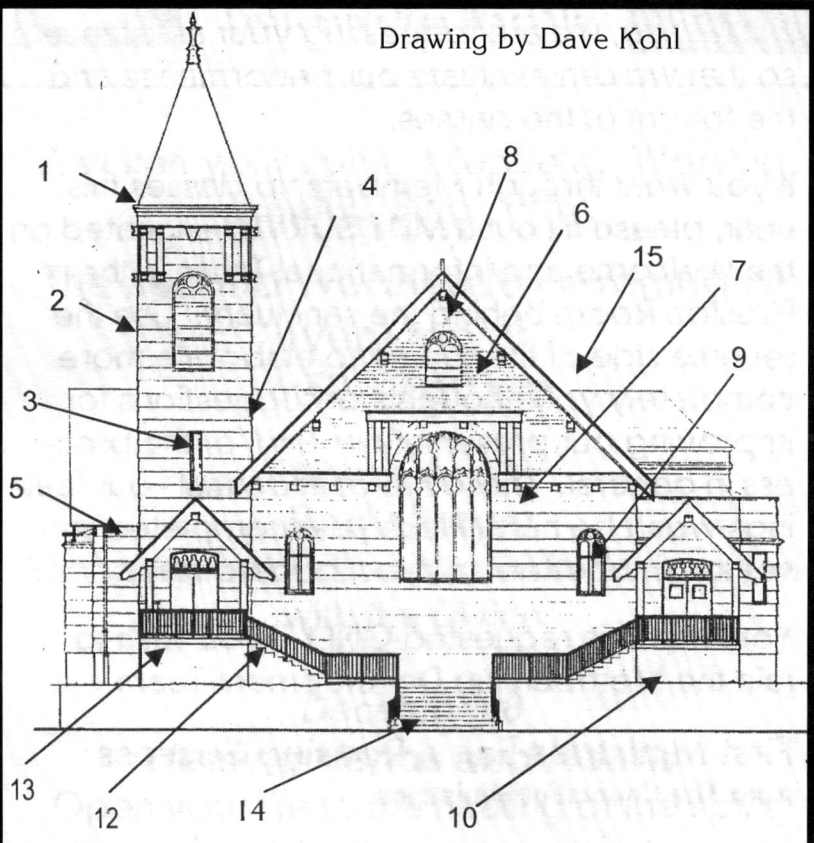

1. No gothic crenellations on tower.
2. Louvered opening instead of stained glass window.
3. No keystone over lancet.
4. No billet molding on roof ridge.
5. Broadway side portal removed.
6. No Victorian "gingerbread" on fascia.
7. Arts & Crafts beams and beam tails added.
8. Round-headed louver instead of keystoned lancet.
9. Stained glass window in place of doorway.
10. Larger portal and double door moved south.
11. Staircase reversed to come to center steps on NE 24th Ave.
12. Staircase reversed away from Broadway.
13. Original staircase going west and north eliminated.
14. Shingle siding added over original stucco cladding.
15. Transept roofs are the same height.

Dave Kohl photo

Interlude: The Church of Good Tidings

3. Wall treatment on N and W facade changed to include large wood expressed (false, or half-timbered) beams, corbels, scroll-sawn beam ends with a scotia cut and a bold Palladian arch motif.
4. Shingled wall cladding added above the wood-beamed Palladian motif.
5. Open eaves with corbelled beams and scroll-cut show rafter tails.
6. Upper window in the west facade replaced with arched louvered vent
7. Gothic buttress motif on facade and tower corners eliminated.
8. Staircase at main tower entrance realigned, split, and enlarged.
9. Crenellated parapet above cornice on tower simplified; trefoil motif eliminated from battlements.
10. Corbelled entablature below tower cornice eliminated; replaced with bracketed wood corbel blocks, wood. Florentine Renaissance arch motif, and scroll-sawn tails.
11. Roof over south transept lowered, roofline altered with a "kick."

Several factors could contribute to the many changes in plans...

A) The original plans are not dated. Hence it is possible that the church may have had these plans for several years before finding the funds and building site. Tastes changed as Victorian revival styles gave way to modern innovative movements in the arts and architecture. The philosophical foundations of the congregation were Foreword-looking innovative, and in the political terms of the day, Progressive. Perhaps traditional Gothic revival romanticism was not seen as appropriate for a group dedicated to community involvement and modernism.

B) The original plans are missing any architect's name. It was a common practice at the time for congregations in far-flung areas to obtain generic church plans from their denominational head-quarters, saving the costs of commissioning local architects for unique buildings. This was the case for Trinity Lutheran Church at N Ivy and N Rodney, built in 1920 from plans sent from Synodical head-quarters in St. Louis. That church was then built by a contractor who was a member of the east Portland congregation, utilizing local materials and installing Povey Brothers Stained Glass windows.

No other Universalist church building is known to have the exact same floor plan or elevation as the Church of Good Tidings, but it is possible that clones do or did exist. It should be noted that the denominational headquarters in Chicago did help the Portland church in its building program, but the specifics of this help are not known.

C) A local architect could have been engaged to "update" the exterior style of the balloon-frame structure. While the "footprint" of the church seems to have remained unchanged, the surface treatment was definitely altered for economic, aesthetic, or philosophic reasons. It would be unusual however, for his designs to lack his signature. The building permit of 1909 only lists the builder as E. M. Rasmussen.

The first decade of the 20th century witnessed several new and innovative architectural movements, some of which originated on the West Coast. A brief explanation of these may prove useful in analyzing the eclectic mix of influences that seem to have playrd on the surface of the church. A parallel to this architectural eclecticism can be seen in the musical movements of the early 20th century when European composers Claude Debussy, Richard Strauss, and Igor Stravinsky were producing radically different styles of music. American music of the era produced works by John Phillip Sousa, Charles Ives, and Scott Joplin.

The architectural styles known as Arts and Crafts, Bungalow, Craftsman, Prairie, and Shingle, were all in vogue, sometimes combined in unique eclectic constructions:

Arts and Crafts–1895–Particularly applied to architecture of homes, this philosophy emphasized a return to quality of construction and exposure of structural elements. Buildings were made of fine quality woods, clay, and stone, handcrafted and polished to emulate historic architecture, as inspired by English design-

OrHi neg 90389   Portland City Archives

Carpenter's Gothic or Queen Anne home in Albina, Prairie style home with broad eaves in Irvington.

Portland City Archives

The sole non-classic building at the 1905 Exposition was the Forestry Building. It was the only building not destroyed when the Fair closed. Note Montgomery Wards building in the background.

Peace House photo

The Cole house, built on NE Tillamook (1905) is an example of Arts and Crafts design, Portland style. With a massive entrance portico and a wrap-around balustrade, it sits majestically on a large corner lot. Hip dormers, and an oriel window on the side breaks its square lines. The house became Metanoia Peace Community in 1987, site of many MCC events.

Interlude: The Church of Good Tidings

er William Morris. His ideals were presented in the U.S. by the Roycroft community in East Aurora, New York and through their Kelmscott Press by 1895.

Bungalow - Starting about 1903, the design of homes primarily with low pitched roof, exposed beams and rafters, utilizing hand-made built-in cabinetry, influenced by one-story colonial and native housing in British India. Two architect brothers in California, Charles and Henry Greene, combined ideas from the Arts and Crafts movement with local woods, stone, stained glass, fieldstone, etc. Sometimes called "Craftsman," they reflect the work and writings of Gustav Stickley in the *Craftsman Magazine.*

Prairie–1904–Midwestern style developed by Frank Lloyd Wright with low-pitched hipped roofs and widely overhanging eaves with a Japanese influence derived from Wright's travels there. Elegant but simple geometric stained glass windows. Facades emphasize strong horizontal lines and bold visual shapes or patterns.

Shingle–1880s–Wall cladding and steep roofing of continuous wood shingles, no corner boards typify this style. Bold extensive porches, often with massive timber supports are common. Palladian windows–two flat-topped windows surrounding an arched central window - were often added for a classic touch. The 1905 Forestry Building of the Lewis and Clark Exposition in Portland shows the influence of the shingle style in that the upper portions of the exterior walls are shingle-clad, and its jettied gables and long eaves were supported with knee brackets.

D) There were several architects practicing in Portland at the time whose style can be perceived in the modernized alterations. A list of candidates includes Ellis Lawrence, Emil Schacht, William Christmas Knighton, and Justus Krumbein. The most likely designer appears to be a German-born architect whose work in Portland includes numerous religious buildings with a strong Italian influence.

Joseph Jacobberger came to Portland from New York in 1900. Born in Alsace-Lorraine, he came to the U.S. as a child, was educated in architecture at Creighton University in Omaha, Nebraska, and worked for years designing numerous homes as well as sanctuaries for the Roman Catholic Church. One of his early Portland works is St. Michael the Archangel at SW Mill and 4th Avenue of 1901. This structure in 20th century Romanesque style displays the identical round headed windows as seen in the Church of Good Tidings. Jacobberger used a Florentine window fenestration in several other Portland buildings, including the Monastery of the Precious Blood on Mt. Tabor and on St. Mary's Cathedral of 1925.

In addition, a brick bell tower or "campanile" at St. Michael's reproduces Tuscan towers of Northern Italy with a large arched area topping the tower, and a single lancet window in the lower tower. A pyramidal roof of tile is topped with a metal finial and cross. Jacobberger used another Italianate tower design on St. Mary's Cathedral, with a three-bay arcade at the top. Again, there is a single lancet window in the lower column, which is also a part of the Church of Good Tidings tower.

Other Jacobberger structures in town include the Monastery and School of the Blessed Sacrament in University Park, the original La Salle High School, the original St. Mary's in Milwaukie, St. Andrew's Parish school and chapel of 1908 on NE Alberta, St. Ignatius at 50th and SE Division, and the Benedictine Convent at SE Mall and Milwaukie Ave. Beyond Portland, he designed Marylhurst College, the 1907 McLoughlin Institute in Oregon City, the First National Bank in Forest Grove, and Condon High School in 1909.

Jacobberger's strong Italian style is likewise evident in St. Phillip Neri Church, which he designed in 1913. This work has large overhanging eaves and exposed beams with identical corbelled supports to the Church of Good Tidings. The facade of this church is dominated by a triple arcade supported on Corinthian columns, nearly identical to the loggia of the choir area of the Church of Good Tidings.

It is conceivable that he could even have been the original architect of the Church of Good Tidings, one clue being the Italianate windows–a

Joseph Jacobberger designed about 30 Portland Roman Catholic churches, including: St. Philip Neri on SE Division (1916;) St. Michael the Archangel on SW 4th (1902) St. Mary's Cathedral (1922) and St. Stephens on SE 41st, near Hawthorne Blvd.

Jocobberger's Portland bell towers show Italian influences.

Three Portland-area churches designed by Henry Dietrich reflecting his Germanic heritage and grounding in medieval and gothic forms. The German Congregational church (below) contains large stained glass windows designed and made by the Povey Art Glass works.

Interlude: The Church of Good Tidings

motif of paired round headed arches with a roundel resting between their apex, within a larger Roman arch. These appear in the original unmodified drawings. Both his Monetary of the Precious Blood and St. Michael's feature these Italianate windows. This parallel to the Church of Good Tidings of both the late Italian Romanesque window style and the Tuscan-style tower could indicate Jacobberger involvement at some level. Another Jacobberger trademark are large extended overhanging eaves, supported with exposed beams and corbels, as seen on his St. Philip Neri on SE Division St.

Jacobberger is credited with at least 30 other churches, mostly for the Roman Catholic Church. His house designs also reflect his incorporation of the traditional and the local contemporary styles. One house built at 2609 NE Hamblet in 1925 exhibits his use of the alladian arch (in this case also a segmental arch), the bold expressed beam work of Arts and Crafts styling, creative corbelling under the porch, exposed rafter tails, and a "kick" roof.

A second candidate for architect of the Church of Good Tidings is Henry Dietrich, also born in Germany, about 1853. In 1890, he came to Portland to work for Whidden and Lewis, and became independent in 1893, designing Portland area buildings until his retirement in 1926. both the Church of the Madeleine and German Congregational Church on SW Clay reflect his German heritage of half-timbering, medieval arches, and a steeply pointed bell tower. The interior of the German Congregational Church has no open beams or trusses in the ceiling, but does have a slanted floor towards a corner altar, as does the Church of Good Tidings.

Other Portland architects did use the Italian or Florentine window motif, most notably W. W. Piper in the Newmarket Theater of 1872. Ellis Lawrence made spectacular use of them in his 1912 design for the Albina Branch Carnegie Library on NE Knott (now the Multnomah County Library Tidal Wave bookstore).

As of this writing, the question of which architect to credit for the eclectic design of the Church of Good Tidings remains open pending any further investigation or discovery.

Interior Floor Plan

Early Christian churches were laid out on one of two basic floor plans. Churches were normally built on an east-west axis, with the facade facing west to the setting of the sun. The first, called basilicas, after the Roman law courts of the same name, were long rectangular spaces, with an altar area or apse usually on the eastern end. At the western end was an entrance area known as the narthex. Over the centuries, additional space was added on the north and south, becoming known as transepts. In doing so these early architects created a cross shape when viewed from above. In the eastern Mediterranean areas of Europe, the transept was most often placed equally distant from each end of the nave, and these became known as Greek-cross shape, with equal length arms. The space thus created usually located the altar in the center, underneath the dome placed at the crossing of the two arms. This style is most often seen in America in Orthodox churches.

The second cruciform option, most often seen in northern Europe, placed the transepts nearer the eastern end of the church, this arrangement being called a Latin cross, the terms Latin and Greek referring originally to the languages of the respective areas. The altar was located under the crossing, while the area behind it, often separated by a screen, became known as the choir. The transepts often became the site of small chapels, while the elongated space for worshippers was termed the nave. There were no pews or seats, so everyone stood. Outside the church, bell towers became part of the complex, sometimes separated from the church as in the campaniles of Italian churches, or connected as the steepled towers of French-influenced church architecture.

The Church of Good Tidings is laid out on a truncated Latin-cross format and oriented with the rounded apse at the east. The transepts are shortened, but still form a cross, which ironically closely resembles the MCC Fellowship cross. Under the north transept is the Fellowship Room, earlier known as the Fireside Room and once dedicated to the memory of Al Williams, partner of MCC-Portland's third senior pastor, Jim Glyer.

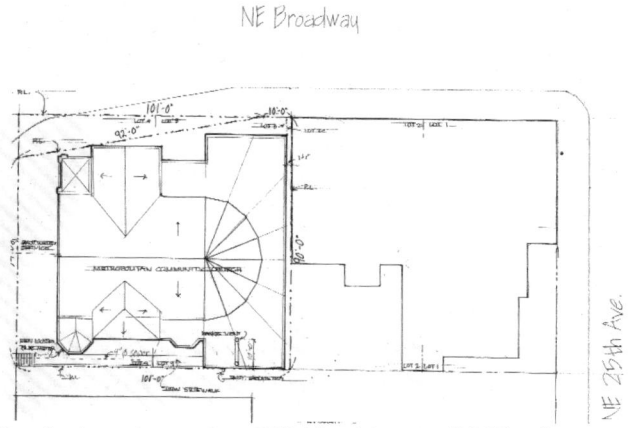

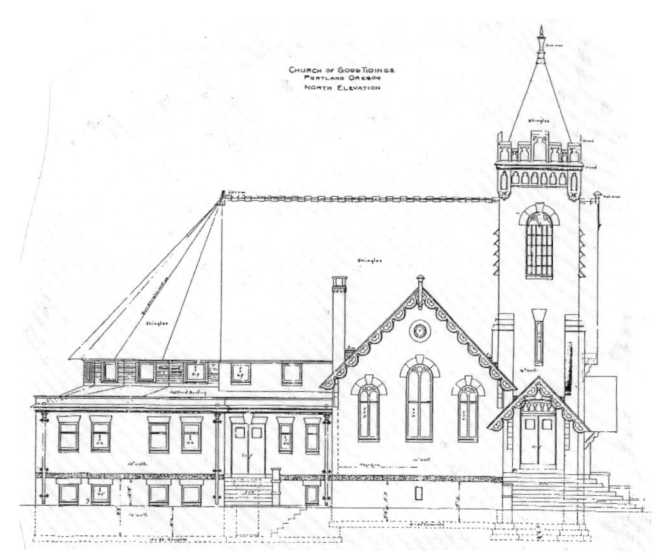

Roof plan drawn by Bill Hawkins in 2005, showing cross shape of nave and transcept.

Unsigned architectural drawings from 1909. Side elevation (above) shows front entrance under the tower and battlements atop the tower, which were removed in 1930. Incised bargeboards were never used. Floor plan shows eight steps approaching the double entrance, the orientation of curved pews towards the angled altar, the partition separating the wedge-shaped Sunday School rooms from the worship space, and space for choir rooms, pipe organ and the office.

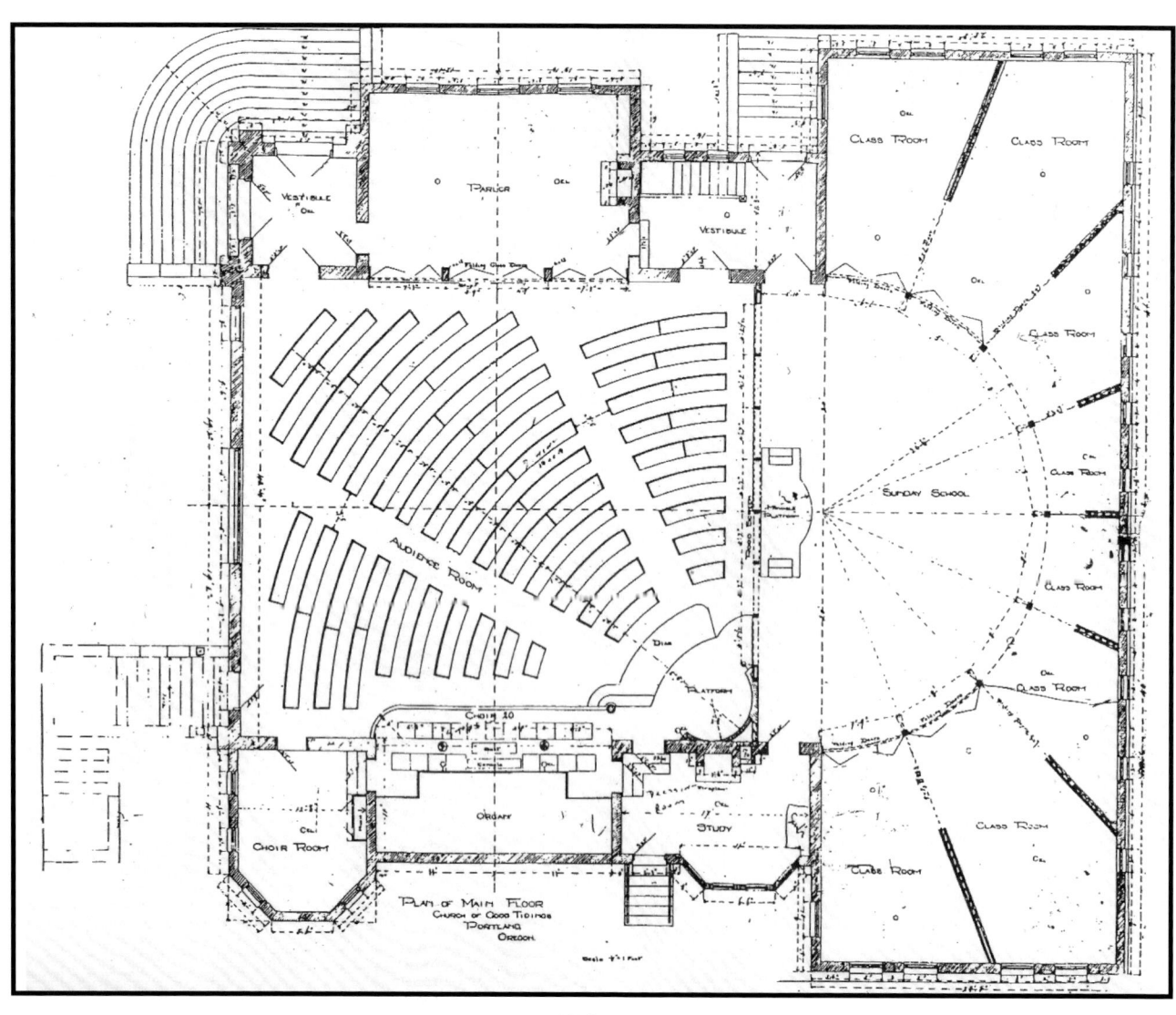

Interlude: The Church of Good Tidings

The southern transept is set off from the main sanctuary with an arcade of three arches set on Corinthian round columns and square pilasters. This area was for years the choir and organ area, and the choir had the small room to the west as its storage and practice area (now it is a liturgical arts storage area), and adjacent to the southern narthex.

Stained Glass Windows

Povey–The original 1910 windows in the church are without question the product of Povey Brothers Glassworks, the primary creative glass works in the Pacific Northwest from 1888 until 1929. Their workshops were located in Northwest Portland on NW 5th and Flanders Street. Povey work is generally categorized as Neogothic, but the designer David Povey was diverse and flexible in order to satisfy changing tastes. He studied at Cooper-Union in New York and was a contemporary of Louis C. Tiffany. Povey specialized in natural and abstract decorative designs. Geometric patterns influenced by Frank Lloyd Wright's Prairie work are also typical in Povey designs.

In the Church of Good Tidings, this simple Prairie-geometric style was utilized in all windows. The glass used was rippled opalescent glass, primarily manufactured by Kokomo Glass in Indiana. Individual glass pieces are held in place with lead caming of various sizes and steel rebar, and in the case of the large west window, a pattern of wood tracery. This pattern reflects a late English pattern of five tall panels, separated by a transom from five lights above. When this window was destroyed in the fire of 1988, most of the glass was shattered and the lead came melted, but the wood tracery pattern was maintained when the new window was installed. (See Schlicker, below.)

While the majority of the large window was a simple geometric pattern, the upper part of the five panels culminate in standard Christian designs in the Arts and Crafts style. The Alpha and Omega are found in the first and fifth panel, two variations of crosses are located in panels two and four, and the central panel depicts the open book. Three central panel designs are filled with the trademark Povey lily pattern, and may also contain another typical Povey design, the dogwood. The central three panels in the upper transom area display shields marked with three Latin cross designs.

The side windows on the west and all of the windows on the north side contain blank shield designs. Two of the smaller windows appear to have been created sometime after the initial construction, perhaps during the remodel of 1930. These are the southernmost window on the west side and the westernmost window in the narthex on the north side. The color of the Kokomo glass is different, the greens having more cerulean blue appearing in the green glass. The color of the shields is also different from the others, and the wooden framing is a different pattern. W. P. Fuller had bought out Povey in 1929 after the death of David Povey, and these two windows are most likely the work of that studio, although several of the Povey artists did work independently in Portland after the firm closed its doors.

The windows are not elaborate, unlike the elegant Povey Windows in other Portland churches of the same period–St. Michael the Archangel, First Christian, First Congregational, and First Presbyterian.

Povey craftsmen designed large "pattern" windows to reflect the elements and lines of a building. They were probably designed as temporary lights to fill spaces until more elaborate windows would have been created as funds were raised, or memorial windows would be given to the church in the future. No records exist of cost, but it is estimated that the original large west window would probably have been priced at $400. The entire set of windows for the Church of Good Tidings probably totaled $1000, five percent of the cost of the entire building.

The Povey Glassworks was working on two other significant jobs around the time of the Church of Good Tidings job–St. James Lutheran Church in the Park Blocks in 1908, and the Pittock Mansion project of 1909-1914. Portland's Old Church (originally Calvary Presbyterian) has a full set of Povey windows completed in 1895. Their earliest work is found at First Presbyterian Church, the job that origi-

Craftsmen pose in 1910 at the Povey Art Glass Company on NW 5th, which closed in 1928. Their work is still found in several area churches and in finer homes throughout Irvington.

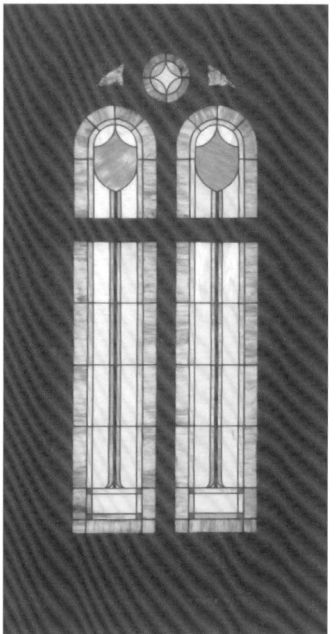

Povery windows in the north transcept, on the west wall, and in the transom over the front door.

Morrison clerestory windows between roofs.

154

Interlude: The Church of Good Tidings

nally brought them to Portland in the 1880s. St. Peter's Landmark Catholic Church in The Dalles also has a remarkable collection of Povey windows, completed about 1898. A fine set of Povey windows exists near the Church of Good Tidings at Mt. Olivet Baptist Church at NE 1st and Schuyler, completed in the 1920s.

Don Meadows, an MCC member and experienced stained glass artist, became acutely aware in 1980 that the clear glass windows above the eastern part of the sanctuary needed to be in stained glass. In architecture, these windows in a wall above one roof but below another are known as clerestory windows. Don vowed to fill all twelve windows with original design glass panels.

His gift to the church took almost two years to complete, finishing by Christmas of 1981. Each design was installed upon completion. They can be easily removed should the congregation ever abandon the existing building. They are to be transferred to any new worship space used by MCC. Each glass panel required 40 to 50 hours of work, involving drawing, cutting selected Bullseye and Kokomo glass, cutting and soldering the caming. These were completed in Don's spare time. Karl Johnson gave him much help in the cutting and soldering, as Don's arthritis was severe. Don Meadows passed away from AIDS in 1985.

Every window consists of a circular format, with a lily placed in each of the four corners, to represent the ministry of Christ's teaching sent to the four corners of the world. Meadows' design for the lilies was based on scraps of original windows in his possession from the destroyed Pantages Theater. (See Chapter 6 for designs) The general style of the windows was selected to reflect the main window at the west end of the church. In addition, many specific designs in the original window are reinterpreted in the Meadows panels. The subjects of the windows are:

1. Chi- Rho Cross–First two Greek letters of Christ's name
2. The Crown–Signifying the Kingdom of Christ
3. The Dove–Signifying the Holy Spirit or Holy Ghost
4. The Ship - Signifying trust in Christ's power
5. The Alpha - First letter of the Greek alphabet–Christ is the Beginning
6. The Testament - Christ has died and has risen
7. The Testament Christ will come again
8. The Omega–Last letter of the Greek alpha bet Christ is the Ending
9. The Burning Bush The power of God's pres ence
10. The Circle of Hands and the Rose of the Family of MCC-Portland.
11. The Chalice–the Host, the Covenant with Christ
12. The Calvary Cross and Robe The Day of Redemption

Schlicker–On Christmas Eve, 1988, a candlelight service was held at the church. Candles were placed along the widow sill of the large west window. Although they were extinguished after the service, apparently one of them reignited and in the wee hours of December 25, burned down into the wooden sill, and ignited a fire, which grew to consume much of the window. Either an alert neighbor walking her dog, or a passing taxi driver (the stories vary) alerted the fire department, and by 4 am, the fire had been stopped with the damage limited mostly to the window and surrounding framing. Lead caming melted and glass shattered.

Black plastic covered the barren opening the next morning when worshippers arrived for Christmas Day service. By February, a proposal for a new window was outlined in a competition announcement. Stipulations of the competition included:

1. The window is dedicated in a life affirming way to the issue of AIDS
2. Any human figures should be both male and female, and not predominantly white
3. Removal of stained glass remaining in the old window
4. Design for a new window following the original window contours, to include

A comparison of the 1910 Povey window destroyed by the 1988 fire and the AIDS Memorial window designed by David Schlicker in 1989. Schlicker's desire was to keep the tracery pattern of the older window and to use similar glass materials and leading techniques. Drawings by Dave Kohl.

The oak altar was shared with the Church of Divine Science when MCC bought the building in 1977. It continues to serve as a more casual worship table. Ministers stand behind it, facing the congregation and the AIDS window. The Bob Jackson Eternal Light hangs near the 30-year-old Rushong cross.

Dave Kohl photos

Interlude: The Church of Good Tidings

glass samples for color and texture

5. Proposal for installation coordination (the artist is responsible for installing the new window)

6. A fee of $400 is provided to help defray the cost of the proposal, which will be applied toward the total cost of the successful bid

7. Total cost of the window and installation not to exceed $15,000

8. Proposals due by March 19; Board of Directors decision on March 22; completed window installed by dedication service September 8, 1989

Three local stained glass artists bid on the project. Winner of the competition was David Schlicker, whose design incorporated an open heart design from MCC member Jimmy Bryant, first used a few years earlier in connection with the AIDS vigil. At the time, Schlicker worked at home, so he had to lay out the panels on his patio, and view the emerging design from his upstairs window for perspective. He maintained the five tall "lights" of the original window design, as well as the transom bar and upper windows of the original wood tracery pattern.

Symbolically, the winning design incorporates the open heart, which was designed to symbolize a soul that can receive. This heart is placed in a field of light blue, over a pattern of healing waters. Unplanned at the time of design, the beveled clear glass outline of the heart projects and focuses an image on the east sanctuary wall in the late afternoon, and the pattern moves across various parts of this wall depending on time of day and season of the year.

Ten doves of different colors in the sky represent spirits, and the multitude of lilies equate with resurrection. There were many lilies in the original window, a trademark of Povey windows. Lilies are symbolic of pallor and chastity, and have been a long time Christian symbol for purity associated with Mary, the mother of Jesus. The Savior referred to lilies in His *Sermon on the Mount*, noting, "Solomon in all his glory was not arrayed like one of these." The many lilies in the Schlicker window also repeat the corner lilies in the twelve clerestories by Don Meadows.

Truss Work

The designer of the church interior created a warm medieval atmosphere through the use of exposed structural timbers supporting the ceiling and roof of the sanctuary. The oak beams are formed into a structure called a "hammer beam" truss. Traditionally, medieval roofs were supported with a combination of vertical and horizontal beams joined together so as to support the weight of tile or lead roofs. Over time, as wider structures were desired, beams long and strong enough to span a wide interior were increasingly difficult to find, so gothic master-builders formulated braced and bracketed truss work with shorter beams tied together to support the heavy weights.

In addition to having a structural purpose, trusses were carved to soften their edges, create elaborate foliage patterns, and terminate with rounded or carved finial endings called pendils. Small notches called a dogtooth were included in the design. Strongly influenced by 19th century English revival gothic design, the "spandrel" cavity between the curved brace and the collar beam are modified trefoil (three leaf) designs at the widest part of the opening. These bear no weight and are purely decorative.

The ceiling of the MCC sanctuary is supported just above the collar beams, with only the lowest portion of the angular struts visible from the interior. Placing the ceiling mid-way from the hammerbeams to the roof ridge allows for more economical use of interior heat, and provides some dead-space for insulating from exterior heat in summer.

Faux Columns

The original choir recess, to the right of the altar space, is separated by a three-bay arcade. The arches are semi-circular or round arches, and are trimmed with a three-band archivolt on the front side. The pattern of a higher central arch is determined by the wider spacing between the two central freestanding round columns. Sometimes this design is called a Palladian Arch, Venetian Arch, or Serlainia. This arcade motif is very reminiscent of early Christian and Byzantine architecture in Italy,

Dave Kohl photo

Open or exposed trusswork gives a gothic feel to the sanctuary. The trefoil spacers have a dogtooth. The beams bear little weight. The exposed collar beam carry the weight of king post and angle struts. The wood appears to be oak.

Corinthian capitals of clustered acanthus leaves top both square pillars and round columns. Columns are wood, covered after 1963 with a faux marbling pattern of black with white streaks. The arcade of three bays carries on the early Christian architectural innovation of placing arches on top of columns. Joseph Jacobberger used that motif in the courtyard of his Monastery of the Precious Blood on the east flank of Mt. Tabor, built in the 1920s. Note his use of Florentine windows (double arch and tondo inside a larger arch).

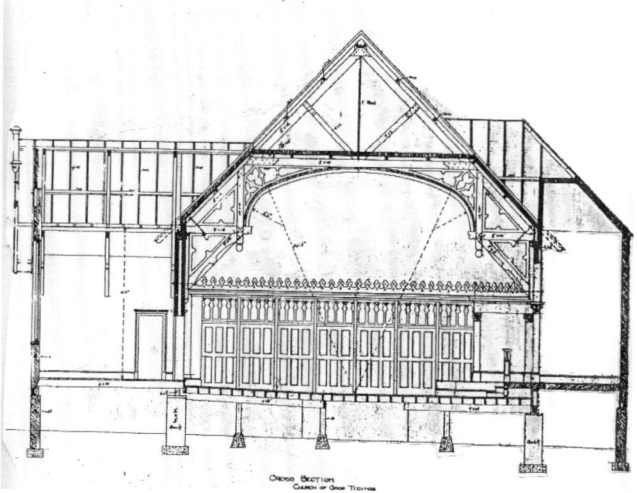

Cross section showing trusswork with hammer-beams and the transcept roof joists.

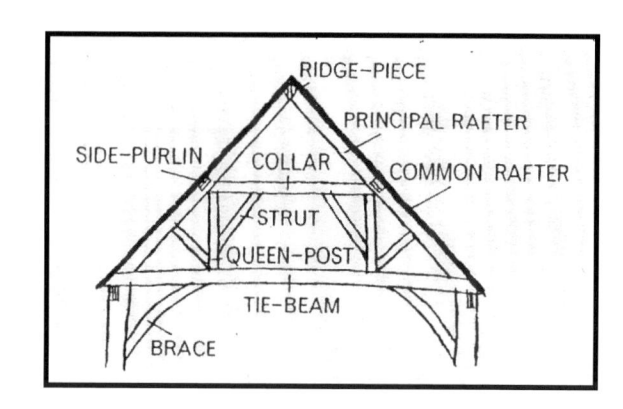

Principle parts of a truss roof system.

Portland City Archives

Dave Kohl photo

Interlude: The Church of Good Tidings

where the Greco-Roman influence was strongest. The square pilasters on the two ends are "engaged" to the supporting wall, as are the pilasters on either side of the altar recess.

Topping the columns and pillars are golden colored capitals, made of a wood core covered with molded plaster. The capitals are in the "composite" order: a combination of acanthus leaves from the Corinthian order and enlarged swirling volutes from the earlier Greek Ionic style. Using such capitals gives an air of nobility or elegance associated with the classical civilizations of Greece and Rome and its revival during the Italian Renaissance. They are the only classic part of the interior and were most likely procured from one of several firms, which manufactured such architectural appointments in the early 20th century.

Above the arcade is a latticed wood screen overlaid with a pointed Gothic arch motif, the only part of the interior that is in the Gothic style. The arches are in the original plans, however, the gothic arches were not indicated. This upper area was most likely the location of ranks of the smaller pipes, and could have contained a swell box, the louvered sound chamber containing some pipes. When the louvers were closed by the organist's foot pedal, the volume was muffled and reduced.

It appears that the hollow wood columns were originally left stained and varnished, as is the lattice screen above the columns and the pediment at the east end of the apse. At some time in the church's history, most likely after Grace Lutheran removed the pipe organ, the columns and pilasters were covered with a faux marble painted finish. The use of thick paint with a textured and feathered over-painting technique to replicate a stone appearance was a practice popular with painters at the turn of the century, creating the expensive look of polished stone. Graining and texturing were skills passed down from masters to apprentices, or learned from textbooks on such techniques. The columns on the ground floor of Portland's City Hall, designed by Whidden and Lewis in 1895, are also painted faux stone designs over hollow wooden cores.

Furnishings and Appointments

Altar–The oak altar, serving table and pulpit are undocumented as to origin, but was in use by the Lutheran congregation. The altar is supported by pointed or Gothic arches, inside of which are cusped trefoil patterns. The four legs are topped with carved foliated capitals, reminiscent of stylized Corinthian motifs. The design on the pulpit and serving table reflects a late Romanesque influence–paired semi-circular arch motif and small foils as borders and feet. MCC has not ever launched any plans to change the altar furnishings. When MCC began their joint use of the sanctuary with the Divine Scientists, no need was felt to change much of anything.

Eternal light–Bob Jackson, member and Deacon for many years, is memorialized in the eternal light, purchased after his passing by several friends from the Theater Arts Team. Without requesting permission to add such a light to the altar area, it simply appeared.

Cherub–Tom Rice and Tony Longo came into possession of a carved alabaster angel that had once been part of a monastery in Italy. After owning it several years, they decided its most appropriate placing would be at MCC. Their donation rests in the southwest corner of the sanctuary, overlooking worshippers as it holds a candle. She has come to be fondly thought of as a quiet peaceful presence by those who notice her at all.

Pews–The oak pews, set in a curved layout, are original. They lack ornament, save for a fine band of thin molding on the upper pew backs. This egg-and-dart motif is a subtle but classic touch of elegance. Pew cushions were made and upholstered by Pat Schwiebert in the late 1980s, out of consideration for the sitting comfort of many members experiencing loss of body mass due to HIV/AIDS.

Crucifix – A promising young sculptress, Liz Konsella, donated the iron and brass processional cross for the 25th Anniversary celebration in 2001. In gratitude for what MCC had meant to her, she consulted with Pastor Roy Cole to design an appropriate piece to be a per-

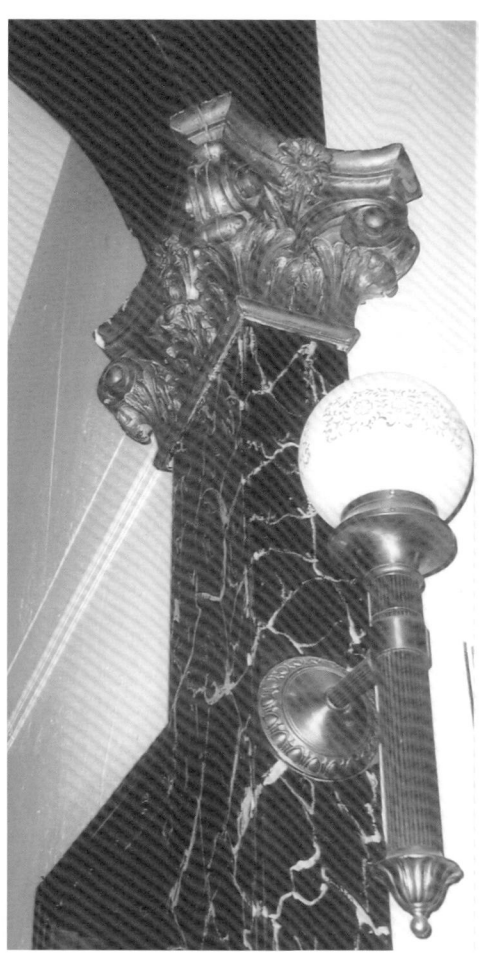

Processional Cross of brass and iron. The Greek column. Faux marble wood pier and gas light.

Detail of original "egg-and-dart" carving on oak pews; cherub from an Italian convent.; baptismal font designed and built by Nance and Estellene, both of the congregation, and donated in 1996.

160

Interlude: The Church of Good Tidings

manent part of MCC. The heart in the center of the crucifix reflects the open heart design of Jimmy Bryan in the center of the large stained glass window.

Communion Ware–An early member donated a complete set of silver communion ware to MCC. Another donation for a set of brown stoneware Communion ware came in the 1980s. Member and potter Dave Kohl made and donated a white stoneware set with several chalices in about 1998. In 2004, Rev. Glenna Shepherd asked him to make eight intinction sets, to aid with a more efficient system of communion distribution. Four more sets were made in time for the congregational retreat of 2005 at Devil's Lake.

Baptismal Font–Roy Cole baptized Jeffrey Forrester in 1996, shortly before his death to AIDS. At the time, the church had no baptismal font, so Roy improvised with a bowl placed on the altar. After Jeff's passing, his family decided to dedicate a font to MCC in his memory. The oak pedestal was designed to harmonize with the older fixtures of the sanctuary, with a stainless steel bowl set under the lid. A brass plaque on the font reads, "In memory of Jeffrey Lincoln Forrester – August 4, 1963 - May 31, 1996"

The Column – Cheryl Hall and Rev. Roy Cole produced a series of 36 cable television programs entitled "*Living Live*" for the Rogers network in 1995. In order to enhance their spartan set, it was decided to purchase a single wooden Doric fluted column from a local builder's supply firm. The white shaft and simple plinth provided the tasteful backdrop for each program. When the series was finished, the column was transported to MCC, where it has stood sentinel in the arcade space in the south of the Sanctuary ever since.

Vestments–Various ceremonial vestments, chasabules, and stoles from various sources have been used over the years at MCC. Care and storage of these has not always been careful, and several have been destroyed due to moisture, mold, and vermin. The most outstanding set of liturgical cloth in the church is the vestments and stoles commissioned by the family of José Montoya. José was a former Roman Catholic brother who became a long-term deacon at MCC until his AIDS related death in 1994. José's openness about his illness and his emotional journey because of it were inspirational to the congregation who dearly loved José and his sincerity in preaching and counseling. The pieces were made by liturgical artist Bryan Paatz of Lake Oswego and incorporate several symbols of resurrection and hope, along with references to the open-heart design of Jimmy Bryan.

Several artworks familiar to early MCC members are no longer in the building. Among them are the two large paintings left by the Divine Science Church in 1977. By the time of Roy Cole, they had become underappreciated and some considered them an eyesore and a distraction during worship. By vote of the Board of Directors, Roy Cole gave them to MCC-Salt Lake City.

Another well-remembered artwork was a plaster sculpture resembling Michelangelo's marble of the seated "Pieta"–Mary lamenting the body of her son, Jesus. The MCC version, about two feet high, depicted a deceased man on the lap of a lamenting male figure. Both figures were unclad, and the emotion of the piece in the time of AIDS was powerful. It was placed in the entry narthex and highly visible. Over time, some members came to feel it was too emotional for grieving friends and families of AIDS patients, and it was removed. Its whereabouts is unknown.

Musical Instruments

At one time, MCC owned two organs and three pianos. The original pipe organ used by the Lutherans was removed by them in 1963, and reconfigured in their new church at NE 76th and Fremont.

The Allen organ used for many years was purchased by Oren Charles and several members. It had originally belonged to the 1st Church of the Nazarene. MCC member Paul Wirth and a "committee" remodeled the organ chambers in 1981. A pre-transistorized instrument, it required a bank of tubes that occupied much of the room adjoining the organ. Heat generated by the tubes kept the space toasty, and Paul often had to improvise replacement tubes and other parts.

Intinction sets used for Communion distribution and golden chalices from Russia. Pipes from the old organ, moved by Grace Lutheran to their new building in 1963. Steven Couch plays the Roland keyboard and Allen organ, assisted by Aharon Madey. Milt Howell plays the Young Chang piano, accompanied by organist Doug Friend. Instrumental duets are the norm for hymn singing at MCC.

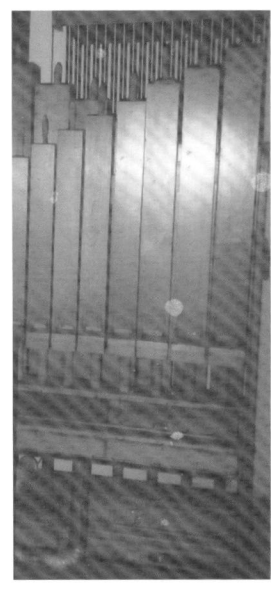

Dave Kohl photos

Interlude: The Church of Good Tidings

A Lowery organ was purchased in 1981 from the family of Allen Beck. Originally valued at $7800, it was sold to MCC for $1650, and used as a back-up instrument for several years. The instrument was capable of producing versatile sounds, simulating various instruments from drums to harpsichords and Hawaiian guitars. Everybody Skate!

When Jack St. John returned to play the Allen for an anniversary service, his exuberant playing, volume and registration did the antique instrument in, literally blowing out a bank of tubes. Even Mr. Wirth had met his match. The current Allen organ was purchased when Dennis Chappell was pastor.

Wendell Gleason negotiated the purchase of a Hammond C-3 organ, purchased in Vancouver in the mid-1980s. It was used occasionally in the chapel area, later to find a home with the Salvation Army.

The Portland Town Council donated an upright piano in 1980, which was located in the basement, and survived four years of use and abuse before its cadence.

Jack St. John and Gary Coleman arranged the purchase of the spinet piano for the Sanctuary in 1980. Tallman's in Hollywood was going out of business and lowered the price 25% to $3000. Two very generous donors came forward to pay for the instrument.

A second piano, a Steinway Grand, was added in 1983. It was a totally reconditioned 60-year old instrument with a player mechanism. Stan Sparks donated the piano and about 200 player rolls, probably as old as the piano. The mechanism was used several times during services. One Christmas evening, a small group assembled during an ice and snowstorm and heard a medley of Christmas tunes, piano-roll style, substituting for the absent pianist.

In 1998, a used Young Chang Concert Grand piano was selected to replace the older instruments. A jolly campaign was launched to purchase the $25,000 prize. Members were encouraged to buy a leg, several keys, the lid, or any other part of the piano, each piece being given a monetary value. MCC members came thru once again!

A Roland electronic keyboard was added in 2003, purchased with funds for the sale of the Kawai piano. Most recently, a complete set of drums was donated to the church, which is mostly used in connection with Elevation.

1980 Haitian refugees flee to America
- Boat lift brings Cubans to Key West
- Ronald Reagan and George H. Bush elected to lead U.S.
- Rhodesia becomes Zimbabwe after 90 years of white rule
- Quebec voters reject separatism
- Eugene Ormandy ends 44 years directing Philadelphia Orchestra
- Mt. St. Helens erupts 40 miles north of Portland
- Dan Rather succeeds Walter Cronkite as CBS-TV anchorman

1981 Sandra Day O'Connor appointed to Supreme Court by President Ronald Reagan
- Washington Public Power Supply System, (WPPSS – prounced whoops) plagued with problems, abandons billion-dollar nuclear plants.
- Two NE precinct Portland Police officers toss dead possums at a black-owned restaurant; brouhaha, demonstrations, and lawsuits follow
- James DePriest, nephew of Marian Anderson, begins 23-year run as conductor of the Oregon Symphony, putting Oregon on the musical map

Chapter Six
Rev. Donald Borbe
September 1979 - January 1981

"Therefore let us not be judging one another any longer, but rather make this your decision, not to put before a brother a stumbling block or a cause for tripping"

Romans 14:13 New World Translation

Reverend Arlene Ackerman filled the four-month gap as Interim Pastor between Austin Amerine's departure to become District Coordinator and the arrival of the new Pastor. In that interim period, about twenty new members joined MCC-P and plans were made for several members to attend the upcoming General Conference.

Deborah Betron and Ann Kenyon were two of the seven members of the pastoral search committee. It became apparent to the women in the church that overall leadership was not yet ready to have a woman serve as senior pastor. Yet the congregation grew to number about 35% women during this period. This is sometimes credited to the fact that MCC had once rented out the sanctuary to a local producer as a venue for a woman's concert. The attendance packed the building, and many women thus discovered MCC and its mission. Several eventually joined.

Additionally, a UFMCC by-law at the time prohibited the possibility of an Interim Minister becoming a Senior Pastor in the same congregation.

For the first time in its congregational life, MCC faced the prospect of finding and hiring a new minister. Church leaders were confused as to their role. Were they to wait for the UFMCC fellowship to take action? How were they to find candidates?

The Search Committee learned that they needed to send out announcements to other pastors in the fellowship about their vacancy with a description of the congregation and its past. Then they waited for responses. There were about ten responses, and after much deliberation, it was decided that Don Borbe should candidate.

Rev. Donald C. Borbe came to Portland from Philadelphia, where he had served MCC Philadelphia since 1975. Born in California, his academic work was first done at Pasadena College. At Point Loma Nazarene College, he completed his education major and religion minor, then taught geography at Southwestern Academy in San Marino, CA, beginning in 1958.

When his mother developed a terminal brain tumor, he returned to Santa Rosa to assist the family and tutor his two younger brothers. He also enrolled in the California Department of Mental Hygiene's Psychiatric Technician program, becoming a certified Psychiatric Technician.

Work Experiences

In 1961-62 he served as director of the Santa Rosa Youth for Christ. Utilizing his experiences with group dynamics, attendance grew from 50 to about 400 persons. He began full-time ministry as an Assembly of God pastor in Santa Rosa and Stockton. When he admitted to

Rev. Don Borbe ministered to the MCC congregation in Philadelphia with Mary Anne Van Fossen. The congregation there supported outreach to people of many denominations and of various backgrounds and sexuality.

Don Borbe photos

Deborah Betron was on Don Borbe's pastoral search committee. She became very active in the local business community, helping form PABA (Portland Area Business Association) in 1992.

Rev. Arlene Ackerman worked with Austin Amerine beginning in 1978. She served in the interim period after Austin's departure, and worked with Don Borbe for about a year. She was instrumental in planning the Portland Candlelight march with Jerry Weller of the Portland Town Council.

Rev. Donald Borbe 1979 - 1981

being gay, he was told that he had no business as a Full Gospel Minister in God's service. Borbe then worked in the executive furniture business in Sacramento. Praying to be made a heterosexual, he married an Assemblies of God woman, with whom he had a son. He soon became owner of a Dairy Queen franchise in Sacramento, and of a Carriage Trade drapery firm designing interiors.

As he evaluated his vocational calling, he had to reconcile his own personality and homosexuality with a call to full-time professional Christian ministry. He spent many hours secretly reading everything published about being gay and Christian, including Troy Perry's *The Lord is My Shepherd and He Knows I'm Gay*. He began attending MCC in Sacramento under Rev. Elder Freda Smith and entered the Exhorter program. Freda became his mentor. In 1974 he was licensed as an MCC clergy and became assistant minister in Sacramento, also working in the music program. The relationship with MCC-Sacramento caused Borbe to come out of his closet to his wife, ending his marriage and the dissolution of their business properties.

Borbe became administrative assistant manager for the chief of General Administrative Services for the state. His challenge was to keep ten women from being dismissed for incompetence. With awareness gained from Freda Smith about women's issues, he helped his employees refocus and assume positive work productivity, saving their own jobs. His last job action before taking a position at MCC-Philadelphia was to hire a full staff for his boss who became the State Energy Commissioner.

MCC-Philadelphia

With his move to Philadelphia in 1975, he once again was a full-time minister, and became active in Center City Clergy, a downtown ministers association. It took several months before this conservative group recognized Don as a gay minister, or the UFMCC as a valid church.

Borbe's work at MCC-Philadelphia was described in a book written to help questioning youth find answers to their questions about being gay. The authors described the programs that he ran with ministerial intern Mary Anne Van Fossen, including movie nights, picnics, bowling, softball, skating, Bible study, and counseling. (Hanckel, Frances, *A Way of Love*, 1979)

Discovering a level of corrupt connections with a local syndicate, Borbe successfully pressed for dismissal of three MCC-Philadelphia board members. He worked with Dignity, a local gay synagogue, and the Christian Association Gay Task Force. Don also became a member of the Fellowship Commission, a local influential organization established to monitor the political discrimination of minorities, including sexual minorities. He hoped to continue participating in local interfaith organizations in Portland.

Noteworthy of his time in Pennsylvania was the increase in female and minority membership at his MCC. Only one black and two women were in the church when he began, whereas four years later the diverse church boasted an equal number of men and women members, about 10 percent of whom were black. Borbe conducted over 200 holy unions during his time in Philadelphia. Although he often received a stipend from the couples, he turned the monies over to the congregation, accounting for over 20% of the church's income.

As part of his work in Philadelphia, he helped found MCC-Atlantic City as a mission effort in 1978, usually riding the bus to his evening worship services there.

MCC Gets Its Second Senior Pastor

Don Borbe came to Portland with the philosophy that the church points toward what a truly inclusive worship of God in Spirit and Truth might be. Distinctions of "straight," "gay," "male," or "emale" have no effect on spirituality, or being created in God's image. God sees our souls, not our physical bodies.

Rev. Borbe was announced as the second senior pastor of MCC-Portland in August 1979. The story ran in the *NW Fountain* and the Portland Town Council Newsletter, which also included an article about an anti-gay religious group called the "Christian Voice." In one year,

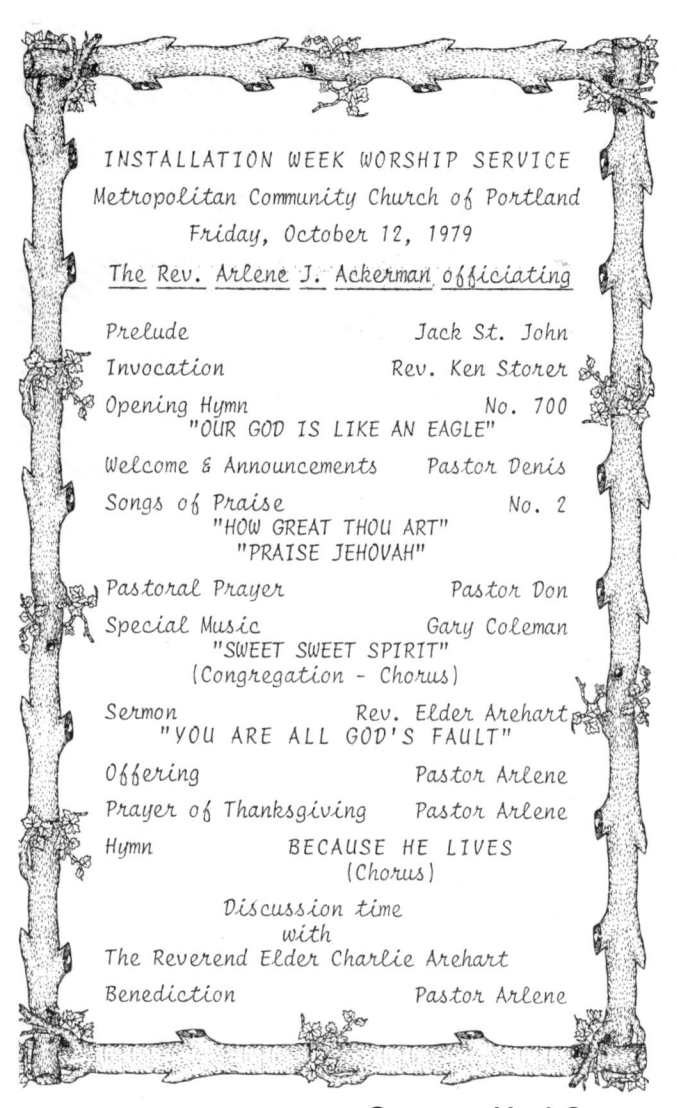

INSTALLATION WEEK WORSHIP SERVICE
Metropolitan Community Church of Portland
Friday, October 12, 1979
The Rev. Arlene J. Ackerman officiating

Prelude   Jack St. John
Invocation   Rev. Ken Storer
Opening Hymn   No. 700
    "OUR GOD IS LIKE AN EAGLE"
Welcome & Announcements   Pastor Denis
Songs of Praise   No. 2
    "HOW GREAT THOU ART"
    "PRAISE JEHOVAH"
Pastoral Prayer   Pastor Don
Special Music   Gary Coleman
    "SWEET SWEET SPIRIT"
    (Congregation - Chorus)
Sermon   Rev. Elder Arehart
    "YOU ARE ALL GOD'S FAULT"
Offering   Pastor Arlene
Prayer of Thanksgiving   Pastor Arlene
Hymn   BECAUSE HE LIVES
                    (Chorus)
        Discussion time
             with
The Reverend Elder Charlie Arehart
Benediction   Pastor Arlene

Courtesy Neal Curry

Note the clerestory windows before Don Meadows designed and made stained glass panels.

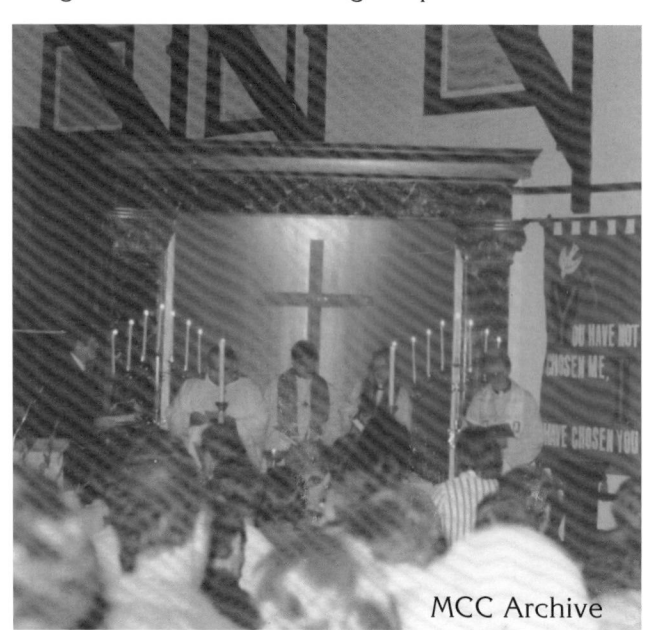

Installation for Don Borbe was also the date for a long-planned Candlelight March in downtown Portland. The Oregon event coincided with the National March in Washington. Jerry Weller of PTC worked closely with MCC's Arlene Ackerman to co-sponsor the event.

Courtesy Jerry Weller

Terry Schrunk Plaza, where the Candle March of about 800 people concluded Oct. 13, 1979.

MCC Archive

Portland City Archive

168

Rev. Donald Borbe   1979 - 1981

this bigoted group had raised $1 million to fight for their three top priorities: An end to equal protection for lesbians and gays, tax subsidies for racially discriminatory "segregation academies" and a lifting of sanctions against the white-dominated government of black Zimbabwe-Rhodesia. Fifteen members of the U.S. Congress were numbered in their ranks, including the notorious homophobe Rep. Larry McDonald, D-GA.

Social life at MCC was in full momentum. Plans were being finalized for attending the General Conference in Los Angeles, August 13-19. Travel agent Roger Bullis arranged inexpensive air fares for delegates Bob Jackson and Susan Starkey. Fall plans also included a Labor Day Picnic at Lewisville Park, the annual open house at the home of Ron Powell and Russ Howerton, a dinner at the Embers later in the month, and the annual Halloween Disco Dance at the Neighbors of Woodcraft.

The new pastor's candidating sermon, "Lookin' good with nothing to say," was presented on August 5. That evening, a congregational forum with Assistant Pastor Arlene Ackerman gave parishioners a chance to meet the pastor and comment on his sermon. MCC staff also included Rev. Denis Moore, who by this time had completed the Exhorter Program and was a licensed UFMCC minister.

Upon arrival, Rev. Borbe immediately began participating in MCC services. Don's partner Richard Pittinger arrived a month later.

Don recommended the continuation of Arlene as Assistant Pastor. Paula Nielsen continued as church secretary and publicist, contributing monthly schedules and articles to the *NW Fountain*. Active members numbered over 200. When Paula Nielsen moved to Eugene, Don chose Pat Cach as the new church secretary, fielding phone calls, scheduling room usage, preparing bulletins, and generally holding things together. She proved to be a responsible support and a healthy communicator, and worked well with Don.

Early on, Don conducted the funeral of member Ron Grimes, whose family was from the Assemblies of God. Several members of the Imperial Sovereign Rose Court came to the funeral. Reluctant at first to have a gay minister conduct the service, after meeting Don the family began speaking in tongues and interpretation. Don had left and did not hear the message. It was directly parallel to, and a reinforcement of, the funeral sermon, which Don had not yet given. He spoke the message that only God can truly know a man's heart. Both Don and the family took this as a sign and miracle of confirming witness.

Installation

October 14, 1979, was the date of the official installation of the new pastor. *The Oregon Journal* carried the story on October 12. A weekend of events included a Thursday reception in the home of Dan Brown for Rev. Elder Charlie Arehart, a special Friday worship service and rap featured Rev. Arehart's message on human sexuality, a Saturday Prayer Vigil and Candlelight Parade in downtown Portland, and the Sunday installation. Rev. Amerine, now District Coordinator, was the officiant, and Rev. Arehart, pastor of MCC-Denver, presented the sermon "A Charge to the Pastor," at the 6 pm service. The Cantor was Rev. David Rich-Miller of the Assyrian Orthodox Catholic Church. Rev. Ken Storer led the prayer of dedication, and Rev. Denis Moore helped celebrate Holy Communion. A reception afterwards featured the culinary creations of MCC's chef-in-residence, Robin Hixson.

The October 13 Candlelight March was not a part of the installation festivities. Rather, it was the long-planned Portland response in support of the National Candlelight March in Washington, DC. Portland's March was a joint venture planned by MCC's Arlene Ackerman and Jerry Weller of the Portland Town Council's Political Action Committee. About 700 marchers from many gay groups met in front of the Portland Art Museum at 9 pm and then paraded down SW Broadway, timed to coincide with the time that several of the Broadway theaters would be letting out patrons. The principal event

The Portland Gay Men's Chorus (PGMC) organized and rehearsed at MCC. Proudly, they formed a democratic organization and spent an entire weekend at the Oregon Coast on a by-laws retreat. Committees were established to govern music selection, performance, and socializing. They insisted that the "G" word (Gay) be part of their name and identity, only the fifth chorus to do so in the U.S. Over 400 gay and lesbian choruses have formed since 1979.

PGMC Archive photo

MCC Archive

MCC Choir Director Gary Coleman became aware of the founding of the San Francisco Gay Men's Chorus, and placed an ad in the PTC Newsletter to form a group to sing for Gay Pride. Many of the original 20 members became leaders in the gay community over the years. The first performance of the group beyond MCC was at the Rafters, above the Embers and Virginia Cafe, on SW Park, in 1980.

Eric Cordingly photos

Rev. Donald Borbe 1979 - 1981

of the march was a pause in front of the Federal Courthouse where Arlene taped a list of demands to the door, somewhat in the style of Martin Luther.

The demands called for repeal of anti-homosexual laws and for the passage of a comprehensive lesbian/gay rights bill in the U.S. Congress. A request was made to ban discrimination based on sexual orientation highlighting cases against lesbian mothers and gay fathers and the protection of lesbian and gay youth. Arlene was quoted in the *Oregonian* as asking, "Why do you persecute us? We are your sons and your daughters!"

MCC continued a strong partnership with the Portland gay community.

Worship Changes

Wednesday nights were designated as mid-week worship or "Sing-spiration." This service became a serendipitous celebration of singing, with many selections being made spontaneously by leaders and worshippers. Scripture readings were interspersed among hymns and spirituals.

Education was a large part of these evenings, with many programs being offered simultaneously. Some programs were single events and others stretched over four sessions. Examples were "Manners, Morals, and Matthew" led by student clergy Ron Bergeron and Phil Crum, "Prayer Power" led by Pastor Arlene, and "Reading for Worship" led by Deacon Bob Jackson.

Beginning October 21, two Sunday services became the norm. New was an 11 am service, now possible because the Church of Divine Science no longer used the sanctuary. Their signboard in front of MCC was finally removed, four years after the building had changed hands.

Portland Gay Men's Chorus

During the spring of 1980, another use was being made of the church's facilities. The music director, Gary Coleman, had recruited some choir members to sing for the Gay Pride event in June. He placed a notice in the Portland Town Council Newsletter to find other singers in the gay community, and 20 men sang in the concert held at MCC during Gay Pride weekend.

So successful was this venture, that the group decided to continue singing and the Portland Gay Men's Chorus was organized. Coleman, Steve Fulmer, and Mark Jones met at Wilde Oscar's one afternoon and penciled out organization and program ideas. Rehearsals became a Monday evening tradition at MCC, although most congregation members were unaware of the group and the impact it would make on the Portland community. That fall, the first official concert of the Portland Gay Men's Chorus was performed at MCC. Other concerts that season were performed at The Rafters and at Dahl and Penne's.

Several initially reluctant MCC singers added to the ranks that first season, eventually including, Coleman, Bill Barry, Dave Dishman, Dean McIntyre, Frank Myers, Eric Callicotte, and Bob Sherwood.

Ever conscious of their independence and political mission, the chorus democratically decided to include the "G" word in its name. Officers were elected, including Steve Fulmer as General Manager, Tom Long as Secretary, Gary Coleman as Business Manager/treasurer, and Mark Weinsoft, Chairman of the music committee. The first co-conductors were Mark Jones and Kevin Walsh. A full set of by-laws was established at a 1980 weekend beach retreat.

New Beginnings

1979 was also the year several long-running gay establishments opened in Portland–the Hot Potato #2, JR's East Saloon, and Cassidy's Restaurant on SW Washington. Glenn Dugger bought the Focal Point from Steve Suss and changed it to Somebody's Place. He moved it to SW 11th in 1983. When he lost his lease in 1985, he moved cater corner to SW 11th and Stark, renaming it Scandals. Glenn began a tradition of showing old movies on Sunday afternoons, creating a friendlier non-bar atmosphere. Favorite films included *Whatever Happened to*

Three early MCC members were active in the emerging leather community. Susie Shepherd has held several titles, Barry C served as host for an early leather contest, and choir-boy-turned-leatherman was Portland's first "Mr. Leather."

Two gay businesses opened in 1979 that are still operating in 2005. Cassidy's restaurant offers quiet dining and bar services. Somebody's started at the Focal Point, then moved to SW 11th in 1981. In 1985 it changed to Scandal's, moving 50 yards south. It moved again in 2006, down Stark Street.

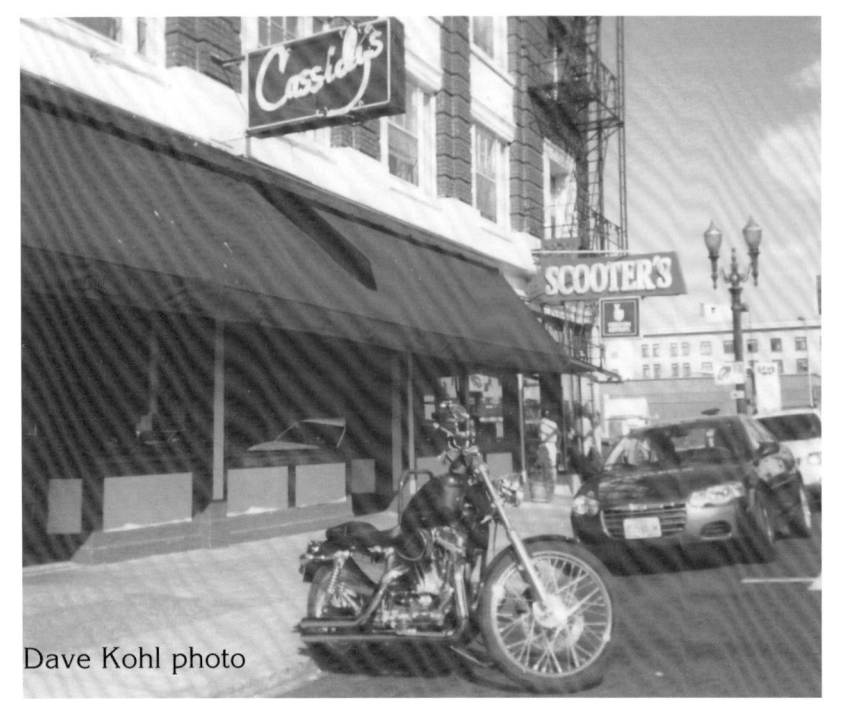

Rev. Donald Borbe 1979 - 1981

Baby Jane, Auntie Mame, and *Boys in the Band*. The informality and friendliness made Somebody's/Scandal's a popular alternative to the S and M ("stand-and-model") practices in most bars.

Rev. Denis Moore completed the requirements to be an MCC clergy in August 1979. His intention was to stay and work with the congregation, but in October he had the opportunity to candidate for pastor at MCC-Honolulu, and moved there in November. He served that group many years, and then led MCC-San Jose until his retirement in 2002. Upon retirement, he returned to Portland and continued to lead classes and study groups, even preaching on request.

At Christmas time, annual events like caroling and a free Christmas dinner continued. The choir presented the Christmas Musical on the Sunday before Christmas. Kathy Walden directed the large choir in performance of quality popular seasonal music. The New Year began with a "Munchie Game Night" and a "Funky '80's Dance."

The following 1980 Easter Season was highlighted with a presentation of the Passover Seder on Holy Wednesday and a musical dramatization on Simon of Cyrene utilizing the talents of Rev. Borbe, Jack St. John, Paula Nielsen, and Bill Samuels on Maundy Thursday. Good Friday's 3-hour service focused on the six miracles of Calvary. Gary Coleman, deacon and music coordinator, preached on "When Jesus Busted Out!" for the 6 am Sunrise service. Another annual MCC-Portland tradition, the Easter Musical, was prepared and presented under choir director Kathy Walden. Entitled "I Know That My Redeemer Liveth," it was an original composition. Both Arlene and Don preached sermons that Sunday.

Troy Perry came to Portland and spoke powerfully (it's the only way he speaks!) at both April 13 worship services. His message proclaimed that homosexuals have a God-given right to be a part of the church as happy individuals who can hold their heads high without shame. He decried the practice of many churches closing their doors to millions of gay people in America, based only on their sexual orientation. His up-beat speaking style motivated nearly everyone, be they religious or not.

Troy also enjoyed participating in the leather community when he came to Portland. Leather was just becoming a part of the gay community and because of the rough appearance of men clad in animal skins and metal studs, their attitude was often misjudged as standoffish. Actually, many leather men report feeling ostracized or at least looked down on by the milder elements of gay society. Ironic.

The newly opened JR's Cell had replaced The Folsom Cell in Old Town, and became the home bar of the leather community before the rise of the Dirty Duck or the Embers. And there was John Adam's new C. C. Slaughter's in the former Rhondee on Stark with its Texas-inspired interior. MCC's own choirboy Gary Coleman competed for and won Portland's first Mr. Leather contest in 1980. Several other MCC leather people have included Barry C, Brad Stephens, Dean McIntyre, and Steven Corpus. Susie Shepherd took the Ms Leather title in 1983. In 2000, Charlie Salt was elected Mr. Portland Leather.

A new gay and lesbian community gathering place opened when Holly Hart began business as the Old Wives Tales. The large restaurant, located in a one-time garage on E Burnside near Sandy Blvd. provided a non-alcohol feminist and gay liberation atmosphere. Inspired by the Mountain Moving Cafe, OWT had a playroom for kids, a simple nutritous menu, and a separate meeting room for groups. A community bulletin board at the entrance has been part of the place, and all local publications are stacked for free distribution on nearby racks. There was a plan to incorporate a bookstore into the OWT, but never materialized. Cooks innovated the use of local ingredients and ethnic tastes, and OWT was the first Portland restaurant to offer a vegetarian selection.

More important than the food was the space provided by Hart for meetings of groups of all causes. Old Wives Tales soon became the place to hold meetings, large or small, announced or

Neil Hutchins photos

THE HALF MOON TAVERN

OrHi neg 98852

Ray Williston purchased the Half Moon Tavern in 1974, located at 122 SW Yamhill in the Franz Building. Fire was the demise of the place, also known as The Tavern, and the building was eventually restored as part of the Yamhill Marketplace. Ray opened his new business as Ray's Ordinary Bar and Grille in 1981. Located on the eastern edge of Old Town, his eatery complimented the relocation of The Embers by Steve Suss just one block away in 1982. Steve, Ray, Darcelle, and Bobby Hoblitt were immortalized by a friend in the Mt. Flushmore painting.

Courtesy Steve Suss

Rev. Donald Borbe   1979 - 1981

informal. For a short time, feminists felt the place should be for their exclusive use and protested Holly's openness to all activist groups. Holly also donated food to various causes and often hauled equipment and food to off-site locations where gay and lesbian causes were holding events.

Fundraising for the Balloon Payment

Paying a scheduled $5,000 balloon payment on the church building became a top priority that spring. Fundraising went into full swing after Troy's visit. Themed "June is Bustin' Out All Over," events included a Champagne Brunch at Jonah's Galley and Pub, owned by two MCC members, Jack Strejt and Jim Nelson. Bar nights were held at The Bushes, Wilde Oscar's, and The Other Side of Midnight. A box lunch social at the church was followed by an auction. Gary Coleman coordinated donated airline tickets, goods, services, and even a lunch with Portland Mayor Connie McCready. The funds were raised and the payment was made!

Community services grew as well. Three gay-oriented alcoholics anonymous groups met regularly. Tuesdays were men only, Thursdays were mixed, and Fridays were for women only. Many other interest groups used the church. Member George DeLand continued leading pinochle and bridge groups and tailored a program for those wishing to learn sewing.

After it became apparent that the new pastor had a good feel for the pulse of the congregation and its program, Arlene Ackerman decided to pursue her career in California, and left MCC in August 1980.

Arlene went on to pastor MCC congregations in Bakersfield and Minneapolis. She is now Rev. Elder Arlene Ackerman, currently serving in the Philadelphia area. Her long-time partner Jacquie Bogle has been with her since they met at MCC-Portland. In 2005, their family was featured as one of four families of faith on a PBS special for the *Religion and Ethics News* Weekly Program. The Public Broadcasters chose four different kinds of families in the U.S. to discuss how their faith influences their lives and family.

Part of the taping was done at Vision of Hope MCC on Mountsville, PA, where their daughter Amanda sings in the choir.

The women's group begun by Arlene continued under guidance from Judi Kiser, Nikki Johnson, and Sue Lantz. They continued the tradition of an annual coffee house evening, featuring a performance by the Fantabulous Jug Band.

The Cuban Refugee Episode

Fidel Castro launched a purge of his Island dictatorship in the fall of 1980 to rid Cuba of homosexuals. The U.S. government encouraged religious groups to adopt the refugees and boat people, and the cause was taken up by Roman Catholics and by a number of MCC congregations, including Portland and Seattle. Members, including George DeLand and Bob Jackson, opened their homes to house some of the 35 men when they arrived in Oregon.

There were some sad situations. One woman brought to Portland had been taken by Cuban police against her will and shipped to Key West, Florida. She was never reunited with her children.

Members hoped to help the Cubans learn English, but the Cubans wanted to teach the Americans Spanish. The need for fluent Spanish-speaking psychologists, psychiatrists and counselors was acute. Pat Cach became the clearing house at MCC for services. Employment was needed. Most of the Cubans were trained in service industries like hotel work, restaurant staff, tailoring and some teaching.

William Temple House also worked closely with the program. Clothing was collected at several gay taverns, including the Hunt Pub, the Half Moon, JR's Saloon, and Somebody's Place.

In many ways, neither group was prepared for the cultural interface. Cubans could not find jobs and became involved in illegal activities. It appears that Castro had grouped many criminals among the gays he no longer

MCC Archive

Eric Cordingly photo

Hal Holt aka Amani Jabari and Don Borbe formed part of a trio to perform at one of MCC's traditional Harvest dinners with Joe Durr. Don is also pictured with several MCC members at Gary Pride, 1980.

OrHi neg 100789

OrHi Neg 20649A

The Bohemian was a long established gathering place. Roman Wydra owned it for its last few years, until torn down in 1973 to become a parking lot. It held many rooms and a basement connected to tunnels beneath the city. Steve's cook was a Japanese man who had cooked there before WW II.

Dave Kohl photo

Bill Dickey photo

Since 1914, the Virginia Cafe has been part of Portland's social scene. Originally it was in the Clyde Hotel on SW Stark. From 1975 to 1982, the space overhead was The Rafters. Many men learned the bar business in both places, including Bill Dickey (center), who later ran The Dakota.

Rev. Donald Borbe   1979 - 1981

wanted as citizens. None of the Cubans were still around MCC after a year.

Another development in Portland was another movement to begin a gay youth center. The Portland Gay Youth Alliance gathered members with help from Outside In and the Men's Resource Center. Connections were made with Ann Shepherd of the Parents of Gays group. Despite such good energy and intentions, no meaningful program for gay youth materialized.

Most gay youth seeking social connections frequented Mildred's Palace, an underage disco operated by Lanny Swerdlow in the Pythian Building, or spent evenings at the Tropique Disco, a dance bar for those 18 and over.

MCC member Hal Holt (aka Amani Jabari) represented the church before the State task force for the White House Conference on Families, emphasizing a multiplicity of definitions of viable family unit structures. MCC joined with 13 other community groups into a coalition to be represented at the Oregon State Conference on Families on February 16, 1980. Among these were the Portland Town Council, the League of Women Voters, the Positive Action Center, Parents Anonymous, Oregon Women's Political Caucus, the American Jewish Commission, and the Oregon Association Concerned for School-Aged Parents.

Exhorters and Deacons

MCC-Portland continued to nurture individuals interested in church work. Several members felt the call to further their knowledge and experience and to consider the public ministry. Rev. Ann Montague from Eugene served from May to November of 1980 as a minister-in-residence. She, like Don, had received early training from Rev. Freda Smith in Sacramento. It was a time of high spiritual energy.

Jack St. John and Paula Nielsen were both in the Exhorter program, working with Pastor Don. Exhorters did individual study, tutored with the pastor, and eventually took a 2-day written exam. They also participated in leading worship and other duties associated with the ministry. Paula was still volunteering as church secretary, and was frequently asked by the pastor to preach the sermons. Many listeners still remember a powerful message she delivered with the theme "You might own the well, but you don't own the water."

Other individuals dedicated to service in the congregation were the deacons. The group in 1980 included Gary Coleman, Bob Jackson, Ron Powell, Glen Scot, Chuck Short, Darl Synoground, B J Wilkinson, and Larry Wormington. Their responsibilities ranged from facilitating the pastor's program, visiting ill and absent members, helping with counseling, meeting as a group to make decisions, and supporting MCC in prayer.

Joyce Baxter and The Legal System

Exhorter and part-time church secretary Joyce Baxter became the focus of a legal confrontation early in 1981. Her history included a 16-year Mormon marriage with seven children in Utah, and physical and psychological spousal abuse. When she divorced her husband, she was awarded custody of the children, one of whom was still an infant. Robbie Coles helped her with childcare and the two eventually realized that they were in love.

Four years later, her ex-husband discovered her new life and filed for custody of their two youngest children. Joyce moved to Southern Washington rather than face the courts. She was found out, and the children taken from her.

MCC congregation members rallied to Joyce's cause with donations and fundraisers to help with legal fees. Don Borbe visited her in the Kelso jail. Nita Gates and Fran Hamilton offered their front yard for temporary residence. Attorney Kathryn English reduced her fees to the bare minimum, but $8000 was still needed.

Events were held at church and at the Embers. After generous donations of the bar by Steve Suss and much organization, only 25 people showed up. Neil Hutchins found the unmailed pile of invitations in his office the day after the event.

The Church Alive

Words and Music by Jack Hoggatt-St. John 1980
Additional lyrics by David Pelletier

♩ = 100

We are the Church A-live, Christ's pre-sence on this Earth; We give God's Spir-it bo-dy in the act of our new birth. As yeild-ed o-pen chan-nels for God's des-cend-ing Dove, We shout and sing, with joy we bring God's all in-clu-sive love.

We are the Church A-live, our faith has set us free; No more en-slaved by guilt and shame, we live our li-ber-ty! We fol-low Christ's ex-am-ple and free-dom now pro-claim, Des-troy-ing myths of doubt and fear in Jes-us' might-y name.

We are the Church A-live, the bo-dy must be healed; Where strife has bruised and bat-tered us, God's whole-ness is re-vealed. Our mis-sion is an ur-gent one, in strength and health let's stand, So that our wit-ness to God's light will shine in ev'ry land.

We are the Church A-live, all praise to God on high. Cre-a-tor, Sav-ior, Com-for-ter, we laud and mag-ni-fy Your name, Al-might-y God of Love, pray give us life that we may be Your church, The Church A-live, for all e-tern-i-ty.

Reprinted courtesy of Jack St. John

Rev. Donald Borbe   1979 - 1981

A Halloween Dance with comic Robin Tyler and music from Full Circle country rock band was held October 31 at the Neighbors of Woodcraft Hall to benefit Joyce and her kids. This time, the invitations were mailed. Even the Empress and Emperor candidates made an appearance. Funds were raised and an out-of-court agreement at the last moment returned Joyce's children. It was a major emotional moment for the entire congregation.

Decision to Dismiss the Pastor

As autumn approached, there was trouble in River City. A shadow of misunderstanding began to develop between some church members and the pastor. Versions of what happened are legion, but several changes in the fall seem to have led to an unfortunate situation. What happened in the late fall is difficult to sort out, but several rumors grew out of proportion (isn't that the nature of a rumor?).

Controversy about Don Borbe exposed not only these unresolved concerns, but became the fuse for some long-simmering issues of trust, communication, and accommodation of differences. As Portland's second senior pastor, he was often compared with his predecessor. Austin had chosen to remain living in Portland and continued attending MCC. Austin had a decidedly evangelical approach; Don's was more mainstream liberal. Predictable factions evolved over each pastor's style and persona. After about six months, Austin heeded suggestions that he relocate in Eugene.

Changes in staffing further reduced the number of collared clergy. Denis Moore had gone to Hawaii, Arlene Ackerman went to Bakersfield, and Ann Montague's time of residency was complete, leaving Don Borbe as the sole minister.

He and his partner, MCC member Rich Pittinger, had decided to split that August. Don soon entered into a new relationship with Jim Murphy who was in a new member class of about 40 people. MCC's other senior pastor, Austin Amerine had not been in a relationship while in Portland, and in the small society of a congregation, these changes assumed significance. The openness of the pastor's personal life had no precedent at MCC.

Misunderstandings began to grow over unsubstantiated rumors related to Don's theology, pastoral care, visiting the hospitalized, and personal life. Some of these were "uncovered" or perpetuated by individuals who felt the pastor needed to go.

The Board felt that Don's attendance at Rev. Robert Schuller's 10th Leadership Conference of the Crystal Cathedral in Garden Grove, CA would be a good thing. Pastor and Roger Bullis flew to California and gained much from the sessions, where other UFMCC pastors like Larry Uhurig were also in attendance. The Board hoped the experience would help with some shortcomings they saw in Don's ministry. These issues had been verbalized, but were not spelled out to the pastor in writing. His experience at the workshop was positive. Borbe returned and began implementing ideas he had garnered.

Pastor also held a liberal Biblical viewpoint regarding acceptance of Christian doctrine and membership at MCC. This was somewhat contrary to Austin Amerine's earlier philosophy of overall acceptance of any individual requesting membership. Austin had built the congregation by being open to many walks of faith and accommodation of anyone interested in membership. While this added significant numbers to the roles, the nitty-gritty of working out differences of belief and tradition had not fully occurred in the congregation. In practice, anyone who accepted Christ as Lord and Savior had been welcome to be a member, and attendees of other persuasions were welcomed as "friends of MCC," the primary difference being the franchise at congregational meetings.

Board members began meeting in Special Session, to discuss performance issues, as stated in the by-laws. With the Pastor left out, this lead to a confrontative situation. One member in particular recruited others on the Board, seeking other reasons for dismissal, taking his position in seeking the ouster of the Pastor. Open and private discussions between Pastor and the Board did not resolve these issues.

Chuck Harvey Archive

Paula Nielsen photo

Nita Gates photo

This symbol appeared in MCC advertisements and on most literature produced by the church.

Joyce Baxter became clergy after years as a student clergy and church secretary. Paula Nielsen was not only secretary to Austin Amerine and Don Borbe, but also performed an act as Portland's Sophie Tucker for a number of years at Darcelle's Old Town Club.

MCC Archive

Early MCC groups found great enjoyment in social activities sponsored by the church. The group above includes Fran Hamilton, José Montoya, Nita Gates, Don Borbe, and Vi Leagjeld. Picnics were held at least three times a year. Paul Tucker, Chuck Harvey, and Phil Krum are in the photo to the right.

Rev. Donald Borbe   1979 - 1981

Because of his years of close ties with MCC, Austin Amerine, although District Coordinator, felt it was inappropriate for him to become involved, and appointed the assistant district coordinator, Gary Wilson, to monitor the Portland situation.

Borbe was invited to an evening meeting with board members, where the Board made a presentation of their desire to seek his resignation. In general terms, they told him he was "not cutting it." Believing that the congregation, and not just the Board hired him, he declined, insisting that UFMCC protocol be followed. He would need to be charged with misconduct.

A congregational meeting was called to address issues, then canceled when it was learned through a phone conference with UFMCC elders in Los Angeles that such a meeting required specific allegations. A generalized list of concerns was then drawn up and presented to the Pastor.

Don and the Board of Directors agreed to hold a special congregational meeting, each feeling they had sufficient support. A letter was sent to all members requesting their presence at this meeting, which followed the regular evening worship that Sunday, January 11, 1981.

It was a meeting most people there would like to forget.

In retrospect, the situation developed into a classic "Evangeline" situation, wherein each party, partially informed with partial truths and with altruistic intentions, successfully missed the stated goal of the congregation to treat each person with dignity and trust, or to follow the admonitions stated in the Book of Acts.

Speakers were limited to two minutes, and were respectful, given the emotions of the day. Rumors had not been checked out with the sources. Accused parties were not included in initial discussions. A "we-they" mentality had evolved. Some people thought the pastor just "didn't get it" while others felt railroaded into a "witch hunt."

A number of new board members had been recently elected. At least one had openly made known his intent to remove the pastor. He drew up a list of 50 areas of concern, although nothing was given to the voters in writing at the meeting. Not all by-laws were strictly followed, pastor was unable to respond in writing to formal charges. Several of the verbal questions, he felt, could not be answered without compromising confidences. Someone challenged and denied the voting status of an individual long-term congregant who technically was not a member, but a "friend." Unkind things were said, and the leadership of Rev. Wilson did little to calm emotions.

Other questions exposed misgivings about Borbe's approach to his job. He had used Tarot cards as part of a social activity, but was accused of relying on them in counseling. A frequent question arose over "is a pastor always a pastor, or is there a time when he is 'off-duty'?"

Don's interest in the Werner Erhardt EST program was also questioned. Part of the "human potential movement," EST (Erhardt Sensitivity Training) was popular especially among individuals trying to find deep honesty about themselves and their past. It was not classified as neither therapy nor religion, for many it did led to a deeper spirituality. EST was later reincarnated as "The Forum," which was popular with many gay men in Portland. Some parishioners felt that these interests were not part of the Christian tradition or necessary in a contemporary and enlightened church. Differing opinions were expressed over how much EST philosophy was part of the Borbe's presentations–was it somehow non-Biblical, or did it even matter.

One attendee charged that there had been a breach of confidentiality when information revealed in counseling sessions with the pastor somehow leaked into the rumor/gossip mill. Some counselees felt betrayed. It had also been Borbe's intent, as a new pastor, to interview all members, with the goal of knowing his congregants better. Some people expressed their feelings that this neared an invasion of their privacy.

MCC Archive photos

Gay Pride in 1980 provided the usual forum for confrontations over gay rights. Several fundamentalist individuals present could not dampen the spirit and resolve of gays and lesbians. MCC pastor Don Borbe walked behind the church's banner, and secretary Paula Nielsen proudly displayed a placard announcing s(he) was out of the closet for good. As Sister Paula, she was a guest on *PM Magazine, Jenny Jones, Craig Kilbourne, Strange Universe,* and *Saturday Night Clive on the BBC.*

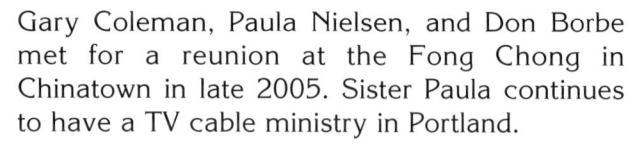

Gary Coleman, Paula Nielsen, and Don Borbe met for a reunion at the Fong Chong in Chinatown in late 2005. Sister Paula continues to have a TV cable ministry in Portland.

Dave Kohl photo

Rev. Donald Borbe   1979 - 1981

Another questioner hinted that Don had at one time shared thoughts of leaving either the congregation or the denomination, casting a shadow of doubt around his motivations.

When the vote was finally called, Rev. Don Borbe became the first pastor in the Fellowship to be asked to resign his post by a majority vote of the members. There had been other pastors removed by church boards, rather than congregational votes.

When asked if he had any further comments after the decision was announced, Borbe simply told the congregation that it had been his honor to serve as their pastor.

There Were No Winners

Borbe's career shifted. Many congregants were disgusted with how the situation had deteriorated. People's differences had been exposed. Several felt that neither Biblical nor legal processes had been followed. An exodus of some dismayed members was one result. So many lessons should have been learned from the episode. A few were.

Borbe moved briefly to Seattle to help friends establish the Ritz Cafe in the Capitol Hill area. But he was encouraged by other friends to return to Portland. With a part-time job selling vacuums at Meier and Frank, he began a study group on *A Course In Miracles*. The group was open to people from all religions and adherence to a traditional creed was not a requisite. Concepts of "sin" and "hell" were seen as antagonistic to spiritual experiences, adopting a blend of Eastern and Western philosophies. They met at the Willamette Center on Front Avenue at Salmon on Sunday afternoons. Seminars were also offered in "abundance and prosperity." Several MCC members attended and supported the group, but it disappeared after a short while.

Don Borbe's UFMCC credentials were not removed, and there was interest in him taking another congregation. Rev. Elder Nancy Wilson offered Don the opportunity to candidate in another UFMCC church, but he chose to voluntarily surrender his credentials at the time. He returned to preach several times at MCC under Rev. Claudia Vierra. Borbe became a member of "The Living Enrichment Center," a church in Beaverton, and later Wilsonville, popular with several gays and lesbians for whom MCC was not the answer to their spiritual quest.

His long-time interests in art and photography resurfaced and he began work with Kodak, leading to a 20-year career in business. Several MCC people who had participated in the congregational meeting later reconciled with him, some remaining fast friends. Two Board members involved later apologized for their role in the affair. Through an EST seminar, Don renewed a close friendship with Roger Bullis. Don has kept occasional ties with MCC, conducting some holy unions and funerals during the AIDS years. He became friends with Rev. Dennis Chappell, and supports the current pastor, Rev. Glenna Shepherd.

He continues to take a keen interest in the health of the gay/lesbian community as it relates to government programs and pressures, and the challenges of Christian fundamentalism. He researches issues of ancient Christianity related to slavery and the enlightened view Christ had of women. He plans to publish his writings in book form as The Tower of Bible.

Rev. Claudia Vierra–
January - September 1981

Rev. Claudia Vierra of MCC-Boise attended the January congregational meeting as a representative of the UFMCC. After the vote was tallied, a meeting was held with the Board and she agreed to shepherd MCC-Portland as interim minister. She would fly in from Idaho three long weekends a month on a special airfare that Roger Bullis was able to secure. Her partner Rev. Beau McDaniels would continue to pastor the Boise church.

One week later, a longstanding MCC founder and board member tendered his resignation with a powerful letter of concern for the "non-Christian" direction he felt in the congregation. He would stay away twelve years.

Dick Burdon photos

Retreats at Boardman State Park on the Columbia River began in 1981, in conjunction with MCC in Boise. Several participants chose to be baptized in its chilly waters, as an immersion experience.

Nita Gates photo

The EXCEL program weekend retreats were powerful spiritual events for participants, who came from several MCC congregations throughout the NW District. Many good friendships resulted.

Chuck Harvey photos

Rev. Donald Borbe   1979 - 1981

Over the following months, over 50 members ceased attending or began attending other churches for various reasons. It was a disaster to the congregation that took several years to overcome. The era of good feelings nurtured by Austin and Arlene was severely compromised. Few ever thought that the occasional quibbling so common in congregations and gay organizations would have led to such an outcome. The event still scars several individuals involved.

Being a commuter from Boise did not inhibit Claudia Vierra's leadership and commitment. She spent three four-day weekends in Portland per month during her seven-month interim.

MCC-Portland had hosted the Fellowship's Ministers' Conference in 1978 and the Northwest District Conference in 1979. At that conference, the choir debuted an original major musical cantata written by Jack St. John and narrated by Paula Nielsen. It was about "Esther the Queen," and was so successful that the choir took the musical on the road, performing in Eugene and Vancouver, BC.

MCC leadership felt ready to host a General Conference and decided to make a bid for one in four years–1985. To do this, an industrious publications committee designed, wrote, and published a 40-page booklet touting the charms of Portland and the history of the congregation. Entitled "Alive in '85" copies were to be distributed to all attendees of the General Conference of 1981 in Houston.

The booklet was a public relations masterpiece. Mary Klepser and Neil Hutchins led the publications committee, which also included Amani Jabari, Jane Sandmeier, Judy Kiser, LaPaula Turner and Bob Jackson. Additional writers were Dave Dishman, Luke Long, Paula Nielsen, B.J. Wilkinson, and Ann Shepherd. Forty-six gay and gay-supportive merchants financed the publication with advertising, and many articles and photos about Portland, Oregon, and the congregation filled its pages.

Unbeknownst to the Portland group was the competing desire of MCC Sacramento to also host in 1985. They prevailed. Although the Portland delegates were disappointed, in hindsight it all worked out for the best in that MCC was between pastors when that conference took place, and it also was a net money loser for the Sacramento hosts.

Sharing Claudia, a close relationship developed between the Boise and Portland Boards and congregations. Meeting geographically halfway, a camp out/conference was held at Boardman State Park on the banks of the Columbia River in August. The weekend was a spiritual and social success, and Boardman Retreats were held annually for 20 years until they morphed into regional retreats now held at various locations. The Boardman Retreat was always a highlight of the MCC year, and well attended. Many friendships and not-a-few relatio grew from these events.

EXCEL

A new adjunct program to the spiritual growth of individuals in many UFMCC congregations began and grew in 1981. EXCEL stood for Exercise in Community Christian Living. Two carloads of members from Portland and Eugene drove to Aptos, near Santa Cruz in California, for the first gathering. Relying on the enthusiastic recommendations of Michael Mank from MCC San Francisco, the caravan travelers knew not what to expect.

The weekend impacted them so strongly that Portlander Chuck Harvey became director of the program for the Northwest team from 1982-86. Autonomous from UFMCC, the EXCEL program of individual and community spiritual growth was based on the Roman Catholic Church's CRUSILL program.

An EXCEL team developed at MCC to include Marguerite Scroggie, Jane Sandmeier, Ron Powell, Russ Howerton, Jimmy Bryant, Larry Foltz, Mary Brady, and Chuck. Trainings were held one weekend per month, building up to an Annual Weekend for returning and new participants. At one time, there were at least 50

The Popsicle-Pineapple conference was a Spiritual Renewal Conference organized to bring together MCC-Portland with MCC-Anchorage and MCC-Honolulu. Through the efforts of Portland member Roger Bullis, a circular airfare bargain was arranged. Participants, including Rev. Troy Perry, flew from Portland to Anchorage for a half week, then on to Honolulu for the remainder of the week. The photo shows the group after arrival in Honolulu. Doug Gay, Nick Eyre, Jack Isbell, Michael Mank, Austin Amerine, and Denis Moore are pictured.

Dave Dishman photo

Pat Cach, one-time church secretary, performs as part of the ladies Jug Band at an MCC dinner. Her life partner Lu El and fiddler Frodo Okalum were part of the act. Frodo became student clergy and was ordained into a women's ministry through MCC. She is the pastor of MCC Sister Spirit in Portland.

By the 1980s, the Universal Fellowship of Metropolitan Community Churches had formalized the organization of the denomination, and adopted this logo as its standard symbol. Centered in the design is the ancient Chi Rho symbol for Christ, surrounded by the Alpha (beginning) and Omega (ending), representing Christ's eternity The cross shape itself is a Greek cross, the shape used in the Eastern Greek-speaking parts of the Roman Empire, as opposed to a cross with a longer leg, used traditionally in western Europe where Latin was the primary language. Hence that shape is called a Latin Cross.

Rev. Donald Borbe   1979 - 1981

participants in these annual retreats from MCC alone. The gatherings built warm camaraderie between the northwest churches. The program continued for six years.

A major Spiritual Renewal weekend happened March 29-31, 1981, opening with a worship service Friday evening with Troy Perry as speaker. Workshops on the "Gifts of the Spirit" Saturday afternoon were followed by banquet and evening worship. Sunday was another worship with Troy Perry preaching, a major brunch and a final worship service, again with Troy Perry. Other participants included clergy from Eugene and Salem and exhorters from the MCC congregation.

Easter Sunrise service was held that April at the Skidmore fountain at 6 am, and breakfast followed at the Plenty Good Grill at SW 16th and Morrison. The 11 am Easter Service at the church featured another cantata, by now a tradition. It was "Alleluia–A Praise Gathering for Believers," by Bill and Gloria Gaither.

In April, the women of MCC participated in the Northwest Women's Conference, the first such conference in the UFMCC. Women nationwide received another cause to celebrate when President Ronald Reagan named 51-year-old judge Sandra Day O'Conner as the first female Supreme Court justice. She would serve until retirement in 2005. There was also the Second Annual West Coast Women's Music and Cultural Festival near San Francisco, featuring Portland's own Dyketones.

MCC participated in the June Gay Pride activities with a Box Lunch Social at Rooster Rock State Park. Social chairman Larry Wormington also organized picnics for the 4th of July and Labor Day, which also included a barn dance.

Although Rev. Vierra had agreed to serve as interim pastor for six months, she agreed to stay an extra 30 days when the pastoral search committee candidated and hired Rev. Jim Glyer to be MCC's third senior pastor, beginning in September 1981.

At the wedding of Alice Myers and Mary Jane Kamm in 1981. Back row: Rev. Austin Amerine, Paul Backus, Ron Raz, and Frodo Okulam; Front row Rev. Claudia Vierra, Alice, Mary Jane, Sally Cohn, Ron Bergeron, Jane Sandmeier, Elliott Dixon, and LaPaula Turner.

Portland MCC delegation at 1983 General Conference in Toronto

1982 First Portland AIDS death, January; *Willamette Week* first mentions AIDS
- Ad firm Weiden and Kennedy score their first big account–Nike
- Fred Meyer stores sold to Kroger
- *Oregon Journal* ceases publication September 4
- Recession hits Oregon; 12.5% unemployment; prime lending rate is 21.5%
- First Lucille Hart dinner, organized by Terry Bean, Jerry Weller, Keeston Lowery Dana Weinstein, and John Baker

1983 Hyster closes its NE Portland plant; neighborhood eventually accepts Fred Meyer
- Former Governor Tom McCall dies of cancer at age 69
- Mayor Frank Ivancie leads Portland Day of Prayer
- Multnomah County Justice Center opens across from Lownsdale Park
- Bhagwan Shree Rajneesh and Ma Anand Sheela shock U.S. on Ted Koppel's *Nightline*

Chapter Seven
Rev. Jim Glyer
October 1981 - June 1983

"He shall feed His flock like a shepherd: He shall gather the lambs with His arm, and carry them in His bosom, and shall gently lead those that are with young".
Isaiah 40:11 (King James Version)

After seven months without a full-time permanent senior pastor, MCC welcomed Rev. James Glyer, beginning his ministry in Portland October 4, 1981. The ensuing twenty months would witness major changes in the lives of the estimated 25,000 gay men living in Portland, which would have ripple effects onto the next generation of Oregonians and of the Nation. A lengthy economic recession would grip America, but most notably, two major cities–Detroit and Portland. Violence against gays would markedly increase, perhaps related to the evolving awareness of a new illness identified with gay men. It would be called AIDS.

Of the eight senior pastors to shepherd MCC-Portland over its 30-year history, James Glyer was probably the most qualified to help the congregation and gay community deal with the shattering of the party-and-promiscuity temperament of the early 1980s. He was the right man at the right time. For a variety of reasons, many gay bars shut down or were relocated. Several popular gathering spots also disappeared. Unemployment in the blue collar and service sectors rose dramatically. Anti-discrimination legislation failed on the state level. Mayor Frank Ivancie disdained "faggots," despite the orientation of one of his children. Anti-gay groups formed in connection with fundamentalist religious groups, and homosexuals were scapegoated as the conduit through which AIDS began to infect the world. During Jim's pastorate, AIDS would evolve from a rare curiosity to a sobering and disastrous epidemic.

Battles within the larger Christian church waged over interpretation of scriptural verse taken out of context. And within the UFMCC, emotional discussions and processes progresse slowly toward the adoption of inclusive language in hymns, scripture, and liturgical references to God.

Jim Glyer, the Man

Twenty-five years of Rev Jim Glyer's public ministry were spent serving upper middle-class Presbyterian congregations in Syracuse, New York, and in Los Angeles. Born and raised in North Dakota, he graduated cum laude from the University of North Dakota with Phi Beta Kappa honors, and was a Rhodes Scholar finalist. Three years later he graduated from Union Theological Seminary in New York City. He was ordained into the Presbyterian ministry in May 1942.

He and his wife raised six children, although his wife was fully aware of his homosexual tendencies. Twenty-eight years of marriage ended with divorce in 1971, and he left the ministry rather than deal with members who would never accept his homosexuality. The pastor felt his 15 years in psychotherapy had been

MCC archive photos

Jim Glyer and his partner Al Williams moved to Portland from Kansas City. Both were immediately embraced by the congregation. The love they shared was obvious to all, and celebrated on many occasions. Jane Sandmeier was the first MCC person to greet them upon arrival at the Portland airport (PDX). She bore a single red rose, symbol of the city.

Rev. Jim Glyer   1981 - 1983

wasted. Two more years of wrestling with "character and determination" to overcome his inability to accept being a homosexual produced no changes. During this period he worked as the administrative supervisor at the Pulmonary Physiology Lab at LAC-USC Medical Center in Los Angeles.

One night he saw a television program that portrayed gays as loving, caring human beings. It was his turning point. The lights went on and he came out of the closet. For the first time in his life, he felt that his life had consistency. He no longer feared being discovered or blackmailed. At the risk of being visible, he felt that gay people needed to be part of society. "Why shouldn't gay people feel the support of the community and of God? Why should we feel that what we are doing is sneaky?"

Pastor Jim then worked on the pastoral staff of MCC in North Hollywood and in 1975 participated in the 7th anniversary celebrations of the mother church–MCC-LA. The same year he became pastor of MCC in Kansas City for five years. Aware of the discrimination he had felt as a divorced person in his former church, he marked the parallel with the judgments leveled on gay people. He grew to strongly encourage gay activism in the fight for civil rights. His hope was that MCC-Portland would play a strong responsible role in the local gay community–to provide leadership and support, and to make MCC's facilities available to the community. He also saw the church's role being that of peacemaker should disputes in the community arise. (How did he know?)

Philosophically, Jim Glyer had arrived at an understanding of the spiritual and cultural path common to many gays and lesbians. "Many gay people have had bad experiences with religion. Many of them felt they had to throw their spirituality out when they denounced (or were denounced) by their religion. Later some gays and lesbians came to realize that spirituality and religion are not identical. The discovery that they are spiritual beings allows them to search with a new freedom. God has many different ways by which we can be led into the truth." (MCC-SF Newsletter, Summer, 1992)

Jim's MCC-Kansas City congregation had been a much more charismatic assembly than the polyglot Portlanders. One of his first series of study groups focused on the nature of the Holy Spirit. The well-attended seminars met for 12 weeks and broadened the knowledge of members. While some critics of MCCs in general say that an MCC congregation is just gays "playing at church," programs like Glyer's and those of every MCC pastor point out the individual search for spiritual understanding and a personal relationship with God.

In the October *NW Fountain*, Pastor Glyer said, "My support system is God. I draw my strength and my peace from daily prayer and meditation. That's mostly where I get what I give." At age 63, he was ready to get involved. At his side was his partner of five years, Al Williams, a mental health professional who quickly found employment in Portland. When they found an apartment near the church, the landlady didn't know whether to be more concerned that they were gay, or that Al was an African-American.

Jim distinctly remembers being overwhelmed when he was met at the Portland airport by Jane Sandmeier carrying a single red rose. Within a month, plans were being made for Jim's December 6 installation. Present would be UFMCC Lay Elder Michael Mank of San Francisco, and Rev. Troy Perry, who would speak Saturday evening. Rev. Elder Nancy Wilson preached at the Sunday morning service. At the 6 pm installation service, Rev. Austin Amerine and Rev. Claudia Vierra represented the Fellowship. Jim preached. Local dignitaries present were Rodney Page of Ecumenical Ministries of Oregon, Virginia Robertson from the United Presbyterian Church, State Representative Gretchen Kafoury, and Mary Wendy Roberts, commissioner of the State Bureau of Labor and Industries. Jerry Weller represented the Portland Town Council.

A renewed enthusiasm and attendance growth followed Jim's arrival. Articles about the change in leadership at MCC appeared in the *NW Fountain* and the *Oregon Journal*. Reported membership stood at 215, about one third of

Don Meadows' twelve stained glass windows were placed over existing windows in the clerestory spaces above the eastern apse of the church, designed to be removed if MCC should ever sell the building.

The Testament windows declare the belief of Christians that Christ died for the sins of humanity. God's victory over evil and death is manifest in Christ's resurrection from the grave. This is the first entry in the Book of Faith, of whom Christ is the Author and Finisher. Christ will return in glory to judge the living and the dead. The glory of heaven promises eternal life with God, release from earthly pain and strife, and an existence in eternal harmony.

The Alpha and Omega symbolize Christ. Just as the Alpha is the first letter of the Greek Alphabet, and Omega is the final letter, so Christ is the beginning and the end of all things. Christ is the source and realization of the Christian faith. The alpha resembles a compass, an attribute of God the Creator. The shape of the Omega is similar to ancient torches, and thus is seen as the fire of apocalyptic destruction–the finality of the life cycle. In Christ, that is hope.

The Ship signifies trust in Christ's power. Passengers trust the small vessel and its crew to bring them safely through storm and calm . The world is a sea in which the Church, like a ship, is beaten by the waves, but not submerged.

The Burning Bush shows the Power of God's presence. God spoke to Moses through the burning bush to tell him to return to a dangerous land. The place of the burning bush was sacred ground, and the wilderness was a symbol of trial.

The Circle of Hands and Rose displays the rose as a symbol from the Romans of victory, pride, and triumphant love. Early Christians made the red rose a symbol of martyrdom. Mary is often called the "rose without thorns." The Rose of Sharon connects MCC-Portland with Portland, the Rose City.

The Dove signifies the Holy Spirit, a symbol of peace since the time of Noah. It brings the olive branch to represent an end to disaster and a return to purity. The dove appeared at Christ's baptism, embodying the third person of the Trinity. The Dove was common on the tombs of Early Christians.

The Crown signifies the Kingdom of Christ. A crown is the visible sign of power and victory with radiating rays of light and spiritual enlightenment. Christ's provenance is a Kingdom where there is both benevolence and justice.

The Chalice and the Host show the Covenant with Christ. The Host or Bread is the body of Christ. Bread symbolizes life. Manna was provided to Israel in the Wilderness. The chalice is the Elijah cup of the Passover. To christians it is the cup of blessing and the cup of Salvation.

The Chi Rho Cross is a design of the first letters of Christ's name in Greek, resembling the Latin "X" and "P" overlapped into a monogram. It is one of the earliest symbols of the Faith.

The Calvary Cross and Robe indicate the Day of Redemption. The empty cross symbolizes Christ's victory over death. It is the emblem of Christ's atoning work.

Rev. Jim Glyer   1981 - 1983

whom were women. Attendance at two services averaged about 180. The congregation was about 90% homosexual, representing doctors, teachers, mechanics, medical staffers, and clerical workers. Some folks were on food stamps and others were upper middle class. Worship reflected the diversity of religious heritages in the congregation, from the use of tambourines, to sermons on the Virgin Mary. A Prayer, Praise, and Healing service was begun on Friday nights.

Through the efforts of House District 19 State Representative Jane Cease of Portland, Pastor Glyer was the State Legislature's guest clergy February 24th. In the morning he gave the Invocation at the opening session of the Senate and in the afternoon he did a similar service in the House of Representatives. It would not be his last trip to Salem.

Rev. Glyer participated in a televised debate in March with two local Biblical scholars from Western Baptist Theological Seminary and Lewis and Clark College. The KATU program ran on a Sunday afternoon with the advertised topic, "Can I Be A Christian and Be Gay?" He also became involved in the Gay Pride Special Events Committee.

Theologically, Jim Glyer stressed that MCC was a Christian church, rooted in the Apostles and Nicene creeds. Most members had drifted away from their home denominations where the subject of homosexuality was a volatile issue over sexual identity concerns. Some people kicked God out of their lives, and then found at MCC that they are acceptable to God, and they could let God back into their lives. Jim counseled 40 to 50 people a month.

MCC was one of seven religious groups advertising in the gay press. While many people came to these groups for spiritual nurturing, they also held the possibility of being good places to meet new partners outside the bars, baths, and bookstores. MCC continued its societal role as a secular and sacred place.

New Windows

Throughout much of 1982, MCC member Don Meadows worked on making a series of twelve 2' x 3' stained glass windows for the Sanctuary. When he had first come to MCC, he spotted the twelve clerestory windows with clear glass panes and determined that he would design and construct a set of colored panels using traditional lead caming and Kokomo glass to match the heritage Povey Brothers glass windows in the rest of the church. He presented his designs originally to Rev. Don Borbe who was enthusiastic about the project. Each window enshrined a different Christian symbol, and took about 50 hours to craft. Suffering from arthritis, Don's hands were easily tired, and Karl Johnson helped in the cutting and soldering process.

The windows were installed so that they could be easily removed, should the congregation ever move to another location. As each panel was completed over a period of about 18 months, it was put into place. His gifts were dedicated at a service June 20, and their photographs were run in the *NW Fountain*. Don's intent was to honor Don Borbe, with whom he had consulted on the designs, but Borbe received the wrong information about service time and missed the ceremony.

Nationally, the UFMCC had applied for membership in the National Council of Churches. A membership of 27,000 worldwide, adherence to a Christian statement of faith with a well-defined church government made UFMCC technically eligible. Nearly 200 congregations belonged to the UFMCC by the spring of 1982. Conservative elements thwarted the possibility of full membership, but a compromise was reached wherein the UFMCC would be seated as non-voting observer delegates. UFMCC's good reputation for work with the Cuban refugees and its phenomenal growth over 14 years greatly enhanced its visibility and credibility.

The United Methodist and United Church of Christ denominations had been wrestling with the homosexual Christian issue themselves. One Methodist Bishop (Melvin Wheatley, Jr. of Denver) was facing a possible heresy trial over statements he made, believing homosexuality not to be a sin. By contrast, a lesbian UCC chaplain in Washington, DC (Anne Holmes) was overwhelmingly supported by her Potomac association. United Presbyterian, Episcopal and

Eric Cordingly photo

Don Meadows design and made all 12 stained glass clerestory windows in 18 months.

MCC archive photos

Jack St. John (left) played organ and composed original music for MCC for 5 years. Pianist Joe Anderson accompanied service and special music at MCC and at Hobos.

Greg Pitts archive

MCC Archive photos

Chuck Hamm and Ron Raz headed the "Feeding the 5000" Sunday lunch program. A prayer circle began the meal, washing dishes ended it.

194

Rev. Jim Glyer   1981 - 1983

Methodist church bodies had taken formal actions recently to bar acknowledged gays from the ordained ministry. In Bangor, Pennsylvania, the first Conference for Catholic Lesbians attracted 110 women from 12 states. It was supported by Sisters in Gay Ministry Associated (SIGMA), the National Coalition of American Nuns (NCAN) and several Dignity groups.

The atmosphere in Portland was more relaxed and accepting. Dignity, the gay Catholic organization, found a new meeting place, moving from Koinonia House at PSU to St. Francis Parish on SE 11th. Masses were held every other Sunday in the evenings. Life Christian Fellowship, pastored by Vaughn Hayden, met weekly at Centenary-Wilbur. MCC was becoming increasingly involved in supporting gay-friendly religious groups, the gay community, and local political action. At a skating party at Oaks Park, Rev. Glyer supported the candidacy of Gretchen Kafoury, along with leatherman Raunchy Robert (Dunn), Presbyterians Ann and Bill Shepherd of P-FLAG, and Commissioner Margaret Strachan.

The climate of Oregon and MCC had also been agreeable to LaPaula Turner, who moved to Portland to complete her licensure work with the UFMCC. After being licensed on May 21, 1981, she participated fully in the ministry, also becoming involved in political action. She grew to believe that it was impossible for her to be Christian without also recognizing her responsibility in politics. She saw Jesus Christ as a Revolutionary going up against the Establishment. When invited to become the pastor at MCC in Columbus, Ohio, she relocated there with her partner in October 1982.

Feeding the 5000

Beginning under Arlene Ackerman, interest in a community food program continued to grow while Claudia Vierra was pastor. Formalized under Jim Glyer as Feed the 5000, an after-worship community lunch was served in the basement fellowship hall. Co-chaired by Vickie Fontes and Ken Ensminger, volunteers ran the weekly meal program by helping with management, public relations, finances, purchasing, and serving. Cooks were led by Ron Raz and his partner Chuck Hamm, assisted by several others, including Vic Winegar and Harry Sherburne. Each Saturday, Chuck would analyze what had been donated that week, take a shopping trip to Costco, then the team would concoct casseroles, stews, soups, and desserts.

Vapors of wondrous cooking often wafted up into the sanctuary during worship. Very few parishioners did not stay to join with neighbors and folks from the street who were invited to join the meal. At one point, about half of the diners were non-members, and the outreach was considered a huge success. A jar was put out for donations, but cash rarely equaled the average $60 expenses of the meal. Attendance ranged from 60 to 100 per meal. Ron and Chuck financed the events as part of their contribution to the MCC ministry.

An appreciation dinner was held in October of 1982–a time to reflect on the contributions of the many people who gave time and services to the congregation. It was decided that this was so successful that it should be repeated every two years.

In combination with other developments, when the Portland city health inspector determined that the church kitchen was in violation of several ordinances, the food program had to end, much to the dismay of all involved. It was never a fancy spread, but it brought people together and added greatly to the body of Christ fellowship. Quite a few unemployed and hungry folk also had benefited from the efforts.

Raising the Roof

A capital funds drive was launched in November 1982 with the goal of fixing the kitchen, making bathrooms ADA compliant and re-roofing and re-wiring the building. "Let's Raise the Roof!" aimed to raise $33,000 over a two-year period. Vic Winegar and Jeri White co-chaired the campaign. Fundraisers involved a concert including Sister Tomato at MCC, a wine tasting at Victoria's Nephew, and a movie night at the Roseway Theater.

Portland's gay mayor, Sandy Director,

The Other Inn was very popular, located on SE Alder near the Grand Oasis and Dahl & Penne's. Mama Bernice tended bar there from 1964 until it closed in 1982, when the Chambers building was torn down. In 1972, the upstairs area was Portland's first Gay Community Center, operated by the Second Foundation

Steve Suss (upper row, left) moved his successful Embers and Rafters Club from SW Park to NW Broadway in 1982. The building originally was a garage. The place soon became known as The Avenue. Embers and its friendly staff have hosted countless shows, fundraisers, and community events, including MCC dinners. The basement housed Esther's Pantry in its early days.

Portland City Archive

Greg Pitts Archive

Neil Hutchins photos

Bartender Cavanall Hoover

Rev. Jim Glyer   1981 - 1983

and several of his commissioners toured the building with Jim Glyer, who pointed out chipping plaster, poor roofing, and the need for paint because of weather damage. Among the guests were Flossie, Louanne Floding, Gordon Abshire, Gary Roberts, and Chuck Harvey. Only $7,000 was raised, and few of the projects materialized, since money was to be in-hand before any work was done. It would be over twenty years before the congregation could successfully bring the kitchen and adjoining washrooms up to the required standards.

Not requiring any kitchen space was MCC's Sunday School. It was introduced to coincide with the 7 pm evening services. Sessions featured handicrafts, puppets, and the use of "flannelgraphs." Average attendance was about five children each week.

Changes

A job bank was begun at MCC by Board member Richard Lusk in July of 1981. The project was aimed at aligning prospective employees with businesses and individuals hoping to hire reliable staff. Finding satisfactory part-time and full-time employment for individuals was done without screening applicants. The task was getting people together and maintaining moral support for those in a job-search.

The Portland Town Council met monthly at MCC. It became the Town Council Foundation and then incorporated its counseling aspects into the entity known as Phoenix Rising. This got confusing enough that even their Board of Directors decided to rename the Foundation as the Phoenix Rising Service Center in March 1982. Through its offices at 408 SW 2nd in the Governor Building, it offered one-to-one counseling sessions; eight-week personal growth programs; housing referrals; public education and a speakers bureau. Additionally they worked to educate public officials on lesbian and gay community needs. The Governor Building became a well-used gay venue. Financing came through donations and it had IRS tax-exempt status. Phoenix Rising, MCC, and the gay community would soon face an unimagined challenge.

A huge number of changes were taking place in the gay business community during the '82-'83 biennium. The economy was in decline (Reaganomics), heavily affected by the downturn in the forestry industry and the cause of the spotted owl. Urban renewal was rapidly changing the configuration of downtown Portland, and homophobia unnerved tenants and several landlords. MCC operated a Job Bank to help unemployed people find meaningful work. No fee was charged. Help came in the form of job referrals, resource identification, job canvassing, résumépreparation, effective interviewing techniques, and psychological support. The service was the project of board member Richard Lusk.

Bar owner Steve Suss lost his lease on the Embers and Rafters, relocating as the Embers on NW Broadway. He designed the back room/dance bar as "The Avenue." The former hardware store and garage (the iron covers in the sidewalk still say "gas only") was decorated with street signs from his previous businesses, and lamp post from the Roaring 20's room of the demolished Hoyt Hotel. Glen Dugger moved Somebody's Place from SW 9th to become part of the newly forming Gay Triangle on SW 11th near Stark.

The Other Inn closed after 10 years of being known as the only bar in the city where you had to wipe your feet when going outside. Supposedly, recreational drug use there was so commonplace that one could snort coke off the residue atop the urinals. The Other Inn was "decorated" with successive layers of holiday decorations, never taken down from the previous season. Equal to the loss of closing the Inn, it meant the disappearance of Mama Bernice Norris. Since starting at Dinty Moore's (her parent's cafe) in 1949, she had become an accepting and caring mother figure to many local gay men and the adored "Imperial Mother" to the Sovereign Court. She had even traveled to other cities to represent the Portland Court. The Knights of Malta celebrated her birthday in grand style with a male stripper show, hosted by Darcelle XV. She told her fans, "I'll be working soon - you'll find me in a dive somewhere." And they did, too.

Annie Skinner's Cafe near SE Hawthorne on 9th.

Wilde Oscars, once called The Filling Station.

Neil Hutchins photos

LuLu's Tavern, originally known as Players Pub, on NW 21st next to Cinema 21.

Sissy's was also Dugos, the Grand Oasis, the Old Towne Legend, and the Rising Moon.

"Uncle Sidney" tended bar at Gail's Dirty Duck in Old Town since 1983.

Marv Almquist (left) ran the 214 on Burnside before opening "mother" Marv's Inn on NE Union.

Rev. Jim Glyer   1981 - 1983

The Grand Oasis flushed the toilet at 243 SE Alder. Then Wilde Oscar's shut down their wonderful courtyard and scrumptious buffets when the rent tripled. The Stark St. Station became Flossie's when Steve had to give up a location farther west on Burnside. The Hunt Club and Tropique succumbed to the economy. The Rising Moon, a women's bar, changed into Sissy's Old Town Legend. At Sissy's, Portland's "Miss Gay Cowgirl" hosted brassy shows combining some "Diamond Lil" with a bunch of "Dolly Parton." A craze sweeping bars at the time was pinochle, and a different bar held a pinochle night each weeknight.

The third point of the "dirty triangle" on Alder shut its doors when Dahl and Penne's surrendered to the wrecking ball in December 1983. The site became the Bank of America Tower. A farewell bash weekend took D and P's down in flames, hosted by The Vanessa, who had helped decorate the place when it opened over 10 years earlier. Once a card room and ten cent beer hall during and after WW II, it became a gay venue when purchased in 1972 by Californians Sam and Gene Landauer. Drag shows in the back "Royal Flush" room were almost as notorious as the shows patrons sometimes put on in the front room. Operated by a straight married couple, it was, ironically, the de facto gay community center of the Portland bar-centric gay culture for over ten years.

Perhaps coincidentally (?), a Canadian tavern opened in Vancouver on Davis Street about this time, named Doll and Penny's. Hmmmmmm.

JR's West and the Cell would fold in 1984. Not as long lived as D and P's, both institutions, upstairs and downstairs in the same building, were notorious for shows on and off stage, in and out of leather and associated gear.

Uptown, Players, and the Lion's Pride withered after short careers. J and J's closing was another loss to the leather and motorcycle crowd. Chuckle's replaced Rosins on NW Lovejoy with a bar and floorshow with dancing boys as well as a quieter restaurant.

New gay bars and businesses made their appearance to fill the void. On SW Stark, John Adams opened a western-themed bar where the Rhondee had operated, and where the Virginia Cafe had first opened. Named after a non-infamous Texas cowboy, Christopher Columbus Slaughter, it quickly became known either as CC's or Slaughter's. Men sported colored bandanas hanging from their rear jeans pockets, using the "hankie code" to display their sexual interests and intents, both active and passive. The Rage Inn opened on SW Washington with a much more sedate English tone.

Gail Kennedy, daughter of Mama Bernice, opened a new leather bar near Union Station to replace the Other Inn. She called it the Dirty Duck. Her mom found the predicted "dive" and poured drinks three more years at her daughter's tavern. Darcelle spoke the eulogy at Mama's funeral. Ray's Ordinary Bar and Grill had just recently opened a few blocks away on NW Broadway, as a resurrection of the old Half Moon.

On the east side. the Helm went under after several years of prosperity. They were a major supporter of MCC's bid to host the UFMCC General Conference. The space is now a Subway. Jerry Quarring bought the Blackhawk, painted over the dingy pink walls, and reopened it as JOQ's (his initials). JOQ's thrived for almost two decades at the Blackhawk's location, where Jerry had added an outdoor garden behind the bar. JOQ's moved east to within a block of MCC, where several members still gather after services, and before evening events. On Tuesday nights, gay men wanting a casual dinner with no attitude met at Annie Skinner's Cafe, run by Ken Forrest at SE 10th and Hawthorne. These were billed as "patrol dinners," and were held in the private banquet room.

There were 19 bars and taverns providing happy hour for the gay community at the end of 1982.

Change evidenced itself in local journalism. After 81 years, the issue of balanced journalism in Portland was dealt an unexpected blow with the final edition of the *Oregon Journal* in

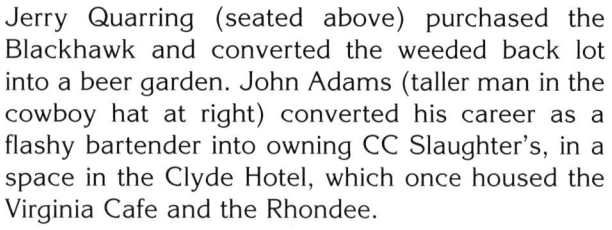

Jerry Quarring (seated above) purchased the Blackhawk and converted the weeded back lot into a beer garden. John Adams (taller man in the cowboy hat at right) converted his career as a flashy bartender into owning CC Slaughter's, in a space in the Clyde Hotel, which once housed the Virginia Cafe and the Rhondee.

ACE Hotel postcard

Neil Hutchins photos

200

Rev. Jim Glyer   1981 - 1983

September 1982. While most staff were absorbed into *the Oregonian*, Portland (and Oregon) basically now had one daily newspaper. Lanny Swerdlow and Neil Hutchins ceased producing the *NW Gay Review* in 1982. Neil then began publishing the *Cascade Voice*. Seven people from MCC were on the *Voice* staff at one time–Neil, Paula Nielsen, Karl Johnson, Joyce Baxter, Pat Kerwin, Mary Klepser and Dan(i) Eaton.

The Northwest Fountain folded in July 1983. Renee LaChance and Jay Brown resurrected it as *Just Out* in October 1983, still going strong under Marty Davis in 2005. The Willamette Week, which began publication the same year MCC formed, continues to serve the alternative cultured and adventurous of Portland. The *Mercury* came along in 2003.

A magazine for gays living a rural lifestyle was published in Oregon. Called *RFD*, it was distributed primarily by mail, wrapped in plain paper. There were only eight subscriptions in Oregon, but it drew the attention of the Oregon State prison censors, who withheld copies of it from inmates who had subscribed. The American Civil Liberties Union filed a suit, and won a judgment on March 22, 1983 against the Prison system. It was seen as part of an effort to stop harassment at the OSP. Jerry Weller and Keeston Lowery of Phoenix Rising worked with the ACLU on the case for years.

In the bookstores, copies of *Lambda Rising's Whole Gay Catalog* were available. This was a comprehensive mail order catalog with over 100 pages of listings, annotated in 26 categories. Copies were available at 23rd Avenue Books and A Woman's Place Bookstore, which also sold a version of Old Maid, the card game, redesigned for light-hearted lesbians as Spinster, with pictured caricatures of stereotypes. Included were Henrietta Hag, Amy Amazon, Phoebe Femme, Softball Sal, Theodora Therapist, Willa Witch, Phyllis Firefighter, Bosom Buddy, and Barbara Blackbelt.

Trouble On the Horizon

A male Portland hairdresser passed away after a short illness related to a rare cancer known as sarcoma in January 1982. The *NW Fountain* of February 1982 ran a small story stating, "A rare cancer has been reported in 95 men across the nation by the Center for Disease Control. It's called Kaposi's sarcoma, and is an opportunistic disease that strikes the body when natural immunological defenses are down." More than 85 percent of the sick men admitted to using "poppers"–drugs like amyl nitrate and butyl nitrate used medically to increase blood flow, and used during sex to enhance sensations (brand names Rush, Aroma, Locker Room, Raunchy Robert Snort, etc.). The death rate exceeded 20% of cases.

In New York City, 40 anti-gay policemen invaded Blue's, a black gay men's bar. They beat, robbed, and sexually abused 20 drag queens and women, sending them to the hospital. Nine days later, the constables returned, locked the doors behind them, and repeated the atrocities. The event galvanized gays locally and nationally. An incensed and angry crowd of 1500 rallied in Times Square two weeks later. Another nadir and crisis.

An increase in violence against Portland gays surfaced in May. "Gay-Bashing" happened several times at Delta Park, a popular cruising venue, and on SW Stark Street in front of several gay bars. MCC became a call center for victims. Jim Glyer and Mary Klepser became part of Police Chief Ron Still's committee on gay violence and harassment. The committee also had representatives from Phoenix Rising, the Imperial Rose Court, and the gay business community. Among other issues, education programs for police officers were proposed.

Guardian Angels, a local branch of the New York City volunteer security patrol, began walking three "beats" in Portland at night– Downtown, The Lloyd District, and the Burnside Triangle (Stark Street). Uniformed volunteers made up the group, which met at several night cafes before going on watch, usually between 10 pm and 2 am. Their program was explained to

Neil Hutchins photos

The *Cascade Voice* began publication in June 1982. At least four staff members were MCC members. Neil Hutchins had also edited the original *Fountain*, the publication of the Second Foundation in 1971. Jay Brown worked with the *Voice*, then started *Just Out* with Renee LaChance. Leatherman Robert Dunn published *the Eagle Newsmagazine* when the *Voice* folded. Typesetter Pat Kerwin was also an MCC musician.

202

Rev. Jim Glyer   1981 - 1983

the PTC by Michael Stoops at their February 1983, meeting at MCC. The program was successful, with 62 Angels in the Portland chapter. Seventeen were women, ten were black, and two were Hispanic. Their presence discouraged confrontations and attacks, and the gay bashing stopped.

A Church of Christ minister directed Operation Nightwatch Portland (ONP) to help patrol downtown streets. Rev. Gary Vaughan organized the group of Orthodox, Protestant, and Roman Catholic clergy who volunteered one night per month to be on the streets and in the downtown bars from 10 pm to 2 am. They did not come to theologize or sit in judgment, but to be a caring presence. Only two gays were in the group, but their goal was to work with the runaways and prostitutes, especially around the Camp. In one year's time, over 100 hustlers, escorts, models, or masseurs had been arrested. This was at a time when Mildred's Palace and other venues for gay youth were not in operation. Coordination with MCC and P-FLAG was suggested at a meeting of P-FLAG at the Old Wives Tales in March 1983.

Local attorney Kathryn English, who was also representing MCC's Joyce Baxter in her child custody battles, wrote and produced a series of detailed and helpful articles for the *NW Fountain* carefully outlining what a person should do if arrested or entrapped by police. Since at least 1979, local police agencies would periodically set-up and bust men on public indecency or sexual abuse II charges. These arrests were made at several bookstores on SW 3rd; in public bathrooms (like at Fred Meyer stores); on the streets of Camp (SW 3rd at Taylor); at Delta Park; and at highway rest stops. At the I-205 rest area in West Linn, men were entrapped in set-ups by the local constabulary. The rest area was eventually closed and bulldozed because of its popularity. It was a situation of aggressive and overzealous surveillance. In those days of Mayor Frank Ivancie and district attorney Mike Schrunk (whose dad Terry had been the previous anti-gay mayor), there was a definite distrust of the police by the gay community. So when gays would be bashed, they usually felt twice disrespected.

In Boise, 350 miles east, certain city fathers were caught doing inappropriate things with youngsters from the Boys Club there and locals vented their disgust against the uninvolved gay population. In support of gays, a march was organized by Claudia Vierra and the local MCC. Portland members Neil Hutchins and Joyce Baxter gathered up a carload of MCC members and drove an overloaded Suburban to Idaho in time to participate in the march and rally.

By April 1982, the *NW Fountain* felt the need to run a double-page spread on guidelines and recommendations for healthy gay sexual activity. Stressing the need for individuals to take responsibility for their own choices regarding health and well-being, the article by Dr. Robert K. Bolan outlined a list of common infections. Included were amebiasis giardiasis, shigella, campylobacter, hepatitis A and B, herpes, gonorrhea (clap), non-gonoccocal urethritis, non-gonococcal proctitis, venereal warts, and syphilis.

Dr. Bolan stressed that people could carry the various diseases without showing any symptoms, hence the need for caution in potential sexual encounters. He encouraged the exchange of name and phone numbers, discussion with partners about health issues, undressing in the light, showering before activity, proper hygiene, and routine and regular testing for venereal diseases. With little understanding of the spread of Kaposi's, experts grappled with the full range of ways the new "gay cancer" could be transmitted.

Throughout the spring, articles and ads in the *NW Fountain* encouraged travel to San Francisco for the Gay Games, scheduled for August 28-September 5. Special travel packages made the trip cheap and fun. Over 4000 gay men and women from 27 countries would converge on Kezar Stadium to participate in 17 sports. Portland athletes held organizational meetings at Dahl and Penne's in April. Competitive events for both men and women included basketball, billiards, bowling, boxing, cycling, golf, marathon, power lifting, physique, rugby, soccer, softball, swimming/diving, tennis, volleyball, and wrestling.

EXCEL weekends were spirit-filled gatherings. Jimmy Bryant, AIDS heart designer, is in the center. Ken Storrer and Mary Brady are in the lower row. Pastor Jim baptized Betty Scott's grandchild.

Bob Jackson was a founding member of MCC. He is surrounded, clockwise, by Jim Gravett, Neal Curry, Frank Myers, Vi Leagjeld, Pat Kerwin, Mary Brady, Benny McAdams, and Harry Sherburne. Bob's career was in TV production with Oregon Public Broadcasting, a skill he shared with MCC. As deacon, he often led worship, served communion, and counseled and befriended many individuals, including Art Dimond, a gifted bass soloist.

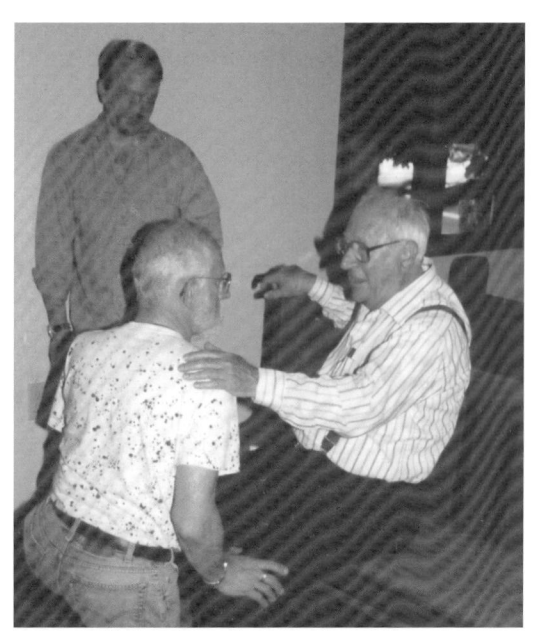

Rev. Jim Glyer   1981 - 1983

A choral festival for gay and lesbian singers was also to be held, called the West Coast Choral Festival. About 20 men from the Portland Gay Men's Chorus proudly donned their red vests and performed, winning a stellar reputation for themselves. The whole week would become a bittersweet memory for some, but a nightmare for others. An estimated 75% of the Portlanders who went on that trip eventually succumbed to the AIDS virus, to which they most likely were exposed while there.

Student Clergy

At MCC, the Exhorter program for clergy-in-training had been redesigned, and those studying for ordination were called student clergy. At least eight individuals were involved, with regular classes conducted by Pastor Jim. Student clergy helped with all aspects of Jim's ministry, including preaching, conducting holy unions, working with committees, and participating in worship with liturgists and readers.

On August 7, two student clergy received the Rite of Blessing, and were conferred the "Portland Stole." While participating in services, student clergy wore a white clerical collar with one vertical stripe sewn onto it. (Deacon collars had two stripes.) MCC developed the practice of making and giving a special liturgical stole for graduating clergy, to be a memento of their time and training in Portland. Joyce Baxter was enstolled in the 10 am service, and Jack St. John was so honored at the 6 pm service. They participated in each other's ceremonies.

It was Jack's farewell service as well. He was to begin his position as Pastor for Outreach Ministries at MCC-San Jose on September 1. Jack observed that MCC was in a twilight zone. The Church was not totally accepted by the gay community because it was a "church" and not accepted by "The Church" because it was gay. His request was that people would see MCC for what is was–a human organization trying to do the best it can at what it feels called to do. Jack said, "When you view the church as a place, you are given the opportunity to serve and a place where you can try to meet others' needs, then maybe you will find a home that won't disappoint you." (*Cascade Voice* October 1982, p 17)

Joyce and Jack were among four northwest Student Clergy who received the Right of Blessing at the Spring 1983 District Conference in Salem at a special service. They would receive their UFMCC clergy licenses at the General Conference in Toronto later that summer.

In March, Rev. Betty Pedersen, once a student clergy, left MCC to take the pulpit vacated by Rev. David Pellatier in Eugene. Palm Sunday of 1983 was her Honoring and Farewell service.

Bob Jackson

While not an official ministry of MCC, work with deaf and gay people flourished under the leadership of Deacon Bob Jackson. Jackson, known to many Portlanders from his television show "Tapestry" on KOAP (later KOPB) public TV, was a leader of the local chapter of the Rainbow Alliance for the deaf. Both of Bob's parents were deaf, and he had been intimately involved with the hearing impaired all his life. Bob tried to help the hearing community appreciate the additional isolation that was part of the deaf and gay experience.

Bob signed most MCC services even when no deaf people were present. Several hearing members of the church took a signing class from Bob. Older gays appreciated this, but Bob reported that the young gays did not like church much. They were tired of being prayed over or patronized. Some churches had treated them badly, or found issue with their "handicap." Deaf people did not like being categorized as handicapped.

Jackson also worked in the larger deaf gay community, signing for the Rosetown Ramblers Square Dance Club beginning in 1982, and at many local gay events. It was hoped that a central social center for the deaf would materialize in Portland, and for ten years plans grew to make this happen. Plans, donations, and Federal and State funding were in place, but the State withdrew its share, and the project only got as far as the drawing board. Deaf men were often seen in Somebody's Place, Slaughter.s, or JR's West signing rapidly amidst

Political friends of the GLBT community: Ted Kulongoski, Ruth MacFarland, and Mike Lindberg.

Gail Shibley (with Terry Bean) was the first candidate supported by the new Gay and Lesbian Victory Fund.

Keeston Lowery (right) was an energetic and creative activist loved by all.

Neil Hitchins photos

The Cascade Voice gave the first newsmakers Awards for gay community leadership in 1982. Honored at The Embers were (l to r) Don(unknown), Mr. Bill, Sandy Director, (unknown), Harold Strong, (unknown), Roger Bullis (MCC), Herb (unknown), Suzie Shepherd (MCC), and John Baker.

Rev. Jim Glyer   1981 - 1983

the chaos of the bars. They especially loved to dance, because of the musical vibrations in the floor. At concerts, deaf people often held a balloon, helping feel the music that way.

The First Lucille Hart Dinner

In the fall of 1982, the Right to Privacy Political Action Committee (RTP-PAC) decided to hold a fundraising dinner in the Mayfair Room of the Benson Hotel. The RPC was an outgrowth of the Portland Town Council led by Jerry Weller. They named the event after a little-known Oregon medical doctor who lived her public life as a man. Her name was Alan Lucill(e) Hart, who grew up in Albany (Oregon), attended Lewis and Clark College, and practiced medicine in Portland as Dr. Alan L. Hart. The Lucille Hart dinner, co-hosted by Weller and Dana Weinstein, presented an impressive array of Oregon political figures who supported gay causes. State Sen. Ted Kulongoski was running for Governor. Others who spoke were U.S. Representative Les AuCoin, U.S. Rep Ron Wyden, U.S. Rep. Jim Weaver, State Labor Secretary Mary Wendy Roberts, and State Senator Ruth McFarland. Among other guests was Chester Brinker, a.k.a. the reigning empress of the Imperial Rose Court Esther Hoffman Howard XXIV.

Tickets were $50. A delegation from MCC sponsored a table. Over $17,000 was raised from 342 contributors. Keeston Lowery, a recent transplant from Tennessee with a strong political will who worked for Commissioner Mike Lindberg, organized the event. Dinners would be repeated annually for years to come until replaced by similar Basic Rights Oregon events.

Another community political event was the 1982 Newsmakers awards, held at the relocated and renovated Embers Avenue. The event was directed by Raunchy Robert (Dunn), Dora Jar, and Fairy Tyler Moore. Metropolitan Community Church received recognition for community leadership. MCC members Susie Shepherd, Roger Bullis, Rev. Jim Glyer, and Bob Jackson were recognized for Community Service. Jack St. John got an entertainment award, and Don Meadows was recognized for his work and donation of stained glass.

Benny McAdams, recently transferred to MCC from Texas, was honored for his work in calligraphy and graphics.

The primary focus of gay politically active Oregonians was the passage of SB 319, a rights bill that would add the words "Sexual orientation" to Oregon's Civil Rights Bill. Governor Vic Atiyeh met with gay lobbyists and supporters, including Bill and Ann Shepherd and Gladys Deitz, wife of Dr. Estil Deitz, the leading Oregon AIDS research doctor. Their son was a member of the gay community. Rodney Page and the Ecumenical Ministries of Oregon also came out in support of Gay Rights and the legislation in January 1983. But Oregon's fifth attempted civil rights bill was defeated 17-13 on the floor of the Senate in October 1983.

The summer was also the softball season, and MCC sported a team to play in the Portland Gay Softball League. The MCC Doves played against teams from PGMC, Somebody's Place, CC Slaughter's, and JOQ's Tavern.

Over Labor Day weekend, Boardman State Park on the Columbia River in central Oregon was the site of the second (and from that time forward, annual) retreat with MCC-Boise. Members from Portland and Boise had such a great experience the previous year that the event grew into a Northwest District Retreat. The theme was "Relationships." The cost for the weekend was $7.50.

Four weeks later, Rev. Elder Freda Smith, pastor of River City MCC-Sacramento, led a special week of Spiritual Renewal services from September 25-29. Of course there was a potluck, workshops, and sermons on "Purple Grass" and "The Return of the Remnant." Evening services were held Monday, Tuesday, and Wednesday. Earlier in the month, she had visited and preached at MCC-Salem, where MCC Exhorter alumni Jodi Mekkers was pastor.

Inclusive Language

Betty Pedersen was an Exhorter who had completed the program. Her guest article appeared in the September 1982 *Cascade Voice*

LaPaula Turner sings at one of many Harvest dinners at MCC.

Jack St. John, Paula Nielsen, and Jim Glyer kept MCC busy.

Betty Pedersen became ordained UFMCC clergy at a service that included John Torres and Wally Lanchester of Seattle. He helped MCC-Portland join the UFMCC in 1976, working with David Rushong and Denis Moore.

Two EXCEL gatherings. The weekend events were well planned by a District committee and held in various locations from Arcata, CA. to Camp Adams in Molalla.

MCC Archive photos

Rev. Jim Glyer 1981 - 1983

explaining the current discussions taking place at MCC over the use of inclusive language. Using gender-neutral pronouns to refer to the Creator, Savior, and Holy Spirit was a hotly debated subject in the congregation and in the UFMCC denomination. She explained the development and rationale for non-gendered images of God in trying to achieve "Unity in Diversity."

The issue of removing male images for God had proven very controversial. When Claudia Vierra was pastor, she had insisted that only inclusive language be used in all aspects of church life. Sexist images placed barriers in the way of worship for some individuals; yet removing familiar terms for the Trinity challenged the worship practices of others. An MCC committee had worked long and hard to gain open dialogue and to discover creative, practical ways to fuse unity and diversity–to honor tradition and be sensitive in the use of "God language."

MCC women in the Northwest held the Annual Women's Spirituality Retreat at Suttle Lake Camp near Sisters, Oregon in May 1982. LaPaula Turner, Sue Lantz, and Nikki Johnson were presenters from MCC. Ann Montague, formerly of Portland, was pastoring MCC–Corvallis and focused her presentation on the 20th Century Evangelist Aimee Semple McPherson. McPherson's work led to the Four Square church. Her Angelus Temple in Los Angeles was a very significant influence on Paula Nielsen, MCC's secretary. Later inspiring her to launch her own radio ministry as Sister Paula. Another Women's retreat was held in February of 1983.

The UFMCC District Coordinator was Rev. David Pelletier, a former Missouri Synod Lutheran. Coming out during his senior year at Concordia's "Seminex" (Seminary-in-Exile) in St. Louis, he had been pastor at MCC-Eugene. He was proud that the Northwest District was the first in the Fellowship to accept and adopt the UFMCC's Task Force Report on Inclusive Language, viewing it as an opportunity to expand consciousness of who God is. The UFMCC adopted guidelines for inclusive language at the General Conference of 1981 in Houston. Pelletier wasn't unaware of how difficult it was to call God by other names, but felt it gave the opportunity for men and women in the church to be sensitive to each other's feelings.

MCC's service bulletins added a note on the back page stating, "At MCC-Portland, we try to use language reflecting the truth that God is no respecter of persons, genders, races, etc. We also recognize that God is greater than any of the limited words or images of our language. If you find that some of the words to hymns are inadequate to express your understanding of reality, please feel free to substitute words of your own. If you find that some words in solos do not express your understanding, please recognize that solos are a time for our sisters and brothers to give us a gift of sharing their own unique experiences of the Creator, Redeemer and Holy Ghost."

The Equal Rights Amendment (ERA) to the U.S. Constitution was a major topic of discussion. The early messages of Gloria Steinem and Betty Friedan still influenced discussions, and the goals of feminists against "sexist" attitudes became embroiled with "separatism." "Separate but equal" parallels to civil rights concepts were confusing.

Language was also an issue in the larger gay and lesbian community. Arguments and impassioned statements in the *Voice* presented many points of view about separating lesbians from gays, using terms like "dyke" and "faggot." Incendiary terms. Historical roots of the Greek "lesbian" traced its origin from "Sappho." (Sappho lived on the island of Lesbos). Scholars pointed out that the "homo," in homosexual came from the Greek for "the same" as opposed to the Latin "homo" meaning man."

Gay Pride celebrations in June were marred by arguments and militancy dividing factions and entrenching polarity rather than unity. A flood of letters to the *Cascade Voice* editor continued for months. A discussion group calling itself TKO. (because the Pride event had been Technically Knocked Out by sexism and bickering) formed to address fears raised that if the issue was not resolved by June, the 1983 Pride events might be the last. A community feedback session was held at MCC on July 12 to

Gay community sports involved the Softball league. The MCC "Doves" played in 1982. Participation in the 1982 Gay Games in San Francisco included over a hundred Portlanders. Art Kranz was a major organizer of athletics in Portland. Volleyball team leaders represented several teams from taverns and emerging gay organizations. Richard Roth, center, led the MCC squad.

JOQ's Tavern mounted the softball squad pictured below, and Rosetown Ramblers danced their "sox" off locally and at national conventions.

Neil Hutchins photos

Dick Burdon photo

210

Rev. Jim Glyer   1981 - 1983

help determine mistakes and successes and to help with future plans. A rose is a rose wasn't a rose in the Rose city.

Liberated groups were just generally uptight about decision-making in the early 1980s. The process was often more important than the end result. Ground rules had to be established before discussions proceeded. Getting things done wasn't as important to many, unless they saw the process as valid. This manifested itself in group discussions composed of both men and women like the Pride committee; in women's groups; and even in the Portland Gay Men's Chorus, where committees were established to make decisions on music selection and seemingly insignificant performance details.

Portland gays and lesbians breached another stronghold of "straight" Americana when they formed a square dance club in 1982. Neil Hutchins and Vic Winegar were determined to establish a club in the Rose City after visiting Seattle's Emerald City Squares. Fighting prejudice on many fronts, the group cast about trying to learn dance moves from 45-rpm records until one open-minded newly-trained woman caller agreed to work with the club. Jan Phips feared her own ouster from the Callers' Association, should she be found to be working with homosexuals.

But as lessons progressed at the NW Service Center, a mutual admiration grew between caller and dancers, who quickly learned the joys of prescribed moves and safe, firm respectful touch. Jan and her husband Mel became proud advocates for the Rose Town Ramblers. Inclusive language became an issue when confusion reigned about how to identify each partner–boy and girl, male and female, lead and follow, gents and ladies? These were confusing references when the vast majority of dancers were all men. Six squares (48 dancers) graduated in February 1983, at Oaks Park followed by a huge dance and party with the Seattle Puddletown club as guests. The Ramblers have continued dancing 23 years and have hosted two International Gay and Lesbian Square Dance Association Conventions in Portland.

Responding to the "Moral Majority"

Fundamental Christians, led by Jerry Falwell, Pat Robertson, and Jimmy Swaggert, launched campaigns to discredit homosexuality as immoral and a threat to family and society. Anita Bryant's messages still influenced mainstream thought. Rev. Troy Perry and the UFMCC Fellowship produced an hour-long television special in 1982 to explain the philosophy of homosexual Christianity and to tell the story of the struggle of gays and lesbians in American society. Entitled "God, Gays, and the Gospel," the program showed the determination of MCC members to bring about change in society as they sought to lead full lives as people, not perverts.

Troy Perry visited Portland that October, showing a "sneak preview" at MCC. He wanted to share the project with all congregations, and was raising funds to complete the project for broadcast to American and Canadian audiences the following spring on commercial and public V stations. For donations over $100, givers received a copy of the finished video and a letter of appreciation from Troy. The program aired in the spring nationally and was lauded for its reasoned and humanitarian approach to the on-going topic of Gays and the Church.

Jim Glyer was the first guest on Vaughn Hayden's Portland half-hour talk show. Called "Gay and Christian," it aired once a month on Liberty Cable, inspired by another cable series called "Troubled Times."

On the Phil Donahue Show in November, Dan Bradley and Ginny Apuzzo of the National Gay Task Force shared the stage with Rev. Falwell to discuss the topic of Gays and the Gospel. The NGTF pair represented the gay issue on the basis of civil rights. Rev. Falwell tried to debate morality and Biblical issues. While Falwell felt gays singled themselves out for special privileges, Bradley countered with the point that gays were standing up and fighting for the basic rights that had been singly denied to them. Falwell's stance on Jews also came to light, after much evading of the issue, when he was forced to declare his opinion that "Anyone

Portland City Archives

Two locations in Old Town attracting a gay clientele included a bath house on NW 4th. The Head Shop is now Cindy's. On NW Broadway, just north of the Broadway Hotel, Spartans Arcade eventually became a restaurant. Today it is Sushi Takahashi.

Neil Hutchins photos

Bobby Hobblit was the last owner of the Family Zoo, a raucous tavern which operated under several names including Derek's, The Tel and Tel, The Annex, The Apartment, and Vince's.

Unknown to anyone there at the time, Bobby Griffith left the bar one evening and, en route to his NW apartment, jumped into the path of an on-coming truck from the Everett St Bridge over I-405.

Rev. Jim Glyer   1981 - 1983

who is not a Christian will not be allowed in heaven." Donahue summed it up saying, "So they, along with all the gays and whoever else doesn't believe as you do, and me along with them, will all be in hell together."

Several well-known theologians contributed to an anthology entitled Challenge to Love: Gay and Lesbian Catholics in the Church. They individually and collectively urged a major reassessment by the Catholic Church, as well as by society at large, of attitudes toward homosexuality. The book also explored the concept of homosexual marriage. The book was edited by Robert Nugent, a priest of the Society of the Divine Savior and co-founder and co-director of New Way Ministry, a national Catholic gay-ministry organization.

Another Christian-positive gay group was Seventh-day Adventist Kinship International. An organization of SDA gay men and women with 500 addresses on its mailing list, tried to help pastors understand homosexuality better and to ultimately treat gay people better in their congregations. Local chapters hosted meetings, dinners, outings, recreational and educational events, and an annual "Kampmeeting."

The Corporation for Public Broadcasting combined funds with the New York Council for the Humanities to produce a 90-minute documentary called "Before Stonewall." A 60-minute version aired nationwide, focusing on the gay emancipation movement from World War II to 1969. The program gave another boost to the education of the nation about 10% of its citizens. Reaction, predictably, was strong both pro and con, but it did elevate a positive interpretation of the issue of gays in America.

In the cinemas, "Making Love" broke new dramatic ground by telling the story of a married man falling in love with another man. The resulting tensions, breakups, resolutions, and conclusion told a then-not-familiar story with sensitivity. It lasted just one week in Portland-area movie houses.

Another boost for gays came when Massachusetts Representative Gerry Studds revealed that he was gay. His home district around Cape Cod was decidedly supportive and interviews with him were carried in many gay and national publications. In a parade in New Bedford, 10,000 fans cheered him. He also reported overwhelming support from his congressional colleagues, although he was eventually censored.

The On-Going Struggle

Individuals still had to wrestle with their upbringing, their church, and deciding the path they would follow. Many individuals found MCC-Portland to be a haven, a place to be refreshed, and a group where they could be themselves and still worship the God they loved. Others found the compromise or accommodation of their religious indoctrination to still be at odds with their sexuality.

A few men wrestling with religious issues became self destructive. News articles documented the higher percentage of gay youth among suicide statistics. One significant case was that of Bobby Griffith in August 1983. Having moved to Portland to be independent of his Baptist roots, he became despondent and lonely. He hung around the Family Zoo, and was known to a few people in Portland. That August night, after leaving the Zoo, Bobby leapt in front of a semi-truck off the Everett St. Bridge onto I-405.

The event received small press at the time. But the story of the family's struggle, the change in his mother Mary Griffith and her efforts to come to terms with Bobby's gayness became the subject of the 1995 book, *Prayers for Bobby* by Leroy Aarons. It addressed his suicide and the misdirected teachings of their church. The story was turned into a musical and performed at the GALA choral festival in 1997. Portland's Gay Men's Chorus presented it to Portland in 1998, with local personality Margie Boule singing the mother's role.

Couples and Holy Unions

Related to the blessings of God on homosexuals and their relationships, MCC churches offered a non-government sanctioned alterna-

Roxy Hart's Memorial Diner was owned by Lenny Borrer and his partner, Peter. Roxy Hart's was just west on Stark Street from 1217, which was The Start Street Station before it was Flossies, now Silverado.

Two variations on MCC logos appeared as MCC churches opened in several foreign countries in the 1980s.

John Phillips and Bill Scott were a couple who also owned JR's East and JR's West on NW 10th in a space that was once known as The Long Goodbye. Beneath the bar was an infamous space, alternately called The Folsom Cell, The Cell, JR's Cell, associated with "Raunchy" Robert Dunn. Business ended in 1984. The Lovely Suzanne later opened it as Blah Blah, and since 1996, it has been Jimmy Mak's.

Rev. Jim Glyer   1981 - 1983

tive to marriage–the Holy Union. A Union was more of a spiritual event, where the couple confesses before God and their friends and family their commitment to each other. Couples wishing to make a public statement about their commitment to each other and their beliefs that their relationship was blessed by The Almighty, invited their friends and family to a ceremony in the church, usually officiated by an MCC minister. Rev. Glyer conducted the Holy Union of Ron Raz and Chuck Hamm to a full church November 13, 1982. Hymns were sung, an orchestra played, I Corinthians 13 was read and three MCC pastors participated. Several other couples proclaimed their love and commitment in this way.

Many other long-term relationships were celebrated at MCC. Ron Powell, a founding Board member and Deacon of MCC has been with Russ Howerton since 1960. Ron actively engages in MCC programs while Russ happily plays the support role. Ron had also been president of the Second Foundation. Another long-term couple was Tom Rice and Tony Longo, also in a relationship almost 40 years before Tom's death in 2005.

Two MCC couples were featured in stories in the December *Cascade Voice*. Ken Ensminger and Ed Walls told their story of meeting in Seattle, being transplanted to Portland by a job, and then deciding to open a crafts business together. Jack Strejt and Jim Nelson had been together four years, and were the co-owners of Jonah's Restaurant. Originally meeting in Vancouver, BC in 1977, both coincidentally had extensive restaurant experience. Jonah's on SW Barbur Blvd. near the Burlingame Fred Meyer Store became a very popular location for MCC brunches and fundraising events for almost 20 years.

Holy Unions were performed by previous ministers, including Frank Fortenberry, Austin Amerine, Arlene Ackerman, Don Borbe and LaPaula Turner. Borbe had performed over 200 such unions during his tenure in Philadelphia. LaPaula wrote a column for the June *Voice*, explaining the church's position on committed relationships. She wrote of the love of two people who want to experience a relationship, depending on God and their own wants and abilities to give to each other all they can. Relationships in a union could be restrictive or open, with it being essential that the mates discuss, understand, and accept the constraint and license of the partnership. Rev. Jodi Mekkers, came from Salem to teach a Wednesday evening series of night classes on "Relationships."

Yet another possibility for couples was a Rite of Blessing. These were different from a Holy Union in that the Rite was performed when the relationship was in its early stages. Usually one counseling session preceded the event, in which the couple was asked to make a commitment to each other to be honest.

While Jim Glyer pastored MCC, there were also several dissolutions of Holy Unions. Reasons for dissolutions ranged from infidelity, to financial situations and geographical relocations. A standard form was completed and signed and dated by the pastor. The explanatory paragraph at the top of the form read: "This is to certify that we, the undersigned, after much prayer, personal effort, and counseling, have determined that we are unable to resolve the extensive differences within our relationship. We affirm that we will be unable to reconcile these differences and that they are having an adverse effect on our Christian growth due to the attitudes that have developed. We further affirm that we now part in Christian Love and without rancor or animosity, resolving to speak well of each other and to cherish the love we have shared as a gift of God."

The Gay Plague

Ten months after the first mention of AIDS in the press, the severity and ominous nature of AIDS was becoming disturbingly apparent. Two years since its first detection, nothing conclusive was known about is cause, method of transmission, treatment, or cure. All that was known for sure was that it was deadly, and that its spread was rapid. The mortality rate was 80%. Gay men made up 60% of the cases, the others being Haitians and IV users. Experts believed that AIDS was sexually transmissible. Amyl nitrate was also suspected as a cause, and

PRIDE celebrations in 1983 were peaceful compared with the contentious PRIDE events of 1982 when divisions between men and women reached past animosity. Jim Glyer was part of the committee facing the challenge of healing bad feelings between the men's and women's communities. Jay Brown, publisher of *Just Out,* is pictured in the center.

Greg Piitts Archive

Portland's own the Dyketones and an amateur group of women musicians gave tone to PRIDE.

Maraget Strachan and the Portland Gay Men's Chorus perform at Tom McCall Waterfront Park.

Neil Hutchins photos

Rev. Jim Glyer   1981 - 1983

use of "poppers" was discouraged. Connections with sexually transmitted diseases (STDs) and Hepatitis B were being studied. Three babies in Los Angeles had died after receiving blood transfusions possibly tainted with AIDS.

Requests for massive government funding to deal with the crisis was called for, but ignored. The Gay Rights National Lobby asked gays to write their congressmen. Without funds, experts could only say "The lack of definitive information surrounding AIDS has many doctors, public health officials, and leaders in the gay community advising caution: fewer sex partners, fewer recreational drugs, 8-10 hours of sleep per night, three healthy meals a day. Basically, stay out of the fast lane, and date, don't trick." (*Cascade Voice*, November 12, 1982, p. 9)

Author Larry Kramer chaired the all-volunteer Gay Men's Health Crisis (GMHC) project in New York City. The group's first research grants arrived in November, totaling $30,000, distributed to five New York area institutions. AIDS cases there had increased from 100 to 319 in one year. Half of all AIDS cases at that point were in New York. Complete recovery from AIDS had not been reported in a single case.

KBOO radio aired special programs originally produced by National Public Radio on specific health problems faced by gay men. Much attention was given to AIDS, hepatitis, amebiasis, and other STDs. At that time the Center for Disease Control in Atlanta reported an average of 3 new AIDS cases daily. Some health concerns were referred to Overeaters Anonymous (OA), relying on a pattern based on the 12-step model.

When the first case of AIDS appeared at a Portland hospital, Jim Glyer received a distressing phone call. The facility did not know what to do with Patrick Cassiday and were anxious about handling him. The pastor was told they were sending the patient to the State Hospital in Salem. There they built a special sterile complex surrounding him at the psych unit. Workers there refused to serve him food directly, and he was treated like an alien.

Portlander Pam Minetti encamped in Salem until obtaining his release. He was brought into Portland by a State vehicle and dropped off downtown with nothing extra to eat or wear, no arrangements for housing, nothing. He walked to where he knew his AA group would be meeting, and when he showed up, people scattered. Darrell DuBois had been diagnosed positive by that time, and knew Patrick. He lived at Darrell's for about four months, until dementia developed. Susie Shepherd brought food on a regular basis. He was placed in a HUD building near Good Samaritan Hospital until his death.

One of Portland's earliest AIDS deaths occurred February 28, 1983. Peter was a well-known businessman who operated Forward Gear leather fashions. As a former worker at the Jelly Bean and The Store, he had been a high profile personality in the gay community.

The reality of AIDS had come home to Oregon. At JR's West, a benefit was held for Phoenix Rising, which had taken a leadership role in providing information and support on AIDS to Portland's gay community. Dr. Estil Deitz, a pioneer in Oregon AIDS research, was invited to speak at the Imperial Sovereign Rose Court's monthly meeting at the Embers in June. Good Samaritan Hospital took the lead in the medical community. Dr. Jim Sampson has been a pioneer in scientific research on the local and national front. Troy Perry came to Portland and made a presentation at MCC on what was known about AIDS at the time. The caring and creative energy of the gay community was about to focus on "the plague."

The sick were leading the sick. And they were sick and tired of being sick and tired. There was little organized care. Individual lesbians came forward to help their gay friends, women like Shepherd, Minetti, and D. J. Dow. They bridged the gender gap and the perceived fragile "gay/lesbian alliance" to set a pattern of almost unconditional help. There was a need for case managers, someone to advocate for the sick, to handle the myriad issues–housing, loss of job and income, health care, psychological and spiritual support, etc.

Empress XXIV Esther Hoffman moved to San Francisco, but returned when he became ill with AIDS. He determined to do all he could to be public about the disease before he passed away. He was a well-loved community leader.

Neil Hutchins photos

ROSE CITY FELLOWSHIP
MCC

MOTTO: "A CHANGELESS CHRIST IN A CHANGING WORLD"
FOR MEN AND WOMEN FROM ALL WALKS OF LIFE

Worship Service
Sunday 6PM
Temporarily meeting at
PORTLAND STATE UNIVERSITY
"KOINONIA HOUSE"
633 SW Montgomery Street at Broadway

P.O. Box 6747 Portland, OR 97228
FOR MORE INFORMATION CALL: 289-0297

WE NEED YOUR HELP FOR MARCH & RALLY "83"

Special Events
Plans all the activities for the week of June 17-June 26, except the march and rally on June 19. Currently ideas for events include:
* Concerts with local and West Coast musicians.
* Performance by the Portland Gay Men's Chorus
* Workshops
* Drag night
* Art show
* Theatre performances
* Sports tournaments

If you can help in any way with any of these events contact Larry at 241-4942 or Carol at 235-7827.

March and Rally
This committee is responsible for these events happening during the march and rally on June 19, including entertainment, speakers, music, booths and organizing the march and facilitating the rally. Please call Renee 232-2515/241-9411 or Stuart 223-5457 if you can help in any way.

Publicity
The publicity committee insures that announcements of events, meetings and all information regarding LGP gets to the media (i.e., radio, newspapers, etc.). If you desire to help call Jay or Lisa at 241-9411.

Community Outreach
This committee differs from publicity in that members will encourage individuals, groups, and organizations to participate in the planning and events of LGP. If you have some time to volunteer call Larry, 236-9839 or Renee, 241-9411 for more information.

Financial
The financial committee takes care of the bookkeeping/accounting and disbursement of funds needed by all the other committees. If you can help call Kathy, 288-0944.

Gay Care
Provides interpreters for hearing impaired, wheelchair access, childcare, and any other special needs of Gays for events. If you can help, call Dennis at 232-5647.

Security
Speaks for itself, maintains security at all LGP events. No one on this committee yet. If you can help, come to a Steering Committee meeting or call any of the above mentioned contact people.

Fundraising
This is the backbone of Lesbian and Gay Pride. Organizes fund-raising events and researches grants and any other funds that may be available for LGP. Unfortunately, no one is on this committee yet. If you want to help, come to a Steering Committee meeting or call any of the above-mentioned contact people

Steering Committee
Consists of two members from each of the work committees (one woman and one man). The Steering Committee coordinates and oversees all the planning and organizing of LGP.

The Steering Committee meets every Monday nights at 7 p.m. at MCC, 24th and NE Broadway. Everyone is welcome and urged to participate.

The theme for this year's Lesbian and Gay Pride week has not yet been determined. A decision will be made by March 14 so that we can get T-shirts, posters, and buttons into production to promote LGP and raise the funds necessary to produce it.

Your ideas on themes and logos are welcomed and encouraged. Contact any one of the people above mentioned, or attend the Steering Committee meeting on March 14.

It is the hope of the Steering Committee that by making the community aware of the various committees, functions, and procedures, that more people will feel inclined to participate in the planning

Please Call NOW

Rev. Jim Glyer   1981 - 1983

San Francisco's Lesbian/Gay Freedom Parade in June of 1983 featured a contingent of marching AIDS patients. AIDS was bringing the gay and lesbian community together there like Anita Bryant had in 1977 and Harvey Milk had in 1978.

There were no reliable drug treatments. AZT was yet to be developed. Acyclovir was used for treatment of herpes. Fuconizol was an often-used antifungal. Pentamital for pneumocystis was only available in hospitals.

One patient died of staph infection after some of his Kaposi's lesions were removed. His partner turned one of his houses into Juniper House, a makeshift hospice where sick men could spend their final days. The house next door was purchased for the same purpose. Jim Case moved in first, and became the de facto "house mother" as others moved in. In one week, Portland lost six men to AIDS. (See Chapter 10)

AIDS smacked the gay community with a full body blow when a former Emperor of the Imperial Rose Court unexpectedly returned from working in Los Angeles in August, 1983, with a diagnosis of AIDS. Chester "Esther" Hoffman Howard had been Emperor XXIV just the previous year, and was well known both because of his charitable work and his dancing skills. Born and educated in Vancouver, BC, he became popular in Portland through his tailoring business and his Leather Bound shop in The Cell. He was very open about his illness, and talked about it in the press, saying he'd rather live five quality days than two frightened and fearful years. A fundraiser was held for his benefit. The illness would silence him nine months later, but not his impact on Portland. (See chapters 8 and 12)

Transition

Jim Glyer announced that he wished to go into semiretirement on his 65th birthday, May 11, 1983. He hoped to cut back his hours, donating 1/3 of his time to the church; taking a 1/3 salary for church work; and doing things he'd been wanting to do 1/3 of the time. A Pastoral Selection Committee formed in February composed of four Board members and four at-large congregational members. A person to serve as a co-pastor or as an assistant pastor was sought. Rev. Jim was destined to be with MCC-Portland for another two years.

Pastor Jim enthusiastically promoted MCC's second annual Spiritual Renewal weekend, September 24-28. Guest speakers were Rev. Elder Nancy Wilson and Rev. Paula Shoenwether. Nancy was the administrator at UFMCC headquarters in Los Angeles. She had served MCCs in Boston and Worcester, MA and Detroit, MI. Paula had been a teacher of English, then founded and edited the UFMCC monthly magazine Journey, and was a founding member of De Colores MCC-Los Angeles, a church with a special ministry to women. Services and workshops were open to all Portlanders, not just gay or Christian people. Issues of emphasis were on women finding their own place of dignity and importance in the church, and on advancing beyond the guilt and shame of external and internalized racism.

Rose City Fellowship

Several MCC members left MCC back at the time of Rev. Don Borbe's dismissal, feeling that issues with him were not handled in a Christ-like way, and that MCC was not living out the type of Christianity that the Scripture called them to practice. The Rose City Fellowship began meeting at the Northwest Service Center at NW 18th and Everett with about a dozen members in 1981. They publicized themselves as an alternative body of worship, meeting the needs of those persons who had no church home and felt comfortable worshiping in a non-political atmosphere, which did not use inclusive language in the services. Ads appeared monthly in the *Cascade Voice*, offering a meaningful worship experience to all Christians, be they gay, lesbian, straight, people of color, white, men or women.

Most of the members of the Rose City Fellowship attended Jim Glyer's installation, dressed in matching dark suits. By Christmas, 1982, they advertised a Christmas Eve service with carol singing, Holy Communion, and a

The Gloria

Jack Hoggatt-St. John

Glo-ry be to God, Cre-a-tor of this world, And to our Sav-ior Christ, Whose death has saved us all. Glo-ry be to the Spi-rit, Whose pre-sence makes us one. Glo-ry be to God, The bless-ed Three In One. A - - men.

Rev. Jim Glyer   1981 - 1983

social gathering to follow. Members of the Portland Gay Men's Chorus were also there. The following spring, they rented space at the former Northwest Baptist Church at NW 18th and Hoyt, holding services at 6 pm. Bill Samuels, Karl Johnson, Ron Powell, Bob Eplin, and Rev. Joyce Baxter were leaders in the church. Application was made to the UFMCC for Study Group status, but the group lost momentum and disbanded sometime in 1985.

Another Portland church drew the interest and attendance of some MCC members. Potters House Ministries, organized in 1983, first met in the home of Nita Gates, as a group calling itself Living Communion Ministries. The living room group grew so that in 1986 they became owners of a building on SE 62nd, near Foster. Rev. Naomi Harvey led the group until 1992 when Rev. Bill Roberts was called from Ohio. He was an Assembly of God graduate from Central Bible College in Springfield, Missouri. Roberts was a part-time pastor until January of 2000. The church regularly advertised in *Just Out* during that period.

For several months after the arrival of his successor, Jim Glyer worked part time at MCC as assistant minister and Director of Christian Education. It became apparent that each minister had their own management style, and that they did not harmonize. After episodes of confusion and misunderstanding, Jim recognized the need to move on. The old adage that emeritus ministers shouldn't stay on in the same congregation held true. Jim and Al Williams gradually became less involved with MCC and transferred their energies to the Rose City Fellowship. After Al Williams died of cancer in 1985, Jim Glyer returned to the San Francisco area. (See Chapter 9)

Portland nom-de-plumes

Amanda B. Reckondwith	Auralee Duall
Olivia Figg	Analee Duall
J.B. Bananas	Misty Waters
Dora Jar	Poison Waters
Mame	Troubled Waters
The Vanessa	Sister O. Mary
Fairy Tyler Moore	Sara Joy Pitts
Helen Gone	Helena Handbasket
Indian Larry	Gloria Hole
Helen Bed	Fonda Knox
Minnie Ann Rivers	Monica Rey
Crymea River	Kissi Dicki
Tallulah	Millie Schwab
Vhy Knot	Dragula
Won Ton Desire	Carlotta
Al Tuna	Bertie Mae
OMONOT	Lady Elaine Peacock
Josephine the plumber	Raunchy Robert
Betty Davis	Auntie Em
The Popette	Blanche Hudson
The Singing None	Fred E. Jar
Screena Dora	Stella Dallas
Freight Train Annie	Felice Merry Merry Jo
Blanche de Portland	Tootsie
Sandra Dee	Sister Mary Rolling Faith
Arlene Frances	Alexis Carrington Colby
Hollywood Greyhound	Juan Hung Lo
Hung Farlo	Rose Window

Signpost at Pioneer Courthouse Square, dedicated in 1985.

1984–*Amadeus* reintroduces Mozart and his music to millions
    •48,637 names appear on brick pavement at opening of Pioneer Courthouse Square
    •Frank Ivancie loses mayoral primary to Bud Clark, owner of the Goose Hollow Inn
    •Hip-Hop debuts at Throw Down '84 at Starry Night; break dancing rules, as does rap

Chapter Eight

Rev. Delores Berry

September 1983 - November 1984

"It's a glorious feeling to be able to unload my heart, to spill out my gratitude in thanks to You, O God. Morning, noon, and night I want the whole world to know of Your love. I want to shout it, to sing it, in every possible way."

Psalm 92: 1-2. (Psalms Now, Brandt paraphrase)

Music dominated the ministry of Rev. Delores Berry. With roots in Methodist, Baptist, Pentecostal, and Jehovah's Witness churches, she incorporated her own solo vocals into nearly every worship service, sometimes in combination with the MCC choir. There was an energetic quality to her preaching that infected nearly all worshippers Sunday after Sunday. Giving concerts and testimonials were part of her ministry. The Portland gay community honored her with a 1984 Newsmaker's Award as a vocalist. She would later become a recording artist, producing several CDs, and touring the nation as a traveling evangelist.

Delores began attending MCC-Baltimore in 1975. During her stay there, she started church outreach to Third World people, and was co-founder of the National Coalition of Black Lesbians and Gays. The first Third World Gay/Lesbian Conference in 1979 was co-organized by Delores. She also organized a gospel choir in Baltimore. She served on the Board of Directors for MCC-Baltimore, and later was assistant pastor there, becoming the first woman to serve as clergy in the Mid-Atlantic District.

In 1981, Delores was called to pastor two churches in Tidewater and Norfolk, Virginia. She reconciled the two churches that had split, aiding the growth from six to about 75 members, and MCC-New Life of Tidewater was chartered before Delores left. When originally contacted by the MCC pastoral search committee, she had turned them down, and she did so again when she met with them at General Conference in the summer of 1983. A third contact found her agreeable to coming to Portland as a "candidate," meeting with the congregation and preaching at morning worship August 19. A congregational forum met after the Feed the 5000 meal. She again spoke at the evening worship.

When MCC-Portland voted September 11 to call Rev. Delores, she was also serving as District Coordinator for the Mid-Atlantic District, a position that she had to resign. She continued as a member of the UFMCC Government Structures and Systems Commission (GSS), The Inclusive Language Task Force, and the team working to gain admittance for the UFMCC into the National Council of Churches. She was nominated to be an Elder in the UFMCC at the Toronto General Conference. She met MCC's Chuck Harvey on the GSS task force.

Deacon Ron Powell organized funding the $3000 moving costs to help relocate the new minister. Senior Pastor Delores Berry arrived in October, along with her mother Inez Berry, and her good friend Terry Snowden. Several housing possibilities were discussed, including a complex of two connected houses off SE 33rd and Belmont that could be developed as a parson-

THIS IS NO FAIRY TALE

ANNOUNCING

DAHL & PENNE

FINAL PERFORMANCE

Dahl & Penne's Boozing, Juicing & Finishing School
Alumni Yearbook Party
or
Kiss Our Ass Good-Bye Party
or
Mame Presents
Tony Mendoza's "I'm Drinking Doubles!" Birthday Party
or
The Cascade Voice 7:00 a.m.
"Is This Any Way to Run An Airline?" Kegger
or
Film to Follow at 11:00
or
Buy A Brick for Dahl & Penne Square Party
or
Buy A Square for Dahl & Penne Brick Party
or
Closing Is Such A Drag Party!

Sunday, December 11, 1983
Closing Forever!

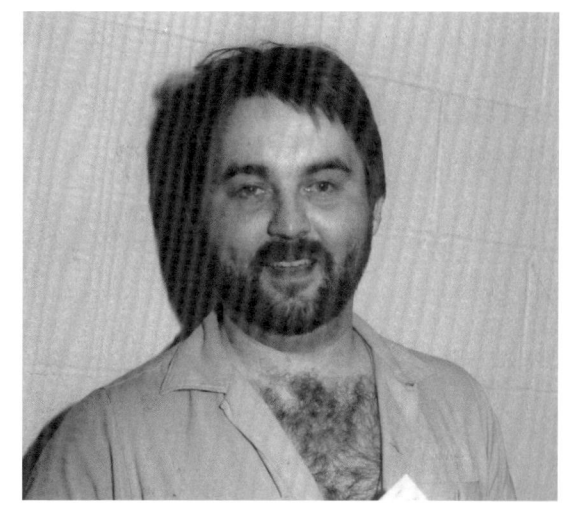

Greg Pitts first came to Darcelle's when barely of legal age. He became a regular bartender at Dahl and Penne's and at other watering holes over the next 30 years. He has kept a remarkable archives of gay bar history and photographs. He wrote regular columns and features as Sara Joy for the *NW Gay Review, City Week,* and other gay publications.

The most significant gay gathering spot in Portland of the past 10 years closed in December 1983. Dahl and Penne's building (Montana Assay of 1884) was torn down, but the place went out in style with major parties. The Vanessa gave her final performance as part of a full weekend of celebrations and bittersweet festivities.

Neil Hutchins photo

Greg Pitts Archive

224

Rev. Delores Berry   1983 - 1984

age and counseling center. Delores became reluctant over legal obligations and the idea was dropped. She first lived near the church on NE 18th and Clackamas, then in Beaverton, in the same complex as Dave Dishman.

Inez and Terry transferred their memberships to MCC. Rev. Jim Glyer had continued to serve full time, despite his retirement in June, and he now assumed the role of Assistant Minister and Director of Christian Education. Linda Tody served the role of administrative assistant and church secretary.

Glen Scott, student clergy, and a very active member and Deacon since helping found MCC, moved to Roseburg in Southern Oregon to pastor the MCC there in October. The Roseburg group had first met and developed with the counsel and help of MCC and Jim Glyer. Glen had edited the Chalice, served on the Board of Directors, and had been a gentle loving influence for eight years. So a connection and commitment to MCC-Roseburg grew with their mutual interests in Glen, who often returned for services and events at MCC.

Glen's formal installation in Roseburg was July 22, 1984, held in the Whipple Theater of Umpqua Community College. It was a celebration with many Portlanders present, including Amani Jabari, Austin Amerine, Nita Gates, Jim Glyer, Fran Hamilton, Betty Pedersen, and David Pelletier, all of whom were involved in the ceremony.

Installation Ceremonies

Installation at MCC has always meant a full weekend of activity and celebration, and the February 4-5, 1984 weekend honoring Delores was no exception. Several workshops hosted by visiting clergy were held on Saturday, followed by a candlelight dinner, held at Judy's. Judy Kiser's restaurant had become a popular gathering place for women and men on NE Broadway, next to Hamburger Mary's just eight blocks west of MCC.

Rev. Candace Naisbitt, pastor of MCC-Seattle delivered the message in the Sunday morning service, followed by a brunch in the basement social hall. Rev. David Pelletier, District Coordinator, and Rev. Sherre Boothman, Dean of UFMCC's Samaritan College, came from Los Angeles. Also present were Rev Elder Troy Perry and Rev Elder Freda Smith of MCC-Sacramento, moderator and vice-moderator of the UFMCC Board of Elders.

Sunday's 6 pm service was occasion for the installation of the new Senior Pastor. Oren Charles and Jeri White played the organ and piano. District coordinator David Pelletier led "Singspiration," the hymn fest before the call to worship. Rev. Mariann Van Fossen led congregational prayers. Delores sang a special anthem with the MCC choir, conducted by Frodo Okulam. Glen Scott, visiting from MCC-Roseburg, read the Scripture with Joyce Baxter. Troy Perry gave the Sermon, and co-celebrated the installation with Freda Smith. Predictably, the service was followed with a potluck reception–smokers in the basement and non-smokers upstairs in the stage area.

Delores was outspoken in her beliefs. As a woman of color, she brought a refreshingly different perspective to the 99% white congregation. She echoed her experiences with the civil rights struggle in her messages of gay pride and the search for Biblical truth.

Delores exhibited a full trust in God. "I never felt disconnected from God because of my sexuality. I don't feel that God frowns on our sexuality. If I believed that, then I'd have to believe that God made a mistake in creating us, and I don't believe God makes mistakes. I don't believe that the Scriptures tell us that our sexuality is negative in God's sight... Remember, the church will do things that God would never think about doing. The problem is–and this is what we have to deal with - that there are people who just cannot believe that God would smile on something that they feel is so "unright". It's just like someone thinking that God could not possibly care for Black people...or God could not possibly care for Jews. That's people's stuff. That's not God's stuff. We need to know what the Scriptures really say. "There will always be a group of people with the need to deny some-

Rev. Delores Berry (center) and her expanded family. Judy Kiser (right) is her life partner, who she met while at MCC. Her mother Inez became part of the MCC family and local women's groups. Their good friend Terry Snowden, came with them from Baltimore. He was an outstanding musician for both MCC and PGMC.

MCC-Bible study groups met in several homes, including Delores'. Groups developed a sense of loyalty and family, strengthening bonds in the congregation. With pride, the MCC banner, made by Nita Gates, was displayed as often as possible.

Rev. Delores Berry 1983 - 1984

one's rights. In the meantime, we can limit the ignorance. It needs to start with our accepting ourselves. We need to deal with self acceptance." (*Just Out*, January 1984 p 20)

Jay Brown and Renee LaChance echoed those statements with a two-page article on homophobia among gays in the July 15, 1983, *Cascade Voice*, pp. 12-13. Noting the Moral Majority's influence on Biblical interpretation, they pointed out how homophobia, like xenophobia, had become an integral part of Western Civilization, afflicting even homosexuals with crippling results. The first conquest for gays was their own homophobia. Because homosexuals had so few positive role models, they had to work doubly hard to maintain self-confidence, overcome fear of judgment and job loss, and reconcile with "Christian civilization," if not their own Christian beliefs. Incidentally, one of the basic principles was to remember that the Moral Majority was neither.

Deacons, Directors, and Programs

A mid-week worship session on Wednesday evenings at 7:30 pm was informal, featuring a variety of themes. Some topics were "Peace," a showing and discussion of the film "*The Day After*"; "*Christian Unity*;" and "AIDS" and prayer for those affected by it." Another worship opportunity became available on Tuesday evenings at 7 pm in the home of Nita and Fran, near the church at 907 NE Thompson These were "led by Rev. Joyce and feeding will be by the Holy Spirit. Let's exercise our spiritual gifts together." (*Chalice*, Jan 22, 1983)

A number of student clergy took classes and met weekly with Delores. This group included Wendy Taylor, Jim Van Camp, Phil Crum, Marguerite Scroggie, and Glen Scott. The Sunday school expanded from 2 children and 2 teachers to 11 children and a division between Beginner (3 years through 1st grade) and Junior (2nd through 6th grade). Ruth Smith coordinated teachers and programs, and hoped to add a junior high level.

The deacons conducted morning worship on any fifth Sunday of a month. Among other programs they sponsored was the Deacon's Pantry, a food bank of donated canned and dry goods available to any members and non-members in need. A clothing exchange was also set up so that people could donate good usable clothing to be shared. Excess clothing items were then donated to the William Temple House, a local charity for the homeless. Sometimes items were given to the Sunshine Division, a police organization helping the poor, especially at holiday time.

Deacons were Bob Jackson, Jean Ringena, Ken Ensminger, Nita Gates, Ruth Halderman, Laura Wilkinson, Sallie Van Helen, BJ Wilkinson, Pat Lynch, Ron Powell, and Ed Walls. Deacons were responsible at various times for preparing sermons, consecrating communion, teaching classes, co-leading the Social Committee, coordinating worship, and providing office help. In addition, deacons took care of hospital visits, made home visits, were part of the Prayer chain, served communion, served as acolytes, and one of them signed for the hearing impaired. Sometimes they made signs and posters, and made sure good bakery items appeared at potlucks. Ken Ensminger also headed the social committee.

MCC had a small bookstore, operated by the Deacons. Various books, jewelry, and other related items were on sale, usually after each worship service. Christian tapes, magazines, and pictures were also available in the basement shop.

Deacons led a Sunday morning adult Bible class at 9 am. Another educational opportunity was Sunday "Discussion Group" led by Rev. Joyce (Baxter) at 1 pm, following the "Feeding of the 5000." Sunday School for children ages 3 through grade 6 began at 5:45 pm and ran through the evening service. On the first Sunday of each month, the pastor presented a children's sermonette.

The Board of Directors included Bob Eplin, Thea Nelson, Dave Dishman, Fran Hamilton, Frank Hiltenbrandt, Steve Read, José Montoya, and Judy Kiser. As Judy and Delores became friends, they developed a partnership relationship and at that point, Judy resigned from the board to avoid conflicts of interest. They are still together in 2006

MCC Archive

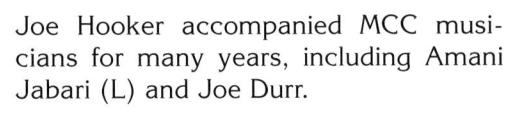

Joe Hooker accompanied MCC musicians for many years, including Amani Jabari (L) and Joe Durr.

Delores returned to sing many concerts, including Vancouver in 2005, where an MCC reunion took place. Dave Dishman, Paul Bartlett, and Justin Vaughn attended.

Sunday school met during the worship service. Children were taught from printed materials and hand-on crafts projects. Sue Lantz and Susan Van Houten often helped.

228

Rev. Delores Berry   1983 - 1984

In addition to controlling the financial welfare of the congregation, and working with the pastors on programs, the Board tried to open channels of communication between themselves and the congregation. In August, they conducted a telephone poll of members and friends to identify areas of interest in the Church, individual needs, satisfaction and dissatisfaction with current MCC organization and services.

"Feeding the 5000" continued every Sunday about 12:30 pm after the morning service. The meal always began with all holding hands in a circle for opening prayer. Meals were substantial, always including a dessert. The donation jar rarely paid for supplies, the difference being covered by the volunteers who also cooked and washed up.

Music and Art

Terry Snowden, a gifted pianist, composer, and singer, was appointed interim choir director in February, replacing Frodo Okulam who was entering the Student Clergy Candidacy. Terry had been a friend of Delores back in Baltimore, teaching at Peabody School of Music, and had moved to Portland when she did. He became active in the local music community, accompanying the Portland Gay Men's Chorus, and composing several commissioned works to be performed by PGMC in concert.

With Terry as director/accompanist and Delores as soloist and preacher, MCC rocked!! Special music became a featured highlight of each service. The choir voted to name itself the "Rose of Sharon" choir, a title suggested by singer Art Shelly. The name tied the City of Roses and MCC to the old Testament image of special beauty in the rose (Rhoda) that grows the Palestinian coastal plain between Joppa and Carmel. Terry arranged "My Redeemer Liveth" an Easter cantata with Jim Simons accompanying on the organ and Ron Powell reading his own narration. The choir practiced twice each week, at 7 pm on Thursdays and on Sundays at 4 pm before the 6 pm service. Terry was nominated for a 1984 gay community Newsmakers Award in September 1984.

Dave Dishman was the music coordinator. The organist rotation included Gene Ellis, Jim Simons, Terry Snowden, and Oren Charles Hornbeck, an eight-year MCC veteran. Pianists were Pat Kerwin and Jeri White. Joyce Baxter was in charge of scheduling Sunday morning soloists for special music, including vocalists Gail Bumula and Amani Jabari among others, and Joe Hooker and Joe Anderson on piano. Anderson was also a popular pianist at Hobo's and other clubs in town. Dori Stubblefield recorded and duplicated sound tracks from each service, and a copy could always be made upon request.

Another musical group that performed for major occasions was the Chamber Ensemble, composed of about eight instrumentalists. Russell Budd was one of several men who performed in MCC groups and also sang with the Portland Gay Men's Chorus.

Benny McAdams, a transfer member from MCC-Dallas, exhibited his detailed "prisma-color" artwork and calligraphy at several local gay-friendly businesses, including Foreword Gear, Cara Amico, and CC Slaughters. His work displayed a fine awareness of natural subjects and sensitivity to spiritual traditions, including those of Native Americans. He was honored with a 1983 Newsmaker's Award.

Pastor Delores wrote two regular columns for publications. One was her monthly notes for the MCC Chalice, covering spiritual topics in depth as thought-provoking material for the congregation. The second appeared in the *Cascade Voice*, distributed to the gay and lesbian community throughout the city, and she quickly became known for her outspoken opinions and challenges. Building enthusiasm for the spirit of Stonewall prior to a Pride celebration, she wrote; "I just wish that for one day in the year, every gay, lesbian and bisexual would turn purple! Bright brilliant shades of purple, whether we wanted to or not. I have been praying for that for several years and I believe in the power of prayer. So just watch out. You might just wake up tomorrow morning a lovely shade of lavender. I guess I just want people to know that they could stand taller if all of us were willing to stand

The Kingston on W Burnside bought Dahl and Penne's liquor license and still is in operation.

Chuckles opened in the former Rosin's on NW Lovejoy in Uptown, often displaying original artwork by local gay artists, including MCC member Benny McAdams. Many of the staff stayed on when it became Silent Partners.

Neil Hutchins photos

Rev. Delores Berry   1983 - 1984

up as one. We don't have to run, we don't have to fear if we would all just take a stance as the wonderful gentle loving, giving people, that we are." (*Cascade Voice*, June 1, 1984, p. 34)

Inez Berry and Delores became active in the Portland P-FLAG chapter. Inez befriended one mother who had both gay and lesbian children and they became good friends. Delores worked on several projects with P-FLAG, finding it a natural extension of her ministry.

Other Churches

On January 21, the local Dignity chapter held a community dinner at St. Francis Parish Hall. They invited representatives from every gay and lesbian organization in the Rose City. Twenty-eight groups were represented. Pastor Delores had worked closely with the women of Dignity in both Maryland and Los Angeles, and hoped to continue connections with the Catholic organization in Portland. MCC was well represented, not just by delegates from the church, but four more MCC members were there representing other groups, which speaks for MCC members' involvement in other aspects of the gay community. Dignity hoped that the function would allow people to establish networks and crossover connections, in order to build the positive forces of so many organizations centered around gay and lesbian issues.

The Dignity dinner was picketed by a group of unhappy Roman Catholics with placards and distasteful signs. They made noises and banged on the closed doors at St. Francis, hoping to disturb the warm fellowship inside, to no avail.

Delores met with Glen Shrope of Dignity on March 31. Several other representatives of MCC and Dignity joined in a discussion around similarities and differences of the churches. Most discussion centered on women and their different roles in the two denominations. Whereas MCCs seemed to attract more women, especially in the clergy, Dignity was almost entirely male in membership. Women historically played a subservient role in the Roman church, although after the 1965 Vatican II council more women were being appointed by bishops where needed to perform marriages, counseling, baptisms, preaching, communion and administration. It was noted that in the UFMCC, women did not abandon their identity as women in order to assume a role formerly held by men, i.e., pastoring.

Another question posed by a resigned priest suggested from his experience with Hispanics that an "oreo" phenomenon often occurs in the church: once a person through education and experience moves up from his oppressed minority group, is he/she not somewhat shunned by his/her minority as he/she joins the majority? Women in the group felt that situation did not apply to women.

Friction between Catholic parishes and gay organizations erupted on occasion. In San Francisco, the Dick Kramer Gay Men's Chorale had its contract to perform in a Catholic church canceled. The Archdiocese overruled local St. Boniface parish resulting in a lawsuit. A similar situation occurred in St. Helens, 10 miles north of Portland, when a P-FLAG dinner and concert of the Portland Gay Men's Chorus, hosted by the local Catholic parish, met with the opposition of their Board. The embarrassed priest moved the event to the neighboring Lutheran church, pastored by his good friend. No need for legal action.

Gay Mormons in Portland made plans to attend the national conference of Affirmation/Gay and Lesbian Mormons in October. Affirmation welcomed inactive and former members of the Church of Jesus Christ of Latter Day Saints and their supportive friends and relatives to the social and self-help group. Education, dialogue, and spiritual development were other goals.

Seventh-day Adventist Kinship International established a chapter in the Portland-Vancouver area in February 1983. A monthly newsletter gave meeting places and offered support in the integration of sexual orientation and Christian experience, alongside spiritual and social interaction.

Indian guru Bgahwan Shree Rajneesh set up his commune in Antelope in Eastern Oregon, but many of his followers spent time in Portland.

Dave Kohl photo

After years as a parking lot for Meier and Frank, the site of the once-glorious Portland Hotel became a new meeting place in the middle of downtown Portland. It was named Pioneer Courthouse Square, after the adjacent antique public building and post office. The Portland Gay Men's Chorus, under the direction of David York, performed at the opening ceremonies. The square is paved with bricks donated for $25 each by local citizens. Their names appear on the bricks. The Umbrella Man (Allow Me) by has become one major symbol for the city, holding his bumpershoot in rain or shine.

Neil Hutchins photo

Portland City Archive

Rev. Delores Berry   1983 - 1984

Muslims and former Muslims had no such support group. In fact, black Muslims in Baltimore picketed at their city hall to protest an anti-discrimination bill, Council Bill 187. Local Muslim leader Ronald Shakir denounced homosexuality as immoral in the sight of (his) Almighty God.

In Eastern Oregon, Indian guru Bhagwan Shree Rajneesh established a spiritual commune espousing free love among and between all sexes. The majority of his adherents were international citizens, which raised suspicions among local Deschutes County citizens when it came time for elections. Sham marriages were often involved in circumventing U.S. immigration policies. References on the status of exclusively gay members are minimal.

From its earliest days, MCC members had expressed an interest in a prison ministry. This took the form of corresponding with men at the Oregon State Prison for a time under Austin Amerine. In June, 1984, Delores Berry, Judy Kiser, Jean Dant, and Larry Hudson visited a friend at OSP, and felt that the outreach program to prisoners should be revived. More visits were made. The issue of homosexual prisoners had been presented in *Just Out*'s March 30 edition. In addition to all the common constraints of penal life, homosexual behavior could be the source of violence and an interruption of the orderly operation of a jail or prison. An inmate accused of engaging in a sexual act with another inmate was subject to disciplinary action and punishment. Proposing sexual activity was also against the rules. Faggots were the butt of jokes and derision. MCC's good intent to help was placed on a permanent hold when Pastor Berry began having health problems.

MCC of the Gentle Shepherd, Vancouver

While Vancouver, Washington, is seven short miles across either of two Columbia River bridges, the drive can be long and the gay community there wanted its own MCC. An early undocumented attempt had not produced a viable group until April of 1984 when things came together. Pat Butler volunteered her house as a venue for a group that had started meeting at the North Bank Tavern for potlucks (someone should write a book on Potlucks in Gay History).

Joyce Baxter, the church secretary, having completed the student clergy program, felt the call to help the Vancouver group and became their first minister. By October 1984, a large group participated in a baptism ceremony, and twenty-five members attended the group's Thanksgiving Dinner, hosted at the North Bank.

Gentle Shepherd did draw about a dozen Portland-MCC members into its flock, some because of geography, some looking for a change, some because of friendship. Over the years, several more MCC women have affiliated with Vancouver. Another student clergy and church secretary from MCC, Teresa Nunn, pastored the group from 1989-2000. Yet another MCC "graduate," Harriet Barschovsky became the minister following Teresa.

While MCC was glad to have a "mission" congregation nearby, there was concern that the loss of members would affect Portland programs. The two congregations have enjoyed exchanges and partnerships, especially when Vancouver hosted District events.

UFMCC Denominational Growth

After 15 years of existence, the UFMCC restructured itself, with an emphasis on decentralization. This was proposed by its Commission on Government Structures and Systems, on which Delores had been a member, and voted on in Toronto at the 11th General Conference. Major changes recognized the need for a Director of Administration, for special outreach ministries to Hispanics, feminists, and international missions. Rev. Troy Perry needed freedom from administrative duties to be able to travel to places with special needs, fighting the Moral Majority, working with the media, etc.

The UFMCC denomination had been expanding the definitions of its mission into 9 countries. International MCC churches grew in England, Australia, and Africa. It was not the sexual issue that brought UFMCC into Nigeria, but rather the prejudice against people within

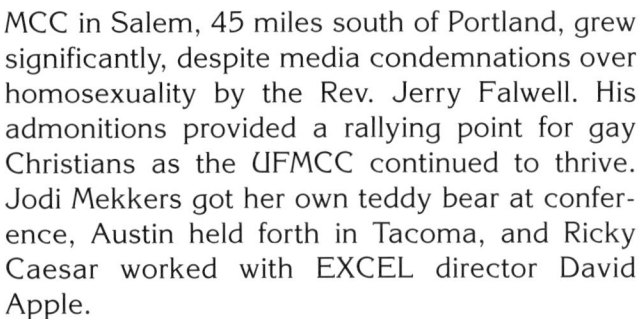

MCC in Salem, 45 miles south of Portland, grew significantly, despite media condemnations over homosexuality by the Rev. Jerry Falwell. His admonitions provided a rallying point for gay Christians as the UFMCC continued to thrive. Jodi Mekkers got her own teddy bear at conference, Austin held forth in Tacoma, and Ricky Caesar worked with EXCEL director David Apple.

Rev. Delores Berry 1983 - 1984

the system there. Specifically, the people of Biafra were the focus, as they had been badly treated in the civil war. The vision was to show the love of God to all people.

The Fellowship was also working through its application to become recognized by the National Council of Churches. By qualifying for membership, UFMCC presented the NCC with a chance to meet gay people in a religious context. Troy Perry felt that three victories had been won in 1984:
  1) The NCC agreed that they sinned, in that they could not come to terms with human sexuality, and that the issue of homosexuality is their fault, not ours;
  2) The NCC postponed the vote on MCC eligibility when they could have denied it; and
  3) The NCC agreed to continue to dialogue with the UFMCC (*Just Out*, March 16, 1984)

Rev. Jerry Falwell railed against the UFMCC on his July 13, 1984 radio, "Old Time Gospel Hour." He said the MCC was "A brute beast... A vile and Satanic system..., which would one day be utterly annihilated and there would be a celebration in Heaven." He later denied his statements and was eventually forced to pay a $5000 defamation settlement in a court case brought by MCC minister Jerry Sloan, who had been a classmate of Falwell's at Baptist College in Springfield, MO in the 1950s.

Spiritual needs of Jewish gays and lesbians were addressed that summer at their 8th International Conference in Miami. Religious services and dinners augmented workshops on "The Future of the Gay/Lesbian Jew in the Brave New World," "Tradition–the Glue that Keeps Us Together," and "Do Your Parents Know Where You Are?"

"Partners in the Gospel" was the theme of MCC's Northwest District Conference in Eugene in the fall of 1984. Only 100 miles south of Portland, MCC members took advantage of the Conference's proximity. Encompassing a diverse geography, almost 200 delegates were in attendance, representing Alaska, Hawaii, Utah, Idaho, Nevada, Oregon, Washington and California.

MCC Social Life

Food and fellowship also often followed the evening worship. Many hands made light work. One month, volunteers who provided food and clean-up included Vi Leagjeld, Jackie Wilkinson, Gerry Ann Hale, Nikki Johnson, Sue Lantz, Stephanie H, Jean Ringena, Melody Hedrick, Laura Wilkinson, Inez Berry, Marty Conway, Cat Granado, Pastor Delores, and Susan Chrusokie.

Several groups were active throughout the month. A men's group met each second and fourth Friday evening. This was basically a support group, providing a forum to share interests and concerns. Weekly support groups on the 12-step model used the MCC facility. Thursdays at 7:30 pm were scheduled for the "On Broadway" AA group. There was also an Al-Anon gathering. The Live and Let Live Club, a group maintained for 12-step as well as social purposes for the Gay and Lesbian community, moved their meetings to their own space at 2707 SE Belmont.

Women met on an irregular basis just for support, but they sponsored and participated in many other programs, seasonal meals, activities and functions. They organized an annual "Coffeehouse" in March, raising funds to send members to the NW District Women's Spiritual Retreat. Coffeehouse evenings were fun-filled presentations of singing, acting, poetry reading, etc.

Bob Jackson's love of theater manifested itself in a Theater Study Group. Not a performance organization, they focused on attending plays, reading scripts, and discussing productions, plots, and performances. The group was large, the laughter contagious, and of course, there had to be food.

AIDS, HTLV-III, HIV, and PALs

Portland's first organized response to AIDS was an ad hoc support group of men in the Portland Gay Men's Chorus, first meeting in February of 1983. Without a name or mission statement, they simply started meeting because they had been diagnosed with the condition, or with ARC (AIDS-related Complex) or PGL

AIDS began effecting Portlanders in 1982. Darrell DuBois (L) was initially diagnosed with Aids Related Complex, and worked with the earliest suppport groups. His friend and fellow member of both MCC and PGMC succumbed, as did local theatric artist Ric Young.

Healing services became part of many MCC events. Other men continued living with AIDS with humor and resolve, like Robert Paul Dunn.

Rev. Delores Berry   1983 - 1984

(Persistent Generalized Lymphadenopathy). There were men whose partners had already died or had AIDS, a mother and her diagnosed son, and men who accompanied their friends who had AIDS. Meeting in various homes, there was the inevitable potluck. The group grew in number to about 25, at least half of who were, coincidentally, MCC members.

Isoprenozine and rivibyran were two experimental drugs rumored to have positive effects on AIDS, but not approved by the FDA. The Tooth Fairy Report, a national underground newspaper, reported that they were available in Mexico. Darrell Dobbs and Jim Case collected $4000 from group members wanting to try the drugs. They then drove to Tijuana, walked across the border, and acquired the pills, bringing them back in shopping bags and wrapped in a serape. In the week that it took to make the trip, two of the group members ordering the drugs had passed away.

Pastor Delores received a phone message from a local hospital about a patient with an unknown disease. He was married, but had revealed his homosexuality to his wife and children, who were supportive. Delores met with the man, his family, and his partner. In spite of his isolation in the ward, he was visited and nurtured constantly through his disease by this group. Delores found a special mission in bringing God's love and assurance to one who felt so isolated. She felt privileged to conduct his funeral at a local mortuary.

Brown MacDonald saw the need for someone in Portland to take a positive step in preventing AIDS. He organized a group to be called the Cascade AIDS Project (CAP) in 1983, specifically focused on education and prevention. Portland physicians, immune deficient patients, and other concerned citizens joined the organization, formed under the wing of the Phoenix Rising Foundation. Reese House took a leading role in initiating discussion and support counseling. Phoenix Rising formed its first AIDS support group and began fundraising to publish information pamphlets.

The scope of CAP did not include services to ill people, but concentrated on getting facts into the awareness of as many Portlanders as possible. When CAP publications were inaccurate in their statements about levels of care and services available, a group of clients took over their offices in the Governor building until CAP leaders agreed to "tell it like it is."

The Fifth National Lesbian and Gay Health Conference gathered 38 separate organizations in Denver in June 1983. They formed a federation of AIDS groups as an information and resource network. The Women's AIDS Network was established at the same conference. Dr. James Curran, overseer of AIDS studies for the Center for Disease Control in Atlanta advised the group to think of AIDS as a health issue first and a political issue second. He recommended developing models of prevention as the highest priority to which health professionals could dedicate themselves.

In the fall, CAP held an AIDS forum in connection with Good Samaritan Hospital for medical professionals and the community at large. Three men with AIDS addressed the group. Jim Case talked about how CAP needed to help physicians in diagnosis and in their presentation to AIDS-positive men first learning of their condition. Darrell DuBois, whose diagnosis at the time was ARC, talked about safe sex techniques and the need for diagnosed men to contact their past sexual partners. A PGMC member talked of the lack of medical treatment, and the need for new and alternative treatments. There were 12 reported AIDS cases in Oregon, and 6 fatalities were attributed to the condition. Connections with hepatitis-B were also being investigated.

By 1984, the AIDS situation was recognized to be epidemic in major cities. Some "experts" felt there was hope for smaller towns, like Portland, to be able to control its spread through education programs. UFMCC and local congregations were actively dealing with the crisis. At that point, this meant raising funds for research and medical help; visiting victims in hospitals; comforting friends and family; and evolving styles of funeral services and memorial celebra-

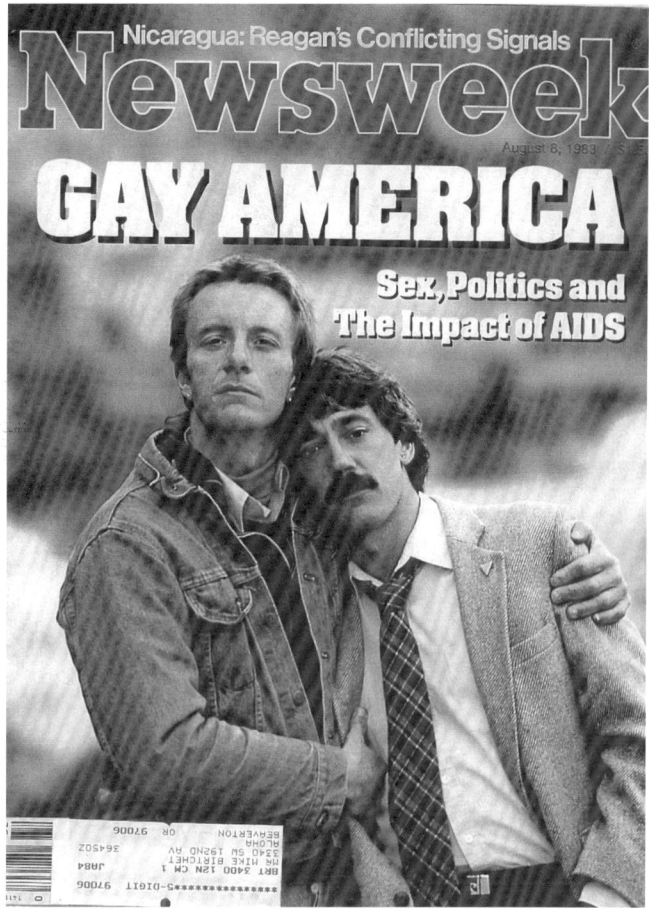

The issue of AIDS drew national attention in 1983 with *Newsweek* cover story. AIDS was labeled originally as the "gay cancer" and became set in the public's perception as a gay disease. Haitians and hemophiliacs were two other groups prone to early AIDS infection.

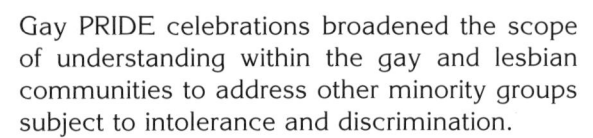

Gay PRIDE celebrations broadened the scope of understanding within the gay and lesbian communities to address other minority groups subject to intolerance and discrimination.

The Bonfire was a popular gathering place for many gay men after work downtown. It was located on the ground floor of the old Imperial Hotel, whose lower mens room was a popular gay rendezvous spot in the 1920s. The Richardsonian brick structure had become vacant and run down prior to its designation on the national Register. Following a long renovation, it is now the Hotel Vintage Plaza.

Rev. Delores Berry   1983 - 1984

tions. Young and middle-aged men were suddenly faced with contracting a fatal disease. Friends, partners and family were tending to the physical and emotional needs of loved ones who could die within weeks. Some healthy gay men felt guilty that they were not sick when their best friends were experiencing a miserable death. Some men were diagnosed with a variant condition called Aids Related Complex (ARC). MCC member Darrell Dobbs participated in an ARC support group formed in 1983 and became an activist advocating locally and in Salem for the needs of persons with AIDS. In 2005, he is the sole survivor from that group of 25.

On April 18, 1984, Department of Health and Human Services Secretary Margaret Heckler made an announcement trying to clarify several new AIDS-related discoveries. A virus had been discovered by researchers in Paris, the Centers for Disease Control in Atlanta revealed research on a different virus, and another discovery was revealed by the National Institute of Health. Dr. Robert Gallo, who first described retroviruses in 1980, had isolated a third variant of Human T-cell Leukemia Virus (HTLV-3), which yielded conclusive evidence leading to an "AIDS Virus." There had been cooperation with French research on Lymphadenopa Associated Virus (LAV), but political motivation within the health bureaucracy had gotten the upper hand over medical fact.

The virus leading to full-blown AIDS became identified at HIV (Human Immuno-deficiency Virus). The discovery of a "prime suspect" offered hope for an eventual diagnostic test, prevention, and cure for AIDS. By July, Portland-based Lazuli Research Foundation was investigating Isoprinosine for its curative properties. These were false hopes.

Former XXIV Empress of the Rose Court Chester Esther Hoffman/Howard Brinker became gravely ill with AIDS in April 1984. Friends rallied to gather donations for the well-known female impersonator. His willingness to discuss and be open about the painful and frightening final chapter of his life brought home the devastating realities of AIDS to Portland. Esther appeared on the Town Hall TV show, in a program called "Humanizing the Face of AIDS."

In advertising the program, KATU had used silhouettes of the individuals who would appear. Darrell Dubois, Brown McDonald, and Esther refused to be over dramatized in that way on the show. Their purpose in appearing was to show that AIDS people are real people, whereas the producers had planned to create a "we-they" situation, using a title of "Are you Safe from AIDS?" The men prevailed. The show presented balanced information.

Esther reentered the hospital, checked himself out of Good Samaritan and returned to his home, where he passed away May 4, at the age of 35.

At David Lee's fundraiser at JR's West it was announced that a new fund would be established, tentatively called the Chester Esther Medical Fund. The fund in his honor would eventually morph into the Brinker fund to help with finances for those with AIDS, and Esther's Pantry, the primary food bank for those with AIDS in Portland. First overseen by CAP, and operated out of the basement of the Embers, then a storefront on NW Broadway, it became an outreach of MCC Portland in 2001. (See chapter 12)

Celebrating its fourth anniversary, the Portland Gay Men's Chorus held a benefit concert to raise funds to benefit AIDS programs. Called "Our Best To You," it presented favorite songs from 20 previous concerts at the June 1984 concert at the Eastside Performance Center. PGMC lost its first member to AIDS when Jim Schelot succumbed the following month. Funds raised were directed toward the start up of the PAL Program, under the 501 c 3 umbrella of Phoenix Rising.

CHESS (Community Health and Essential Support Services) also came about because of Chester Brinker's death. Honoring Chester's deathbed wish to do "something," Steve Fulmer donated funds to start a program which provided direct services to people with HIV or AIDS, coordinating with the PAL program. Steve had been active in the gay community since the days of the Second Foundation, and was a founder of PGMC. In 1986, CHESS and the PAL program merged with the Cascade Aids Project (CAP).

Bar owner and neighborhood activist Bud Clark decided to challenge the incumbent Mayor Frank Ivancie and launched a successful campaign. He brought his campaign to the gay community at the Dirty Duck, where he is seen with MCC member Keith Nofziger. Well-known for his laugh and flexability with public art, he was the anti-thesis of his opponent. Bud appeared at Hobo's for a fundraiser, shown here with Rosey Waters (aka Robert Hill). After his victory, one of his celebrations was held at the Dirty Duck, where he danced with Linda Norris as her mother, Mama Bernice, looked on.

Neil Hutchins photos

Rev. Delores Berry 1983 - 1984

Personal Active Listeners (PALs) were volunteers trained over 44 hours to become support persons for AIDS patients. A PAL was paired with one patient or client and shared and supported that person throughout the AIDS process, helping by listening, advocating, filling out forms, driving them to medical visits, helping with domestic tasks, and whatever else that came up. It was an exhausting process for many PAL but one that they would come to see as an invaluable and life-changing experience.

When "Raunchy" Robert Paul Dunn assumed responsibility for owning the *Cascade Voice*, he firmly declared a manifesto in his first editorial. "We will harbor no unwarranted radicalisms that deliver only the messages of self pity and destruction and defeatism. We will strive to analyze what the world is handing us about AIDS, our most deadly disease. We will continue to work in and with other media that serves the lesbian and gay community... We will continue to probe and search out the intricate and intimate and intelligent ways we relate to ourselves, each other and all the segments of society." (*Cascade Voice* September 1, 1984 p 3)

Bud Clark and Political Changes

Amidst all the disconcerting health developments, Portland's gay community supported the candidacy of a renegade neighborhood activist and local tavern owner in the 1984 May primary mayoral race. Bud Clark, the dark horse, won a resounding victory over entrenched incumbent Frank Ivancie. His landslide primary victory eliminated the need for a fall campaign. Earlier mayors Neil Goldschmidt and Connie McCready had been far more gay-friendly than the homophobic Ivancie.

Clark's campaign mushroomed from grass roots interest groups and the overwhelming support of the gay community. He had spent years as a neighborhood volunteer, working with Meals on Wheels and the Northwest Neighborhood Association, and creating the *Neighbor*, one of the better community newspapers in the city. His NW Portland neighbor Vera Katz gave him moral support. Campaigning at several local gay spots, he held rallies at his own Goose Hollow Inn, a dinner at Hobo's, a Chinese auction fundraiser at JOQ's, and held a victory celebration at the Dirty Duck. Darcelle, his 1949 Lincoln High school classmate, was master of ceremonies.

In 1978 Mike Ryerson had snapped a photo behind Bud wearing his usual bicycle boots, shorts, and trench coat in front of a Portland street sculpture. A contest was held with a $25 prize to name the photo. In those racy days of streakers, the winning title was "Expose Yourself to Art." It became an instant bestseller, and along with Bud's signature "whoop-whoop," assured his reputation.

The significance of Clark's victory was that a grass roots campaign had unseated an old Portland icon. The gay community had rallied for a cause beyond their immediate concerns. There was hope for more triumphs at the ballot box. Governor Victor Atiyeh was still pledging to veto any gay civil rights legislation, and Ivancie had hoped to run as the next governor. Power to the People!

In the fall elections, former Multnomah County Commissioner Gladys McCoy won a seat on the Portland City Council. Along with Representatives Vera Katz and Gretchen Kafoury, Gladys boldly led battles to overcome racial and sexual discrimination policies for years to come. Another friend of the gay community, Barbara Roberts was elected Secretary of State, and would one day be Governor.

Jerry Weller, who for seven years had served Oregon's lesbian and gay community by leading the Portland Town Council, Town Council Foundation, Phoenix Rising Foundation, and the Right to Privacy PAC, moved to Washington, DC to work with the National Gay Task Force. He named Metropolitan Community Church as one of the outstanding supporters of political and health projects in the community.

From the nations Capitol, he continued to work for AIDS awareness, working for the only organization lobbying Congress on behalf of 25 million lesbian and gay Americans. He worked with Senator Gary Hart (D-CO) to co-

Neil Hutchins photos

Incomparable hamburgers and a laid-back atmosphere was the hallmark of Hamburger Mary's at SW Park and Taylor. It was the first place in Portland to offer coffee cream in baby bottles with sawed-off nipples.

MCC member Dave Sorber opened the Hunt Pub on SW Morrison in the old Lincoln Hotel, where Gregory's had previously operated.

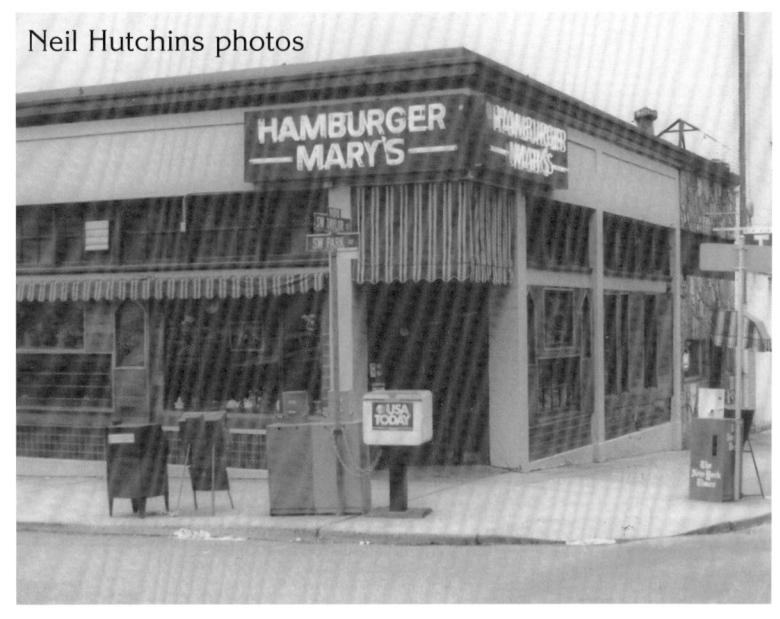

Portland City Archives

242

Rev. Delores Berry   1983 - 1984

sponsor SB 430, the Senate fair employment bill for lesbians and gays in 1984. Senator and former astronaut John Glenn opposed the bill, and asked for special Secret Service protection in fear that his stand against the gay bill would make him a target for assassination.

Youth Issues

Gay fathers met in a support group, led by David Callentine, an MCC member. The group existed primarily to support the educational and social needs of dads in various degrees of coming out, divorcing, or fighting for custodial rights. Several MCC-Portland members were among the 45-member association. There were socials involving the kids, Halloween parties, picnics, and even an overnight trip to the Goldendale (Washington) observatory in combination with a lesbian mothers group. Bonnie Tinker's Love Makes a Family group was addressing gay family communication issues. Parents, however, still couldn't bring their kids to the All City Picnic, sponsored by The Forum at McIver State Park in July 1983.

The needs of gay youth in Portland were still a much debated topic throughout the community. The Counseling Center for Sexual Minorities did not serve underage people, but recommended they socialize at the Metropolis, a Burnside Street disco. This place advertised itself as an all age club, but was adjacent to a bar where older men ogled the youth and made approaches on occasion. The Met was the reincarnation of an older club for underage youth called Mildred's Palace. Mildred's had begun in the Pythian Building, set up by Lanny Swerdlow in 1973 as a safe place for kids to socialize. He named it Mildred's as a subtle dig on conservative City Commissioner Mildred Schwab, who did not support the gay community. Mildred's Palace had moved into the Burnside location when it lost the Pythian Building lease and advertised its state-of-the-art disco sound system, but management had apparently relaxed its standards of supervision.

Lanny reopened his venture as The City Nightclub at a new location on SW 13th. No longer sharing a space with alcohol burners, he was able to regulate admission to the club and guarantee the safety of his young customers from prowlers. His $4 admission charge did discourage some youth, and the street crowd drifted to the nearby Outside In.

Controversy over the North American Man/Boy Love Association (NAMBLA) became public in July 1985. Ignoring Oregon State Law, the group condoned physical relationships with or between consenting underage youth. While some boys stated their interest in such relationships, it was illegal and considered unwise for boys under the age of consent. While not advocating these relationships, Lanny Swerdlow took up the cause of frustrated youth who had no legal avenue for full sexual expression. He voiced his irritation as "most of the time, the gay community refuses to even acknowledge the existence of gay people under 21 (let alone under 18) and just wishes that people (at least gay people) didn't become sexually active until they are old enough to legally drink...kids are simply ignored by the rest of the gay community." (*Just Out*, July and October 1985, p.3)

Even the issue of touch became debated. Specialists noted that touch-deprived individuals usually develop doubts about their self-worth and attractiveness as an explanation for the lack of affection. Parents, teachers, and coaches were caught in a "Catch-22" between normal affectionate touching as opposed to sexually-motivated "grooming."

Windfire, a weekly rap group for gay, lesbian, and bisexual teenagers began meeting at Old Wives Tales in 1982. The adult facilitator was Frank Jenkins, who had been contacted by Jim Glyer after a young man reported the pickup situation at the Metropolis. Windfire was self-directed, and organized dances, movies, plays, hikes, and potlucks (a perfect choice for "gays-in-training!"). Attendance ranged from 10 to 60. Windfire also held workshops, often coordinating with P-FLAG and Ann Shepherd. Young gays sought different role models from the adult bar scene and its exploitive nature, and from the "separatist" nature of both the lesbian and gay communities.

Those Attending Must Be 18 or Over

WINDFIRE

Page 5 Cascade Voice, February 3, 1984

MILDRED'S PALACE

Windfire offered one of the most positive social outlets for gay and lesbian youth who were underage. Members who stayed with the program were eligible to be in the Bridge group, a mentor program to help the younger people. Mildred's Palace, named in honor of long time City Commissioner Mildred Schwab, was a nightclub operated in various locations by Lanny Swerdlow. Lanny walked a narrow line between trying to work with underage kids and under suspicion of being a chicken-hawk by the gay community.

Community efforts to help Delores Berry with medical and moving expenses united several groups in presenting an evening of fundraising. Although in Portland a relatively short time, Delores had a major impact through both her activism and her music.

March 10th   8 PM

Raising Funds for Rev. Dolores Berry

at

Darcelle XV

Jeff Ditzler and Raunchy Robert Your Co-Hosts

Entertainment will feature:

Members of Portland Gay Men's Chorus
Dyketones
Lady Elaine Peacock
Terry Snowden
Misty Waters
Rev. Dolores Berry
    and many others

We're raising funds for Rev. Berry's moving fees back to her home. We hope to see you there.

Introducing the O.K. Choir

Chinese Auction — please bring items to the EAGLE Newsmagazine Offices by March 6th for donation

$4.00 per person door

244

Rev. Delores Berry 1983 - 1984

Windfire spawned the Bridge Group, a peer support club of those aged 18-29. There was an intentional overlapping of ages between the two groups so individuals had the option of swinging between them. Most Bridge members, like its leader Randall Parfiet, were former Windfire participants, though the group addressed different issues. An article in the *Eagle* devoted itself to GALYA (Gay and Lesbian Youth Association) activities, reinforcing that gay youth were interested in and capable of committed relationships. No mention, however, was made of their Portland leaders or meeting place.

MCC ran a Sunday school for the children of adult members, but did not have a program as such to help gay youth. As in other gay organizations, even at MCC, an older adult who might socialize or befriend a new young attendee was suspected of being a "chickenhawk." This "Catch-22" added to the difficulty of incorporating younger new members.

Difficult Decisions

As autumn approached, Rev. Berry's health became a major concern to herself and the congregation. Long periods of ill health had caused her absence from the office and pulpit. Encouraged by the Board of Directors to make a decision, she decided that in her best interests, she should resign the pulpit and take care of her own needs. She continued living in Portland many months before returning to the east coast with her mother Inez, and with her partner, Judy Kiser.

MCC's era of spirited gospel music did not end, but it took a major hit from the loss of Delores' dynamic singing and presentations. Terry Snowden continued on as organist and Choir director, maintaining the high standards of the Southern Gospel heritage.

The congregation entered a 16-month journey of self-sufficiency and pastoral search generally known as the Lay Interim.

OrHi file 1810

OrHi neg 68515

1985 Mayor Bud Clark appoints Penny Harrington first woman police chief in the country
- Anti-police sentiment boils when innocent Lloyd Stevenson killed with a "sleeper hold"
- First HTLV-III screening tests offered to gays apprehensive of their health and privacy
- Portland Building, first major Post-Modern style office building, completed and opened

1986 Dark Horse Comics put Milwaukie on the art map, and collaborates with filmmakers
- Tri-Met debuts first MAX light rail line; 200,000 riders packed first weekend to Gresham
- Old Paramount Theater re-opened as Portland Center for Performing Arts

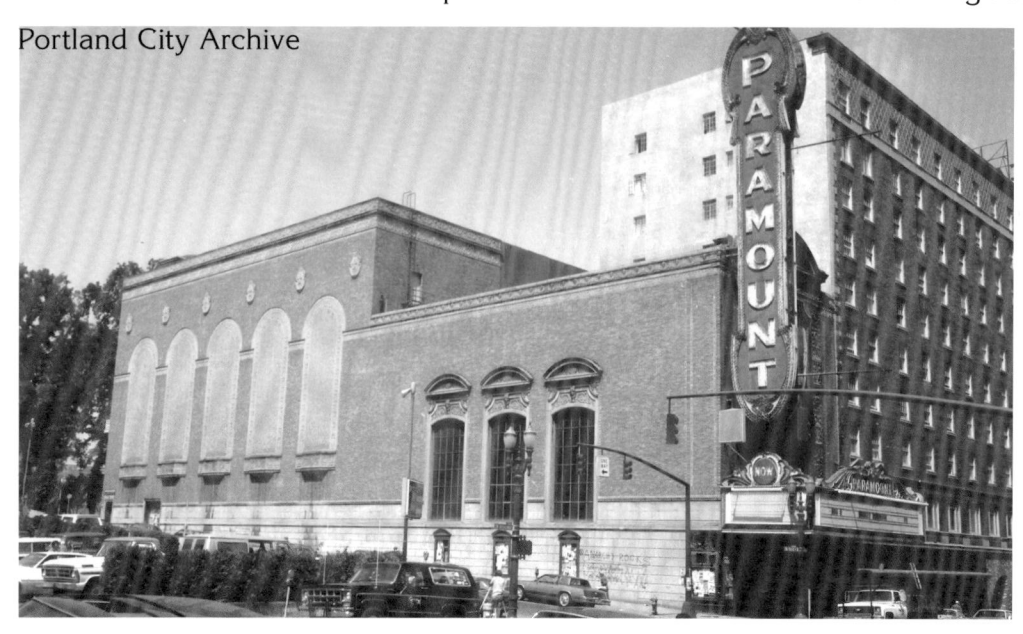

Portland City Archive

246

Chapter Nine
Laity Leadership
December 1984 – March 1986

"Now look around among yourselves, dear brothers, and select seven men, wise and full of the Holy Spirit, who are well thought of by everyone; and we will put them in charge of this business."
Acts 6:3 (The Living Bible)

Sixteen months is a long period for any organization to exist without a leader, and the Metropolitan Community Church of Portland could easily have deteriorated into chaos. The Board of Directors appointed two individuals as Worship Coordinators to pilot the congregation through the challenges of seeking a new pastor while maintaining productive order. Dave Dishman was appointed by the Board as lay pastor, a role that he successfully fulfilled for about seven months. He was followed by Marguerite Scroggie.

Dave Dishman's qualifications for MCC worship coordinator were not so much theological as they were organizational. He had inherited a deep commitment to MCC through his initial joining of MCC while Austin Amerine was pastor. He sang in the choir, participated on boards and committees, and drew upon his business experience in finance. Approaching burnout after an intense seven months, he turned over leadership of the congregation to Rev. Marguerite Scroggie, who had been a student clergy under Jim Glyer. Everything and every process were done according to the by-laws. Even when Marguerite was to be out of town for the month of January of 1986, she formally turned over the duties of Worship Coordinator to Dishman with an official letter.

MCC was embarking on an interlude that would utilize past strengths of the congregation, and establish patterns of leadership among lay people that would become an asset in future periods of vacancy. That same spirit of survival and independence would also present a few challenges to future pastors.

A pastoral search committee was formed when Pastor Delores Berry resigned her position in November of 1984. Perhaps it was ironic that only two months before this, a piece had been published in the Chalice which read:

The Perfect Pastor...

"Results of a computerized survey indicate that the perfect pastor preaches exactly 15 minutes. The pastor condemns sin, but never embarrasses anyone, and works from 8 am until midnight, and is also the janitor.

"The pastor makes $60 a week, wears good clothes, drives a new car, and gives $50 a week to the poor, plus tithing a full 10%. The pastor is 28 years old, has been preaching for 15 years, is wonderfully gentle and pleasing to the eye, loves to work with teenagers, and spends countless hours with senior citizens. He/she makes 15 calls daily on parish families, shut-ins, and hospital patients, and is always in the office when needed."

Changes in the building environment of Portland in the mid-1980s included the construction of new commercial centers. Fred Meyer stores expanded into large complexes, eliminating several smaller neighborhood locations such as this store at SE 36th and Hawthorne, now the Cup and Saucer Cafe. A larger Fred Meyer opened on Hawthorne at SE 39th

Downtown on SW 3rd, urban renewal continued to take blocks of older buildings and transient hotels. The large site became the Justice Center and jail, at the foot of the Hawthorne Bridge, across from Chapman Park. The Lennox Hotel to the north disappeared a few years later to become the Mark Hatfield center. The Broadway Theater was torn down to become the Broadway building. In the Northwest Industrial area, Bridgeport Brew Pub opened in an old cordage warehouse on an unused rail spur, signalling the beginning of development into what would become The Pearl District.

OrHi neg 005936

Portland City Archives

Laity Leadership   1984 - 1986

"If your pastor does not measure up, simply send this letter to six other parishes that are tired of their pastors, and put your parish at the bottom of the list.. Then bundle up your pastor and send to the church at the top of the list. In one month, you will receive 1643 pastors. One of them should be perfect."

Seeking candidates for a new minister fell to the committee composed of seven active members, headed by Dave Dishman. The procedure to secure a new minister involved obtaining lists of candidates from the NW District and from the UFMCC Fellowship. The committee created an information packet about MCC and its needs, to be sent to interested candidates.

Some critics of the congregation quipped that MCC had a reputation of taking in new pastors, chewing them up, and spitting them out. It was an unfair criticism from outsiders, but four pastors in eight years may approach some kind of record. Robert Dunn editorialized in the *Cascade Voice* about perceived MCC troubles and shortcomings, perpetuating rumors and gossip about insensitive treatment of Delores Berry and her health. Responses from former pastor Jim Glyer and member Sally Cohn in the next edition, which was actually the first issue of *The Eagle*, set the record straight about how the situation had been handled, and explained more about MCC and the Board of Directors. Dave Dishman wrote that it was negative for *The Eagle* to run stories about the internal operations of any organization, and that the community criticizing each other in the press was inappropriate. (*Eagle*, January 1985)

Farther east in Antelope another religious organization was in turmoil. Indian guru Bhagwan Shree Rajneesh had established his Rancho Rajneesh near the Oregon town in 1981, bringing wealthy new age enlightened individuals from around the world to live on the 64,000 acre commune. They attracted the negative attention of Federal and Deschutes County officials with immigration concerns. When the Rajneeshees first attempted to poison voters in The Dalles at a salad bar with salmonella, then plotted to kill the U.S. District Attorney in Portland, the free-love guru returned to India.

His spokesperson Ma Anand Sheela became a notorious laughing-stock in the news and on a top-selling 45-rpm recording. The Big Muddy Ranch was up for sale, and the place thereof knew the Bhagwan no more. (*Oregonian*, September 27, 2005, p 1A)

Maintaining The Semblance of Order

Going back to the days of Austin Amerine, MCC had a well-developed congregational framework, with committees to organize programs, deacons to look after the spiritual welfare of the congregation, and pastors-in-training (exhorters and student clergy). The calendar of the Christian year and the regular 3-year lectionary cycle provided the liturgical structure. With four pastorates over eight years, long-term members had a fund of experiences and examples to draw upon. Many individuals had stepped into a variety of roles when called upon to do so in the past, and that spirit of involvement grew during the interim.

Countless members volunteered to usher, read scripture, lead prayers, and help with communion. Several former ministers in the congregation from various denominations delivered sermons. These included Reverends Dick Burdon, Jim Glyer, Marguerite Scroggie, Teresa Nunn, Frodo Okulam, and Joyce Baxter. David Callentine and Jeri Lee-Hostetler were Student Clergy. Deacons occasionally wrote and delivered the homily. Services continued to be held at Coffee Hour following services continued to be hosted by "The Bagel Committee." The Chalice was reduced to a single newsletter sheet, distributed weekly along with the service bulletins.

Christmas was celebrated with a Cantata, directed by Terry Snowden, accompanied by PGMC pianist Stuart Zimmerman. Soloists were David Callentine, Bob Sherwood, Frodo Okulam and Art Shelley. The usual candlelight service was held on Christmas Eve, and a Christmas day gathering and dinner fed a crowd in the basement Social Hall.

The congregation's 9th anniversary was celebrated in January, 1986, with a 3-day spiritual renewal weekend. Founding Pastor Austin

MCC Archive photos

Anniversary celebrations marked the 9th year that MCC was chartered. The festival theme was "Nine Years in the Vineyard." Founding pastor Austin Amerine returned. Speakers included Dave Dishman. Mel Hart and Ron Raz displayed the anniversarybanner. Student Clergy Frodo Okulam performed a solo with the MCC choir, and at the basement reception, veteran member and cake creator Mel Hart crated a sheet cake adorned with several Christian symbols.

250

Laity Leadership   1984 - 1986

Amerine was to preach five times on the renewal theme "Nine Years in the Vineyard." Jack St. John returned to provide his special music. The reunion spirit of the two former worship leaders was infectious. Invitations were sent to former members and MCC congregations in the Northwest District. Of course, there was a dinner, a spread prepared by Vic Winegar.

Vi Leagjeld and Ron Powell were appointed by the Board of Directors as Interim Board Members, filling vacancies created by the resignations of Judy Kiser and Fran Hamilton. Holy Unions were performed for Ray Hecox and Ed Walls, Marty and Betty Lostheart-Hale, and several other couples.

Programs and schedules continued at MCC with little interruption during the Lay Leadership Interim. Lesbian and Gay Pride committee meetings were held every Thursday evening. Twelve-step groups continued to use the facility. The usual bake sale was held around Christmas time. The monthly budget was $5568.

Anticipating the Easter celebration, living room groups meet during the six weeks of Lent. Most groups met in homes, the rest at MCC. Leaders included Dick Burdon, Ruth Halderman, David Callentine, Allen Epp, Rod Abernathy, Betty Hale, Jean Conner, Vi Leagjeld, Rick Baker, Pat Kerwin, Don Whittaker, Jill Frankie, Sunny Travis, Bob Jackson, Richard Lusk, Laura Wilkinson, and Vic Winegar. Good Friday worship was put together by Joe Hooker, Jill Frankie, Marguerite Scroggie, Nikki Johnson, and Sue Lantz. An extensive Easter Vigil was held.

Rev. Joyce Baxter, former MCC student clergy, now pastored MCC of the Gentle Shepherd across the Columbia in Vancouver and wrote a regular column for the Eagle, with thoughtful Christian messages and reminders bordering on counseling. MCC member Jean Dant became Religion Editor, keeping religion and MCC in the public awareness. Paula Nielsen continued to contribute feature columns as well.

A popular MCC pianist was Joe Anderson, well-known performer at the old Embers since 1975. A volunteer pianist and accompanist at the church, he celebrated 20 years in the Portland Gay community with regular shows at the Fish Grotto's Outrigger Room.

Terry Snowden, once MCC's organist and choir director, took up a similar post at St. Philip The Deacon Episcopal Church. He continued his friendship with MCC, and performed a recital there to benefit the music program on May 17, 1985. He also produced a music cassette with former minister Delores Berry, which boasted a national distribution. Terry also composed original works for the Portland Gay Men's Chorus.

MCC's EXCEL in the Spirit Team sponsored "Christmas in July." Singing holiday carols with the church family in the heat of an evening service seemed incongruous, but proved to be celebratory.

Dealing with AIDS

Lifestyles for most gay men changed radically with the growing AIDS situation. The *Homosexualization of America* (Dennis Altman, 1982) had just proclaimed that the gay movement had shifted the debate from behavior to identity. The polymorphus term "homosexual" described many practices and beliefs of both genders. With the appearance of AIDS, the progress made in recognizing gay identity and rights was seriously challenged.

A government proposal to compile lists of patients exposed to AIDS, or with any sign of exposure to AIDS-related viruses confirmed the fears in the New York Gay Men's Health Crisis organization that the government was only concerned about protecting the population at large, and not with the male homosexual population. President Ronald Reagan cited the Judeo-Christian tradition in marriage as a social relationship to be protected against erosion by alternative sexual expression.

San Francisco gay bathhouses were closed by city order in a move to protect public health. There was also talk of placing a quarantine on diagnosed individuals who remained sexually active. The city of Armistead Maupin and his Tales of the City was becoming the battleground of desperate people. The Castro was becoming a ghost town, and Baby Cakes had no where to go. Some Portlanders were reluctant to

PGMC Archive

Gary Coleman photo

Neil Hutchins photo

Barbara Roberts requested that the Portland Gay Men's Chorus sing at her inaguration as Secretary of State in the Capitol Building in Salem. She never minced in her loyalty to justice and diversity (and PGMC).

John Adams, owner of CC Slaughter's, opened a second bar on Stark Street in 1984, calling it the Eagle. It held several private spaces, a loft, and an unusual fountain just inside the door.

Dave Kohl photo

Laity Leadership   1984 - 1986

get too close to gay visitors from the Golden Gate.

New York State followed suit within a year by attempting to ban all sexual activity except standard heterosexual intercourse (whatever that meant). The four "tubs" in Portland open in 1985 were the Continental, the Majestic, and the two Olympics–Downtown and Uptown (the Workout Baths).

The legal and governmental response to AIDS around the world was grim. In England, doctors were authorized to "detain" AIDS sufferers in hospitals. In Sweden, AIDS was debated as a quarantinable disease. The World Health Organization considered travel restrictions on citizens from countries where AIDS was prevalent.

PGMC appeared prominently for the Swearing In Ceremony for newly elected Oregon Secretary of State Barbara Roberts in January. In June, they sang at MCC for Father's Day. On June 28, the Chorus performed for the first time in the newly refurbished Arlene Schnitzer Concert Hall (originally the Paramount Theater). The concert was a combination event with the Gay Men's Chorus of Los Angeles. The spirit of the concert was a much needed boost to spirits sagging under the weight of the growing AIDS epidemic. Music in the concert addressed issues of love and loss with upbeat songs from the 1940s. They finished with "I Am What I Am" and "The Best of Times," from La Cage Aux Folles. The 140 men sang at the Seattle Opera House the next day with the men's choruses from Seattle and Vancouver, BC.

Personal legal issues were also emerging into the awareness of young men having to do with end-of-life legalities. Even in 1980, Christopher Street had featured a young man whose life partner had died unexpectedly, and his lack of legal standing to inherit any of the estate, or even keep their apartment. Portland men in their 20s and 30s suddenly needed to concern themselves with putting property into joint tenancy with the right of survivorship. Lawyers like Ben Merrill were consulted on establishing power of attorney. Wills were written dealing with naming executors, disposition of bodily remains, and disposition of property. Changing the named beneficiary on life insurance policies meant more forms to complete.

There was progress in identifying the role of "T-helper" cells in the immune system. The working of a retrovirus like HTLV-3 was explained in May, noting that the genetic material RNA genome could be copied into DNA, a process called reverse transcriptase. The resulting disappearance of T-cells would leave an individual defenseless against so-called opportunistic diseases such as pneumocystis carinii pneumonia and Kaposi's sarcoma. The virus had finally been traced to origins in Uganda, where cases of Kaposi's had been on record for 25 years. Detection of HTLV-3 had proven so difficult because by the time a patient was symptomatic, viral shedding had rid the body of the original retrovirus. (*The Eagle,* May 1985, p. 62)

The only known method of preventing AIDS was (and still is) to avoid exposure. Living according to the laws of health decreased the likelihood of serious illness. The problem was that many people had very little idea what the laws of health might be. So *Just Out* named them: Family Genetics, Good nutrition, regular exercise, handling stress, avoiding unnecessary drug use, getting rest, and relaxation; maintaining a positive attitude with faith and love; and maintaining mental and emotional health. (*Just Out,* June 1985 p 18)

NBC television aired the movie "*An Early Frost*" on Veteran's Day, 1985. Starring Aidan Quinn, Ben Gazzara, and Gena Rowlands, the film portrayed an American family responding to their son's AIDs diagnosis. Praised and promoted nationally by AIDs service organizations, local "*Frost Watch*" parties were held in Portland. Guests were asked to contribute $10 to Cascade AIDS network and the Community Health Support Services/PAL Project. An estimated 75 million viewers saw the program nationwide. It brought

Several consequences resulted from the emergence of AIDS. Signs appeared on busses and in newspapers, sponsored by CHSS, spreading information about the disease. In the basement of the Cornelius Hotel, the Continental Baths closed despite its 10-year history and friendly staff. Owner Dick Lawson soon opened a replacement location in the Majestic at SW 12th and Burnside. An overwhelming crowd participated in the first AIDS run.

Hugging doesn't cause AIDS.

Portland City Archives

Neil Hutchins photo

Neil Hutchins photo

Laity Leadership   1984 - 1986

the health crisis into stark reality for mainstream Americans who had not been aware of the severity of the health crisis.

Portland bathhouse operators met with Bob DeWalt of Phoenix Rising and Reese House of Cascade Aids Project to discuss procedures, which would better educate and protect tub clientele from AIDS. There was talk in San Francisco and other cities of closing the baths altogether to prevent the spread of AIDS. The Majestic baths survived, but the Club Continental Baths drowned in 1985.

PAL Project and CHESS

Originally dubbed the "Chicken Soup Brigade" after a similar organization in Seattle, the Community Health Support Services (CHESS) coordinated emotional and social support services for lesbians and gay men facing terminal or life-changing illnesses in Portland. The motto was "acceptance, not rejection." CHESS modeled itself on the Shanti Project in San Francisco, organizing under the umbrella of Phoenix Rising and funded with $2400 from the PGMC benefit concert. Many gay organizations in Portland contributed funds and energy to the project, including MCC. After 10 months of intense organizational activity, peer counseling activities began in April of 1985 with 34 "matches." One hundred caring men and women were sought for the next round of trainees. (*Eagle*, June, 1985 p 5)

Additional funding for CHESS/PAL was donated from fundraisers presented by City Nights Group. These volunteers staged theatric evenings, which helped persons with AIDS through the funds raised from tickets. Their first event was called the Sylvester Summer Party, in July, 1985, raising about $11,000.

CAP also received funding that summer, notably a $19,860 award from the U.S. Conference of Mayors. The grant was specifically given to help implement programs to educate Portlanders about misconceptions of AIDS and its transmission. Five hundred gay community volunteers were to be trained to deliver information about AIDS and safer sex on a formal and informal basis to peers. CAP operated as a committee of Phoenix Rising, the non-profit counseling cooperative. CAP held a "Bartenders' Seminar" in June. Realizing that bars and bartenders were both a source of entertainment and social interaction for gays, they were also to be utilized hopefully as a feeding ground for information about AIDS and AIDS-related issues. Continued help from the gay community was also needed.

GMT (Gay Men Together) continued meeting Wednesday evenings at Portland State as it had since the early 1970s. Topics shifted from political interests and coming-out issues to discussions around safe sex, emotional stability, and anxiety over health concerns. Politicians like County Commissioner Gretchen Kafoury and Keeston Lowrey met with the group, as did representatives from P-FLAG. Attendance usually numbered over 60 men.

Abigail Van Buren, writing her nationally syndicated newspaper advice column since 1959 as Dear Abby, often wrote positively about gays and questions about homosexuality. In 1985, the 2000-member Gay Fathers Coalition International gave her the group's "Image in Media" award. She had also given hope to thousands of men in parenting roles. She accepted the award in person in Los Angeles, May 31. Her sister, Ann Landers, also supported reason and caring over emotional hostility for families learning about their children's gay/lesbian orientations.

Al Williams

Jim Glyer's partner had been with him since they met when Jim pastored the MCC he founded in Kansas City. Al became involved in many aspects of the congregation while working in the health care profession. His jovial nature and kindheartedness won him instant friendships. In both Kansas City and Portland, he received the honor of being voted an honorary lesbian...not a distinction to be taken lightly!

Al became terminally ill with prostate cancer and passed away in April 1985. He had been lovingly cared for by Jim and, for a time, by Al's former wife. After eight years together, Jim chose to follow Al's wishes, and distributed

Popular places of entertainment in the 1980s included the Jefferson Theater on SW 12th and newly opened Slabtown, a bar in the once provocative Sonny's. Slabtown later became the Primary Domain, especially popular with women.

From 1982 through 1985, Glen Dugger operated Somebody's Place on SW 11th, after he had to move out of what had been the Focal Point on SW 9th. Somebody's featured a small dance floor, a wonderful balcony, and Sunday after- noon films. The staff was especially friendly. Glen moved into the old Rainbow Galley at SW 11th and Stark in 1985, with a parade of customers carrying the furniture. He is the fellow on the far left of the lower right photo.

Neil Hutchins photos

256

Laity Leadership   1984 - 1986

Al's ashes off the lower bridge at Multnomah Falls in a morning ceremony. Good friends from both MCC-Portland and Rose City Fellowship were there for support. Ron Powell and Russ Howerton hosted a breakfast afterwards on their North Portland houseboat. Glyer's son David had flown to Portland for the event, then helped his dad pack up the apartment near MCC and drive to a new home in Piedmont, across the Bay from San Francisco. After a time, Jim became involved with MCC-San Francisco. There, as an assistant minister, he conducted support groups for people with AIDS and other long-term illnesses.

At MCC, the Fireside/Friendship room north of the Sanctuary was redesigned and dedicated as the Al Williams Memorial Chapel, with funding donated by Jim Glyer and many MCC friends.

Rock Hudson

Shock was the national reaction when legendary Hollywood actor Rock Hudson died of AIDS October 2, 1985. When he had returned unexpectedly from medical tests in France on July 30, speculation was quelled that he had contracted the disease through homosexual contacts. Only in his final days had the gaunt film star spoken about AIDS. Many gay men were disappointed that Hudson had bypassed the opportunity to bear witness to the issue of AIDS research funding and care systems.

The Eagle editor/owner Robert Dunn (yes, that's "Raunchy" Robert of JR's Cell fame) had written a powerful editorial in his August issue. Excerpts include:

"Dear Rock Hudson...We are faced with the most vile attempts by the vicious right-wing religious fanatics to use a lethal disease as an excuse to persecute us even as we struggle with death. The rights we believed so smugly we had won in the '70's are not as sound as some of us thought...There is no purple paint (remember Delores Berry's dream?) to show everyone how many of us there really are. We had no visible means of identification...but now we have this disease that is sorting us out regardless of where we have chosen to settle in the spectrum of social visibility...the duties that life finds for us are not often those we would have asked for. It would seem to me that the contribution you could make at this time...is one of contributing to the quality of Life for those Gays and Lesbians from whom you have separated yourself all your professional life. To be bold and courageous enough to claim your identity and to proclaim our need for basic human rights, health support and research; to contribute to an end of discrimination and vitriol; and to seek honest understanding of mutual existence and growth is not an easy task under the best of circumstances. I ask you to remember those who have done so before you...You have an opportunity to make this ugliness still one more performance on the stage of Life for an audience that desperately needs an image of inspiration and respect...I urge you to take this step with what strength you have." (*The Eagle*, Aug, 1985 p. 6)

The week of Hudson's death, "Portlandia" was transported and positioned on the Portland Building on SW 5th, with parades and much fanfare. Portlanders were fascinated with the hammered copper image of the City personified in the 38-foot-high sculpture by New York artist Raymond Kaskey. It is set on Portland's only example of post-modernist Michael Graves' architecture.

Survival Issues and Tactics

Right wing and conservative religious folks challenged the Multnomah County Charter's human rights ordinance of 1984. Concerned Citizens of Portland were headed by former State Representative Drew Davis, frustrated that their anti-gay mayoral candidate Frank Ivancie had been so soundly defeated by Bud Clark. The County Commission itself repealed the ordinance and replaced it with a resolution, which would not be subject to a referendum threatened by a signature-gathering group soon known as the Oregon Citizen's Alliance (OCA). Fueling emotions was the current showing of *The Times of Harvey Milk* in Portland-area theaters, reminding viewers of the slain gay San Francisco commissioner.

It was a demoralizing time for the gay community. Mysterious and lethal diseases were

MULTNOMAH COUNTY OREGON
BOARD OF COUNTY COMMISSIONERS
DISTRICT FIVE

COUNTY COURTHOUSE
PORTLAND, OREGON 97204
(503) 248-5213

GORDON E. SHADBURNE · MULTNOMAH COUNTY COMMISSIONER

November 14, 1985

Dear Christian Leader:

From time to time, I believe it is important for my office to give you information which affects our community, and the Christian community in particular. Enclosed is such information.

The Metropolitan Human Relations Commission is jointly funded by city and county dollars for the specific purpose of helping reduce racial and minority tension. I believe this particular newsletter contains important information as to how the gay community sees themselves and lays out from their leadership, the plan of action for the future. You will note that the authorship of these articles is written by them. Keeston Lowery was a key contact for Commissioner Kafoury's office with regard to denying the "right to vote" on the sex orientation ordinance of Multnomah County.

This raises the question of Christian ministry in this area. Most recently, I talked to a local pastor, Rev. Mays, and his wife, who have assisted in facilitating a local chapter of Homosexuals Anonymous, a support group that has some Christian base. As you recall, I had a meeting in my office over a year ago, suggesting that the Christian community realize the need to take the offensive, in love, to reach out from the people within our church to members of the gay community and with the love of Christ, challenge this stronghold of Satan. I said at that time that I feared for our community because of the present apathy of the church.

I would like to encourage you to do what you can as a church leader in this great home-mission field. If you are interested in this type of ministry or if I can be of assistance to you, please feel free to contact my office.

Sincerely,

Gordon E. Shadburne
Multnomah County Commissioner

GES:jh

Encl.

Gordon Shadburne's letter, not meant for public circulation. It caused quite a stir.

Laity Leadership 1984 - 1986

attacking bodies while spirits were barraged with slogans about God's judgment and vigilante crusaders were threatening civil rights.

Multnomah County Commissioner Gordon Shadburne used official County letterhead to write to 100 area Christian churches on November 14, warning them that the gay Portland community was a "stronghold of Satan," and called for the establishment of a local chapter of "Homosexuals Anonymous." This stirred the pot of public opinion, resulting in a rebuke from the Metropolitan Human Relations Commission when they adopted a long-awaited policy on gay/lesbian rights on December 17, 1985.

During the only three hours when the rooms were unoccupied, the offices of the *Eagle* in the Mylar Building were burglarized on June 27. Thieves removed the entire TRS-80 four-computer system, plus discs containing all *Eagle* records and several typeset discs. Monetary value was placed at $12,000. But the loss of morale and momentum, and the delay in production of the Gay Pride issue, was far more costly. Culprits were never found, nor was any of the equipment or software. The *Eagle* stopped its soaring in August.

Medical insurance coverage was in tatters. Some companies refused to pay AIDS-related claims. Some employers refused to provide medical coverage for employees with AIDS. Coastal Insurance Company, of Santa Monica CA, offered AIDS Medical Expense Insurance policies for an annual premium of $194. Other companies devised Reverse or Viatical Insurance, paying medical expenses for AIDS patients, drawing down the pay out value of life insurance policies.

AIDS wasn't the only topic on the minds of lesbians. The Lesbian Aging Project (LAP) formed from a group originally calling itself the Old Dyke's Home. Some older lesbians didn't like the idea of aging in a heterosexual retirement home, and began working for a house of their own where they could have total control of everything, right down to the colors. Women reported that "old-style dykes are hiding out," and finding older lesbians was a challenge for LAP members. LAP knew of similar projects in Florida, New York, and San Francisco.

Portland police chief Penny Harrington appointed Deputy Chief Tom Potter to be police liaison to the gay community. He was a strong believer in civil rights, and volunteered for the position. His first action was to meet with the Lesbian and Gay Pride Steering Committee. The police had forgotten to send escorts to the 1985 PRIDE parade. Oops!

Actually, the parade took place without any mishaps or confrontations anyway. Potter participated in later Gay Parades with his lesbian policewoman daughter Katie. Their father-daughter relationship would be written about in a book on open families (Robert Bernstein, *Straight Parents, Gay Children*, 1995), and would be the subject of several *Oregonian* articles. Twenty years hence, Tom Potter would be elected mayor of Portland (See Chapter 13)

Diversions

MCC-Salem member Patricia was Empress V of the Salem Imperial Sovereign Court in 1985. She and Emperor V Bob hosted a Christmas show featuring the MCC "Celebration Singers," performing part of their Christmas Cantata. Food donations from the Knights of Malta were distributed to MCC-Salem for distribution by Rev. Jodi Mekkers in that city. The event represented a coordination of the Court, community organizations, and the church.

Several existing gay and lesbian social groups provided continuity for individuals feeling lost, alienated, angry, despairing, or just plain lonely in a changing culture that had been at one time so cavalier. The Rosetown Ramblers square dancing group, founded in 1982, continued to hold regular classes and dances, often traveling to Seattle or other cities for "fly-ins" and conventions. The safe touching possibilities in dancing was particularly appealing. The gay hiking group maintained their momentum of planning outdoor events. Darcelle continued her ribald entertainments, sometimes hosting guest performers including Paula Nielsen, Portland's own "Sophie Tucker."

MCC Archive photos

Members from MCC continued to participate in District and Fellowship events during the period of laity leadership. Conferences in Modesto, Arcata, and Eugene were well attended. Larry Foltz continued making presentations at EXCEL events, often held at Camp Adams in nearby Molalla.

Laity Leadership   1984 - 1986

Recently arrived New York writer Jim Anctil noted the reaffirming presence of the Cascade Guild and its subdivisions for professionals, medical workers, and teachers. He marveled at the support of the deaf community, and of leaders like Hank Stack and MCC's Bob Jackson. He complimented the Men's Resource center, the Gay Pride Committee, and community leaders like Sandy Director and Keeston Lowery, along with elected leaders like Herb Cawthorne, Bud Clark, and gay advocates in Salem.

Looking for non-sexually charged social outlets, and loving the cooking and eating of food, several potluck groups emerged in the mid-1980s. "PIGS" was the Portland International Gourmet Society. Another group called itself the "Blue Collar Guys." Probably the most successful was "Cookboys," a group that rose in March 1985 at the home of Dave Kohl. Kohl named the group after the kitchen servants he knew of from seven years of living in Hong Kong. The group swelled from eight founders to over 100, with an average attendance of about 40, meeting in the homes of various members. "No agenda, No attitude, Good Food" became the theme. Members brought a dish in the spirit of the host's announced theme–spring, Valentine, cylindrical, Latino, Chinese, etc. Mailings were handled by Kohl for the first 10 years, then Dick Walker, another MCC attendee, took over the task. Phil Joslin volunteered to continue arrangements when the group switched to e-mail notices. Without a business meeting, board of directors, or mission statement, they celebrated their 20th anniversary in 2005.

David Gernant, a quiet lawyer type, put together a different food-oriented group in 1983 that met at several local restaurants. Called "Rendezvous," members paid in advance for a set menu, which David had arranged with a restaurant of interest. Usually 50-75 men would pre-register and attend. Involving more work on the leader part, the actual events were no-agenda enjoyable social events where men of various ages and backgrounds could mix and network in a pleasant environment. The Alexis Restaurant on W Burnside was by far the group's favorite with the attendance there reaching 95 for one dinner. "Rendezvous" continued for about 10 years.

Another dinner possibility was the 4th annual Lucille Hart fundraiser on October 4, 1985, at the Benson Hotel, with Oregon Speaker of the House Vera Katz as master of ceremonies. She would go on to be elected 3 times as Portland's Mayor, beginning in 1992.

And in February of 1986, Mama Bernice celebrated her 76th with a major party at the Dirty Duck. Sadly, it would be her last. That same month, Performing Artists for Life held a benefit performance for the Cascade AIDS Network at the Schnitzer with members of the Oregon Symphony, the Choral Consortium, the Civic Theater, the Pacific Ballet Theater, and the Woody Hite Big Band. The City Nights group produced a second benefit to raise funds for people with AIDS on March 22 at the Masonic Temple.

On the international level, it was the year of the disastrous explosion at a Chernobyl nuclear power plant in the USSR. The fallout, literally, affected much of Ukraine and beyond. The political fallout–concerns about pollution and radiation–eventually shut down Trojan, Oregon's only nuclear power plant, just north of Portland in Rainier, WA.

Candidate Dennis Chappell

The pastoral search committee had successful communication with Rev. Dennis Chappell, pastor of Christ Chapel MCC in Orange County, California. MCC flew Dennis to Portland for a week of "candidating." He preached at the July 14 (Bastille Day!) services and met with the congregation for a question-and-answer session in the evening. He also met with the board and became acquainted with Portland and MCC.

He left Portland having given a verbal commitment to return. However, the health of his partner in California caused him to reconsider and eventually decline the Portland pastorate. A discouraged but understanding search committee started the process all over again.

Neil Hutchins photos

The Imperial Sovereign Rose Court elected Kim Chichester as its first Emperor. Dora Jarr (aka Bernie Sanford) became Empresse XXVI-II. The Court and individual drag performers staged numerous shows, donating the proceeds to political causes and organizations, which provided major financing for several gay rights causes pioneered by the Portland Town Council.

Dani Diamond (MCC member Dani Eaton) volunteered for many years in the operation of Esther's Pantry. Gary Benoit was Emperor X, and in 2005 was re-elected as Emperor XXXI. Van Richards (The Vanessa) was a fixture at Dahl and Penne's during its 10-year life span.

262

Laity Leadership   1984 - 1986

Politics

The City Open Press replaced the *Eagle* Newsmagazine, after just eight editions, in October 1985. COP's high minded goals were stated: "to establish a gay press of distinction, both editorially and graphically; to provide an open forum for discussion and exchange of ideas on topics relative to our lifestyle; to instill a sense of pride for what is positive about our community...to campaign violently against the AIDS crisis that is darkening our future both as individuals and as a credible minority in the world community" (*COP* October 25, 1985, p .3).

Edited by T. Distel, the staff included gay community regulars Ray Southwick (of JR's), Sallee Huber and Dave "Hutch" Hutchison (of *The Voice*) Keeston Lowery (Commissioner Mike Lindberg's aide), well-known bartender Greg Pitts (aka Sara Joy, aka Zazu Pitts), and Sanford Director (Portland's gay mayor.)

Forty-nine open or closeted ex-Catholic nuns were featured in a new book in 1985 titled *Lesbian Nuns: Breaking Silence,* edited by Rosemary Curb and Nancy Manahan. Whether active or celibate, the women and their stories were a revelation, discussing historic and current references to convent love. The women described their struggles between their own sexual drives and the Vatican's Declaration on Sexual Ethics of December 29, 1973 which stated "...homosexual acts are intrinsically disordered and can in no case be approved of." Sisterly back rubs sometimes led to erotic feelings and overt activity. One of the nuns anticipated that the book would be a catalyst, and all hell would break loose in some communities, religious and secular. It did. Over 400 people filled PSU's Lincoln Hall to hear the two ex-nun editors speak, opening Gay Pride week June 14, 1985.

A quasi-religious phenomenon emerged in Portland around mid-year. Jack and Sherry Reynolds, a self-appointed "god-squad" began a spray painting campaign, painting "TRUST JESUS" in aerosol lettering on walls, bridges, and overpasses. The anonymous vandals were eventually found, arrested, and fined.

Memories of the man with a dream were rekindled when Portland and the nation recognized the 57th birthday of Dr. Martin Luther King Jr. with a public holiday and observation of his tragic assassination at age 38 in 1968. All sexual minorities took heart in his messages demanding civil rights and freedom for all oppressed peoples. *The City Open Press* editorialized: "With the onslaught of the New Right and this two-term (Reagan) administration, AIDS and the ignorance surrounding it, we cannot allow ourselves to be caught unaware. The security and new-found freedom stemming from Stonewall has just been a euphoria due to our great step forward in declaring the fact that we, too, have rights. After coming out of the clouds we need to realize that these newfound rights need to be enacted into law. We, too, deserve our equal rights and the protection "(and limitations) provided by the law. (*COP,* January 1986)

Candidate Gary Wilson

A familiar figure to MCC-Portlanders was Rev. Gary Wilson, who had been the assistant NW District Coordinator in the early 1980s. He was currently pastor at MCC-Seattle, and it was there that MCC contacted him regarding their vacancy. Gary accepted the offer and candidated in March 1986, ending the longest period of pastoral vacancy in MCC's history. His would be the second longest pastorate in MCC history.

Gary Wilson and Marguerite Scroggie

1986 City Commissioner Gordon Shadburne calls homosexuality the "stronghold of Satan"
- Claymation innovator Wil Vinton generates California Raisins in his NW Portland studio
- Reagan administration secret deal of Oliver North's "weapons for hostages" exposed

1987 Portland volunteer engineer Ben Lindner killed by Contras in Nicaragua
- Portland Performing Arts Center opens Schnitzer, Intermediate, and Newmark Theaters

1988 Multnomah County opens Inverness Jail
- Sex scandal fells homeless advocate Michael Stoops
- Burnside Community Council closes Baloney Joe's homeless shelter
- Skinheads kill Ethiopian immigrant Mulugeta Seraw; Tom Metzger sued to pay $12.5 million
- Measure 8 approved 53%, removes gay civil rights; later overturned by the Court

1989 Gus Van Sant films Matt Dillon in Portland for *Drugstore Cowboy*
- Protection of Northern Spotted Owls triggers recession for timber industry
- Equity Foundation begun by Terry Bean, Karen Keeny, Jim Vigher and John Grigsby

1990 *The Simpsons* debuts Jan 14 on Fox TV; satirizes everything in American culture
- Barbara Roberts elected Oregon's first woman Governor; Measure 5 limits tax base
- Springfield passes ordinance to strip gays of equal rights; PGMC sings there anyway

1991 Van Sant does it again with Keanu Reeves and River Phoenix in *My Own Private Idaho*
- Video Poker introduced by the Oregon State Lottery, draws $77 million its first year
- U.S. troops reclaim Kuwait and invade Iraq; Operation Desert Storm stops short

1992 Vera Katz elected Portland Mayor
- Measure 9 denouncing homosexuality is defeated; OCA vows to target small towns
- Oregon's U.S. senator since 1968, Bob Packwood, charged with sexual harassment

Chapter Ten
Rev. Gary Wilson
March 1986 - February 1993

"For I am not ashamed of the good news, for it is God's power for the salvation of everyone who trusts, of the Jew first and then of the Greek."
Roman 1:16 (The New Testament in the Language of the People)

One of the most challenging eras in MCC-Portland history became the lot of Reverend Gary Wilson. During his seven year tenure, individuals and the congregation as a whole would experience the devastation of Acquired Immune Deficiency Syndrome, commonly called AIDS. Healthy robust men could sicken and die within six months. So many left so quickly.

The Oregon gay community would also be challenged as never before with two battles at the polls–Ballot Measures 8 and 9. Financially draining, the fight to preserve guarantee constitutionally-guaranteed freedoms would sponge up funds that could have been used to fight AIDS.

A Christmas Eve fire in 1988 nearly destroyed the 80-year old frame church building, but damage was confined to the west wall and large stained glass window. The event precipitated repairs, restoration, and the advent of a new symbol for the church.

Membership first rose, then began a precipitous decline to a core of about 35 people. Dissension over politics, privacy, and prayer divided members. It was not the best of times.

Gary Wilson was 46 years old when he arrived in March 1986. He had a diverse background, having volunteered for two years in Ethiopia in John F. Kennedy's Peace Corps. He then taught mathematics for 8 years in Castro Valley, near San Francisco. He began his ministry at MCC-Oakland in 1973. After almost three years, he next pastored at MCC-Anchorage for three years, then at MCC-Seattle as assistant and interim pastor for six years.

"Pastor Gary" had first come out as gay in 1966, "when there was little to come out to." He attended MCC-San Francisco services in 1969, and was first licensed as an MCC clergy in 1973. Wilson received a UFMCC lifetime ordination in 1976. With its strength of commitment to social justice for all, he saw viability in the denomination, but he also believed the UFMCC had compromised some of its initial potential by adopting questionable standards of the world church. Clergy should dress in blue jeans rather than formal stilted clerical attire, according to his philosophy.

Once settled into Portland, Gary began assuming the leadership responsibilities from the lay people who had led the church over the previous 16 months. He reported in the City Week, a neighborhood tabloid, which he felt the congregation had done an incredible job, especially keeping financially healthy. Wilson soon established three major goals for the congregation. He wanted MCC to be an active presence in

"Three Queens for a Day" reads the banner. Rev. Gary Wilson's good sense of humor spilled into the congregation as he celebrated January birthdays with Bob Jackson and Neal Curry. Bob served in many capacities over the years, primarily as a deacon, and Neal served as treasurer for decades.

Sue Lantz photos

Gary Wilson had served as Northwest District Coordinator before accepting the position to minister at MCC-Portland. He became active in local politics and in issues around human rights.

Sue Lantz photos

266

Rev. Gary Wilson 1986 - 1993

the community. He hoped to restore the confidence that had been lost in the church. And Wilson hoped to have the church be a constant voice for human dignity. Wilson saw himself as a facilitator and resource person, to help people understand their gifts and strengths. He vowed to stay two years.

Installation

Gary's installation service was the evening worship on June 29, 1986. Joe Hooker performed on the piano and special music was sung by BJ Wilkinson and Amani Jabari. Deacon José Montoya said the Prayer of Installation followed with a sermon "Only Through Love," delivered by Rev. Marguerite Scroggie. She had served as Worship Coordinator for the previous eight months as the search committee narrowed the number of candidates for the senior pastor position. Dave Dishman, the previous Worship Coordinator, read words of installation, and Teresa Nunn lead prayer.

At the installation, Board Treasurer Neal Curry spoke his thoughts to the congregation saying, "It has been a long, difficult, and rewarding last year and a half, for the Church and for myself. We have had to dig down deeper than we ever thought, rely on ourselves, and truly come to believe that 'with God, all things are possible.' And now, today formalized by this ceremony, MCC-Portland moves forward on a new path, to once again become one of the vehicles in the UFMCC and the Portland area for bringing the love and message of God to all people, for the Church is not the building, but the people."

A list of people who helped make the Installation weekend a large success include Mary Brady, Grace Schaefer, José Montoya, Bob Carter, Bob Jackson, Vicki Girardin, Gloria Sumpter, BJ Wilkinson, Gail Bumala, Teresa Nunn, Stephanie H, Sallie VanHalen, Sue Lantz, Marilyn Richmond, Alan Dickson, Gayla Williams, Vic Winegar, and Don Brooking.

Six months after Gary's installation, the congregation celebrated the 10th anniversary of its charter on January 24, 1987, calling the festivities a "Homecoming." Tom Koberstein, director of the Cascade AIDS Project, was special speaker at the Saturday evening Gospel concert. The group "Sojourn" and the MCC choir provided the music. Sunday's services featured Claudia Vierra preaching at the 10 am service, and Gary Wilson at the 5:45 pm worship.

Congregational Leadership

Leading the church was the Board of Directors. Members included Retha Garrett, Wendell Gleason, Amani Jabari, Sue Lantz, Vi Leagjeld, José Montoya, and Stephanie H. Gary's presence rounded out the composition of the Board with the clerical and administrative element that had been absent for 16 months.

Deacons were Mary Brady, who at one time had been Roman Catholic; Bob Jackson, hailing back to the days of Denis Moore and Austin Amerine; and BJ Wilkinson, who also delighted worshippers with her special music and chalk talk presentations. At the time, Fran Hall was a deacon candidate. It was the task of the deacons to look after the spiritual and counseling needs of members, taking some of the responsibility from the pastor so he could do other jobs. Mary Brady wrote articles for the Chalice explaining liturgical practice helping congregants understand the various objects used in worship, such as communion ware and paraments.

The Board of Directors included three women–Holly Beyer, Casey Elliott, and Gayla Williams. Men on the Board included Bob Basque, Jonathan "Rick" Cantu, Jimmy Bryan, Dick Burdon, Larry Foltz, Rocky Rudy, and Pastor Gary Wilson.

A spirited group of student clergy served the congregation, including Gail Bumala, Ashan Nelson, Wendy Taylor, Sallie VanHalen, Kate Zon, and Teresa Nunn, who also volunteered as the pastor's administrative assistant. Kate Zon later became a clergy on staff by 1991. Teresa Nunn was appointed to pastor MCC-Vancouver by District Coordinator Rev. Ed Sherriff.

Jimmy Bryan, a member with artistic and design skills, was the editor of the revived

Music has always been a major part of MCC activity. including an infamous jug band featuring several MCC luminaries. After a concert, Bob Eplin and Stephanie Holloway share the moment.

Gail Bumala strums before singing; Lu El enjoys the show, as does Nikki Johnson (above).

Sue Lantz photos

Rev. Gary Wilson   1986 - 1993

Chalice, while also remaining very active with the Imperial Sovereign Rose Court. Dick Burdon, a former Methodist missionary and minister, participated in several committees, and kept the congregation informed on other denomination's attitudes towards homosexuality and AIDS. He was also one of several MCC members dancing their feet off weekly with the Rose Town Rambler Square Dancing club.

Music

Terry Snowden continued playing organ, piano, and directing the choir for several years. He gave benefit recitals for Our House, and also had a music ministry at St. Stephens Episcopal on SW 14th. In September 1990, he announced his resignation so that he could pursue his interests in composing religious music reflective of the AIDS crisis and the lesbian/gay experience. Eventually, he spent time in Spain as part of his ministry before succumbing to AIDS in September 1995, passing away at Our House at age 48.

Larry Moad moved from Spokane to Portland in 1984 with his partner, Mike Austin. He learned about MCC in 1986, and spent a few Sundays as a "drive-by"–hesitant to actually stop, park, and cross the threshold of a gay-friendly church. He had played piano for East Spokane Baptist Church for many years, a mega-church with a fleet of 26 busses, and was saddled with a fundamentalist church background. When he did make the decision to crossover, his involvement at MCC was rapid. He began playing the offertory during services. His playing was a wonderful mixture of flamboyance, spiritual, and jazz, with a little cocktail lounge thrown in for good measure. He performed for social functions in addition to his regular job, much like Joe Anderson. The Steinway instrument was nearing its life's end, and volunteer Kevin Campbell tuned it constantly.

A rotation of three regular pianists shared keyboard responsibilities–Wendell Gleason, Larry Moad, and Gary Patton. Each man represented a different performance style. Unknown to anyone in the congregation, Gary enjoyed performing wearing just his robe and shoes. Larry's style was pretty hard on the old player Steinway. The donated instrument could hardly hold tune, and Larry played with a touch ranging from tender to brutal. One Sunday as he played variations on "*It is Well with My Soul*," his final cord snapped one of the lower strings. It was found after the service several feet away from the piano under a pew! Time for a new piano.

Larry accompanied the choir, directed by Jeri Harvey. Soon, a men's quartet formed called the "Pastel Tones." The group would perform at several of the AIDS vigils. A group composed of Frank Myers, Dan McNeil, Rose Morgan, and Claudia Johnson sang deeply spiritual pieces for offertories. Amani Jabari assembled another Gospel-style group, composed of Jodie, Joe, Joe's cousin, and Amani. Cleverly, they called themselves "Three Guys and a Girl."

Terry Bonnett volunteered to make a series of large banners for the sanctuary. These provided color while adding symbolism, and partially covered the walls between the hammer beam trusses. They hung in place for several years but were taken down when the wording on them was deemed politically incorrect, since they were not inclusive.

Balloon Payment Campaign–1987

Looming 18 months after Wilson's installation was a balloon payment on the building. This was to be the final payment, due in September 1987, 10 years after the purchase of the property at 24th and NE Broadway. The mortgage balance was $30,000.

Repairs and renovations were also needed, and a list of projects was drawn up. The needed repairs involved roofing, plumbing, interior repairs, and covering the large stained glass window to aid in its preservation. Two major projects were in long need of redress – remodeling the restrooms in the basement to make them handicapped accessible and remodeling the kitchen to accommodate the feeding program which had been curtailed by city health and building officials. The estimated costs for these projects were set at $20,000, giving the campaign a $50,000 goal.

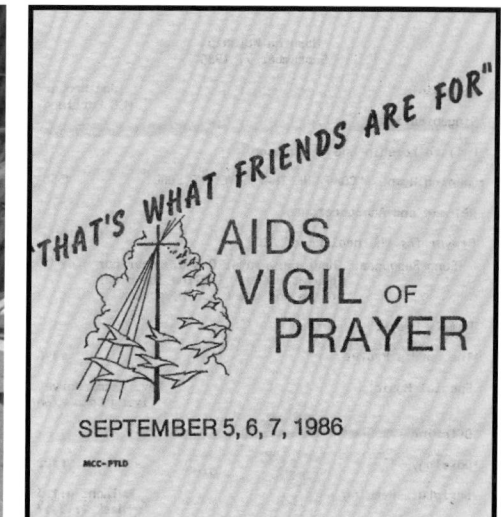

MCC held its first AIDS vigil in 1986. In 1987, the community was included in planning and implementing AIDS vigils, which continued for several years. Phoenix Rising helped with counseling.

270

Rev. Gary Wilson 1986 - 1993

Brochures were prepared, which gave a bit of history, a listing of the projects, and a strong statement of the church's self-concept. It read, in part:

"The doors of MCC have been opened to provide assistance to the homeless and needy through its feeding and clothing programs. It has also served as a meeting place for community and neighborhood groups. Many existing groups had their start at MCC. It has offered referral services for housing, counseling, and employment. The church has also provided workshops, discussion groups, and spiritual support around the issue of AIDS. Through its continued endeavors, Metropolitan Community Church personifies its belief in being a place of worship for all people. MCC is a Christian church that is proud of its diversity....The full purchase of the building will be another historic step; it will make the MCC building the first property in the community to be owned, free and clear, by a Lesbian/Gay organization."

Several special fund-raising events brought in funds. A cruise on the Willamette River was held in conjunction with the Cascade Aids Project. Intercultural Gospel concerts garnered free-will offerings. There was a Valentine's Dance with the Lesbian Community Project. The business community was solicited for tax-deductible donations and there were articles and appeals printed in *Just Out* and *Willamette Week*.

The campaign fell short of its goal. Some payment was made, and the contract renegotiated for a final payment due in 1993.

Troy Perry spoke at MCC-Portland during a weekend spiritual renewal program, November 20-22, 1987. The weekend addressed the role of the church in human and civil rights causes. Another timely topic of the weekend was the Christian response to the AIDS epidemic.

The Wellness Candle

No one seems to remember exactly when a new feature was added to MCC worship practice, but the Wellness Candle has become a major significant focus of worship for nearly 20 years. At each regular service, a single large candle is designated to be lit as part of a prayer request related to healing and wellness.

In the midst of the AIDS crisis when the practice began, an individual spoke a short message related to healing, comfort, or a request for God's blessing on a situation. After the verbal presentation, the candle, placed on the altar, is lit as a symbolic reminder of the prayer. While originally begun as a response to AIDS, the scope of requests and thanksgiving have grown far beyond AIDS. The lighting of the Wellness and Liberation candle continues in practice each week, reminding the congregation of the need for prayer and praise.

AIDS Vigils

MCC-San Diego Pastor David Farrell invited various community groups to participate there on December 1, 1985 in a 50-hour prayer vigil and series of workshops. He had become frustrated with the rate of AIDS deaths in the San Diego gay community, the growing need for counseling and support services, and the severe lack of government attention to medical funding. MCC-San Diego had become a physical and emotional care center, which Rev. Farrell had encouraged.

The UFMCC fellowship asked Rev. Farrell to lead an international campaign to sponsor similar events in other MCCs, and in main-line denominations. MCC-Portland thus held its first AIDS Vigil in December 1986. Amani Jabari headed up the planning committee. The first Portland Vigil was an emotionally powerful event, gathering over 200 attendees, and it was resolved, that the following year, the event should be expanded to include people and churches throughout the Portland area. Hence began an annual community tradition that continues still, in a slightly reformatted identity as World AIDS Day.

The 1987 event was planned by a committee including MCC leaders Wendell Gleason, Larry Foltz, and Kathy Stout. Feeling they had to do something about losing so many friends, the MCC committee tried to get a wide cross

Always on the look out for good food and warm atmosphere, several eateries were available in the mid-1980s, including the Brasserie Montmartre (formerly Zorba the Greek's) and the Chocolate Moose, both in downtown Portland. The Moose was in the corner space, now occupied by the Shanghai Tunnel. On the eastside, Starkey's opened on SE Stark in 1987. It became immediately popular with MCC members for Sunday brunch. Vying for popularity has always been the Village Inn, 10 blocks west on Broadway. Susan VanHouten and Sue Lantz enjoy brunch anywhere.

Rev. Gary Wilson   1986 - 1993

section of involvement from the larger community. Supportive congregations and organizations within the gay community were invited and participated. A much larger vigil was the result.

Jimmy Bryan designed an open heart graphic design to symbolize the Christian spirit in time of AIDS. The dry-brush outline of the heart was not complete, leaving an opening near the bottom, symbolizing the passage of energy and love both into the heart, and out from the heart. Entitled "*A Time to Heal*" the 50-hours included far more events than the previous vigil. Gil Gerald, director of minority affairs of the National AIDS Network, shared Friday's opening ceremony honors with Kristine Gebbe, the Oregon State Heath Division administrator. A reception and concert followed. There were workshops, concerts, meals, and discussion panels all day Saturday. Sunday brought worship, an open discussion about ministering to people touched by AIDS, and a closing candlelight gathering in Terry Shrunk Plaza.

An ironic side issue within MCC was solved over the AIDS vigil of 1987. Two strongly opinionated camps contended over the issue of cigarette smoking at church. Smoking inside the building was the issue, and a de facto agreement relegated smokers to the basement. It was agreed that there would be no smoking within the building during the AIDS vigil for health reasons, and soon thereafter, all smokers migrated outside the building.

By 1989, the organization and planning had grown through experience. Gary Wilson put out a directive of suggestions to the planning committee detailing whom to contact where, when, and for what. He named the preachers who had agreed to speak. He included from the past what worked and what didn't. People of Color United Against AIDS was to play a significant role along with the co-sponsors, Ecumenical Ministries of Oregon under Rodney Page. Gary's final thought to the committee was "plan away; enjoy yourselves; grow in the experience; and depend on God, not on yourselves or me."

Gregory Franklyn coordinated the 1989 Vigil, 10 years after the first report of AIDS. Vigils were about grieving, learning, growing, and celebrating. Dr. Estil Dietz, local primary care physician who had specialized in work with HIV patients was honored at a reception. Lady Elaine Peacock Empress XXIX, the reigning Empress Velvet Monet XXXII and other members of the Imperial Sovereign Rose Court lead a program about the art of female impersonation at 3 in the morning, followed by a 10 am Sunday worship service. Amani Jabari, member and local PWA and activist, delivered the closing message, along with Jimmy Bryan, designer of the Portland AIDS Heart.

The Portland Gay Men's Chorus performed several concerts during these years trying to present sensitive compositions relating to AIDS. Several Gay Choruses across the country began commissioning original works telling the story of grief and love in a compassionate way. Attending GALA (Gay and Lesbian Association of Choruses) conferences in Seattle (1989) and Denver (1992) exposed the chorus to these new pieces. Many were then conducted by Jon Rollins, himself a person with AIDS, for Portland audiences.

Among these pieces was Grammy award winner John Corigliano's *Of Rage and Remembrance*, a haunting, and jagged, angry work with lyrics like, "Was there a time before the sorrow?" and "Is there life outside the terror?" In another concert, "Left Behind" was sung, while country dancing men disappeared gradually from the stage until there was just a sole dancer on the empty stage. Yet concerts were always programmed to ultimately uplift audiences. Works didn't dwell on despair, but followed a progression from anger to acceptance and an exhortation to life and a celebration of relationships. PGMC concerts were often an emotional experience, and some audiences chose to stay away rather than expose themselves to reminders of lost friends or their own illness.

Esther's Pantry

Following the death of Chester Brisker in 1985, efforts were begun to establish a food source for men afflicted with AIDS. Chester was Empress Esther Howard Hoffman XXIV, well known and loved in the gay community, and

This storefront on NW Broadway housed Esther's Pantry for several years. It was just 2 blocks north of the Embers where the pantry had been located. No large sign or information of any kind marked the location, protecting the privacy of clients. Food donations came from individual, groups, major events, and gifts of funds from several groups, including the Imperial Sovereign Rose Court, Portland Gay Men's Chorus, and Metropolitan Community Church. Women donated hundreds of hours in service and organization, especially Babaloo, who stayed involved 20 years.

ESTHER'S PANTRY
2nd Annual Shopping Cart Parade

"REMEMBERING ESTHER" Show
SUN. — JULY 17th!!
Parade Starts — 5:45 pm
Show Time — 7:30 pm at EMBERS
For More Details Call **231-0843**

just out • 15 • July 1988

Entertainers, professional and amateur, all joined in to help raise funds to help AIDS patients and to finance education campaigns across the city and state. Foxy Ladies held parties and the Dyketones gave several concerts.

Rev. Gary Wilson 1986 - 1993

very public about his AIDS status. The gay community contributed funds to pay for his care, but after his death, the family wanted the funds used in an ongoing way. The costs of medication and treatment often devoured entire life-time savings. Without the ability to work, men soon became destitute and dependent upon family, friends, or charity. A food bank for people with AIDS was first established in a vacant storefront next to the Dirty Duck, facing NE 3rd.

The second permanent home of Esther's Pantry was in the basement of the Embers on NW Broadway, in space provided by owner Steve Suss, who served on Esther's board for many years. While there was adequate subterranean space for storage and display, many ill men could not muster the emotional energy to return to a place where they had celebrated life so heartily just months earlier. It was emotionally draining and many found it downright embarrassing. While grateful for the food and supplies, returning to a once happy place proved devastating in their thinking.

It was decided to move Esther's two blocks north on Broadway into another storefront, directly across from Ray's Ordinary Bar and Grill. Being at street level was a bonus, and this location served for many years, with no outward markings, or large signs advertising the nature of the place.

Food for the pantry was donated through canned food drives and events. Operated by the Imperial Sovereign Rose Court, the Court garnered money from shows and donations from bar owners. There was no paid staff. Originally, most of the volunteers helping with daily operations were clients themselves. It would help them feel involved and they often worked until too weakened by their own disease to be of service. MCC members were early clients. Dani Eaton structured the volunteer scheduling and Ricky Caesar volunteered as manager for several years. Food was donated, or purchased for the Pantry with federal funds through the Ryan White act. White was a young hemophiliac who had contracted AIDS through a transfusion and died, probably gaining more attention than all of the gay AIDS deaths to that point.

Clients requesting food simply needed a diagnosis of AIDS to qualify, as confirmed by a medical doctor. Qualified men could then visit Esther's once per month, leaving with a large amount of canned and dry foods, paper supplies, and toiletries. Bubbaloo set up a system so that as they selected items, a "shopper" assistant would accompany them, to be sure they received a balanced supply. Volunteers talked with clients about pacing their use of the items so that they could stretch their supplies, which were often supplemented by food stamps from the State. Both volunteers and clients were often old friends, who had once partied together in various bars and homes before they got sick, and Esther's thus functioned as an ongoing support group. Some volunteers have survived 18 years of losing friends to the incurable disease.

MCC assumed management and ownership of Esther's Pantry years later, when Roy Cole was Pastor. Esther's is now a ministry of the congregation. (See chapters 12 and 13)

From All Walks of Life

Begun in 1987, CAP held an annual fundraiser called "From All Walks of Life." It was a walk-a-thon, routed through downtown Portland on a Sunday. Peter Walters led MCC participation in the event on August 7, 1988.

Another soon-to-be-annual event first took place in the Rose Garden of Washington Park that summer. Lady Elaine Peacock, a drag queen and dancer at Darcelle's, hosted the event when she was Rose Empress XXIX. Performances gave people a chance to see drag outside of the bar scene. "Peacock in the Park" raised money to fund the Audria Edwards Youth Scholarship, named after Lady Peacock's mother. The annual event would be staged for 19 years, the last event being in 2004.

Peace House

Lincoln Street Methodist Church, near SE 50th, began offering a "hard times" supper to members and neighbors in 1981. Rev. John Schwiebert and his wife Pat started the program, which grew too large for the small white frame

Panels from the *Names Project Quilt* were displayed in Portland in 1988 at the University of Portland. On another visit, panels were displayed at the memorial Coliseum. AIDS Vigils grew into citywide events. Many men, like early MCC member Eric Callicote, were able to continue normal activity years after diagnosis.

Peace House has provided hospice for people with AIDS and for others who can no longer take care of themselves. After Bob Jackson suffered a stroke, he chose to move into Peace House, hosting a large reception for his MCC friends, even while on oxygen

276

Rev. Gary Wilson   1986 - 1993

church. In 1984, they moved the free suppers to Centenary-Sunnyside Methodist, where the remnants of Centenary-Wilbur had relocated after its closure in 1980. Pat was an active member at MCC, and soon many volunteers from the church were involved in her program. As more poor and vagrant people gathered for free meal opportunities, neighbors became vocal in their concerns about neighborhood stability. Negotiations to continue the suppers were fodder for the news media. Several compromises were reached and the feeding program was allowed to continue with yellow-vested security guards and foot patrols to keep the migrants off of lawns and walkways.

With a quiet but committed zeal to build a worshiping community, the Schwieberts organized a joint effort of seven adults to form Metanoia Peace Community United Methodist Church in 1986. They met temporarily at Wilshire Methodist, Centenary-Sunnyside, and AME Zion churches.

Twenty-seven other friends made short-term loans to provide the cash to acquire an old neglected house at NE 18th and Tillamook, about a half mile west of MCC. Two couples, the Schwieberts and Bruce and Ann Huntwork, sold their own properties, donating proceeds to the project. The property was deeded as a gift to Metanoia Peace Community. Residents became stewards of the property, rather than owners, making clear that this venture was no private investment, but the medium for an ongoing ministry to a larger public constituency. Extensive renovation, upgrading, and painting restored the Irvington home to its former glory. It has become a significant place in the life of MCC-Portland for receptions, celebrations, discussions and meetings, concerts, funerals, and memorial events.

A three-alarm fire broke out in the frame house on June 25, 1987, and destroyed the entire third floor. Water damage was extensive throughout the rest of the structure. Good neighbors on the street opened their homes for six months to the residents of the charred dream while rebuilding began. With insurance funding, financial contributions, and thousands of hours of volunteer labor, the reconstruction was completed in time for an open house and service of edication on June 25, 1988–the first anniversary of the fire.

The stated mission of Peace House is to live into the kingdom (family) of God by cultivating community, and publicly demonstrating and advancing God's peace. As the AIDS crisis expanded into the Portland community, several men sought and received end-of-life care at Peace House. 10 MCC members number among the 15 residents who have died there of AIDS, including Ron Raz, Bob Carter, and José Montoya. Terminally ill people with other ailments were also cared for at Peace House in their final days, including Don Strausbaugh and Bob Jackson. These men hosted celebrations of their life for friends and MCC members, while hooked up to oxygen tanks. At Don's celebration, he had his entire 30-year collection of Christmas decorations displayed and for sale, with profits going to the MCC music program.

Metanoia Community is a worshiping community as well, with weekday Bible study and meditation and Sunday gatherings. Darrell DuBois, has been a participant in those services for 16 years, in addition to attending MCC with his partner, Larry Culkins. Average attendance on Sundays is about 25.

Pat Schwiebert's sensitivity to the needs of AIDS patients even led to a special project at MCC. The 80-year old hard wood pews were difficult to sit on for patients who had lost much of their body mass to the disease. Pat's solution was to upholster the seat portion of every pew in the sanctuary, seating for 200 people.

With changes in medications and treatments for AIDS in the early 21st century, at least one client originally moving to Peace house for terminal care, was able to regain health and strength and move out! The community and Pat celebrated Darrell DuBois as her finest "failure!" Praise God! He moved into Peace house planning to die there in November 1993 and moved out in September of 1997. The theme is "long-term vision, not long-term care."

A new mission for Peace House emerged in 1990 when several member/residents created

Response to AIDS took many forms. Juniper House was the first hospice where men could be cared for during their final days.T house and the adjoining one were linked and became the last home to many people with AIDS in the mid-'80s. Our House grew from this humble beginning through campaigns and fund-raising events. Barbara Roberts lent her support to the efforts of long-time activists like Tom Norton.

Marchers in Washington, DC brought the lack of governmental action to national attention. The time gap between the advent of AIDS and any significant government action delayed research and education programs. The gay community, supported by the efforts of many lesbian friends had to provide emotional and financial support during the maelstrom. Gay magazines faced the situation head on, with articles on research, health care, AIDS prevention, and the emotional impact of the plague.

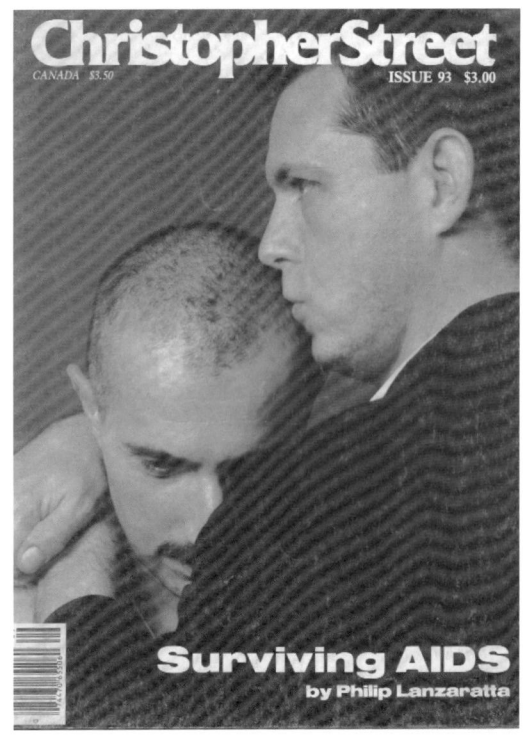

Rev. Gary Wilson   1986 - 1993

a new concept called Grief Watch, incorporating a form of grief support ministry as the Perinatal Loss Program. Pat worked to join Peace House efforts with the Oregon Health Sciences University Foundation. The primary ministry is to parents who are experiencing grief following the death of an infant. Pat wrote *Tear Soup*, a full-color illustrated book telling a story of grief and how it can be experienced. Sale profits still benefit Peace House.

MCC's AIDS Care Team

Grappling with the emerging understanding of AIDS and its pervasiveness in gay society nationwide, the UFMCC began providing emotional, spiritual, and educational support early on. MCC-North Hollywood Rev. Stephen Pieters wrote the first pamphlet used by the denomination to present a Christian response to the disease. The publication gave responses to frequently asked questions...What is AIDS? What does the UFMCC say about AIDS? Where is God in all this? Can AIDS be healed? What is it like to have AIDS? What can we learn from PWAs? What can local churches and individuals do? How can we be less susceptible? A list of reading materials was included. and several scriptural references were also suggested:

> Psalm 13
> Psalm 23
> Isaiah 41;10
> John 9: 1-3
> Romans 6:3-9
> Romans 15:13
> I Corinthians 15: 51-57
> II Corinthians 4: 7-18
> Matthew 6: 25-34

As the AIDS crisis materialized, MCC set up an AIDS Care Team. They received a $10,000 grant, and with those funds, the church provided almost anything the individual needed except medical and nursing care. Over 50 people in the church volunteered to work on the care team, and would go to visit and listen to clients, to clean house, to walk the dog, or to go grocery shopping with or for the client. Pat Schwiebert, Rich Kibbons, and Betty Nelson were three active leaders of the team. There was some case management and advocacy with government agencies, but most of the help was simply "hands-on" help and a lot of listening. Help was individualized to whatever need was current, and volunteers were pooled so that almost any volunteer could help almost any client. When men's conditions deteriorated to the nearness of their life's end, they were generally moved into Peace House with Pat Schwiebert.

Our House of Portland

A great need was developing in the AIDS community for places beyond hospitals for long-term care of the ill and dying. A house at SE 20th and Ankeny was donated by a man whose partner had died of AIDS. Called "Juniper House," volunteers soon had the place modified as a hospice for the care of six clients. The house next door was purchased and called Assisi House. A deck was built to join the houses. Even so, the houses soon were overcrowded and a better solution was necessary.

Rev. Gary Wilson, Rosemary Anderson and Rick Shurz formed a group chaired by Pat Schwiebert to support a larger hospice. This was when Pat first became acquainted with MCC-Portland. A 2-story house was donated, but the group soon realized that a one-level building was necessary. A former women's convalescent home on SE 27th was leased, and it was called Our House by the first clients, who saw it as their place. MCC cleaned, painted, and decorated one of the ten rooms; nine other community organizations did the same. Annette Guido became the first physician-in-residence, and Carolyn Ofiara was the first nurse. Everyone was in a learning mode about how to care for clients, involve them in the community, treat their conditions, and provide support for them, their families, and friends. Clients took up residence and died at the rate of one per week. The monthly $800 stipend per client from the State was far insufficient to cover expenses, and soon Providence Health Systems became partners with Our House.

MCC's Terry Snowden gave weekly benefit piano recitals at MCC with the free-will offerings donated to Our House.

Portland's mayors, Bud Clark and Sandy Director supported the gay community any way they could. Cookboys started as a no agenda pot luck group, and became a networking and support group for men from all cuts. Thanksgiving at Wendell Gleason's was an MCC tradition.

Barbara Roberts continued to support the gay and lesbian community, becoming involved in Lucille Hart dinners and other events. Her husband Frank was an Oregon State Senator. They became good friends with Sandy Director, gay business man and honorary gay Mayor of Portland.

Rev. Gary Wilson 1986 - 1993

By 2005, over 400 PWAs had spent their final days at Our House. As medicines and care progressed, not all entering patients were terminal. The role of Our House shifted, and the building underwent a total renovation for a new philosophy. (See Chapter 13)

The Oregon Citizen's Alliance and Measure 8

National culture was being controlled more and more by cable television. Rupert Murdock's new Fox network debuted "The Simpsons" in 1990. As a flawed 20th century secular "every man," Homer Simpson and his dysfunctional family presented humorous and satirical programs incorporating characters that were clowns, CEOs, South Asian immigrants running a convenience store, inept in-laws, and a Bible-thumping do-gooder neighbor. Episodes explored morality, commitment, and infidelity, but rarely homosexuality. Ned Flanders, the Christian neighbor, attributed his success to the three C's: Clean living, chewing thoroughly, and a daily dose of "vitamin church." Ned is spirituality in bondage, a model of righteousness gone wrong. He captures the image of the fundamentalist, and in Oregon, the stereotypical member of the Oregon Citizen's Alliance (OCA).

Organized in 1987, the Oregon Citizens Alliance came together to support "traditional American values." Baptist, Rev. Joe Lutz, defeated in the 1986 senatorial elections by Bob Packwood, rallied his supporters to "give conservatives an effective political voice." Fellow conservatives Lon Mabon, TJ Bailey, and Dick Younts formulated a credo to support a strong military, school prayer, and capitalism. They would oppose abortion and gay rights.

Lon Mabon, of rural Keizer, just north of the State capitol at Salem, became chairman of the group when Lutz left his wife and moved to California with another woman. (*Oregonian*, July 28, 1991, p.1 A)

Governor Neil Goldschmidt, a former liberal Portland mayor, passed an executive order in 1987 that prevented State agencies from discriminating against individuals based on their sexual orientation. The outraged Mabon and the OCA began a petition drive to have the order repealed. The war cry was "No Special Rights." Enough signatures were gathered to get the proposal to rescind the Governor's order onto the 1988 fall ballot as Measure 8.

MCC decided to no longer do business with the Christian Supply Company after strong anti-gay statements were made by several fundamentalist church bodies served by Christian Supply. The alternative was Ecumenical Church Supply located at 2829 SE Stark, very near a favorite gay restaurant and lounge, Starkey's. Even as the church took this token action, Gary Wilson was in dialogue with pastors at Hinson Memorial Baptist Church, hoping to discover and develop ways MCC could relate and treat others as Christians, regardless of theological differences.

The gay community tried to mobilize, amazed that such a proposal could garner the required signatures to get onto the ballot, much less muster a majority of votes to pass it. Feeling financially drained and emotionally distracted with AIDS and caring for sick and dying friends, the gay community was challenged to publicize their cause much beyond their own community.

During the pre-election summer of 1988, Oregonians for Fairness formed to oppose the OCA and its drive to revoke the Governor's Executive Order concerning the rights of gay citizens. The campaign kicked off with a rally July 8 at Terry Schrunk Park. A boycott against Alpenrose Milk protested their anti-gay stance.

Statewide, Oregon citizens did not benefit from the Portland-area dialogues and demonstrations, giving the OCA a 53% statewide victory in November, with Measure 8 passing 586,311 votes to 518,953.

Gays felt disenfranchised; they realized they had been disorganized. Some were even more encouraged to come out. Inclined to criticize the "No on 8" campaign (Oregonians for Fairness) leadership, gays soon realized it did no good to trash their own leaders and began

Significant individuals in the history of the Equity Foundation include Terry Bean (L) shown with Senator Ron Wyden (D); Rev Matt Nelson, first executive director of Equity; and Linda Traeger, current Executive Director, shown with youth advocate and activist Norm Costa.

Political buttons from the collection of Greg Pitts.

Rev. Gary Wilson   1986 - 1993

positive steps to strengthen their community and its organizations, including the entry of a gay and lesbian float for the first time in the Rose Festival Starlight Parade in June, 1989.

Equity Foundation

Jim Vegher and John Grigsby responded to the misinformation and stereotyping by Measure 8 backers. Taking an unprecedented and positive action, they organized a philanthropic organization with some members from the Right to Privacy Board. The mission of the Equity Foundation was and is "to assure the prosperity of gay and lesbian health, cultural and service organizations, and to promote a positive image of gay and lesbian people by making visible our contributions to the wider society." (*Just Out*, October 15, 1993, p. 15)

The founders were a collection of people who had an impassioned commitment to provide support to lesbian and gay organizations, especially those regularly bypassed by traditional grant-giving foundations. Under the early leadership of executive director Thomas Aschenbrener, funding has also been granted to non-gay causes that merit the support of the gay community. Grant application was made as simple as possible, but also required accountability and followup reports for use of funds granted.

Funds managed by Equity come from individual estates, planned giving, endowments, outright gifts, and several workplace giving campaigns including the City of Portland, Metropolitan Services District, Multnomah County, Tri-Met, and the State of Oregon. Employees at these places requested the inclusion of Equity as a recipient of their funds.

Christian Churches Take A Stand... Or Don't

Dialogue in many Christian churches over homosexuality was sparked by the ballot measure, and was the subject of an *Oregonian* article on July 10, 1988. With a photograph of MCC worshippers raising their arms reciting the Lord's Prayer, the article focused on the division of devout believers on both sides of the issue.

Ecumenical Ministries of Oregon director Rodney Page noted that all denominations were struggling with the issue. The EMO had not taken a stance the previous year on a proposed Oregon Senate's gay rights bill.

Episcopalians had rejected a measure condemning homosexuality as a contradiction of Christian ideals. Their bishops did endorse traditional and Biblical teachings of chastity and fidelity. The Greater Portland Association of Evangelicals supported the OCA, since it had supported similar measures in the past. A group of evangelical educators, pastors, and businessmen called the "Saltshakers," believed that Scripture condemned homosexuality in no uncertain terms, and discrimination against its practitioners was justified.

Citing the story of Sodom, and "proof texts" in Leviticus and Romans, Western Conservative Baptist Seminary taught that homosexuality was a sin. Rev. S. Bowen Matthews, senior pastor at Hinson Baptist, held similar views but urged churches to avoid becoming scenes of political standoffs. "Churches that become scenes of political confrontation may seriously compromise their ability to provide understanding and respect," he said. (*Oregonian*, July 10, 1988, pp c1, 7)

United Methodists weren't united on this topic. While affirming all individuals as having "sacred worth," they prohibited the ordination of self-avowed practicing homosexual ministers. Some Methodist congregations voted to become "open and affirming" in support of gay members. "Affirmation" was growing as a group of United Methodists concerned about full inclusion of gay men and lesbians in the church. Paul Nickell, active in the group, said "We believe it's possible to love God, to love Christ, to live a Christian life and to have a sexual life."

The newly united Evangelical Lutheran Church in America debated the ordination of "openly gay" seminarians. A professor from the Lutheran School of Theology in Chicago suggested that perceived Biblical condemnations were more likely means of distinguishing Jews and Christians from pagans during scriptural times. A nationwide caucus of gay Lutherans

Inclusive Language as printed in an MCC Brochure from 1987

Since its inception, the Universal Fellowship of Metropolitan Community Churches has been committed to inclusivity in its life and faith.

In the 1970's and continuing in the 1980's, the issues of inclusive language (in worship, scriptures, publications, speech) came to the forefront of the whole Christian Church and to the attention of the universal Fellowship. In 1979, the Board of Elders appointed an Inclusive language Task Force whose report to the 1981 General Conference in Houston, Texas, was passed overwhelmingly after some amendments were made. That final report forms the Policy base for the Universal Fellowship and its local churches regarding the use of inclusive language. Major portions of that report are presented in this pamphlet.

The Preamble of the report deals with the question: Why Inclusive Language?

"The reason we need to find and use inclusive language in our church life has been widely misunderstood. Inclusive language has often been urged upon congregations on grounds that the use of traditional, non-inclusive language upsets and angers some who then avoid the church. As Christians we need to be concerned about the feelings of others; however, if the only reason we use inclusive language is that it keeps some people from getting upset, then what of those who find the use of inclusive language disturbing because of its unfamiliarity? The principle, which guides the life and practice of the Church cannot be "what do most people find comfortable, but rather, 'what is God's will and purpose?.'" The reason we need to use inclusive language is not because we want to keep a particular group happy, but because it is necessary to promote justice, reconciliation and love, the agenda to which we Christians have been called.

A World of Division

"Because of human sin," we live in a world of division and oppression. Groups which have traditionally exercised control over other groups inevitably and often unconsciously seek to preserve that superior status by denying the same access to power and privilege to others that they themselves enjoy. Such denial may be blatant in the form of discriminatory laws or customs, or it may be hidden but even more potent in the form of oppressive concepts or language. The insidious nature of language which serves to emphasize one group as the norm or standard is that it reinforces that group's primacy and importance every time we think or speak, thus, it becomes automatic or 'natural to ascribe greater weight to that group. Justice, reconciliation and love demand that we overcome oppression wherever it exists and we cannot exclude the oppressive structures of our language from this task.

Widening Our Hearts

"The use of inclusive language does more that overcome a barrier to equal access. It frees us to apprehend and convey the wider truth. Paul urges the Corinthians to widen their hearts that they might fully experience the gospel (II Cor. :13. In the same spirit, he might urge us to widen our understanding so that we might better grasp the richness and fullness of God as well as of our own humanity. It is our openness to move beyond comfortable and familiar images that enables us to grow in our relationship with God. The importance of inclusive language is that it serves to liberate everyone."

The Introduction to the guidelines provides a perspective on Christian faith and language and the prophetic task that challenges the Church:

Not So Simple

"Language is not so simple a matter as it might first appear. How we speak about something not only describes the experience, but often shapes and creates it. The power and significance of language, words, the word, was clearly understood by the authors of Scriptures which identified the act of creation with God's Word, God's speaking. The imagery of God's interaction with humanity is consistently expressed in terms of God's Word or speaking. The early prohibition against uttering God's name was recognition of the power that a name or word holds.

Indeed, God's delegating to humanity the authority to name the birds and animals was an act of empowerment. Thus, when we head with language in general and God language in particular, we are venturing into an area of the deepest significance, and it is important that we proceed with care and caution.

Change is Constant

"At the same time, both the Biblical tradition and the history of the faith community reveal that one constant in God language is that of change. And how could it be otherwise? For it is a living God whom we worship and respond to. Both as individuals and as communities, our understanding and experience of this God grows as we grow and growth inevitably brings change.

"The Bible in its present form evolved over a period of many centuries. Beginning as stories of faith passed by word of mouth from generation to generation, these stories were eventually written down and added to.

Different generations of faith communities shaped, edited and retold these stories in light of their own understanding and experience of God. Still other communities later on discussed and debated which stories and versions would be included, as scripture and which would not.

Rev. Gary Wilson   1986 - 1993

was organized as "Lutheran Concerned."

Concordia Publishing House, of the Lutheran Church-Missouri Synod, published a 38-page adult Bible Study entitled *AIDS, A Christian Response,* in 1987. Through six chapters, the study group was educated about what was known of AIDS medically; what were important issues to persons with AIDS; what were the opportunities for ministry to AIDS patients and their families; how to deal with feelings of guilt; how to offer forgiveness and hope; and a look at responsible sexual behavior. Prayer over the study and open-minded interpretation of multiple scriptures was encouraged.

While not dwelling on a traditional condemnation of homosexuality, the booklet offered "when we confront people by telling them about their sin (such as homosexual behaviors, promiscuous heterosexual practices, or sinful use of drugs) we are speaking Law...As we speak God's law, Satan will tempt us to speak lovelessly and judgmentally. However, such confrontation may drive the person to despair or rebellion against the Law. God desires that we speak the Law for the sake of the Gospel, to lead to sorrow over sin, repentance, and acceptance of God's forgiving love in Christ..."To the brokenhearted, not a syllable containing a threat or a rebuke is to be addressed, but only promises conveying consolation and grace"(C.F.W. Walther, in AIDS - A Christian Response, St. Louis, 1987 p. 29)

In October, 1985, Catholics held a "Servants of the Good Shepherd" Mass on Saturday afternoons at MCC. The Vatican issued a 1986 statement describing homosexual orientation as against natural law, a grave depravity, and intrinsically disordered. But the Oregon Catholic Conference remained neutral. Taking a position would have confused the broader community about the church's stance, because the local Catholics did not want to support any discrimination against gays in employment and similar areas. Renegade gay Catholics continued to meet as "Dignity" where sympathetic priests allowed them to assemble with respect and dignity, primarily at St. Francis parish on SE 12th where they continued their annual community dinners through 1988.

Unitarian-Universalists held an opposing viewpoint, believing that committed and loving relationships can exist between same-sex people. Metropolitan Community Church remained firm in its special mission to lesbians and gays, whether they were Christians or of other spiritualities. MCC was to gain a greater visibility throughout the State for its stance on the gay rights issue with voters. The United Churches of Christ, later to become supportive of the UFMCC, was not mentioned in the 1988 news article.

At Koinonia House on the PSU campus, a Mass in Time of AIDS began in January, 1987. The city-wide AIDS Vigil in September, 1987, involved several local churches, and raised the visibility of AIDS and homosexuality in public awareness. It was covered by local news media, especially the closing Candlelight Vigil ceremony at Terry Schrunk Plaza downtown.

The 1988 Vigil, another 50-hour event held September 9-11, was co-sponsored by Ecumenical Ministries of Oregon and Metropolitan Community Church, raising AIDS visibility even more during the heated election season. Several workshops were held at Grace Memorial Church, eight blocks west of MCC. The theme of the weekend was "The Healing Continues." Gary Wilson had been attending EMO meetings even though MCC was not officially admitted into the organization. His enthusiasm and participation earned him a position on the EMO Board, leading to the co-sponsorship.

Other religious organizations raised their visibility in 1988, including the gay and lesbian Mormon group called "Affirmation," and the "SDA Kinship," a support group of Seventh-Day Adventists. An MCC Friday night prayer group, which had begun in 1982, evolved into Living Communion Fellowship led by Pastor James Sconce, Nita Gates, and Judy Allen. They became a separate group when Rev. Delores Berry resigned from MCC and bought a church on SE 62nd near Foster, with Naomi Harvey as pastor. The group split in 1989 into Crown of Praise Ministries and The Potter's House. Crown of Praise identified themselves as a gay and les-

The MCC choir sang Christmas Carols at Eastport Plaza as part of the church outreach program. Three of those singers had no problem with national Coming Out Day. What you can't change, you can't hide.

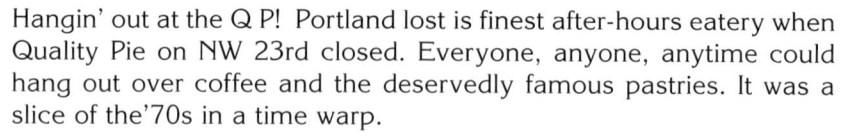

Hangin' out at the Q P! Portland lost is finest after-hours eatery when Quality Pie on NW 23rd closed. Everyone, anyone, anytime could hang out over coffee and the deservedly famous pastries. It was a slice of the '70s in a time warp.

Rev. Gary Wilson   1986 - 1993

bian charismatic church. The Potters House was led by Rev. Bill Roberts along a more fundamental path. The Sacred Band was another group advertising itself as dedicated to exploring spirituality.

At MCC-Portland, "Hallelujah" was the theme of a spiritual renewal in June, 1988. Guest presenter was Rev. Elder Jeri Ann Harvey, a passionate presenter and healer. Her challenge to the congregation was to accept the wholeness offered to humanity by Christ...in the midst of plague and politics. Weekend events included workshops on "Living with Loss," "Healing and Evangelism," and "The 12 Steps and Spirituality." Souvenir hankies with "Hallelujah" imprinted on them were sold to raise funds. There was, of course, a potluck, and three opportunities for worship.

National Coming Out Day

October 11, 1988 was the first national Coming Out Day. For some gays, it was a confusing time; for others, it was a time to take a visible stand, singing with the PGMC. "I am what I am, I am my own special creation...so it's time to open up your closet!" The Portland chapter of the National Leather Association held its first meeting and 36 people attended. Phoenix Rising became the first gay and lesbian organization in Oregon to join the United Way Campaign.

It is probably no coincidence that a large number of gay and lesbian social groups formed in the years around Measure 8. The Lesbian Community Project first met in 1987 and had over 600 members within a year. QUAC (Queers United Against Closets) organized, as did GENESIS, a group for men with AIDS looking for healing through positive imagery, affirmations, unconditional love, and camaraderie. The Gay Men's Pagan Circle was also formed, as was the Jewish Lesbian Daughters of Holocaust Survivors. The Portland Frontrunners initiated the annual Stonewall Run, a 2-mile or 10-K benefit run for CAP (Cascade AIDS Project).

The NAMES project, honoring deceased AIDS victims with uniquely designed and sewn panels, gave friends and families the opportunity to memorialize loved ones to be part of the 1987 National AIDS Quilt. The Oregon Chapter became official in February 1989. The Quilt came to Portland twice and was displayed at the Chiles Center at the University of Portland and at the Memorial Coliseum. The Portland chapter dissolved when membership fees in the national organization became prohibitive.

Portland also honored its fallen son, Ben Lindner in April 1988, who was murdered in Nicaragua a year earlier as he worked on a humanitarian water project in a remote village. The Portland-Corinto Sister City Association began meeting, and by February, the Portland Central America Solidarity Committee was functioning.

The Fire of 1988

After the Christmas Eve candlelight service, one small votive candle apparently reignited and burned down into the wood window sill upon which it had been left. Liquid wax and 80-year old wood fueled flames, which eventually spread to the wood tracery of the large five section stained glass window and then into the west wall.

Flames were spotted by a passer-by. Stories credit either a watchful neighbor or a cab driver who reported the fire. Firefighters were able to confine the blaze to the west wall and eaves. The window was a total loss: the structure was compromised, and water damage inside the church ruined carpeting and stained the old yellow walls.

Gary Wilson lived nearby on NE 31st and was soon on the scene. With pastoral concern, he greeted Christmas day worshippers with the sad news. The firemen had cleaned up sufficiently that Christmas day service was held in the church, with a large black plastic sheet flapping where the Povey window had once filtered light.

Services were held in the disheveled sanctuary for six months, as repairs were finished, replacement carpeting installed, and painting was done. The Board of Directors and congregation met soon after the fire to decide the future course of rebuilding. As meaningful as the historic window design was with flowers, open bible, crosses, and colored glass, the deci-

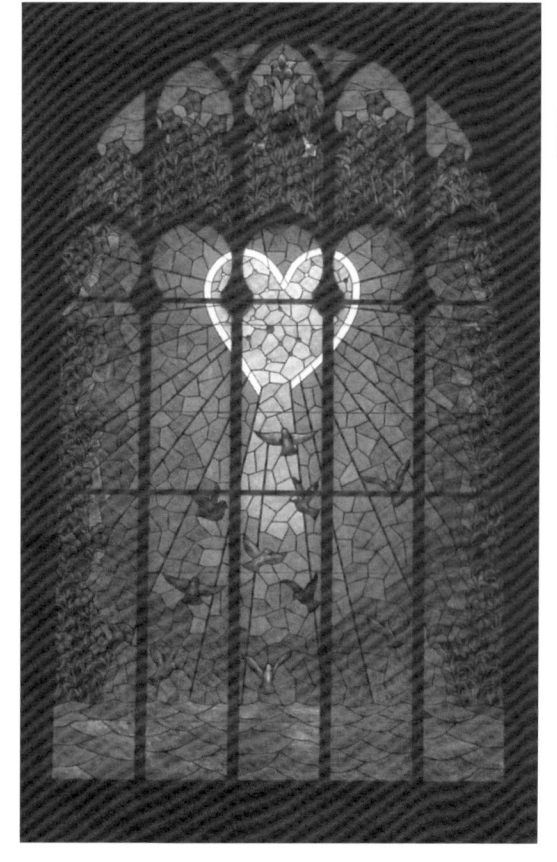

David Schlicker was one of three artists who submitted designs to replace the window destroyed by the Christmas Eve fire of 1988. Having repaired many of the historic Povey windows around Portland, he was able to use some of their techniques and materials, including Kokomo glass. He used beveled glass pieces to surround a heart design based on Jimmy Bryant's AIDS Vigil design. Those faceted pieces focus late afternoon light on the east wall of the interior. The effect is the lighted heart.

Rev. Gary Wilson   1986 - 1993

sion was made to have an image in the new window that would reflect the history and vision of MCC as a worshiping family. By Washington's Birthday, parameters for a commission were sent to potential stained glass artists. Most importantly, the new design was to be dedicated, in a life-affirming way, to the issue of AIDS. Human figures, if any, were to be both male and female and not predominantly of the white race.

David Schlicker, a young Portland artist in glass, was one of three artists to submit detailed plans and color schemes. Advocates for each of the designs spent hours in discussion before the final vote gave the nod to Schlicker. In the center of a blue field is a heart design with rays of light emerging from the lower side. The design honors the open heart design of Jimmy Byran, created a year earlier for the 1987 AIDS Vigil, and symbolizes an open heart—one that can receive as well as give. The blue field represents the world, and flying in this field are ten birds, each of a different color, symbolizing diversity. Framing the design is green foliage with lily and dogwood blossom designs, reflecting the heritage of the original Povey window. In Christian iconography, the lily represents purity.

He also had experience in repairing Povey windows and in his work was able to use several Povey Brothers' techniques. Lacking a full studio, he produced the window in sections and was only able to view the emerging full project by laying it out in his backyard patio and surveying the window from his second floor. (See chapter 5)

May 1989, was already selected as the date for the spring Northwest District Conference to be hosted by MCC-Portland. As Schlicker's work progressed, it seemed conceivable that the window could be done and installed in time for the conclave. The church building was closed for a week and church was moved to the Red Lion Hotel at Jantzen Beach. This allowed a very hardworking crew headed by Rocky and Harriet Rudy to put scaffolding in place and paint the entire sanctuary. The custom-mixed color chosen was "Rose of Sharon," now a Sherwin-Williams blend. Whether the color was chosen for its name or tint is not known, but the pre-fire dirty yellow walls were definitely improved with the new dusty pink (Rose of Sharon) paint.

Schlicker's window arrived and was installed. The congregation soon had a "wow" experience. Unexpectedly, people were amazed at a unique phenomenon. The beveled glass outlining the central heart design of the window directs a bright heart-shaped image on the east wall on the late summer afternoons. Participants in events between 5 and 7 pm can usually watch the progression of the image as it moves across the sanctuary wall while the sun lowers to the horizon. During a funeral one time the image landed on the face of a woman whose mother was being celebrated.

Before the altar alcove was moved in 1995, the light-shaped heart occasionally centered directly on the old Rushong cross above the altar. This only happens from the spring to autumn equinox, and is not present during the winter months.

Truth, Justice, and the American Way?

Barbara Roberts, a good friend of the gay community, won the 1990 gubernatorial election. Her election culminated years of community involvement and elected office, beginning when she felt her handicapped son was not receiving proper services and ran for her local school board. On the same ballot was Measure 5, which reduced property taxes supporting government and public school support. For the next several years, any budget cut or reduction in services was blamed on Measure 5. It almost became a state mantra.

Janice Wilson was Oregon's first out gay judge. She began holding court in March 1991. Another gay judge was appointed in 1993, and since then there have been at least 10 more openly gay justices in Oregon, including Portlanders David Gernant, Sid Galton, Michael McShane, and Alicia Fuchs. Other judges were appointed in Marion and Lane Counties. Rives Kistler was appointed to the Supreme Court by current Oregon Governor Ted Kulongoski.

Dave Kohl photo

First Congregational UCC not only has a landmark Italian Gothic tower, they have a landmark philosophy of welcome and affirmation. Rev. Pat Ross led the congregation through discussions in 1992 to adopt their statement of beliefs. Rev. Paul Davis is Asst. minister, and a member of PGMC. Their church's Povey window exhibits this philosophy–Christ with the Woman at the Well.

Sue Lantz photo

Rev. Frodo Okalum created Sister Spirit which is affiliated with MCC-Portland as a special ministry to women.

Dave Kohl photos

Rev. Gary Wilson 1986 - 1993

AIDS funding from the Oregon Health Division was reduced by two-thirds because of Measure 5. Fundraisers became even more important for CAP and other organizations. New methods were initiated of publicizing safe-sex and positive images of the "gay lifestyle." PGMC teamed with the Health Division through the efforts of MCC member David Lane to promote AIDS education. Outreach concerts were performed in outlying towns across the state in support of local P-FLAG and county health chapters. Many rural Oregonians saw their first "out" gay brothers on stage at a local junior high school, church, or community college. Rows of tuxedo-clad proud harmonizers often brought tears to eyes and standing ovations in crowds of people whose only references to homosexuals had been negative news coverage.

Sister Spirit MCC

Frodo Okulam joined MCC in 1977 at age 24, when there were about a hundred men in the group, and less than 10 women. She found Austin Amerine's energy infectious and his message of welcome to anyone seeking to know Christ inviting at a time when she was leery of both men and religion. When she experienced Betty Nelson giving her communion using the words "mother/father God," Frodo felt she was "home."

At a women's retreat with Arlene Ackerman, she was baptized. When Claudia Vierra led the congregation, Frodo enjoyed her teachings about female images from the Bible. Claudia's partner, Beau McDaniels exposed Frodo to the female leather culture, and became another mentor. The women joined with groups from MCC-Boise and MCC-Portland to participate in a candlelight march in Boise during the NW District Conference in 1980, a week after Rev. Jerry Falwell had stirred up public emotions there.

Entering the student clergy program under Jim Glyer, Frodo grew in her awareness of the needs for social justice, inclusive language, and an outreach to alternative spiritual groups, especially Wiccans. She performed on the violin, directed the MCC choir, and completed her requirements for licensure in 1985. She was ordained in 1989, and in 1991 felt the need to start the special ministry to women, to be known as Sister Spirit.

Frodo approached the UFMCC Home Missions Board with a proposal for her group, and was granted approval. Despite the misgivings of several MCC Board members, she was ultimately given the blessing to begin her mission. The all-woman assembly continues to meet in a small space on SE Belmont, and Frodo remains connected with MCC, occasionally preaching or participating in musical events.

Sometime during this period, Kate Zon also completed requirements of the Student Clergy program, and became an assistant minister to Gary. Her participation at MCC included all aspects of the ministry.

First Congregational UCC Pioneers Openness and Affirmation

The General Synod of the United Church of Christ in 1985 called for individual congregations of that denomination to explore and develop interpretations of scripture and actions in regards to homosexuality and the church. In Portland, First Congregational Church, second oldest existing church in the city, established "The Open and Affirming Task Force" of ten members to study the issue and develop a policy for the congregation. Charles and Rita Knapp, who had 15 years earlier help found P-FLAG, were members of the committee.

On January 26, 1992, the congregation declared itself "Open and Affirming," with a special service and written statements of a covenant. This set a model for other UCC congregations in the region, and for other denominations to follow, which eventually led to the establishment of the Community of Welcoming Congregations. (See chapter 13)

In summary, First Congregational stated that they were a diverse people who knew and were affirmed by God and one another, differences in education, race, ability and orientation

Button from Greg Pitts Archive

Ballot measure 9 in the 1992 election would have declared homosexuality to be perverse and promised to deny basic civil and human rights to non-straight people. Religious and political leaders declared that the Measure would be regressive. Rallies, meetings, editorials, and statements from the office of Governor Barbara Roberts combined to defeat the proposal.

Marty Davis photos

notwithstanding. As committed Christian people, they sought the end of continuing injustice of institutional discrimination, and setbacks in civil rights protection of gays and lesbians. As part of the body of Christ, they felt called to love one another, to do justice, to bring release to the oppressed, and to walk humbly with God. Sexuality was seen as a gift of God, which enriches lives and touches our humanity–it is part of the image of God in which we are created.

The Covenant of 1992 listed four affirmations:

1. We celebrate the image of God in every person, we rejoice in the sacredness of life, and we affirm all relationships of support that are founded on the principles of love and justice.
2. We condemn all acts of discrimination and violence against persons because of their sexual orientation, just as we condemn such acts against people because of race, age, gender, religion, ethnic background, or physical/mental disabilities or limitations. We pledge to support advocacy efforts designed to assure that homosexual persons enjoy the same rights and privileges as heterosexual persons
3. We affirm that lesbian, gay, and bisexual persons are welcome within the community of believers upon making the same affirmation of faith that all other members make. We encourage all members to share their talents, gifts, and energy in the liturgy, life, employment, and leadership of the congregation.
4. We pledge ourselves to support and honor committed partnerships of lesbian, gay, and bisexual people, recognizing the difficulty of maintaining such partnerships in the absence of the social validation and legal frameworks which do support heterosexual unions.

Ballot Measure 9

The first Gulf War began January 15, 1991 with the U.S. invasion of Kuwait to drive back oil-thirsty Iraqi occupation forces. Later in the year, the Portland City Council adopted a civil rights ordinance that banned discrimination in housing, employment and public accommodation based on sexual orientation. It was a victory for Keeston Lowery, Commissioner Mike Lindberg's aide, but inflammatory to OCA leader Lon Mabon. By May, he had begun another petition drive, gathering signatures to place a new ballot measure on the 1992 ballot. He succeeded in July 1992.

Measure 9 was titled "Amends Constitution: Government cannot facilitate, must discourage homosexuality, other 'behaviors'."

The Question was: "Shall Constitution be amended to require that all governments discourage homosexuality, other listed 'behaviors,' and not facilitate or recognize them?"

And it was summarized as: "Amends Oregon Constitution. All governments in Oregon may not use their monies or properties to promote, encourage, or facilitate homosexuality, pedophilia, sadism, or masochism. All levels of government, including public education systems, must assist in setting a standard for Oregon's youth which recognizes that these "behaviors" are 'abnormal, wrong, unnatural, and perverse,' and that they are to be discouraged and avoided. State may not recognize this conduct under 'sexual orientation' or 'sexual preference' labels, or through 'quotas, minority status, affirmative action, or similar concepts'." (Young, Pat, Measure 9, PSU thesis, 1997)

Scot Lively, spokesman for the OCA commented that "granting civil rights to deviant sexual behavior...is an insult to every moral citizen of this nation." MCC's Gary Wilson countered, saying, "anything that assaults people, anything that denigrates people, anything that seeks to make some people ok and other people not ok is never a blessing."

Gary challenged Roman Catholic Bishop William Levada over that church's interpretation of peace and justice issues. After a letter writing campaign, the two men met in person to discuss the topics. In 2005, the conservative Levada became part of the Vatican, leading the congregation for the Doctrine of the Faith under Pope Benedict XVI.

The summer and fall were filled with rhetoric, radio and TV ads, and a wide variety of tactics. Ground work by the gay and lesbian community led to a successful campaign. In June, a

Rallies and candlelight marches were part of campaigns to defeat anti-gay measures proposed by Oregon Citizen's Alliance efforts. Energy to defeat the measure drained needed finances that could have gone for AIDS work.

The Northwest Industrial area began its transition to respectability in the late 1980s. Portland maintained its equestrian unit and neighborhood policing. Abandoned warehouses, similiar to Meier and Frank's on Everett, were converted into loft condominiums. Near the approach to the Fremont Bridge, Bridgeport Ale opened their brewpub in a former cordage warehouse. The second of the white buildings west of the I-405 became Slabtown, then The Primary Domain.

294

Rev. Gary Wilson   1986 - 1993

two-week march of 150 miles was organized as the "Walk Against Hate," ending June 20 in Portland by joining in the Gay Pride Parade. Gary Wilson was one of the marchers. It was the largest PRIDE parade in Portland history. Rallies continued throughout the summer. On July 20, two hundred opponents gathered at the Capitol in Salem. A week later, 1,500 gathered at Tom McCall Waterfront Park, and on October 4, an estimated 10,000 people assembled at Pioneer Courthouse Square, site of the old Portland Hotel, to rally and protest.

Most politicians opposed Measure 9, led by Governor Barbara Roberts who likened the potential results to a Nazi-like situation. Democratic leaders Les AuCoin, Elizabeth Furst, and Ron Wyden were vocal opponents, as were several Republicans including Senator Bob Packwood. The Portland City Council and Corvallis City Council were opposed to the measure.

Religious groups were also opposed. When Rodney Page of Ecumenical Ministries of Oregon presented the merits of the issue to Archbishop William Levada, the Roman Catholic leader agreed that the measure would deny civil rights due any American. He agreed to write a position paper and statement opposing Measure 9. The 17 denominations of the EMO voted unanimously to oppose the measure, and Ellen Lowe became the EMO's spokesperson. It should be noted that the Bishop became the first Roman Catholic priest to participate in a Jewish service when he co-led worship with Rabbi Emmanuel Rose of Temple Beth Israel a few years later.

Jewish leaders denounced Measure 9. Denominations from the Evangelical Lutherans to the Presbytery of the Cascades, the Oregon-Idaho Conference of the United Methodist Church, the Episcopal Dioceses for Western and Eastern Oregon, and the Unitarian Church all made stands against the measure. Vandalism occurred at several churches, including spray painted hate graffiti at MCC and at St. Matthew's Catholic Church in Hillsboro.

At First Congregational Church on October 24, Dr. James B. Nelson, Professor of Christian Ethics from United Theological Seminary of the Twin Cities, New Brighton Minnesota, delivered two powerful lectures and a sermon the next day. All dealt with sexual orientation, the Church and human sexuality, and the lessons gay people have for straight society. Ecumenical Ministries of Oregon co-sponsored Nelson's visit. The weekend also included thirteen workshops dealing with homophobia, AIDS, and what it means to be open and affirming. (See Appendix)

MCC became one of several focal points in the divisive campaign. As a Christian denomination, many in the community sought out answers from MCC clergy, leaders, and members. The old familiar litany of Biblical interpretation called for renewed education about what scriptures really say about what aspects of same-sex relationships. Some church members were not initially interested in once again exposing themselves and coming out. However, a transformation in thinking and resolve emerged over the course of the campaign. It was not MCC as a congregation, but rather individuals within the body who became motivated and involved themselves in campaign activities. For some, this meant donating funds or wearing a No on 9 button at all times.

Gary Wilson had been a political activist for years, and he saw the Measure 9 campaign to be one calling for social Christian action. He had joined in opposing the petition drive. He joined a group called "Bigot Bashers" that worked to stamp out injustice. He walked as a representative of MCC in the Walk Against Hate. Flyers and brochures were readily available at several spots in the church building, and Gary often referred to the campaign from the pulpit, to the adulations of some and the distress of others. United only in their determination to defeat the ballot measure, members were divided on what to do, how to do it, and how visible to become.

Press photographers sometimes appeared at services, wanting shots of worshippers in action to show the response of gay community to OCA onslaughts. MCC members not wanting to be photographed sat in a separate section, which the photographers agreed to avoid.

HOMOSEXUALITY & THE CHURCH

The most beautiful word in the Gospel of Jesus Christ is "whosoever." All of God's promises are intended for every human being. This includes gay men and lesbians. How tragic it is that the Christian Church has excluded and persecuted people who are homosexual!

We are all created with powerful needs for personal relationships. Our quality of life depends upon the love we share with others, whether family or friends, partners or peers. Yet, lesbians and gay men facing hostile attitudes in society often are denied access to healthy relationships. Jesus Christ calls us to find ultimate meaning in life through a personal relationship with our Creator. This important spiritual union can bring healing and strength to all of our human relationships.

Not a Sin, Not a Sickness

For many centuries, the Christian Church's attitude toward human sexuality was very negative: sex was for procreation, not for pleasure; women and slaves were considered property to be owned by males; and many expressions of heterosexuality, like homosexuality, were considered sinful. Such tradition often continues to influence churches today. Many teach that women should be subordinate to men, continue to permit forms of discrimination against peoples of color, and condemn homosexuals. They say that all homosexual acts are sinful, often referring to their interpretation of scripture.

Other churches today are influenced by a century of psychoanalytic thought promoted through a powerful minority in the field of medicine. They see homosexuality as some kind of sickness. Although this view has now been soundly discredited by the medical profession, some churches and clergy continue to be influenced by the idea. They say that homosexuals are "imperfect" and in need of "healing."

The good news is that, since 1968, when Metropolitan Community Church was founded, the emergence of a strong lesbian and gay community, and the conclusions of new scientific studies on homosexuality have forced the Christian Church to reexamine these issues. A growing number of biblical and theological scholars now recognize that Scripture does not condemn loving, responsible homosexual relationships. Therefore, gay men and lesbians should be accepted–just as they are– in Christian churches, and homosexual relationships should be celebrated and affirmed!

ABOUT THE BIBLE

The Bible is a collection of writings which span more than a thousand years recounting the history of God's relationship with the Hebrew and Christian people. It was written in several languages, embraces many literary forms, and reflects cultures very different from our own. These are important considerations for properly understanding the Bible in its context.

There are vast differences in doctrines between various Christian denominations, all of which use the same Bible. Such differences have led some Christians to claim that other Christians are not really Christians at all! Biblical interpretation and theology differ from church to church.

Biblical interpretation and theology also change from time to time. Approximately 150 years ago in the United States, some Christian teaching held that there was a two-fold moral order: black and white. Whites were thought to be superior to blacks, therefore blacks were to be subservient and slavery was an institution ordained by God. Clergy who supported such an abhorrent idea claimed the authority of the Bible. The conflict over slavery led to divisions which gave birth to some major Christian denominations. These same denominations, of course, do not support slavery today. Did the Bible change? No, their *interpretation* of the Bible did!

New Information Refutes Old Ideas

What influences lead us to new ways of understanding Scripture? New scientific information, social changes, and personal experience are perhaps the greatest forces for change in the way we interpret the Bible and develop our beliefs. Scientific awareness of homosexual orientation did not exist until the nineteenth century.

Most Christian churches, including Metropolitan Community Church, believe the Bible was inspired by God and provides a key source of authority for the Christian faith. Therefore, what the Bible teaches on any subject, including sexuality, is of great significance. The problem, however, is that sometimes the Bible says very little about some subjects; and popular attitudes about those matters are determined much more by other sources, which are then read into the biblical statements. This has been particularly true of homosexuality. But fortunately, recent scholarship refutes many previous assumptions and conclusions.

UFMCC Brochure 1992

Rev. Gary Wilson   1986 - 1993

Associated Oregon Industries, a large and significant business lobbying group, came out against the measure in August, stating that the OCA was trying to make religious doctrine part of the Oregon Constitution. The AFL-CIO and eight other unions agreed in October. Sexual abuse therapists derided the assumption that homosexuality was equal to pedophilia.

OCA campaigners resorted to door-to-door leaflet campaigning, and to the use of slanderous videos purporting to portray homosexual acts as the inevitable result for Oregon, should their initiative fail. Spending about $400,000, the OCA relied primarily on donations, but received large out-of-state donations, such as the $20,000 donated by television evangelist Pat Robertson and the Christian Coalition.

When Portland Police Chief Tom Potter marched with his lesbian policewoman daughter Katie, in the Gay Pride Parade, OCA leaders condemned his actions and unsuccessfully asked for his resignation. In July, the OCA decided that the Oregonian's coverage of the campaign was biased and called for a boycott of the newspaper. It was not successful.

Few ballot measures in Oregon's history have had such an impact on individual citizens as did the Measure 9 campaign. Not only were individual rights being tossed about, but the very personhood of people was called into question by OCA statements declaring, "we believe we are fighting for the moral absolutes of our universe." Once passive and diminutive, legions of gays and lesbians were forced to take a visible stand with family, friends, co-workers, neighbors, and fellow Christians. Many Oregonians found out for the first time just how many homosexual people they actually knew (or had known for years).

It became a quality of life issue for many folks, realizing that the hatred espoused in the measure could lead to job loss, and a rise in violence, and harassment. Some MCC members had received anonymous hate messages on their telephones, and some believed that the atmosphere was ripe for violence as homosexuals were being stripped of their humanity though labeling and judgment. Gays and lesbians began walking with a partner or in a group, even between the bars on Stark Street. Less socializing downtown meant less exposure to hate groups. Some in the church sensed a change in public attitudes that created an atmosphere that made them fear for their own safety. Some felt pressure to change their lifestyle or habits, making sure they did not put themselves in situations where they could be victims of violence or verbal abuse. (Jansen, Michael, Surviving Measure 9, U of O thesis, 1993)

On October 4, the MCC church building was broken into and vandalized. Ransacked offices were first discovered when the Fallen Angel Choir, a popular community comedic singing group came to their regular rehearsal. Once Gary Wilson was called and came onto the scene, he noted desk drawers and files had been riffled and that a container holding prayer requests had been opened. Papers were scattered, making immediate analysis of damage difficult. The police arrived and surmised that the office door and the pastor's office door had been both forced and broken. About $60 was taken from the safe, and the altar had been vandalized.

Most significantly, the master mailing list was gone. It contained names, addresses and phone numbers of both regular members and anyone who had attended the church and signed their name within the past six months. The only method available to contact those on the list was to make a public announcement of what had happened. Television and newspaper coverage spread the information to the public.

There were at least two significant results. A chill of anxiety swept the congregation, when members realized that the possibility of violence was possible. Several members did receive disturbing phone messages hinting at judgment and implying violence. The safety and anonymity of the church was breached, and there was legitimate concern over harassment and invasion of privacy. Once the church lost its ability to be a safe place and offer refuge from community negativism, many people were frightened away. Attendance dropped by about one-third. Some attendees later returned, especially after the election, but some were never to be seen again at MCC.

GENESIS 19:1–25

What was the sin of Sodom? Some "televangelists" carelessly proclaim that God destroyed the ancient cities of Sodom and Gomorrah because of "homosexuality." Although some theologians have equated the sin of Sodom with homosexuality, a careful look at Scripture corrects such ignorance.

Announcing judgment on these cities in Genesis 18, God sends two angels to Sodom, where Abraham's nephew, Lot, persuades them to stay in his home. Genesis 19 records that "all the people from every quarter" surround Lot's house demanding the release of his visitors so "we might know them." The Hebrew word for "know" in this case, *yadha*, usually means "have thorough knowledge of." It could also express intent to examine the visitors' credentials, or on rare occasions the term implies sexual intercourse. If the latter was the author's intended meaning, it would have been a clear case of attempted gang rape.

Horrified at this gross violation of ancient hospitality rules, Lot attempts to protect the visitors by offering his two daughters to the angry crowd, a morally outrageous act by today's standards. The people of Sodom refuse, so the angels render them blind. Lot and his family are then rescued by the angels as the cities are destroyed.

Several observations are important. First, the judgment on these cities for their wickedness had been announced prior to the alleged homosexual incident. Second, *all* of Sodom's people participated in the assault on Lot's house; in no culture has more than a small minority of the population been homosexual. Third, Lot's offer to release his daughters suggests he knew his neighbors to have heterosexual interests. Fourth, if the issue was sexual, why did God spare Lot, who immediately commits incest with his daughters? Most importantly, why do all the other passages of Scripture referring to this account fail to raise the issue of homosexuality?

What was the Sin of Sodom?

Ezekiel 16:48–50 states it clearly: people of Sodom, like many people today, had abundance of material goods. But they failed to meet the needs of the poor, and they worshipped idols.

The sins of injustice and idolatry plague every generation. We stand under the same judgment if we create false gods or treat others with injustice.

LEVITICUS 18:22 & 20:13

Christians today do not follow the rules and rituals described in Leviticus. But some ignore its definitions of their own "uncleanness" while quoting Leviticus to condemn "homosexuals." Such abuse of Scripture distorts the Old Testament meaning and denies a New Testament message.

"You shall not lie with a male as one lies with a female; it is an abomination." These words occur solely in the Holiness Code of Leviticus, a ritual manual for Israel's priests. Their meaning can only be fully appreciated in the historical and cultural context of the ancient Hebrew people. Israel, in a unique place as the chosen people of one God, was to avoid the practices of other peoples and gods.

Hebrew religion, characterized by the revelation of one God, stood in continuous tension with the religion of the surrounding Canaanites who worshipped the multiple gods of fertility cults. Canaanite idol worship, which featured female and male cult prostitution as noted in Deuteronomy 23:17, repeatedly compromised Israel's loyalty to God. The Hebrew word for a male cult prostitute, *qadesh*, is mistranslated "sodomite" in some versions of the Bible.

What is an "Abomination"?

An abomination is that which God found detestable because it was unclean, disloyal, or unjust. Several Hebrew words were so translated, and the one found in Leviticus, *toevah*, is usually associated with idolatry, as in Ezekiel, where it occurs numerous times. Given the strong association of *toevah* with idolatry and the Canaanite religious practice of cult prostitution, the use of *toevah* regarding male same-sex acts in Leviticus calls into question any conclusion that such condemnation also applies to loving, responsible homosexual relationships.

Rituals and rules found in the Old Testament were given to preserve the distinctive characteristics of the religion and culture of Israel. But, as stated in Galatians 3:22–25, Christians are no longer bound by these Jewish laws. By faith we live in Jesus Christ, not in Leviticus. To be sure, ethical concerns apply to all cultures and peoples in every age. Such concerns were ultimately reflected by Jesus Christ, who said nothing about homosexuality, but a great deal about love, justice, mercy and faith.

UFMCC Brochure 1992

Rev. Gary Wilson   1986 - 1993

Division in the congregation created two camps of thought. Discomfort with Gary Wilson's activity over the years coalesced into open criticism of his political activism by a group frustrated over the break-in and its aftermath, as opposed to a smaller faction that backed Wilson and supported his visibility in the community and in the No on 9 campaign. His opponents felt that he had exposed the church and its members unnecessarily, and that MCC should not be in the business of politics. He continued his political activity despite the increase in criticism and calls for him to tone down his rhetoric and involvement.

MCC received a ominous phone call four days before the vote, threatening that if Measure 9 failed on election day, a number of gunmen would come into the church on the following Sunday with uzis and "get a whole bunch of f - - king queers." While the church had fielded phone threats and graffiti messages in the past, this one seemed to have a greater impact, with an actual date for action.

Measure 9 failed at the ballot box. For the moment, the gay and lesbian communities could breathe a little easier. For the moment.

A self-appointed committee took its own action the following Sunday at MCC, posting unarmed "guards" at two entrances, locking another door that was usually open on Sundays, and staying in contact with another member outside with walkie-talkies. Fortunately, there was no confrontation.

Wilson was angry with this committee, as they had not included him in their planning, apparently fearing his tendency to down play such threats. His planning for that Sunday had included working out some sort of plan with the police which included monitoring of the situation. These two approaches to the threat typified the division and erosion of communication and trust at the church between parishioners and pastor. Gary was convinced of the correctness of his actions and political involvement. He had only a small number of supporters. Some people remained loyal to the church, but not to Gary.

Confrontation and Resignation

Although the early years of Gary's ministry saw a renewed spirit and energy in the congregation, the later years witnessed a decline in membership. When Gary arrived, a core of about fifty members were maintaining the congregation. Attendance grew to nearly 200 in the late 1980s, but by 1992, the number of worshippers on Sundays averaged fewer than fifty. On September 13, 1990, 65 attended the morning service and 35 people were at the evening worship; seven months later on April 14, 28 people were at the only Sunday service. Many factors converged to precipitate these lower numbers.

Foremost among these seems to have been the mounting impact of the AIDS epidemic. Although the AIDS vigils, beginning in 1986, provided both consolation and resolve, the accumulated sorrow of so many deaths was profound. The core of Christian believers at MCC continued in their faith to accept death as part of the eternal cycle, but this did not fully assuage grief over friends departed and careers and relationships cut short by painful and debilitating illnesses without cure. For some marginalized believers, the challenge proved too great, and they chose to drop out. Grief counseling both within and outside the church proved inadequate to meet the needs of so many processing the loss of so many. Others found the worship space and some of its artwork too painfully reminiscent of funerals and memorial experiences.

Onslaughts and attacks from religious and social conservatives reappeared partially as a result of AIDS. The political attacks of the OCA and Ballot Measure 8 and 9 campaigns were demoralizing, financially draining, and time and energy consuming. Some took deeper comfort in the church, while others felt exposed and unsafe with the higher visibility of the homosexual issue caused by media attention. When the church offices were vandalized, this was the final straw for several members who felt vulnerable.

Gary Wilson often preached a theology of oppression. While some tribulations could be seen as a parallel to the Biblical Job, frequent references to suffering in sermons became tiresome. Some members tired of singing what seemed to be the

ROMANS 1:24–27

Most New Testament books, including the four Gospels, are silent on same-sex acts, and Paul is the only author who makes any reference to the subject. The most negative statement by Paul regarding same-sex acts occurs in Romans 1:24–27 where, in the context of a larger argument on the need of all people for the gospel of Jesus Christ, certain homosexual behavior is given as an example of the "uncleanness" of idolatrous Gentiles.

Does this passage refer to *all* homosexual acts, or to *certain* homosexual behavior known to Paul's readers? Romans was written to Jewish and Gentile Christians in Rome, who would have been familiar with the infamous sexual excesses of their contemporaries, especially Roman emperors. They would also have been aware of tensions in the early Church regarding Gentiles and observance of the Jewish laws, as noted in Acts 15 and Paul's letter to the Galatians. Jewish laws in Leviticus mentioned male same-sex acts in the context of idolatry.

What is "Natural"?

Significant to Paul's discussion is the fact that these "unclean" Gentiles exchanged that which was "natural" for them–*physin*, in the Greek text–for something "unnatural," *para physin*. In Romans 11:24, God acts in an "unnatural" way, *para physin*, to accept the Gentiles. "Unnatural" in these passages does not refer to violation of so-called laws of nature, but rather implies action contradicting one's own nature. In view of this, we should observe that it is "unnatural," *para physin*, for a person today with a lesbian or gay sexual orientation to attempt living a heterosexual lifestyle.

Romans 1:26 is the only statement in the Bible with a possible reference to lesbian behavior, although the specific intent of this verse is unclear. Some authors have seen in this passage a reference to women adopting a dominant role in heterosexual relationships. Given the repressive cultural expectations placed on women in Paul's time, such a meaning may be possible.

The homosexual practices cited in Romans 1:24–27 were believed to result from idolatry and are associated with some very serious offenses as noted in Romans 1. Taken in this larger context, it should be obvious that such acts are significantly different from loving, responsible lesbian and gay relationships seen today.

UFMCC Brochure 1992

Rev. Gary Wilson 1986 - 1993

same 40 "blood songs" for hymns, whose words focused on sacrifice but not on redemption. Wilson conceded that his style of ministry was unacceptable to some, "My preaching is designed not to give answers but to provoke appropriate questions." (*Oregonian*, Jan 9, 1993 p. C1)

Services grew in length due to extended periods of community prayer, during which individuals expressed their own petitions to God. Common topics were health, finances, employment, family, cars, and pets. While worshipful in theory, without some type of regulation these often became therapy sessions for the supplicant while the remainder of the congregation listened sympathetically but increasingly impatient. When service time exceeded two hours, attendance dropped considerably. A 1991 newsletter spoke to the issue of shortening some parts of the service, but with little effect.

The division among members about the mixture of politics and theology at the church and from the pulpit really split the congregation. For some, MCC was a rallying place, but for others, it needed to be a place away from the fray. Gary seemed unable to accommodate a compromise on the situation.

With reduced attendance and involvement, financial contributions also dropped significantly. At one point, a letter was sent from MCC to several other faith-based organizations in the city requesting donations to help with the monthly budget. The larger community was also experiencing a recession in 1992.

At a board meeting in late 1992, members confronted Gary with the demoralizing situation. Gary Wilson resigned, effective January 1993. Aged 53 at the time, he had served 19 years in the ministry. In his own words, he resolved to continue to fight for gay rights and to be a leader in the post-Measure 9 healing process. But he felt he could not muster the "strength and energy to deal with problems in the church in a really compassionate way." He acknowledged that the Measure 9 debacle had contributed to rifts in MCC, yet he claimed to not be embittered by the bruising of the Measure 9 battle.

Wilson also felt detached from the strategy adopted by the No on 9 Campaign, which emphasized the broad constitutional and civil rights effects of the Measure. The committee's down play of the proposal's impact on the lives of gays and lesbians was evidence of the gay community's own homophobia, in his view. It was his intention to remain in Portland and continue participating at MCC. He was quoted, "I hope in terms of human equality issues, someday we may not need a Metropolitan Community Church."

Wilson later moved to California, where he completed his career as a teacher, retiring in 2005.

MCC PORTLAND OUR NEXT PASTOR?

Part of a flyer inviting the congregation to see and hear the candidate.

1993 Intel unveils the first pentium processor wit 60 MHz
- Senator Bob Packwood continues defending his name amidst sexual harassment charges
- Charles Moose, Portland's first black Chief of Police, appointed by Mayor Vera Katz
- *Willamette Week* cartoonist Matt Groening gains national attention with *The Simpsons*
- Highest AIDS infection rate in Oregon reached, nearing 800 cases in 1993

1994 University of Oregon "Ducks" play in the Rose Bowl after 32 years, lose to Penn State
- Clackamas ice queen, Tanya Harding linked to attack on rival Nancy Kerrigan
- Oregon voters approve "Death-with-Dignity" (physician-assisted suicide) Ballot Measure,
- Thomas Lauderdale forms Pink Martini to help rally morale after Measure 9 divides voters
- 100 Yellow Bikes donated to needy kids by activists Tom O'Keefe and Joe Keating

Chapter Eleven
Rev. Dennis Chappell
September 1993 – March 1994

"Continue to love each other like brothers, and remember always to welcome strangers, for by doing this, some people have entertained angels without knowing it. Keep in mind those who are in prison, as though you were in prison with them; and those who are being badly treated, since you too are in the one body."
(Hebrews 13:1-2 (Jerusalem Bible)

Following the resignation of Gary Wilson, a leadership team was assigned by the Board of Directors to continue the momentum of worship and social activity while a search for a new pastor was launched. A separate committee headed a campaign to pay off the church debt. Dennis Chappell candidated for the position of senior pastor and was hired, but he resigned after seven months of positive restorative work. Austin Amerine was asked to fill in the ensuing vacancy period until another candidate was found. Flexibility remained the name of the game for many months.

Interim Leadership Team

Upon Gary Wilson's resignation, effective January 1993, the Board of Directors needed to designate a minister to lead the congregation through the vacancy period ahead. Rev. Mary Frantz, who had completed her student clergy work under Gary Wilson, was appointed Clergy on Staff. Deacon Bob Jackson was designated the Pastoral Coordinator, and Chuck Harvey became the Lay Administrator (Secretary). The Board voted to pay a stipend to Bob and Chuck, but did not provide one for Mary. While there wasn't much money involved, the men tried to cover the oversight by designating part of their stipend for Mary. The oversight was never rectified.

Mary Frantz had lived for a while in Salem, and while there, became friends with a man named Don Strausbaugh. Don was a retired district manager from Northwest Natural Gas, and was the gardener at the Oregon State Fairgrounds there for over 20 years. She told him about MCC, and when he moved to Portland, he began attending, and was soon totally involved in programs and leadership committees, serving for many years. (See Chapter 12)

Amazing things happened under this leadership team. Attendance and participation began to rise. The Deacons continued providing the Pantry to distribute donated food items. Diana Hill and Eddy Sullivan coordinated another massive garage sale in the church basement on August 7th.

The church sent delegates to the UFMCC General Conference in Phoenix. Members looked forward to the annual retreat with MCC-Boise and other northwest MCCs at Boardman State Park over Labor Day weekend. The theme was, "You are the Gift."

In addition to a pastoral search committee, another committee formed in April 1993, to spearhead a final fundraising drive to pay off the church mortgage. They were the "Mortgage Burning Committee," and they pursued their goal with fervor.

Larry Moad became involved in the music program at MCC shortly after joining the church. He's accompanied worship, and performed solos and offertories as well as conducting the choir.

Eddy Sullivan (L) and Larry Moad were two of the "Destruction team" that spontaneously began remodeling the family room. Don Strausbaugh and José Montoya were both deacons, doing just about any task that needed to be done.

Dave Dishman (L), Don Rogers, and Denis Moore reunited at a conference. Dave served as music chairman for several years. Denis played both piano and organ originally with the Portland Community Church and the first several years of MCC history.

Rev. Dennis Chappell   1993 - 1994

Weekly announcements informed members and the public about "The Church ALIVE." This program aimed at highlighting all the aspects of MCC's community ministry and outreach. "A healthy church supports all ministries as well as support groups ministering to a diversity of human needs," read their literature. The weekly news inserts grew to include news items of community, not just church interest, and outside groups were encouraged to consider using MCC's facilities. The community was also approached for help in raising the funds for the final payment. Nay-sayers were quieted as the fund neared its goal.

Rev. D. Dennis Chappell

After a seven month search process, the pastoral Search Committee announced on June 20 that their choice for MCC's sixth senior pastor was Rev. Dennis Chappell. At the time, he was the director of AIDS Ministry at MCC-San Diego. This was the same Dennis Chappell who had candidated in 1985 and had turned down Portland's call. Rev. Chappell's theological background was consistent with the requirements of the American Lutheran Church, considered liberal for a Lutheran denomination. He rated his personal beliefs as conservative to orthodox. Dennis was first licensed as an MCC minister in 1978. He had served in Los Angeles, Jacksonville, and Santa Ana before taking on the AIDS ministry in San Diego. His partner was Keith Elder.

His week of candidating was July 5-11, 1993. During that week, he participated in a Independence Picnic at Laurelhurst Park, lunches with the Interim Leadership Team and other area MCC pastors, dinners with the deacons and the Coordinating Council/Finance Committee. A reception at the church for community groups and businesses was held at lunchtime on that Saturday, with an open house potluck dinner at the church followed by a question/answer forum. On Sunday Dennis gave the sermon and consecrated the Communion. At the congregational meeting following that service, members voted to extend a call to Dennis Chappell.

During this entire week, a special outreach was made to the Portland gay and lesbian community at large to participate in the events getting to know Dennis Chappell. Former members were invited to participate, and a special emphasis was placed on accumulating funds to pay off the 15-year mortgage on the building.

On September 7, 1993, the church treasurer wrote the final mortgage payment check, and a mortgage-burning ceremony was planned to coincide with the installation of the new pastor in October. It had been almost exactly fifteen years from the initial date of signing the contract to buy the old Church of Divine Science.

Dennis had arrived in the late summer before all preparations were ready for his appearance. Mary's church office was instantly converted into the senior pastor's study in one afternoon, and she was quickly without an office (in either sense). The office remodeling continued well into the fall. As Dennis assumed pastorial duties, Mary recognized that her services were no longer essential. She continued helping to lead services through the Christmas Season, then went on hiatus for several years, returning to serve as Sunday service coordinator when Marsha Dempsey and Roy Cole were pastors in 1998.

By September 19, 1993, Dennis was in full leadership of the congregation. While his installation was still a month away, he launched into a full program of preaching, meeting with the Board, and implementing several changes in leadership and worship. Average Sunday attendance when he arrived stood at about 35 people. Curiosity about the new pastor coaxed new and returning members into the church, inching attendance up to 53 in a few weeks. Some of the changes Dennis made did not please everyone, and a few folks left, but 170 people attended his installation.

Installation

The largest crowd to fill MCC since the 1987 AIDS Vigil showed up for Dennis Chappell's installation on October 24, 1993. Eleven pastors participated. Jack St. John returned to perform at the organ, two guest trumpeters from the Gay Freedom Band per-

Choices in cinematic entertainment varied at several low-budget theaters. *Deep Throat* played for years at the Aladdin on SE Milwaukie near Powell. Third Avenue video businesses were shut down by modernization, but the Aval;on persists to this day. On Hawthorne, "Can We Talk" was a short-lived bar, now called the Bar of the Gods, just west of the Mt Tabor, now a music club. Other visual entertainment was sold at the Book Bin.

Rev. Dennis Chappell 1993 - 1994

formed Purcell's Trumpet Voluntary in D Major, Larry Moad conducted the PRISM choir and Gail Bumala sang the special music. Mary Frantz led the Call to Worship and Denis Moore (then at MCC-San Jose returned to give the Invocation. Frodo Okulam of MCC-Sister Spirit read the Old Testament lesson; John Schwiebert, co-pastor of Metanoia Peace Community read the Epistle; and Metanoia's other co-pastor, Joyce McManus, read the Gospel.

In the buildup to the sermon, the official "miracle of the mortgage burning," was enacted, with Dave Dishman grasping a burning copy of the official document over a large basin as five senior MCC pastors looked on–Austin Amerine, Donald Borbe, Jim Glyer, Gary Wilson, and Dennis Chappell. An audible gasp swept the audience as the Xerox copy of the document ignited.

Kenneth Martin, co-pastor of MCC-Austin, TX, then gave the sermon on "What's Past and What's Possible!" based on II Corinthians 12:4-8. The text refers to St. Paul's humility in himself, but his pride in the Gospel.

Teresa Nunn, pastor of MCC-Vancouver, led in the Confession of Sins and gave the Absolution and Pardon. The Lord's Prayer was sung by the Congregation. Dennis spoke the Words of Institution, and after the distribution, proclaimed the Acclamation of Faith so familiar to MCC people:

> "Christ has Died
> Christ has Risen
> Christ will come again
> Hallelujah"

Rounding out the weekend of celebrations was a dinner and festive evening at Darcelle XV's club in Old Town on Saturday evening before the installation. MCC had the place to themselves and filled the club with well over 100 people.

Getting to work

After the grand installation weekend was complete, several groups began working toward new goals. AIDS Vigil weekend was scheduled for Dec. 3-5, 1993, and the Diaconate, headed by Deacons Bob Jackson and José Montoya, assembled a planning committee. Among other events and services, panels for the AIDS quilt were to be blessed, and a play was to be performed. A "mini-display" of the Quilt had been on display in Portland at Pioneer Place earlier in October.

Bob Jackson formed a new theater group expressly to produce the AIDS play, entitled Adam and the Experts. A full crew of actors, technical staff, box office, and promotion people was needed in order to pull off the major presentation in just six weeks. Sister Paula was to make a cameo appearance in the play, in addition to her secretarial duties at MCC.

Although not a direct ministry of MCC, Sister Paula energetically continued her tele-evangelistic programs. Her 30- and 60- minute specials aired on Paragon Cable, Columbia Cable of Oregon, Columbia Cable of Washington, and Willamette Falls Television in Oregon City. She often interviewed local and national guests, including Troy Perry. She also visited other cities as part of her evangelistic work.

Dennis Chappell invited congregation members to his home on Tuesday evenings as part of a "get acquainted" plan. Members scheduled with Sister Paula so that a reasonable number of people would show up on any given evening. A new membership class began in November.

Dennis also hoped to gain a high profile for MCC in the gay business community, and attended several PABA (Portland Area Business Association) lunches with Dave Dishman and Larry Foltz. The Association held monthly luncheons to hear timely guest speakers, learn about gay community projects, and generally schmooze and network to build a strong coalition of gay and lesbian business people.

MCC networked with several other alternative churches in the Portland area, including the Metropolitan Ministries Commission. MCC-Sister Spirit continued meeting in the Governor Building on SW 2nd, and across the Columbia MCC-Vancouver coordinated programs with the

Three popular meeting spots included the Dirty Duck, with a picture window view of the Steel Bridge. Formerly Hippo's Hardware, the bay-windowed business on SE 12 became a restaurant, then morphed into 3 Friends Coffee house. Sedately set back on NE Everett is Inner City Hot tubs, with two open-air pools and a sauna.

Artistic creativity appeared in various versions of street art about the same time that the "Trust Jesus" artists were adorning bridges and retaining walls with that slogan. Bob Jackson took a higher road, directing the *Seven Lively Arts* program for Oregon Public Broadcasting.

Rev. Dennis Chappell 1993 - 1994

Portland church. Potter's House ministries, started by three former MCC members, flourished with about 40 members at 3830 SE 62nd, with Ohio pastor Bill Roberts. Metanoia Peace House under Pat and John Schwiebert met for light suppers at 5 pm and worship at 6 pm on Sundays; and Shalom ministries met at Lincoln Street United Methodist Church at SE 52nd. Shalom was a United Methodist Ministry of education, justice and empowerment for lesbian, gay, and bisexual people. Trinity Episcopal Church held a "healing evensong" service once each month at 5 pm. for those affected by HIV/AIDS, with a light supper afterwards.

Music programs rejuvenated themselves. Larry Moad not only performed on the piano with style and expression, he conducted the MCC choir, which took on the name PRISM. Joe Gray served as organist, and on some Sundays, a third accompanist, Tom Fields, joined the keyboard ensemble. Individual soloists volunteered to present special music, vocal or instrumental, solo and in duet.

Pastor Chappell modeled organization. His sermons were clear messages, presented well, and not too long. What wasn't generally known, was that he overcame his dyslexia by typing out his entire sermons with large double spaced type. The next week's sermon topic would be printed in the Sunday worship folder. Monthlong sermon series were announced in separate mailings to congregants. Coordination with community and religious groups was obvious by the long list of announcements in the weekly service folders.

Dennis continued several MCC worship traditions. The Wellness and Liberation Candle became an integral part of the Order of Worship. Jack St. John's 1978 *Gloria* was always sung after the reading of the Gospel. *The Lord's Prayer* was always sung by the congregation as part of the communion preparation. The statement about MCC Communion policy was always printed in the folder: "MCC practices an open communion. All who know, or seek to know Jesus, the Christ, are welcomed at God's table" Dennis brought a breath of fresh air to MCC with an upbeat attitude and a can-do philosophy. It didn't hurt that he was an attractive man with a youthful appearance and professional demeanor. Average attendance continued to rise steadily into the new year, approaching 80 people at the single 10 am Sunday service each week. Several weekday activities were offered, including a women's group on the 1st Wednesday of each month and a men's group on the 3rd Wednesday of each month. The MCC choir rehearsed each Tuesday.

Living With AIDS

AIDS was still the overriding concern of gay men. And the disease was becoming more prevalent in other segments of the population, National news focused on Ryan White, a young hemophiliac infected due to his need for frequent transfusions. AIDS expanded its domain to include intravenous drug users, women that were not part of the sex industry, and children born of infected women. Obituaries became a regular part of the Alternative Connection newspaper. The U.S. Postal Service issued an AIDS awareness commemorative stamp on World AIDS Day, December 1, 1993.

Trinity Episcopal Cathedral at NW 19th and Everett began a monthly healing service of evensong for those affected by HIV/AIDS in October, 1993. Services on the second Sunday at 5 pm were followed by a light supper in the Parish House. Clergy and parishioners of Trinity made the event open to all, whether Episcopalian or not. Caregivers, partners, families, friends and anyone affected in any way by the disease were welcome.

The MCC AIDS committee presented an all-day legal forum at the church. Included topics were, "Wills and Estate Planning; power of attorney, relationship contracts, living wills, etc. On the committee were Betty Nelson and José Montoya. Betty brought a professional counseling background and José had trained for the Roman Catholic priesthood.

José Montoya came to MCC in 1980, and soon brought his partner Bob Carter, a quiet but humorous man who also had two young sons. José and Bob participated in a gay fathers group initially set up by another MCC dad, David Callentine. José often shared the story of his

Laymen have made up to the core of congregational leadership over the years. Rich Kibbons is a community activist, involved in the PRIDE committee, Board member of the NAMES Project in Portland, and most significantly for MCC, the head of the Gardening Team. His work has made the church property an outstandingly beautiful site on NE Broadway. Dave Dishman (L) and Austin Amerine (Pastor emeritus) coordinated in leading the congregation after Dennis Chappell resigned.

Long serving and long-suffering deacons Bob Jackson (R) and José Montoya (L) remained steadfast in providing sermons, communion, and spiritual guidance. Bob's deep and melodious voice was also heard on Oregon Public Broadcasting's "Seven Lively Arts." José survived several years after the passing of his beloved Bob Carter. He lived with AIDS publically, honestly, and spiritually.

310

Rev. Dennis Chappell   1993 - 1994

journey from being "hidden" in a New Mexico monastery community. He prayed about his homosexuality and struggled to find guidance from God. One of José's nightly duties was to secure the monastery chapel. On a certain evening as he was closing up, with his prayer on his heart, José found a button on the floor. When he picked it up, there was message on it that said "it will be alright." José knew this was his answer, and he left the monastery.

José and Bob were each diagnosed with AIDS, and both men were open about their condition and their love for God and their fellow worshipers. In his role as Deacon, José never flinched from honesty or about sharing his story, especially after Bob passed away in 1990. José continued as an active and positive Deacon until shortly before his own passing in April 1996.

Emotional responses to AIDS began to fall into predictable categories. HIV or AIDS affected uninfected men in mental and emotional ways, often manifesting in physical symptoms, unsafe behaviors, and even suicide. Emotions often swayed between anger and helplessness. Another response was the conviction that their own infection with AIDS was inevitable, Some people became nihilistic, feeling destructive towards themselves or the world-at-large. This could mean sexual dysfunction, celibacy, or unsafe activity.

"Survivor guilt" emerged wherein uninfected men somehow laid blame on themselves for the illness of friends. The blame came from an idea that to remain uninfected meant to be "against" those who were infected. Guilt among these men who had HIV-positive friends could lead to binging on unsafe sex, ignoring the wisdom of prevention research. In some, a feeling of being left out or unimportance became a reaction to the attention given their sick friends by AIDS service organizations and care teams. These responses seem manifestly ironic, yet they became a clear reality to some, and had to be addressed. This would lead to the "brother-to-brother" program in 1993 and "Mentalk" in 1996, both programs of CAP.

One positive response in the larger community over the years when AIDS was becoming a central focus for most gay people was the emergence of community social resources and organizations. While some had been in existence for years, by 1993, listings for such groups filled two complete pages in the Alternative Connection, and included:

  Hot lines - 10
  AIDS/Heath Support Organizations - 12
  Counseling Organizations - 6
  Newspapers/Magazines - 7
  Professional Groups - 7
  Spiritual Organizations - 14
  Service Organizations - 8
  Social and Interest Groups - 43
  Sports and Hobby Groups - 17

and listings for Ashland, Bend, Coos Bay, Corvallis, Eugene, Klamath Falls, Medford, North Bend, North Coast, Roseburg, Salem, and Longview/Kelso, WA, as well as statewide resources. (See Appendix for a more complete listing of these groups)

Among the many AIDS deaths in 1993, the loss of Keeston Lowery was especially devastating to the Portland gay community. Keeston had been the energizer bunny of activists, enthusiastically supporting every gay cause socially and politically. He had worked on Bobby Kennedy's campaigns, and in Dade County against Anita Bryant in 1977. Keeston's charm and dedication won over critics and he was a master at harmonizing factions with differing positions. Keeston loved helping people, which he was able to do admirably as Commissioner Mike Lindberg's assistant. Keeston had been instrumental in establishing the Right to Privacy PAC and the Lucille Hart dinner tradition. Oregon Governor Barbara Roberts and former Governor Neil Goldschmidt gave tributes at his memorial service in the Washington Park amphitheater, September 2, 1993.

It wasn't all doom and gloom. In additional to the many social organizations in town, local travel agents organized a gay Disneyland weekend. Organizers recruited 22 revelers on the SW Airlines excursion.

Destruction Derby

A spontaneous decision by Larry Moad and Kimberly Brown in 1993 to renovate the

The Gardens of MCC-Portland

In the beginning ... the church was getting a fresh coat of paint in the late fall of 1995 when we began the church gardens. The quest was to put some of the church's inner beauty on the outside, where passersby might see.

A dozen King Alfred daffodils were planted near the Broadway entrance door while the painting scaffolding was still in place.. Tulips, hardy fuchsias, fernleaf bleeding hearts, French Lace Cap hydrangeas came next ... unique, colorful, individual ~ just like us!

Bit by bit the MCC-Portland gardens have grown. First there were small beds to dig in front of the hedges and along the front steps. The grass was removed so pansies, marigolds, hollyhocks, and roses might show off under the great west window. Hydrangeas like a bit of shade, so they grow on the north, in the raised beds. One can find old-fashioned bleeding hearts, azaleas, snowballs, and violets growing there. And hardy fuchsias! What masses of color! Color all year long.

Soon the two front grassy slopes also became flower beds ... each some 30 feet long, perhaps 15 feet deep. In 2001, cottage stones became retaining walls and reduced the incline of the front beds. A magnolia tree and a "China Doll" white dogwood now thrive in the mid-day sun. Hardy annuals and new perennials stick their toes into the soil and show off their colors of purple, blue, green, yellow, orange, and red.

The grass along the church's north side needed refreshing. Once the turf was dug, we had to mix peat moss and sand into the remaining soil and slowly moisture stopped running off the surface. Ice plant's bright purple blooms and tiny succulents changed the texture of the higher beds. Lacey-leafed "Peter Pan" began presenting it's cherry rose blooms amongst the purple and green.

A wedge of grass at the corner of NE 24th and Broadway became a moss garden in 2003. Irish and Scotch moss grow in rows that might appear as crashing waves of the ocean ... the deeper green of Irish moss giving an illusion of deep water over which the lighter green of Scotch might flow.

Roses are always a part of any garden. Beloved deacon José Montoya grew yellow roses for his patron saint, Our Lady of Guadalupe. "Midas Touch" and two other yellow roses were planted in 1997 for José. We didn't know why José grew yellow roses. No one thought to ask him, "why yellow roses." In 2004, we discovered "Mary's Flowers, Gardens, Legends and Meditations" by Vincenzina Krymow, and it provided the answers.

We honour Mary in so many ways ~ among them, using flowers and herbs as symbols to enhance spiritual life. Memories of Mary, mother of Jesus, are celebrated through meditations using the language of plants to hold Mary in their life. A Mary's Garden may be as small as a pot and as large as a city block. Among the messages of Saxifraga granulata {Lady's Featherbeds}, Chrysanthemum balsamita {Mary's Coin}, Coix lacryma-jobi (Job's tears), we found José's purpose. Three colors of roses are especially appropriate in a Mary Garden: red roses to symbolize the sorrows of Our Lady, white to symbolize her joys, and yellow to symbolize and herald her glories.

As all gardens grow and change, so, too, do the MCC-Portland Gardens. The large mass of grass along 24th is changing too. An "abstract" linear garden curves its way across the view. Half of an "8" with a break in the middle, looks like a "hook" that might snare passersby to join our celebrations. Starting at the north of the bed, blooms of red, orange, and yellow, then a break, continuing with green, blue, and finally, purple complete the abstract rainbow garden.

A new element was added to the garden in celebration of the church's 30th anniversary when a member donated three varieties of bamboo, now planted on the Broadway side, east of the street level entrance. Soaring 30 feet is a phylostachys vivax, a tall timber bamboo from China. Close by is a medium height "nigra," or black bamboo. It's culms grow green the first season, turning to a leopard-skin texture the second, and to black the third and subsequent years. The third variety is a shorter golden strain. Bamboo in oriental cultures symbolizes beauty and wisdom. The gangly but graceful plants wisely bend and give under heavy weight, snow or ice, rather than fighting the weight and breaking under the stress. Stalks then return to their own stance when the weight or pressure is removed. These can be a lesson for individuals and groups struggling to survive and thrive.

Rich Kibbons, gardener

Rev. Dennis Chappell   1993 - 1994

dilapidated "Founders Room" at the southeast corner of the main floor resulted in months of volunteer activity to replace dry rot, reseal windows, resurface and repaint walls, and carpet the space. Kim, Larry, and their partners, Gail Bumala and Eddy Sullivan, headed the efforts. They became known as the "Destruction Team." Barriers were erected to keep in the dust and keep out the curious. Only volunteer workers were allowed to see the progress and transformation. The space, which had become a catch-all for old books, theater props, costumes, choir robes, extra pews and furniture, was unveiled amidst much ceremony on Easter Sunday 1994, complete with a costumed, full-chorus, rendition of songs from the Woopie Goldberg film, *Sister Act*.

At some point during this era, food began disappearing from the pantry under suspicious circumstances. Exploration under the Sanctuary revealed a family of at least three "street-people" who later confessed to having lived quite comfortably beneath the church for several months, enjoying the relative warmth of the finished basement areas, after the church was locked up at night. Other uninvited residents have included a colony of rodents in recessed basement areas A small contingent of pigeons regularly entered the attic space through the louvered opening in the western facade. Several services were disturbed (or augmented?) with pigeon cooing and an occasional errant feather descending towards the pews. Eddy Sullivan was volunteered to climb into the attic and seal off the louvers with chicken wire.

Disappointment and Resignation

In March, a non-member who had sought counseling from the Pastor reported that the Pastor had made uninvited sexual advances. The Board of Directors quickly called a meeting with Dennis and when confronted with the accusations, the Pastor offered to resign, although he maintained his innocence. Church lawyer and board member Kimberly Brown procured the proper legal forms and the pastorate of Dennis Chappell ended.

The resignation shocked the congregation, just beginning to feel comfortable and energized under a popular leader. Investigation revealed that Rev. Chappell was also about to be censured by the UFMCC denomination over charges originating at an earlier parish. MCC had not been informed of this situation during the candidating process. In California, Austin Amerine had just retired from his full-time ministry, and MCC-Portland contacted him about serving as Interim pastor during the search for yet another new pastor. Deacons Bob Jackson and José Montoya agreed to help lead the congregation's worship program.

The Vacancy

Long-time members were delighted to once again have Austin Amerine preaching and leading worship. Since leaving MCC in 1979, he had been NW District Coordinator, and had then founded MCC-Spokane. When that church was well established, he relocated yet again, to found MCC-Overlake in Belleview, WA. He later moved to MCC-River City in Sacramento where he worked in the music ministry under Rev. Elder Freda Smith until his hoped-for retirement.

Austin pastored MCC for about fou months, preaching his last sermon on July 26, 1994. He requested that B J Wilkinson be the guest singer for the service. He preached on the topic, "Now is the Time." No frogs this time!

Local pastors graciously filled the vacant pulpit after Austin left. Rev. Steve Torrence flew into Portland for PRIDE Sunday's service. Delores Berry returned for a Sunday service and concert. John Schwiebert of Peace House also preached, as did Bill Roberts from The Potter's House Ministries.

One well-known speaker who preached at MCC during the vacancy was Mel White. Dr. White was Dean of the MCC-Cathedral of Hope MCC of Dallas. His national fame came from his history as a one-time ghost writer for Dr. Billy Graham, Rev. Jerry Falwell, and Rev. Pat Robertson prior to coming out as a gay man. His book Stranger at the Gate, published the same year, told a powerful story of fundamentalist Christians stonewalling one of their own after he came out. White spoke on the message "How to Survive the Days Ahead" on September 11, 1994.

In the Midst of New Dimensions

In the midst of new di-men-sions, in the face of chang-ing ways,
Through the flood of starv-ing peo-ples, war-ring fac-tions and de-spair,
Through the years of hu-man strug-gle walk a peo-ple long de-spised,
We are Black and we are A-sian, In-di-an, His-pan-ic, White,
We are man and we are wo-man, all per-sua-sions, old and young,

who will lead the pil-grim peo-ples wan-der-ing their sep'-rate ways?
who will lift the o-live branch-es? Who will light the flame of care?
gays and les-bi-ans to-geth-er fight-ing to be re-al-ized.
we a rain-bow co-a-li-tion, all of va-lue in thy sight.
each a gift in thy cre-a-tions, each a love song to be sung.

God of rain-bow, fier-y pil-lar, lead-ing where the ea-gles soar, we, thy peo-ple,

ours the jour-ney now and e-ver, now and e-ver, now and e-ver-more.

Rev. Dennis Chappell   1993 - 1994

UFMCC moderator Rev Elder Troy Perry came to Portland to offer advice and counseling to the dismayed church and the pastoral search committee. There was also news of a young Episcopalian minister in Reno, NV who was interested in serving an MCC congregation, and communications were begun with Rev. Roy Cole.

Being somewhat accustomed to changes and challenges, most church ministries continued during the vacancy. MCC participated in the annual Lesbian and Gay Parade on July 9.

Efforts to finally open a Portland Lesbian/Gay/Bisexual Community Resource Center led to incorporation and registration of the name in 1994. Plans were made for a common social and reading area, meeting rooms, and a referral desk. No physical space was ever rented, but a fund raiser was held at La Luna (the same Centenary-Wilbur space that once housed MCC in its infancy - see Chapter 3 and 4) The Queer Night part of June 27th was supported by MCC and held as a benefit for the Center.

Members voted unanimously on September 4 to call Rev. Cole as senior pastor. His first Sunday in Portland would be October 3. The collective sigh of relief was audible. The congregation had elected the man who would turn out to serve MCC longer than any other minister in its history.

Exhorters and Student Clergy since 1976

Harriett Barshofski (sp?) - pastored at MCC Gentle Shepherd, Vancouver
Joyce Baxter - pastored at MCC Gentle Shepherd, Vancouver
Ron Bergeron - served in Quebec; deceased
Jacquie Bogle - did not finish the program; became part of Arlene Ackerman's ministry
Gail Bumala - stayed in Portland; did not complete
Gary Coleman ?- MCCP Choir Director & Music Coordinator
Phil Crum - Lay pastor at River of Life MCC, Tri-Cities (WA)
Jean Dant - did not finish
Mary Frantz - Stayed in Portland; Worship leader at MCC during 84-86 Interim
Dan Hoggatt
Steve Jordan
Dorothy Kipps
Jodi Mekkars - Pastored in Boise, Eugene, and Salem
Denis Moore - Pastored MCC Honolulu and MCC San Jose; retired but still associate at MCC- Portland
Ashan Nelson - went to Hawaii
Paula Nielsen - 10 years MCCP church secretary, Cable Access Television ministry as Sister Paula
Teresa Nunn - MCCP church secretary - pastored MCC of the Gentle Shepherd, Vancouver, 12 years
Frodo Okulam - Pastor of Sister Spirit in Portland
Betty Pederson - pastored in Eugene and SF Bay area
Ron Powell - did not finish program; became leader @ Living Enrichment Center, Portland
Glenn Scott - Pastoral leader in Roseberg
Jack St. John - major musical involvement at MCCP; exhorter under Amerine, Borbe and Glyer; Assistant pastor at MCC San Jose 1983; musician at Maranatha MCC Hayward; MCC San Francisco 1986-90; became a nurse; part-time musician MCCSF 1997-2002; Interim Director New Spirit Community Church (joint MCC/UCC) Berkeley.
Ken Storrer (Jamshaid) - MCC of the Valley; now staff and sufi at Breitenbush Retreat Center, Detroit (OR)
MargueriteScroggie (Mark MacKenzie) - pastored at MCC Eugene
Wendy Taylor - became a UCC Pastor
LaPaula Turner - became pastor at MCC Sacramento and MCC Anchorage
Kate Zon - Pastored at MCC Tacoma

1995 Critical Mass bicyclists win right to tie up Portland rush hour traffic once a month
- Lucille Hart dinner picketed by transsexuals, demanding its name be changed
- Salvation Army closes Baloney Joe's homeless shelter on East Burnside
- Oregon mails the Nation's first vote-by-mail primary election ballots

1996 9,000 year old Kennewick man fossil found on the banks of the Columbia
- Torrential rains and snow flood Willamette; Vera Katz urges sandbagging; it works
- Bill Sizemore's Taxpayers United pass bill limits annual property tax increases to 3%

1997 British return Hong Kong to China, British Crown Colony becomes the S.A.R.
- Oregon Regional Primate Research Center successfully clones two Rhesus monkey
- Portland Power women's basketball team takes 2nd in league; fans are 40% lesbian
- Oregon's "Death with Dignity" ordinance becomes legal; first used in 1998

1998 Springfield Thurston High freshman Kip Kinkel kills parents, two students; wounds 22
- West side MAX Light Rail opens 18 miles of tracks through Beaverton to Hillsboro
- Wyoming student Matthew Shepherd murdered, giving gay hate-crime an identity

1999 Blitz Weinhard ends 143 years of brewing; McMenammins, Widmer, and Bridgeport hop in
- Millennium fever hypes the end of (computerized) civilization as we know it
- New Carissa runs aground near Coos Bay, refuses to be towed, blown up, or sunk

2000 Y2K fever fizzles; clocks, computers, and nervous programmers all survive Jan 1, 2000
- Portland Classical Chinese Garden opens, revitalizes Old Town/Chinatown/ Pearl
- Qwest adds 971 area code, introducing ten-digit dialing in the 503 area code
- Enron powers energy crisis and whopping electricity rates, aluminum plants close
- Bush II squeezes presidential victory from Florida; "W" needs supreme court win
- Skate boarding legalized in downtown Portland

2001 The Dalai Lama speaks in Pioneer Courthouse Square
- Whitaker declared a "sick" Middle School, with radon, carbon dioxide and toxic mold
- Four terrorist airplanes destroy World Trade Towers and damage Pentagon on 9-11

Chapter Twelve
Rev. Roy Cole
October 1994 - October 2001

"You are the earth's salt, but if the salt should become tasteless, what can make it salt again? ... You are the world's light— it is impossible to hide a town built on the top of a hill."

Matthew 5:14 (Phillips' Modern English Version)

Roy Cole brought pastoral energy into MCC-Portland that it had not experienced in a decade. Under his leadership, projects that had been put off for 15 years were addressed. New campaigns to refurbish the building were implemented. The historic structure was repainted in an attractive scheme. The grounds were reconfigured and planted with an aesthetic and spiritual plan. Mundane repairs were made and a new sewer line was dug.

MCC's involvement with the community blossomed once more as Roy became involved in community organizations, became part of the Outside-In Board of Directors, made the final effort which led to MCC's acceptance into the Ecumenical ministries of Oregon, assumed a leadership role in a program for gay and lesbian youth, and celebrated two anniversary milestones of the congregation - the 20th and 25th.

To the joy of long-time members, attendance and membership rose to the levels of the founding years. MCC launched a strategic growth initiative program, and was recognized by the UFMCC denomination as the fastest growing congregation in the fellowship. "Rose of Sharon" MCC-Portland felt like it had come through the valley of the shadow.

Beginnings

Warner-Pacific College on SE Division was Roy Cole's undergraduate alma mater in 1984. While there, he also served a yearlong internship at Mt. Scott Church of God. He also earned a Masters degree in Counseling Psychology from the University of Nevada, Reno, a Diploma in Anglican Studies from the General Theological Seminary, a Masters in Sacred Theology from the same Seminary, and a Diploma in Ancient Near Eastern Studies from Jerusalem University College in Israel.

When Roy returned from his Israel studies in 1985, he became pastor at the First Church of God in Reno, NV, until he came out as gay in 1987. Since the Church of God would not accept him as an openly gay minister, he began attending Trinity Episcopal Church in Reno, and it was during that time that he explored the possibility of priesthood, but was dissuaded.

Rev. Ed Sheriff, the NW District Coordinator for the UFMCC heard about Roy and persuaded him to become pastor of MCC-Sierras in Reno. Roy was not credentialed at that time with the UFMCC. At the time there were only five members meeting in a basement room with a ceiling so low that there was but 5' space above his head. However, it should be noted that Roy Cole stands 6'5" tall! MCC-Reno moved their meetings to Temple Sinai, a Reformed Jewish Congregation where they continue to meet in 2005.

In 1993, he was among the applicants for the MCC vacancy left by Gary Wilson. He reapplied in 1994. One of the letters of recommen-

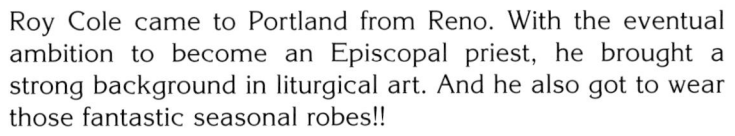

Roy Cole came to Portland from Reno. With the eventual ambition to become an Episcopal priest, he brought a strong background in liturgical art. And he also got to wear those fantastic seasonal robes!!

Call them administrative assistants, clerical staff, or church secretaries, efficient office staff have been essential in the effective handling of daily and weekly chores. Vance Van Cleve held the post initially under Roy Cole, to be succeeded by Terry Van Gelder (lower right), shown with his partner Russ Stoneman.

Rev. Roy Cole   1994 - 2001

dation on Cole's behalf came from Rev. Elder Freda Smith of MCC-Sacramento. She wrote "I truly believe that Roy is one of the most outstanding young clergy persons in our fellowship, I expect great things from him. I believe that he is a church builder, he's musical, he's brilliant, he's very well educated, and he's extremely well versed in the Bible. I believe that with him as pastor, Portland probably has the potential of passing every church in the District as far as attendance and building the congregation."

Roy Cole was 38 when he accepted the call to MCC-Portland Since he was not yet credentialed, approval was requested and given by the Northwest District committee of the UFMCC. He was installed October 30, 1994. Nine days later, Oregonians were to vote on yet another ballot measure (13), which would prohibit state or local governments from extending specific anti-discrimination protections to homosexuals.

Ten ministers participated in Roy's installation service. Rev. Elder Freda Smith gave the address "God will never lead you where God's grace will not keep you." A communion paten and chalice were presented as gifts by Denise Cordova, who later became pastor at Roy's former MCC-Reno congregation. Rev. Janet Suess-Pierce represented the NW District. Other ministers offering greetings and support were Rev. J. A. Barber, Director of Development, OHSU (Oregon Health Sciences University); Dr. Michael Fitting of MCC-Reno; Pastor Patricia Jackson of Sweet Spirit MCC-Salem; Rev. Don Magill, NW District AIDS Representative from the UFMCC; Rev. Teresa Nunn, pastor of Gentle Shepherd MCC-Vancouver; Rev. Frodo Okulam, Pastor of Sister Spirit, Portland; and Rev. John Schwiebert, Co-Pastor of Metanoia Peace Community United Methodist Church and Peace House of Portland.

Joe Gray performed the organ prelude and postlude, and Larry Moad provided his unique special music on the piano. The choir sang the anthem Make Us One. Congregation leaders Kimberly Brown, Gail Bumala, Dave Dishman, Chuck Harvey, Bob Jackson, and Pat Schwiebert also participated in the ceremonies.

Roy Arrived With Several Agendas

Topping the list was his commitment to help the congregation deal with Measure 13 and its implications. He hoped that the ministry of MCC-Portland would be a force promoting the truths that Christ taught–justice, understanding, and inclusion of all individuals in the full rights of society. "As a pastor, I publicly stand opposed to groups such as the OCA. To me, its very important that the church take a leadership role in the community." "What we are seeking is to be treated just like everyone else is treated in the United States." (*Oregonian*, October 29, 1994)

Measure 13 was defeated in the November election. There would not be any more ballot measures challenging the gay and lesbian community during Roy's tenure at MCC, yet much energy would be expended on keeping the OCA at bay. MCC would work closely with Basic Rights Oregon and other Political Action Committees.

Roy also hoped to transform MCC's membership composition, realizing that 90% of the current 65 attendees were men. "I really want to see that change, because I think lesbians can offer so much to gay men, and gay men can offer so much to lesbians." Women always participated in services and he made a commitment to keep women visible. Roy planned a service honoring women, and extended an invitation to gay and non-gay Christians to attend all services.

He was aware of the various reasons MCC attendance had dropped so low, and felt that MCC had lost much of its impact in the community because gays and lesbians were staying away from the church. "Many gays and lesbians, in their journey to accept themselves, have been rejected along the way by the Christian church. Many believe that God no longer loves them because of their sexual orientation. That's what they're told by their religious leaders. It takes time to get over that hurt and to realize that's not true. One of MCC's roles is to reach out to lesbian and gay men and help them reclaim their spiritual heritage." (*Just Out*, December, 1994)

Activities and Events Team-This was the fun squad, providing safe, healthful, and friendly opportunities to mix new and existing members, to build friendship and communication, headed by Pam Lyster.

Administrative Team- Assistance to the pastor, Board of Directors, and other ministry teams was this group's focus - secretarial and archival duties on a volunteer basis, headed by Terry van Gelder.

Building Team - Repair and maintenance of the building in good physical condition was the challenge to the painters, plumbers, and handymen of Rich Kibbon's crew.

Care Team - This ministry provided services to assist in maintaining the dignity and independence of people living with AIDS at the highest possible level. Roy Cole, Rich Kibbons, and Pat Schwiebert coordinated this team, which numbered over 40 volunteers. A separate Congregational Life Team emerged in 2000, which carried on caring ministries, but avoided using the "Care" name in their title, since the word had become associated specifically with AIDS care. See below.

Christian Education Team - Kimberly Brown and the Sunday School teachers exposed children and youth to the inclusive Christ, encouraging them to explore their spirituality in an environment which respected both traditional and non-traditional families.

Sanctuary and Garden Ornamentation Team - Cut flowers for the altar, potted plants, and plantings around the building were grown, pruned, cut, and arranged by Don Strausbaugh and his crew throughout the year.

Television Productions Team - Bringing the message of hope, wellness, and liberation to a cable TV audience was accomplished by producing a series entitled "Living Live." Cheryl Hall coordinated volunteers at Mt. Hood Community College in this creative endeavor.

Publications Team - Weekly bulletin inserts, the monthly newsletter, *Here and Now*, press releases, handbooks, and brochures explaining MCC news and programs were all generated and published by Bob Jackson's very ambitious team of writers.

Sanctuary Choir - Directed by Jim McGinnis, the choir was to provide opportunities to enhance worship experiences through regular performance in church services and special programs. The goal was to have a gender balanced group reflecting the demographics and talents of the congregation and community.

Social Hour Team - Coffee, juice, donated snacks and the ever-present possibility of a potluck were the provenance of this group, which organized the social time before or after worship. Marvin Gray and Rich Kibbons joyously headed this epicurean team.

Strategic Planning Team - The mission, under Don Strausbaugh's leadership, was to use the insight and experience of members to develop the strategies necessary to accomplish the mission and vision of MCC-Portland. Members included Tom Rice, Arlie Adam, Dave Dishman, and Betty Nelson.

Usher Team - The practical aspects of setting up for worship, distributing bulletins, welcoming members and visitors, guiding people to communion, and yes, taking the offering with an awareness of security issues, were all part of Jim Cornwall's squad.

Rev. Roy Cole   1994 - 2001

The new pastor also made the effort to reach out to Dennis Chappell, who had continued to reside in Portland. Chappell passed away from a heart attack a few years later.

Roy made the decision to base worship services on the liturgy of the Presbyterian Book of Common Worship. Utilizing the heritage of a strong universal Christian order of service provided the structure common to most members' own church backgrounds without using worship practices unique to any individual tradition. This proved to be a wise decision. Every new MCC pastor to date heard supplications about using this or that piece of liturgy from this or that tradition, and each pastor evaluated the situation and made decisions under advisement but without favoritism.

Roy pulled elements from the Anglican Book of Common Prayer for many funerals, and after the 1997 UFMCC Sydney General Conference, began using parts of the New Zealand Prayer Book. He also found the Affirmation from the United Church of Canada to be a valid and inclusive alternate to the Apostle's Creed. (See Appendix)

Another item on Roy's list was to attain full membership for MCC in the Ecumenical Ministries of Oregon. Representing 17 denominations and about 2000 congregations in the State, EMO was a vital Christian link to the community, involved in AIDS ministries and several other service projects. Dialogue with Rodney Page of EMO dated back to the days of Austin Amerine, at which time there was opposition to MCC membership from several conservative EMO members.

At the time of his interview with the MCC pastoral search committee, Roy was convinced that he would not receive the call because his top agenda item, if called, would be too costly. This was to restore the historic building to its former glory. He noted that the grass on the non-landscaped grounds was brown, some of the outside wood was rotten, it was painted a depressing chocolate brown, there was dry rot, and it was not a place to be proud of. The church was paid off, but it was an eyesore. It didn't seem to be a fit representation of the philosophy or pride of the congregation. MCC hired him anyway!!

Roy's last agenda item was for the church to nurture a growing involvement with the Portland community, gay and otherwise. He noted with pride that four MCC churches in Oregon worked to educate people about homosexuals. At the time, the other MCC congregations were located in Eugene, Salem, Sister Spirit in Portland, and Vancouver, WA.

So many programs emerged or were reinvigorated that MCC-Portland quickly became known for its vibrancy, especially in the face of ever-mounting AIDS deaths, which reached a peak in 1994-95.

Structure and Infrastructure

At the first Coordinating Council meeting, Roy proposed changing the bylaws and standard operating procedures in order to align with other UFMCC terminology. The Council eventually became the Board of Directors.

A team structure developed for the purpose of accomplishing the various tasks, projects, and outreach ministries of the congregation. These were listed and explained thoroughly in a 20-page booklet called, *Guide to Ministries and Service* printed in 1998. The names, leaders, and mission of each team was explained.

The ministries teams held a Team Ministries Fair in January, usually the same day as the annual congregational business meetings when voting on budget and by-laws took place. The Council of Ministries often met at Peace House for special meetings and planning sessions

Building with Our Community – Capital Campaign 1995-98

MCC-Portland had managed to burn the mortgage in 1993, but the building was anything but a showplace. That situation began to turn around with the energetic renovation of the Family Room under the leadership of four members–Kimberly Brown, Deacon Gail Bumala, Larry Moad, and Eddy Sullivan. It began as a classic, "Its easier to seek forgiveness than per-

BUILDING WITH OUR COMMUNITY:

A PLACE FOR THE COMMUNITY

Roy Cole made good on his vow to restore the church building, initiating a 3-year capital campaign to raise funds. Scaffolding was in place for repairs and a new paint job by autumn, seen in this photo from the *Daily Journal of Commerce*, November 16, 1995.

Rev. Rodney Page (R) of the Ecumenical Ministries of Oregon, was extremely supportive of the request of MCC to join the EMO. When the vote was tallied, the 17-member group unanimously accepted not only the Portland congregation, but by extension, all MCC churches nationwide. His friend, South Africa's Bishop Desmond Tutu is also in the photo.

Rev. Roy Cole   1994 - 2001

mission," project when they sealed off the derelict room full of stored pews, books, and general detritus with black plastic. For months efforts of many volunteers were hidden from view as they replaced rotten supports, added new sheetrock, painted and carpeted the space, and revealed their work on Easter Sunday, 1994.

Their work inspired the congregation, and the new pastor, Roy Cole, to launch a campaign to renovate and restore the rest of the facility. A dinner at Peace House kicked off the fundraising among members and strong supporters. That night, $150,000 was pledged, inspired by a $10,000 donation from Deacon Don Strausbaugh. Although more was needed, with funds in hand, the result was action. Architect Bill Hawkins III, who had designed the restoration of the Old Church (Calvary Presbyterian) into a community performance venue, was hired by the congregation to make recommendations, analyze structural elements, and design new uses for old spaces. Three other architecture firms had also submitted bids.

A second fundraiser was addressed to the larger gay and straight community, with mailings and a festive dinner at the Red Lion Lloyd Center. Featured speaker was Donna Red Wing, the National Field Director of the Gay and Lesbian Alliance Against Defamation (GLAAD). Christian lesbian gospel songwriter Marsha Stevens was the featured entertainment along with the Portland Gay Men's Chorus. Oregon State Representative Gail Shibley was the special guest. All had a good time, however, the fundraising goal of $400,000 was not accomplished. About $15,000 was added to the fund from the dinner.

A sincere but humorous memo was set out It stated:

" Building Cleanup Needs"
Kitchen cleaned and dishes...boxed
Toilet...cleaned
Men's toilet urinal don't flush - either fix or turn off and cover
Furnace Room and Hall...dump
Unclean front basement stair...????
Old Coke machine...OUT
Old Dishwasher...OUT
Small Coffee Heater in Kitchen by water heater...OUT
Shelves for Books in Social Hall...out

In other words, open all doors of church, put truck close and tilt building!

First the scaffolding went up around the church in November 1995. Then the roof was repaired. Two sides of the tower had to be completely re-shingled. To find matching rake shakes, contractors located a small supply in Canada. Then the new 3-tone color scheme was applied. When the scaffolding came down, the results were convincing. Enthusiasm rose for several other projects.

The wheelchair lift did not comply with ADA requirements. Studies were launched to sort out the best solution. The unreliable elevator was relocated near the Broadway entrance, and replaced with its own atrium for $10,000. Several friends of the church and a grant from the Blanche Fisher Foundation provided most of the funding. Office walls were then moved, ceilings and walls replaced and painted, new lighting added, and carpeting completed the job. Moving the office usurped a small area behind the stage once called "The Kids Space," but Sunday School leader Kimberly Brown relocated the education program to the much larger family room. In 1998, accessibility to the altar area was made possible with construction of a ramp.

The third phase involved removing a partition wall in the sanctuary, opening the worship space. The altar was moved against the wall, but the volunteer committee, headed by member Gordon Branstator, kept all historic parts and finishes intact. The dismantled partition doors were used to panel the old choir loft wall, keeping the antique varnish finish consistent with communion rails, altar, and pew finishes.

There was a free bonus to this last phase. The eastern curved wall clerestory windows, atop the curved eastern wall, suddenly became a major part of the worship space. Designed and made in stained glass and lead came 18 years earlier, Don Meadows' volunteer work of 1980-

MCC rchive photos

Gordon Branstator headed a work crew to reconstruct the retaining wall on the NE 24th side of the church property, defining large flowerbeds.

Portland City Archives

Portland had its own impromptu building project in the winter of 1996 when early snowmelt and heavy rains flooded the Willamette. Water under the Hawthorne Bridge rose to the level of Tom McCall Waterfront Park. Mayor Vera Katz called on volunteers to help reinforce the top of the seawall. President Bill Clinton visited and praised Portland citizens for their volunteerism.

Rev. Roy Cole   1994 - 2001

81 now added both brilliance and symbolism to the enlarged nave. Combined with new halogen lighting, the once-dingy interior assumed a different tone and atmosphere. No one had realized the confining and darkening effect that the old partition had caused since its construction in the original building of 1910.

The "Lift Project" and other work of the "Renovation Team" was recognized as "sweat equity," saving over $5000 on construction estimates. Thanks were expressed to Jack Alleckson, Gordon Branstator, Lela Collver, Jim Cornwall, Steve Dondanville, Sue Evans, Rich Kibbons, Tony Longo, Marna McComb, James McNall, Larry Moad, Ron Rasmussen, Tom Rice, Sam Richardson, Jim Sconce, Eddie Sullivan, Kathleen Swain, Phil Wagoner and Fred Willcox.

Roy Cole also made a commitment to remain long term in Portland when he became the first MCC-Portland pastor to purchase a home. He found a Craftsman house at 4006 NE 10th at Shaver and started making mortgage payments, intending to settle for years in the Rose City. While he preferred to keep the home as a place of privacy, he did host the occasional committee meeting in the house.

Garden Ministry

Shortly after the scaffolding was removed from the exterior, a member approached Roy about the possibility of planting a few flowers amongst the dry grass and gangly shrubs outside the building. With a little trepidation, Rich Kibbons was given the okay. This seemingly mild request changed so much more than a few petunias and cedars.

With very few dollars from the budget, Rich planted, fertilized, grafted, rooted, and pruned plants on the sloping ground into amazingly beautiful and colorful fields of blooms, programmed to add color from February to November. Convinced of the merits of sprucing up the "front yard," a crew of volunteers headed by Gordon Branstator and Rich Kibbons graded the entire front slope, building a moderate retaining wall to contain and frame Rich's plantings. The hidden south side of the church became the nursery and potting area where Rich and his small team nurtured future plantings. They even sold off their extras at several church garage sales.

When trying to describe where MCC is located to friends and possible visitors, several members report that if they say the church is located where Broadway and Weidler come together, someone inevitably says, "Isn't that the church with all the flowers?" The church building was transformed from neighborhood eye sore to neighborhood landmark!

Roy and several others knew about Rich's congestive heart failure condition and worried about him doing so much. After several scoldings from concerned and loving friends, Rich wasn't about to change his habits, and continues working almost daily on his knees, landscaping what he now calls the "Mary Garden." Thank you, Rich!!

Music Ministries

Roy Cole had a commitment to the ministry of music and its place in worship. MCC-Portland had a long tradition of outstanding music and volunteer musicians played the organ, sang in the choirs, performed special music during services, and accompanied singing on piano. All musicians fulfilled their duties gratis. Larry Moad, Milt Howell, and Kelly McFarland emerged as core musical leaders.

Larry directed the choir, which increased in numbers as enthusiasm for participation in outstanding worship grew. Jim McGinnis volunteered as new choir director and continued building the group. He had moved from North Carolina and wanted to get involved in a church where he could be completely open, and where he and his partner could worship together. His work paved the way for the eventual hiring of a full time director of celebration and worship. In 1998, the choir included:

Small group performers also presented special music. One group included Kimberly Brown, Gail Bumala, Dave Dishman, and Marvin Gray. Many groups and quartets formed for a single event, then disbanded.

Bass I	**Bass II**	**Tenor II**	**Tenor I**
Gordon Branstator	Jack Alleckson	Alex Casareno	Dave Dishman
Don Lonsborough	Glenn Hiner	Jim McGinnis	Michael Demaree
Jim Strouse	Steve Dunn	Marvin Gray	Jerry Maytorena
Cheryl Hall	Rick Woodrum	Phil Scholze	Maury Evans
Vince Irelan	Milt Howell	Art Shelly	Jonathan Carusoe
	Wayne Shull		

Soprano I	**Soprano II**	**Alto I**	**Alto** II
Mark A Brown	Ron Goodsell	Liz Konsella	Carolee Erickson
Kelly McFarland	Lela Collver	Al Lucero	
Dennis Carter	Lance Duncan	Liz Lucero	
	Donna Snoke	Lark Jarvis	
	Catherine Lewi		

The "Rose of Sharon" Choir grew to its largest numbers under the direction of Jim McGinnis. Small groups formed for special occasions. The "Falsettos" included Darcy White, Rick Edmundson, Mark C. Brown, and Tony Stroh. Gary Newton is in the right photo. Tony Stroh also worked with PGMC. Milt Howell, on the bench, has been the regular organist over ten years.

Rev. Roy Cole   1994 - 2001

Attendance grew significantly under Roy's leadership, justifying the hiring of a part-time minister of music to perform and coordinate the various musical aspects of the church. Rev. Eugene McMullen from MCC-San Francisco was hired as the first Director of Celebration and Worship. Despite his best efforts, there didn't seem to be a good match between him and the congregation, and McMullen returned to San Francisco after several months. A national search was launched for a replacement. When the best candidate was located, it turned out that Mark C. Brown was already living in Portland, serving as music minister at First Christian Church on the South Park Blocks!

Jonathan Carlyle, Gene McMullen, Mark Brown became part of the staff in 2000 as Director of Celebration and Worship. He assumed directorship of the choir, replacing Jim McGinnis. Larry Moad continued playing the communion hymns during distribution. He played awesome offertories, quite often selecting his choice during the sermon as Roy's message came into focus. He didn't think he was seen flipping pages, but he was. Milt Howell, with a Church of the Nazarene background, had become the regular organist in 1994. Kelly McFarland also played keyboard, but especially thrived in a tight harmony men's trio called "Joyful Sound," in combination with Dennis Carter and Mark A. Brown. Yes, it's confusing –there are two Mark Browns, both outstanding musicians.

Attendance rose when word got out about the energized music program. More than ten new members first appeared in the choir, long before introducing themselves to the Pastor. About 100 new members joined in the year following Mark's hiring. A new supply of musicians led to a symphony orchestra of about 10 players, with Mark selecting music and personally writing arrangements to fit the skills of his instrumentalists. As the skills of the musicians improved, Mark wrote more complex arrangements. They performed biweekly, often giving the prelude and post service music, as well as accompanying hymn singing.

Mark also organized theatric presentations in harmony with the Bob Jackson Drama team, and formed at least one quartet. Mark's efforts culminated in the 2004 production of Stephen Sondheim's Into the Woods. Mark knew the singers and actors in the community and cast them into a highly successful production.

Sunday School and Youth Ministry

There had been no Sunday School program at MCC since long before Gary Wilson's tenure, and more single and partnered parents were showing up with young children. Roy was keen to reinstate Sunday School, and Kimberly Brown let it slip one day that she was interested in ministry in some form. That was it.

Curriculum materials from the United Churches of Christ were ordered, for both youth and adult education programs. The UCC lessons were lectionary based, following prescribed readings for each Sunday of the church year. Part of each lesson involved a crafts or hands-on project. Sunday School class started after opening announcements were made in the service. Children would go into the family room with Kimberly, and usually return to be with their parents in time for the Communion.

Several members helped with the initial program, including Liz Konsella and David Jones. For the first two years, they simply showed up every Sunday and hoped there would be children to work with. Usually there was at least one youngster, and slowly the program grew into a core of 5-6 regular kids. Volunteers often were discouraged when no children came, and Kimberly ended up being the mainstay of the program until Roy left in 2001. Sometimes she didn't have time to try out the crafts project first, and kids often ended up with some very unusual objects to take home. But they were happy.

Food Ministries

When celebrating...eat! When stressed... eat! When fund-raising....eat!

Although rarely without an excuse for a potluck, the pace of food-related gatherings at MCC increased soon after Roy Cole arrived. In the two-month period of May and June, 1995,

Member Dani Eaton not only did some gender bending, he also worked tirelessly for many years to guarantee the success of Esther's Pantry. Much of the food distributed to PWAs (Persons with AIDS) came through the Ryan White Act. Ricky Caesar was another long-running volunteer. A separate entity was Todd's Closet, collecting and distributing clothing to the AIDS community.

Rev. Roy Cole   1994 - 2001

there was "Spaghetti and Bingo evening," a garage sale and potluck, a potluck dinner/gay and lesbian film night, a Pride Festival Luau dinner, and a Gay PRIDE parade and picnic. Easter meant an Easter breakfast. Sometimes a dessert buffet was served between the two morning services, especially at Christmas time. Marvin Gray supervised many of these. After regular worship, there were always snacks and coffee, provided for years by the Broadway Coffee Merchant and member Rick Edmondson. Then there was the Harvest Dinner, a huge annual event with food, fun, fellowship, and fundraising auctions.

Food for dinners could not legally be cooked in the basement kitchen after it was deemed substandard by city inspectors, but creative minds and hands whipped up some fabulous meals, including the ongoing gourmet leadership of Robin Hixson, Vic Winegar, and Rich Kibbons. Pat Schwiebert could always be counted on to do food, either at church or at Peace House.

The deacon's pantry, supplying canned and dry food upon request to homeless and underfunded visitors continued as a community service. When the supplies ebbed, a call for donated food and funds always topped up the supplies.

Esther's Pantry Changes

MCC major commitment to feeding others materialized in 2000, when the congregation assumed management and ownership of Esther's Pantry, the food bank for people with AIDS. The Pantry was originally set up in 1986 by friends of Esther Hoffman Howard, Empress XXIV, aka Chester Brinker. Dignity had jump-started the pantry with a successful food drive the first year. Jean Babaloo donated a large cash "start-up" fund. Donations came from the Rosetown Ramblers, several gay bars, other groups and individuals, and the court, which one year raised $8000. Esther's was managed by the Imperial Sovereign Rose Court for the next 18 years. Additional food was collected at dances, bingo, roller skating, bowling, even haircuts and shoe shines. A cooperative arrangement developed with the Oregon Food Bank. Many individuals even helped with clipped coupons.

Esther's received nonprofit status with the state of Oregon in 1991 and served about 300 clients. By 2000, administrative burnout and a lack of volunteers threatened to end the all-volunteer charitable endeavor. Nearly 300 men received monthly food supplies from the Pantry at the time.

When Roy Cole got wind of Esther's possible closure, he met with Esther's Board and the MCC Board of Directors. It was agreed that the work at Esther's was vital, and could not be allowed to disappear. The Board of MCC was ready to take on a larger role in the community with an off-site project. The Pantry saved $4600 a year by moving to NE 28th and Halsey, walking distance from MCC and adjacent to the Fred Meyer store built on the site of the old Doernbecker Furniture plant in Hollywood West.

Long-term volunteers Dani Eaton and Ricky Caesar provided continuity. Derek LePak did not have a title, but was the main man keeping things running onsite. Like most men there, he had started initially as a client. The all-volunteer staff reorganized procedures and physical aspects of the Pantry, personally helping each "shopper" access and supply their food needs. Some clients feared that they would be preached to, but Roy stressed that there would be no religious overtones. Volunteers combined friendship, support, and some casual counseling for the "shoppers," which grew to include some women and children.

Esther's had benefited from being a part of the National Ryan White Act, which honored the young hemophiliac who had died of AIDS. U.S. Department of Health and

Human Resources funding was reduced, and the use of funds for groceries was eliminated. Roy asked Dave Beckley to write up a grant proposal, seeking other government funding. With the support of Sen. Gordon Smith, who had known Beckley when he was mayor of The Dalles from 1994-98, an initial grant of $45,000 was received in 2000. The next year, the funding was $25,000.

Originally limited to clients with a diagnosis of AIDS, Esther's widened its scope in

Cheryl Hall joined MCC while Roy Cole was pastor. With experience in film and TV, a decision was made to launch a series of 36 cable shows with Roy. One worker from the Midas shop facing MCC often talked with Roy about the shows.

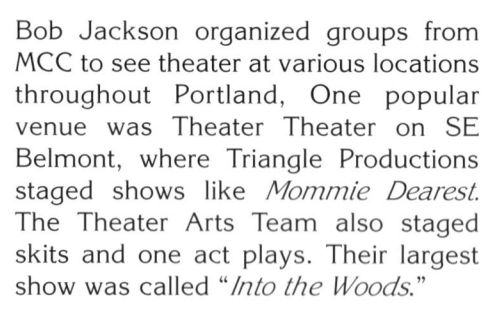

Bob Jackson organized groups from MCC to see theater at various locations throughout Portland, One popular venue was Theater Theater on SE Belmont, where Triangle Productions staged shows like *Mommie Dearest*. The Theater Arts Team also staged skits and one act plays. Their largest show was called "*Into the Woods*."

330

Rev. Roy Cole   1994 - 2001

2005 to include HIV positive clients as well. (See Chapter 13)

Theater Arts Team

Founding member and deacon Bob Jackson had a deep background in the arts, especially theater. He worked for many years for Oregon Public Television, offering a program called the *Seven Lively Arts*. He was totally involved with MCC and his infectious enthusiasm galvanized many individuals to form a group dedicated to producing theatrical presentations at church as well as attending other productions throughout the city. They worked up skits for the Harvest Dinner, generated chancel dramas to aid worship, and mounted full-scale theater evenings, usually with a minimum of props and a maximum of creativity.

After Bob passed away in May 1999, the group renamed itself the Jackson Theater Arts team and produced many more events, keeping spirits high in the congregation after Roy Cole left. In 2001, Bob was also honored with a gift to the congregation of an Eternal Light, reminiscent of Bob's constant light and energy for the church. The gift came from the Theater Arts Team. Mark C. Brown worked with the Theater Arts Team people to produce *Into the Woods* at which time the entire Sanctuary was transformed into a sylvan atmosphere. Roy Cole returned from New York for the presentation.

Many more productions were mounted during the interim period pastored by Mike Nikolaus. Consistently faithful members of the team included Marvin Gray, Dennis Carter, Donna Snoke and several others. (See Chapter 13)

Living Live

Snickers LaBarr, a popular gay cable TV host(ess) interviewed Roy Cole in 1995 for her show. This led to Cheryl Hall, Bob Jackson, Terry VanGelder, and Roy Cole initiating a series of 36 television programs from 1995 to 1997. Episodes were filmed at Mount Hood Community College and presented on cable. Using a minimalist set, Roy conducted the programs and Bob did the voiceovers against a setting of a single fluted classical gray column, a plinth, and a set of stairs.

The programs were aimed at the general community, proclaiming a message of hope and positive outlook. So many people seemed to feel that their lives were at a dead end, or that they were just "treading water." Cheryl and Roy designed presentations to let people see the multitude of opportunities that were alternatives to just existing without a goal.

Three of the hour-long segments were nominated and voted the top religious show on cable in the area. From time to time people would recognize Roy somewhere out in the community and tell him that they had seen an episode, and how much they appreciated it. One consistent fan of Living Live was the co-owner of the muffler shop across NE 24th from the church. He would often remark that he and his wife had watched and enjoyed the show. The program elevated MCC's profile in the public eye.

Sister Paula continued her cable TV ministry, which had begun in December, 1987. Her programs aired on Paragon Cable Channel 21 and Rogers Cable Access Network Channel 11. Paula's hour-long special July 25, 1994, featured her interview and discussion with Troy Perry. Both individuals had blazed their own trail of faith during the era of "flower power," hippies, and Stonewall. On the program, they shared and compared their stories. Although not a direct ministry of MCC, and receiving no funds from the church, the Paula connection with MCC was nearing 20 years.

Rainbow Youth and SMYRC

The Urban League of Portland approached Roy in 1995, requesting a meeting space for their GLBT youth program. Young people of color hesitated to hold meetings at the Urban League, risking being seen by someone who might know their families. Secrecy and confidentiality were still very much essential for these youth to meet and discuss their issues and interests. The group was successful at MCC, but after about a year, the Urban League was unable to continue funding the program. By way of a Multnomah County grant, MCC was able to assume control of the program, and it grew for a number of years. Facilitators for the group were

Family and youth concerns were successfully addressed through the work of several groups, including Love Makes a Family, led by Bonnie Tinker. MCC assumed leadership of a Rainbow Youth group started by Brother-to-Brother. This group transitioned into Sexual Minorities Youth Resource Center (SMYRC). Mike Whitcomb (center below) has co-moderated the Gay Dad's Group, founded in 1995. TIME magazine devoted a cover story to issues around the sexual interests and practices of young people in 1997.

Marty Davis photos

Dave Kohl photo

funded by the county grant. Roy's role was primarily administrative, although he did occasionally visit groups and got to know several of the members. There was a plan to connect the group with the Brother-to-Brother organization, but that did not happen.

The same old issues concerning adult gays trying to support the needs of underage questioning and gay people were still evident, and there was not much interaction between MCC membership and the Rainbow Youth. Adults were still self conscious or reluctant about being perceived as "chicken hawks." Community perception that gays "recruited" or that gray men were pedophiles was still influenced by OCA propaganda. Once again the opportunity to really bridge the age gap became mute. The program ceased about the time Roy Cole departed Portland.

MCC did host a Friday night youth drop in center. It had marginal success but helped Phoenix Rising move forward with plans to develop a free-standing fully funded center, which became SMYRC (Sexual Minority Youth Recreation Center). When Phoenix Rising faced closing the center because of insufficient financial support, Roy was asked to assume the presidency of the Phoenix Rising Board. He led the negotiations in merging Phoenix Rising with Network Behavioral Health Care (now Cascadia Behavioral Health Care). Part of the negotiations were to ensure that SMYRC would continue and that l/g/b/t people in Portland would have access to mental health services through NBH.

Roy's activism led him into another Portland arena for working with homosexual and generally disenfranchised youth when he became involved with Outside-In. During his tenure on the Board there, a grant application was made to the Bill and Melinda Gates Foundation for funding a new permanent day facility and residential quarters. A normal, nondescript envelope arrived months later containing a single piece of paper –a check for $1 million, dedicated to the building project. The new facility on SW 13th opened in 2003.

For several Christmas seasons, MCC members helped brighten the holidays for Outside-In youth. A Giving Tree was displayed in the MCC sanctuary during Advent, covered with gift tags that described a bit about one homeless youth and a gift that the person had requested. Members took a tag, bought the requested gift, and brought it, unwrapped, to MCC a week before Christmas. Outside-In staff did the wrapping and distribution of the anonymous gifts for their Holiday party.

Fun and Fundraisers

Gordon Branstator, a choir member, handyman, and retired florist, took charge of the annual rummage sale. He advertised, picked up, priced, and arranged a basement full of items each year with help from dependable volunteers. Some years the choir was the beneficiary. Other years' profits became part of the building fund, general fund, or some other project. But if there was a rummage sale, Gordon would be somewhere close by.

Police Activity

Tom Potter, former Portland Chief of Police and one-time police liaison to the gay community, was featured in a 1995 book with his daughter Katie about straight parents and their gay children. When the author, Bob Bernstein, did a presentation and reading that August at 23rd Avenue Books, "Supercop" Tom and Katie were part of the audience during the discussion, sponsored by P-FLAG. (Robert Bernstein, *Straight Parents, Gay Children*, 1995)

Bernstein later stayed in the Potter home in 1997 while visiting Portland and doing research on another book about community policing, a concept and practice implemented in Portland when Tom was Chief of Police under Bud Clark in the mid-1980s. (See Chapter 8)

Tom and Katie took the bold step of appearing together, in uniform, in the 1999 Gay Pride parade through downtown Portland. There was little doubt where the Chief stood on Gay rights issues. Five years later, he would emerge from "retirement" to run for and be elected Mayor of Portland.

Relations with the gay community and the City of Portland continued harmoniously although Mayor Bud Clark decided no to seek a

Porrtland CityArchive

Dave Kohl photo

Portland's City Hall presents a warm classical facade on SW 4th. Two blocks closer to the Willamette is the Justice Center, housing the Police Bureau built near the site of the Transfusion Inn.

Police Chief Mark Kroeker (R) presented an award to MCC member Norm Costa. He also conducted an open forum at MCC when there was community concern about an historic comment he had made about gay people.

Portland's shortest Mayor, Vera Katz, posed with Portland's tallest drag Queen Snickers LaBarr, at a PRIDE celebration. Vera supported the gay community and pioneered an ordinance guaranteeing access to public rest rooms for transsexuals. Her aide for eleven years was Sam Adams, who successfully ran for City Commissioner in 2004, after Vera's retirement. He has led the campaign for a GLBTQ community center, Portland's first in 30 years (to be called the Q Center).

Rev. Roy Cole   1994 - 2001

second term. His friend and neighbor Vera Katz was elected in 1994 and carried forward a spirit of respect and diversity for twelve years. Her assistant for eleven of those years was young political scientist Sam Adams, an openly gay and partnered man who became the liaison with the gay community. He would be elected as one of Portland's five city commissioners in 2004. His City Hall office is currently downstairs from the suite of Mayor Tom Potter. (See Chapter 13)

Growth, Acceptance, and Recognition

Picking up the pieces left by Gary Wilson and the foundational rebuilding begun by Dennis Chappell, Roy was able to fulfill his goal of building MCC attendance and membership. Roy and the congregation embarked on the "Strategic Growth Initiative" program headed by UFMCC Elder Rev. Don Eastman.

MCC was one of the targeted congregations selected to be part of this innovative program from the Fellowship. Lead by Rev. Don Eastman, a partnership developed using growth strategies similar to those in the business world. It was a very successful partnership. Whereas it took three years to reach a membership of 100, that figure doubled in 18 months. The next 100 were added within a year, the same year that Mark C. Brown joined the staff. Roy became a SGI trainer under Don's mentoring and later worked with Emmanuel MCC-Spokane for about a year and a half.

In recognition of this rapid growth, Roy was honored at the 1997 UFMCC General Conference XVIII in Sydney. The Pastor and the congregation were given the "Phoenix Award" for leadership in church renewal. The award recognized the vision and leadership Roy brought to revitalizing the life of MCC-Portland.

The Sydney Conference was the first to be held outside the United States, signifying the growth of the denomination into 19 countries. Nearly 1000 worldwide delegates were present. MCC-Portland sent the pastor and congregational representatives Dan Brown, Dave Dishman, and Chuck Harvey. Their first stop was in Hawaii, where the Northwest District Conference was hosted by MCC-Ke Anuenue O Ke Aloha.

Several other MCC members joined the delegation, including Deacon Bob Jackson, as they visited Australia for the General Conference, followed by various amounts of sightseeing.

The momentum of membership growth seemed to increase geometrically, until MCC-Portland was recognized by the UFMCC as the congregation with the highest number of new members in a given quarter. Seventy-five new members joined MCC between December 2001 and March 2002! That season, MCC-Cathedral of Hope in Dallas had gained 71 people, and in third position was MCC of the Resurrection of Houston with 47.

Ecumenical Ministries of Oregon

In a separate but parallel development, Roy Cole was doing intense work with the Ecumenical Ministries of Oregon. At the time of his arrival in 1994, he met with EMO director Rodney Page. Gary Wilson had worked closely with Rev. Page on several committees, including, AIDS vigils and World AIDS Days. At the first meeting, Roy and Rodney both agreed that the climate within EMO was still too divided to consider an application from MCC-Portland for membership.

However, Roy became active in EMO activities not requiring membership, and was appointed to several committees. As local church leaders got to know Roy, and see the commitment of the congregation to many issues of social justice, the tide of opinion began to turn. With new leadership in the late 1990s, the fullness of time had come, and MCC did apply for membership. After months of discussion a vote was taken. The vote was unanimous for acceptance, with the Greek Orthodox abstaining, and the Roman Catholic representative not in attendance.

The net result was that EMO recognized not only MCC-Portland, but also the entire Universal Fellowship of Metropolitan Community Churches into membership. EMO only accepted membership by denomination, not by individual congregation. At the 2001 UFMCC General Conference XX in Toronto, Pastor Cole was awarded the Ecumenical Award In recognition of his efforts.

Some MCC members became very involved in NW District (later called Region 1). Dave Dishman is shown with Roberta Booth of Tacoma. Mark McKenzie (aka Margaret Scroggie) is at s Spokane Conference with Harriet Meric of Eugene and Connie Staff from San Francisco. Chuck Harvey held office in the UFMCC, shown here at the 2001 Sacramento Conference with Rev. Freda Smith and Kathleen Meadows.

Ever friendly, MCC continued to participate in Boardman Retreats and to welcome guests at. home.

Rev. Roy Cole   1994 - 2001

Community involvement

With emerging pride, MCC-Portland began getting involved with the Irvington neighborhood. On Sunday, May 21, 1995, MCC members participated in the "Out on Broadway Stroll," a casual afternoon of walking much of the length of NE Broadway, getting to know the numerous shops, restaurants, and institutions which were gay and lesbian owned. Advertised in *Just Out* and Willamette Week, it turned out to be a large and successful neighborhood event. MCC hosted an Information Fair that day from noon to 4 pm, with many gay and lesbian community groups setting up information tables, distributing literature, and informally chatting with visiting neighbors.

That evening was the 12th International AIDS Candlelight Memorial and Mobilization in the South Park Blocks at First Congregational Church.

Gay Pride celebrated its 20th year in 1995 with the annual Saturday parade through downtown Portland. Although splattered by occasional cloudbursts, dignitaries Mayor Vera Katz, Police Chief Charles Moose, state Rep. George Eighmey, and former Police Chief Tom Potter and his daughter Katie all took part. Portland Fire Bureau personnel manned a recruiting booth, but disappointed marchers when there was no fire truck present. Contingents from Dykes on Bikes, Bad Girls, and Darcelle XV's female impersonator squad contrasted with more vanilla delegations. Radical Women marched in their T-shirts, which read, "Stonewall was a riot - now we need a revolution."

Roy Cole had clipped his mullet hairstyle, losing his identity as "Pastor Bee Gees." He was unaware of his reputation as Portland's answer to Andy Gibb until after he got his locks off, and someone was brave enough to tell him. He energetically led the MCC-Portland delegation of about 40 members in the gay march, joined by UFMCC District Coordinator Janet Suess-Pierce.

In that parade, the United Church of Christ sent contingents from 13 congregations who had declared themselves "open and affirming." Gay Catholics, Seventh-Day Adventists, and Episcopalians also participated. There was a noticeable lack of religious protesters in the 1995 event, although same-sex marriage was a current topic, owing to the eminent movement in Hawaii to legalize gay marriages. The OCA did have several anti-gay rights initiatives in the hopper for 1996. (*Oregonian*, June 18, 1995, p. D1, 8)

As part of the 1997 Pride weekend, MCC held a worship service at Pioneer Courthouse Square just before the annual parade. It was an ecumenical service, with participation from several other ministers. The 1997 Pride celebration was officially sponsored by Coors Brewing Company, known years earlier for their homophobia.

The Shepherd's Award Dinner

Honoring the dedicated volunteer work of Portland's most influential activists, MCC-Portland held the first Shepherd's Award Dinner at the Portland Hilton Pavilion Ballroom on April 12, 1997. Roy and the Board determined that with MCC's return to a vital place in the gay community of Portland, that it needed an annual visible community-wide event. They chose to honor local or regional leaders with a fundraising event that would be a benefit to all. Roy asked Ann Shepherd if she would allow her name to be attached to the dinner title. She was delighted. and surprised when she herself received the first award.

Ann and Bill Shepherd, parents of two lesbian daughters, had stood up for gay and lesbian rights since Ann's first appearance before the State Legislature in 1975. Her subsequent involvement with the Governor's Task Force led to the establishment of Parents of Gays under the leadership of Chuck and Rita Knapp. That group evolved into P-FLAG. Bill Shepherd, a lawyer, and Ann, a journalist, continued their activism with numerous state and local task forces, various speaking engagements, and virtually any opportunity that allowed them to defend the rights of the lesbian, gay, and cross-gender community. Even after Bill's passing in 1995, Ann had remained a vital force. Their daughter Susie was an early MCC member, and

Portland's de facto gay mother was Ann Shepherd. Once on the Governor's task force, she and husband Bill worked with Charles and Rita Knapp to found what became the P-FLAG chapter in Portland. Roy Cole honored her by establishing the Shepherd's Award Dinner, and surprised Ann with the first honor. She also founded the "Class Act," raising funds for scholarships for students in gay law careers.

338

they spoke often and eloquently at services and rallies at the church. Ann even preached a Mother's Day sermon back in the days of Austin Amerine.

MCC commissioned the making of a 17-minute documentary film, directed by Matthew Levin, about the contributions of the Shepherds. Entitled *Bill and Ann Shepherd, A Life's Work,* it was shown at the Awards Dinner, and later included as part of the Portland Gay and Lesbian Film Festival at Cinema 21 four months later.

Dinner attendees purchased tickets, which included a large donation to the church. The recipient of the award was given a beautiful Waterford Crystal bowl mounted on a stand, an engraved plaque, and $1000 to be donated to a charity of their choice. Remaining funds would be directed into the Capital Campaign for use in MCC building renovation.

The dinner event was to be an annual affair, honoring top Northwest community activists, but it would remain named for the Shepherds. The event was also part of a fund-raising program for the MCC Capital Campaign, raising funds to rehabilitate the church building. Future recipients of the award would include Darcelle, Rep. Gretchen Kafourey, Rev. Troy Perry, and Roey Thorpe. Roy Cole was honored for his seven year's leading MCC back into a dynamic congregation.

Living with AIDS

Almost 800 new cases of AIDS were reported in 1994, and more than 350 people died from AIDS that season. Drug therapy was revolutionized in 1996 with the development of the "triple cocktail," combinations of drugs (protease inhibitors), which greatly slowed the development of the disease, forestalling an inevitable death. Indinovir, Retonavir, Sequinavir, and Neifinavir became familiar in the battle to reduce the amount of virus in the blood (Viral Loads) while keeping the T-cell count above 200.

Much experimentation was required to find the "cocktail" that worked best for each individual, and the meds could cost over $2000 a month. Not everyone could pay to keep themselves alive, even though the Oregon Health Plan pioneered by Governor John Kitzhaber, himself a medical doctor, covered the cost of the cocktail for many Oregonians.

In Washington, DC, White House security personnel donned rubber gloves before admitting a delegation of gay politicians, including Oregon's Rep. George Eighmey, to a meeting in June 1995.

Progressive local needle exchange programs helped keep Oregon's infection rates below the national average. CAP continued its educational programs, and the Oregon State Health Division continued supplying free condoms, distributed at bars, baths, bookstores, and in the men's room at MCC-Portland.

CAP tried several new programs to energize support groups and educational events. Mentalk was a CAP program, which established smaller chat groups in various neighborhoods for convenience. Other groups were based on age. Mark Elliott, who had begun a gay dad's support group independently, arranged to have that group meet under the auspices of CAP. There was also coordination with Bonnie Tinker's Love Makes a Family organization. On Friday evenings, CAP sponsored the "Lavender Lounge" meeting at various coffeehouses including Zing's and Utopia, both in SE Portland. This was a social networking group that ranged in attendance from two to 20 men. Changes in CAP priorities and funding later pulled the support from these groups, and only the Gay Dad's group continues, with two meetings each month.

Our House of Portland was filled with clients in various phases of AIDS. Many volunteers helped with cooking, housekeeping, grounds work, and general support of clients. Sister Paula was a volunteer cook, but was also well-known to clients from her cable show. She told a touching story in her June 1994, newsletter:

"A client saw me in the hallway and told me his lover had been placed in Room 8. 'He would like to see you. He has been a fan of your TV show and is real excited about meeting you

John Kitzhaber, a former emergency room doctor, became Oregon's Governor for two terms. Concerns about AIDS were also voiced by Oregon Senator Gordon Smith (center). Fifty hour AIDS Vigils were incorporated into International AIDS Memorials. David Lane, a frequent attendee at MCC, worked with the Oregon State Health Division on AIDS education and outreach.

Panels from the NAMES Project Quilt visited Portland in 1987. It was paraded on SW Broadway displayed at the Chiles Center of the University of Portland. It has been in Portland several times. At MCC, a wall in the Al Williams Chapel/Fireside Room held smaller panels for members lost to AIDS.

Rev. Roy Cole   1994 - 2001

in person.' So before leaving that day, I ventured down the hall to Room 8 and visited and joked with Dave, a handsome young man in his 20's. Outside of the room, as I was leaving, Dave's lover thanked me and said: 'Sister Paula, you put the first smile on Dave's face in months.'

"Every week thereafter, I made it a point to stop in and visit with Dave. And each week, as with all of the clients of Our House, I noted Dave's condition deteriorating. Toward the last, his mind wandered and he was not always able to respond although he was aware of who I was and the fact that I was there. Whenever I came into his presence, a smile always came on to his face.

"One day, his bed was empty, with the traditional flowers, Dave's cap, pictures of Dave throughout his childhood, and a note from his lover saying; 'Good bye, Dave,' I'll always love you and miss you." I wept. And I thanked God that Sister Paula was counted worthy to be used to put a smile on a dying young man's face."

A Candlelight Memorial and Mobilization service at MCC-Portland on May 18, 1997 tied in with the 14th Annual International AIDS Candlelight Memorial. At that service, a sculpture entitled Healing Hands of Love was on exhibit. It was the work of Debra Beers for ART/AIDS, and was the gift to MCC-Portland by the Friends of Bess Kaiser Medical Center. The plaster work was strongly influenced by Michelangelo's Pieta, and graphically displayed the care of one man for a weakened brother, held in his arms. Its impact on viewers was instantly emotional, and it was displayed in the narthex for many years. At one point, it was removed, and, sadly, its current location is unknown.

The Care Team

Over 1500 hours of volunteer time was logged by about 20 individuals in 1997 alone to help people with AIDS at MCC. Organized by the Care Team, they offered as much, or as little, help as requested by PWAs. They would help with transportation, moving, grocery shopping, laundry help, cooking, and sponsoring the International AIDS Candlelight Memorial. They also helped with "Fabric of Life," a funding source to local agencies providing HIV/AIDS services. Thirteen Care Team members volunteered to help with Fabric of Life fundraisers.

The Care Team produced its own newsletter, often a supplement in the quarterly Here and Now. It contained the latest news on AIDS medications, listed community resources, and publicized the NAMES project and news about the Quilt. There were even healthy recipes and cooking/household hints included.

Ray Kincade created the role of Parish Nurse. He was an energetic member of MCC and the Congregational Life Team, whose services expanded to include a regular column in the Here and Now, as well as work with individual situations. Office space was found behind the stage area and Ray established a professional presence with regularly scheduled hours.

AIDS Events

The AIDS Vigils of the late 1980s had become interfaith community-wide events. As World AIDS day, they were sponsored by the Regional AIDS Interfaith Network, the first such day being December 1, 1988. Growing in magnitude, the observances increased understanding of the global epidemic, with an emphasis on promoting action and sound policies to prevent HIV transmission. The Joint United Nations Program on HIV/AIDS (UNAIDS) coordinated research revealing a shift by 1997 that 70% of new HIV infections came from male-female sexual contacts and that 5-10% of new cases resulted from male-male contact.

Portland's 1997 observance of World AIDS Day highlighted the tremendous price paid in human life because of HIV/AIDS. Attention was focused on the often neglected populations of youth, people of color, and women, seeking education on prevention, and on the effect of cuts in programs and services. Although the infection rate of gay men in the U.S. was dropping, people needed to be reminded that the pandemic was not over, and that the price in lost human lives would continue to be paid daily until a cure was found. MCC, the Urban League of Portland, and the Portland Area Business Association (PABA) co-operated in planning and financing the event.

Just Out photos

The national march on Washington was a landmark event. Scott, an MCC attendee, was there.

In Portland, AIDS and HIV information were made available in bars, baths, and at gay PRIDE. The local candlelight march was celebrated at MCC. Vigils were also held in the South Park Blocks. At MCC, a pieta-like sculpture donated by the staff of Good Samaritan Hospital brought out a full range of emotions from anguish to comfort. It was also displayed at Peace House.

MCC Archive photos

Rev. Roy Cole   1994 - 2001

In an unexpected manifestation of the fear and loathing felt by some straight men over homosexuality and AIDS, a young gay student was found tied to a fence outside Laramie, Wyoming. Matthew Shepherd, 21, a gregarious 5'2" gay college student was lured outside the Fireside Lounge, robbed, pistol-whipped with the butt of a .357 Magnum, and left to die, tied to the fence several miles from town. He was near death when he was found the next day., he died later in a hospital. Prayer vigils and death watches had formed spontaneously across the nation when news of the incident was reported.

Matthew Shepherd's death crystallized the risk and fear that gay men and lesbians in small-town America were forced to live with daily. With no public places to gather, the Wyoming gay community had resorted to dinner parties, casino nights, and camp outs. But with a false bravado, some gays hoped to infiltrate into communities and meet other men, especially in college towns. Many men reported spending time in cowboy bars in Casper or Cheyenne, picking up "straight" men who were far into the closet, some even married. Shepherd had probably depended on his "gaydar"–the sense of how gay someone might be, based on clues of speech, demeanor, or dress. His two assailants had led him to believe that they, too, were gay.

A national outpouring of grief and disgust over the following months produced a backlash against gay hate crimes. Shepherd was eulogized in several songs commissioned by various gay choruses, and in the 2002 documentary drama by Moises Kaufman, *The Laramie Project*. It chronicled people of the town in the year following the killing. In 2005, its presentation at a local Beaverton high school created a confrontation, when followers of the anti-gay Kansan Fred Phelps protested the production.

Keeping the Faith

Just Out ran a cover story on December 18, 1998, looking at the faith life of 10 local individuals with diverse belief systems. Front and center were photos of Roy Cole and Frodo Okulam. Also included in the article was Jerry Deas, national secretary of the Dignity organization of gay and lesbian Catholics. Rev. Cecil Prescod, ordained minister with the United Church of Christ spoke of faith in the face of homophobia, despite his own African American heritage. Rick Hernandez and Henry Miller had recently been involved in the 20th annual conference of gay Mormons, Affirmation, held in Portland. Alex Villarreal declared himself a gay Christian, but expressed fear that homosexuals will not enter heaven.

Nelly Kaufer described herself as a "Ju-Bu" (a person born to Jewish heritage who has strong Buddhist leanings) and an active member of B'nai Or, a Jewish renewal congregation. She had written the book *A Woman's Guide to Spiritual Renewal* (Harpers, 1994), and described spirituality as making a deep connection with yourself and something greater. Partners Rev. Berdell Moffett and Rev. Casey Chaney led a congregation at The God Connection in Beaverton, describing 75 members as "lightly traditional. We allow people to make (God) who they need Him to be. We don't believe in literal hell. We believe the essence of all people is good, not evil." (*Just Out*, Dec. 18, 1998 p. 21)

Although the *Just Out* article did not mention it, Roy Cole was deeply committed to bridging the gap between various Christian tradition s regarding homosexuality. He was a guest at Concordia University's popular triennial homosexuality seminar, organized by Dean Chuck Kunert. In his seven years at MCC, Roy spoke at three seminars, a tradition carried on by current pastor Glenna Shepherd. Demystifying Biblical references traditionally interpreted as opposing homosexuality, and reminding the audience of God's overall loving message toward all people, gave seminar attendees a fresh point of view, and a new reference point for discussion.

Roy also welcomed students from local Bible colleges and from George Fox University, a Quaker school in Newberg. His own former Warner-Pacific professor Rev. Irv Revlinger taught a comparative religions course at GFU, and brought groups of students to MCC Sunday worship on at least two occasions. Dialogue and open conversation with the student groups took place following worship. Many of the scholars

Marty Davis photos

The PRIDE parades always give a window into the wide support the gay and lesbian community has from various mainline church groups. Along with MCC in Portland and Vancouver, church groups witness their support of diverse communities. United Church of Christ congregations each decide their policy. Worshiping Catholics formed Journey Faith Community after the demise of Dignity. Counter Balance supports Christian gay youth in Yamhill County, 30 miles west of Portland..

Rev. Roy Cole 1994 - 2001

expressed amazement at the traditionally organized worship and the intensity of faith they experienced in their visit. Doors of understanding and acceptance were opened.

Unbeknownst to parishioners, Roy also had an informal agreement with a local sex therapy clinic, allowing one or two men who were in the legal system for sex-related offenses to attend services at MCC. It would otherwise have been impossible for them to attend a church. Each man had worked out a detailed safety plan with his probation officer, the director of the clinic, and Roy, to guarantee proper behavior and to have no contact with anyone under age 18. No one in the congregation was aware that these men had a past, or had been accused of improper behavior. The agreement made it possible for several gay-questioning men to experience participation in a friendly church where their sexuality was not an issue. It was the closest to any type of prison ministry at MCC since the days of Delores Berry. There was never a problem.

Changes in Congregational Life

During a Sunday service in 2000, Roy Cole invited the deacons of the congregation up front to be honored for their dedicated services. Deacons were congregation members who by their demeanor, dependability, and caring nature were appointed to the position of deacon by the Pastor, usually for terms of three years. In the early days of MCC, the melding of various Christian traditions had caused some confusion over the role and duties of deacons, although the position was established by Austin Amerine already in the days at Centenary-Wilbur.

Deacons included David Sorber, Don Strausbaugh, Bob Jackson, Dan Brown, Arlie Adam, Gail Bumala, Andrea Toye, Mary Welch, and Julie Christian. They were divided into four teams of two, so that a pair was present at every worship service. Deacons wore a distinctive deacon's collar and a black shirt when on duty, followed rules of protocol, took care of the sacraments, kept altar objects clean, and often participated in speaking from the pulpit. They also oversaw outreach programs, served communion, and visited the ill in hospitals or at home.

A decision was made to change the structure. The 2000 recognition was also a farewell to the diaconate. The Congregational Life Team was assigned and assumed the duties of the deacons. Harriet Barshofsky and Marsha Dempsey had been instrumental in establishing the team in 1999.

Known as the CLT, members practice a division of labor. The Prayer team coordinated all prayer requests, public and private. Several congregation members also volunteer and pray regularly over requested situations from the CLT. The Emergency Medical Fund is supported by designated giving and donations, and monies are made available to members and regular attendees who lack insurance for medical emergencies. CLT members also visit the ill in hospitals and make home visits. There is a large referral service, helping those in need find community services. And at least one CLT member is assigned to be at each worship service. This structure has continued to successfully relieve some responsibilities from the pastor to this day.

What had been called the "Deacon's Pantry," has become the "People's Pantry," with donated food items sorted into shopping bags of mixed items, enough to supply requests from homeless and needy persons for a few meals. Not really under the scope of any ministry team, it has become the special project of several individuals, currently organized by Gail Bumala.

MCC-Portland hosted the 2000 Northwest District Conference at the Greenwood Inn in Beaverton. Planning had begun three years earlier, but the MCC-Tri-Cities had then hosted two conferences in a row. Planners were Mary Frantz, Kathy Martin, Chuck Harvey, and Dave Dishman. Arlene Ackerman was the presenter, giving workshops on Church Planting. Author Christian de la Huerta and a Yoga expert, Darren Main, were also guests. The Gay Swing Band provided music for an evening dance at the hosting Greenwood Inn in Beaverton, and Arlene preached at MCC on Sunday. Harriet Barshofsky was ordained at one of the evening services.

Probably the most significant event of the conference was Saturday night, when a special service was held downtown at First Congregational

Rev. Marsha Dempsey brought a delightful Tennessee wit and accent to the ministry at MCC. Her work focused on congregational life. With her partner Amy Kussmann, she became especially involved in work with women's groups. At her farewell were Amy, Lorrie Borgio, Donna Snoke, Marsha, and Reggie Snyder.

Rev. Roy Cole   1994 - 2001

UCC Church. There in special ceremony, MCC and all Metropolitan Community Churches, were formally welcomed into the Ecumenical Ministries of Oregon. Groundwork laid by Rodney Page, Austin Amerine, and Roy Cole over 15 years had led to MCC's acceptance by the other 17 denominations.

Rev. Marsha Dempsey

With membership growing, the need for a second pastor became apparent in 1997. Applications were sought from UFMCC pastors worldwide, and Rev. Marsha Dempsey from Oklahoma was selected and came on board in 1998 as the Director of Congregational Life. She added a caring and joyous element, providing personal pastoral care that Roy had less time for as he became increasingly involved with administrative and community duties.

Harriet Barshofsky joined the worship team as a student clergy. She completed her master's degree and coordinated with Roy and Marsha to work with the Congregational Life Team, consecrate communion elements, and preach occasionally. She later became pastor of Gentle Shepherd MCC-Vancouver when Teresa Nunn retired.

When Roy joined MCC in 1994, Sunday worship attendance averaged 35, with an occasional spike for holidays at 70. Roy felt that getting more women into the life of the church was critical. He constantly involved Gail Bumala, Betty Nelson, and Pat Schwiebert in visible roles such as reading the Lection and lighting the Wellness Candle. By 1999, the Sunday average was 207. Even with two Sunday services, it seemed that the building was nearing its maximum capacity for comfortable seating. This was a delightful problem.

Discussions ranged over possibilities for physical growth. The renovated building looked better, functioned better, and felt better than it had in 25 years. Some felt it was fine, although the kitchen and bathrooms downstairs were still woefully inadequate. There was an element of members who advocated for a move to a suburban setting with more land and parking. Beaverton was suggested. Pastor Cole felt that if the church were to relocate, it should be closer to the urban core. The corner of Burnside and Martin Luther King, Jr. Blvd., a prominent location where Baloney Joe's stood abandoned, would be a perfect location for a gay community center and church, with commercial space and apartments as part of the complex. It was a vision ahead of its time.

Harriet Barshofsky completed her student clergy experience in spring, 2000, working with Roy and Marsha. Her pastoral application package was completed with the video taping of her sermon on March 11, entitled *To Journey Toward Home*. Having been an active participant at MCC for several years, she had hoped to continue as an Assistant Pastor, but that did not work out. Within a short time she assumed leadership of MCC-Gentle Shepherd in Vancouver.

Rev. Mary Frantz had rejoined the congregation, and had become worship service coordinator. She also held a Women's Bible Study Group with Kathy Martin. One of their resource books was *Bad Girls of the Bible*.

Anniversaries

During Roy's tenure, MCC-Portland celebrated both its 20th and 25th Anniversaries as a congregation. The Sunday, January 21, 1996 service celebrated the 20th year since Austin Amerine began the Portland study group. Congratulations were presented by several community leaders, and Rev. Michael Piazza, from Cathedral of Hope MCC-Dallas, represented the Fellowship and gave the message, "Dreams Really Do Come True."

Scaffolding had been removed and the building looked better than it had since MCC bought it. Inside renovations were in process and spirits were high. Austin came from Sacramento and enjoyed the festivities. He would soon move into retirement in Bellevue, WA. He transitioned from this life into the eternal rest of God's love on November 21, 1998. Troy Perry spoke the message at his memorial gathering in the church he loved so well on December 5. An ice cream potluck followed in the basement, a party he would certainly have enjoyed.

Five years later, there was even more to celebrate in 2001. Sanctuary renovations had

MCC's 25th Anniversary was an occasion to bring all living former ministers to celebrate the quarter century. Dave Dishman hosted one service, honoring Rev. Troy Perry (center). Banners of all sorts filled the arcaded old choir "loft." Mark Brown conducted a choral extravaganza. In addition to regular Sunday worship, a festival celebration was held at First Congregational UCC. Roy Cole received the UFMCC Phoenix Award the previous year, recognizing MCC Portland's remarkable growth.

Roy also participated in the Governor's prayer breakfasts.

Ticket

Governor's Prayer Breakfast

with

Governor John Kitzhaber

Friday, April 25, 1997

Eight o'clock

Portland Hilton Hotel

921 S.W. Sixth Avenue

Portland, Oregon

Rev. Roy Cole   1994 - 2001

removed the partition wall; new lighting, carpeting and paint made a better worship atmosphere; and Marsha Dempsey and Mark Brown had joined the staff. Member Dave Kohl designed a 25th anniversary logo honoring both the UFMCC connection and the uniqueness of the church tower.

The service of celebration was held at First Congregational United Church of Christ on the South Park Blocks, anticipating a larger crowd than would fit at MCC. Troy Perry returned to give the sermon. Representatives from the greater Portland faith community along with gay community leaders spoke, gave congratulations, or conducted part of the service.

A new and special award was begun in honor of the 25th anniversary. Called the "Silver Anniversary Award," it was a recognition of one congregation member's outstanding contribution to the congregation, and was designed to be an annual award. The first recipient was Gordon Branstator, who had tirelessly and efficiently led volunteer groups through several remodeling projects, including rebuilding the retaining wall on NE 24th and removing and repositioning the divider wall, altar, and alcove. He worked daily for many weeks, often solo, to get the jobs finished with quality.

In future years, Rick Nye (2002), Chuck Harvey (2003), and Betty Nelson (2005) would be honored with similar awards. Their names are engraved on a large plaque near the side church entrance.

Just Out devoted more than a half page to an interview with Roy and photos of the church, Cole, and Austin Amerine. The January 19, 2001, article pointed out the healthy role lay people played at MCC, stressing the priesthood of all believers. The equality of women, inclusive language, and democratic decision making processes were noted as contributing to the uniqueness of the congregation. The article recognized MCC's leadership in being open and affirming, of welcoming diversity, and in promoting spiritual healing for minority communities. Congregational leaders Dick Burdon, Dave Dishman and Chuck Harvey were also quoted in the article, which did publicize the 25th anniversary celebrations.

Honoring the Inner Voice

During the summer of 2001, Roy took his summer vacation and some weeks of leave to take courses at San Francisco Theological Seminary, a part of the Graduate Theological Union. He was accepted into the D. Min. program at SFTS, which had an extension program at Marylhurst University, 11 miles south of Portland. While in San Francisco, he found the Episcopal church had altered its position on homosexuality, and he made the decision to actively pursue the possibility of becoming an Episcopal priest. This would mean full time course work.

With reluctance to leave MCC-Portland, but a commitment to be an openly gay priest within an American mainline denomination, he announced his plans to leave MCC-Portland. Roy felt he had accomplished the goals he had set with the congregation in 1994. He had stayed the course, serving longer than any other MCC pastor. Attendance had risen, community involvement had grown, the physical facility was restored, and the congregation was in the admirable place of having to make decisions based on abundance. His last Sunday at MCC was October 14, and he moved from Portland in January, 2002, to do work at San Francisco Theological Seminary in San Anselmo. He was the first pastor since Austin Amerine, 22 years earlier, to leave MCC for a higher calling.

Its appropriate to conclude Roy Cole's chapter with the benediction he spoke at the close of nearly every service he conducted at MCC-Portland:

"Remember, You are a Child of God, Precious and Cherished in His Sight"

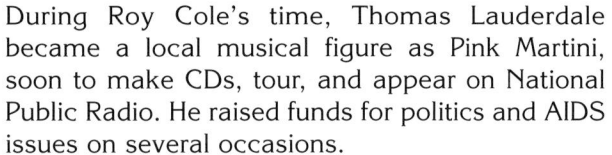

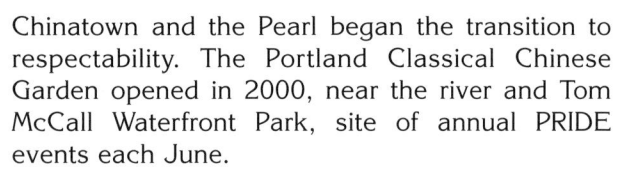

During Roy Cole's time, Thomas Lauderdale became a local musical figure as Pink Martini, soon to make CDs, tour, and appear on National Public Radio. He raised funds for politics and AIDS issues on several occasions.

Chinatown and the Pearl began the transition to respectability. The Portland Classical Chinese Garden opened in 2000, near the river and Tom McCall Waterfront Park, site of annual PRIDE events each June.

Rev. Roy Cole 1994 - 2001

MCC Music History partial listing (as collected by interview and from bulletins & newsletters)

Organists:
- Jack St. John
- Wendel Gleason
- Oren Charles Hornbeck ('76-'84)
- Denis Moore
- Gene Ellis
- Jim Simons
- Alan Beck (deceased - AIDS)
- Terry Snowden (deceased-AIDS)
- John Phillippi (deceased)
- Joe Gray
- Kelly MacFarland
- Milt Howell
- Eugene McMullen
- Doug White

Pianists:
- Austin Amerine
- Joe Anderson
- Mark C. Brown
- Joe Hooker
- Milt Howell
- Pat Kerwin
- Kelly MacFarland
- Larry Moad
- Jeri White
- Gary Van Horn

Soloists - Vocal
- Amani Jabari
- Mark A. Brown
- Mark C. Brown
- Steven Couch
- Teresa Demarest
- Rick Edmondson
- Casey Elliot
- Carol Lee Erickson
- Jill Frankie
- Vicki Girardin
- Kirk Herring
- Kelly MacFarland
- Jack St. John
- Kate Shimasaki
- Frederico White
- B J Wilkinson

Choir Directors:
- Mark Brown
- Gary Coleman
- Steven Couch
- Rick Edmondson
- Michael Hanks
- Pat Kerwin
- Jim McGinnis
- Larry Moad
- Frodo Okulum
- Gregg Nelson
- Terry Snowden
- Jack St. John
- Gary Van Horn
- Kathy Walden
- Claudia Johnston
- Jonathan Carlisle

Soloists - Instrumental
- Luke Avani (Violin)
- Joyce Baxter (Flute)
- Russell Budd (Flute)
- Tony Garrett (Piano)
- Stan Laskey (Piano)
- Larry Moad (Piano)
- Frodo Okulum (Violin)

Duets and Groups
- Falsettos
- Kim Brown & Gail Bumula
- Joyful Sound
- Pastel Tones
- Rainbow Review
- Rose of Sharon MCC Choir
- PRISM
- We Three

Spiritual Renewal Retreat at the B'nai B'rith Camp on Devil's Lake, Spring 2005.

2002 Gresham beauty Katie Harmon becomes Miss America 2002
- John Ashcroft charges 7 local Muslims as terrorists under the new U.S. Patriot Act
- Ashley Pond and Miranda Gaddis murdered, found on Ward Weaver's Oregon City land
- Occupation forces in Afghanistan can't find nemesis Osama Bin laden
- Rev. Mike Nikolaus agrees to a 3 month as interim MCC pastorate; stays 10 months

2003 Satyricon, longest running punk rock club on the West Coast, closes after 20 years
- Seeking weapons of mass destruction, George W. Bush sends military forces to Iraq
- Glenna Shepherd becomes 8th senior pastor at MCC-Portland

2004 3000 same-sex couples granted marriage licenses by Multnomah County
- Retired Police Chief Tom Potter elected Mayor; Sam Adams elected Commissioner
- Portland Archdiocese gets Chapter 11 bankruptcy protection due to sex-abuse cases
- December 26 Indian Ocean earthquake and tsunami kills thousands, destroys towns
- Tri-Met opens North Interstate MAX yellow line after success of its Airport Red line

2005 Hurricanes Katrina, Rita, and Wanda wreak havoc, death, and destruction in the South
- MCC Spiritual Growth retreat stimulates 100 members, inspires "Rebuilding"
- Pope John Paul II succeeded by Cardinal Joseph Ratzinger as Pope Benedict XVI
- UFMCC founder Troy Perry retires, Rev. Nancy Wilson becomes 2nd UFMC Moderator
- MCC launchs "Rebuilding Our Home and Our Mission"; History Project researchs book

2006 Assistant minister Wes Mullins chosen to join MCC staff
- Portland Archdiocese continues resolving priest sex-abuse and liability issues
- *Brokeback Mountain* tells a story of two Wyoming cowboys who love each other in secret
- 30th Anniversary weekend reunites former ministers and many returning members

Chapter Thirteen
Rev. Glenna Shepherd
February 2003 -

"Do what is right to other people. Love, being kind to others. And live humbly, trusting your God."

Micah 6:8 (New Revised Standard Version)

"Shepherd of the flock" took on a new meaning to MCC-Portland with the arrival of Rev. Glenna Shepherd from Tampa in February 2003. An interim committee and interim pastor Mike Nikolaus had kept the momentum of Roy Cole's work moving forward for more than a year. The congregation had maintained its good spirits; the drama team had continued producing outstanding and entertaining productions; the potlucks, bazaars and harvest dinners had not stopped. Neither had concern for the ill, nor management of Esther's Pantry.

Glenna pumped up the action several notches with her enthusiasm and can-do attitude. Changes in organization were initiated and the new minister energized congregants. The predictable 5% stopped attending, replaced with new members attracted to Glenna's high energy and thoughtful preaching.

Within months of Glenna's arrival, close work with Basic Rights Oregon seeking legal recognition and marriage equality for same-sex couples culminated on March 3, 2004, with the issuance of over 3,000 Multnomah County marriage licenses. Predictably, a backlash across Oregon resulted. Ballot Measure 36 proposed to re-define marriage between one man and one woman, and an intense campaign followed. The measure was approved in November 2004. Legal juggling and intense action at the State capital brought passage of a "gay-rights" bill through the house during the summer of 2005. The bill was stonewalled in the senate and the issue remained unresolved when the session closed.

Rebuilding neglected areas of the 95-year old building and refocusing the mission of the 30-year-old congregation occupied energies, committees, and finances during 2005, the 30th year of congregational life.

In the community, changes in terminology and communication brought about the resurgence of the term "queer," self-applied to encompass the various incarnations of the sexual minority community. Once a term used derisively, "queer" evolved as the catch-all category for gay, lesbian, bisexual, transgendered, intersexed, questioning people and their allies. Online dating and the instant communication possibilities of cell phones and blogs began altering long established social patterns. Pilots were now electronic planners and blackberries miniaturized computer use. I-pods replaced Walkmen and Discmen.

Gay characters in film and television, reality TV, and the new category of "metrosexuals" added to the increasing climate of diversity. Drug usage, especially of methamphetamines, brought about serious social and personal changes. The country was united by the terrorist invasion of September 11, 2001, and divided

Historic areas of Portland experienced great transformations as the old industrial Northwest became the Pearl. The old Armory was excavated into a new theater space. The Fox Tower rose south of Pioneer Courthouse Square. The street car connected downtown to NW 23rd and the old Hoyt Freight Depot was reconditioned into condominiums in the heart of the Pearl District.

JOQ's Tavern, 45 steps east of MCC, is a popular stopover spot, and especially popular after MCC resorted to porta potties during the 2005-06 rebuilding project.

Rev. Glenna Shepherd - 2003

by drawn-out wars in Afghanistan and Iraq. Natural disasters abroad and at home challenged emergency response systems and worldwide charity.

Interim Activity

With Roy Cole's departure to pursue seminary work, MCC's pulpit was filled with several guest ministers for more than a year. David Beckley accepted the position of Church Administrator during the vacancy. One of his tasks was the scheduling of several area pastors which meant there was always a quality message being preached.

Several church members were lined up to preach during the fall of 2001, including Rev. Harriet Barshofsky, Rev. Kelly McFarland, and Kimberly Brown. Sister Paula filled the pulpit on several occasions. Rev. Cecil Prescod of "Love Makes a Family," was an honored speaker. Rev. Dale Rhodes, Spiritual Director of the Interfaith Spiritual Center gave sermons twice. Rev. Bill Roberts from the Potter's House also spoke twice. Other guest preachers included Rev. Mark Reid, co-pastor of Sunnyside Centenary United Methodist Church; Rev. Wayne Bryant, retired pastor of First Christian of Portland; and Rev. Shama Southerin, visiting UFMCC clergy from Gallup, New Mexico. Rev. Hector Lopez, conference minister for the United Church of Christ, formed a bridge with MCC and Ainsworth UCC, where his wife Rev. Lynn Smouse Lopez is minister. Rev. Bernie Turner, a retired Baptist minister from McMinnville and strong advocate for a Baptist reconciliation with gays, spoke twice. In 1996, this congregation had sponsored Counter Balance, a gathering of gay Baptist young people.

The Theater Arts team took an active role in producing an outstanding Harvest Festival on November 17, 2001. This drama group acted out "The Dining Room" in March 2002. All ministries of the church continued functioning. Steve Dondanville produced and edited the weekly service folders and the *Here and Now*. Dale Boss continued as church bookkeeper. A pastoral search committee began publicizing the church's need for a new minister.

When it became apparent that MCC would not have a new pastor in time for Easter, David Beckley phoned Rev. Mike Nikolaus at MCC of the Valley in North Hollywood, CA, about conducting and preaching Easter Sunday celebrations. The Maundy Thursday worship featured The Living Supper, an enactment of the Last Supper set to music performed by Maurice Evans and Mark Brown. The MCC orchestra and singers enriched the Easter Sunday celebration. Cheri Fromm and Rick Edmundson sang solos. It was Mike's first trip to the Pacific Northwest.

Mike entered into discussions about possibly returning to accept an interim position at MCC. Shortly after his return to Los Angeles, Mike received a phone call from David Lomnicki, then the MCC treasurer, offering the interim pastoral vacancy. Mike was interested, but the "sticky wicket" was his two dogs, which he did not want to leave behind.

With a Roman Catholic background, Mike had an MA in Pastoral Ministry from St. Thomas University in Miami. He pastored at Christ MCC-Miami there for nine years - 1987-1995, and took an interim assignment at MCC-Boca Raton, FL. He was at West Hollywood when the invitation from MCC arrived. He had just authored a book of devotions titled *Tugs of War*.

Greg Curé, then the coordinator of Esther's Pantry, provided accommodation for Mike and his two canines. From May 2002 until February 2003, Mike preached most Sundays, but also allowed innovations in the Sunday programs. One such non-traditional Sunday featured member Dave Kohl, who presented a sermon on clay while throwing a large clay pot on a potters wheel set up in front of the pulpit. Several analogies from scripture regarding clay emerged with gooey clay spinning through his hands in a graphic demonstration of Jeremiah's visit to the potters house. (See Jeremiah 18: 1-6)

Mike was new to the Pacific Northwest, and became fond of the spectacular natural beauty. Being an avid cook, he took advantage of the variety of fresh berries in the summertime, as well as enjoying Northwest cuisine. He especially enjoyed the atmosphere at JOQ's.

The Portland Gay Men's Chorus celebrated its 25th Anniversary in 2005. Conductor Bob Mensel is shown with *Just Out* publisher Marty Davis. PGMC commissioned several unique programs and song cycles since their founding, but two especially memorable presentations were the "Millenium Mosaic" dedicated to gay youth issues, and the Vintage Voices concert. In that program, older gays and lesbians were honored. Several local persons were interviewed and their stories put to music. Honored were Irv Ewen, a quiet activist, dresser for the Portland Opera, PGMC rehearsal manager, and an MCC member. Darcelle laughed it up with Gibby Clarke, a career military veteran and softball player, as was Mary Beth and her partner, recent emigrants from Florida.

The chorus numbered over 100 singers for its 25th anniversary concert at Reed College, one of several halls PGMC has used in Portland.

Rev. Glenna Shepherd - 2003

Originally, the feeling was that the stint at MCC would be about 3 months, as the pastoral search process was under way. Instead, it turned into a 9-month term. All churches that have experienced the loss of a long-term pastor go through the process of grief, anger, confusion, resolution, etc. MCC-Portland was no different, and worked with the regional elder in the self-search process. During the vacancy period, the congregation was involved in an evaluation process. The interim period provided a time to reevaluate strengths of the church, and to identify areas where changes and improvements were desired. This helped define the kind of minister the congregation was seeking. Mike's assignment did not include involvement with the search for a new minister.

The Sunday of July 4th weekend featured music played by members of the Sandy Christian Church High School Marimba Band. They were part of a reunion of Hong Kong International School alumni in Portland that weekend. Dave Kohl had invited them to worship at MCC, and 50 American and international guests had their first experience at a gay church that Sunday. Anyone at that service vividly remembers the amazing sounds, spirited singing, and infectious rhythms. Mike Nikolaus commented that it was one of the five "top" services of his career.

Board Members during the transitional period were Anna Brouns, David Lomnicki, Charles Donald, Lorrie Borigo, Gordon Branstator, Marie Kennedy, Liz Lucero, Kelly McFarland, and Dave Nichols.

Although not a member of the Drama Team, Mike created a small drama when he collapsed suddenly while distributing communion on January 5, 2003. Paramedics took him to Providence Medical Center where it was discovered that his HIV had advanced very rapidly and that his immune system was almost totally depleted. He had declined medical insurance, but the Board of Directors volunteered to cover the large medical bill, for which he remains very grateful.

Mike regained his health, and stayed long enough to welcome the chosen pastoral candidate, Rev. Glenna Shepherd. Upon return to Los Angeles in February, he hooked up with a successful HIV program. He has since served a year as interim pastor of MCC in the Valley, gives guest lectures, and has an online cookie business. Yes, cookies, the baked kind.

Pastor Glenna

Glenna Shepherd and her partner Kermie Wohlenhaus moved to Portland in February 2003 to begin an energetic and intense ministry of proportions that neither the pastor nor the congregation had anticipated. Within a year of getting to know each other, the church and pastor embarked on pioneering ventures in the community and within the congregation that propelled both into spheres of activity and involvement with high visibility in the gay and straight communities.

Glenna's background includes a childhood in East Tennessee, a heterosexual marriage and raising two children, work with homeless and prison ministries for women, and several positions of teaching and Christian ministry. Her great love of music had meant her involvement with music ministries at a Methodist church; as Minister of Worship and Music at the Cathedral of MCC-Hope in Dallas; a career in teaching high school choir in Minnesota, North Carolina, and Georgia; conducting choirs at several regional and general UFMCC conferences; and doing some recording with Contemporary Christian music artist Marsha Stevens.

Glenna's academic preparation includes a Master of Divinity from Candler School of Theology at Emory University, a Master of Music degree from the University of Tennessee, and her Bachelor of Music degree from the same Knoxville institution. She has completed all but her dissertation for the Doctor of Ministry at Pacific School of Religion in Berkeley.

Most recently, she had been the Interim Pastor of MCC-Tampa, and previously, Interim Pastor of All God's Children MCC-Minneapolis. One major career accomplishment was the founding and nurturing of Christ Covenant MCC-Decatur, GA, which she founded in 1992 and served until 2000. She had been, and still is, on several UFMCC national committees.

Rev. Glenna T. Shepherd

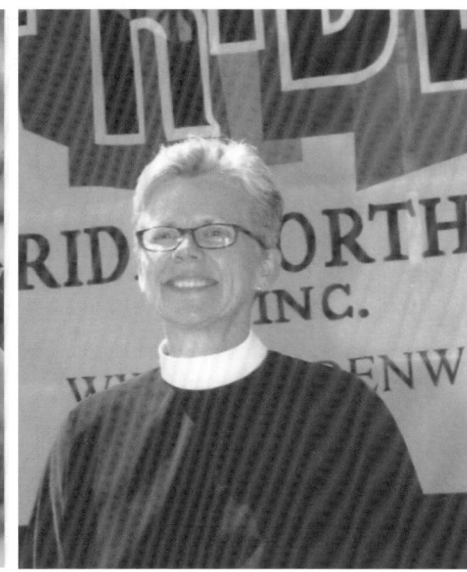

Glenna Shepherd brought a renewed energy to MCC with her cheerfulness, her enthusiasm for the community, and a desire to help members grow in their faith. She also represented MCC to the community, leading the MCC contingent in the PRIDE parade four months after her arrival.

Rev. Kermie Wohlenhaus supported Glenna's work at MCC while developing her own ministry. Her work in angelology is recognized as a special ministry of MCC-Portland. And she juggles! Mark A. Brown continued working half-time with the music program several months into Glenna's ministry. When his work load presented conflicts, it became necessary to seek another minister of music. Steven Couch joined the Portland ministry in January 2004. Before that, he concertized on the staff of Cathedral of Hope in Dallas Texas. He enjoys writing and arranging music as well as performing on keyboard and wind instruments. Milt Howell provided continuity at the organ and piano, especially enjoying opportunities for self-expression at Christmas eve family celebrations. Milt has volunteered his musical services since the days of Gary Wilson.

Rev. Glenna Shepherd - 2003

Kermie Wohlenhaus

Kermie had also been in the MCC Fellowship since 1979. Coming from a Methodist background, she described herself as a "closet" Jesus freak in her youth. She began attending MCC of the Rockies in Denver, and with the mentoring of Rev. Charlie Arehardt, she entered and completed a Master of Divinity program at Iliff School of Theology. She was ordained in 1996 and became pastor of MCC of the Living Spring in Eureka Springs, Arkansas, a tourist community with a large gay population. After a year there, she felt the Spirit moving her to relocate to St. Petersburg, FL, where she enrolled in the College of Metaphysical Studies (CMS). There she learned the structure of metaphysics, benefited from experts in non-traditional spirituality, and did her dissertation in Angel Studies. Upon receiving her PhD she requested a "special works" ministry from the UFMCC Southeast District. This did not materialize and she voluntarily surrendered her credentials.

She first met Glenna Shepherd when she was in Arkansas, but became reacquainted at a Marsha Stevens Concert. Their relationship blossomed and Kermie accompanied Glenna to Portland when she candidated in January 2003.

Kermie found employment in occupational therapy in Portland, supporting Glenna's ministry at MCC and continuing to grow in her own ministry. In May 2005, her UFMCC credentials were reaffirmed, recognized by UFMCC Region 1 as Clergy doing Angel ministry, sometimes described as Christian new thought spiritualism.

With co-producer Kimber Phillippo, she began a cable TV program, *Kermie and The Angels*, in December 2004, which aired on three local cable systems. Kermie opened the School of Angel Studies on January 1, 2005, meeting in a space at 2625 SE Hawthorne. Seven part-time instructors lead courses exploring the mystical experience with the Divine.

New Beginnings

Every pastor, after evaluating their new situation, suggests changes and makes modifications to an existing infrastructure. With great relief, David Beckley was able to transfer leadership responsibilities to new administrative assistant Eric Cordingly in 2004. Committees and teams were able to benefit from the advice and experience of an ordained minister once again.

After 18 years of male pastoral leadership, MCC once again had a woman as senior minister. Gender issues arose among a small number of members. Some leaders, disappointed over the pastoral selection process, chose to leave MCC. Some found a new church home at Ainsworth UCC, a nearby church in the Community of Welcoming Congregations. Ainsworth also houses the HIV-AIDS Day Center in cooperation with CAP.

Glenna's passions for pastoral ministry are preaching and worship, congregational development, stewardship and economic growth, building alliances with other organizations, and clergy development. She believes that the church is called to build and sustain congregations for service to the community, local and beyond. This means building strong, loving faith communities that offer healing, education, and development of spiritual practices, and offering our gifts in service to the larger community. The gospel and the call of the Holy Spirit urge the giving of lives to work for wholeness, peace, and justice. Glenna notes that many MCC congregations and individuals get stuck at the healing phase, and need to reach beyond fixing people to serving others. Glenna notes with joy the remarkable spiritual growth she has seen in MCC members.

Her belief is that spiritually vital congregations will emphasize meaningful worship, fervent prayer, and programs of significant outreach meeting community needs.

Using the template of a Council of Ministries, more than a dozen ministry teams were formed to do the work and mission of the congregation under Glenna's mentorship. With some alterations, three were teams originally envisioned by Roy Cole. Glenna developed a full program, based on team involvement and leadership. They were summarized in her 2004 Annual Report as:

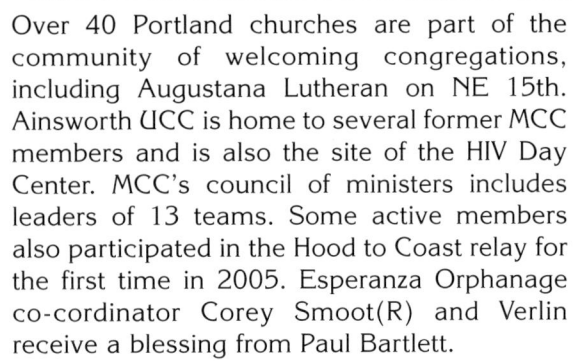

Over 40 Portland churches are part of the community of welcoming congregations, including Augustana Lutheran on NE 15th. Ainsworth UCC is home to several former MCC members and is also the site of the HIV Day Center. MCC's council of ministers includes leaders of 13 teams. Some active members also participated in the Hood to Coast relay for the first time in 2005. Esperanza Orphanage co-cordinator Corey Smoot(R) and Verlin receive a blessing from Paul Bartlett.

The Fred Meyer Hood to Coast Relay 2005

Rev. Glenna Shepherd - 2003

Advertising–Choosing new logos, working with community groups, advertising in publications including *Just Out*, Willamette Week and El Hispanic News, originating HTML advertising, and "branding" the church - Bill Barry, facilitator

Altar Guild– Performing many tasks formerly done by deacons, assuring preparation of sanctuary and altar areas, caring for altar linens, maintaining the sacristy, scheduling floras, and maintenance of communion ware and supplies - Jack Kipp, facilitator

Children's Ministries–Managing the Sunday school for children ages 3-12, acquiring meaningful curriculum materials, planning family social events, and maintaining a pleasant and positive meeting space with adequate crafts supplies - Kimberly Brown, facilitator

Congregational Life–Supporting individual members in need with prayer; organizing the prayer team; giving personal contacts and support; making hospital visits; helping people relocate; administering the Emergency Medicine Fund; and finding transportation for members who need it - Betty Nelson, facilitator

Front Lines–Ushers and greeters trained to help every person feel welcome and part of the MCC community; distribution of service bulletins, collecting the offering and regulating communicants to the altar area - Leigh Harper and Gen DuPre, facilitators

Gardening–Beautifying the church grounds with annual and perennial flowers, mosses, and grasses; designing a scheme of year-round attractive plantings; fertilizing, weeding, replanting, pruning, and propagating new plants - Rich Kibbons, facilitator

Health and Wellness–Organizing opportunities for social and physical health and wellness such as weekly gym nights, Pedal with the Pastor 20-mile bike ride, bowling, church picnics, participation in Portland Marathon and Hood-to-Coast run - Reggie Snyder, facilitator

Liturgical Arts–continuation of the Bob Jackson Theater Arts Team; presentation of plays at Congregational dinners, chancel dramas during services, and Seder presentations connected with Maundy Thursdays - Donna Snoke, facilitator

Membership Development–Acknowledgement of visitors during the worship service; informing visitors about MCC ministry; follow-up letters and contacts for those expressing interest; organizing New Member classes three times a year; and a review of membership listings - Dave Dishman and Lorrie Borgio, facilitators; neighborhood outreach facilitated by Chuck Harvey

Spiritual Development–Organizing and providing thought-provoking and spiritually uplifting classes and Bible studies; generating innovative worship ideas, implementing all-church retreats; hosting smaller retreats separately for men and women - Nicole Highhouse, facilitator

Website–Finding host companies to provide space for growth and new abilities; listing with major search engines; joining the MCC WebRing; updating site information; expansion of information pages, and inclusion of weekly pastoral messages and sermons - Barbara Pfieffer, facilitator.

Young Adult Ministries–involving members under age 30 in hikes, movie nights, volleyball, potlucks, and a white water rafting trip. PSU campus ministry involving opportunities for spiritual conversations; expanding outreach to young adults; developing the Elevation service - John Huff and Lianna Mechanic, facilitators

Other ministries were in formation - the MCC History Project, Animal Welfare Ministries, a Discipleship Program, a Healing Team, and Outreach Ministries to people in need.

Installation

Thirteen active and retired ministers participated in Glenna Shepherd's installation ceremony on July 20, 2003, four months after her arrival in the Rose City. In addition to ten MCC ministers, Rev. David Dornack from Rose City Park Presbyterian, Ms. Toni Tortorilla of the Portland Interfaith Spiritual Center, and Rev. Steve Witte, the Director of the Oregon Farm-

Johnny Kraus photos

Dave Dishman confers the church stole on Glenna Shepherd as her partner Rev. Kermie Wohlenhaus looks on. Ministers from several MCCs and area churches were invited to lay hands on Glenna and pray for her success. Members of the congregation also participated in the rite.

The Sunday School program was revitalized with new leadership. Several parents began attending when this became known. Many traditional and GLBT families are part of MCC.

Rev. Glenna Shepherd - 2003

worker Ministry were involved. Roey Thorpe brought greetings from Basic Rights Oregon. Marsha Stevens, her long-time friend and a Contemporary Christian musician, sang a pre-service concert, representing BALM (Born Again Lesbian Music) ministries.

Music and Music Ministry

Mark C. Brown continued to lead the music program and work with the Theater Arts Team through the interim period. Mark wanted to develop another career path, and needed to cut his halftime position still further. With the church in need of more rather than less musical leadership, Glenna accepted his resignation, although he still does some singing at MCC. This created the need for a new person in the part-time role, and Texan Steven D. Couch visited Portland, auditioned for the position, and was hired. Formerly, he had been on the musical staff at Cathedral of Hope MCC-Dallas. His initiation to Oregon was being stranded several days in Eastern Oregon during the worst snow and ice storm in five winters, waiting for the Interstate-84 to be reopened.

Steven's gifts include performance as well as composition, and he has written several original pieces for congregational singing and for the choir, which he directs. He also joined the Portland Gay Men's Chorus briefly, but has since concentrated on writing instrumental and vocal arrangements for performance by PGMC. With Kirk Herring, he wrote a major musical titled *FlipSide,* performed in August 2004, at Montgomery Park and at Miracle Theater, as a fundraiser for Esther's Pantry. The production was a gender-bending journey through Broadway's best music, with a reversal of gender roles adding irony and humor.

Sunday School and Kids' Space

Kimberly Brown had stepped away from leadership of the Sunday School program during the Interim. A renewed interest in children's ministry was stimulated with the arrival of several new couples and single parents with younger children. Parents brought their youngsters to Sunday School, where they were taught and led through activities before returning to their parents in the sanctuary about the time of Communion. Lessons were most often planned in relation to the sermon topic of the day. Children learn songs and have their own special experience with "church."

Glenna initiated the Children's Christmas Service, a time for families to share the message of Christ's birth at a special service. Glenna gathers the children around her on the chancel, adding a personalized aspect to the children's celebration in a service designed especially for them.

The need for a well-defined quiet and protected space just for a Sunday School classroom became apparent when attendance neared 20 on some Sundays. A section of the basement nearest Broadway was allocated. The old concrete ramp from the defunct first elevator was taking up a lot of space, so Jane Ellis, Kimberly Brown, Bill Barry, and others spent a day with a jackhammer cracking, crumbling, and carting away a cubic yard of broken cement and gravel. Volunteers built an enclosing wall with a door and window, painted the space, and created a mural of Jesus and children on the west wall.

Additional volunteers came forward to help with the teaching and management of the multi-level class, including Beverly Harger, working with the primary level children, and Victor Salinas, working with older students. Other folks help as needed, including Olivia Brigance, Michael House, and Dana Catt.

Parenting and adoption issues on a larger scale were topics the U.S. Supreme Court refused to hear. Potential adoptive gay and lesbian parents had hoped for success in a challenge to a Florida law that bars gays and lesbians from adopting children. In Oregon, regulations are less restrictive, and several MCC couples and at least one single man did adopt successfully. A new national magazine, *And Baby,* appearing in 2003 also gave support and practical advice for same-sex parenting.

Esperanza Orphanage

Missionaries Dale and Marta Johnson decided to visit an MCC worship service in 2004, when they were on home leave from their work at an

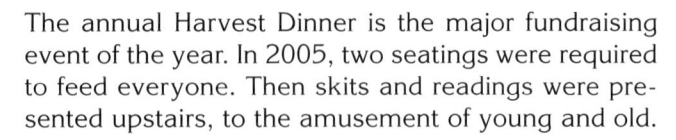

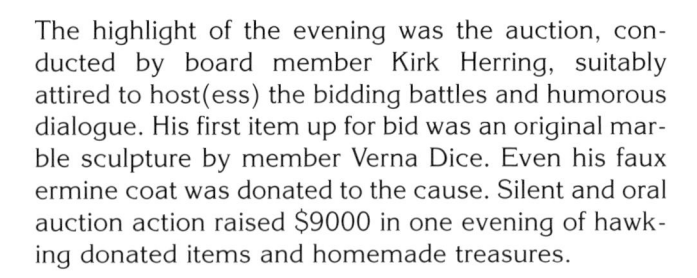

The annual Harvest Dinner is the major fundraising event of the year. In 2005, two seatings were required to feed everyone. Then skits and readings were presented upstairs, to the amusement of young and old.

The highlight of the evening was the auction, conducted by board member Kirk Herring, suitably attired to host(ess) the bidding battles and humorous dialogue. His first item up for bid was an original marble sculpture by member Verna Dice. Even his faux ermine coat was donated to the cause. Silent and oral auction action raised $9000 in one evening of hawking donated items and homemade treasures.

Dave kohl photos

364

orphanage in the Dominican Republic. They felt the Holy Spirit's direction to become MCC members and approached MCC-Portland about becoming a partner and sponsor of their work with orphaned children at their Good Samaritan Orphanage. The Johnsons work with about thirty boys who have been orphaned or abandoned. Their parents, if living, are usually AIDS-infected, are prostitutes, or are in poverty. Boys attend a nearby public school until old enough to go to private school.

MCC member Corey Smoot volunteered to be the liaison with the Dominican project. Monies for the orphanage are collected in a designated fund, and forwarded regularly. Another area of service was to collect shoes needed by the boys for school. When the need was announced to the congregation in the summer of 2005, over 100 pairs of shoes was donated, as were many new toys. Dale Johnson, on leave in Portland, was able to bring them back in his luggage.

The Johnsons encourage volunteer groups to come to the orphanage between January and July when there are no hurricanes. Volunteers serve for a week to work with the boys on a personal level, offering friendship and help with studies. Volunteers are usually college students on break or doing an interim experience. The first small group from MCC is scheduled for January 2006.

3000 Weddings

It wasn't long before Glenna became acquainted with Roey Thorpe and Basic Rights Oregon. BRO had become the most active political group in Portland, Oregon, advocating gay rights, having taken that role from the Right to Privacy Political Action Committee. In 2003, Glenna represented MCC in a BRO group called "Love Welcomes All," a campaign and conference organized to counter the message being preached by a weekend convention of ex-gays in Portland. That gathering was called "Love Won Out," inspired and funded by Rev. James Dobson's Focus on the Family.

Concerns for the progress of same-sex marriage issues had been mounting for several years. Since the founding of the UFMCC, holy unions and other forms of commitment ceremonies had been performed in all MCC congregations, although none of them carried legal status with any state.

Several scholarly books and articles on the subject appeared locally and nationwide. At the most intellectual level were two books by a gay professor of history at Harvard University, John Boswell. His first book *Christianity, Social Tolerance and Homosexuality* (1980) presented scholarly research showing how modern society had become saddled with intolerant attitudes toward homosexuality disguised as articles of religious faith. In the early Christian era, homosexual love was as acceptable as heterosexual love, and there was no word equivalent to homosexual in the languages of classical and Biblical writers. His second work, *Same-Sex Unions in Pre-modern Europe* (1994) expounded on the church's acceptance of same-sex unions. Little-known rites expressly for same-sex matrimonials were known and used by the church through the 12th century.

The topic of same-sex marriage equal in all social and legal aspects had simmered in America at least since the 1960s. Public recognition of a loving relationship, the ability to show affection anywhere, and equality with heterosexual couples were social issues. Spousal consent on medical situations, rights of survivorship and inheritance, ability to adopt children, tax benefits, and access to over 300 government programs were legal concerns. Using the term "marriage" pushed buttons for religious conservatives, concerned that America would abandon morality and the raising of healthy children. Should gays and lesbians be allowed to use the same term? Distinctions between a civil union required by the state and the religious vows made with the church accentuated the heat of rhetoric. Historically, clergy act as agents of the state when performing marriages. Hawaii and Massachusetts stirred the pot when same-sex marriages were recognized in those states.

The story leading to March 3, 2004, is a tale of planning, opportune moments, key political leaders, coordination, timing, and guts.

March 3, 2004 was the date Multnomah County began issuing marriage licenses to same-sex couples. Many ministers and officials were present, including Rev. Tara Wilkins of the Community of Welcoming Congregations and MCC's Glenna Shepherd.

Just Out and publisher Marty Davis strongly backed the progress on marriage issues, and their cover story celebrated the event. At First Congregational, the Gay Men's Chorus and several other groups sponsored a celebration of marriage service which packed their sanctuary.

Rev. Glenna Shepherd - 2003

Roey Thorp was in communication with the Multnomah County Commissioners over the granting of marriage licenses. She felt the need to keep quiet about their interest, while still trying to enlist support from groups such as the Metropolitan Community Church. County Chair Dianne Linn consulted with county attorneys about interpretation of the Oregon Constitution. The question arose over recognizing same-sex marriage as a legal option. When she was informed that the county could actually be in violation of the state Constitution by not issuing licenses, she made the decision to grant requests and issue marriage licenses to same-sex couples on March 2. Fellow commissioners Maria de Rojo Steffey, Serena Cruz, and Lisa Naito backed her. Retired Oregon Supreme Court Justice Betty Roberts would conduct the first official lesbian wedding ceremony.

The decision appeared as a news item on the 11 pm newscast. By the time the courthouse opened March 3, couples were lined up around the building, awaiting their destiny with history and marriage. Over 400 marriage licenses were issued on that day, and spontaneous weddings were performed on the street, in the court house, in judge's chambers, at several churches, and in the massive space of the Civic (Keller) Auditorium, a few blocks south of the courthouse.

Roey had included Glenna in her phone calls to supporters March 2, and the pastor was at the Courthouse early the next day. There, she performed 16 weddings, and nearly 100 more at Keller Auditorium over two days. Several local judges, two rabbis, and ministers from Unitarian, UCC, and other churches also performed weddings. A number of other ministers stood silently nearby in affirmation, unable to perform the ceremonies themselves lest they violate policies of their own denominations.

An MCC couple asked if Glenna could marry them back at the church, and she responded that anyone who wanted to get married at MCC could meet there at 6 pm and she would officiate a ceremony. Eric Cordingly and Steven Couch spent an intense day calling in florists, decorating the church, selecting music, and designing a program. Fourteen couples were wed in front of friends and family in one ceremony that March 3. Overall, she officiated at over 200 weddings in a period of six weeks. More than 3000 couples were married in the days and weeks to follow, in courtrooms, at MCC, and at several other churches in the Community of Welcoming Congregations.

Community of Welcoming Congregations

Oregon and SW Washington religious groups wanting to act on their support and affirmation of the GLBTQI community began to form an association as early as 1992. By 2004, their association was the Community of Welcoming Congregations, defined as religious and spiritual congregations that welcome and affirm people of all sexual orientations. The report testified to hearts and minds open to the possibilities of God's unfolding creation and the transformative power of the Spirit. Each congregation proclaimed welcome to all wishing to join them in the journey of faith, respected and-beloved of God. Rev. Tara Wilkins became CWC Executive Director in 2004.

Membership in the CWC is by individual congregation, and each congregation has gone through its own process of research, discussion, and resolution. Methodist congregations dealt with the issue through their own study groups, eventually naming themselves as "Reconciling Congregations." UCC Congregations vote to become "Open and Affirming." Presbyterians followed the "more light" movement, studying the issue, holding classes, and having congregational meetings.

Three pages of religious communities advertised in the 300-page "gay yellow pages" published by the Portland Area Business Association. In the group listing for CWC in 2005 are five Catholic churches, three Episcopal churches, five Jewish congregations, three Lutheran churches, two Presbyterian congregations, eleven United Church of Christ congregations, four United Methodist churches, four Unitarian Universalist congregations, two Quaker meetings, and single listings for MCC, the Church of the Brethren, Disciples of Christ, Mormon, New Thought, Pagan, and several independent groups.

The Community of Welcoming Congregations represents 45 area churches that welcome and affirm people of all sexual orientations. Despite their presence, not everyone at the 2005 PRIDE celebration agreed that homosexuality is not a sin.

Several young new members were baptized in the fall before declaring their intent to become full members of MCC. The nation and Portland continued to debate issues around sexual orientation and practice. At MCC, the Elevation service attracted new college-age women and men.

Rev. Glenna Shepherd - 2003

The United Churches of Christ developed advertising for a national campaign of openness and acceptance. One phrase was "Our faith is over 2000 years old. Our thinking is not." The CBS-TV network refused to carry their ads, on the grounds that gay Christianity was a taboo topic for broadcast. The resulting flap produced far more good publicity for the open and accepting denomination than advertising dollars could possibly have purchased.

Worship That Lifts

During the first year of Glenna's Portland ministry, she found an increasing number of college-age and 20-something people coming to worship. Some of these people expressed the desire for a Sunday evening service with a non-liturgical format and contemporary music. Glenna called a meeting of interested folks and those who had worked with younger members. They were stimulated with the opening topic: Design a church.

Conversation indicated several trends. People wanted anything but a morning service. They hoped for a high-energy worship experience, one centered on a topic rather than a scripture lesson. They wanted something culturally relevant, perhaps dealing with movies, or bands. They wanted to discuss spirituality, sexual ethics, and their own experiences.

A simple format emerged, and so did an entire musical ensemble. The evening slot of 6 pm was selected, and Elevation came into being. Participants worked on selecting the name Elevation, on a logo, and on distinctive color scheme for shirts and posters. The service template has become two opening songs, followed with prayer. Two additional songs most often lead to a reading, then a message from Glenna. The offertory is another song.

A ritual, often but not always communion, precedes the closing. This ritual commonly involves something tangible. It may be an object. Or it could be a writing activity, but is always something to reinforce the message of the day. Following the closing song is the Elevation equivalent of the ever-present potluck ...pizza and social time.

Victor Salinas, a student at Portland State University, attended several Elevation services. Seeking a way to outreach to gay Christian college students, he followed University procedures and filled out paperwork to become a recognized student organization on campus in 2004. Minimal funding therefore comes from PSU student fees. The MCC-PSU mission is to give students an on-campus opportunity to explore spiritual and sexual issues. Monthly meetings, hosted by Glenna and Victor, have drawn a few interested and curious students.

A large fundamentalist presence on the PSU campus is connected to Campus Crusade for Christ. Koinonia House continues to offer traditional worship opportunities on the downtown campus. A large number of international students attend PSU, representing spiritualities from Muslim, Buddhist, and Hindu to Wiccan and Native American. The MCC-PSU ministry is sensitive and respectful of other campus religious organizations, and reevaluates its goals frequently. The goal is to harmonize with the other ministries, offering discussion and support for GLBT students, and for those with questions about their sexuality and spirituality.

Another community group working with college-age youth is the Equality Coalition, a group composed of Portland Community College students and representatives from Love Makes a Family. Bonnie Tinker founded the nonprofit Love Makes a Family in 1992 as a grassroots social movement, blending rights for queer families with the anti-war movement philosophy. The group developed programs to build community with gay and lesbian families, and to help parents and children communicate, socialize with other non-traditional families, and to validate all family groupings. MultiQueer was developed as a program geared toward queer youth of color, and a Middle School Transitions Project was also proposed, then shelved for lack of funding.

AmeriCorps volunteers have worked with the group, and it has received operational grants from several charities, including Equity Foundation, Seattle's Pride Foundation, Black United Fund of Oregon, Rosenberg Fund for Children, McKenzie River

Two new worship formats developed under Glenna Shepherd's leadership. Based on discussions with many parishoneers, Elevation is a Sunday evening service of contemporary music, readings, and worship style. One Wednesday evening each month, a Taize-style meditative experience offers a contemplative atmosphere for more individual spiritual growth and insight.

With great enthusiasm, the 2005 campaign of "Rebuilding Our Home and Our Mission" called on volunteers to dig the church dirt, hand-digging, and emptying 175 five-gallons buckets of soil into three pickup trucks. Norm Costa and Corey Madey conquered their fear of the axes of evil, and a thermometer-type chart was elevated in the sanctuary to keep everyone posted on fundraising progress, towards a goal of $150,000.

Rev. Glenna Shepherd - 2003

Gathering, and the Meyer Memorial Trust. In addition to coordination with MCC and BRO, Love Makes a Family networks with the Gay Dad's group, P-FLAG, and any other group that works with parent, family, or kid interests.

The Inner Experience

During Glenna's second year at MCC, she became aware of another need within several members for a contemplative group experience, for a quiet experience without a lot of words, allowing the spirit to speak through silence and music.

Wednesday evenings have become those times, and a candle-filled sanctuary is the setting for worship called "The Inner Experience." Using a model from the Taize ceremonies first begun in France by Brother Roger, an experiential climate of caring, healing, and meditation is provided. Individuals experience the Spirit in their own way, within a rubric of love in this world and of this world.

Corporate meditation is not an experience common to many traditional Christians, and some MCC members probably view the non-traditional "smells-and-bells" atmosphere as a nostrum, Yet both the Inner Experience and Elevation have found small but faithful adherents as Glenna and worship leaders explore alternative routes to spirituality.

Rebuilding Our Home and Our Mission

Shortly after observance of the congregation's 29th anniversary, the January 2005 congregational meeting directed the path of the church into unanticipated ventures. Following the traditional discussions about budget shortfalls and complaints about inadequate bathrooms, a dysfunctional kitchen, and parking frustrations, an unexpected proposal was made, seconded and approved overwhelmingly. Simply stated, the proposition directed the Board of Directors to either start seeking a different church location or implement a program to fix up and modernize the current building.

With a few months of research into real estate values, the Rubicon was crossed, and the decision made to stay put at NE 24th and Broadway. MCC would launch a major campaign to take care of the existing building... to make it functional for an expanding membership and a revitalized program of services to the congregation and the community.

At the Spring Congregational Retreat and Spiritual Renewal held at Devil's Lake, a lot of conversation and interest was expressed over improving the church, in structure and Spirit. Many individuals made informal commitments to help with labor and finances to see the church up-graded. An enthusiastic spirit was palpable.

Family Day on June 12 added more interest in the project. This second annual celebration combining Mother's Day and Father's Day recognized the variety of family groupings at MCC with a focus during worship and a reception and refreshments in the basement. Such events, filling the undercroft with happy faces, cavorting playful kids, marvelous munchies, and conversation gave a vision of how the space could once again become a center of congregational socializing.

Cory Madey, building maintenance team facilitator, began exploring what specifically needed to be done to the physical structure. With research from historian Dave Kohl and digging through dusty files by office manager Eric Cordingly, plans were found from the proposed 1997 remodel. A visit to the City Planning Office inspired the team to recontact Bill Hawkins III, architect of the 1997 plans. A designated donation of $5000, made in 1997 from an organization known as "Fabric of Life," had been specifically assigned to a kitchen upgrade, and was used to draw up a set of plans.

A coincidental visit by Roy Cole helped unearth details of already-existing new sewer and water lines. Paul Bartlett, with a background in contracting, came on board as de facto project manager, bringing an air of energy and enthusiasm.

Several heating contractors were contacted about bidding for a replacement of the

Dave Kohl photos

The Board of Directors manage financial dealings and programs of the church, meeting twice a month. Ministry teams, such as buiding maintance, get the dirtier jobs, like remodeling basements.

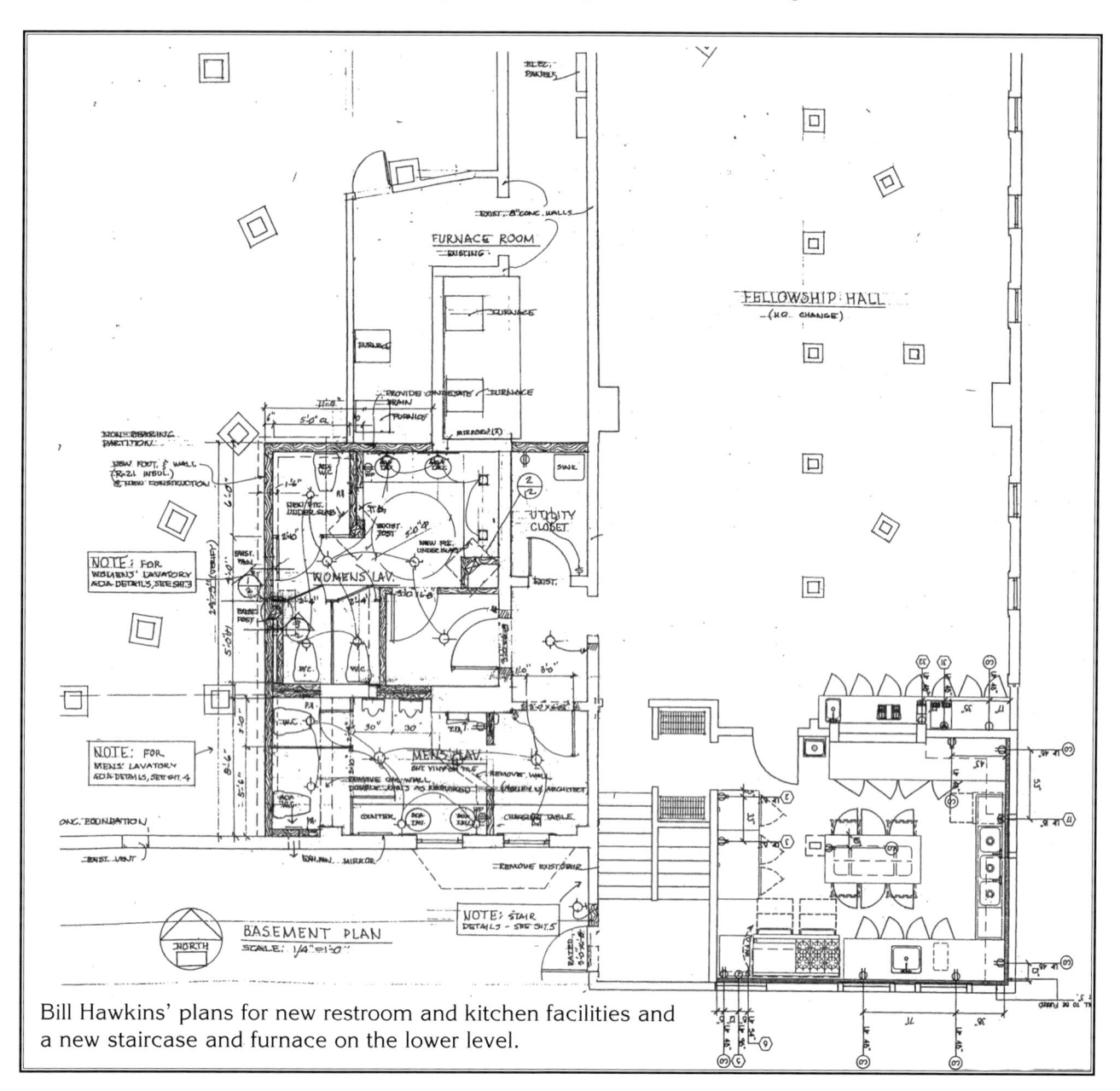

Bill Hawkins' plans for new restroom and kitchen facilities and a new staircase and furnace on the lower level.

Rev. Glenna Shepherd - 2003

ailing 95-year-old furnace system. Once a woodburner, the oil-slurping basement behemoth was found to be less than 30% efficient. The two small bathrooms, near the furnace area, were inadequate, a condition noted by the Lutherans when they bought the structure in 1918. Bill Hawkins recommended that if the bathrooms were to be redone, it made sense to take on the kitchen, long deemed problematic and out of code. Between those two areas ran a narrow stairs upwards to the area behind the altar. At the base of the stairs was an exit door, opening to a stairwell below ground level, which often flooded during Portland's annual rainy season(s).

The net result of these and other discoveries was a total renovation plan for the southwest quarter of the lower level–furnace, bathrooms, kitchen, and stairs. Estimates ran to over $150,000, even with anticipated volunteer labor for digging out several cubic yards of dirt under the sanctuary, demolition, framing, and hanging sheetrock.

The parallel interest in fixing up the physical plant and finding renewed spiritual growth were combined over the summer into a campaign called "Rebuilding our Home and our Mission." Launched September 11, 2005, over $100,000 in financial pledges was made and $25,000 of that materialized in cash donations by October 1. $22,000 seed money had been donated to the church from the estate of deceased member Jim Warden. In a surprise to all, one member offered to match any donations that were made during the 11 am service on October 2., bringing in over $14,000.

The first phase of the renovation began with the replacement of the antiquarian furnace. Twelve volunteers dug 1.5 tons of earth out from around the old furnace one Saturday, hauling out 175 five-gallon buckets of soil. Deluxe Heating Company replaced the furnace with four units ducted in a zonal pattern to different parts of the building. A fifth pre-heating furnace was added at the requirement of city inspectors. Doubters were greeted with clean efficiently filtered warm air for worship on October 23 the day 23 new members were received into membership.

During the remainder of the fall, two weeks of hand digging removed four drop boxes of soil and rock, which had lain dormant beneath the southern part of the sanctuary since 1909. New walls and wiring were put into place. Porta-potties sat outside the church for a few weeks while destruction and construction marked out new men's and women's restrooms. Restroom facilities more than doubled. To the outsider, it may not have seemed very significant, but to long-time MCC patrons, this was quite the deal. Women had three toilets to choose from, rather than one. Men gained an additional urinal, making three, plus two commodes.

Designs for efficient use of the kitchen were drawn up by the Bargreen Ellingson kitchen design firm. The ailing commercial gas range was hauled away in pieces to Metro Metals, to be replaced with a more efficient unit. A center prep and serving island made for efficient utilization of space. The new water heater was located beneath the new stairway, with its intermediate landing. Aligned with the outside ground level through the newly moved south exterior door, everything now complies with City codes.

The goal was to have as much work completed as possible so that 30th anniversary festivities could be hosted in the new Congregational Life Center in the renovated lower level, displaying for members, alumni, and visiting dignitaries, the results of the first major remodeling in nearly ten years, accomplished with five months of planning and five months of contracted and volunteer labor.

Spiritual Renewal

For several years, there had been no "off-campus" getaway retreat experience for the congregation. In former days, the annual Labor Day Boardman retreat had offered members a chance to leave town and focus just on growing spiritually and getting to know fellow congregants in a pleasant social setting. Kelly McFarland, musician and experienced retreat planner, took charge of organizing a Spiritual Renewal Retreat, April 29-May 1, 2004.

Kelly had teams set up for worship, entertainment, child care, set-up, and even the

Over 100 MCC members spent a weekend of spiritual growth and networking at Camp B'nai B'rith near Lincoln City. Volunteers cooked and served outstanding meals and snacks. Pat Schweibert organized and led the cooks. She also manages Peace House.

Bill Barry photos

Rev. James Mitulski came from Los Angeles to lead the workshops and worship.

Mary Lee got to know Rev. Marsha Dempsey in Eugene and became a member of MCC-Portland in 2005. Roger Troen, persistant animal rights activist, proposed and established an animal advocacy ministry, doing all things possible to prevent euthanasia through adoptions and spaying. Roger helped publish Portland's first gay newspaper, *The Fountain*, in 1971 in his basement printshop.

Rev. Glenna Shepherd - 2003

bonfire. Pat Schwiebert led the cooking crew. Scholarships were handled by Betty Nelson, enabling people with low finances to fully enjoy the event. Participants were divided into eight small groups, each facilitated by a pair of leaders.

The three day experience at the B'nai B'rith camp on Devil's Lake in Lincoln City was a very successful event on several levels. The guest presenter was Rev. Jim Mitulski, UFMCC Director of Leadership Development and pastor at City of Angels MCC-Claremont Jim piloted the group through "Making Connections," a series of discussions that led to closer understandings and friendships throughout the weekend. Healing stories grew out of listening activities and people became involved in the history and emotions of others. Ultimately, people could share their dreams and future goals and giving thanks for all experiences.

While the weekend anticipated the growth of friendships and corporate involvement with the church, an additional unexpected outcome was a determination by most participants to actively get involved in the physical renovation of the building and a renewal of the fellowship aspects of congregational life. The seeds for the "Rebuilding our Home and our Mission" were planted and germinated.

Animal Advocacy

For over two decades, Roger Troen tried to elevate the congregation's awareness of animal rights. Through a bulletin board dedicated to animal issues and occasional discussions, he tried to educate members to the plight of research animals, euthanasia of unwanted animals in shelters, and the abandonment of unwanted pets in hostile environments.

Although never given the opportunity to light the Wellness and Liberation Candle on animal issues, he was able to invite guest presenters to do so. Not everyone understood or appreciated Roger's passion, and he had difficulty tolerating what he perceived as insensitivity from a group that had itself experienced insensitivity. This changed in 2005, when a clearer definition of what a church's involvement with animal issues was agreed upon between Pastor Glenna and Roger. For the first time, MCC established an Animal Ministries Team as part of the Council of Ministries. The team provides information, clarifies issues, and advocates for humane treatment of all animals. They also take an active role in networking with potential homes for abandoned pets. A strong emphasis is placed on Spaying and neutering as a solution to animal overpopulation.

A History of the History

Retired educational missionary and art teacher Dave Kohl began volunteering as an office Angel in 2003. Becoming more familiar with the daily workings of the office and the people using the church, he became appreciative of both the longstanding service of several members, of the local entanglements of the congregation, and of MCC's place as a de facto community center for the gay community. Several reliable longterm members recently had passed away and the church's 30th anniversary was just over a year away. In addition, the historic church building was nearing its 100th season in just a few years.

Dave made an effort to contact former members and invite them to the 29th anniversary service in January 2004. Richard Lusk, John Rushong, Barry C, Mel Hart, Nestor Perala and several others returned for the service. Interviews were set up and a 20-page written history was planned, to be printed on the church's copy machine.

With eight pastors in 30 years and the various comings and goings of boards and individuals, no complete organized set of minutes, bulletins, newsletters, or photographs existed at the church. Not archivally oriented, several zealous committees and crews over the years had discarded most potentially historic materials. The church has been more interested in making space to initiate new projects rather than dwelling on the past. An all-call was made for any old church materials and photographs from anyone's scrap books, and photos came in from Dave Dishman, Chuck Harvey, Johnny Krause, Eric Cordingly, Bill Barry, Sue Lantz, Nita Gates, and Rich Kibbons.

MCC historian Dave Kohl (L) met with about 200 people, including David Bernhard, whose grandpa was Pastor in the 1940s. Bud Clark gave great insights into the Portland of the 1980s.

Marty Davis/*JustOut* photo

ESTHER'S PANTRY
Give. Serve. Empower.

Esther's Pantry got a new logo in 2005. An annual dinner at Starkey's honors the volunteers who help with everything from greeting to stocking and shopping.

Dave Kohl photos

376

Rev. Glenna Shepherd - 2003

Dave Dishman, Chuck Harvey, and former member Dick Burdon brought in several boxes of unsorted bulletins, newsletters, and memorial materials. Kohl approached Neal Hutchins, one-time member and former editor of the *Cascade Voice* in an effort to find copies of the 20-year-old paper. Neal produced and donated all of his archival copies of the paper, plus a large unsorted bin of photographs used in the paper's paste-ups.

Over 200 interviews were conducted, including contacts with local gay leaders from the 1970s, and suggestions were made about researching the Second Foundation, Portland Town Council, Portland Gay Men's Chorus, the Imperial Sovereign Rose Court and Cascade Aids Project. As the field of investigation widened, Dave became familiar with GLAPN (Gay and Lesbian Studies of the Pacific Northwest). Tom Cook, former GLAPN chairman, and Rob Douglass, the current chairman, were extremely helpful and supportive. Investigating the GLAPN collection, housed at the Oregon Historical Society, Dave was led to the discovery of extensive photograph collection at the OHS, including most of the photos ever used by the *Oregon Journal* and *The Oregonian*.

Local businessman Bill Dickey, a specialist in promotion and printed materials, was approached about the possibility of printing a book of up to 200 pages. He offered to do the job for the church at cost! Former MCC member Larry Foltz introduced Dave to Suzanne Deakins, a local publisher specializing in spiritual books. She volunteered to act as publisher and to donate her services. The book became a fundraiser for the church's "rebuilding" program when donations from several local individuals and groups basically covered the printing costs.

At Glenna Shepherd's request, Dave began writing a weekly column in the Sunday service folder on historic discoveries, patterns, and artifacts he was unearthing. With constant reminders of the church's heritage, many members discovered a pride in membership and a greater interest in the historic building they had so taken for granted. The collected materials from Dave's research will eventually be housed permanently at the church, and a more systematic approach used in the future to catalog new donations.

Esther's Flips

Steven Couch accepted the half-time position of Esther's Pantry Director when he arrived in January of 2004. This complemented his half-salary as Music Director. Several changes were made to both the physical space and to the structure and program of the food bank. The Director's position entails interfacing with the support community, writing grants, and coordinating finances and personnel.

Several new shelving units and display cases were added, giving the Pantry the appearance and feel of a small grocery store, with pleasant displays of all available foodstuffs. Clients shop with the assistance of a volunteer and together client and host figure out the needs and tastes of the "shopper." Many volunteers are also clients, and the mutual nurturing and friendship gives a friendly ambience to the place.

Walls were completely repainted in the summer of 2005, and new carpeting added comfort and a touch of class to the former warehouse space.

Mark A. Brown serves as the on-site manager, coordinating volunteer schedules, picking up supplies, and coordinating the unloading and storage of weekly shipments from the Oregon Food Bank. Paul Bartlett takes care of ordering and other paperwork. About ten percent of food items are donated, the rest coming from community sources, and purchased from the Oregon Food Bank. At least three volunteers are scheduled when the Pantry is open, which is on Tuesdays and Thursdays. Nearly 280 clients qualified for Esther's services in 2005. About 200 actually utilize the program monthly.

New directions of service opened in November 2005, when the Esther's program was opened not only to AIDS clients, but also to individuals with a bona fide HIV positive status. This change made the Esther's program available to an enlarged client base of several thou-

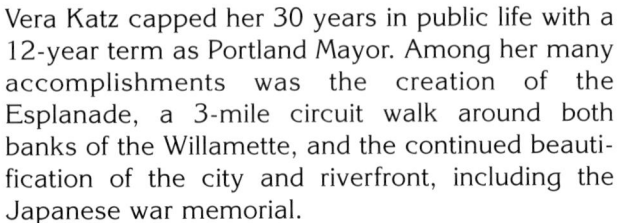

Vera Katz capped her 30 years in public life with a 12-year term as Portland Mayor. Among her many accomplishments was the creation of the Esplanade, a 3-mile circuit walk around both banks of the Willamette, and the continued beautification of the city and riverfront, including the Japanese war memorial.

Tom Potter was elected mayor in 2004, appealing to the common man and making many appearances in the gay community, including a forum at MCC. He gave a citation to Darcelle at her 75th birthday party. His daughter Katie and her partner have made him a proud grandparent. Sam Adams became the first gay city commissioner in 2004.

Rev. Glenna Shepherd - 2003

sand men, women, and children with HIV status, rather than several hundred AIDS-diagnosed people.

Encouragement from City Hall

Portland's GLBT community has benefited from the leadership of open-minded and supportive Mayors since the election of Neil Goldschmidt and his replacement, Connie McCready. Frank Ivancie wasn't as supportive, but Bud Clark and Vera Katz were adamant in their programs of diversity, equality, and support of minority causes. Bud Clark continued the appointing of a liaison from City Hall to the Gay community. Vera Katz' assistant for 11 of her 12 years in office was Sam Adams, an openly gay man who kept the mayor connected with the gay community. MCC member Norm Costa sits on the Portland Police Bureau's Sexual Minorities Round Table, which meets monthly to coordinate and inform city and gay community representatives about programs, problems, and possibilities.

Tom Potter came out of retirement in 2004 to run for and be elected to the office of Mayor. He made several appearances in the gay community during his campaign, including a forum at MCC-Portland. Elected on the same ballot was Sam Adams, one of the five City Commissioners. Among his other duties (Transportation Division), he has supported the organization and planning of a proposed Gay Community Center. The "Q-Center" would be the first gay community center in Portland since 1973, and anticipates having a space in time for PRIDE 2006. Included in the center would be meeting rooms, coffee bar and lounge area, recreational facilities, a library and archival center, and office spaces for several local GLBT organizations.

Discouragement From the Voters

The November 3, 2004 election included Ballot Measure 36. The initiative was generated hastily in response to the granting of marriage licenses in March by the Portland City Commissioners. The proposal banned same-sex marriages, amending the State Constitution to specifically deny such unions.

Autumn was dominated with radio, TV, newspaper, and pulpit campaigns arguing both sides of the issue. Several forums were held, including one at Multnomah School of the Bible where six panelists in front of a standing-room only crowd calmly discussed differences of opinion and interpretation on homosexuality and same-sex marriage. Glenna Shepherd was one of the three panelists with a GLBT-positive stance.

The state-wide vote passed the Measure by 59%. Eleven other states across the country also had similar issues on their ballots, but Oregon came the closest to defeating such a proposal. Hurt, anger, and resolution in the GLBT community were the result. Gay rights leaders across the nation were divided over what strategy would best advance the cause. Aggressive advocates believed that marriage rights were the key to winning fundamental equality for the queer community. Others suggested modification of goals and rhetoric, seeking more accommodation and revision. The gay marriage debate had galvanized straight and gay people more than any other recent social issue, even President George W. Bush's efforts to change and privatize Social Security.

BRO, Basic Rights of Oregon, vowed to take the issue to court, and terminology was changed from marriage to union. A case was filed and arguments presented. On April 14, 2005, the Oregon Supreme Court decision was announced, upholding Measure 36's straight definition of marriage. Mayor Tom Potter issued a statement reading, in part,"Today is a sad day not just for Oregonians, but for anyone who values individual dignity and the absolute right of two people to share their love with their families, their friends, and their community. To deny two people the basic legal rights that every American in a loving, committed relationship enjoys simply because of their gender is a slap at the core moral values that shaped our country, and a denial of our collective humanity."

Multnomah County refunded the $60 filing fee paid by each couple for their license, and many creative plans were advanced for a coordinated use of the fees, which would total nearly $180,000. Many couples forwarded their

Sir Robin Hixson, who has master-minded MCC banquets since the days of Centenary-Wilbur, administered the old iron stove its extreme function in October 2005 for the harvest dinner, before the old cooker was wheeled to an ignominious date with the Metro Metals scrap yard.

Paul Bartlett acted as contractor for much of the re-building project, especially enjoying the hands-on destruction aspect. Eric Cordingly coordinated control of the padlock key for the Honey Buckets placed strategically on the sidewalk by the Broadway entrance. Over the old bathrooms, evidence of a 1923 fire was found behind the lath and plaster ceiling. Live "knob-and-tube" wiring was also found. Architect Bill Hawkins measured progress and kept it all in code.

Dave Kohl photos

Rev. Glenna Shepherd - 2003

refunds to Basic Rights Oregon, the Human Rights Campaign, Lambda Legal Funds, the ACLU, and the Portland Gay Men's Chorus. A few simply framed their refund checks as historic mementos (which also passively fouled up the County's accounting).

During the same period, the State legislature was addressing Governor Ted Kulongoski's SB 1000, an anti-discrimination Bill which also proposed civil unions for same-sex couples. In the summer, the Bill passed the State Senate and was headed for probable approval in the House. Many appearances and demonstrations were made in Salem in support of the Bill. Speaker of the House Karen Minnis stymied progress on SB 1000, and it failed to reach the House for a vote before adjournment, thus dying for lack of action.

So the 3000 marriages in Multnomah County of 2004 were denied registration and legal status. The couples still regard themselves as married, as do their families and friends. Couples continue to hold Commitment Ceremonies or holy unions. But recognition from the State is still in the future.

Rev. Elder Nancy Wilson - UFMCC's Second Moderator

By 2005, the Universal Fellowship of Metropolitan Community Churches had grown to over 42,000 members, in about 300 congregations in 19 countries. Troy Perry had been the first and only moderator of the Fellowship. In addition to guiding the denomination spiritually, he had represented the causes of the GLBT community nationwide. He led marches, went on hunger strikes, conferred with presidents, and spoke to political groups large and small. As he neared the age of retirement, Rev. Nancy Wilson was elected to be the second moderator of the UFMCC at the Calgary General Conference in July.

Nancy Wilson became involved with Boston's MCC in 1972, while doing graduate studies at Boston University's School of Theology to be a Methodist minister. Within weeks of joining, she had consecrated communion and preached at MCC, thus coming out of her closet at the school. She found joy in the ministry with Rev. Larry Bernier and excitement in realizing MCC combined religion, activism, lesbianism, and feminism. She became the pastor of MCC-Los Angeles.

She advocated inter-religious affiliations for the Fellowship and by 1981 was urging the Board of Elders to apply for membership in the National Council of the Churches of Christ in the USA. After being rebuffed by the NCC, a Department of Ecumenical Relations was formed, co-directed by Nancy and Adam DeBaugh. While the gay church did not need the recognition from the National Council, UFMCC realized there could be a "gift exchange." UFMCC could offer the gift of a new Christian reality, less restrictive than a narrow theology of deified heterosexuality. Instead, a broader, more inclusive understanding of sexuality, love, inclusiveness, and acceptance of diversity came from the UFMCC. The gift from the NCC would be recognition, cooperation, and acceptance by fellow Christians.

UFMCC met all five requirements for membership in the NCC: 1) a Christian theology; 2) a stable corporate identity in the USA; 3) cooperation with other communions; 4) responsible church government and ministerial training; 5) at least 50 congregations and 20,000 members. Nancy Wilson headed UFMCC representation in 1983 when the NCC voted to postpone indefinitely any vote on eligibility. Stalemate ...or limbo?

Rev. Wilson was installed as the second moderator of the UFMCC in the National Cathedral in Washington DC on October 29. Special banners were hung from the high gothic arches and the joyous ceremony was attended by representatives of all major church denominations as well as ministers from most large UFMCC congregations. The gathered ministers participated in a conference the following week. Glenna Shepherd and Roy Cole represented Portland. In 38 years, the UFMCC had grown from the little pink house in Huntington Beach to the National Cathedral!

Thirty Years

Any excuse for a party is good, but especially anniversaries with nice round numbers...like 30. A planning committee of Dave Dishman,

Denis Moore, John Rushong, Bill Barry, and Ron Powell were among the founding members who reunited for the 29th anniversary in 2005.

Rev. Harry Knox of the Human Rights Campaign spoke at several services in the fall. He worked with Glenna on several national committees.

Rev. Elder Nancy Wilson was installed as second moderator of the UFMCC in Wash-ington's National Cathedral in October. Rev. Troy Perry then became retired.

Dave Kohl photos

As MCC experienced substantial growth in program and attendance since Glenna Shepherd's arrival, the need for a second minister became obvious. Rev. Wes Mullins (L) agreed in January 2006 to accept the position, focusing primarily on Media and Youth ministry.

Dave Kohl photo

UFMCC photos

382

Rev. Glenna Shepherd - 2003

Dave Kohl, Steven Couch, and Glenna Shepherd began discussing plans six months before the event, scheduled for January 27-29, 2006. A weekend of returning friends and pastors will make the event a family affair. Concerts, book signings, receptions, and guest preaching from retired founder of the UFMCC, Rev. Troy Perry will bring the celebration full circle.

As the congregation marks the 30-year plateau and looks forward, change is in the air. Spiritual awakening and growth are happening in parallel with long-awaited physical improvements to the building, which is the base of operations. Change means discomfort and doubt and well as hope and expectation - that's the nature of human beings in shifting situations. How the congregation grows and stretches spiritually, how each individual becomes more open to the call and work of God, and how each person searches their own heart for the will of the Spirit will determine the journey and mission of the congregation.

The possibilities in Portland for a dynamic ministry continue. The journey ahead for the congregation and for each member means healing wounds, taking on the cause of those without voice or power, bearing witness to God's love and acting as enlightened people of Spirit in the Portland, in the Northwest, and in the World.

O Lord God,
    Who has called Your people
    to ventures of which we cannot know
    the ending,
    by paths as yet untrodden,
    and through perils unknown,
Give Us Faith
    To go out with good courage,
    not knowing where we go,
    but only that Your hand is leading us,
    and Your love supporting us, through
    Jesus Christ out Lord,

Amen

Postlude

To God's chosen people who live as refugees...you were chosen according to the purpose of God the Father, and were made a holy people by his Spirit, to obey Jesus Christ and be cleansed by his blood"

Presuming, dear reader, that you have followed the progress of this tome somewhat faithfully, please bear with the writer for one more installment. Using the format of the book as a church service, we now come to the postlude, that composition which sums up the e-motions and message of the service and sends worshippers on their way with fulfillment, hope, and a tune in their brain.

In Germany, congregations traditionally sit and meditate during the performance of the postlude. It is a part of the service, a completion of the experience called worship. They hear the musical tune or theme, and experience its variations building to a coda or finale. Allow me introduce Johann Sebastian Bach's Triple Fugue in *E flat major* BWV 552 as the paradigm. In this Baroque masterwork, there are three musical tunes. The first represents God the Creator, and resembles the tune called St. Anne (Oh God Our Help In Ages Past). The second theme is a dance tune, signifying Jesus (Lord of the Dance?). The third motif embodies the Holy Spirit with a stately melody. Each tune gets introduced, receives expanded variations, and eventually is intertwined with the other themes into a composition of beautiful harmonic complexity, and majesty.

With humility, this chapter is presented as a wrap-up, a summary, and it is hoped, a sending. The views and observations expressed are totally those of the author, and do not reflect opinions or theories of MCC-Portland, the Universal Fellowship of Metropolitan Community Churches, nor any of its former or current pastoral staff or Board of Directors.

The role of a historian is to step out of his own experience and see larger trends, give them a name and form, and present them to his contemporaries for discussion. One of the joys (?) of taking oral histories and trying to sort out the stories is unearthing different versions of the same event and endeavoring to harmonize the versions, especially if accounts of the same event are also in print. Newspapers print facts as the reporter and editor see them, as revealed by their sources. It's a dicey business, but somebody has to do it.

After living with the story of MCC-Portland, the gay community, and issues surrounding homosexuality and the Christian church for over a year of research and writing, I would like to submit the following observations, using the same three categories or "gospels" which Rev. Troy Perry originally set forth in 1968. Think of them as the three intermingling themes from Bach's *Fugue*.

Salvation

Perhaps Roy Cole said it best in the winter 1997 *Here and Now*, "The success of this

Postlude

church is measured only one life at a time, as that life is transformed out of despair, loneliness and isolation into wholeness, community and service." This is the first major theme of the congregation's existence, if we follow the analogy of the Fugue and variations.

Many people have come through MCC's doors with emotional wounds and scars, some self-inflicted, others administered by ministers, churches, families and "friends." It's an easy platitude for MCC to claim that it is a place of healing. A hospital is only a building unless it is properly staffed with trained professionals following a philosophy of healing. A repair shop is only a shed unless it is staffed with knowledgeable mechanics and experienced parts staff. The church is not the panacea, it is the forum. It is a refuge and redoubt but not a hide-away.

Bob Jackson said, "I want to think things through for myself. My needs are mine. All I ask my church to do is to point me in some possible directions, and I will build my own spiritual life. I need to build strength for my journey. Isn't that a good reason to come to church?" The Deacon wanted a "thinking-for-yourself" church, rather than a denomination with prepackaged answers. A catechetical approach, with predictable questions and preordained answers did not fit his character.

Likewise, current pastor Glenna Shepherd notes that MCC is a Biblical church, not a creedal congregation, allowing for individual exploration of what God means in their life, rather than relying on any particular historical Christian creed as the major definition of one's beliefs, or their experience of God.

The UFMCC and many other churches have addressed the issues surrounding harmonizing homosexuality and other forms of sexual variation with proof texts used by opponents of gay rights. It is so important to keep in mind that Christ said not one word regarding what we call homosexuality, and that He Himself interpreted the sin of Sodom as inhospitality. It gives perspective to note that there are 362 admonitions on heterosexual behavior in Scripture, and six that speak to same-sex relationships.

References are to why and how people relate sexually, not with what gender. Individual counseling and group classes have helped individuals come to realize that God loves them, made them to be who they are, and holds a place for them in eternity.

But the devil is often in the details...specific challenges and situations still arouse doubts - health and political issues, but also economic reverses and relational failures often put frail and fallible humans into an emotional tailspin until we remind ourselves of John's message. "For God so loved the world that He gave his only Son, that whoever believeth on Him should not perish but have eternal life. God did not send his Son into the world to condemn it, but to save it." (John 3:16-17).

Nineteenth century Lutheran theologian C.F.W. Walther taught the proper distinction between Law and Gospel. Sin, abomination, disobedience, addiction, irresponsible behavior, and judgment are the law concepts that the historical church has used to demonize wrongdoing, to point out each person's "evil twin." But once each person recognizes their need for redemption, Walther says the time for law is done, and the gospel of Jesus Christ redeems the accepting believer, giving new Life, Hope and Promise. Individuals experience their own "exodus" from "how should I believe?" to "I see God in my life." Each person is on his or her own progression from a condition of internalized poverty to an awareness of overwhelming liberation. St. Paul said, "I can do all things through Christ," and "By the grace of God, I am what I am." (I Corinthians 15:10)

Community

Troy Perry's concept was that MCC should be, or could be, the optional replacement for lost family ties. So many individuals have been shunned, rejected, physically shut out and emotionally cut off from their biological families over their homosexuality. Each UFMCC congregation has had the opportunity to develop as a family and community, and MCC-Portland certainly has most of the characteristics of a typical family, for good or ill.

Postlude

MCC has functioned best when things were great, or when things were terrible. At zenith, the momentum of committees and individuals has resulted in wonderful events, successful outreach, and enthusiasm for new ideas. There have been times when after the initial rush of excitement, the hard work has fallen on a few individuals. The glue that holds a volunteer organization together is commitment, which comes in many forms and sizes.

In the worst of times, the congregation members have had to circle up the wagons, hunker down, and muddle through poor finances, misunderstandings, AIDS, and the challenge of outsiders who would restrict the rights and freedoms of GLBT people. MCC-Portland has been a place to exchange strengths and to build up each person for the chutzpah needed to move forward. There's nothing like a crisis or a challenge to rally the troops!

One essential link that is missing at MCC-Portland is a published directory of members. While most churches have these readily available, issues concerning privacy have clouded the process of getting a published congregational directory into the hands of members. This precipitates a breakdown in member communication. The 1998 directory contained photographs and listings for members who felt they could be public with their affiliation. The church needs to solve the privacy issue, or put out a listing of those members comfortable with being listed as a member of a gay-friendly church. What a sad commentary that this is still an issue in 2006 Portland!

There certainly have been times when the MCC family has been dysfunctional. Many people do come to the church with emotional baggage, and the need for healing. Spiritual experiences can reopen emotional wounds and dreg up forgotten feelings. Boxes of Kleenex are set on every pew, and the church may set some kind of record for the number of tissues used per capita!

Finances have been of the trickiest aspects of this congregation. Some members donated generously, consistently, for years. A few quiet benefactors at one time made sure that there was enough funding to balance year-end budgets. They are gone. Some faithful folks contribute the Biblical 10% tithe, or, more often, some smaller but regular percentage. There is a noticeable trend one pastor termed a "low-level infection of personal and systemic poverty." This is the self-inflicted belief that giving much money to the church will negatively impact a family budget. They miss the joy of giving and sharing.

Another identifiable trend has been the withholding of donations or pledged giving because of disagreements with the pastor, Board, committee, individual, or church program. Ironically, this position doesn't make the withholder feel much better, and quite often the targeted person or program is not even aware that they are the subject of a grudge.

MCC asks its members to make a financial pledge at the beginning of the fiscal year and then waits hopefully for the promised donations. Communicating about money is problematic - few people like to request money, and fewer enjoy being asked to provide it. Members not fulfilling their pledge seldom explain why, and the church rarely checks into why someone is behind on their promised giving. Since no one likes to talk directly about their monetary conundrum, generalized pleas fail to resolve deficit situations. No one is very happy, and unnecessary bad feelings or frustrations result. If a member leaves or transfers, they universally take their unmet financial pledge with them, further complicating feelings and clouding emotions.

Some people have quit MCC over real and perceived disputes - sometimes doctrinal, but more often procedural, political, or emotional. Some have left after one or two visits because they felt pressured to become socially or sexually involved with others. Some have come specifically looking for a datable person with out the predictable baggage of someone they might meet in the bars, baths, or at the beach. They often left after an initial survey, or stayed on when they found MCC to be more than a higher class pick-up venue.

Postlude

Dwelling on the past, feeling sorry for one's self because real or perceived persecution, and sitting on a "pity pot" of self-sorrow has yet to produce one positive outcome. Gary Wilson's "theology of oppression," while perhaps aimed at giving comfort, sent folks away from services sometimes feeling worse than when they arrived. Glenna Shepherd said it well when she reminded the congregation that staying adrift in a pool of hurt causes people to stagnate without moving forward in their emotional "swim." Part of the journey as spiritual people is "growing up" into all God wants us to be, including emerging from woundedness in our past, giving up that which we kept in the God-position in our lives, and getting past the oppression-sickness that has marked us so deeply (October 16, 2005, *Here and Now* p.9).

"If your primary goal is to avoid pain, then being human isn't the best way to attain it. Any time you care about something, anything, you've set yourself up to get hurt. (Carolyn Hax, September 22, 2005 *The Oregonian* p E 2).

Sadly, some long-term members leave because of burnout or hurt feelings after long periods of service in leadership positions. Folks with intensity and energy have sometimes felt unsupported when others did not rally to their particular cause with equal enthusiasm. Fortunately, some have returned after a period of non-involvement, with a new perspective.

In retrospect, it would have been better for all parties if most pastors, once out of office, would have disaffiliated with the congregation for a period of time (The standard at Westminster Presbyterian is two years). Although well-intentioned, it is conventional wisdom that the former leader gets out of the way for the new person, so that person can assume leadership. Lingering loyalties from members and even the emotional attachment of the former minister to the congregation and some members has not always produced healthy situations.

Ministers, by their very position, function as friend, parent figure, problem-solver, spokesman, and spiritual coach. Intense loyalties have developed between members and pastors. While their training and experience creates a caring leader and theological speaker, parishioners sometimes forget that their pastor is still a standard-issue human being with the full set of accompanying individual qualities and quirks. Members sometimes want the pastor to be available at their beck and call, or feel that their crisis must be more important than anything else the pastor may be currently doing. When pastors don't perform exactly in a preconceived way, feelings are frequently hurt.

The role of pastor is an amalgam of at least ten job descriptions. In the case of MCC it involves the predictable preparation for worship, a quality homily each week, counseling, administration, coordination of teams or committees, and management of the facility. Add to that the demands of a quality representative to various civic functions, liaison with gay community groups, oversight of Esther's Pantry, dialogue with local religious organizations, and involvement with the larger UFMCC community. Oh yes, they need a personal life, and are generally held to be models of civilized and proper behavior.

An age-old question at MCC has been "Is the pastor always a pastor?" St. Paul outlined a template of behavior, trying to cause no offense to anyone, working with the Jew and the Greek, endeavoring to be all things to all people for the sake of the Gospel. While most congregations hold their minister to a more strict code of behavior and demeanor, the risk of passing judgment on our fellow believer merits St. Paul's query, "Why do you criticize other followers of the Lord? Why do you look down on them? The day is coming when God will judge all of us...and so each of us must give an account to God for what we do." (Romans 14: 10-12).

We have been blessed, and challenged, by generally high-key ministers with lots of ideas and often holding strong beliefs about how things can best be accomplished. While this seems an admirable situation, it's way too easy to "chew up" a pastor, use them till they stay too long or run out of energy. Alternately, we have watched pastors "burn out" from overextension,

Postlude

either by expecting them to be able to handle everything, or by their own inability to say "no" to their own or congregational imposed projects. Most pastors have been able to share the load with assistants or student clergy. The congregation is too large to have just one pastor.

The smallest good work is worth more than the grandest intention. The church has had its share of back-pew critics...folks who always have an opinion yet rarely, if ever, come forward with either a positive solution or commitment to get involved in rectifying a poor situation. Not to be confused with work righteousness or legalism, James' treatise on the actions one takes because of their belief in God makes some very practical suggestions for congregational living. Simply put, "Just as the body is dead when there is no spirit in it, so faith is dead if it is not the kind that results in good deeds." (James 2:26, Living Bible)

Action and visible progress have done much more to build fellowship, camaraderie, and loyalty to friends and the church. People are happy doing what they do best with their hands - digging, constructing, painting, designing, sewing...cleaning. The 2005-06 experience of members volunteering to help dig out the basement for enlarged bathroom facilities has been a good case in point. Folks with a few hours of available time showed up to dig and haul dirt, moving 37 cubic yards of earth, saving $ 4300 from the contractor bid. Not only did many hands make light work, it gave individual members a tangible sense of ownership in the project, and provided a different kind of opportunity to make a donation "in kind."

Likewise, a predictable pattern at MCC has been that people who do things for others are almost universally happier than people who seem to primarily live unto themselves. Individuals having a greater purpose in life than theirs own material happiness have become volunteers with commitment and positive energy. As joyful givers of time and money, they are members willing and anxious to participate in worship leadership and ministry teams, and just about anything else that needs to be done.

MCC brings out passionate loyalty in many members. For many, it has been the place that brought them back to God. For some, it was just because a "real" church for gays and lesbians existed. For many, it was the caring and family atmosphere they detected in their earliest visits. For some it has been movingly spiritual, for others, grandly social.

Rodney King probably said it best: "Can't we all just get along?"

Social Action

Churches have taken on social issues and causes since the earliest days of Christianity. Christ spoke to the issue when he said "Render unto Caesar the things that are Caesar's and unto God the things that are God's." But sorting out that distinction has taken on different form over the centuries.

Paramount to the interests of most MCC members has been the status of gay rights, social justice, diversity, recognition of marriage, physical and emotional health, care for the ill and dying, and bringing God's message of acceptance to those do not feel accepted.

The distinction needs to be made that many individuals from MCC have taken on significant roles in the Port land community as committed individuals, but not directly as part of their MCC involvement. Establishing the Portland Gay Men's Chorus; founding P-FLAG; involvement with State, County and City committees; work at Our House, Peace House, Cascade Aids Project; the Imperial Sovereign Rose Court; and a myriad of other involvements have been coincidental to membership at MCC. It does definitely speak to the personal philosophies of these individuals, that their lives involve service and commitment to causes and programs of social merit. I believe it is tangential that they are also people of faith.

From the days of Austin Amerine, the church has endeavored to stay apolitical, yet support causes that are just, and significant to the lives of GLBT people. The church's exempt

Postlude

status under Section 501 (c) (3) Federal tax law requires the non-endorsement of candidates, and imposes some limits on political advocacy.

The congregation participates in Gay Community programs with representation in the Gay Pride Committee, the Portland Area Business Association, and Basic Rights Oregon.

In the religious community, MCC values highly its memberships in Ecumenical Ministries of Oregon, and Community of Welcoming Congregations, and of the Universal Fellowship of Metropolitan Community Churches.

Probably the strongest involvement in social action is the ownership and management of Esther's Pantry. Assuming responsibility for the food pantry was a huge step for the congregation, committing to the practical day-by-day operation of a large budget and highly visible service. Esther's operates with little visible connection to MCC and cannot and does not proselytize there in any form. As the client base expands in 2005 to include those diagnosed with HIV, far more women and children will quality for the program, meaning a greater mingling of straight and gay people, and mixing of healthy and diagnosed people.

As of 2006, it was estimated by the United Nations that 40 million people were living with AIDS, worldwide, and that 25 million have been killed by the disease since 1981 when it was first recognized. UNAIDS tallied 3.1 million deaths and 4.9 million new cases of HIV in 2004. New drug therapies have enabled many to live longer and productive lives after infection. There is still no vaccine to prevent HIV, only the wisdom and discipline of safe-sex practices in all communities. The disease will continue to impact the foreseeable future, and MCC and all Christian churches will need to continue to find avenues of ministry to those effected by HIV and AIDS.

Historically, MCC has been an outreach to gay and lesbian, bisexual and transgendered people of faith. Within the recent past, several distinctions in sexuality have become less significant. The gay community said for years that it was working for the breaking-down of barriers between gay and straight. Changes in attitude and definition have occurred through American society in the past decade. TV programs include, or focus on, gay and lesbian characters. Significant role models such as Rock Hudson, Greg Louganis, Billie Jean King, Leonard Bernstein, Ellen DeGeneris and countless others have made it more acceptable to be sexually different. Music groups have bent genders, blurred categories of sexual interest, and poked enough fun at rigid sex roles to create an atmosphere once called unisex, then metrosexual, intersexual, or questioning.

For much of younger society, sexual identification is almost a non-issue. This foments several changes in society, but for MCC, it opens the doors ever wider as the church attempts to reach spiritual people of all sexuality. Issues and roadblocks typical of the 70s and 80s are less significant, and the church needs to seek out and define what the issues of significance are for the current generation of young adults. Secondary students are far more comfortable with identifying themselves as sexually different, and society in general is far more accepting of them. Over 3000 Gay-Straight Alliance chapters exist in high school across the U.S. in 2005. (*Time*, October 10, 2005)

The struggle over gay rights is far from over. Whether this is part of the larger Civil Rights Movement or not, Christians on both sides of both issues will struggle to find appropriate meaning in the same Holy Bible. Some observers note that the gay rights movement is about 30 years behind the cause of racial civil rights. Parallels in the role of music, charismatic leaders and sympathetic legislators are common elements in the progress towards equality. More confrontations inevitably lie ahead.

MCC is overwhelmingly white by composition. The very few Asian, Latino, and Black members are most welcome, but their racial issues are not noticed, due to their low numbers. Similarly, MCC has made accommodation for blind, hard-of-hearing, and wheel chair bound members, yet it's difficult for most non-disabled members to identify with or comprehend the

Postlude

issues around being different, and somehow less than "well-bodied." Gay men in particular seem able to find more flaws than positive qualities in other men. The Congregational Life Team helps when help is needed or requested, but the majority of MCC members are disengaged from these many minorities within a minority.

A church that does not study contemporary society cannot hope to serve it. If the congregation resists anything new - technology, Biblical scholarship, social issues, biological discoveries, or national trends and advances in family and individual living, it takes the risk of standing firm on the wrong issues. Stability and growth will proceed from community involvement, individual growth, and care for each other. Should MCC ignore its mission, it runs the risk of becoming an atrophied institution like those we established ourselves to replace.

We are always the same, yet always different. This makes the joy of finding refined meaning in Scripture an adventure. And one more principle needs to be remembered...a new philosophy doesn't have to be a challenge to an existing practice.

So, in early middle age, MCC-Portland celebrates all the past that has made it the organization it is at 30 years - the sum total of the highs and lows, joys and sorrows, feast and famine - praising God and marveling that we have survived, sometimes in spite of ourselves, with a tune in our head, and hopeful of living out our mission as God's curious and peculiar people.

Historic Project Patrons

To a few of my beloved freedom fighters who have passed.
Their lives taught us all about love and courage.

Greg Wagner

Mike Honochick

Bill Sloat

Chuck Holmes

Randy Klose

Steve Endeen

"There is no easy walk to freedom anywhere, and many of us will have to pass through the valley of the shadow of death again and again before we reach the mountaintop of our desires"....................

Nelson Mandela

Compliments of Terry Bean

Historic Project Patrons

"Never doubt that a small group of thoughtful, committed citizens can change the world. Indeed, it's the only thing that ever has."

Margaret Mead

"Each generation has but one chance to be judged by future generations...and this is our time."

Governor Barbara Roberts, Governor's Inaugrural Speech January 14, 1991

"There are too many people and too many great activities to count up. The heroes are for the most part everyday people who are doing something–anything–about AIDS... We have had an extraordinary journey the last two decades. It has been a trail of tears. We have buried our dead and then manned the barricades of liberty."

A Series of Quotes by David Mixner

"I still hear people say that I should not be talking about the rights of lesbian and gay people, and I should stick to the issue of racial justice. But I hasten to remind them that martin Luther King Jr. said 'Injustice anywhere is a threat to justice everywhere.'" I appeal to everyone who believes in Martin Luther King Jr.'s dream to make room at the table of brother-and sisterhood for lesbians and gay people."

Coretta Scott King

"Where, after all, do universal human rights begin? In small places, close to home—so close and so small hey cannot be seen on any maps of the world. Yet they are the world of the individual person...Such are the places where every man, woman and child seeks equal justice, equal opportunity, equal dignity without discrimination. Unless these rights have meaning there, they have little meaning anywhere. Without concerned citizen action to uphold them close to home, we shall look in vain for progress in the larger world."

Eleanor Roosevelt

"There is no such thing as part freedom...Your freedom and mine can not be separated... For to be free is not merely to cast off one's chains, but to live in a way that respects and enhances the freedom of others."

A series of quotes... Nelson Mandela

Compliments of Terry Bean

Historic Project Patrons

Ransom Blackman LLP

A Portland law firm working to balance the scales of justice

since 1977

Dave Dishman

Thank You, MCC, for being my second family

since 1979

WITHAM & DICKEY
PRINTING · PROMOTIONAL PRODUCTS · DIRECT MAIL

since 1996

EQUITY FOUNDATION
Investing in Dignity

Chip Mayhue Memorial Fund

Since 1987

In fond memory of departed members and friends of MCC

an anonymous MCC couple

Spirit Press

Words are the Breath of Life

In loving memory of Stephen Mark Graham and all of his departed friends..

Since 1998

Historic Project Patrons

Scandal's — Since 1979

CC Slaughters — Since 1981

Portland's Gay Yellow Pages — since 1998

The Embers Avenue, Portland, OR. — since 1972

JJQ's Tavern — since 1981

Silverado

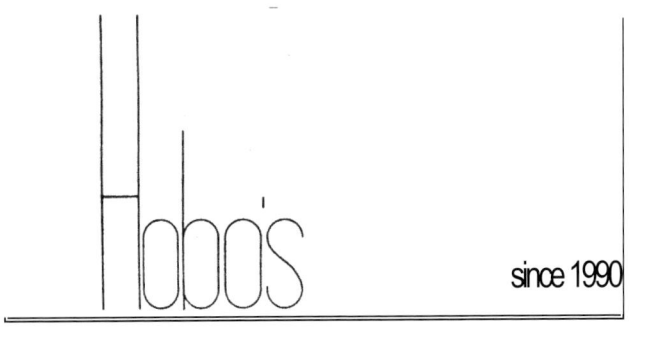

Historic Project Patrons

Beaumont Market
since 1988

Cook Boys
good men... good food... no agenda
since 1985

Dad's Support Group
Offering support and friendship
since 1996

The Imperial Sovereign Rose Court of Oregon
Since 1958

MCC METROPOLITAN COMMUNITY CHURCHES
MCC Region One
Congratulations from your District coordinator
Debbie Martin,

Paul & Jerry Poirier
Real Estate Brokers
Placing your needs and goals first.
Simple, isn't it?
Windermere
since 1928
since 2005

Portland Gay Men's Chorus
since 1980

OMEGA Funeral & Cremation Service
Portland Area Business Association

Hobo's
since 1990

A²
Allen² Law, LLC

396

Historic Project Patrons

the ROXY
"In the Heart of the Glamour District"
since 1998

Starky's
since 1987

PABA
Portand Area Business Association
Your GLBT Chamber of Commerce
since 1992

STEAM PORTLAND
since 2003

Mug Man

Potter to the
GLBT Community

since 1982

Q center
A COMMUNITY CENTER for us.
www.pdxQcenter.org
Opening 2006

Pine Street Studios
lKenton Wiens

opening 2006

Historic Project Patrons

Cadillac Cafe - supporting the GLBT community since 1989
Darcelle XV and Roxy Neuhardt
Dick Burdon
Charles Donald
Irving Ewen - In memory of departed loved ones
Fosler Portland Architecture LLC /Steve Fosler
Terry Furman
Charlie H
Cheryl Beatrice Hall, Member MCC, President ISRC
Ted Hax and Jim Bartlett
Healing Waters and Sacred Spaces
James S. Heuer and Robert C. Mercer
Robert Hogg
Old Wives' Tales
Portland Gay Men's Chorus Bass Section
Periodicals and Books Paradise
Richard Lawson
Windermere/Community Commercial Realty - Richard Levy
Robert Douglass
Ryan Stotts
"If God sends me, God will equip me" - The Hawthorne/Madey family
David W. Owens PC & Associates - Supporting the community since 1975
Bruce Richards
Joy Safstrom
In loving memory of Matthew Jason White - Romans 8:38-39
In Memory of Aaron Kohl
Typemasters - Bob and Vickey

In fond memory of:
Eric Callicote
Ernie Conte
John Paul Dillard
JR Franklin
Keith Nofziger
Steve Witt
Bob Jackson
Don Strausbaugh
Jose Montoya
Bob Carter
Hutch
Bob McKinney

Historic GLBT Venues In Portland

Public "Rendezvous" Locations
Meier & Frank downtown - (2nd floor & 10th floor) b. 1909; 1915; 1930
Camp - general vicinity of SW 3rd and Taylor
Old downtown YMCA - 831 SW 6th & Taylor (1909-1973) - demolished
PSU (Portland State University) - Gym & Locker rooms (current) Smith Center & Cramer Hall ('70s) Lincoln Hall main floor restrooms - before '60s remodel
Fred Meyers - pick one...any location... any year
Frederick & Nelson Dept Store - 506 SW Washington - (now Fifth Avenue Suites) b. 1912 as Lippman, Wolfe, & Co Department Store
Pioneer Courthouse men's latrine - (closed mid '80s)
Greyhound Bus Depot - lower level restrooms – 509 SW Taylor - demolished; b. 1939 as Central (Union) Bus Depot
Trailways Bus Terminal - SW 6th; later NW 6th
Nordstroms - 701 SW Broadway - after 1978
Imperial Hotel - - 400 & 422 SW Broadway (1st floor men's room); b.1894 - later renamed Plaza Hotel; now Hotel Vintage Plaza
Multnomah Hotel Bar - 319 SW Pine - (early 1900s) b.1911 - now Embassy Suites Hotel
Benson Hotel - London Grill - 309 SW Broadway ('60s) b. 1912 as Hotel Oregon
Galleria (formerly Rhoades Dept Store)- 3rd floor men's room ('90s – '00s) b. 1910 as Olds Wortman & King Dept Stone
Old St. George Hotel - 118 W. Burnside ('70s) demolished
Hotel Joyce - 322 SW 11th - Hourly rates in the 50s-70s
Rich's Cigar Store - 734 SW Alder ('61-'81) – 820 SW Alder ('81 - current) previously 539 SW Washington before '61
Imperial (Roller) Skating Rink - 419 SE Madison @ SE end of Hawthorne Bridge
Oaks Amusement Park - Sellwood - 1 SE Spokane b.1905
Princeton Club - 614 SW 11th (1101 SW Washington) ('80s-'90s)
Lloyd Center - NE Multnomah - 2nd Floor restrooms outside the **Aladdin Restaurant**
Breitenbush Hot Springs - OR HWY 46, Detroit, Oregon
Seaside Promenade - lower restrooms - beach level, Seaside, Oregon

Parks -
Portland City Parks
Mt. Tabor Park
Couch Park
Laurelhurst Park
Holladay Park - prior to Lloyd Center, c 1960
Plaza Blocks –
  Chapman Park
  Lownsdale Square - men only from 1924-1975
Restrooms @ 100 SW Park - 1920s
O'Bryant Square Shelter - opened 1973
North Park Blocks - also Gay Pride assembly area

Washington Park - ("Fruit Loop") - and restrooms
Delta Park West - "The Force"
Parks Outside Portland
  Dodge Park – Gresham
State Parks
  Dabney State Park
Claclamas County Parks
  Milo McIver Park (site of Vortex I)

Rest Areas –
I-5 Wilsonville;
I-205 West Linn (closed 1983 due to "activity")

Beaches:
Willamette River: (Sauvie Island), St Johns,
Columbia River: Rooster Rock, Jantzen Beach Hayden Island (Bare Buns),

Performance & Community venues
Ainsworth United Church of Christ -2941 NE Ainsworth (HIV Day Center)
Atkinson Memorial church - Oregon City
Augustana Lutheran Church - NE 15th @ Knott
Benson Hotel - Piccadilly room - 309 SW Broadway
Centenary-Wilbur Methodist Church - 215 SE 9th @ Ash ; b. 1928 - architect Walter E. Kelly
First Congregational Church UCC - 1126 South Park (on the Park Blocks)
First United Methodist Church - 1838 SW Jefferson
Lincoln Street Methodist - Shalom Ministries – 5145 SE Lincoln
Living Enrichment Center - 9372 SW Beaverton-Hillsdale Hwy; later Wilsonville
Old Church (Calvary Presbyterian) - 1422 SW 11th
Metropolitan Community Church -1644 NE 24th – 2400 NE Broadway after '95
Piedmont Presbyterian Church - 5760 NE Cleveland
St. Francis of Assisi church – (Dignity) 303 SE 12th & Pine;
St. Philip Neri - 2408 SE 16th & Division
St Stephen's Episcopal Church - 1432 SW 13th Av
Sunnyside Centenary Methodist Church - 3520 SE Yamhill
Trinity United Methodist Church - 3915 SE Steele
YWCA - 1111 SW 10th - empowering women, eliminating racism, life skills, health/wellness

Bradley-Angle House - shelter & advocacy for battered women
Friendly House - 2617 NW Savier - Keeston Lowrey 1988
HIV Day Center - 3835 SW Kelly; begun by EMO 1990, OHSU clinic added 1991
Hopewell House (EMO), formerly **Hospice House** – 6171 SW Capitol Hwy (1988)
House of Light - 597 NE Dekum - Aids hospice & care center (1992)
David House - 1st AIDS hospice
Juniper House - SE 20th & Ankeny
Lambda House - 1867 SW 14th
Our House - 2727 SE Alder St; previously at SE 26th &) (1988-)
Peace House - 18th Street Peace House - 2116 NE 18th (1986-)

Historic GLBT Venues In Portland

Swan House - 4764 SE Logos Rd, Milwaukie - AIDS Foster care for low-income individuals
Gay Community Center - 258 SW Alder ('72-'73)- in Chambers building b.1897
Gay Community Center – 1973 - Pythian building – 918 SW Yamhill
Gay Community Center - 33 NE Killingsworth - Villa St. Rose HIV hospice
Portland Center for Gays - 33 N Ainsworth & 24 Hour help line (1978)
Men's Resource Center - 3534 SE Main; 2036 SE Morrison
Multnomah County Health Clinic "County Clap Building" - SW 5th & Burnside
Out of the Closet - Phoenix Rising Thrift Store – 2857 SE Stark (c1986)
Outside In - 1132 SW 13th
Stairs Down - PDX Youth Alliance Community Ctr & Nite Club - 615 SE Alder 1970s
Women's Place Resource Center 1431 NE Broadway

Benson Hotel - Mayfair Room - 309 SW Broadway; b. 1912 as Hotel Oregon
Convention Center - NE Martin Luther King JR Boulevard - Georgia-Pacific Room
Eastside Performing Center - SE 14th & Stark; b. as Washington High School
Echo Theater - SE 37th near Hawthorne
Hilton - Pavilion Room - 921 SW 6th
Hoyt Hotel - 614 NW Hoyt
Liberty Hall - 311 N. Ivy
Mallory Hotel – Driftwood Bar - 729 SW 15th
Mark Spencer Hotel- 409 SW 11th - Peter & Alix Nathan (1976-)
   Bowers Hotel (1911)
   b. 1907 - Nortonia Hotel
Masonic Temple -1118 SW 9th @ Main b. 1927
Melody Ballroom – Eastside Commercial Building – 615 SE Alder
Metro Police Club - PPAA Ballroom - 618 SE Alder D J Crystal's Country Jam
Neighbors of Woodcraft - 1410 SW Morrison - now the Tiffany Center
NW Neighborhood Cultural Center - NW Service Center - 1819 NW Everett
Pioneer Courthouse Square - SW Broadway at Morrison Dedicated 1985;
   site of Portland Hotel (1889); demolished for parking structure in 1951
Pythian Building - 918 SW Yamhill - Site of Second Foundation Community Center, MCC, etc; b 1907 as Ancient Free & Accepted Masons Temple–
Portland Center for Performing Arts & Arlene Schnitzer Concert Hall - 1037 SW Broadway b. 1927 Portland Public Theater; Portland Theater; Paramount Theater

Bossanova Ballroom - 722 E. Burnside
Melody Ballroom - 615 SE Alder
Wonder Ballroom - 128 NE Russell
Fez Ballroom - SE 11th
Helen's Pacific Costumers - 1036 SW Burnside

• **Theaters** *Film*:
Guild - 829 SW 9th - also NW Film Institute b.1927 part of Studio Bldg
Broadway - 1008 SW Broadway;-demolished/rebuilt Hippodrome; Broadway "Peacock" marquee added 1931; b. 1926 Keller-Boyd Bldg
Cinema 21 - 616 NW 21st NW Gay Film Festivals
RKO Orpheum (1929-76) - Now Nordstroms on Broadway
Pantages (1926-29); Empress; Pangtages (1912-26) now Alderway Building SW Broadway @ Alder
Circle- 518 SW 4th ('50s)...two balconies, right for men only) - demolished
Blue Mouse - 626 SW 4th - demolished
Capitol Theater - 828 SW 4th - demolished
Fifth Avenue - SW Hall (by PSU)- no longer a theater
Round Up Theater - 339 SW Morrison - demolished 1977; b. 1917 as The Rex Theater
Liberty Theater on SW Broadway
Oregon Theater - 3530 SE Division
Hollywood - 4122 NE Sandy b. 1928
Music Box - 801-819 SW Broadway – demolished; rebuilt as the Fox Tower; b. 1924 as Broadhill Bldg
Movie House - 1220 SW Taylor – (1973–2003);West End Theater; b. 1923 as Portland Women's Club
Jefferson Theatre -1232 SW 12th
Oriental - 822 SE Grand - demolished 1970 b. 1927
Egyptian - 2511 NE MLK JR - closed 1963 – now New Song Community Church; b. 1924
Irvington - 1337 NE Broadway - now a restaurant
Walnut Park - 5029 NE MLK JR Blvd) – redeveloped
Bob White Theater - 6423 SE Foster
Erotic Film Fair -933 N. Russel l- (1stheld Oct,1974)
Hart's X Movie Arcade - 330 SW 3rd – (1991)
Film Follies - 915 SW 3rd
Aladdin - 3017 SE Milwaukie -Gellers Theater
Clinton Street - 2522 SE Clinton; The Encore

• **Theaters** *Live*:
The Tom Kat (Theater) ("Beaver Hall") - 425 NW Glisan- also film
Capitol - 626 SW Broadway (balcony for men) – demolished John Becker & Tempest Storm '53
Fox - 833 SW Broadway - demolished - now the Fox Tower; Mayfair Theater
   as Heilig ('20's vaudeville & female impersonators)
Paris - 6 / 10 SW 3rd - Also called the Storefront Theater; Star (1938 -?) Third Ave Theater (1930); Union Theater (1922); Fritz Theater Concert hall
Roseland - Starry Night - 8 NW 6th;
   b. 1922 as Apolostic Faith Temple
Starr Theater - 9 & 13 NW 6th
   b. 1911 Star Nickel Theater; Princess Theater
La Luna - Pine Street Theatre - 125 SE 9th @ Pine; b. 1928 as Centenary-Wilbur Methodist Church
Portland Civic Theatre - 1530 SW Yamhill (gone)
Echo Theatre - 1515 SE 37th
Milagros Theatre - 525 SE Stark
Sumus Theatre - 13 NW 13th
Theatre Theatre - 3430 SE Belmont – Triangle Productions! (1989-current) (Don Horn)
Fireside Theater - 1436 SW Montgomery

Historic GLBT Venues In Portland

Baths, Spas, etc

Aero Steam room (in the **Aero Club**) - 808 SW Taylor - demolished - now Paramount Hotel b.1920 as Knights of Columbus Club

Aero-Vapor Steam Bath -1237 SW 3rd (1958-1972)) - demolished - now Terry Schrunk Plaza

Olympic Vapors - 509 SW 4th - under the Greek Cusina; Downtown Olympic Baths

Portland Steam b.1903 McMahon's Baths ('20s-60s)

Bath and Massage Institute - 3133 NE Union (1940)

Benton Baths (in the basement) - 812 SW Washington (1940-3)

Hot Springs of Portland (Brown's Hydropathic Institute)(1928); Brown Hydropathic Institute (Women only T & F); b. Stevens Building

Civic Auditorium Baths - SW Market (eliminated in the '60s remodel?); b. 1918

Club Portland - 303 SW 12th - Majestic Club baths (1970s - current);"Zippers" playroom below; b. 1911 as Majestic Hotel

Club Glory - 415 SW 13th - Fred Morris; Club Xes

Continental Baths - 531 SW Park ('78-'85); b. 1908 as Cornelius Hotel & Coffee shop

Dekum Building Baths - Evelyn LaBende (1920) Bessie Hayes - (1940)

Finlandia Spa - SW Montgomery between 4th & 5th demolished mid-'80s

Finnish Baths - 304 NW Flanders - under the Seaman's Center at the Royal Palm Hotel

Franklin Baths - 1320 SW Washington (1975)

Hanson's Baths - (1920-8) - SW 6th @ Yamhill b. 1889 - Portland Hotel

Inner City Hot Springs at Common Ground – 2927 NE Everett

Jacob Jacobson's Finnish Baths - 3750 N Montana

Japanese Baths - NW 3rd & Everett (in basement under a steam laundry)

Ladd Finnish Sauna - 1715 SE Hawthorne (1965)

Multnomah Hotel Turkish Baths (in the basement) – (1920 - 43?); b. 1912

Nordic Saunas - 2146 NE Broadway (1965)

Olympic Sauna & Bath - (original location) – 359 SW Morrison

Sanitary Steam Baths - 1005 N. Failing (1928-56)

Silvers Russian Turkish Hot Salt Water Baths & Vita Glass Solarium (1920) - 595 Front

Steam Portland - 2885 NE Sandy (2003 to current)

Thompson's Mineral Bath Parlors - 305 Main (1928)

Workout Baths - 531 SW 12th (1968-79) **Uptown Olympic Baths** (1979-1983); previously the Camp Fire Girls PDX Area offices

Viking Sauna NW - 1135 SW Salmon

Viking Sauna Studio - 1217 SW Morrison

Bath House - Adults Only - 2 NW 4th (now Cindy's)

Restaurants - West Side

Roman's Tavern & Supper Club - 949 SW Stark – (1969-71) Roman Wyrda

Bohemian - 910 SW Washington (1920's -'69) – (1970-'71) - Roman Wydra - now parking lot

Chaco's Restaurant (1981-84?) - 820 SW Stark

Mamie's Diner (1979-1981?)

Fish Grotto - 1035 SW Stark (1960 -) - Part of "The Complexx" - Don Sexton; Dan Zielke
The Outrigger Lounge
The Quarter Deck (The Deck) (85)

The Roxy - 1121 SW Stark -(1994-);The Lovely Suzanne
Lone Star Texas Cafe
Roxy Heart's Memorial Diner - Lenny Borer & Mark Adrian b. as Fairfield Hotel

The Buick Cafe-1239 SW Washington - (1949-'60s) b. 1910 - Drake Hotel

Aura Restaurant - 1022 W Burnside

Hot Potata #2 -422 SW 13th @ Burnside & Stark (1979) - Daniel Moore & Charles Walker

Cassidy's - 1337 SW Washington (1979 -); b. 1912 Hotel Ramapo; later Taft Home for the Aged

Shanghai Steakery - 16 NW Broadway (1999 -) Broadway Cafe & Sealander Lounge - women's bar California Café; b. as Broadway Hotel

Jolly Joan - SW Broadway - Morgan Building

Cafe Potpourri - 213 SW Broadway

The Abbey - 223 SW Stark; now Abu Karim Lebanese Restaurant (1985 - current)
Bishops House

Louvre Cafe - 275 SW Alder @ 4th - (1907-1913); in Belvedere Hotel

Metro - 911 SW Broadway (1980s) Union Carriage Garage

Demetri's - 1650 W. Burnside
Konnie's Korner

Hamburger Mary's - 840 SW Park; 239 SW Broadway (1978); moved to NE Broadway

Dakota Cafe - 239 SW Broadway - Bill Dickey

Cascades - 333 NW 23rd

Virginia Cafe - 725 SW Park (originally 1014 SW Stark)(Clyde Hotel)

Quality Pie - 1111 NW 23rd or 2316 NW Northrup - **Plenty**

Good Grille - 1609 SW Morrison
Manion's Restaurant- Steve Manion & Curt Burgess in the Commodore Hotel

Sambo's - NW 23rd & Burnside

Bonnie's Burgers - NW 19th @ Kearny

Cafe Babana - 1231 SW Jefferson - Jon Murray, then Barry Allen & Rick McCoy

Purple Parrott - SW Barbur (?)

Jonah's - 7425 SW Barbur Blvd - Jim & Jack Streijt

Campbell Hill Cafe - 2261 W. Burnside - Bill Farrar & Doug Miller

The Red Herring - 1231 SW Jefferson

Veritable Quandry 1220 SW 1st - (1967 - current) b.1885 as Portland Marble Works

Victoria's Nephew - 409 SW 2nd; 212 SW Stark - now Mother's Bistro - Rob Sample

Wilf's Restaurant - 800 NW 6th in Union Station; b. 1895

Jerry's Gable - 618 SW Grant - steaks & seafood

Denny's - SW Broadway by Portland State University

Boulevard Cafe - 7958 SW Barbur Blvd.
The Crab Bowl

International House of Pancakes - 722 SW Yamhill

Huber's - 320 SW Stark

Bonnie's Burger Drive-In - 932 NW 19th

Henry Thiele's - 2305 W. Burnside

Valhalla Cafe - 7 NW 3rd

The Lamplighter - near PSU - Goose Hollow

Historic GLBT Venues In Portland

Sisters of the Road Cafe - 133 NW 6th
Mississippi Pizza Pub - 3552 N Mississippi
Porky's Pub - 835 N. Lombard
Vitis Enoteca - 535 NW 16th
Coffee
Agora Coffeehouse - Koinonia House Basement – SW Broadway (1966-1972)
Black Rooster Cafe - 424 SW 10th; (2004-)
Ninth Street Exit Coffeehouse - Centenary-Wilbur Methodist Church - 215 SE Pine
Stairs Down Coffee House - 615 SE Alder (1973-5)
Outside In Coffeehouse - SW 13th
Jackman Joe Coffee - 1111 NW 16th - 2003 - Keri Jensen
Let's Do Coffee - 19373 SW Willamette Drive, WL -(2004-05); Craig Shannon & Brad Day

Westside Bars/Taverns
•**Camp** (vicinity of SW 3rd & Taylor)
Transfusion Inn - 1139 SW 1st - working class lesbian bar (1959 to 1964) - Milton Buck
   Silver Slipper
   Rockaway Cafe
   Mt. Shasta Restaurant (1936-1959)
       LaSalle Tavern - 1223 SW 1st (1940)
       Winner Cafe - SW 1st
Harbor Club - 736 SW 1st & Yamhill (1946-1965) – Re-opened at The Riptide - Johnnie Honegger
Half Moon Tavern - 74 SW Morrison (1958-1960) – Lester Kennedy, jr.
The (Half Moon) Tavern - 122 SW Yamhill - (1960-1975) – Lester Kennedy, sr. b. 1880 – Frantz Block
   The Tavern - 122 SW Yamhill (1975-1981) – Ray Willitson - relocated at Ray's Ordinary
Wilde Oscars - 318 SW 3rd (1976-1983) -Earl Wright – ("Hat Box" shows) - now the Red Sea
   The Filling Station
   The Crystal Pistol
   Turtleneck Tavern (1970)
   Rigoletto Tavern (1940)
Embassy Club - 309 SW 3rd
Town Pump - SW 2nd & Salmon
Dahl & Penne Tavern -604 SW 2nd (19'72-83) - Gene & Sam Landauer -(now B of A Building)
   Dahl & Penne Inc., Soft Drinks (1916 - 1971)
   The Alder Cafe (1912 - 1916)
   The Manhattan Club (1911)
   b. 1884 - Montana Assay Building
Lotus - 932 SW 3rd - (1928 - current) 1961 - Peter & Mrs. Kathleen Traypen; b. 1906 - Hotel Albion
Dinty Moore's - 924 SW 3rd - Mama Bernice tended bar since 1949 - Carl Wilson; b. 1895 - Auditorium Bldg
The Reed - 901 SW 3rd or 236 SW Alder (1952-59)
   The Beach Comber (1960)
   Taylor Tavern (1943)
The Rose City Club Tavern - 917 SW 3rd (1930-1975)
Mama B's Inn - 1228 SW 3rd (1964-1966) – Arthur Brannen - attempted to re-open at 736 SW 1st
   The Phoenix Cafe (1954) - Nicholas G. Polechrones
W.C.'s Watercloset - 424 SW 4th - upstairs dancing('75)
   Polyesther's
Eli's - 424 SW 4th - street level ('early 80's)
   …VIPsRestaurant
   Up the Down Staircase… now City Sports Bar
   b. 1890 New Mayer Hotel; Canadian Hotel
Wallbangers (across from PGE bldg?- closed after 1974 fire
Little Brown Jug - 908 SW 4th (1951?)
Buddies Post Tavern - 926 SW 4th (1962-1968) - Sadie Balmer; Wm Bullard
Old Glory Tavern - 118 SW Madison (1950s-1967) - Roy Cope; Gordon S. McKay

Other Inn - 242 SW Alder - leather bar (1964-1982) – Jim Franz - Mama Bernice tended bar
   The Arizona; b. 1897 Chambers Building
Grand Oasis Tavern - 243 SW Alder - (1979-83)
   The Last Resort

Cafe Trieste - SW 12th & Montgomery - Walter Cole
   Way Out
   Cafe Espresso
Model Inn (women only) - 1536 SW 1st - (1956-67) – Olga then son Nick Polechrones; 1940s

Westside Bars/Taverns
•**Gay Triangle**
Family Zoo - 820 SW Oak (1971-1985) Bobby Hoblitt Salvation Army "Green House"; now Janus
   The Annex- (1965-1971)
   Dereks (1963-1965)- Derek L. Akerson
   Oak Street Tavern
   Tel & Tel - (1957-1962) - Robert Lloyd Saunders
   Vince's - 1957
   Saunder's Tavern; b. 1907 as the Lintnon Trolley Station
The Escape - 333 SW Park - all age club
CC Slaughters -1014 SW Stark (1982-1997)- JohnAdams; John Houston & Bruce moved to NW Davis
   The Rhondee ('79-'81)
   Julie's Supper Club
   Virginia Cafe (original location - now 725 SW Park)
   b. 1912 as Clyde Hotel; Ben Stark; Ace Hotel (2005)
Boxes & The Brig - 330 SE 11th - "The Complex" - Don Sexton, Dan Zielka
   b. 1912 as Treves Hotel; Hotel Joyce
Red Cap Garage - 1025 SW Stark
Panorama - 341 SW 10th -
Somebody's Place - 319 SW 11th - (1983-85) - (relocation of The Focal Point) - Glen Dugger
   Roxy's Leopard Lounge
Scandals & The Other Side Lounge-1038 SW Stark (1985-2005) (moved to" 6 tits") - Glen Dugger
   Express it Coffee House & Art Gallery
   Rainbow Gallery…in the Clyde Hotel
Three Sisters - 1125 SW Stark (1963-2005) - original bar on 14th - Georgia
   Scandals in 2006 - Glen Dugger
   b.1911 as Blackstone Hotel; Fairfield Hotel; Kent Hotel
Silverado - 1217 SW Stark - Don Sexton & Tommy
   Flossies' (1983) - Stephen Boden
   Stark St. Station (1982) & Edy's Eatery
   The Bushes
   Riddles (1976-77)
   Kuchina Lounge
   Pied Piper
   The Mocambo (1960) - Robert Lloyd Saunders
   Desert Room (1959) -hangout for pimps, madams & safecrackers - Nate Zusman
Roman's Riptide (Lounge) - (1969-1973) — 923 - 949 SW Stark; - Trevor Roman Wydra
   The Riptide (1965-9) - succeeded the Harbor Club – John Honeggar;
   Bali Hai Supper Club
PDX Eagle -1300 SW Stark @ 13th - Fred Morris
   The Eagle - John Adams
   Le Cuisiner (1300 W. Burnside)
   The Curtain Call (1300 W Burnside)
   Maus Haus (1300 W. Burnside)
The Alley - 1135 SW Washington (1971?) - go-go boy bar
   Axe Handle (1974
   Timber Topper (1954)
   Yen Ching
   Stephanos
   Bettie Ford's Clinic

Historic GLBT Venues In Portland

b. 1912 as Washington Hotel
Ritz Disco - 1116 SW Washington (mid '70s)
    Flight 181 (1976)
    b.1907 as Waldorf Hotel; New Ritz; Hotel San Marco
Gay Cock Inn - 1039 SW Washington (1940)

Westside Bars/ Taverns
• Downtown
Music Hall Nightclub - 413 SW 10th - 413 1/2 SW 10th
    (1937-1950) - Leonard Schneiderman
    Zebra Super Club (Zebra Club) - (1947-1950) – Paul
      Schneiderman
    Backstage & Lucien (upstairs)
Clover Club - 923 SW Taylor @ 10th (1941)
Roman's Bohemian Restaurant - 910 SW Washington –
    Roman Wydra
Rage Inn - 330 SW Washington - British Pub atmosphere –
    (1982) - Terry Davis
    Coach House
    Running Fox
Red Carpet Lounge (in the Greyhound Depot) - 840 SW 6th
Cartwheel - 1223 SW 5th (1958-62) - PSU lesbians
    Hannah Brown - (Papa Jay Scott, bartender)
The Masthead - 1415 SW 6th
Somebody's Place – 728 SW 9th (1979-1983) – Glen
    Dugger; now The Mercantile
    The Fiddlers Three (1974-79) - John Chaney
    The Focal Point (1971-74) - Steve Suss
Roman's Tavern 739 SW 9th (1969-71) - Roman Wydr
    Embers Supper Club (1971-82) & The Rafters (1975-......82)
    - Steve Suss
Sidedoor - 811 SW Yamhill (1971-2) - Yamhill side exit of
    The Embers
    Zombie Zulu - (1940's & 50's)
Zorba the Greek - 626 SW Park (1971-1976)
    Brassarie Montmarte
    The Eaton Bldg
Mildred's Palace - 918 SW Yamhill (mid-70s) - moved t0
    Dante's (1 SW 3rd) & 316 (Metro)
    Pythian Building
Agostino's - 725 SW Alder (1965-68)
    b.1928 as Alderway Bldg (Pantages Theater)
Castaways Lounge (Disco) – 901 SW Salmon (1974) –
    Steve Suss
Candlelight Décor – Jazz Club – SW 5th @ Lincoln
Cupboard – 620 SW Salmon – (Broadway Theater)
    The Pantry
The 19th Hole – 1002 SW Broadway – Broadway Theater
    b. 1926 as Keller-Boyd Building
Hunt Pub – 1021 SW Morrison - (1983) – Dave Sorber
    Gregory's
    b. 1903 Lincoln Hotel
Club Rhumba (1949-1952) – 722 SW Taylor - basement
    The Rathskeller Beer Parlor (1936-1949) – (Mike) Kokich
    Moonlight Inn (1933-1
Bear Hall -1116 SW Morrison; - now MAX turnaround
    The Metropolis Saloon
    Tropique (underage) – 1980
The Happy Hare – 1730 SW Taylor (1966) – Swiss Chalet
    décor – Sidney Smith
North Dakota – 225 SW Broadway ('80s)
City Nite Club (underage) - 13 NW 13th (1989-1997;
    originally 624 SW 13th (1983-989)
    Re-opened 1997 as Evolution (Lanny Swerdlow)
The Escape – 333 SW park
Evolution – underage club SW 2nd
Brass Duck – 1128 SW Jefferson – Darold Hamilton

1201 Club – 1201 SW 12th
    TAC's
    The Westside
Stone Balloon – SW Broadway near PSU?
Rod & Reel (across from Embers)
Kelly's Olympian – 420 SW Washington (1902-current)
    b.1906 as Scott Bldg; Buchanan Bldg; Bullier Bldg
Frontline – SW Washington @ 12th
    Steffano's
    Bettie Ford Clinic (2005)
Westside Barb / Taverns
• Old Town
Multnomah Hotel (now Embassy Suites) 319 SW Pine–
    Jester Bar
The Met - 1 SW 3rd - drag shows (1982)
    Dante's
Key Largo - 31 NW 1st; (Lesbian bar next door 1997?)
Chocolate Moose (1972-) & Steak Cellar (1977-)- 50 SW
2nd (211 SE Ankeny) Chuck Council
    Mary's
Anchors on Ankeny - SW 2nd & Ankeny ('80s)
214 Tavern - 214 W Burnside (1985) - Marv Almquist
C. H. Teasers - 309 W. Burnside (1985)
    Valhalla - Sandy Director
Aunt Fanny's - 208 NW Couch (1975)
Limbo Lounge - 316 W. Burnside
    Metropolis –
    Mildred's Palace (all age)(83?) Lanny Swerdlow
    Single Guitar Tavern (1974)
    Tash's (1969-74) American Museum Restaurant – Ron
      McCarty
    316 - (1974) - No men allowed
Hobos - 120 NW 3rd - 1978 - Lynn Ellis; 1989 - Harriett &
    Andy Guthrie
    Old Town Strutters' Hall
Fox and Hounds - 217 NW 2nd (1990 to current)
    Dobie's Old Town
CC Slaughter's (New) - 219 NW Davis - (relocated 1997)
    John Adams JR.; (2003) -John Houston
    The Odyssey
    Greek Restaurant
    Daisy Kingdom (original location)
Darcelle XV - 208 NW 3rd. classy drag - (1969 to current)
    Walter Cole
    Demas Tavern (1965-68)
      b. 1911? Foster Hotel (F & H; CC's & Darcelle's all in
      the same building)
Dirty Duck - 439 NW 3rd - (1983- current) Mama Bernice
    helped pour till 1986 - Gail Kennedy
Hoyt Tavern - 521 NW 6th - Walter & Nettie Sweek
Dugo's - 413 W Burnside
    Grand Oasis - Joe Powers
    Sissy's Old Towne Legend - (1982-85)
    Angela's (1985)
    Rising Moon - 1978-82 - women's bar - Sally Bird
Magic Garden - 217 NW 4th -("the "Plastic Fern") - lesbian,
    then strip club (1975 -current)
    Club Northwest (1968-1972) James Cleve
Mildred's Palace 1 SW 3rd & 316 W Burnside
    Metro
    Dante's
    Chang's Mongolian Grill
Ming Lounge - 222 NW 4th (1951-) in the Republic Cafe
Roseland Grill - 8 NW 6th - under Roseland Theater
    Starry Night
      b. 1928 as Apostolic Faith Temple
Sportsman's Inn (Jim's) - 15 NW 6th (1972)
Shanghai Steakery - 16 NW Broadway (1999-current)
Embers Avenue (new) - 110 NW Broadway (1982-)
......(relocated from SW 9th) - Steve Suss

Historic GLBT Venues In Portland

Ray's Ordinary Bar & Grill - 317 NW Broadway (1981-1999) - Half Moon successor - Ray Wiliston
   Tiger Bar
Hoyt Hotel & Roaring 20's Room - 614 NW 6th & Hoyt (1941-72) - Harvey Dick - demolished 76
Caboose Room - 638 NW 6th (1962) - Jack Eckstrom (site is new Greyhound Bus Station)
Depot Tavern (1940) north of the Hotel Rainier
JR's West - 300 NW 10th - (1981- 1984) -Ray Southwick & John Phillips; Bill Scott
   Jimmy Mak's
   Blah Blah (1993) - The Lovely Suzanne
   E Street Tavern
   The Long Goodbye
The Cell - 300 NW 10th (basement) - (1981- 1984) Robert ("Raunchy") Paul Dunn
   The Folsom Cell
   Close Encounters
   Ram's Down Under (1994)

WestsideBars / Taverns
*****Uptown** - Vaseline Flats (Swish Alps) (S & W of I-405 Stadium Freeway)
Flossies - 1981 W. Burnside - (1982) - moved to 1217 Sw Stark
Milwaukee Tavern - 1535 W. Burnside (1963-1964) lesbians bar - Edna Jorhal
J & J Tavern - 1719 W. Burnside (1978-81) - Leather & Motorcycles
The Kingston Saloon - 2020 W. Burnside (Dahl & Penne's liquor license)
   New Moon Inn
Slabtown - 1033 NW 16th
   Cal Sport
   Primary Domain (1984)
   & Maximillian's - formerly Olivia's Diner
   Magar Magar
   Sonny's Topless Bar
Vitis Enoteca restaurant/bar - 535 NW 16th
Silent Partners - 1810 NW Lovejoy
   Chuckles & Rib Tickler Restaurant (1982)
   Rosins
   Oak Pit
JJ's Backroom - NW 17th & Lovejoy (part of Chuckles'/Silent Partners?)
Lulu's Tavern - 612 NW 21st - (1983-); now Muu Muu's
   ...Muu Muu's
   Player's Pub (1982) - Chris & Mickey
Lion's Pride - 721 NW 21st (1980-81)
   Al's
Goose Hollow Inn - 1411 SW 14th (1967-) - Bud Clark
   Ann's Tavern
Driftwood Room - Mallory Hotel
Purple Clown - NW 21st Bar & Grill
Dandelion Pub - (1983)

East Side - Restaurants/Coffee
Hot Potata #1 on SE Foster
Sambos - 909 E Burnside (now The Galaxy Restaurant)
Cadillac Cafe -1801 NE Broadway after 2002-); previously 914 NE Broadway
Moon Star Bar & Grill - 7410 NE MLK Blvd –
Blend Coffeehouse - 2327 E. Burnside -
Hollywood Espresso Bar - NE 41st & Sandy - 1998-2004)
   Randy Darby
Windows - on top of the Cosmopolitan Hotel – now Red Lion, on NE Grand
Village Inn - 1621 NE 10th (60's to current)
Old Wives Tales - 1300 E Burnside (1980 -) (Holly Hart)
   Pizza Keg
   Martini's Spaghetti House
Duchess of Burnside - 2924 E. Burnside
Dugan's- 1441 NE Broadway ('85 -?) - Now Peet's Coffee
   Hamburger Mary's East
Dugan's Stage Door - 1431 NE Broadway
Cafe Mocha - 4108 NE Sandy
Touchstone Coffeehouse - 7631 NE Glisan - Becky Bilyeu
Cafe Destino - 1330 NE Fremont - 2001 - Cahntal Zinn
Tik Tok - 1230 E. Burnside
Waddle's - 11900 NE Union (MLK)
Yaw's Top Notch - 2001 NE 40th
Starkey's III - 2913 SE Stark (2004-) - Joe Waldriff & Greg Simshaw (originally a gas station)
   Starkey's (1987-2004) - Carl & Archie
   Starkey's III (1984-1987) - Andy, Carl, & Archie
   D'Angelo's Italian Restaurant - Nick D'Angelo
   Original Soft Serve Ice Cream Parlor (1930s)
Cup 'n Saucer Cafe - 3566 SE Hawthorne
Tabor Hill Cafe - 3766 SE Hawthorne
Common Grounds - 4321 SE Hawthorne
Stairs Down - 615 SE Alder - underage club/coffee house; offshoot of 2nd Foundation (1974)
Haven Coffeehouse - 3551 SE Division - Dale Schiff
Jackman Joes -1111 NW Marshall & 16th- Kari Jansen
Halocene - 1011 SE Morrison
3 Friends Coffee - 201 SE 12th (2000) - Randy Rappaport
Cooper's Coffee East - 4500 SE Stark -2002 – Michael McRae
Ninth Street Exit (@ Centenary-Wilbur) - SE 9th @ Pine
Mountain Moving Cafe -532 SE 39th - (1975-1979)
Annie Skinner's Cafe - SE 9th & Hawthorne - (1979)
Crema Bakery & Cafe- 2728 SE Ankeny –(2004 -)
   Brent Fortune
Foster Grounds - 5532 SE Center - 2003 - Lynne Getzlaff
Zing's Coffee - 3584 SE Division (1997-2002)
Dingo's Taco Bar - 4612 SE Hawthorne
Jonah's – (1st location)SE McLoughlin – Jack Streijt
Bertie Lou's Cafe - 8051 SE 17th Ave (1943 -)
Windy City - 3766 SE Hawthorne (1981) - Russ & Bob
Aladdin Restaurant (Meier & Frank) 1100 Lloyd Center

East Side Bars / Taverns:
JOQ's - 2512 NE Broadway; formerly at 1422 NE Broadway - Jerry Quarring
   Blackhawk Tavern (1961 -) - Richard Larkin
The Helm -1301 NE Broadway (1981 - 82)
   Ray's Helm
Judy's - 1431 NE Broadway (10/83 to 1/85) – major fundraising & musical events (Judy Kiser)
Frolic - 1447 NE Sandy
Marv Inn - 2216 NE MLK (Union) (1995)Marv Almquist – Mother Marv's Inn
   Egyptian Tavern
Champagne Claudia's - 3278 NE Sandy & Halsey
HR's - 5827 E. Burnside - women's bar
Doug Fir - 830 E. Burnside – Jupiter Hotel (2004-)
   Pa's Cellar (in the basement) (1983-85) Linda Lee & Co
Moon Star Bar & Grill - 7410 NE M L King Jr. Blvd
Code Blue - lesbian dance bar @ SE Pine St Theater (1991) and other moveable locations
Club 927 - 927 SE Morrison (1980 -90) - Yassolino Bros.
Zero 'N Eight Saloon - 018 SE 8th (1985)
Other Side of Midnight - 426 SE (1983-85)
   The Ramp- 1970
The Sunnyside - SE 35th @ Belmont (1974-80) (became a coffee shop)
Women's Bar and Disco (about SE 39th & Powell?)
JR's East Saloon - 4036 SE Hawthorne (1979-1984) John Phillips & Ray Southwick; now Omega
   Carol's

Historic GLBT Venues In Portland

Raven's Nest
Happy Tavern (1940)
Coachlight Inn - 2140 SE Sandy
Egyptian Club - 3701 SE Division - Kim Davis (1995-)
...Eastside
Aaron's Place - Disco Tavern - SE 39th & Holgate
Charlie Brown's
Can We Talk - 4801 SE Hawthorne - (1985) –
Bar of the Gods
Crow's
Varsity Tavern - 3531 SE Division – (1961)- Wm & Lenora Dension
Goodfoot Lounge - 2845 SE Stark
Choices (1988)
Hospital Pub

Night Scene clubs (2000's)
•**Westside:**
Aura - 1022 W. Burnside
Bar 71 - 71 SW 2nd
Baracuda - 9 SW 2nd
Berbati's - 19 SW 2nd
Blue Moon - 432 NW 21st
Carlyle - 1632 NW Thurman
Chart House - 5700 SW Terwilliger
Crystal Ballroom - 1332 W Burnside
Dante's - 1 SW 3rd
El Gaucho - 319 SW Broadway
The Escape (All Ages) 333 SW Park
The Gilt Club– 306 NW Broadfway
The Green Room - 2280 NW Thurman
Higgins - 1239 SW Broadway
H2O - 240 SW Yamhill
Lola's - 740 NW 23rd
The Matador - 1967 W. Burnside
McFadden's - 529 SW 4th
Portland City Grill - 111 SW 5th - 30th Floor
Ram's Head - 2282 NW Hoyt
The Red Sea - 318 SW 3rd
Ringler's - 1332 W. Burnside
The Roxy - 1121 SW Stark
Saucebox - 214 SW Broadway
VooDoo Lounge - 53 NW 1st
XV - 71 SW 2nd

•**Eastside**:
Acme Food & Drink - 1305 SE Eighth
Bar of the Gods - 4801 SE Hawthorne
Bossanova - 722 E. Burnside
Club 21 - 2035 NE Glisan
Colosso - 1932 NE Broadway
CRUSH - 1412 SE Morrison
Doug Fir - 830 E. Burnside
Dune's - 1905 NE Martin Luther King JR. Blvd
Holocene - 1001 SE Morrison
Kennedy School - 5736 NE 33rd
Mint - 816 N. Russell
Nocturnal - 1800 E. Burnside
Paragon - 815 NE Killingswworth
Rabbit Hole - 203 SE Grand
- 4570 SW Lombard (Beaverton)
Bookstores
•**Legitimate:**
Random Strands - 933 SW Park (1970s)
Gai Pied - 2544 NE Broadway (closed 2004)
Skidmore Village Paperbacks - 223 SW Ash
Brian Thomas Books - 921 SW Morrison (Galleria) (1970s)
(Andrea's)
Twenty-Third Avenue Books - 1015 NW 23rd

New Renaissance Books – 1338 NW 23rd
A Woman's Place Books - 1431 NE Broadway (1973-1990) - earlier at 706 SE Grand; 2349 SE Ankeny; 1533 E. Burnside (1974); 1300 SW Washington (1977) **Cat**
Bird Seat - 933 SW Broadway; earlier at 1231 SW Washington
Jelly Bean - 721 SW 10th (The Store); formerly at 802 SW 10th; and 3534 SE Hawthorne
Laughing Horse - (non-profit cooperative) - 3652 SE Division; formerly at 1322 NW 23rd (1985)
Ladd's Addition Bookstore - 1864 SE Hawthorne
Looking Glass Books – 318 SW Taylor
It's My Pleasure - NE 64th & Sandy ('97) - lesbian, gay, bi-sexual-, & transgender- books and "toys" (1991-current) formerly located at SE 43rd & Hawthorne ('95); originally at 4526 Hawthorne ('91)
In Other Words - (non-profit cooperative) - 3734 SW Hawthorne (1993 - current)
Powell's - 1005 W. Burnside & 3747 SE Hawthorne
Plain Brown Wrapper - (open Jan 83) - Chris Tolley & Stewart Benson

Bookstores/Arcades
•**Multi purpose:**
The Book Bin – 213 SW Taylor
Fantasy - 3137 NE Sandy Blvd
Ecstasy Books - 1520 SW 37th
Star Theatre - 13 NW 6th
Cindy's Adult Books & Arcade - 8 NW 4th
Scorpios Adult Books - 209 SW Taylor
Sin City Books - 835 SW 3rd
Book-a-Rama - 820 SW 3rd
Pink Cat Bookstore - 523 SW 3rd
Harts "X" Movie Arcade - 330 SW 3rd
Hard Times - 926 SW 3rd - 311 NW Broadway
Lombard Theatre - 842 N. Lombard
US Distributing - 626 E. Burnside
Eros Theater - SW Taylor (between 3rd and 4th)
Eros Adult Books - 837 SW 3rd
Eros Adult Discount Books - 725 SW 3rd
Film Follies - 915 SW 3rd
The Adult Flick - 24 NW Broadway ('70s)
Hawthorne Adult Book Store (1984)
Fat Cobra - N Interstate & Ainsworth

Historic GLBT Organizations In Portland

* - indicates women's group

Journalistic Publications:

The Alternative Connection (1991-) Ray Southwick & Elwood Johnson
Cascade Voice - (June '82 - Dec '84) - Neil Hutchins, ed., sold to Robert Dunn
City Open Press (COP) (Oct '85-'87?)
City Week - (Oct '85 - ?); Oregon Gay News; Portland Monitor; Chris Smith & Jerry Weller, ed
The Eagle Newsmagazine - (Jan'85-Aug '85) – Robert Dunn, ed
Flash
The Fountain - (Mar '71- Oct '73) - Niel Hutchins, ed
The Fountain Northwest - (Nov-Dec '73) -
The Northwest Fountain (Apr '78-July '83) – David Porter, ed; Jim Bird
*Lavendar Network-(Feb'86-Oct'94)- Ron Zahn, publ
Just Out - (Oct '83 - Nov '92) - Renee LaChance & Jay Brown, publ; Marty Davis editor/owner 1999;
NW Gay Review - (Feb '74 - '82?) - Lanny Swerdlow, ed., & Neil Hutchins
Oregon Gay Rights Report (PDX Town Council Newsletter) (Jan '75-Oct'82)
Oregon Rainbow Magazine - 123 NW 2nd (1977)
Portland Scribe - (1974 - 1978)
*Rag Times (A Women's Place Newsletter) - 2349 SE Ankeny(? '80 - July '82)
Willamette Bridge - Gay Liberation Front - (1970) – Chuck Wilkerson, ed
Willamette Week - (1979 - current)
*Womanspirit - (Fall '74 - Sum '84) - Magdalen Farm, Wolf Creek, Or

Broadcast:

KBOO - "Queersville" - Howie Baggadonutz - (early '70s till mid 80s)
    "Woman Soul" – (women's music -'80s)
    "Bread & Roses" - weekly feminist lesbian public affairs ('80s)
    "51%" - Women & Society
    "Detour" - International gay and lesbian public affairs ('88)
    "Nightrap" - Gay and Lesbian concerns, Tues @ 10pm (1984)
    "Out Loud" - queer news & public affairs (2005)
    "This Way Out" - International queer show (2005)
KOAP (KOPB) – National Public Broadcasting (NPR)
    Seven Lively Arts - Bob Jackson
    "God, Gays, & the Gospel" - MCC Special with Rev, Troy Perry - April 1988
Cable Access Ch 11, 27, 33
    Sister Paula - America's Trans-Evangelist – Paula Nielsen
    Slightly Bent News (1988)
    Nightscene –(1989) Rosey Waters, Lanny Swerdlow, Robert Hillas, Shan Leslie -
    Living Live - Cheryl Hall, Roy Cole, Bob Jackson, Terry VanGelder ('95)
Snickers La Barr Show - Jerry K

Gay, Lesbian, Bi-Sexual Video Access Project – facilitating training in public access TV
Clackamas County Government Cable - *Vortex I* Documentary - 2005
Cable systems Pacific Channel 28 - Gay Pride 1983

Political Organizations

ACT-UP (AIDS Coalition to Unleash Power) – Pdx Chapter (1988)
BRO - Basic Rights Oregon
Equity Foundation
Imperial Sovereign Rose Court – 1958
    The Forum
    Knights of Malta - 1981
Lesbian Democratic Club; Lesbian/Gay Democratic Club (1992)
Lesbian Political Caucus
Oregon Women's Political Caucus
Peacock in the Park (1987) benefits Audria Edwards Youth Scholarship fund
PFLAG - Parents and Friends of L:esbians and Gays (1976) - POG - Parents of Gays (1975)
No on Hate - grassroots group working to defeat the OCA (Oregon Citizens' Alliance)
*Old Lesbians Organizing for Change (OLOC)- 60+ women confronting ageism
OFF Oregonians for Fairness)1988 against Measure 8
Phoenix Rising (came from Town Council Foundation 1979)
Right to Privacy PAC - Human Rights Campaign – Lucille Hart Dinners (1982)
Portland Association for Gay Equality (PAGE) – Prisons, Public Ed, Literature& Civil Rights (1975)
Portland Gay Liberation Front (GLF) - (1970)
Portland Town Council - (1974) - PTC-PAC (77) – Town Council Foundation ('79)
PRIDE:
    Lesbian and Gay Pride (1982)
    Gay Pride Day (1977)
    Gay Pride Fair (1975)
    Gay Pride (1971)
Q-LAND - Queer Love Action Network for Discovery - HIV/AIDS prevention & resources
QUAC - Queers United Against Closets – Inspired national ACT-UP group (1988)
Queer Nation:Portland - multiracial, polygender group fighting homophobia & heterosexism
Rights for Domestic Partners - public & private employees coalition working for equal benefits
Second Foundation (1970-74) - counseling, support, social action, community center
Sexual Minority Roundtable-Mult Co Sheriff, Pdx Police & Community discuss GLBT law issues
SOC PAC - Save our Communities Political Action Committee (1993); fought son of 9 and 13
UEK - United Ebony Kingdom - black equivalent to Imperial Sovereign Rose Court ('60s-'90s)
Walk for Truth, Justice and Community (2005) – Salem to PDX walk publicizing social, civil & economic issues - organized by Rural Organizing Project, Oregon Action, and CAUSA

Social Organizations:(dates uncertain - single year indicates citing in community events columns)

Historic GLBT Organizations In Portland

Service Organizations:
American Civil Liberties Union - Commission on Lesbian and Gay Concerns
American Friends Service Committee - Gay and Lesbian Project (Dan Stutsman) (1988)
HUB - facilitating community resources for sexual minorities
*Lesbian Community Project - sponsors variety of social, political & educational activities
Metropolitan Human Rights Commission
Phoenix Rising Foundation - Gay and Lesbian counseling and wellness support center
Pride of the Rose Scholarship - Provides academic funds for G/L/B/Ts, and their children
Portland Forum - Charitable and assistance organization
Portland People's Fund (1988)

Physical activity & Sports:
Adventure Group - year round hiking/walking/skiing/rafting/mtn biking club
*Amazon Dragons Paddling Club – dragon boat team
Bicycle Decide and Ride
Cascade Flyers - G/L/B/T private/professional aviators FITS - bowling league for gay men and women, ABC/WIBC sanctioned
*Florists - Lesbian softball team – national champions (Lind & Pomeroy Club) - (1937-1965)
*FOREST - Feminists of Oregon Really Excited about Seeing Trees
Oregon Gay Softball League - Art Kranz
Gay Hiking Group
Gay Board Sailors Group
Gay Scuba Group ('90)
*Gay Women's Golf Club
K-9 Club - gay men and their dogs
*L-9 Club - lesbians and their dogs
Lavender Winds Kite Club - G & L kite flyers; member American Kitefliers Assn
Lesbian & Gay Volleyball League - Richard Roth
*Lesbian Equestrian Group
Northwest Big Mountain Support Group
Out Dancing - same-sex country, swing, tango, cha-cha dancing
Out Kayaking Northwest - sea kayak group
Portland Avengers
Portland Coast Boating Club
Portland Gay and Lesbian Swim Team
*Portland Power - basketball
*Lavender Menace - (1972)
Pacific Coast Boating Club - promoting safe boating
Portland Community Bowling Association - Tom Geil
Portland Front Runners - Stonewall Run
Portland Gay Games Team II
Poder Latino - non-profit outreach to GLBTQ Latinos and Latinas; at Outside In
Rosetown Ramblers Square Dance Club (1982)
*RCSA - Rose City Softball Association – Silver Streaks (women's softball team)
Ruby Red Flippers - gay and lesbian scuba Divers
SOAR - Shared Outdoor Adventure Recreation
Team Oregon - prep for Outgames 2006 (Montreal) & Gay Games (Chicago)
Team Tennis - at University of Portland
Wrestlers - Wrestling Club of Oregon
*Women's Wilderness Institute NW

Health, Counseling, and Recovery:
AIDS Forum - weekly AIDS survival programs (1992)
*Ample Opportunity - Health group for fat women
ASAP Treatment Services - counseling organization for alcohol & drug treatment
Bottoms Up - support group of men with hemorrhoids, warts, cysts, prolapsed colons (1983)
Cascade AIDS Project (1983);
    Brinker Trust Fund - providing financial & food support for persons with AIDS/ARC - 1988
    Camp Starlight - safe & caring camping experiences for children affected by HIV/AIDS
    Esther's Pantry - Food Bank; now owned by MCC
    The Link - weekly group of HIV positive men for movies, dinner & social/education events
    Mentalk - community-based discussion groups for health & changing unsafe sex habits
    Oregon AIDS hotline - anonymous information, testing, referrals - 1988
    PAL (Personal Active Listeners) (1986); Partnership Project
    Pride of the Rose Scholarship - academic help for gays, lesbians & children - 1988
    Todd's Closet - clothing for persons with AIDS
CHAT - Catholic Charities AIDS Ministry
CityGuys - Cascade AIDS Project safe-sex information group
City Nights - fund raising entertainment evenings benefit AIDS organizations
Co-Ed Recovery Group
Community Clinic Defense Coalition
Daily Bread Express - home delivered quality meals for HIV positive individuals
Extended Family-queer-friendly Alcoholics 12-step
Friends of PWA's Foundation - volunteers assisting persons living with AIDS
Gay Alcoholics Anonymous - (1971)
Gentle Giants of Oregon - fat men and their admirers
*Hambleton Project - support services for Lesbians with life-threatening illness
Live and Let Live Club - 12-step meetings & recovery community - 2940 SE Belmont
Lunch Bunch - queer-friendly Alcoholics Anonymous
Multiple Sclerosis Self-Help Group – providing information & support
Overeaters Anonymous for Gay Men
Phoenix Rising Foundation - gay and lesbian counseling and wellness and support
Portland GLBTQ Yoga Alliance - Yoga teachers of sexual minority classes
Portland Area HIV Services Planning Council – county decision-making for PWAs re Fed $$s
Positive Link - Free, anonymous phone support and information for HIV+ people
Project Quest Integrative Health Center - nutrition, sports, recreation resources for PWAs
PWA (Persons with AIDS) Support Group - (1983)
Rush Hour Reprieve - open Alcoholics Anonymous

Historic GLBT Organizations In Portland

meeting- 1210 SE 7th
*Women with Heart Fighting AIDS

Spiritual Organizations:

Affirmation - Latter Day Saints (Mormon) support group (1988)
Affirmation - United Methodists for Gay and Lesbian Concerns
ANAWIM (Wounded Spirit) –(2000) –(Pat Moore)
Aktinson Memorial Unitarian Church - 710 Sixth St Oregon City welcoming Congregation
Alternative Spirituality Association - Pagan group celebrating Goddess and God (1988)
Bridgeport United Church of Christ – welcoming congregation - 621 NE 76th
Christian gay and Lesbian singles Bible study/social group
Community of Welcoming Congregations - Rev. Tara Wilkins
Congregation P'nai Or (Faces of Light) – egalatarian Jewish renewal (@PSU Campus Ministries
Congregation Neveh Shalom - sponsors GLBT outreach program (1992)
Crown of Praise Charismatic Church - 2300 NW 30th (Pastors Nita & Judy)
Dignity - Gay Roman Catholics (1969); met @ St. Phillip Neri; St. Francis; St. Andrews
Eastrose Fellowship Unitarian Universalist- Gresham welcoming Congregation - 1133 NE 181st
Eastwood Community Church (1976) - 3950 SE Lincoln - Rev Frank Fortenberry after PCC
Eckankar - Religion of the Light and Sound of God – 7904 SE Milwaukie
Enneagram Community of Portland
Faith United Methodist Church – 27400 SE Stark Troutdale welcoming Congregation
First Congregational United Church of Christ – welcoming Congregation - 1126 SW Park
First Congregational United Church of Christ – Hillsboro affrirming & open - 494 E. Main
First Unitarian Church - open & affirming liberal religions community - 1011 SW 12th
Gay and Lesbian Outreach (GALO) at St. Philip Neri 2408 SE 16th
Gay Mormons
Gay Wiccan Support Group
Gentle Shepherd Metropolitan Community Church – Vancouver, Washington
Integrity -gay & lesbians in the Anglican Communion St. Stephen's Episcopal
Interfaith Spiritual Center - honors various world religious traditions
Journey Catholic Community - SW 13th @ Clay
Keshet - Kosher queer Jewish group
Kinship International - Gay and Lesbian Seventh Day Adventist organization
Koinonia Catholic Community - ecumenical and Catholic in tradition - @ Bridgeport UCC
Lazarus Community - spiritual resource for PWAs
*Lesbian Witchcraft Weekend Intensive
*Lesbian Christians (Lesbian Community Project)
Life Christian Fellowship - 9th St Exit, 215 SE 9th – Vaughn Hayden
Living Communion Church - 3830 SE 62nd
Living Enrichment Center met in Beaverton, then Wilsonville till 2004
Mass in Time of AIDS - Weekly at PSU Campus ministries ("K" House); later at HIV Day Center
Metanoia Peace Community - Peace House, 2116 NE 18th; previously at 3520 SE Yamhill
Metropolitan Community Church of Portland (1971 & 73; 1976 - current) - 2400 NE Broadway
MCC of the Gentle Shepherd - 2200 Broadway, Vancouver, WA
MCC - Two Rivers - 1166 Oak St, Eugene
Nichiren Buddhist Temple - 2025 SE Yamhill
Our Lady of Grace Chapel - Old Catholic, viable Catholic alternative - 5917 N. Michigan
Pagan Spiritual Group
Peace Church of the Brethren - welcoming Congregation - 12727 SE Market
Portland Center for Spiritual Growth – inclusive philosophy similiar to 12-step
Portland Community Church (1972; 74 - 75)
Potter's House Ministries - evangelical & charismatic church 3830 SE 62nd
Radical Faeries - alternative spiritual community
Reach Out - group for former Jews and Mormons
Rose City Park Presbyterian - welcoming congregation - 1907 NE 45th
Sacred Band
St. Andrews Catholic Church - meeting place of post-Dignity Catholics - 806 NE Alberta
St. James Lutheran – 1315 SW Park; a reconciled in Christ congregation
St. Michaels & All Angels Episcopal - 1704 NE 43rd
St. Steven's Episcopal Church welcoming congergation since 1863 - 1432 SW 13th
SDA Kinship - 7th Day Adventists support group
*Sister Spirit - celebrating women's spirituality – 3430- SE Belmont
Soul Quest - exploring woul, spirit, inner transformation & authentic living
Southminster Presbyterian Church – Beaverton welcoming congregation - 12250 SE Denney Rd
That's What Friends are For -Friends for gay/ Lesbian concerns- Quaker group
Trinity Episcopal Cathedral - welcoming & affirming congregation
*Turning Point - spiritual weekend for lesbians by Dr. Lynn Grabhorn
Unitarian Universalist Community Church of Washington County - 22785 NW Birch, Hillsboro
Unitarians for Gay and Lesbian Concerns (1988)
United Church Coalition for Lesbian/Gay concerns – United Church of Christ
United Methodists for Gay & Lesbian Concerns
Unitarians for Gay and Lesbian Concerns
Unity Church - 4525 SE Stark - positive & practical Christianity honoring all spiritual wisdom
University Park United Methodist Church – open progressive faith community 4775 N Lombard
Waverly Heights United Church of Christ - open/ affirming congregation - 3300 SE Woodward
WWHOH - Witches, Warlocks, and other Assorted

Historic GLBT Organizations In Portland

Homosexuals
*Women in the Woods" 4-day retreat @ Breitenbush Hot Springs
Wy'east Uniterian Universalist Congregation - open/liberal congregation - 3300 SE Woodward
Zion United Church of Christ - open & affirming congregation - 22025 NE 23rd Av, Gresham

Sexuality:
*Bi-sexual Women's Group- for all bi-positive women
Cascade Bears (92-95)
Co-Ed Bi-Sexual Group
Coqsure - social group for female-to-male, genderqueer, drag kings & friends
Love Tribe - bi-sexual
Men Massaging Men
Northwest Gender Alliance
OMEN - Oregon Men Enjoying Nature
ORGAN - Oregon Regional Gay and Naked
PAGAN - Portland Area Gay and Naked
PRIDE Oregon - transsexual counseling and support
Portland Jacks
Portland Polyamory Circle
Renegade Bears (95) - Oregon Bears (95)
Sex Addicts Anonymous - 12-step recovery from addictive sexual behaviors - 909 NW 24th
Tara foundation - non-profit helps with $$$ for reassignment surgury(2004)
Trans/Identity Resource Center - physical, emotional, educational support for trans people
Transforming Us - Education, support, counselling, $$ planning for male-to-female trans(2004)

Parenting & family:
Continuity Guild (1980) (MCC) - Vi Leagjeld & Jackie Wilkinson
Fathers Support Group (8l)
Gay Dads (96- current) - originated as part of CAP Mentalk (1997)
*Lesbian Mothers Support Group (1988)
Love Makes a Family(1975?) (Bonnie Tinker)
Oregon Education Assn (OEA) G/L/B/T Caucus – protecting teacher & students
PFLAG - Parents and Friends of Lesbians & Gays
POG - Parents of Gays(Knapp/Shepherd)

Transfamilies - family & friends of transgenders
*Women w/ adolescents support group
*Women w/women and children
YWCA - 1st gay & lesbian Parent Camp Out 1998

Youth:
The Bridge Club - social and discussion group for persons 18-25.
Gay, Lesbian and Straight Education Network (GLSEN) - seeking value & respect in schools
Gay, Lesbian & Bi-Sexual Student Alliance
Outside In - clinic, counseling & transitional housing for homeless & HIV youth
*Lesbian Youth Group
Park Avenue Social Club - social & discussion group for young men ages 19-25 at 1st Congregational
Portland Awakening – GLBT Youth Group

Pride Project - queer and questioning youth of Washington County
Sexual Minority Youth Resource Center (SMYRC) – support for glbt kids under 23 - 2100 SE Belmont
Special Kids - children of GLBT parents (1983) - Friends Institute
Windfire - under 21s rap group meeting at Old Wive's Tales in the 80s – Frank Jenkins

Leather / Cycles:
Black Out Leather Productions
Black Rose Levi Leather Club (80)
Black Leather Wings (89-97)
Border Riders (1969-current)
Chaps (93-96)
Columbia River Motorcycle Club (78-82)
Harley Strokers (88-94)
Knights of Malta: Cascade Chapter (81-96)
Knights of Malta: Black Rose Chapter (72-82)
Leather Night Social (98) – Dirty Duck Social Nights
The Leather Syndicate (81)
Masters & Slaves Together (2002)
Oregon Bears
ORGASM - Oregon Guild of S & M - 1st pan-sexual educational & social S&M club)
Portland Leathermen (87) - pot luck socials
Rain Riders Motorcycle Club (2002-   )
Rose City Discussion Club (93) - S&M Seminars
Sisters of Perputual Indulgence

Leather / Women: -
*The Group (80-82)
*Catharsis (82-84) - S&M women's playground at JR's Cell
*Defenders of Mithra - (84-88) -Women's Leather, levis & lace
*Portland Power & Trust (86-92;95; 98-   ) met at Primary Domain - Sallee Huber
*The Bad Girls (87-91; 93-current)
*LuLu's Pervy Playhouse (96-current)

Age-related groups:
Continuity Group - meeting needs of older gay men & women (1978)
Elder Resource Alliance - Elder GLBT Outreach Committee (2001)
*Late Awakenings - support group for lesbian coming out later in life
*LAP - Lesbian Aging Project
*Lesbians over 40: Lesbians over 35; 50 + lesbian social group
Men Over 40
Primetimers- older men & those who appreciate them
SHARE - Senior Housing & Retirement Enterprises planning senior housing

Ethnic groupings:
Asian-Pacific Islanders group
Black and White Men Together
Black Lesbians and Gays United (1981)
Brother to Brother - support / advocacy for African Am men & families; PDX Black Pride (2002)
MACT - Men of All Colors Together - multi-racial social and support group

Historic GLBT Organizations In Portland

Issues – oriented:
American Civil Liberties Union - Commission on Lesbian and Gay Concerns - 1988
American Friends Service Committee - Gay and Lesbian Project - 1988
Bisexual Community Forum (1985); Bi-Sexuality Exploration Group (1982)
D.A.F.T. - Dykes and Faggotts Together – mixed group for positive social M & F activities (1982)
*Downtown Dykes (1990)
Deaf & Hearing OUT Reach (DHOR) - for deaf and hearing queers and their allies
Feminist Gay Men
*Freedom - lesbians committed to living outside limits of monogamy (1990)
*Funny Ladies Afternoon Tea and Posey Society – lesbians over 35 & friends
GALA - Gay and Lesbian Alliance
GMT - Gay Males Together (1971); Gay Men Together - discussion and support group at PSU
Gay Mayor's Commission - 1988
Jewish Gay Men's Group
Jewish Lesbians & Feminists
*LABIA - Lesbian Access to Babies Inseminated Artificially
Lesbian and Gay Pride (Steering Committee)
*Lesbian Discussion & Social Group
*LENS - Lesbians Enjoying nature and Science
*Lesbian Forum - Lesbian Business Fair – Lesbian Community Project
*Lesbian Garden Club - viewing gardens; exchanging ideas, plants, & seeds
*Lesbian Peer support group
*Lesbian Vision
*Lesbians with Degrees -group for intellectual women
Men of All Colors Together - multi-racial social and support group
New Jewish Agenda (1990)
*Network of Entrepreneural Women
*NOW - National Organization of Women
Northwest Scenic Cruisers - gay & lesbian car club
Northwest Veterans for Peace - Queer-friendly vets
Oregon Safe Schools and Community Coalition
*OLOC - Old Lesbians Organizing for Change
*Oregon Women's Conference - (1977)
Pinnochle Group
*PDX Lesbo Nerds - intelligent women over 35 playing board games
Pride at Work Oregon - AFL-CIO affiliate supporting GLBT & workplace issues
*Portland Bi-Sexual Women - discussion and support

Portland People's Fund– GLBT Emergency assistance
PSU Gay Student Union - Gay Liberation Front
*PSU Women's Union
*Portland Women's Counseling Collective - (1981)
*Portland Women's Crisis Line - 24-hour hotline
Pride of the Rose Scholarship - academic scholarship for lesbians, gays, and their children
QLAND - Queer Love Action Network for Discovery - wellness & STD prevention
*Radical Women
Rainbow Coalition

Reed College Lesbian, Gay, and Bi-Sexual Union
Rose City Discussion Club - pansexual/alternative safe/sane sexuality club
Safe Street Alliance - (1980)
*Support Group for Abused Lesbians
*Tea & Lesbians - Funny Ladies Afternoon Tea & Posey Soc. - (women over 35)
Trans/Identity Resourse Center
Transsexual Support Group
*Uncoupling Group for Women - helping those experiencing the loss of a love
Veterans for Human Rights - GLBT Vets & friends offering support, socials and services access
*Westside Organization of Women
*Wetomachek - social women (name comes from indian word for "friends")

Musical:
*Ursa Minor (1974); Izquierda Quartet (1978)
*Dyketones (1977)
The Fallen Angel Choir
Gay and Lesbian Bagpipe Band
Gay and Lesbian Marching Band
NW Passage Gay Freedom Band
PGMC - Portland Gay Men's Chorus   (1980)
    Subgroups: The Other Side - Stark Street Singers – Tri-Met Transfer - Cascades - Express
Portland Lesbian and Gay Community Band
*PLC - Portland Lesbian Choir (1986)
Portland Women's Jug Band
Rose City Freedom Band - Rose City Swing Band
Bridges (1985-2004)
Confluence - The Willamette Valley Mixed GALA Choruses
*The Chase - all women's band
*Women's Musicians Network Coalition
Women's Percussion Workshop

Food & Socializing:
Blue Collar Guys - men's potluck group
Cook Boys - men's potluck group (1985-current) Dave Kohl, Richard Walker, Phil Joslin
FLATPS - Funny Ladies Afternoon Tea & Posey Society - Tea and Lesbians (women over 35)
*Gourmet Cooking club - women only
*Kinky Women's Welcoming Munch
*Lesbian Welcome Wagon - Lesbians Wishing Welcome
Metro Club - Prime Timers
Park Avenue Social Club - under 30 gay social & potluck club
PIGS - Portland International Gourmet Society
Rendezvous - met at pre-arranged local restaurants for quality dining {David Gernant}
Richmond Dining Society - progressive dinner group for couples
*Second Sunday Brunch Group - lesbians at the Dakota
SoyBoys (2004 - current)
Tuesday Night Patrol

Educational & Cultural:
Art Association of Gay and Lesbian People

Historic GLBT Organizations In Portland

Babble-On Toastmasters (2004-   )
Classic Car Club
Creative Connection - The Real Connection – men interested in the Arts
Gay Bridge Club
Gay Pinochle Group
GLAPN - Gay and Lesbian Archives of the Pacific Northwest - collecting historical documents
Gay and Lesbian Writers
Garden Friends
*Lesbians Enjoying the Sciences
*Lesbian Gardening Club
*lez.com group (1990)
Metro Artisans Guild - Gay and Lesbian artists support and social group
Oregon Safe Schools and Community Coalition – helps create safe schools & communities
*Portland Womens Theatre Company
Silver Screen Club - support NW film & Video Center
Sumus Theatre Ensemble
Store Front Actors Theatre
*Women's Book Group
*Women's Bridge Group
*Women's Reading Group
*Women Writing - Journal Writing for Women

Professional Groups:
BPA Lesbian, Gay, and Bi-sexual Employees – mutual support for Bonneville Power staff
Cascade Guild - at zenith, incorporated 12 sub-groups, including:
    Cascade Business Network - Original Cascade Guild - 1980)
Cascade Union of Educators (CUE)
    Health Care Chapter
    Gay Public Employees Federation of Oregon (1973); - Portlandia's Pride
    Data Processing Group
    Realtor Group
    Legal Services Group
    Women in the Workplace
EAGLE (Employee Association for Gays and Lesbians) (US West)
Gay, Lesbian, and Straight Teachers Network (GLSTN) (1996)
OGALLA - Oregon Gay & Lesbian Law Association education, visibility, advocacy & social
OEA Gay, Lesbian, Bi-Sexual & Trans- Caucus – protecting teachers & students
OHSU "All Hill" Lesbian and Gay Alliance
*Oregon Tradeswomen - promotes women in construction & trades careers
PABA - Portland Area Business Association – networking business professionals - Larry Foltz
*PPOW - Portland Professional Organization of Women

What is Metropolitian Community Church-Portland?

Metropolitan Community Church is a progressive community of faith, welcoming all people, with special outreach to the gay, lesbian, bisexual and transgender communities of the Portland area. The church is part of the larger denomination founded in 1968 to meet the needs and challenges of people of faith who had been alienated by their own home churches because of their sexual orientation. By the mid-20th century, the times were right for correcting misperceptions about the issue of being both homosexual and Christian.

Troy Perry, a Pentecostal preacher and married father of two sons, was denied his pulpit because of his homosexuality. After a stint in the military, a failed relationship, and years of prayer and study, he began a house church in October 1968 in Los Angeles while making a living working at Sears. The initial group of twelve grew rapidly, meeting in the Los Angeles Women's Club, the Echo Theater, and then buying an old church building, which they renovated and beautified. They inspired start-up congregations in many American cities and formed the Universal Fellowship of Metropolitan Community Churches in 1971. It is the fastest growing denomination, with over 300 congregations, worldwide.

What has enabled this growth is the blessing of the Holy Spirit and the hard and determined work of sexual minority Christians to stand up for what the Bible says and does not say about being a person of faith.

What does the Hebrew Bible say?

Scripture is markedly silent on the topic of same-sex love. There are classic examples of men who loved each other - David and Jonathan, and women who loved women - Ruth and Naomi.

Directions about the care of the poor are given over 3000 times in the bible; comments about the misuse of same-sex practice appear five times; comments about misuse of heterosexual practices appear over 400 times.

The most common incident cited in the Old Testament about sex is the story of Sodom. Both Ezekiel and Christ told their followers that Sodom's sin was inhospitality, ignoring a very important component and merciful practice of the nomadic desert culture. Rejecting the visitors and wanting to rape them, as a sign of submission was hostile and the exact opposite of using sexual activity to promote a loving relationship between two people. Sadly, GLBT people have been the victims of the true sin of Sodom.

Other references speak to the misuse of sex. Leviticus sets out morality for the Israelites. Men were not to betray their trust in God by participating in the fertility rites of the neighboring Canaanites - having sex with pagan priests to ritually fertilize their fields. Worship of the phallus and sexual unfaithfulness was condemned in the story of the Golden Calf. Upon reentering Israel from Egypt, God's people were not to associate with, or adopt the sexual rites of the idol and phallus worshiping peoples of The Levant.

Sexuality in Scripture

The Bible is filled with incidents about sex. Adam and Eve were instructed to be fertile and multiply, which they did. Abraham wanted an heir so badly that his wife allowed her maid to become a concubine and bear his child, Ishmael. A harlot helped the spies sent to Jericho to accomplish their mission so that the Israelites could conquer and reenter Israel.

In the practice of the day, King Solomon had multiple wives. Solomon created erotic and sensual poetry in praise of beauty and sexuality. His son David so lusted for Bathsheba that he made sure her husband was killed in battle. David also wrote verse-praising love for his friend Jonathan, whom he loved more than women.

Jacob so loved Rachael that, even after he was tricked into marrying her sister, he worked seven additional years for Laban so that he could marry and love the woman of his heart.

Joseph resisted the approaches of Pharaoh's wife, risking the political advantages that could have been his,

The prophet Hosea was told by God to marry a harlot, as an example of how sincerely God wants to rehabilitate humanity.

What does the New Testament say?

Most significantly, Jesus says nothing about same-sex love in any of the Gospels. It is clear that He loved both men and women, setting examples constantly in His friendship with the marginalized of society - prostitutes, cheats, widows, prisoners, and the poor. His parables revealed honest and caring living, wisdom, stewardship, and faithfulness. Christ taught against love of material goods, love of self, and misuse of power.

In the Greco-Roman society, the philosophic and social education of young men was commonly assigned to a mature man, who became tutor, coach,

What is Metropolitian Community Church-Portland?

and sexual confidant until the youth reached adulthood. Christ made no references to this practice.

Paul speaks about morality in his letter to the Romans. While not an enthusiastic advocate of marriage, he says it is a better alternative than being alone. He is more vocal about controlling passion, and presents more of a Jewish legalist interpretation of sexuality.

The disciples are never referred to as sexual people, although at least one (Peter) was married. They all left family in order to travel with and learn from Jesus, and the apostles did the same as they journeyed to establish communities of faith from Rome to Alexandria.

What are Gay Christian issues?

The first major realization is that we are people of God, created in the image of God, to live lives celebrating the goodness of God, and God's creation in anticipation of reunification with our Creator.

God loves us and Christ teaches that we do not have to be separated from God. We are asked to accept this eternal gift, and to live in harmony with all people on earth, loving our neighbor as ourselves.

If the church body of your faith does not accept sexual minorities because of their history or doctrinal interpretations, the choice comes down to a few options:

1. Stay in that church and remain silent about the truth of one's sexual being.

2. Participate in that church and live openly, preparing to encounter criticism, hostility, or attempts to change one's sexual orientation and practice.

3. Reject all church activity and assume that God is either irrelevant, or does not love you either.

4. Denounce church involvement and become an independent spiritual being, finding your own path.

5. Accept atheism or agnosticism as an ultimate solution to a temporarily misunderstood issue.

6. Join with other GLBTQ and straight Christians in a community of faith, celebrating God's gifts, rejoicing in friendships, working to change social practices, and participating in a community of faith.

What does MCC Portland offer?

We are a vibrant congregation of men and women - single and paired - gay, lesbian, straight, trans, bisexual, and questioning. We are a community of faith, welcoming all people in the name of God, especially of Jesus who was foretold in the Hebrew Scriptures and proclaimed in the Gospels and Epistles.

Several of our founders from 1976 are still members. Our Sunday school of about 20 youngsters ages 3 to 14 meets during 11am worship services. All age groups are represented in our congregation of 300+ individuals.

Sunday Worship services happen at 9am
- Sung worship and Praise
 11am - Traditional liturgical format
  6pm - Elevation contemporary music

A different message (sermon or homily) is presented at each worship. Holy Communion is a part of each worship experience, and all who accept God's healing are welcome.

Music is a strong component of each worship experience. Congregational singing, soloists, choirs, and various instrumentalists all play a part.

Taize meditative worship takes place on two Wednesday evenings each month.

Our Healing team members are available at each service to provide individual prayer.

What else happens at MCC?

In addition to worship services, MCC offers a program of enrichment sessions, including a Course in Miracles, a look at the Metaphysical Option, interpretations of the Da Vinci Code, and offerings on prayer.

Living in the Spirit is a 5-month look at the Five Components of the Spiritual Life, co-led by two pastors.

Bible Study with the Pastor happens on Tuesday Mornings - the current study is The Book of Galatians.

Individual members are invited to join one of the ministry teams. We do the work of the church in teams because we value a diversity of gifts, skills, and experience. Teams meet monthly to carry out the various missions of the congregation:

What is Metropolitan Community Church-Portland?

Advertising and Public Relations
Children's Ministries
Membership
Altar Guild
Healing Ministries
Health and Wellness
Young Adult Ministries
Congregational Life Team
Gardening and Grounds
Liturgical Arts - Drama & visual arts
Maintenance - Building upkeep
Frontliners - Ushers & Greeters
Congregational Life Team

We extend the hand of peace to all who worship with us. Members are invited to also participate in worship as readers, greeters, ushers, and in distribution of the Eucharist.

A Brief history of our Church

In 1976, a group of 20 gay, lesbian, and straight Christians and Jews invited an MCC pastor from San Francisco to move to Portland and help them grow into a congregation. These people had been meeting for two years in an upper room at a liberal Methodist church in SE Portland, at a time of social unrest and change.

By January 1977, the group of 60 members requested a charter with the Universal Fellowship of Metropolitan Community Churches Nine months later, the growing church purchased the historic Arts & Crafts wooden sanctuary at NE 24th and Broadway, built in 1909 with a cornerstone laid by President Taft.

Since 1977, the building has been a center for the Portland GLBTQ community, offering spiritual support, meeting space for several groups including the Portland Gay Men's Chorus (which was founded here), three 12-step groups, a trans support group, a toastmasters group, and many more. We help support an orphanage ministry in the Dominican Republic and are developing an outreach program at Portland State University.

MCC has been deeply involved in issues of GLBT people, including the HIV-AIDS crisis, political challenges, and the rights of all people to live as God's children and to love and marry according to their orientation. We manage "Esther's Pantry", a foodbank for qualified persons living with AIDS.

Our 30-year history as a church and social force is being researched and written in time for our anniversary celebrations, January 22-29, 2006.
Pastor: Rev. Glenna T. Shepherd
Adjunct clergy: Rev. Denis Moore
                    Rev Dianne Shaw
Director of Music: Stephen Couch
Administrator: Eric Cordingly
Board Chairman: David Dishman
Esther's Pantry: Mark Brown
Historian: Dave Kohl

Come visit us!!
What Jesus said about Homosexuality
By Rev. Joyce Baxter, MCC Minister, Vancouver, WA - 1985

(All Scriptures used have bee iclusified and are from the Revised Standard Version of the Bible unless designated.)

Perhaps you have seen the interesting pamphlets that are often passed amongst the crowds at Gay Pride parades...they are usually entitled something like 'what Did Jesus Say About Homosexuality?" You open the pamphlet and a blank page stares at you. Nothing. That's what Jesus said about "homosexuality." Very impressive...or very disappointing, depending on your viewpoint. I remember, five years ago, how disappointed I was when I opened such a pamphlet. I was hungry for some assurance about myself. I was desperate to know what Jesus Christ had to say about my condition and the condition of the person I loved..NOTHING>

Since that time, after much study and searching, I am happy to report to you that I have discovered for myself that Jesus really didn't say anything about homosexuality that is recorded in Holy Scriptures. Homosexuality as we know it today, as we of the Lesbian/Gay communities of the world understand it, did not have a designation. It did not have a definition. Jesus didn't talk about "homosexuals" and their life-styles. He did talk about what many Bible scholars feel is the closest description of a Gay male in Hebrew culture at that time. He talked about "eunuchs."

In Matthew 19:1-12, curiously enough, following a discussion that the Savior had with Pharisees who were trying to trick Him into speaking against the Mosaic law concerning divorce in heterosexual marriage, Jesus says this: "Not all people can receive this saying, but only to those to whom it is given. For there are eunuchs who have been so from birth, and there are eunuchs who have been made eunuchs by

What is Metropolitian Community Church-Portland ?

others, and there are eunuchs who have made themselves eunuchs for the sake of the kingdom of heaven. Those who are able to receive this let them receive it."

The term "eunuch" in the Greek language of the New Testament means "keeper of the bed." The term is sometimes translated as "chamberlain." The translation comes from "eune"- bed, and "echo" of "cheo" - to hold. It also meant, by extension, an impotent or unmarried man; and by implication, it meant a valet, especially of female's apartments, an officer, or a minister of state. Eunuchs were used as especially trusted servants in royal and wealthy household in the Middle East at that time, and in ancient times they were "holy men" & "holy women" (qadesh, qadeshah) who participated in rites of worship other than Hebrew (Canaanite, especially) that the Hebrews called "idol worship" or going after "strange gods." But castration was not something that the Hebrews did to their own people, since castrated persons were not allowed to enter the congregation. (Deut 23:1) "He whose testicles are crushed or whose male member is cut off shall not enter the assembly of the Lord." Thus, to the Hebrew, a man who was "blemished, one who was castrated, or one who was unmarried, or impotent, the eunuch was someone who was kept away from the religious life and forbidden to enter the temple (Lev. 21:1:24)

Jesus did not busy Himself with long commentaries about eunuchs or cult prostitutes. But it is fascinating to discover that in preparation for the last Supper that He would spend on earth with His friends and disciples, which came during Passover, Jesus DIDTHIS: (Mark 14:12-16) He sent two of his disciples into the city of Jerusalem to find a man carrying a jar of water. The were to follow this man and wherever he entered, they were to ask the householder, "the teacher says, 'where is my guest room where I am to eat the Passover with my disciples?'" The disciples did as they were instructed and found the man, bearing the jug of water. William Barclay, an imminent Bible scholar, says that the fact of a MAN carrying a jug of water, which was WOMEN's work, was most unusual...it was something that the disciples could not have missed. Matthew (26:17-19) describes the same incident in this way: Jesus said, "Go into the city to a certain one, and say to him "The Teacher says, "My time is at hand:" I will keep the Passover at your house with my disciples." (The King James Version of Matt 26:17-19 say us "Go into the city to Such a Man..." The Greek word for such is "Deina" - carries the idea of "forgetting" the name of one so designated because it is "fearful" or "strange." (It is remarkable here that the Hebrew word for "Strange" or "stranger" is "goy") "Deins" comes from the root word "deilos" which means dread, timid, fearful, and faithless. The Greek word for MAN in this context is "anthropareskos" - man-courting, i.e. fawning, man-pleaser.

There are other implications here. The bearer of the water vessel carried the receptacle of life-giving liquid for the family in the Hebrew culture. The man, a "stranger" was the householder. He was a timid, fearful person that was not publicly practicing the Hebrew faith. But Jesus, in preparation for His last mean with His friends and disciples, chose to eat and share Himself doing things of great intimacy with them, such as washing their feet and praying with them...in the house of a man who did not conform to gender roles of the culture.

No, Jesus didn't say, "Go into the city and find Thaddeus the Faggot. But the evidence is startling. "Not all people can receive this saying...Those who are able to receive this, let them receive it."

unmarried man; and by implication, it meant a valet, especially of female's apartments, an officer, or a minister of state. Eunuchs were used as especially trusted servants in royal and wealthy household in the Middle East at that time, and in ancient times they were "holy men" & "holy women" (qadesh, qadeshah) who participated in rites of worship other than Hebrew (Canaanite, especially) that the Hebrews called "idol worship" or going after "strange gods." But castration was not something that the Hebrews did to their own people, since castrated persons were not allowed to enter the congregation. (Deut 23:1) "He whose testicles are crushed or whose male member is cut off shall not enter the assembly of the Lord." Thus, to the Hebrew, a man who was "blemished, one who was castrated, or one who was unmarried, or impotent, the eunuch was someone who was kept away from the religious life and forbidden to enter the temple (Lev. 21:1:24)

Jesus did not busy Himself with long commentaries about eunuchs or cult prostitutes. But it is fascinating to discover that in preparation for the last Supper that He would spend on earth with His friends and disciples, which came during Passover, Jesus DIDTHIS: (Mark 14:12-16) He sent two of his disciples into the city of Jerusalem to find a man carrying a jar of water. The were to follow this man and wherever he entered, they were to ask the householder, "the teacher says, 'where is my guest room where I am to eat the Passover with my disciples?'" The disciples did as they were instructed and found the man, bearing the jug of water. William Barclay, an immi-

What is Metropolitan Community Church-Portland?

nent Bible scholar, says that the fact of a MAN carrying a jug of water, which was WOMEN's work, was most unusual...it was something that the disciples could not have missed. Matthew (26:17-19) describes the same incident in this way: Jesus said, "Go into the city to a certain one, and say to him "The Teacher says, 'my' time is at hand: I will keep the Passover at your house with my disciples." (The King James Version of Matt 26:17-19 say us "Go into the city to Such a Man..." The Greek word for Such is "Deina" - carries the idea of "forgetting" the name of one so designated because it is "fearful" or "strange." (It is remarkable here that the Hebrew word for "Strange" or "stranger" is "goy") "Deins" comes from the root word "deilos" which means dread, timid, fearful, faithless. The Greek word for MAN in this context is "anthropareskos" - man-courting, i.e. fawning, man-pleaser.

There are other implications here. The bearer of the water vessel carried the receptacle of life-giving liquid for the family in the Hebrew culture. The man, a "stranger" was the householder. He was a timid, fearful person that was not publicly practicing the Hebrew faith. But Jesus, in preparation for His last mean with His friends and disciples, chose to eat and share Himself doing things of great intimacy with them, such as washing their feet and praying with them...in the house of a man who did not conform to gender roles of the culture.

No, Jesus didn't say, "Go into the city and find Thaddeus the Faggot. But the evidence is startling. "Not all people can receive this saying...Those who are able to receive this, let them receive it."

What is Metropolitian Community Church-Portland?

Historic MCC Mission Statements
1988 MCC Portland Vision Statement:

MCC is a community coming together to proclaim through word and action the message of God's loving presence in all creation.

We are called, by the radical Jesus, to experience an Exodus, away from unjust rules and traditions to what is new, uncertain, perhaps uncomfortable. We celebrate each one's journey toward wholeness, each one's seeking to know and be known.

MCC provides a sanctuary while challenging us to use our freedom, to grow through participation, and to become God's intentional people.

1998 - MCC Mission Statement

Metropolitan Community Church of Portland is a Christ-centered community of faith which welcomes all people and has a primary outreach in the gay, lesbian, bisexual and transgendered communities. We provide love, acceptance, well-being and self-respect, and inspire a spiritual transformation through celebration, community and commitment so that lives are enhanced by the presence of God.

Vision: Metropolitan Community Church of Portland will be regarded as:
    A leading advocate for the greater respect and acceptance and inclusion of gay, lesbian, bisexual and transgendered people in churches and society;
    A center of resources and support for the needs of Portland's gay and lesbian, bisexual and transgendered community
    A model teaching church for other churches in the region

2006 - MCC Vision Statement

Mission:
Metropolitan Community Church of Portland is a Christ-centered community of faith, which welcomes all people and has a primary outreach in the gay, lesbian, bisexual and transgendered communities. We provide love, acceptance, well-being and self-respect, and inspire a spiritual transformation through celebration, community and commitment so that lives are enhanced by the presence of God.

Vision:
Metropolitan Community Church of Portland will be regarded as:
...A leading advocate for greater respect and acceptance and inclusion of gay, lesbian, bisexual and transgendered people in churches and society;
...A center of resources and support for the needs of Portland's gay, lesbian, bisexual and transgendered community
...A model teaching church for other churches in the region

Core Values:
We affirm:
...We are all beloved children of God.
...We value diversity and inclusion in all that we do.
...We are a safe and affirming place to worship, to learn, to grow, and to share God's love.
...We share God's gift of love and welcome all with unconditional acceptance.
...We extend a healing hand to our sisters and brothers through love, concern and support.

Drawing by Dave Kohl

In Memoriam

Deceased members/participants of MCC Portland
    Also a member of the Portland Gay Men's Chorus

Andy Accunero
A. Austin Amerine (Rev)
Richard Avilla
Matt Bailey
Oliver Bankster
Wyn Belfield
Curt Benson
Ron Bergeron (Rev)
Jimmy Bryan -
Russell Budd
Roger Bullis
Wally Burke
Bernie Busse
David Callentine (Rev)
Eric Callicote
Brooks Campbell
Connie Caputo
Mike Carey
Bob Carter
Patrick Cassidy
Barbara "Coach" Chapman
Dennis Chappell (Rev.)
Don Cline
Steven Corpuz
Phil Crum (Rev)
Craig Culver
Jim Davis
Bob DeMaree
Jimmy Dickinsen
Dennis Dickson
Terry Dillon
Art Dimond
Dennis Dixon
Elliot Dixon
Audria Edwards
Casey Elliott
Ken Ensminger
Bill Fitzgerald
J.R. Franklin
Russell Fridley
Daniel Fromhertz
Jim Les Gardner
Bill Godeck
Jim Gravett
Fran Hamilton
Mel Hamilton
Kelso Jim Hanson
Frank Harper
John Harteloo
Vaughn Hayden
Roger Heib
Bill Hickok
Frank Hildenbrandt
Howard Hill
Michael Hoffmann
Oren Charles Hornbeck
Ray Horning
Mark Hutchinson
Amani Jabari
Bob Jackson
Bill Johns
Jay Johnson
"Mom" Mary L. Kamm
Jim Kelso
David Kidoo
Wayne King
Bill Knapp
Mark Knodell
Art Lee
Barry Long
Pat L:ynch
Shaun Lynch
Randy Magee
Wayne Marple
Lee Marvin
Buzz Matthews
George McGovern
Don Meadows
Penny Menashe
Harlow Mills
Jose Montoya
Don Mott
Don Morrison
Gregg Nelson
Jim Nelson
Keith Nofziger
Hugh Owens
Ken Paris
Mark Parkinson
John Phillippi
Gary Pierson
Richard Pittenger
Louise Plagge
Marvin Polokow
Tulsa Pritt
Paul Province
Ron Raz
Steve Reed

In Memoriam

Tom Rice
Lonnie Ray Riley
David Rushong
Michael Russell
Patrick Santiago
Pat Savage
Mark Scheurman
Jonathan Schneider
Robert Schwartz
Tom Simonds
Steve Skuzeski
Tom Slevin
Phil Sims (Rev)
Gary Slavins
Terry Snowden
Jason Stebins
Brad Stevens
Jim Stewart
Russell Stoneman
Don Strausbaugh
Jack Strejc
Jim Swank
Norman Thomas
Andrew Tilton
Gary Van Horn
Steve Wanvig
Jim Warden
Mary Welch
A. Leonard Westberg

Dan Wheeler
A. Leonard Westberg
Al Williams
Mark Wilson
Vic Winegar
Clay Wing
Ken Wood
Darrell Zabell

Community of Welcoming Congregations

Roman Catholic
Journey Catholic Community - Portland
www.journey-catholic.org/
Koinonia Catholic Community -
St. Andrew's Catholic church - Portland
www.standrewchurch.com/
St. Francis of Assisi Catholic church - Portland
rkrueger@hevanet.com
St. Philip Neri Gay & Lesbian Outreach - Portland
www.stphilipneripdx.org/

Christian
Cross Roots Ministries - Vancouver
crossrootsministries@comcast.net

Church of the Brethren
Peace Church of the Brethren - Portland
www.peacecob.org/

Disciples of Christ
Mallory Avenue Christian Church - Portland
Episcopal
St. Stephens Episcopal Parish - Portland
lsfalkowski@comcast.net
Trinity Episcopal Cathedral - Portland
www.trinity-episcopal.org/

Jewish
Congregation Beth Israel (reform) - Portland
bethisrael-pdx.org/
Congregation Neveh Shalom (conservative) -
Portland www.nevehshalom.org/
Congregation Shir Tikvah (liberal) - Portland
www.shir-tikvah.net/
Havurah Shalom (reconstructionist) - Portland
www.havurahshalon.org/
Keshet Jewish Group - Portland
www.gayjewishportland.com/

Lutheran
Augustana Lutheran Church - Portland
augustana.org
Mt. Carmel Lutheran Church (ELCA) - Portland
www.mtcarmellutheran.com/
St. James Lutheran Church - Portland
www.stjameslutheranportland.org

Universal Fellowship of Metropolitan Community Churches
Metropolitan Community Church of Portland
www.mccportland.com/
MCC Two Rivers - Eugene
www.mcctworivers.com'
Mormon
Affirmation (Queer Mormons)
www.affirmation.org

New Thought
Portland Center for Spiritual Growth
www.portlandcenter.org

Pagan
Sister Spirit - Portland   home.tele-
port.com/-sistersp/index.html

Presbyterian
Rose City Park Presbyterian Church - Portland
www.rosecityparkpres.org
Southminster Presbyterian Church - Beaverton
www.southmin.com/
St. Mark Presbyterian Church
stmarkpres.org/

Quaker
Fanno Creek Worship Group - Beaverton
eda@acm.org
Multnomah Monthly Meeting - Portland
www.multnomahfriends.org

United Church of Christ
Ainsworth United Church of Christ - Portland
www.uccwebsites.net/ainsworthusportland.html
Beavercreek United Church of Christ - Beavercreek
www.beavercreekucc.org/
Bridgeport United Church of Christ - Portland
www.bridgeportucc.org
Christ the Healer United Church of Christ -
Beaverton Gabrielle@cthgathering.org
Clackamas United Church of Christ - Milwaukie
macinola@comcast.net
First Congregational United Church of Christ -
Corvallis www.ucc-corvallis.org/
First Congregational United Church of Christ
pdxfirst@aol.com
First Congregational Church of Vancouver
www.vancouveruss.org/
Forest Grove United Church of Chist - Forest Grove
fgucc.org
Hillsdale Community United Church of Christ -
www.hillsdaleucc.org/
Kairos-Milwaukie United Church of Christ -
Milwaukie http://kairosucc.org/
Lake Oswego United Church of Christ - Lake
Oswego www:loucc.org
Meridian United Church of Christ - Wilsonville
www.meridianucc.org
Zion United Church of Christ - Gresham
www.uccwebsites.net/zionuccgreshamor.html/

United Methodist Church
East Vancouver United Methodist Church -

Community of Welcoming Congregations

Vancouver joyburton@aol.com
First United Methodist Church - Portland fumcpdx.org/
Metanoia Peace Community United Methodist Church   www.tearsoup.com/metanoia/
Morningside United Methodist Church - Salem revkarenc@msn.com
University Park United Methodist Church - Portland www.upumc.net/
Corvallis First United Methodist Church - Corvallis www.corvallisfumc.org

Unitarian Universalist
Atkinson Memorial Church - Oregon City atkinsonchurch.com/
Eastrose Fellowship Unitarian Universalist - Gresham www.eastrose.org/
First Unitarian Church - Portland   firstunitarianportland.org
Michael Servetus Unitarian Universalist Fellowship - Vancouver www.msuuf.org
Unitarian Universalist Fellowship of Corvallis - Corvallis www.uu.corvallis.uua.org

Affiliated Members
Act for Action - Theater for all - Portland   www.artforaction.org/
City Church - Portland
Interfaith Spiritual Center - Portland www.interfaithspiritualcenter.com/
Justice & Witness Ministry Team - UCC - Portland
PFLAG Portland www.pflagpdx.org/
Clackamas County PFLAG - Oregon City www.clackamaspflag.org/

Bibliography

Bibliography:
   * references to GLBT spirituality

Books:

*Aarons, Leroy, *Prayers for Bobby*, Harper Collins, New York, 1995

Abbott, Carl, *The Great Extravaganza*, Oregon Historical Society, Portland, 2004

*Anderson, Ron, *The Truth shall make you free*, New Freedom Press, Quincy, Il, 1983

Arndt, William, *Does the Bible Contradict Itself?* Concordia Publishing House, St. Louis, 1955

Ashcroft, Ida, comp, *The Book of the Century - St. James: The First 100 Years*, Binford & Mort, Portland, 1990

Balcomb, Raymond, *Portland's First Church - the Sesquicentennial History, First United Methodist Church*, Portland, 1996

Bender, David, pub, & Leone, Bruno, ed, *Discrimination, Opposing View-points Series*, Greenhaven Press, Inc, San Diego, 1997

Bernstein, Robert, *Straight Parents, Gay Children*, Thunders Math Press, 1995

*Berzon, Betty, Ed, *Positively Gay*, Mediamix Associates, Los Angeles, 1979

Boag, Peter, *Same-Sex Affairs - Constructing and Controlling Homosexuality in the Pacific Northwest*, University of California Press, Berkley, CA, 2003

Bock, Fred, gen. ed., *Hymns for the family of God*, Paragon Associates, Inc., Nashville, 1967

*Boswell, John, *Christianity, Social Tolerance, and Homosexuality*, University of Chicago Press, Chicago, 1980

*Boswell, John, *Same-Sex Unions in Premodern Europe*, Vintage Books, New York, 1995

*Boyd, Malcolm, *Are You Running With Me, Jesus?* Avon Library, New York, 1965

Briggs, Martin, *Everyman's Concise Encyclopaedia of Architecture*, Readers Union, J. M. Dent, London, 1962

Carley, Rachel, *The Visual Dictionary of American Domestic Architecture*, Henry Holt, New York, 1994

Cirlot, J. E., *A Dictionary of Symbols, Philosophical Library*, New York, 1962

*Classen, Chris, *Troy Perry - Pastor and Prophet, Metropolitan Community Church*, Los Angeles, 2004

Cook, Thomas, *A Walking Tour of Downtown Portland: A Century of Gay, Lesbian, and Transgender Historic Sites*, Gay and Lesbian Archives of the Pacific Northwest, PO Box 3646, Portland, OR 97208, June 1999

Cook, Thomas, *The Role of the Newspaper in Oregon's Gay Liberation*, Gay and Lesbian Archives of the Pacific Northwest, Portland, 2001

Corning, Howard, *Dictionary of Oregon History*, Binford & Mort, Portland, 1989

Corning, Howard McKinley, *Willamette Landings - Ghost Towns on the River*, Oregon Historical Society, Portland, 1973

Copper, Baba, *Over The Hill - Reflections on Ageism Between Women*, The Crossing Press, Freedom, CA 95019, 1988

*Crimmins, Cathy, *How the Homosexuals Saved Civilization*, Jeremy P. Tarcher/Penguin, New York, 2004

Cruikshank, Margaret, *The Gay and Lesbian Movement*, Routledge, New York, 1992

Culp, Edwin D, *Stations West - The Story of the Oregon Railways*, Caxton Printers Ltd, Caldwell, ID, 1972

Cummings, Charles A., *A History of Architecture in Italy, Vol 11*, Houghton Mifflin, & Co. The Riverside Press, Cambridge, 1901

Curtain, Cait, *The Grand Lady of Fourth Avenue - Portland's Historic Multnomah Hotel*, Binford & Mort, Portland, 1997

Cyclopedia of Architecture, *Carpentry, and Building*, American School of Correspondence, Chicago, 1908

Deterding, John G, *Living for Jesus, A History of St. Lorenz Lutheran Church*, St. Lorenz Historical Society, Frankenmuth, MI, 1995

Downing, A. J. *The Architecture of Country Houses* (1850), Dover reprint, New York, 1969

Downing, A. J. *Victorian Cottage Residences* (1873), Dover Publications Reprint, New York, 1981

*Duberrman, Martin, *About Time - Exploring the Gay Past*, Meridian, New York, 1991

Duberman, M., Vicinus, M., & Chauncey, G. Jr., *Hidden from History: Reclaiming Gay and Lesbian Past*, New American Library, New York and Ontario, 1989

Ferguslson, James, *A History of Architecture in All Countries*, Dodd, Mead & Co, New York, 1907

Ferguson, George, *Signs and Symbols in Christian Art*, Oxford University Press, New York, 1954

Ferriday, Virginia Guest, *Last of the Handmade Buildings - Glazed Terra Cotta in Downtown Portland*, Mark Publishing, Portland, Oregon 1984

Fletcher, Banister, *A History of Architecture on the Comparative Method*, Butterworths, London, 1987

Bibliography

Foye, Joseph Francis, *A Treasure of Promises Kept - A Centenary History of Queen of the Most Holy Rosary Priory & Parish - Portland*, Oregon 1894-1994, Turner Publishing, Paducah, KY, 1999

Granata, Fred A., J. D., *The 100th-year Celebration of the Church of Saint Michael the Archangel*, Dynagraphics, Inc, Portland, OR, 1994

*Glaser, Chris, *Coming Out to God*, Westminster John Knox Press, Louisville, 1991

*Glaser, Chris, The Word Is Out - The Bible Reclaimed for Lesbians and Gay Men, Harper, San Francisco, 1994

*Goss, Robert E., and West, Mona, ed,, *Take Back the Word - A Queer Reading of the Bible*, Pilgrim Press, Cleveland, 2000

Gwilt, Joseph, *The Encyclopedia of Architecture - Historical, Theoretical, and Practical*, 1867, Reprinted by Bonanza Books, New York 1982

*Hall, H. Laron, *No Darkness At All - A Collection of Sermons*, First Methodist Church, Portland, OR 97201, 1994

*Hanckel, Frances, & Cunningham, John, *A Way of Love, A Way of Life - A Young Person's Introduction to What It Means to Be Gay*, Lothrop, Lee & Shepard Books, New York, 1979

Handlin, David P., *The American Home - Architecture and Society 1815-1915*, Little, Brown & Co, Boston, 1979

Harris, Daniel, *The Rise and Fall of Gay Culture*, Hyperion, New York, 1997

Hawkins, William J,III, & Willingham, William F., *Classic Houses of Portland, Oregon - 1850-1950*, Timber Press, Portland, 1999

*Herdt, Gilbert, ed, *Gay Culture in America*, Beacon Press, Boston, 1992

Hopkins, C. Howard, *History of the Y.M.C.A. in North America*, Association Press, New York, 1951

Hudson, Rock, and Davidson, Sara, *Rock Hudson - His Story*, Wm Morrow & Co, New York 1986

Johnson, Sidona V., *A Short History of Oregon*, A. C. McClurg, Chicago, 1904

King, Bart, *An Architectural Guidebook to Portland*, Gibbs Smith, Layton UT, 2001

Kinsey, Alfred C, *Sexual Behavior in the Human Male*, W. B. Saunders, Philadelphia, 1948

Knuth, Priscilla, *"Picturesque" Frontier: The Army's Fort Dalles*, reprinted from Oregon Historical Quarterly, Oregon Historical Society, Portland, 1967

Kurlansky, Mark, *1968 - The Year that Rocked the World*, Ballentine Books, New York, 2004

Labbe, John T, *Fares, Please! Those Portland Trolley Years*, Caxton Printers, Ltd, Caldwell, ID 1980

*Larue, Gerald, *Sex and the Bible*, Prometheus Press, Buffalo NY 1983

Lee, Martin A, and Shlain, Bruce, *Acid Dreams - The Complete Social History of LSD*, Grove Weidenfeld, New York, 1985

Love, Matt, *The Far Out story of Vortex I*, Nestucca Spit Press, Pacific City, OR, 2004

Lowenstein, Steven, *The Jews of Oregon 1850-1950*, Jewish Historical Society of Portland, Oregon, 1987

Lubke, William, *Geschichte Der Architektur*, VBerlag von E. A. Seemann Leipzig, 1870

MacColl, E. Kimbark, *Merchants, Money and Power - The Portland Establishment 1843-1913*, Georgian Press, 1988

Makinson, Randell L., *Greene and Greene - Architecture as a Fine Art*, Peregrine Smith Books, Salt Lake City, 1977

Mars, G. C., Ed., *Brickwork In Italy,* American Face Brick Assn, Chicago, 1925

Massey, James & Maxwell, Shirley, *Arts & Crafts Design in America*, Chronicle Books, San Francisco, 1998

McAlester, Virginia and Lee, *A Field Guide to American Houses*, Knopf, New York 1988

McArthur, Lewis A, *Oregon Geographic Names*, Binfords & Mort for the OHS, Portland, 1944

McDonald, Roxanna, *Illustrated Building Glossary*, Butterworth/Heinemann, Oxford, 1999

McNeil, Robert, *Valiant for Truth - Clarence True Wilson and Prohibition*, Oregonians Concerned about Addiction Problems, Portland Oregon, 1992

Medved, Michael, and Wallechinsky, David, *What Really Happened to the Class of '65?* Ballentine Books, New York, 1976

Miner, Rev. Jeff, *The Children are Free - Reexamining the Biblical Evidence on Same-sex Relationships*, Jesus Metropolitan Community Church, Indianapolis, 2002

*Mueller, Howard E, *AIDS: A Christian Response - Study Guide for Adults*, Concordia, St. Louis, 1987

Nelson, Donald, *Progressive Portland on the Move*, Donald R. Nelson, Portland, 2004

O'Donnell, Terance, & Vaughn, Thomas, *Portland - A Historical Sketch and Guide*, Oregon Historical Society, Portland, 1976

Painter, George, *The Vice Clique - Portland's Great Sex Scandal*, Portland, unpublished, 2005

Parker, John Henry, *A Concise Glossary of Architectural Terms*

Bibliography

(1896), Crescent Books, New York, 1989

*Pennington, Sylvia, *But Lord They're Gay,* Lambda Christian Fellowship, Hawthorne, CA, 1978(?)

*Perry, Troy. *Don't Be Afraid Anymore*, St. Martin's Press, New York, 1990

*Perry, Troy, *The Lord is My Shepherd and He Knows I'm Gay*, Liberty Press, Austin TX, 1987 (Nash, 1972)

Phillips, Steven J., *Old House Dictionary*, The Preservation Press - NTHP, Washington DC, 1994

Pintarich, Paul, *History by the Glass - Portland's Past and Present Saloons*, Bars, & Taverns, Bianco, Portland, 1996

Pratt, Laurence, *I Remember Portland - 1899-1915*, Binford and Mort, Portland, 1965

*Piazza, Michael, *Holy Homosexuals - The Truth About Being Gay or Lesbian and Christian*, Sources of Hope Publishing, Dallas, Rvised Edition 1997

Priestley, Harold, *The English Home*, Garden City Press, Letchworth, UK, 1977

Pugin, A. and A. W., *Gothic Architecture - Selected from various Ancient Edifices in England, 1821-1838*, reprinted by Lincoln Press, Cleveland, 1923

Ritz, Richard Ellison, *Architects of Oregon*, Lair Hill, Portland, 2002

Roth, Leland, ed, *America Builds - Source Documents in American Architecture and Planning*, Harper & Row, NY 1983

Schwantes, Carlos Arnaldo, *Long Day's Journey - The Steamboat & Stagecoach Era of the Northern West*, University of Washington Press, Seattle, 1999

Sill, Gertrude Grace, *A Handbook of Symbols in Christian Art*, Collier Books, Macmillan, New York, 1975

Smith, Mary Ann, *Gustav Stickley - The Craftsman*, Dover, New York, 1983

Snyder, Eugene, *Early Portland - Stumptown Triumphant*, Binford and Mort, Portland, 1970

Stanford, Phil, *Portland Confidential - Sex, Crime, and Corruption in the Rose City*, West Winds Press, Portland, 2004

Stein, Harry, Ryan, Kathleen, & Beach, Mark, *PORTLAND - A Pictorial History*. Donning, Virginia Beach 23462, 1980

Steinman, Ron, *Inside Television's First War - A Saigon Journal*, University of Missouri Press, Columbia, 2002

Stewart, James, *An Archaeological Guide and Glossary*, Phoenix House, Ltd., London, revised Ed, 1960

Sweet, William Warren, Ed, *Religion on the American Frontier - 1783-1840, Vol IV, The Methodists,* University of Chicago Press, Chicago, 1946

Taylor, John & Joy, *Old Timer's Tales of Oregon*, John & Joy Taylor, Bloomington, IN, 2004

Teal, Donn, *The Gay Militant*, Stein and Day, 1971

Tinniswood, Adrian, *The Arts and Crafts House*, Watson-Guptill, New York, 1999

Todd, Mary, *Authority Vested: A Story of Identity and Change in the Lutheran Church-Missouri Synod*, Wm Erdmans, Grand Rapids, 2000

Vaughan, Thomas, & McMath, George, *A Century of Portland Architecture,* Oregon Historical Society, Portland, 1967

*Via, Dan, & Gagnon, Robert, *Homosexuality and the Bible*, Fortress Press, Minneapolis, 2003

Wesson, Kath, *Families We Choose,* Columbia University Press, NY, 1991

Wollner, Craig, *The City Builders - 100 Years of Union Carpentry in Portland*, Oregon Historical Society, Portland, 1990

Wong, Marie Rose, *Sweet Cakes, Long Journey: The Chinatowns of Portland, Oregon,* University of Washington Press, Seattle, 2004

Yarnes, Thomas, *A History of Oregon Methodism,* Parthenon Press for Oregon Methodist Conference Historical Society, n.d. (1958?)

Young, Pat, *Index of Just Out Coverage of Portland 1983 - 2003*, unpublished, Portland

Young, Pat, *Measure 9: Oregon's 1992 Anti-Gay Initiative*, Thesis for Master of Arts in History, Portland State University, 1997

Zimmer, R. Allen, ed, *A Catechism of Christian Worship*, Concordia Publishing House, St. Louis, 1961

Translations of the Holy Bible:

Cyclopedic Indexed Bible, *Authorized or King James Version*, John A Hertel, Chicago, 1926,1946

The Dartmouth Bible - An Abridgement of the King James Version, Houghton Mifflin, Boston, 1950

The Everyday Bible - New Century Version, Guideposts, World Publishing, Dallas, 1988

Extreme WORD, *New King James Version*, Thomas Nelson, Nashville, 2001

Good News Bible - *Today's English Version,* Thoman Nelson, American Bible Society, New York, 1976

Holy Bible, *Authorized or King James' Version of 1611*, Holman, Philadelphia, 1942

Holy Bible, *Contemporary English Version*, American bible Society,

Bibliography

New York, 1995

The Jerusalem Bible, Darton, Longman & Todd, Ltd, London, 1966; Doubleday, Garden City, 1968

The Living Bible - Life Application Bible for Studens, Tyndale House, Wheaton, IL, 1992

New International Version (NIV), New York International Bible Society, New York, 1978

New Oxford Annotated Bible - *New Revised Standard Version*, Oxford University Press, New York, 1991

The New Testament and Psalms - *An Inclusive Version*, Oxford University Press, New York, 1995

The New Testament in the Language of the People, A private Translation by Charles B. Williams, Moody Press, Chciago, 1950

The New Testament of the Inclusive Language Bible, Cross Cultural Publications, Notre Dame, IN, 1954

New World Translation of the Holy Scriptures, Watchtower Bible and Tract Society, New York, 1961

Psalms/Now, Paraphrase by Leslie F. Brandt, Concordia Publishing, St. Louis, 1973

Revised Standard Version Greek-English Interlinear New Testament, Alfred Marshall, Regency Reference Library, Zondervan, Grand Rapids, MI, 1958

Newspapers:

Cascade Voice (Portland)

Dec 16, 1983, p21b, "A Message of Love from Rev Delores P. Berry"

The Capitol Forum (Salem, Or)

November 1982, p8, "Troy C. Perry"

The City Open Press
March 14, 1986 p. 14, c3 "The Cop and the Gay Mayor"
May 15, 1986, p5 c1, "The Naming of Lesbian/Gay Pride"

City Week

Dec 26, 1986, Vol 2, No 12, p6-8, "The Year in Gay Review"

The Fountain (Second Foundation, Portland)

Just Out (Portland)

*December 18, 1998, Vol 16, No 4, p1 "Keeping the Faith"
Jan 7, 2005, Vol 22, No 5, p 20-23m "Our Years with Vera."

NW Fountain (Portland)

NW Gay Review (Portland)

December 1974 p 18 "Mame"
*November 1975, Vol 2, No 10, p6 "MCC Seven Years Old"
*Jan/Feb 1976, p8 "M.C.C. returns to Portland"
June 1977, Vol IV, No 5 - Special Issue "Portland from WWII to Stonewall"
July/August 1977 Vol IV, No 6, P 21 "Portland Community Church" Ad

Oregon Gay News

Vol 3 No 25 Issue 117 April 6, 1988, p 10, "Community Resources

Oregon Journal (Portland)

October 3, 1909, Several Articles and Photographs
October 4, 1909, Several Articles and Photographs
November 21, 1912, p1, c 5, "E.J.S. McAllister Arrested on Way into California"
August 29, 1920, p1, c2, "New Church Dedicated Today"
July 3, 1963, sec 2, p3, "Grace Lutheran Church Sells Building"
October 12, 1963, "Congregation Sets Opening"
*Apr 16, 1973, p5, c1 "Church set for Portland Gay People"
May 6, 1975, p2, c6, "Homosexual bias....."
June 22, 1976, p6, c1, "Gays claim Harrassment...."
June 23, 1976 p11, c2, "Gays have work to do...."
January 6, 1977, p2, c4, "Homosexual civil rights sought...."
January 19, 1977, p4, c3, "Task Force urges legal...."
*June 25, 1977, p1, c4, "Portland Parents of Gays...."
March 27, 1979 pMW2, c3, "Police vow to end pandering"
October 12, 1979, p 7, c3, "MCC to Install its New Pastor"

The Oregonian (Portland)
April 5, 1909, p8, "Ground is Broken...."
October 3, 1909, Several Articles & Photographs
October 4, 1909, p1 "15,000 People See Cornerstone Laid," " Taft Wields Silver Trowel"; "Church Gets Taft"
April 10, 1910, Photo of nearly finished church
April 17, 1910, Sec 2, "Costly Homes Erected - Corby's Manse"
May 28, 1917, p 13, "Dr. Corby Remembered""
October 20, 1917, p 1, c2, "Pastor Enters New Field"
October 3, 1985, p 1, c5 "Rock Hudson Dies of Aids"
*July 10, 1988, p C1, 7 "Denominations Struggle do deal with issue of homosexuality"
January 9, 1993, Sec C p 1 c4, "Activist pastor resigns"
June 18, 1995, Sec D p.1,8 "Thousands put best foot ahead for gay pride"
March 16, 2004, Sec A, p 6, "Oregon's Gay Rights Fight"
January 9, 2005, Sec E, p 1, 8, "Far Out - How a Portland writer became obsessed with Vortex
May 27, 2005, A & E, p 11, "Party Animals" by Lee Williams
July 5, 2002, Sec C, p 3, "National Lampoon's legacy sinks to gross-out level" by Jake Tapper
August 14, 2005, Sec C, p 5, Obituary of Channing Matthew Briggs

Portland Mercury (Portland)

June 02, 2005, p. 55, Dan Savage, "Savage Love"

Willamette Week (Portland)
July 16, 1987, Vol 13, No. 37, P 1 "The New Crusade Against Gays"
Periodicals:

Bibliography

The Advocate, Liberation Productions, Los Angeles,

Barrett, Jon "The Lost Brother "(Matthew Shepherd) Issue 773, Nov 24, 1998, pp 26-30

Alternative Living, City Voice Productions, Portland, Or,

Vol 1 Number 1, Dec, 2004 (AltLiv@yahoo.com)

Christopher Street, That New Magazine Inc., New York,

*Ortleb, Charles: An Interview with John J. McNeill, S.J. "God and Gays: A New Team?" Vol 1, No 4, Oct 1976 p 25-33
*Dlugos, Tim, "Gay Windows: What happens When Your Lover Dies?" Vol 4, No 6, Feb 1980

Dragazine, West Hollywood, CA Lois Commondenominator, Publisher

Dickmann, Ken, "Wanna Buy An Illusion - Charles Pierce," (Vol 1) No 7, pp13-17

GQ (Gentlemen's Quarterly)

*"Can there be a Gay Gospel-Singer?" April, 2004

Instinct, JR Pratts, pub, Sherman Oaks, CA

Perry, Joel, "Gay Rights & Civil Rights - Are They The Same Thing?" July 2005, pp 71-2

Mandate, The International Magazine of Entertainment & Eros

Devere, John, " Dave Kopay, I Know Who I Am," Vol 3, No 25, May 1977, pp 5-7
Devere, John, "Portrait of the Artist (Rudolf Nureyev)," Vol. 3, No 29, Sept 1977, pp 41-3
Hartinger, Brent, "The History of Gays on Television," Vol 14, No 12, Dec 1990, PP 39ff
Llewellyn, Michael, "Next Stop, Greenwich Village," Vol 3, No 25, May 1977, pp36-40
_____, "Gay Hustle: For Love and/or Money," Vol 3, No 32, Dec, 1977 pp. 5 ff

The New Yorker

*Boyer, Peter J, "A Hard Faith", May 16, 2005, p 54-65

Newsweek

Morganthau, Tom, et all, "GayAmerica in Transition," August 8, 1983 pp 30-40

Oregon Historical Quarterly

Boag, Peter "Does Portland Need a Homophile Society?" Vol. 105, No 1, Spring 2004, p 6 ff
Boag, Peter, "Sex and Politics in Progressive-Era Portland and Eugene - The 1912 Same-Sex Vice Scandal", Vol 100, No. 2, Summer , 1999, p 158ff
Nicoll, G. Douglas, "The Rise and Fall of the Portland Hotel," Vol 99 No. 3 Fall 1998, p 298 ff

Pacific Historian

Wahl, K. Jane, "The Raiders from Sullivan's Gulch", Summer 1971, Volume 15, pp 12-16

Portland Monthly

Abbott, Carl, "200 Years in Words & Photographs", Vol 3, Issue 9, pp 55-84; 85-105

Psychology Today

Freedman, Mark, "Homosexuals may be healthier than straights" March 1975, p 28ff

Stained Glass Quarterly

Barclay, Melissa, "Povey Brothers Revisited", Vol 98 No 4, Winter 2003 p 294-5

Time Magazine
Cloud, John, "The Battle Over Gay Teens," Vol 166 No 15, October 10, 2005, pp 42-51
Gibbs, Nancy, "How Should We TeachOur Children About Sex?" Vol. 141 No 21, May 24, 1993, pp 60-66

Vector - The Gay Experience, Society for Individual Rights, San Francisco, 1974

Klein, Satya, "The Heterosexual World," Vol. 2, No 10, Oct. 1975

Websites:

*www.gerberhart.org (Gerber/Hart Library, Chicago)
*www.glbthistory.org (GLBT Historical Society, San Francisco)
*www.lesbianherstoryarchives.org (Lesbian Herstory Archives, New York)
*www.lgbtran.org (LGBT Religious Archives Network)
*www.lgbtran.org/Exhibits/CRH/Exhibit.asp (Council on Religion and the Homosexual in SF)
*www.mccchurch.org (Universal Fellowship of Metropolitan Community Churches)
*www.mccportland.com (Metropolitan Community Church of Portland)
*www.nypl.org/research/chss/spe/rbk.faids/igic.html (Int'l Gay Information Ctr Archives, NY)
*www.oneinstitute.org (One National Gay & Lesbian Archives, Los Angeles)
www.pridenw.org (Portland PRIDE)
*   www.st-francis-lutheran.org (St. Francis Lutheran Church, San Francisco)
www.stonewall-library.org (Stonewall Library and Archives, Fort Lauderdale)
*www.trettercollection.org (Tretter Collection, Minneapolis)
*www.yale.edu/lesbiangay (Larry Kramer Initiative for Lesbian & Gay Studies, New Haven)

Maps:

1852 - Federal Township Survey Map - Metro Region 2040 Project, redrawn by Ruth Cotugno & Emily Weid
1860 - Original Platt of Portland

Bibliography

1871 - Portland - Showing Additions on both banks of the Willamette
1880 - Portland, Showing proposed Grand Union Depot
1881 - Portland, Albina, and East Portland
1887 - East Portland
1890 - Nickel Map - All Lands on the Willamette & Columbia River Peninsula
1891 - City of Albina
1894 - Paving Map of the City of Portland, Jan 1st, 1894
1894 - Sewerage Map of Portland - showing flooded District of June
1894, Pacific Coast Abstract Company, 147 First St, Portland, Oregon
1901 - Portland and Vicinity, 1901, Front & Stark Sts, Portland,Oregon
1905 - USGS Topographic Sheet, 15' series, Edition of July, 1905, Portland, Oreg. Quadrant
1908 - Map of Portland and Vicinity, Rowland and Fortiner, Portland, Ore, 1908
1915 - Map of Pacific Northwest showing Trade Districts Tributary to Portland and Puget Sound, 1915
1918 - Graphic Sketch of Track-system of Portland Railway Light and Power Co., Portland City Lines
1920 - Metskers Map of Portland and Vicinity, 1920
1922 - City of Portland Paving Map, Department of Public Works, showing paving before 1920, and paving in 1921
1928 - School and Park Map of Portland
1930 - Metsker's Map of Portland and Vicinity, 1930
1936 - Metsker's Map of Portland and Vicinity, 1936
1958 - Chevron Portland Street and Vicinity Map, H. M. Gousha Company, Chicago, 1958
1990 - USGS 7.5 minute series, U S Dept of Interior Geological Survey. Portland Quadrangle
2003 - AAA Portland Oregon City Series, GM Johnson & Associates, Ltd, Burnaby, BC V5C 4C1
2005 - Topographic and selected streets map of Portland, Commissioned for "A Curious and Peculiar People," Metro

Bibliography

Interviews with

- Arlene Ackerman
- Sam Adams
- Vivian Allison
- Marty Appell
- John Baker
- Scott Baker
- Kathy Bambeck
- Bill Barry
- Joyce Baxter
- David Beckley
- Gary Benoit
- Delores Berry
- Deborah Betron
- Jacquie Bogle
- Mary Brady
- Gordon Branstator
- David Bernhard
- Barbara Bernstein
- Lille Brock
- Dan Brown
- Kimberly Brown
- Mark A. Brown
- Richard Brown
- Don Borbe
- Z. Arthur Buck
- Gail Bumala
- Dick Burdon
- Barry C
- Pat Cach
- Bud Clark
- "Gibby" Clark
- Sally Cohn
- Roy Cole
- Walter 'Darcelle' Cole
- Gary Coleman
- Tom Cook
- Eric Cordingly
- Norm Costa
- Neal Curry
- Paul Davis III
- Jerry Deas
- Marsha Dempsey
- William Dickey
- Dave Dishman
- Dwayne Downing
- Joe Dubay
- Darrell DuBois
- Glen Dugger
- Dani Eaton
- Bill Findlay
- Larry Foltz
- Mary Franz
- Steve Fulmer
- Terry Furman
- Nita Gates
- Joe Gimarelli
- Wendell Gleason
- Jim Glyer
- Joel Godby
- Holly Hart
- Chuck Harvey
- William Hawkins III, AIA
- John Herbst
- Michael Hibbard
- Charles Hinkle
- Robin Hixson
- John Houston
- Milt Howell
- Russ Howerton
- Don Howse
- Wallace Huntington
- Neil Hutchins
- Steve Jordan
- Mary Jane Kamm
- Rich Kibbons
- Judy Kiser
- Wally Lanchester
- Sue Lantz
- Dick Levy
- Andy Mangels
- Debbie Martin
- Michael Marx
- Kelly McFarland
- Robert McNeil
- Larry Moad
- Denis Moore
- Ann Mussey
- Frank Myers
- Alix Nathan
- Betty Nelson
- Will Neumann II
- Roxie Neuhardt
- George Nicola
- Paula Nielsen
- Tom Norton
- George Oberg
- Frodo Okulam
- Kathy Oliver
- Rodney Page
- George Painter
- Nestor Perala
- Greg Pitts
- Troy Perry
- Lloyd Porter
- Jerry Quarring
- Ron Rassmussen
- Susan Remmers
- Bruce Richards
- Harper Richardson
- Jack Rickli
- Barbara Roberts
- Bill Roberts
- John Rushong
- Mike Ryerson
- Jack St. John
- Jane Sandmeier
- Frank Schreckenberger
- Pat Schwiebert
- Glenna Shepherd
- Susie Shepherd
- Harry Sherburne
- Bruce Silverman
- Robert Smith
- David Sorber
- Darrell Standley
- Steven Stone
- Harold Strong
- Mike Susa
- Steve Suss
- Roey Thorpe
- Roger Troen
- Paul Tucker
- Joe Waldorf
- Kenton Wiens
- Jerry Weller
- Mike Whitcomb
- Frederico White
- Jim White
- John Wilkinson
- Larry Wormington
- Pat Young
- Dan Zielke

Abridged Index

Index (abridged)

Adams, Sam
AIDS
Baker, John
Barry, Bill*
Bean, Terry
Berry, Rev. Delores*
Bernice, Mama
Blue Mouse Theater
Borbe, Rev. Don*
Brown, Dan*
Buck, Rev. Z. Arthur*
Burdon, Rev. Dick*
Camp, The
Cascade AIDS Project
Chinatown (Portland)
Circle Theater
Clark, Bud
Cadillac Cafe
Cole, Rev. Roy*
Coleman, Gary*
Community of Welcoming Congregations
Cook, Tom
Cordingly, Eric*
Curry, Neal*
Dahl & Penne's
Darcelle XV
Director, Sandy
Dirty Duck Tavern
Dishman, Dave*
Dubay, Rev. Joe
Dugger, Glen
Ecumenical Ministries of Oregon
Embers
Equity Foundation
Flossies Tavern
Foltz, Larry*
Fox & Hounds Tavern
Fred Meyer Stores
Fulmer, Steve
Gay & Lesbian Archives of the Pacific Northwest (GLAPN)
Gay Liberation Front (GLF)
Glyer, Rev. Jim*
Goldschmidt, Neil
Half Moon Tavern
Harbor Club
Hart, Holly
Hart, Lucille
Harvey, Chuck*
Healey, Kiernan
Hinkle, Charles
Hoyt Hotel
Hutchins, Neil*
Imperial Hotel
Imperial Sovereign Rose Court (IRSC)
Jackson, Robert*
Jonah's Restaurant
JR's Tavern
JOQ's Tavern
Kafourey, Gretchen
Katz, Vera
Kibbons, Rich*
Knapp, Rita
Kulongoski, Ted
Lee, Dorothy McCullough
Lindberg, Michael
Mattachine Society
MCC-Boise
MCC-Hollywood
MCC-Indianapolis
MCC-Kansas City
MCC-Los Angeles
MCC-North Hollywood
MCC-San Francisco
MCC-San Jose
MCC-Seattle
MCC-Spokane
MCC-Tacoma
MCC-Tri-Cities (Richland, Pasco, Kennewick, Wa)
MCC-Vancouver(Wa)
MCC-West Hollywood
McCoy, Gladys
McCready, Connie
McNeil, Rev. Robert
Meier & Frank's
Montoya, Jose*
Moore, Rev. Denis*
Multnomah County Library
Multnomah Hotel
Nelson, Betty*
Nicola, George
927 Tavern
Oberg, George
Old Town (Portland)
Old Wives' Tales Restaurant
Oregon Historical Society
Oregon Liquor Control Commission (OLCC)
Other Inn Tavern
Other Side of Midnight Tavern
Page, Rev. Rodney
Perry, Rev. Troy
Pioneer Courthouse Square
Pitts, Greg
Portland, City of
Portland Gay Men's Chorus (PGMC)
Portland Hotel
Potter, Tom
PRIDE
Redwing, Donna
Richards, Bruce*
Richardson, Rev. Harper
Riptide
Roberts, Barbara
Ross, Rev. Patricia
Roxy Hart's (The Roxy)
Scandals Tavern
Schwiebert, Rev. John
Schwiebert, Pat
Second Foundation
Shepherd, Ann
Shepherd, Rev. Glenna
Shepherd, Matthew
Shepherd, Susie
Silverado Tavern
Slaughters (CC's) Tavern
Smith, Gordon
Society for Individual Rights (SIR)
Somebody's Place Tavern
Star Theater
Starkeys
Stonewall
Strausbaugh, Don
Suss, Steve
Transfusion Inn
Universal Fellowship of Metropolitan Community Churches (UFMCC)
Weller, Jerry
Wilde Oscars
Wilson, Rev. Gary*
YMCA (Portland)

Endings

Colophon:

Headings set in 18 pt Papyrus
Text set in 11 pt Korinna
Formatted in QuarkExpress
Printed on Spicer 80# Discovery Dull
with soy-based Ink

Printed and bound in Portland Oregon USA
Witham & Dickey, Printers
Softcover binding by Rose City Bindery
Hardcover binding by Grossenbacher Bros
January 16-26, 2006

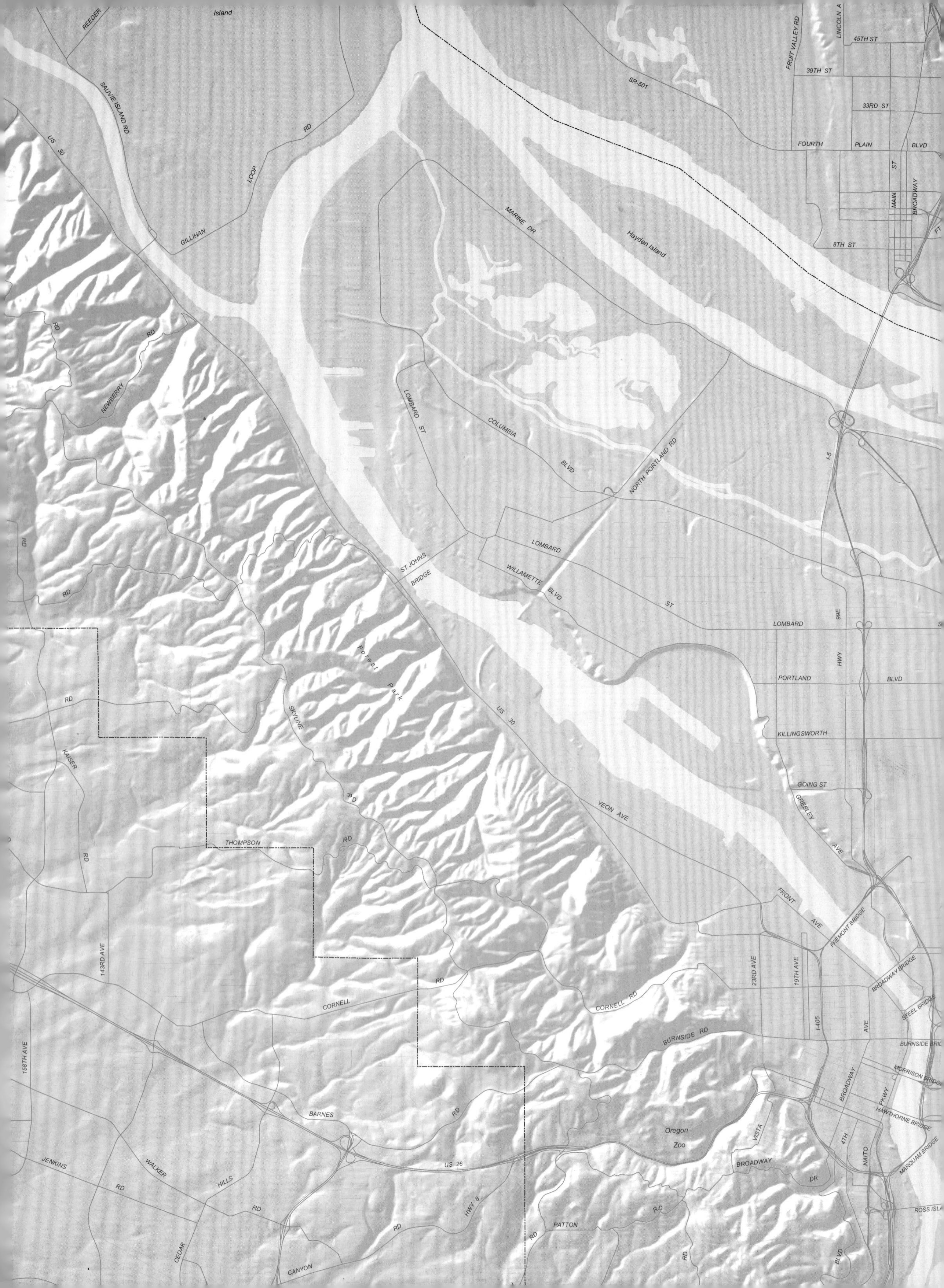
REEDER
Island
SAUVIE ISLAND RD
US 30
RD
LOOP
GILLIHAN
SR-501
FRUIT VALLEY RD
LINCOLN A
45TH ST
39TH ST
33RD ST
FOURTH
PLAIN
BLVD
MAIN
ST
BROADWAY
8TH ST
FT
MARINE DR
Hayden Island
RD
RD
NEWBERRY
LOMBARD ST
COLUMBIA
BLVD
NORTH PORTLAND RD
I-5
RD
RD
ST JOHNS
BRIDGE
LOMBARD
WILLAMETTE
BLVD
ST
LOMBARD
99E
HWY
Forest Park
PORTLAND
BLVD
RD
SKYLINE
US 30
KILLINGSWORTH
KAISER
RD
GOING ST
GREELEY
AVE
YEON AVE
THOMPSON
RD
RD
FRONT
AVE
FREMONT BRIDGE
23RD AVE
19TH AVE
BROADWAY BRIDGE
143RD AVE
RD
CORNELL
CORNELL RD
STEEL BRIDGE
I-405
AVE
BURNSIDE RD
BURNSIDE BRI
158TH AVE
MORRISON BRIDG
BROADWAY
PKWY
HAWTHORNE BRIDGE
BARNES
RD
Oregon
Zoo
VISTA
4TH
NAITO
MARQUAM BRIDGE
JENKINS
WALKER
US 26
BROADWAY
DR
RD
HILLS
RD
HWY 8
R-D
ROSS ISLA
RD
PATTON
CEDAR
RD
RD
RD
BLVD
CANYON